# Southwest Humboldt Hinterlands

The Press at Cal Poly Humboldt
Cal Poly Humboldt Library
1 Harpst Street
Arcata, California 95521-8299
press@humboldt.edu

Copyright © 2022 Jerry Rohde

This book is licensed under a Creative Commons Attribution-NonCommercial-4.0 International License.

Cover Photo: Briceland (HCHS, colorized by JR).

Original copyright holders retain all copyright over images used in this book, and are thereby excluded from provisions granted by Creative Commons license.

Cover design and layout by Maximilian Heirich, Sarah Godlin
Interior layout by Maximilian Heirich, Sarah Godlin

ISBN: 978-1-947112-83-4

# Southwest Humboldt Hinterlands

Jerry Rohde

The Press at Cal Poly Humboldt

**History of Humboldt County People and Places series**

*Both Sides of the Bluff*
*Southern Humboldt Indians*
*Southwest Humboldt Hinterlands*
*Southeast Humboldt Hinterlands*

# Expressions of Gratitude

*Southwest Humboldt Hinterlands* can trace its roots back to the first book my wife Gisela and I wrote, *Humboldt Redwoods State Park: The Complete Guide*, which was published in 1992. Information that we collected then has been resting in my file cabinet for 30 years and has now been called again to active duty. Most of the persons whom we interviewed for the earlier book have passed on. I still treasure the time I spent with them. They recalled a past that is now difficult to imagine, but thanks to their accounts we can still gain some sense of what southern Humboldt was like as far back as the 1910s and 1920s. If I wore a hat, I would tip it in their memory.

So, for what they shared with me three decades ago, I give thanks to Darrell Beasley, Bill Beat, Roberta Curless Beat, Verda Chadbourne Bishop, Dave Chadbourne, Richard Childs, Robert Childs, Velma Childs, Max Crismon, Harold Fisher, Jane Bryant Fisher, Don Gould, Linda Moore Hillbrun, Dorothy Rose Baxter Johnson, Al Lewis, Ed Lewis, Mel Martin, Lloyce Moore, Marie Moore, Carol "Mori" Morrison, Geraldine Stockel Myers, Susan Pritchard O'Hara, Henry Perrott, John Perrott, June Ruggles, Margaret Pritchard, Angus Russell, Blanche Lewis Tompkins, Clara Luke Trapier, James Trapier, Lucille Vinyard, Hershell Wheeler, and Irving Wrigley.

Three persons Jan Anderson provided expert proofreading. Maximilian Heirlich created yet another beautiful layout and skillfully combined all the materials for the book. Kyle Morgan, Scholarly Communications and Digital Scholarship Librarian of the The Press at Cal Poly Humboldt, masterfully supervised the completion of the book.

Many others subsequently offered their help in providing material that found its way into this book. At the Humboldt State University Library I benefitted from the expertise of Erich Schimps, Joan Berman, Edie Butler, and Carly Marino. At the Humboldt County Historical Society I was guided to sources by Matina Kilkenny, Linda DeLong, Deb Meador, and Jim Garrison. At the Ferndale Museum Ann Roberts frequently found important items for me. As the director of the Humboldt Redwoods Interpretive Association, Dave Stockton was a font of information and perpetual enthusiasm. Jack Irvine, Steve Lazar, and Rusty Goodlive all generously shared their postcard collections with me. Don Tuttle gave me access to the extensive photo collection he had accumulated. Susie Van Kirk continually shared pieces of pertinent information she had found during her long career as a researcher. Mary Ann Machi and Laura Cooskey not only provided information about Shelter Cove and the Mattole Valley, respectively, but they also reviewed the chapters I had written about those areas. David Heller answered countless questions about southern Humboldt history. Ben Schill responded to inquiries I had about the Phillipsville area. I have worked with three archaeologists—Bill Rich, Nick Angeloff, and Jamie Roscoe—who all shared their knowledge of local Indian history. Diane Hawk located obscure accounts about far southern Humboldt. Jerry Scott shared stories about the Whitethorn and East Branch areas. Melinda Wilson provided extensive information about Bear River and took us on a tour of the valley.

George Cockman recalled historical locations in the East Branch drainage. JoAnn Bauer told me about the back to the land movement in Salmon Creek. Darlene Magee shared her knowledge of the George Burtt family. Janet Barton and Joyce Blueford of the California Nursery Company generously granted permission for the use of images from the company's collection related to Albert Etter. Steve Matson kindly permitted the use of his photo of *Astragalus agnicidus*, aka the "Lambkiller," while Frank Callahan graciously let me use his image of the Council Madrone. I have included several images that are now out of copyright and I thank the archives that hold them and the archivists who collected them. If I have omitted mention of anyone who helped me, I have not done so intentionally.

Three persons helped bring the book to completion. Jan Anderson provided expert proofreading. Maximilian Heirlich created yet another beautiful layout and skillfully combined all the materials for the book. Kyle Morgan, Scholarly Communications and Digital Scholarship Librarian of the The Press at Cal Poly Humboldt, masterfully supervised the technical work on the book. I am fortunate to have had their help.

Finally, I thank my wife Gisela for the help and enthusiasm she has always provided for my work on the history of Humboldt County. I write for her, first of all.

# Acknowledgements

The places described in this book lie within the ancestral homelands of what are commonly called the Bear River (Nekanni), Mattole, and Sinkyone tribes. In the 1850s and 1860s numerous whites committed genocide against these peoples, killing many of them, sending some to reservations that were often little more than concentration camps, kidnapping others and forcing them into slavery, and driving a few into hiding. By the late 1860s whites claimed possession of all of southern Humboldt County. No payment was ever made to any Indian for the taking of their land nor was any reparation offered for the murders, rapes, kidnappings, and other atrocities that were committed. This book describes some of these events, and the previous volume in this series, *Southern Humboldt Indians*, provides additional accounts.

Telling what happened so far in the past can, of course, never right the wrongs that took place. The perpetrators cannot be held accountable, for they are all dead. The victims cannot be compensated, for they, too, are dead. But the information nonetheless has value. It revises the reputations of the perpetrators, and it honors the lost lives of the victims. And one thing further: by bringing the truth of the past into the present, these accounts provide us with an understanding that may help heal the wounds that were inflicted so carelessly, so needlessly, so many generations ago.

# Key to Photo Credits

The photo captions use initials to designate the sources. I colorized numerous black and photos using both the colorization feature at myheritage.com and Photoshop Elements 2021, and I have noted this at the end of the relevant captions.

BL = UC Berkeley, Bancroft Library

BLM = Blue Lake Museum

CDV = California Division of Highways

CE = United States Army corps of Engineers

CEFP = California Ethnographic Field Photographs. UC Berkeley: Phoebe A. Hearst Museum of Anthropology; the photographer is Pliny E. Goddard

CPH = Cal Poly Humboldt Library Special Collection

CNC = California Nursery Company - Roeding Collection, Fremont, California

CSP = California State Parks

DPR = Department of Parks and Recreation. State of California: the Resources Agency

DTC = Don Tuttle Collection

FC = Frank Callahan

FM = Ferndale Museum

FMC = Fritz-Metcalf Photograph Collection. UC Berkeley: Bioscience & Natural Resources Library; the photographer is Emanuel Fritz

GH = Gordon Hewes

GR = Gisela Rohde

HCHS = Humboldt County Historical Society

HRSP = Humboldt Redwood State Park

IA = Internet Archive

JIC = Jack Irvine Collection

JNL = J. N. Lentell, Map of Humboldt County, 1914

JR = Jerry Rohde

JRC = Jerry Rohde Collection

LC = Library of Congress

LI = Leigh Irvine's *Humboldt County California*

MCNAP = Merriam (C. Hart) Collection of Native American Photographs. UC Berkeley: Bancroft Library; the photographer is C. Hart Merriam

MVHS = Mattole Valley Historical Society

MWC = Melinda Wilson Collection

RGC = Rusty Goodlive Collection

SLR = Save the Redwoods League

SM = Steve Matson

THPO = thehumboldtproject.org

UP = University of the Pacific

USGS = United States Geographical Survey

WM = Wikimedia

WP = Wikipedia

# Preface

The world is too much with us; late and soon,
Getting and spending, we lay waste our powers;—
Little we see in Nature that is ours;
We have given our hearts away, a sordid boon!

—Wordsworth

And what would we have seen of Nature, had we visited the world of southwestern Humboldt County in the early 1900s?

A flat of some 200 acres that stood above a protected harbor—Shelter Cove—a place where ships unloaded the cargoes that supplied southern Humboldt and loaded the cargoes that paid for the supplies.

Hills filled with vast stands of tanoak, the trees rapidly reduced in number as their bark was taken for its tannin, an agent prized by the state's many leather tanneries.

A single road that led south, mostly near the coast, winding and climbing and dropping and twisting through terrain so daunting that only necessity brought travelers upon it.

Towns that often were but a cluster of houses, huddled around a store and saloon, with perhaps a small school to provide distinction to some deeply rural place.

Redwood forests that crowded the river canyons, shading streams that each year filled with salmon in the fall.

The imprint of the Indians from six different tribes, who lived in harmony with their surroundings until the onslaught of white newcomers sent most of them to the land of shadows.

Read on, and perhaps learn what else the land waits to tell us.

# Introduction

This book is the third volume in my "History of Humboldt County Peoples and Places" series. It covers 24 areas in the southwestern part of the county, running from Bear River on the north to the Mendocino county line on the south and from the Pacific Ocean on the west to the drainage of the South Fork Eel River on the east. It generally reports on the time period from 1850, when whites first began taking over the region, to 1964, when the huge Christmas flood rearranged much of the local landscape.

Each chapter tells the story of a particular place, generally presented in chronological order. Certain significant events and processes that are described in detail are placed within sidebars or appendices that speckle the work. The main illustrations are mostly photographs or postcards. If the original image was in black and white, I have colorized it using MyHeritage software. Several maps appear at key points in the text. These are mostly based on a 1916 United States Army Corps of Engineer series that I have not seen anywhere in print.

As with the other volumes in this series, I have tried to link every factual statement with one or more sources upon which the statement was based. This results in a lengthy set of endnotes. In evaluating the accuracy of sources, I have followed what I call a "hierarchy of reliability." In this system I generally place the highest value on reports that originated at the time of an event, while being mindful of possible bias by the reporter. I also try to find other sources that corroborate such reports, especially when they are of a controversial nature. I usually have less faith in the veracity of accounts given some time after an event, even if provided by one of the observers or participants, since the corrosive effects of time sometimes affect the accuracy of the recollections.

This book, along with next one, *Southeast Humboldt Hinterlands*, in part represents a continuation of the accounts given in volume 2 of the series, *Southern Humboldt Indians*. That volume described the ethnogeography of the southern Humboldt area as it appeared in early 1850, the time of stability for the local tribes, and it also provided certain accounts of Indian history after the arrival of the whites. The two hinterlands books contain further reports on the local Indians, which are now localized to the chapter that covers the area where specific events occurred.

Some streams of activity transcended connection with a single place. The construction of the Redwood Highway and the creation of state redwood parks are two examples of this. In such cases, the main story appears as either a sidebar or an appendix within one of the chapters whose location is closely related to the subject.

The sources upon which I've based my account were acquired during more than 30 years of research. For some locations this has resulted in the collection of ample information, but for a few places there is less coverage than I had hoped. I offer what I have found, knowing that it is only part of the story, but hopefully the most important part.

# Chapter Locations

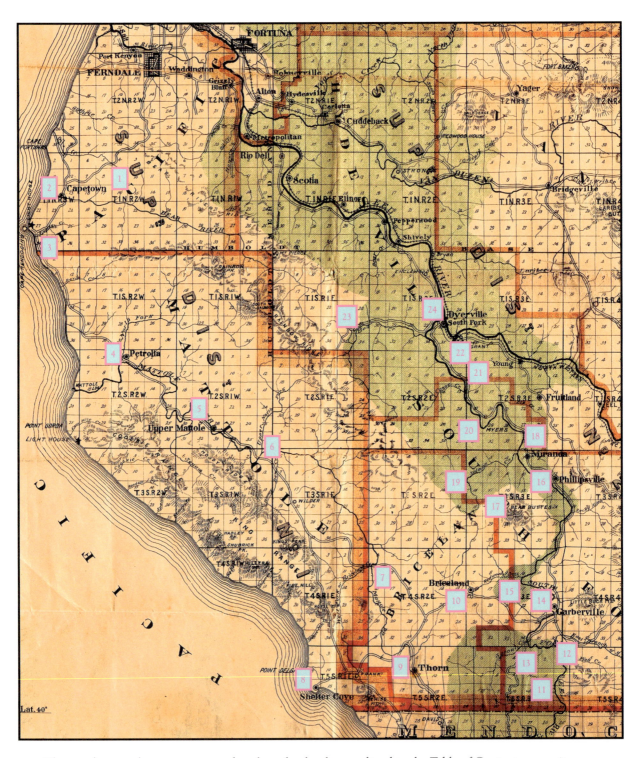

The numbers on the map correspond to those for the chapters listed in the Table of Contents, opposite.

# Table of Contents

| | |
|---|---|
| Acknowledgements | vii |
| Key to Photo Credits | viii |
| Preface | x |
| Introduction | xi |
| Chapter Locations | xii |
| 1. Bear River | 1 |
| 2. Capetown | 23 |
| 3. Cape Mendocino Area | 39 |
| 4. Petrolia | 61 |
| 5. Union Mattole & Upper Mattole | 91 |
| 6. Honeydew | 103 |
| 7. Ettersburg | 109 |
| 8. Shelter Cove | 117 |
| 9. Whitethorn | 143 |
| 10. Briceland | 153 |
| 11. Richardson Grove | 167 |
| 12. Benbow | 177 |
| 13. Sproul (Sprowl) Creek Area | 189 |
| 14. Garberville | 197 |
| 15. Redway | 215 |
| 16. Phillipsville | 221 |
| 17. Bear Buttes | 241 |
| 18. Miranda | 253 |
| 19. Salmon Creek Area | 263 |
| 20. Myers Flat | 271 |
| 21. Burlington | 281 |
| 22. Weott | 287 |
| 23. Bull Creek | 297 |
| 24. Dyerville | 323 |
| Sources | 349 |
| Endnotes | 389 |
| About the Author | 411 |

# Chapter 1
# Bear River

> Bear River . . . is not of great length nor of much value in itself, but flows through a region excellently adapted to stock-raising and dairy purposes, and to some extent to agriculture.[1]
> —Owen C. Coy

In August 1851 the *Daily Alta California* carried an account of the Eel River valley, noting that one of the local residents, a "Mr. Dobbins," had just "explored a stream to the southward."[2] "Dobbins" was probably Kennerly Dobyns, from the Alton area.[3] His report found

> . . . the country to be not less beautiful than any he has seen, abounding in elk and in "grislys," feeding about, in his own words, like hogs. The stream which, for this reason, he calls Bear river, debouches into the Pacific among the rocks just north of Cape Mendocino."[4]

If Dobyns had inquired of the Indians who inhabited the area, he would have found they already had a name for the river: "Tcalko."[5] But that term, like their name for the tribe itself—Nekanni[6]—was washed away on a torrent of white words, and today Tcalko is referred to almost exclusively as Bear River, just as the Nekanni tribe is now known as the Bear River Indians.

Despite Dobyns's glowing report, it appears that no other whites visited the Bear River area until the summer of 1852. Then Silas Morrison, Silas Hoagland,[7] Robert M. Williams, and an unidentified fourth man "camped on Bear River Ridge for a while and then returned to Trinity County." Silas Morrison's grandson, Clyde, indicated that

> . . . Silas rode from the camp to a point on Olympia Ridge just above the present [1962] Olympia Ranch. Here he sat on a large rock and looked out over the valley. From this point he could see much of the land that he later acquired. The view was enchanting, so quiet and restful. A small stream meanders lazily westward toward a wall of interspercing [sic] ridges. Here and there are sprawling benches set at varying elevations that are in turn hemmed in by steeply rolling hills and at no point is the valley floor more than three quarters of a mile in width. To the north for most of the year the tawny coloring of the open range dominates the scene with some intermingling of grays and greens of small clumps of trees. To the south the deep green of the thickly wooded slopes blends into a dark blue in the distance. All this could easily create in a land hungry emigrant a deep sense of longing to be a part of it.[8]

Regardless of such manifold enticements, Morrison did not return to Bear River immediately. Meanwhile, others arrived.

In the fall of 1852 Joseph Russ purchased a herd of cattle in Placerville, driving them all the way to Bear River Ridge. There he grazed the beeves[10] before taking them to sell in Eureka.[11] That same year Barry Adams drove his own herd

In 1852 Silas Morrison would no doubt have seen a similar view, minus the road and the buildings of the Green Pond Ranch (JR, colorized by JR).

to Bear River, whereupon he went into partnership with Russ. Adams and Russ brought over "a large number of beef cattle" from Sacramento in the fall of 1853 and thus supplied, the men opened the first meat market in Eureka.[12] Adams then "engaged in the butcher business in connection with stock raising for twenty years."[13] Russ sold his half interest in the meat market to Adams in 1855,[14] relocating to Forks of Salmon, where he opened a market. In the spring of 1857 Russ went to Oregon, bought another herd of beef cattle, drove them to Bear River, "and again opened a meat market in Eureka." Soon Russ "commenced to invest in grazing lands."[15] He probably began by preempting "a cattle range on the cape ridge between Capetown and Ocean House." Here Russ established the first of his many ranches, which his windswept wife Zipporah named "Spicy Breezes."[16]

Whether Russ and Adams were the first ranchers to graze cattle in the Bear River area is unclear, but others soon came to the valley. The *Humboldt Times* noted in July 1855 that:

> Some five or six families, with large stocks of cattle, have lately removed into the county, and settled on Bear River. They are old farmers, and will form quite an addition to our populations. In addition to the number of families lately settled in the place, we hear that four or five more are expected to arrive by the next steamer, from San Francisco.[17]

One of the arrivals that year was Seth Kinman, a peripatetic Pennsylvanian who had recently reached Humboldt County and established a ranch on Table Bluff. Kinman then took up land on Bear River Ridge to use "as a grazing place for stock. It was a lovely place and the grass was as tall as you could reach and of the most nutritious kinds." He calculated that he "was some 14 or 15 miles distant from neighbors," who had ranches near the mouth of Bear River.[18] Seth's property was high atop the eastern part of the ridge; his water source still bears the name Kinman Pond.[19]

In 1856 a small flood of newcomers washed up on Bear River. John Lewis Southmayd, a New Hampshirian, started ranching above the south side of the river. He is credited with building the first house and establishing the first dairy in the vicinity.[20] William T. Olmstead moved a cattle herd from Tehama County to Bear River that June. He also moved his family to Hydesville and started a meat market in Eureka.[21] For five years, Knyphausen "Foss" Geer worked at Olmstead's Bear River ranch. It was there, claimed Geer, that he produced ". . . the first butter that was made on Bear River." Geer also took out a claim for his own 160-acre property.[22]

Also in 1856 Silas Morrison at last returned to Bear River, where "he took up government land and engaged in the stock business."[23] That same year George Williams drove a herd of cattle to Bear River and in 1857 he went into partnership with Morrison, a connection that lasted 49 years.[24] Morrison ran the ranch, while Williams spent over a decade in Weaverville and then moved to Hydesville, where he operated a meat market for 18 years.[25]

Another 1856 arrival in the Bear River area was the Johnston family: Richard, Mary, and their two children. Twenty-six years later, Richard wrote a "Narrative" that told of the tribulations of being a small rancher in a valley dominated by a big rancher. (See sidebar 1.)

The Johnstons had reached Bear River just after the area's first reported incident between

Charles Henry Southmayd left Bear River in 1885, but he left his name on a local landmark (JR).

## 1. Ranchers Rich, Ranchers Poor

In December 1856, Richard Johnston and his family reached Bear River Ridge, where Richard "dairied" W. T. Olmstead's[26] cattle for several months, finally selling enough butter to net him about $300. As Johnston lamented, the money constituted the proceeds from

> . . . about seven months [sic] work which did not make us very rich. Be that as it may, we moved down to Bear River about the middle of June 1857. Employed a man by the name of John Wilson to build a log house for us, 14 x 20, with a shed roof 10 x 20, which was to answer as a kitchen and dairy. When completed, took all my money.[27]

Events progressed quickly:

> I think in July, or the beginning of August, our house was ready for us to move into and by September we had a corral made so that we milked a few cows that fall. In October, my dear wife give [gave birth to] another daughter. I had to act as Dr. and midwife, but she got along very well, as she was, and still is, a very healthy woman.[28]

Johnston, along with an unnamed partner from Weaverville, then essentially sharecropped, or rented, a herd of milk cows:

> All of the cows that ever Mr. Swales furnished me was 50 cows, American, good, bad and indifferent, and 25 Spanish cows with horns nearly a yard and a half long that no one would try to milk but myself. Such was my first dairy on Bear River. I was to raise all the calves and give one third of the Butter, which did not make either of us very rich. I got some in debt that year, and have never been out of debt more or less since. My Weaver friend made a lucky escape.[29]
>
> . . . Another friend traded me a cow for chickens, which was the first cow I owned in Humboldt Co. It was uphill work to make two ends meet as there had to be improvements made and every thing of the kind was new to me. We had no sawed lumber nearer than Eureka, and that was out of the question. In the first place, the distance (35 miles) was so great with no roads, and what was still worse, no money to buy

with, so that every thing in the shape of board had to be split out and as that a kind of work I had never done until I did it here.

In fact, every thing that I did was done by main strength and awkwardness and had I not been young, strong and determined, I never would have succeeded and, as I had left the mines never intending to return, I had to stick it out.[30]

And stick it out, more or less, the Johnstons did. Their family grew until they had six children, whose welfare was a great responsibility. Many of the local ranchers became worried about an Indian raid on Bear River. Although Johnston claimed he "had no fear of an Indian attack," he wanted to be cautious. In December 1863 he accordingly moved his family to the Eel River valley, where his four oldest children could attend school. Ironically it was there, at Alton, that Indians indeed attacked two children: one of the victims was his oldest daughter, Ellen, whom they wounded severely and left for dead.[31]

But Ellen Johnson survived, and in March 1865 the family returned to Bear River. Soon a brief oil boom hit the area, with the result that the Dick Johnston Company was formed, a derrick raised on the Johnston Ranch, and a well sunk about a hundred feet. It gushed nothing but expenses, leaving Johnston with no oil and a deficit of about $470.[32]

Johnston's financial struggles continued. He bought 360 acres of land to fill in a gap between his two existing ranch properties. This cost $1,080, for which Johnston had to give a mortgage.[33] He fenced part of his property at a cost of about $800.[34] Johnston bought into a butcher shop in Eureka, but he had difficulty selling his beef, since an unnamed neighbor, who was actually Joseph Russ,[35] "had the butcher business monopolized for years."[36]

Johnston wanted to sell his beef to the local lumber companies, but because Russ was there first and offered a better price, only two potential purchasers were interested. One was the Occidental mill, whose owners "graciously" accepted Johnston beef as payment for lumber. The other was John Vance. As Johnston explained it, "Mr. John Vance, a man of varied peculiarities could neither be bought nor induced to trade at the other shop as long as I owned a butcher shop in town, although he was offered beef and etc. a cent a lb. less than he was paying me for it."[37]

Johnston seemed unable to avoid further financial misadventures. He offered security to James D. Henry Brown[38] for a lawsuit Brown brought against mill men and loggers on Elk River. Brown lost the case, leaving Johnston with a security pledge of $1,995. Brown said he would make good on the debt but never did. Johnston had to take out a second mortgage to clear the pledge.[39]

The last pages of Johnston's narrative continue to chronicle his growing indebtedness. He borrowed money from one of his brothers-in-law, but then Joseph Russ foreclosed on the property. Still refusing to use Russ's name in his account, Johnston refers to "his neighbor" as a "miserable two faced hypocrite," someone whose "avariciousness and greed got the better of him when he seen he had a good plausible pretext for making a clean sweep of all that I had into his own purse."[40] After much haggling and maneuvering, Russ and Johnston finally made a new agreement, in which the "interest only changed from ten to twelve per cent per annum."[41]

Johnson concludes his narrative in 1882 with a final reference to Russ: "But enough of this, I am nearly done with him and wish him or his no harm and would not harm if I could."[42]

Joseph Russ died four years later, in October 1886. His laudatory biography in Leigh Irvine's *History of Humboldt County* claimed that:

> So systematically did Mr. Russ plan his undertaking, and so thoroughly were his plans blocked out, that many of them were practically self-operating for years to come. . . .[43]

Richard Johnston, perhaps contemplating life's difficulties (CPH, colorized by JR).

Such was the case with his loan to Richard Johnston. According to one of his descendants, Johnston, not having read the fine print in the loan agreement, failed to fulfill one of its requirements. Russ's widow, Zipporah, thereupon foreclosed on Johnston, who forfeited half his ranch to her as a result.[44] In March 1894 Johnston gave up 1,860 acres to pay off two mortgages totaling $15,924.60,[45] proof that Joseph Russ's plans were indeed "self-operating for years to come."

Indians and whites. A perceived crime by the Indians provoked a massive retaliation that ended in a massacre. (See sidebar 2.)

During the early 1860s several Bear River whites reported various hostile acts by Indians, none of which resulted in either injury or death. There are no known accounts about what the whites did to the Bear River Indians during this time, but elsewhere the record shows repeated acts of "ethnic cleansing" by genocidal white vigilantes and military units, the most notorious being the series of at least a dozen massacres in late February 1860 that included the mass killings on Indian Island.[46]

On July 2, 1860, Seth Kinman's dwelling on Bear River Ridge was reportedly burned by Indians.[47] Kinman, whose tales were often among the tallest, claimed that "three different

---

### 2. The Just and the Dead

Although Bear River ranchers feared trouble with the Indians, the biggest known conflict that occurred there was caused by the whites. There are various versions of what happened, but the most plausible account came from Silas Morrison. It was handed down to his son, George, and then told to, and recalled by, Viola Russ McBride.

According to the Morrison-McBride story, in late 1856 a group of whites that included Silas Morrison descended from Bear River Ridge, intending to cross Bear River and explore the southern slope of the valley. With them was a late arrival, an Australian named Charles Hicks. The group was doubtful about letting Hicks join them, and only agreed to do so after he promised to "be SURE not to make any trouble."[48]

But Hicks broke his promise.

The group crossed the river and went by an Indian camp, which was located on the future site of the second Bear River School.[49] The men "passed the encampment peaceably enough, but as they did, Hicks apparently spied an attractive Indian girl." The whites camped about half a mile south of the Indians. Hicks announced that "he was going hunting to see if he could get some meat."[50]

He had a different quarry in mind. Soon the whites "heard a commotion down the hill at the Indian encampment and then, after a bit, a gun shot!" Hicks never returned. The next day the whites rode to the Indian camp and indicated they wanted Hicks back. Then they rode back up to Bear River Ridge.[51]

Hicks, it turned out, "had gone straight to the Indian camp and tried to get the Indian girl. The chief and other men objected, and there was a struggle during which one Indian was knifed and killed." An Indian from Eel River managed to wrest Hicks's gun from him. Hicks ran for the river and was half way across when the Indian fired at him, hitting Hicks in the shoulder. Hicks managed to reach the other side of the river and crawl out of sight.[52] Then:

> The next day, the Indians did the best they could. They sent some squaws across the river with water and food. The squaws, when they found him, treated his wound by packing it with herbs and made a litter for carrying him.[53]

The Indian women hollered until they caught the attention of the whites on the ridge. The women then left Hicks. The whites came down and got Hicks and took him to their camp, where he died.[54]

The *Humboldt Times* soon printed a letter from someone calling himself "Eel River" that told a different story. In this version, several whites were hunting on Bear River. One of them, Charles Hicks, went to a nearby Indian rancheria, where he was "attacked by about fifteen diggers. . . ." In the melee that followed, Hicks and an Indian were wounded.[55]

The *Times's* account is similar to that of Knyphausen Geer's. Geer continued the story, stating that Hicks was attended by a doctor[56] but that he died from a severed artery. After Hicks's burial, Thomas Hawley, who was his trapping partner, exclaimed, "Who'll go with me? I can't eat or sleep in peace until I kill a God Damned Digger."[57] Hawley, Geer, and several others accordingly set off after the Indians, who had fled northeast over Bear River Ridge and then down Price Creek. The pursuers finally located them near Grizzly Bluff. The whites gathered local reinforcements and in the morning eleven men attacked the Indian camp. According to Geer, "we fought and killed quite a lot. . . . They never resisted."[58]

Another version comes from Seth Kinman, whose story is similar to Geer's: an unprovoked attack on Hicks by a "whole squad of Indians." Kinman's conclusion to the incident was more graphic than Geer's: "We slaughtered Indians in piles and the work of slaughter and revenge went on."[59]

For years the "bad Indian" accounts of the *Times*, Geer, and Kinman were the only reports available that described the Hicks incident. The Morrison-McBride version of the Hicks story was not published until 1995.[60] Only then was it revealed that a large group of Indians were killed simply because they tried to prevent one of their women from being raped. Such was the white vigilantes' version of justice.

times did the Indians burn my cabin. I was engaged in dairying—making butter—and a large quantity of this was stored under the cabin in a kind of a cellar and it melted and ran down the hill, a distance of 200 yards."[61] Kinman failed to mention that these attacks may have been retaliatory, for he was known to have shot Indians on sight.[62]

In October 1860, John Lewis Southmayd and his partner, Osgood, returned to their ranch to find their house burned, "no doubt," as the *Humboldt Times* put it, "set on fire by Indians."[63] The following June, not having learned their lesson, the two ranchers left their house again; they were gone only a few hours but that was long enough for them to be ". . . robbed by Indians of every portable article of furniture, as well as clothing, blankets and provisions." It was the third invasion of Southmayd and Osgood's property, and although ". . . the cash value of the property stolen did not exceed, probably, two hundred and fifty dollars, . . . the annoyance arising from the coercive familiarities is not to be reckoned with in dollars and cents. . . ."[64]

Other "coercive familiarities" may have occurred. Referring to the early 1860s, Historian Owen C. Coy claimed, without citing his sources, that "the ranges on Yager Creek were those most seriously affected during the earlier years of the war, with the result that a large part of the stock was removed to the coast region near Bear and Mattole rivers. These valleys became overstocked and likewise were infested by hostile bands."[65]

According to Viola Russ McBride, the Russ ranch house was twice approached by Indians when Joseph Russ was gone and his wife Zipporah left with the children. Once, an Indian boy who was raised by the Russes foiled the attempt when he persuaded Zipporah to shoot a hawk from a tree. This feat so impressed the Indians that they promptly left. In the other instance, John Mackey from the Mattole Valley rode up to find the Russ house surrounded by Indians. He approached with gun in hand and

The Southmayd Ranch house, 1900 (DTC, colorized by JR).

the Indians fled. Mackey entered the house to find one of the Russ children hidden "under an overturned washtub and the rest under her [Zipporah's] skirts."[66]

As the above reports indicate, Indians in the Bear River area had burned houses, stolen or ruined goods, and frightened people. In apparent response to such acts, Captain William B. Hull of the Second California Volunteer Infantry received, in early 1864, "orders directing me to take the field and capture or *kill* all Indians found between the northern boundary of the Mendocino Reservation and Bear River, in Humboldt County."[67] [emphasis added] Apparently no one at the time questioned the use of deadly force against a group of people accused of no more than theft and vandalism.

That March, a detachment of soldiers from Company E, First Battalion, California Mountaineers, pursued Indians over much of southwestern Humboldt County. The unit's commander, Lt. W. W. Frazier, reported Indians "killing horses and cattle on Bear River." He also noted that his troops had recovered "several articles of clothing, supposed to be taken from Mr. Russ' house when robbed by them [the Indians] some time since."[68] In early April the same soldiers nearly caught an Indian raiding party, which left behind "frying pans, milk pans, earthenware, cups and saucers; property they had stolen from the citizens on Bear River. We also found the remains of cattle, potatoes and pumpkins."[69]

And this appears to be the worst the Bear River Indians had done. According to Viola Russ McBride, the rapist Charles Hicks was the "only white man killed on Bear River by Indians."[70] When, a few years later, the Indians went on a potato and pumpkin rampage, the response was for the state militia to attempt to "capture or kill" all the Indians.

In the accounts of the early white settlement of Bear River, there is no mention of the permanent Indian villages that had long occupied the north side of the valley. There had, in fact, been several, as noted by two ethnographers: Pliny Goddard's informants named six villages[71] on the lower river, and Gladys Nomland, with information from a different interviewee, mapped eight.[72] The process by which this string of Indian communities was converted into ranchland has never been fully described, but the search and destroy tactics of the state militia must have removed most or all of the village inhabitants from their homeland on Bear River.

This removal was apparently still in progress in 1864, for in that year it appears that many white residents of Bear River, imagining themselves to still be under dire threat by the Indians, had vacated their properties; in the presidential election that fall only four votes were cast in the local precinct. Come the following year, however, many whites had returned, since a state and county election drew thirty-two local voters.[73]

And by 1865 almost all of the land in the lower Bear River valley and its north slope up to the ridge had been patented.[74] No mention is made of how title of the land was transferred from the previous owners, the Bear River Indians. The next ten years found land patenting of smaller areas south and northeast of the river.[75] Despite these acquisitions, the white community in the valley experienced population stasis; the 1875 election found twenty-nine voters present, three less than a decade earlier.[76]

Then came 1876, and the bright eye of Nellie Wildwood, new correspondent to the *West Coast*

*Signal,* focused upon Bear River. Calling the area a "little paradise," Nellie noted, however, the dominating (and sometimes deleterious) influence of the topography:

> Bear River valley lies between some of the hills of the Coast Range, and does not exceed half a mile in width at the widest point. The main river, or North Fork, takes its rise some seventeen or eighteen miles inland, just southeast of Mount PIERCE, more familiarly known as "The Monument," and empties into the ocean. It is as full of kinks and turns as an old maid's temper, and in ascending a distance of five miles, one has to ford it about twenty times. The wagon road lies in the bed of the river often, as the banks are so perpendicular it is impossible to go on the land. The whole valley is used for dairying purposes, the hills making fine ranges for the cows.[77]

A year after Nellie's trip came another newcomer–innovation. In the fall of 1877 A. D. Spear, who had located on Bear River Ridge, announced plans to manufacture cheese. Butter was something Bear River had aplenty, but Spear, "an experienced cheese maker," saw the opportunity to expand the scope of the area's dairying operations. He accordingly constructed two buildings for cheese processing, piped in "cold water from mountain springs," and introduced "all the modern improvements which have made cheese making a success in the Eastern States and Canada." Spear was hoping to offset the ". . . statistical fact that California has never yet produced enough cheese for home consumption. . . ."[78]

As Spear worked during the winter on his cheese factory, a January storm disrupted the valley's transportation, wrecking Clark, DeLasseaux & Company's ferryboat. Another boat of unspecified function, Captain Brown's *Black Rover,* was left as the only "vessel afloat in this vicinity."[79]

During these years Joseph Russ assiduously accumulated land throughout much of Humboldt County, a large part of which was in the Bear River area. In 1881 Elliott's history noted that:

> . . . Joseph Russ owns thousands of acres which he has divided into suitable ranges, and he is still laying out new farms on Cape and Bear River ridges, where the largest dairies are situated. Mr. Russ is fitting up a dairy in the heart of the Bear River country, which will be one of the largest in the county. All this country is well supplied with spring water for stock and dairy use.
>
> Of the eighty-one dairies[80] in the Bear River country, Mr. Russ owns twenty, nineteen of which are leased. On these eighty-one dairies, 4,580 cows are milked, being an average of a trifle over fifty-six cows to the dairy. These 4,580 cows yielded 732,800 pounds of butter for the season of 1881, being an average of 160 pounds to the cow. . . . The great bulk of this butter is shipped to Eureka and San Francisco markets.[81]

With 81 dairies, butter was king at Bear River, but it rested on a tottering throne. (See sidebar 3.)

Elliott's 1881 history caught agricultural activity in Bear River at, or near, its peak.[82] It was also a time of high tide for the area's largest landowner, Joseph Russ. Humboldt County assessments for that year showed Russ owning

Four-footed cheese factories at the Bunker Hill Ranch (CPH, colorized by JR).

### 3. A Better Place for Butter

Richard Johnston, who was embroiled with Russ in their loan dispute, provided some specific information about dairy operations:

> A good milker will milk twenty cows in two hours and a half, or three hours at the farthest. . . . We churn every day by horse power, wash the butter thoroughly with water in the churn. . . . [The butter] is either moulded into what is called two pound rolls, or put down solid . . . [as] one hundred pounds of butter. . . .
>
> A dairy of 100 cows requires the labor of five men for about five months,[83] and four men for another month, and three men until the cows are dried up, except when they feed. The milking season lasts in Humboldt County on Bear River, seven months. On the Mattole from five to six months. On the farming land in the valleys, longer.[84]

Other dairy workers described the milking process. It wasn't a picnic. In the early days on Bear River milking was not done in a barn but in an open corral. A cowboy drove the herd into the corral at about 3:00 A.M. and milking began in the dark. The milkers carried a lantern, a bucket, and a stool with them, moving from cow to cow. Each milker had his own string of cows that he would milk in the same order every day. The corral was covered with crushed rock, but on rainy days the surface still turned to mud, so that "it wasn't unusual for a cowboy to lose his boots" as moved through the corral.[85] There is no report about how much mud and rainwater wound up in the milk buckets.

Johnston described Bear River dairying at its high point in the early 1880s. He also alluded to a problem with the area's forage:

> . . . [O]n most of the dairy ranches on Bear River, a cow can be kept on every four acres. The valley or farm land, which is a rich alluvial deposit . . . , can be made to keep a cow to the acre.[86]

Johnston may not have foreseen the day when hand milkers would be replaced by machines, but his statistics suggested another change that was coming. "Rich alluvial" land in the Eel River valley and elsewhere could provide four times as much forage, per acre, as that at Bear River. Gradually Eel River bottom land was cleared and wetlands reclaimed, while potato and grain growing there was reduced. Dairy cows increasingly occupied the lower Eel, their milk creating products that, starting in 1884, could be easily shipped by rail to Humboldt Bay. Bear River, remote and offering less fertile land, could not, in the long run, compete. Yet it held out for a time, perhaps because of its reputation. J. A. Mulcahy stated that:

> From 1904 to 1908 each year I made a trip to Bear River to purchase a year's supply of butter for the Korbel, Riverside and Glendale lumber manufacturers. The Bear River Dairymen were fine Swiss people who knew their business. The butter they made would keep much better than the Creamery butter made in Humboldt County. They would deliver the butter in 50 and 100 pound kegs to Singley Station. I would go there, test the butter and ship it to Arcata. I recall the last shipment was in 1908 when 11 tons was shipped to Arcata and distributed from there.[87]

This represented the end of Bear River's dairying heyday:

> The dairies began to fade in the early 1900s. Some stayed in operation but not many. Sheep came in to replace the dairy cows and beef cattle took the place of other stock. . . . The Bear River country went into the raising of sheep, selling wool and lambs of a quality second to no other place in the state.[88]
>
> Nearly a century later, in 2002, dairy operations were concentrated in the Eel River valley and the Arcata bottom.[89] Of the 81 dairies that once occupied Bear River, nary a one remained. Humboldt ranchers had found better places to make butter.

or co-owning property valued at over $380,000, more than twice as much as his nearest rival, William Carson.[90] Russ was assembling a land empire that would exceed 150,000 acres[91] and would include a collection of some 30 ranches, most of them in the Bear River area. One reviewer of Russ's business transactions reported that "between 1857 and 1886, the Recorder's Office lists 296 land transactions with Russ as the grantee, plus 44 patents."[92] He was serving in the state assembly when in July 1882 the *San Francisco Call* announced that "Hon. Joseph Russ, of Ferndale, Humboldt County, is mentioned as a candidate for Governor on the Republican ticket."[93]

But Russ was not nominated for governor. Instead, he was implicated in a gigantic land fraud scheme that attempted, and partially succeeded, in illegally securing thousands of acres of prime timberland on Redwood Creek and Prairie Creek.[94] He died in October 1886, five months after the district court in San Francisco quashed the indictment against him.[95]

The Russ ranches in the Bear River Ridge-Bear River-Cape Ridge area were numerous and often either poetically or enigmatically named. "Lone Star" and "West Point" were outdone by "Bunker Hill" and "Central Park," which in turn were eclipsed by "Dublin Heights" and "Mazeppa."[96]

As Elliott's history indicated, by 1881 all but one of the twenty Russ ranches in the Bear River area were leased. A notable number of Italian-Swiss dairymen put in time at Bear River as lessees or workers. Many of them came from a single canton in Switzerland. (See sidebar 4.)

By the end of the 19th century, everyday life in Bear River had receded from the headlines of the county's newspapers. In the early 1900s reportable excitement transpired only occasionally.

Two such instances involved animal attacks and occurred within a year of each other. In November 1903, Fred Richardson, who lived on the north side of Bear River Ridge,[97] found a "wild cat" trying convert a turkey into dinner. Richardson seized the only weapon available, "an ordinary hammer . . . and entered the fray, and with one or two well directed blows, killed the cat and saved the turkey."[98] It was a timely rescue, since it occurred just before Thanksgiving.

The next year, across the Bear River valley to the south, a panther inspected the Dublin Heights Ranch, found that the two-year-old son

# Bear River

The prosaically named Green Pond Ranch lies but a few ridges away from the blue Pacific (JR).

of Cipriano and Theodorlinda Ambrosini[99] was available and carried the child off preparatory to "eating it at its leisure." According to the newspaper account, Cipriano

> ... was taking care of morning milk in the dairy, when startled by the fearful scream from his child, he rushed out to see his baby in the jaws of a ferocious panther, who, hampered by the weight of the child was prevented from making rapid progress in the direction of the woods.

Cipriano grabbed a stick and immediately gave chase, pursuing the panther for nearly a mile before the fatigued feline "finally dropped the child and escaped into the woods." Remarkably, the little boy was unhurt, suffering only the tearing of his clothes. A posse of men and dogs were soon after the panther but failed to catch it.[100]

Like catching a panther, reaching the ranches in the middle section of Bear River was never an easy task. As Nellie Wildwood noted in 1876, going up the valley from Capetown required numerous river crossings, which could not be made in times of high water. By the 1920s an alternate route had appeared on the map: it left Bear River Ridge Road about two miles southeast of the junction with the Wildcat Road. From there it seemingly dropped off the edge of the earth, twisting southward down a spur ridge past the Bolivia and Green Pond ranches to reach Bear River on the Walter and Audrey Ambrosini property.[101] After passing the Ambrosini house the road crossed the river on a covered bridge.[102]

The Bear River bridge caught the attention of bridgeologist S. Griswold Morley,[103] who was compiling a book that ultimately listed 29 California covered bridges, 12 of which were in Humboldt County. Morley, who was also a

### 4. The Switzerland of Humboldt County

Canton Ticino is the southernmost state in Switzerland, the only one that has Italian as its sole official language.[104] It lies in a beautiful section of the southern Alps and includes parts of Lake Lugano and Lake Maggiore. Yet Ticino has had its difficulties. A geographer in the early 19th century, Conrad Malte-Brun, was harsh and brief in describing the area: "The canton of Tesino [Ticino] is the poorest, and the people the most ignorant of any in Switzerland."[105]

Poor the Ticinoians might have been, but ignorant they were not. By the late 19th century they had devised an effective method for ending their poverty: migrate to Humboldt County.

Records are incomplete, but between 1875 and 1914, more than a score of men from Ticino arrived at Bear River to engage in dairying, many on ranches owned by the Russ family.[106] Perhaps the first of this group was Bernardino

What they left behind: stone hut in Canton Ticino (WM, partly colorized by JR).

# Bear River 17

> Genzoli, who came from the town of Lodrino in 1875 and "immediately found work in a dairy on Bear river ridge." Nine years later, Bernardino joined forces with his brother, Morello, and leased the Harken Ranch near Capetown. There followed a progression of other Genzoli ranches—at Bear River, Elk River, and Arcata bottom, the latter of which Genzoli was operating in 1915.[107]
>
> Martin Ambrosini also emigrated from Lodrino, arriving in Humboldt County in 1882. He "commenced his career with humble employment in dairies on Bear River Ridge and near Ferndale. When he had accumulated considerable means by faithful work and wise economy, Mr. Ambrosini . . . in 1895 purchased twenty acres . . . [near] the town of Ferndale. This he has improved to great extent, and has engaged in the dairy business there since that time."[108]
>
> Fedele Guglielmina's biography sums up the experience of many of the transplanted Ticinoians:
>
>> . . . his early training among the Alps mountains in Switzerland has combined with favorable conditions in this region [Humboldt County] to win him success in the line which has been his life work [dairying] up to now. His prosperous career speaks well for the land of his birth and for the land of his adoption. Reared in a region noted for the productiveness of its herds, he became familiar with the care of dairy cattle from boyhood. But he was ambitious for greater returns than the intense competition and small areas of his own country made possible, and settled in the new world, which has indeed proved a land of promise in his case.[109]
>
> Although Bear River was considerably lower than the Alps, it became a welcoming place for Italian-Swiss dairymen with lofty aspirations.

professor of Spanish at University of California Berkeley, in 1938 noted the interesting approach to the bridge he called "Ambrosini's":

> To reach . . . Ambrosini's ranch, six miles above Capetown, you must drive fourteen miles south from Ferndale, over one of those tremendous long rounded hills or mountains which are a specialty of Humboldt County. The gravel road is unfenced, one of those aimless modified cart tracks that seem to have laid themselves out on the line of least resistance. No signposts mark the forks, and if you fail to heed carefully the last rancher's directions, you are as likely as not to land ten miles away from where you aimed, and find no soul to set you on your way. But if you follow the rule "Take every right-hand turn," you will meander for a

The Bear River covered bridge (MWC, colorized by JR).

distance along the hippopotamus back, and then, after having opened and shut at least five cattle gates, drop down by second-gear zigzags into the valley of Bear River. There you will come to a small brown bridge, obviously new, with iron roof and board sides. The stream, modest in autumn, flows lazily under the flooring. The twelve-by-twelve truss timbers are in part new and sawn, in part old and hewn. The hewn ones were evidently taken from an earlier structure. Steep twenty-seven-foot plank approaches, uncovered, follow the fashion of this region. Near by lies Ambrosini's, not so isolated as you might think, for he has many neighbors up and down Bear [River]Valley.[110]

Years later, Audrey Ambrosini indicated that Morley had underestimated the ranch gate count, claiming that there were about seven gates to open and close, thereby requiring fourteen car stops. Ambrosini was living nearby when the bridge was built, and she "saw it taken out by Bear River in 1955."[111] Afterwards state highway engineer John Canfield was sent in to build a replacement bridge out of logs. Canfield had his crew construct a large center pier for the bridge. Walter Ambrosini, who was observing the work, told Canfield, "I am afraid you've made the center pier too wide. It will be too much of an obstruction during flood stage." Canfield responded with a polite demurral. It then rained heavily for two days. When he subsequently checked the bridge, the pier had vanished. Canfield indicated that:

> A week or so later, when the river was reduced in volume where it could again be diverted to one side, we rebuilt the pier. This time I consulted with my rancher friend and followed most of his advice. . . .

I later learned that this log bridge remained in place for about five years before it was replaced by a permanent concrete structure.[112]

Both Morley and Ambrosini would have likely complained about another route to the valley floor. This was a private road that left the Wildcat Road a couple of miles west of the Bear River Ridge Road junction and made at least 11 switchbacks as it descended through Russ and Morrison ranches to reach the river about two miles west of the Ambrosini bridge.[113]

East of the bridge, the Bear River valley narrowed to a canyon. Brothers Victor and Ferdinand Ambrosini ranched an opening above the river on the slopes of Bear River Ridge. In the valley below them the Teichgraber family had steep hillside property that stretched across both sides of the river. The Ambrosinis reached their ranch from a road that descended from Bear River Ridge west of Kinman Pond. A half-mile upriver from Teichgrabers was the Barbettini Ranch. Although part of it was on the river, the ranch was accessed by a road from Bear River Ridge.[114] The last ranch up the river canyon belonged to Alice and Arthur Chase, who homesteaded the Monument Ranch in the 1870s.[115] Their property was about a mile east of the river and a mile west of Mount Pierce, a landform more recently known as Monument Peak.[116] (See sidebar 5.)

When Mabel Lowry arrived in the valley in 1931, she found "there was no telephone, electricity or school."[117] Bear River had not always been schoolless, however. In 1868 the first school in the area was established on the Johnston Ranch, about halfway between the center of the Bear River community and Capetown. Then, in 1879, Capetown started its own school and the Bear River School moved to a new location upstream, on the north side of the river.[118] An elderly Indian[119] would help the younger southside students cross Bear River on a log to reach the school. Sometimes the students crossed on their own, once with almost dire results. (See sidebar 6.)

### 5. A Monumental Task

In 1853 Deputy Surveyor Henry Washington came north to establish the "Initial Point" for the cadastral survey[120] of northwestern California. Washington had already used Mount San Bernardino as the initial point for southern California (Mount Diablo became the initial point for central and part of northern California). Washington, whose political leanings are not known, named the northwestern initial point for Franklin Pierce, who was President at the time.[121] Pierce, as a "Doughface" Democrat, was one of a series of 1850s presidents who, although from the North, sympathized with the South on the slavery issue.[122] He supported the Fugitive Slave Act and has consistently been ranked as one of the country's worst presidents.[123] Unsurprisingly, Mount Pierce soon came to be called Monument Peak, a politically neutral name that merely described its function.[124]

> ### 6. "An Act of Bravery"
>
> One day in May 1889 Georgie Morrison, 13, was riding to the Bear River School in company with Amelia[125] Meyer (no age given), the school teacher. When "opposite the Geer place Georgie rode across the river to bring Jennie Lowry over."[126] The first crossing went okay, but on the way back things became difficult. Georgie had Jennie, age nine, behind him on his horse,
>
>> . . . and when in the middle of the stream the horse began to rear and plunge, throwing the girl, who clung to Georgie, and they both went into the river, which was pretty high and running swift. She lost her hold of him in the fall, but the brave boy seized hold of her clothing, and they both were carried quite a distance down the river. The girl seemed to be perfectly helpless, but the boy struggled manfully until he reached the shore, and dragged his friend after him, who was nearly as heavy as himself. Miss Meyer tried to ride to their rescue, but her horse refused to go to them, and all she could do was to give them words of encouragement. They got out on the opposite side from where the teacher was. As soon as the boy got to shore he looked back at the teacher and took off his hat and waved it over his head. What a grand subject for an artist, to see the little hero standing by his prostrate and almost lifeless friend, and waving his hat over his head. After he had regained his strength he lifted the girl to her feet and held her until she was able to stand. Georgie cannot swim, but he thinks the oil coat he was wearing buoyed him up.[127]
>
> Surely it was an instance of spreading an oil coat over troubled waters.

Bear River School #2 was washed out in 1905 by a flood, whereupon school #3 was established in an "old Indian hut" on the south side of the river that had probably belonged to the students' river-crossing escort. This school closed in 1932. It was "later used as a sheep shed and a horse barn until it fell to pieces and was burned." In 1938 Bear River School #4 was built about a quarter mile upstream from the forks of the river, on the south side of the main branch. The creation of the fourth school required a lot of work. First, the local parents had to produce enough kids to meet the minimum enrollment requirements. This the Lowrys, Ambrosinis, Morrisons, and McBrides did, contributing eight young children among them.[128]

Second, a new school house was needed. Will Lowry, Mabel's husband

> . . . obtained permission from Joe Russ to tear down an old abandoned dairy on the Comisto Ranch and haul the lumber

Bear River School #4 (JR).

down to the river to use to construct the school house. The lumber was sound and well worth using. Shingles, windows, nails, etc., were still needed. Seven families of the valley gave a lamb barbecue complete with salads, bread, coffee, dessert, all donated. Tickets were sold for 75 cents each in Ferndale and the surrounding area. The people came and approximately $150 was cleared. The money purchased the needed materials and work began. Sundays found most of the neighborhood helping under the direction of Walter Ambrosini as head carpenter. The men sawed and hammered and the women furnished a picnic lunch.[129]

The school was provided with the desks, blackboards, etc. from the Bunker Hill School at the top of the ridge, which had closed. Bear River's fourth school operated until 1947, when only one student, Joe Ambrosini, was left. Joe then finished his elementary education in Ferndale. The schoolhouse later became the home of Mabel Lowry.[130]

In 1945 the valley witnessed two signal events, one an addition and one a subtraction. That fall, the local ranchers made an agreement with Pacific Telephone and Telegraph: the ranchers would furnish and install phone poles, and the company would wire them and connect the system with the company's main line that reached the outside world.[131]

That October, as Ed Sacchi was digging holes for the poles, a fire broke out on the old Williams ranch, which lay high on the north side of the valley just below the Wildcat Road. Various "men on the ridge and from the valley fought the fire and thought it was contained." The next day, however, "... a high wind came up and the fire spread from ranch to ranch. It came [down] nearly to the river. Concha Morrison had made sandwiches for the men on the fire line. Her aunt tried to take the food up to the men but they yelled at her, 'Go back! Go back! You'll be burned up.' She left the sack of sandwiches and the bottom was burned out of it."[132]

The ranchers from Bear River fought the blaze by backfiring and using wet gunny sacks to beat the flames back when they approached a house or barn. A call went out for regular fire fighters, but they were all busy with other fires in the county. Another call was made to Petrolia, and "a dozen or more men" assembled and went over the ridge to fight the western end of the Bear River fire. Bob Morrison, Concha's husband, later called the roll of burned ranches: "about half of Seattle . . . plus all of Olympia, Bonanza, Morrison, Smith, Upper Johns[t]on, Central Park, Lower Eastern . . . [it] was stopped on the Peters Place just before reaching the Capetown ranch."[133] It recalled the big fire of 1889, when the Russes' Bolivia, Seattle, Olympia, What Cheer, and Green Pond burned, along with several others.[134]

Despite the diversion of the fire, the phone line was completed. All the ranches were on a single line, and all the phones rang whenever there was a call. Finally, in November 1982, Bear River entered the modern world when dial service was established. No longer would an early morning call wake everyone in the valley when "some rancher [was] making arrangements for lamb shipping or sheep shearing."[135]

In earlier days, the valley's tanbark was peeled and sold. Then, in the 1950s, logging commenced in the timber on the valley's south side. Infrastructure accordingly improved. The road from the ridge to the valley received a coat of black top. A road was built to the timber claim, "allowing trucks with their trailers to come in and go out with their huge loads of logs." Ranchers also used the new road for their stock trucks. The stock changed over time. Starting in the late 1970s, ranchers, concerned about predators, replaced many of the sheep flocks with cattle.[136]

Other alterations affected the valley, but some things remained the same. John Southmayd's ranch, which dated from 1856, became part of the Russ domain. It was given to Viola Russ McBride by her father as a wedding present. When he died in the 1930s Viola took over "all his enterprises," and she and her family were forced to live closer to Ferndale. "In later years, however, Viola spent much of her time at Southmayd, painting and writing and enjoying leisure life in the country." The millennium came and went, and the ranch still had neither telephone nor electricity.[137]

# Chapter 2
# Capetown

Capetown was not an especially appropriate name for the small community that developed some three miles from the nearest cape and a couple of miles even from the ocean, but it was an improvement over an earlier designation—Gas Jet—which commemorated a stream of escaping natural gas that for a time helped to illuminate the vicinity. It took a while for the improvement to be made. For over eight years, April 1868 to July 1876, letters sent from the town's post office were postmarked Gas Jet.[138] Then the post office closed, jettisoning Gas Jet. When the pseudonymous Nellie Wildwood rode through in October 1876, she noted the nearby "ocean with its dancing waves," but she failed to mention the apparently now nameless community at the crossing of Bear River.[139]

Nellie also was silent about the actual gas jet, which she would have reached just south of the bridge over Bear River. There stood a pipe, some six to eight feet high, that spewed flames into the sky, a spectacular but inefficient use of the combustible material that was later improved upon when the gas became the lighting source for the Capetown hotel.[140]

Once the Gas Jet post office closed, it appears that residents for a time received their mail at the distant False Cape Post Office, which was located several miles up the coast at Centerville.[141] This facility closed on January 7, 1879, the same day that the Capetown Post Office opened.[142] The latter served until 1937, when it merged with the Ferndale office.[143]

Long before the whites were trying to permanently name their community, the Bear River (Nekanni) Indian tribe had a village at the mouth of the river and another on or very near the later location of Capetown. The ethnographer Pliny Goddard stated that the village of "atcanco xebi" was located "where the store and hotel are."[144] Another ethnographer, Gladys Nomland, gave this village's name as "Chil-sheck."[145]

By the mid-1850 whites had settled at several locations in the Bear River valley. It is unclear which of them first occupied the Capetown area, but there are two pairs of leading candidates. According to their biography, Martin and Rachel Branstetter arrived on lower Bear River in 1854, where they "improved a large ranch of government land . . . and engaged in general farming and stock raising. They experienced the customary exciting and dangerous times of the early settlers in this vicinity, but prospered and both lived to a good old age. . . ."[146] But Nellie Wildwood contradictorily claimed that "the first settlement was made in 1855 by Mr. O'Dell and his partner, Mr. Fred Cassins. They had a stock ranch first, though now it is used as a dairy."[147]

When the Surveyor General's office mapped the area in 1858, there was no indication of either the Branstetters or of O'Dell and Cassins; the only residence depicted was "Swale's [sic] house," located in the vicinity of the later business district of Capetown.[148] "Swale" was probably Thomas Swales, who in 1863 wrote out a most interesting will, which stated in part:

> It is my will, that my two Indian boys, if they stay with me till my death (Sam and

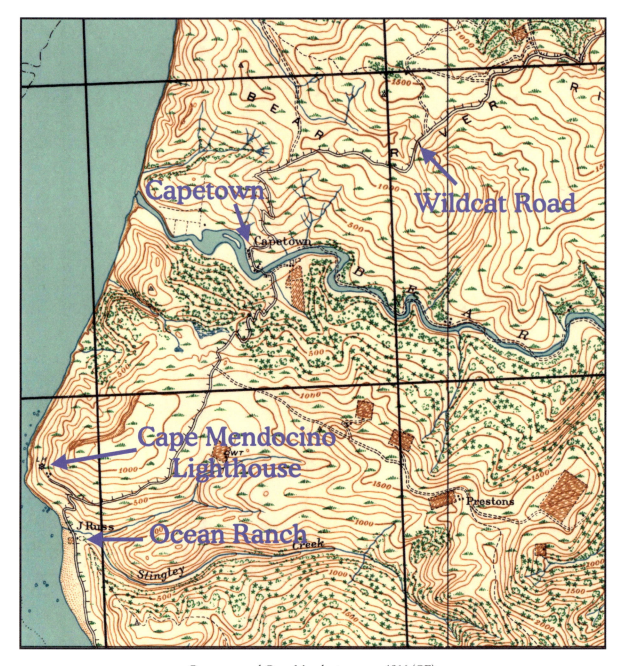

Capetown and Cape Mendocino area, 1916 (CE).

Peter), or are released by terms of their indenture, shall receive each a good horse, saddle and bridle, two good suits of clothes, and $50 in money.

I bequeath to my son John William Swales, one dollar, he not being a good boy.

I bequeath to my daughter, Mrs. Mary Ann Leach, one dollar she having already received her share.

I bequeath to my illegitimate son, Robert Batty, now in Morgan County Illinois, two fifths of all my property....[149]

A traveler with the signature "W" reported on the increased population in the area in November 1859, noting that:

Bear River Valley is finer agricultural country than I expected. It is narrow, there being about enough room between the mountains for respectable sized farms, gardens, houses, corrals, dairies, etc. On descending the mountains to the valley a beautiful view is presented. The farms of McGregor, Swales, Webster, Carson, O'Dell and others are visible, and the mountains, the grade of which is so gradual that a wagon and team could be driven up it any place is covered with stock.[150]

The first official Humboldt County map, from 1865, shows not only properties belonging to Branstetter and the O'Dell-Cassin partnership, but also places T. S. Watts's parcel between them.[151]

Somewhat later Thomas Stewart ranched near the Capetown Post Office. A biographical sketch indicated that he was a very persistent hunter:

> At one time he undertook to rid the county of grizzly bears, being engaged for that job by Mr. Russ for two years; he slew a great many, and found them to be tough customers; into one of them he had to fire thirty-two bullets before he brought him down; it proved to be a very fat specimen.[152]

Certainly this was an exceptional exploit, yet one that was arguably exceeded by the wife of Grant Johnston, who resided several miles upriver. When F. J. Preston caught a 400-pound "cinnamon bear" in April 1904, Mrs. Johnston, "a plucky little woman," rode several miles through a terrible wind, walked up to within 15 feet of the bear, and shot him dead.[153] Plucky, indeed.

Thomas Stewart added to his resume by becoming the postmaster at Gas Jet in 1870,[154] operating the town's first hotel,[155] and then, in 1878, donating land for the Capetown School. Stewart was a picturesque individual who "wore a long beard, reputed to reach his waist, but [he] always kept it buttoned inside his shirt. . . ."[156] When but six years old Stewart, who was born in Scotland, started service as a cabin boy on his uncle's ship, running away at age 18 to become a sailor on the Great Lakes. He next mined coal in Illinois, "was financially ruined" in Missouri, and came west by wagon train, arriving in Hydesville in 1864. Stewart then took up dairying and established himself at Capetown.[157] Eventually, the siren song of the called sea again, this time with disastrous results; Stewart set off towards the blue Pacific in a small boat and promptly disappeared at the mouth of the Mattole River.[158]

Stewart's land donation for the school site came a decade after the start of another school some two miles upriver on the Johnston Ranch. Beginning in 1868, the latter school attempted to serve students from the entire lower valley. The road that ran up the canyon from Capetown, however, was subject to the fluvial fluctuations of the river, and it "could not be traveled in the winter time."[159] This periodically prevented the attendance of certain students. When the Christian Anderson family arrived at the Spicy Breezes Ranch, south of Capetown, in 1878, the event solved the problem; the Andersons had such a large family that it became possible for Capetown to have its own school. Accordingly, Chris Anderson and Ben Flint hauled lumber down the Beach Road from Centerville and built the compact but serviceable structure that still stands at the roadside today.[160]

An article about the Capetown School

The Capetown School had a very tall flagpole (DTC, colorized by JR).

generously names two individuals as the first school teacher. At one point it gives the honor to William Keefe, about whom it says nothing further. Later the other nominee, Charles Harkins, is provided with a brief biography:

> He was a powerful man, as broad as he was long. He raised tobacco on his ranch, and of this he was said to have chewed aplenty. Another of his specials was "Peachblow Potatoes,"[161] reputed to be a little less in size than a ten pound pail. He was unmarried, but a niece and nephew were among his first pupils.[162]

In 1896 Sadie Flowers became the Capetown School teacher. She taught about 30 students scattered over 10 grades. The highest grade had an advanced curriculum: algebra, geometry, physics, literature, and bookkeeping. Flowers also taught English to young male immigrants from the Azores, who had been brought to Capetown by Frank Peters, a dairy rancher who lived across the river from the school.[163]

Flowers taught for six years at Capetown before she left the profession to marry Joseph Russ Jr.[164] During her tenure, only one student, Margaret Sanders, graduated from the school; most of the others left before finishing to take up jobs.[165]

For years the Russ family offered much of the local employment. Their ranches spread across the lower Bear River area, and up onto Cape Ridge and Bear River Ridge. By 1886, the year he died, Joseph Russ Sr.'s name stretched across the county map from the ocean to near the headwaters of Monument Creek south of Rio Dell, along with outpost properties near Bald Mountain, on upper Redwood Creek, and in the vicinity of Showers Pass.[166] In March 1884 the editor of the *Ferndale Enterprise* visited Mazeppa, one of the Russ ranches north of Capetown. He found that the place required using his descriptive powers at full throttle:

This is one of Mr. Russ' principal dairy ranches. Here they have their own blacksmith shop, carpenter shop, butcher shop, harness shop, and in fact almost every trade is represented that would be required in a colony depending entirely on its own resources. This ranch boasts of one of the largest barns in the county, presenting all the conveniences of a smaller structure. Some 150 cows are milked during the milk season and employment given to 20 men. . . . On this evening everything was bustle and stir, preparing to receive friends. . . . The day had been rather blustering, but as the king of day surrendered himself behind the horizon of the briny waves and the somber robes of night were encircling this western hemisphere, the misty vapors were dispelled as if per magic and once more poured forth their effulgent rays on the balmy evening air. . . .[167]

Some 20 couples danced the somberly robed night away at Mazeppa, "till the Woodland Echo(ed) [a pun on the name of another Russ ranch] the approach of the orb of day. . . ." And then, for the 20 ranch hands at least, it was back to their labors; as the *Enterprise* put it, "each man having his allotted work to perform."[168]

In the late 19th century any dairying area needed containers for transporting butter, so it was no surprise that the Eel River valley, Bear River, and Petrolia all had cooperages that slowly and carefully hand-built firkins[169] and barrels to hold solidified butterfat. In the Bear River area there were once three cooperages, one at the Mazeppa Ranch, one at the False Cape Ranch south of Capetown, and one in downtown Capetown across from the school. Frank Peters started the last after he emigrated from the Azores in 1871 and began ranching at Bear River. Frank's brother, William, subsequently took over the cooperage and then sold it to Gus Bernardasie.[170] Gus employed Ted Francis, who was known for his speedy work. In top form, Ted could assemble "12 butter kegs a day." The last reported operator of the Capetown cooperage was Julius Albonico, who built barrels and finished firkins "until at least 1915." Albonico was known to be "notoriously short-tempered," and he confirmed this evaluation at a Capetown dance in 1906 when he attacked Josh Preston, one of the musicians, "first with his fists and then with a hatchet."[171] Perhaps Preston had refused to play "Roll out the Barrel."

In September 1885, "McTavish," writing to the *Humboldt Standard*, provided readers with a detailed account of the Capetown area that updated Nellie Wildwood's report of a decade earlier. McTavish started with the

> BEAR RIVER HOTEL, which is exceptionally neat and well kept. . . . In the vicinity there is excellent fishing and hunting and the climate being superior in all respects, many persons seek this favorite location for rest and recreation. Mr. Rodgers owns, at this point, 570 acres of land, upon which are kept 70 cows besides other live stock. Each cow will produce annually 200 pounds of butter, a market for which is found in Eureka. . . .[172]

Near the hotel was the Capetown School, which was examined thoroughly. McTavish found it was "supplied with a choice library, charts, both geographical and historical, [and] with other convenient appliances to facilitate

A squad of Capetown males appear to be waiting for something—
perhaps for the Capetown females to show up (colorized by JR).

the advancement of pupils." The teacher, Jennie McCarthy, had come from San Jose.[173]

McTavish also noted the nearby ranch of C. Harkins, who held 815 acres between the county road and coast, on most of which he ran sheep. Upriver was M. Brazil's dairy ranch, which he rented from the O'Dell estate. This represented the easternmost precincts of Capetown. Beyond that was Richard Johnston's ranch and others of what was called the Bear River area.[174]

Correspondent "E. B. C." provided readers of the *Enterprise* with an update on Capetown in March 1892, stating that:

> The Bear River section, in the springtime especially, is a perfect paradise. The hills and vales present a lovely appearance, clad in their coat of green, and the dairy cows and stock cattle are in excellent condition.[175]

E. B .C. noted that Gus Bernardasher[176] was "busily engaged in turning out butter barrels at the Capetown cooper shop," while up the hill to the north Ted Francis was "still turning out barrels at the Mazeppa cooper shop." Charles Harkin's ranch, near the ocean, was "still conducted by the Genzoli brothers, who are excellent dairymen," while "Frank Peters has greatly improved the Odell [sic] ranch since he took charge of the same." Travelers were afforded a choice between the "Capetown Hostelry," which proprietor Hunter was making into "a popular stopping-place," and Flint's "Myrtle Grove Hotel and Feed Stables," which was deemed "a first-class stopping-place," apparently for both man and beast.[177]

# Capetown

The presence of two hotels in the small community was not surprising, given the transportation conditions of the time. Capetown was "a full day's ride" from Ferndale[178] and a slightly shorter distance from Petrolia. For ranchers bringing cattle from the Mattole to Fernbridge, the trip took three days.[179] Capetown lay in a valley on either side of which were high ridges with horse-tiring grades. It was the perfect location to stop and rest from the wearying labors of the road. Petrolia resident T. K. Clark recalled that:

> Everything being normal, a two horse buckboard or a light spring wagon with two horses pulling would leave Ferndale and Petrolia each morning except Sunday. Their departure each morning would be at 7 o'clock or shortly thereafter. Usually these horses weighed in the neighborhood of 1000 to 1200 pounds. This is the weight that could trot along on level ground and down hill. Sometimes these rigs had two seats so that four or five people could be passengers. A big load could cause the male passengers to be called upon to walk up the steep hills if they were able-bodied.
>
> By noon time these mail and passenger rigs would meet at Capetown. . . .
>
> After the stage drivers and their passengers had been fed . . . they would continue on to Petrolia or Ferndale behind a fresh team.[180]

So things stood for years, and then decades. A new century began, and with it came the Advent of the Automobile. Eventually even far-flung Capetown felt its effects, most dramatically when Governor James Gillett's motorcade came through in August 1907, having left Ferndale only 45 minutes earlier.[181] No longer would travelers need to stop overnight on their way to and from Petrolia.

Another of the several hotels that at various times welcomed travelers to Capetown (DTC, colorized by JR).

Speedily approaching Capetown by car from the north (FM, colorized by JR).

Three years after Gillett's whirlwind tour,[182] the peripatetic pedagogue Delmar Thornbury[183] motored through Capetown and found that it

> ... consists of a feed stable, postoffice, hotel, store, blacksmith shop, school house, hall, a dairy and its necessary buildings. It has but one broad street, lined by eucalyptus trees.... Cape Town is a trifle over a mile from the ocean and travelers and their teams generally stop to get something to eat. After a very good dinner, we fed the automobile with fifteen gallons....[184]

The Capetown that Thornbury described was not to last much longer, but first there came a day that etched the community onto the consciousness of all Humboldt. (See sidebar 1.)

After the excitement of the Bear, calm

---

### 1. The *Bear* Comes to Bear River

It is well-known that salmon and other anadromous fishes implacably return to the stream of their birth. Therefore it should have come as little surprise when, on June 14, 1916, a bear attempted to return to its namesake river. Except that in this case the entity involved was not a creature but instead was the *S. S. Bear*, bound for San Francisco from Portland. The steamer did not complete its trip and even fell slightly short of its apparent alternate destination—Bear River.

The evening of June 14 was marked by a party at the Bismarck Hansen ranch, which was located about two miles inland from the mouth of Bear River. As midnight approached, some of the revelers thought they heard a ship's whistle in the distance and wondered if it might be a distress signal. Then the sound was heard no more and everyone returned their attention to the party.[185]

The next morning it was the sound of a telephone that alerted locals to what had indeed been a nautical disaster. Mrs. L. P. Branstetter took the call at the Cape House Hotel in downtown Capetown. It was a reporter from the *Humboldt Standard* asking for details about a shipwreck in the area. The Humboldt Bay lifesaving station and a tugboat company had received a distress call by wireless the previous night, and the *Standard* wanted an on-the-scene report.[186]

Mrs. Branstetter could not immediately comply with request as she knew of no such wreck, but she promptly set about finding out. Her method would not be wireless communication or phone, but rather the U. S. Mail, which was present in the person of Robert Frost, the local carrier, who at that moment was loading mail and goods to take northward to Ferndale. Frost changed his itinerary, mounted a horse and rode west toward the mouth of the river.[187]

Frost never made it to his destination. Rounding a hillslope at a bend in the river, he saw in the distance a large object wallowing in the surf. It was too big to be a beached whale, so he correctly concluded that it was a grounded ship. Frost immediately reversed course for Capetown.[188]

After trying to reach Japan, rolls of newsprint
have rolled in on the surf (CPH, colorized by JR).

Once back in town Frost sounded the alarm and "a group immediately gathered, hitching wagons and buggies, loaded with clothing, blankets, [and] stimulants and headed for the wreck." The rescue party was kept busy taking 29 waterlogged survivors back to the Branstetters' hotel as "doctors, nurses and neighbors in Ferndale rushed to the scene" to help.[189] Offshore, they were assisted in their efforts by a small armada of rescue vessels that included the tug *Relief*, the Coast Guard power boat *Venturesome*, the steamship *Grace Dollar*, and the battleship *Oregon*.[190]

Another vessel, less mobile, played a major part in the rescue. The Blunts Reef Lightship, anchored about five miles offshore,[191] became a temporary haven for most of the ship's passengers and crew. Fourteen lifeboats reportedly left the distressed steamer, which of course was the *S. S. Bear*. Of those, nine boats were steered westward to the safety of the lightship, two had their occupants rescued by the appropriately named tug *Relief*, two managed to land near the mouth of Bear River, and one capsized in the surf.[192] The bodies of five persons washed ashore, but the rest of the 210 passengers and crewmen survived.[193]

The previous afternoon had found the *Bear* steaming south. With the approaching dusk came fog. A sounding was taken that indicated at least 200 fathoms (1,200 feet) of water beneath the ship, with no discernable bottom. But seven minutes later the *Bear* itself found the elusive bottom by grinding

*Bear* passengers rescued by the *Grace Dollar*, (THPO, colorized by JR).

Bringing ashore boxes of Carnation Condensed Milk. The instructions on the cartons have not been followed (CPH, colorized by JR).

onto the ocean floor about a mile north of the river.[194] As one account put it, the ship "suffered internal injuries of a fatal nature."[195]

For a few days the newspapers provided accounts from the various participants in the wreck, but the excitement soon diminished. Then a new story developed that involved the disposition of the cargo. The first chapter concerned members of the crew, most especially winch operator Walter H. Villemeyer, who was found to have in his possession a suitcase containing, among other things, "a camera, two razors, a manicure set, . . . two gold bracelets, . . . a woman's ring and other articles"—not the usual items found in a sailor's kit. A Mrs. Beckwith, who had recently survived the breakers at the mouth of Bear River, identified these and other items as belonging to her, a disclosure that resulted in the arrest of Villemeyer.[196]

Besides razors and manicure sets, the Bear also contained other items of value, not the least of which was several hundred tons of newsprint packaged into six-foot-diameter rolls. J. H. Crothers, co-owner of the *Humboldt Times*, offered $500 for the lot, but the owners of the *Bear* turned him down. Subsequently the paper was dumped overboard in an attempt to lighten the ship enough that it could be towed off the beach. The huge rolls, despite weighing over 1,000 pounds each, promptly began floating towards Japan. Suddenly Crothers's offer was accepted. He quickly engaged some of the local ranchers

*S. S. Bear* near its namesake river (THPO, colorized by JR).

to bring their teams to the beach. There they waited for the incoming tide to return the peregrinating paper to the shores of California, whereupon they hauled it above the high-water mark.

So far, so good, but there was a lot of paper. It took months to gather all the rolls of newsprint and stack them on the beach, and the long row (some of it double width) that resulted stretched more than a mile and a half, all the way from Bear River to Cape Mendocino. A road was cut from the beach and a bridge put across Bear River; this allowed horse teams and wagons to move the paper as far as Capetown. From there it was transferred onto "hard-tired motor trucks" and hauled to Eureka. There it was stored in the old Eureka Foundry building at the foot of S Street.[197]

The Times Printing Company cut the newsprint into sheets of several sizes. Most of the cut paper was sold to schools and local newspapers. Requests were made "for envelopes, business cards, etc.," and entrepreneur Crothers decided to form the Humboldt Paper Company. He purchased the former Margarita Theater, which was located on E Street between 3rd and 4th streets, and converted the square tower at the back into a four-story paper warehouse, complete with hand-operated elevator. By 1922 the company "had a very good stock of fine paper for printing and coarse paper for all other lines of supply." All went well until a fire in 1931 burned the roof off the storage building and damaged the stock. It took about 50 days of cutting to salvage the undamaged paper. In 1936 the Humboldt Paper Company was sold to the Zellerbach Paper Company, the new owners probably unaware that their new business acquisition had been created by a shipwreck 20 years earlier.[198]

While the rescuing of the newsprint was an impressive accomplishment, another part of the *Bear* salvage operation was absolutely spectacular. It was determined that the *Bear's* boilers, six in all, could be recycled at a profit, if only they could be hauled to Eureka. And that was a big "if"—each cylindrical boiler was 14 feet in diameter and 14 feet long and weighed 44 tons,[199] give or take a few hundred pounds. It was at best a questionable operation, but Arthur Way, who later served as Eureka mayor and in both the state assembly and senate, was undaunted by the prospect and took the job.[200]

The boilers were too heavy and cumbersome to transport by the Wildcat Road, which climbed steeply into the mountains on its way to Ferndale. Accordingly, Way proposed to move them by beach, barge, and bay, an ingenious but complicated transportation system. Phase one involved skidding the boilers across railroad ties that had been laid on the beach. A wire rope was placed around each boiler, and the other end attached to a steam donkey, which provided the motive power. Stream crossings were bridged using the smokestack funnel from the *Bear* as a mobile culvert.[201]

Arthur Way finds a way to move the Bear's boilers (CPH, colorized by JR).

> In this way the ambulatory boilers made their way northward to the mouth of the Eel, a distance of about 12 miles. There the launch *Cornelia* waited with a barge to pull the boilers, steam donkey, chuck wagon, and "all sorts of gear" across the mouth of the Eel and up onto the Eel's north spit. Once again the donkey, wire rope, and ties were utilized as the boilers were dragged to the southwestern edge of Humboldt Bay, whence the Cornelia and her barge took everything to Eureka. From there, the boilers "were loaded onto a steamer and transported to Shanghai, China, to be installed in a ship being built there."[202]
>
> And so, far across the Pacific from the site of her demise, a part of the *Bear* lived on.

The long-retired Capetown School (JR).

returned to Capetown. Thornbury's 1910 auto trip through town proved to be a harbinger of the community's changing status. A decade later the Branstetters' hotel closed,[203] as more motorists discovered they could leave Ferndale after breakfast and be in the Mattole Valley by lunch.[204]

Only the Capetown School remained as a community building. It lingered until the 1950s, but by then its importance had diminished so completely that the exact year of its closing can no longer be recalled.[205]

Today Capetown has neither cape (which it never possessed) nor town. Branstetter's hotel building, now the family's ranch house, reposes near the barn and a row of eucalyptus trees. The schoolhouse, its sides a faded red, still stands on the opposite roadside. Not realizing they have encountered a historic setting, motorists speed by without a thought of stopping. One day a year, however, the townsite becomes a focal point of activity, for it lies at mile 86 of the 100-mile "Century Ride" Tour of the Unknown Coast, a bruising bicycling race called (by its sponsors) "California's toughest century."[206] Capetown lies in the trough between the ride's two most demanding climbs, "The Wall" that ascends Cape Ridge and the "Endless Hill" that goes up Bear River Ridge. Thus strategically positioned on the bike route, Capetown would appear poised to annually regain its glory, if only for a day. But such is not to be. The ride summary tells of a more prosaic reality:

> Mile 86 UNSTAFFED AID STATION at CAPETOWN. Porta potty, water, snacks at the side of the road.[207]

What a change a century makes. Imagine the survivors from the Bear, staggering (unaided) up from the beach to find only an UNSTAFFED AID STATION instead of Branstetters' welcoming hotel. Perhaps they never find their destination, for the murky night is no longer penetrated by the illumination of a GAS JET. *Sic transit gloria*[208] Capetown.

# Chapter 3
# Cape Mendocino Area

According to a 17th century Spanish friar named Ascension, Cape Mendocino was home to a deadly miasma that plagued mariners returning from the Philippines. The Spanish galleons followed a route that often brought them close to the coast at or near the cape. No sooner had the sailors espied the promontory than "a terrible sickness seized them," which quickly, and mercifully, ended in death. Padre Ascension asserted that the malady thus "struck down more than forty men of Cabrillo's own fleet."[209]

Over time Cape Mendocino's meteorological malevolence apparently changed modes, for there was nothing miasmatic about the southwester that ripped across the cape in January 1886 at 144 miles an hour. The contrast prompted the claim that "so, after all, Cape Mendocino is rather a peculiar place," a conclusion that the ensuing decades have done nothing to eradicate.[210]

One of the first landward reports of the area came in November 1859, when "W" confused the cape with its offshore companion, Sugarloaf Rock:

> The Cape is a round rock which I should guess is near three hundred yards in circumference at the base and over one hundred feet high. It stands about two hundred yards from low water mark in the ocean, and is surrounded by many smaller rock. The most attractive feature of this locality, to this traveler, is the appearance of hundreds of sea lions,[211] which perch their uncouth carcasses upon the low rocks, within a stone's throw of shore, and salute the passer by [sic] with their terrific howls. . . . These huge monsters keep up a continual roaring in their rocky home, which may be heard for miles above the roar of the surf.[212]

To the roaring of the wind and the roaring of the sea lions was added an even more disturbing unpleasantness—the hull-shredding effects of the offshore rocks and reefs as they tore through the undersides of unsuspecting ships. The first mile of ocean west of the cape is dotted with obvious obstacles—Off Rock, Twin Rock, Sharp Rock, and a score of smaller protrusions—while about four miles farther westward lurks Blunts Reef, described in 1909 as "the outermost danger off Cape Mendocino. It consists of two small, black rocks, awash at high tides. . . ." Southward three-fourths of a mile is the Great Break, which lies, with concealed menace, about 25 feet beneath the surface. The *Coast Pilot* warned mariners that "eastward of Blunts Reef and the Great Break are a number of dangerous rocks and sunken ledges, a description of which is unnecessary. Vessels should not attempt passage between Blunts Reef and the cape under any circumstances."[213]

But often vessels did, so that the dangerous shortcut was "pretty generally used by coasting steamers and schooners,"[214] and soon the sea between the cape and the reef splashed over the wreckage of ships whose captains had challenged the wisdom of the *Coast Pilot* and lost. The first to make the news was the *Northerner*, Captain Dall, which scraped over the reef in January 1860, tearing open her hull, and,

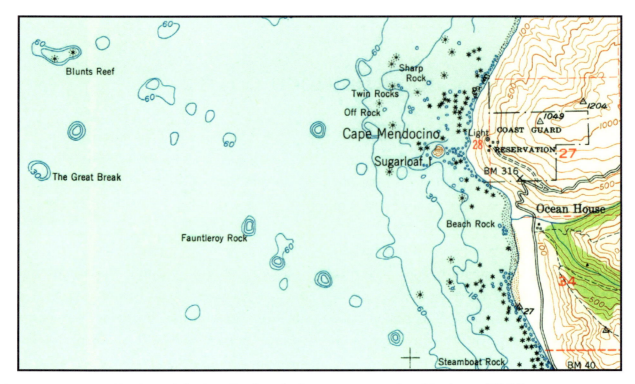

Blunt's Reef, the Great Break, and other menaces near Cape Mendocino (USGS).

although fatally wounded, managed to reach the beach near Centerville. A fierce storm raged as the passengers and crew tried to abandon ship. Thirty-eight died.[215] In 1877 the *Kittie Stevens* hit the reef, tearing away part of her keel; however, "a friendly sea following immediately after the vessel struck, lifted her over the rocks and into deep water." She made it to the Humboldt Bar, "was towed in nearly waterlogged . . . [and] was laid on the beach down near the shipyard."[216] The schooner *Anna Nermine* went ashore near the cape after losing her rudder in June 1885.[217] Five years later the steamer *Ajax*, Captain Donaldson, struck Blunt's Reef but managed to sail south to within ten miles of Shelter Cove before sinking; everyone on board made shore in lifeboats.[218]

In 1867, seven years after the *Northerner* disaster, work started on the Cape Mendocino lighthouse. It was not without incident. That August the side-wheeled lighthouse tender *Shubrick* safely landed a work crew and a "full cargo of materials for the lighthouse building." All was well so far, but the following month the *Shubrick* was steaming north with more men and supplies for the project when she struck a rock off Big Flat, some 30 miles south of her destination. The ship was beached and "everything was . . . saved from her that it was possible to get ashore." A week later the schooner *Good Templar*, which was "discharging materials for the lighthouse buildings" was forced by a heavy wind "to up anchor and put to sea. In effecting this she narrowly escaped being wrecked, and only escaped by picking her way out between numerous rocks that exist in that locality."[219]

Despite the mishaps, work continued so that "within a year, a two-story brick duplex, a carpenter shop, and a barn were completed." When it came time to transport the material for the lighthouse itself, including its Fresnel lens, the equipment was prudently shipped first to Eureka, in the summer of 1868, and then moved overland to the cape by wagons.

In the early 1860s the Singley family sold their ranch, which lay just south of the cape, to Joseph Russ, who was busily aggrandizing his net worth by acquiring agricultural property throughout much of Humboldt County. Nicholas Singley reportedly had

> . . . some good farming land . . . but quantity rather than quality appears to have governed him in his buildings, and they seem to have been thrown together more with a view to economy than comfort and durability."[220]

So it came as no surprise when Russ proceeded to build what he called Ocean House, which "became a second headquarters for the Russ ranching empire." The ranch associated with the house took the building's name.

In 1878 S. S. Johnson took charge of Ocean House,[221] providing for the needs of travelers. The *Ferndale Enterprise* was on the scene in 1881, commenting first on the approach to the stopping place:

> Down the winding grade that runs around the southern side of the ridge we go, with nothing but the "break" on our light wagon between us and the canyon a thousand feet below, or eternity, the two being, in this case, synonymous terms.[222]

Having survived the harrowing descent, succor was subsequently found at Ocean House, where the cosseted riders were able to "rest over night on a couch of down plucked from the breasts of the wild sea birds that have their homes in the haunts of the ocean. . . ."[223] The following day the Ferndale travelers rode their first six miles southward "along the ocean beach over a road as fine as any Jehu[224] could wish for . . . ," before turning inland to run through the Zanone Ranch on their way to the fair precincts of Petrolia.[225]

Ocean House and occupants (colorized by JR).

They traveled south of Ocean House past spots of significance to the earlier inhabitants. The whites observed an offshore rock formation, which, when seen from the south, prompted them to call it Steamboat Rock. But earlier, Indians viewing it from the north saw not a steamboat's smokestack but an Indian leader standing above a rank of rowers and called it the Canoe.[226] The type of vessel was in the eye of the beholder.

A nearby rock formation, known as the Devil's Gate, also had an earlier name. According to the Wiyot Indian Amos Riley,

> . . . before the white people came . . . there was always a big draft of wind going through there, it blows so hard . . . we call that place . . . [the] curlew.[227]

Farther south at Davis Creek was the site of a major battle involving several Indian tribes, including the Mattoles, Bear Rivers (Nekannis), Wiyots, and others.[228] The creek formed the boundary between the Bear River and Mattole tribes.[229] Travelers who had spent the night at Ocean House likely passed the battlefield with no knowledge of what had occurred there a few decades earlier.

The dangers the *Ferndale Enterprise* noted on the descent to Ocean House if anything multiplied to the south, for in the early days travel was not by road but on the beach. For a time Rusty Greig and Jack Smiley were the drivers for G. M. Brice's Ferndale-Petrolia stages. Then one night Smiley was sent from Ferndale to take a nurse to a Petrolia resident. Smiley attempted to drive the stage around the rocky protuberance of Devil's Gate and the rig turned over on the beach. The nurse was pinned under the coach with her face in the mud. Smiley could not get her out and she died. He gave up driving after that.[230]

The Curlew, aka Devil's Gate (JR).

# Cape Mendocino Area

Just up the coast at Cape Mendocino, the lighthouse had its series of excitements. In November 1882 came one of the cape's frequent gales. Sergeant John McLean, who maintained the weather station there, had a lot to record on November 30. The previous night's storm had shaken his table so much that he could barely write out his report. He complained that "the hurricanes crept around the corner at umpty-ump miles per hour," a statement that lacked precision but conveyed his frustration at spending a sleepless night in a flooded office. Switching to red ink, McLean wrote "damage to government property," describing how, upon going outside in the morning, he first and foremost "found the water closet gone." All the rain spouts on the east side of the building were also missing. Later in the morning McLean "found the pieces of the water closet scattered over the mountain 300 yards from its original site [but] the rain spouting has disappeared entirely." He did not document what he substituted for the wayward water closet.[231]

Coinciding with part of McLean's tenure at the Cape Mendocino weather station was Andrew Marble's time as the keeper of the cape's lighthouse. Marble's stay could appropriately have been recorded in a gossip column. (See sidebar 1.)

---

### 1. The Multiple Marriages of Andrew Marble

The saga of Andrew P. Marble began inauspiciously enough when he brought his first wife, Hannah Maria, to Eureka in 1853. There Hanna lasted only two years before fleeing both the town and the marriage, leaving her husband with a two-year-old son. In 1862, while temporarily unmarried, he made the news when a general court martial at Fort Humboldt found Sergeant A. P. Marble guilty of "mutinous conduct." He was sentenced to:

> . . . be confined at hard labor wearing a twenty-four pound ball and chain for the balance of his enlistment; to forfeit all pay now due and ten dollars a month during the term of his enlistment; and at the expiration of the period of his confinement to be drummed out of the service.[232]

Despite this blot on his record, in 1867 Marble found work with another branch of the government, becoming assistant keeper of the Humboldt Harbor Lighthouse on the Samoa Peninsula. Then, eight years after wearing a real ball and chain, he donned a figurative set of the objects when he married his second wife, Mary Elizabeth Burke, in 1870. Over the next nine years she bore at least a half-dozen children and was appointed second assistant keeper of her husband's lighthouse. She died in 1879, cutting short what nonetheless proved to be Marble's longest marriage. Perhaps a few eyebrows were raised in 1882 when Marble wed Nancy J. Matthews, who thereby became his third wife, and took her to the Cape Mendocino Lighthouse, which by then was his windswept place of work. In 1886, with Nancy now "out of the picture," an arrestingly opaque characterization, Marble wed wife number four, Emily Irene Reid, who died at the lighthouse in 1891. By this time chroniclers of conjugal catastrophes were paying attention. It was well they did because Marble's fifth union, to Louise Harding, commenced in August 1891, just six months after Emily Marble's death, and lasted exactly nine days, at which time Louise booked passage on the steamer *Los Angeles*, escaping both her 60-year-old husband and the winds of the cape. Marble marriage mavens then had to wait nearly six years before adding a final tally to their scorecards; Gertrude C. Thayer became Andrew Marble's sixth, and last, wife, in July 1897. Gertrude held out for a month, which was less than average, and then left both her husband and Humboldt County. By then Andrew Marble had retired and was living in Eureka, where he remained, never again to wed, until his death in 1901.[233]

No one knew for sure whey Marble had such difficulty staying wed, but perhaps the problem lay in his middle name, which was Philander.[234]

Cape Mendocino light on a calm day. (JIC, colorized by JR)

Marble's matrimonial misadventures almost ended abruptly in December 1893, when a hired horse and buggy he was renting plunged over the side of the Wildcat Road, crashing down the embankment for more than 300 feet before reaching the bottom of a gulch, with the result that "the horse was killed instantly and the buggy demolished into kindling wood." Marble survived without a scratch but had no explanation for his miraculous escape.[235] Nine years passed, and then—guess what?—Cape Mendocino was connected with another escape escapade. (See sidebar 2).

In 1904 *Lightship 83*, a 135-foot steam-powered vessel, was launched at Camden, New Jersey.[236]

She sailed to the West Coast "around the Horn," and came north, finally halting about five miles west of Cape Mendocino.[237] Here, in 1905, she ceased to be a number and instead became the Blunt's Reef Lightship, complementing the light-

### 2. The Rejected Captain

On the morning of January 2, 1902, the French bark *Max* was sailing off the Humboldt coast about ten miles west-southwest of Cape Mendocino.[238] So was the Pacific Steamship Company's *Walla Walla*, which had 160 passengers and crew on board. During the night the weather had thickened, and the two ships were moving through a heavy fog and light rain. Several members of the *Walla Walla's* crew were on watch. Everyone else was asleep, including Captain A. L. Hall. At 4:10 A.M., however, Hall was "awakened by an awful crash," and his "bunk was struck and thrown across the room." These events rendered Hall wide awake, and he immediately ordered the crew to "man the lifeboats and rafts," adding that they should try to save the baggage, but this latter command "was given up, however, the vessel filling at such an alarming rate that there was no thought of anything but the safety of the passengers."[239]

The steerage quarters were in the *Walla Walla's* bow, right where the *Max* had hit. Hall went there and discovered that the jolt from the collision had jammed one of the doors shut. He forced it open and found a family of seven inside, with two girls "pinioned beneath fallen timbers." Hall managed to release them, and the family hurried to the deck.[240]

All of the *Walla Walla's* lifeboats and rafts were put to sea, but two of the boats were smashed and their passengers dumped into the water. They all, however, made it to the life rafts. Hall made sure that everyone had gotten away, and then, good captain that he was, entered the *Walla Walla's* social hall and prepared to go down with his ship.

It was now 4:45. The *Walla Walla*, with a large hole in her bow, had stayed afloat for 25 minutes, but her time was up. As the ship sank beneath the waves, her boilers exploded, causing spectacular but unexpected results. Crewman George A. Reise watched from one of the lifeboats as "pieces of the vessel [flew] in every direction."[241] One piece, however, was larger than the others; it was the social hall, which was propelled intact to the surface, allowing the ship's bruised but unbowed captain to swim to one of the life rafts "where,"

The S.S. *Walla Walla* (Wikimedia Commons, University of Washington (WM, colorized by JR).

in one of the more dramatic accounts of the incident, "the hands of three survivors reached down to pull the brave skipper from the ocean."[242]

The steamer *Dispatch*, Captain Johnson, had arrived at the wreck at about 8:30 A.M. and spent all day rescuing survivors. Early that evening the *Dispatch* came alongside Hall's raft, and the captain and the other occupants were brought aboard. Meanwhile, the *Nome City* picked up survivors from another lifeboat, and the tug *Ranger* towed one boat to Eureka. Two boats floated up the coast, one going ashore at Trinidad and another traveling all the way up to Dry Lagoon. The steam schooner *Acme* located the *Max* and towed the culprit to San Francisco. When the *Walla Walla*'s survivors left Eureka at the end of the week, they cheered Captain Hall as he went up the gangplank. He was among a very select group of skippers who not only went down with his ship, but came back up afterward.[243]

house with a warning light west of the dangerous reef.

Delmar Thornbury visited the area in 1908 and hiked to the lighthouse, which was a little more than a mile from the county road and 327 feet above the sea. Thornbury was more impressed with the wind at the lighthouse than the water below it. He noted that the location

# Cape Mendocino Area

was "a wild place and wild scene even on a mild day as the wind reaches forty miles an hour some time during each day." When a storm strikes, however, "the place becomes a veritable maelstrom." Thornbury indicated that

> The keepers of the light do not venture out at such times as they would be blown off the Cape. Marvelous tales are told of the strength of the wind playing around Cape Ridge. In heavy storms the teams are obliged to stop and lay over until the wind abates, sometimes as long as two or three days. In other words, rather than being blown backward while trying to make headway against the winds they quit hauling supplies over Cape Ridge. Often times the bridles are torn from the horses' head and the searching zephyrs unharness the teams.[244]

The wind was also pretty powerful offshore. By the time of Thornbury's 1908 trip the Blunt's Reef Lightship had been "dragged off station in heavy storms" six times.[245] When the winds abated the lightship was still not safe. In January 1910 she was rammed by the *S. S. Del Norte*, a lumber schooner with a high deckload of wood that so obscured the helmsman's vision he could not see an object whose very purpose was to be visible.[246] In January 1916 the winds were back toying with the lightship, with 110-mile-per-hour gusts moving her two miles off station. Fortunately the weather was calmer that June, when the *S. S. Bear* grounded on the ocean floor near the mouth of Bear River. Some 155 victims were brought by lifeboats to the lightship, where they remained until rescue vessels could take them to Eureka.[247] Dealing with the wreck of the *Bear* proved to be just a warmup for a more demanding disaster that occurred in 1921. (See Appendix A.)

Changes came to the area in the late 1930s. The original Ocean House was torn down

Building the Petrolia road in the Devil's Gate area. It was a difficult project but eliminated the dangers of the earlier route, which went along the beach (HCHS, colorized by JR).

shortly before World War II and replaced by Ocean House #2, which still stands.[248] In 1939, the Coast Guard took over operation of the Cape Mendocino Lighthouse,[249] which proved to be a timely transition, for soon the coast needed increased guarding. (See sidebar 3.)

Once the war ended, the pulse of activity in the Cape Mendocino area ebbed. The big news in early 1947 found the Blunt's Reef Lightship temporarily off duty, as it went to San Francisco for an overhaul. It was relieved by another vessel, appropriately named the Relief. A newspaper article carrying this news also described life aboard the lightship, where the 18-man crew faced "one of the loneliest, and most disagreeable jobs that [the] service offers." The ship "either rolls in [the][250] trough of the ground swell or pitches when frequent storms toss it." Except for the challenge of staying upright in rough weather, there was little excitement. One crewman complained that "I've spent months fishing from this ship without catching a single fish." Another crewman noted that "we always get along with each other. We have to on a 130-foot ship that never goes anywhere."[251] No one pointed out that the Blunt's Reef Lightship had just gone somewhere: a thrilling 250-mile trip that ended with a long stay in drydock.

When the Navy created some excitement in the area later that year it came by air, not by sea. (See sidebar 4.)

Few locations were less hospitable to humans than Cape Mendocino. It is likely that few tears were shed when the lighthouse's Fresnel lens was replaced by a rotating aerobe-

The Blunt's Reef Lightship (HCHS, colorized by JR).

Cape Mendocino Area

### 3. The Ship That Wouldn't Sink

On the afternoon of December 20, 1941, Boatswain's Mate Walter G. Muenter was on lookout duty at the Cape Mendocino Lighthouse. A message arrived from the Naval Radio Station at Table Bluff, stating starkly that the "STEAMSHIP EMIDIO OFF BLUNTS REEF LIGHTSHIP NEEDS ASSISTANCE AT ONCE." Muenter scanned the ocean and reported back that there was a tanker in sight rounding Blunt's Reef Lightship and headed inshore, but that she did not appear to be in trouble and no other vessels were in sight.[252]

Next came a report from the Blunt's Reef Lightship to the Coast Guard cutter *Shawnee*, stating that the tanker was proceeding in a northerly direction. Coastal lookouts noted that the ship was continuing to head north. She passed the mouth of Humboldt Bay at about 3:25 P.M. There had been no radio contact with her.[253]

Subsequently the Eureka Section Patrol Base, which had been receiving all the messages from the lookouts, reported that there was no vessel in distress and that the mystery ship was the *Emidio*.[254] The report was not entirely correct. While the vessel was indeed the oil tanker *Emidio*, she was actually in grave difficulty. Earlier in the day she had been fired on and then torpedoed by the *I-17*, a Japanese submarine. The *Emidio*'s crew had abandoned ship, and for the last several hours the damaged tanker, with no one left on board, had nonetheless been navigating her way up the Humboldt coast.[255]

Two weeks earlier, on December 7, the *I-17*, skippered by Commander Nishino Kozo, had patrolled the waters northeast of Oahu, Hawaii, ready to torpedo any American ships that escaped from the attack on Pearl Harbor. On December 9 the *I-17* sighted a carrier and two cruisers off Oahu and pursued the carrier but was unable to attack it. The *I-17* then proceeded to the West Coast of the United States where it was assigned to patrol off Cape Mendocino. On December 18 it spotted the lumber steamer *Samoa* about 12 miles off the cape. The sub fired several shells from its deck gun and launched one torpedo at the *Samoa*, but the steamer escaped undamaged. Then, on December 20, the *I-17* found the *Emidio*.[256]

At about 1:30 P.M. the *Emidio* was approximately 20 miles from the Blunt's Reef Lightship. Sailors on board the tanker sighted a vessel about a quarter-mile away, which was briefly mistaken for a fishing boat. It was actually the *I-17*, which made "remarkable speed" and was soon identified

World War II comes to the Humboldt coast.

more accurately. Captain Clark Farrow of the *Emidio* ordered "full speed ahead" and began a zig-zagging evasive maneuver. The gun crew on the *I-17*'s deck opened fire. The first shot, aimed at the *Emidio*'s radio antenna missed, but the second shot tore away the antenna, which meant that *Emidio*'s radioman, W. S. Foote, had only been able to send a single SOS. Captain Farrow ordered his crew into the lifeboats as the *I-17* fired four more shells at the ship. One shell hit the davits that held a lifeboat, spilling three crewmen into the sea, where they drowned.[257]

Suddenly a PBY Catalina flying boat flew overhead and dropped depth charges on the *I-17*. The sub crash-dived and avoided the explosives. Meanwhile, all but four men had left the *Emidio*. Radioman Foote was still on board; he had rigged a temporary antenna and was preparing to send another SOS when a torpedo from the *I-17* hit the *Emidio*. Foote stayed at his station, calmly tapping out his SOS and adding "torpedoed in stern." Then, his job finished, he went to the main deck and jumped over the side.[258]

The other sailors still on board were in the engine room. Oiler B. F. Moler watched as the *I-17's* torpedo tore through the bulkhead and exploded on the other side of the engine room, killing fireman Kenneth Kimes and third engineer R. A. Winters. Moler, with three broken ribs and a punctured lung, "somehow swam and climbed up to the upper deck and jumped overboard." Both Moler and Foote were picked up by the lifeboats.[259]

The *Emidio's* survivors rowed all night before reaching the Blunt's Reef Lightship. Shortly thereafter the Coast Guard's *Shawnee* arrived and took the men to Eureka.[260]

The *I-17* left the area. Commander Nishino had seen the tanker settling rapidly by the stern and incorrectly decided she was sinking.[261] Three days later the *I-17* struck again, firing four shells at the tanker *Larry Doheny* some 80 miles southwest of Eureka. Once again, a patrol plane flew overhead and the *I-17* crash-dived. Then the *I-17* returned to periscope depth and fired a torpedo at the tanker. This time, however, the torpedo exploded prematurely and only managed to blow off the tanker's chartroom door. The *I-17* then went back to the western Pacific. The submarine returned to the California coast in early 1942. It fired shells at the Bankline oil refinery near Santa Barbara and tried, unsuccessfully, to blow up three oil tankers, including one off Cape Mendocino. The submarine subsequently saw combat at numerous locations in the Pacific. In August 1943 the *I-17* was sunk off Australia when a depth-charge attack by American aircraft was finally successful.[262]

The *S.S. Emidio*, trying to get into Crescent City's harbor (JIC, colorized by JR).

> Unlike the *I-17*, the *Emidio* never sank. Continuing to chart her own course up the California coast, with a gaping hole in her side, she passed Patrick's Point, Split Rock, the mouth of the Klamath, Footsteps Rock—onward and northward—until, on Christmas Eve, she arrived at the entrance to the Crescent City harbor. A slight turn to starboard, and the *Emidio* would reach the welcoming wharves that she had traveled towards for four days and four nights.
>
> But sailing the open seas was one thing, navigating the rock-dotted harbor mouth another. A pilot was needed for this final quarter-mile of the *Emidio*'s valiant voyage. But the helm stood empty, as it had for the entire 85-mile trip, and the tanker, a steamship, in a final appropriate gesture, grounded on Steamboat Rock.[263]
>
> Hope that she could complete her voyage rose later in the week when a storm hit. But instead of releasing the *Emidio* from her rocky perch, it broke the tanker in two, leaving both pieces still stranded. There the *Emidio*, stern and bow, spent the rest of the war, a rusting steel sentinel warning of the dangers lurking in the offshore waters. Only in 1950 did the tanker leave her resting place, removed by two salvage companies from southern California.[264]
>
> A small portion of her did not go south. A section of her steel hull was moved ashore, where it resides to this day in Crescent City's Beachfront Park, the county's—and perhaps the world's—only monument to notional navigation.[265]

acon after the end of World War II.[266] The retired lens was moved to Ferndale in 1948 and the lighthouse decommissioned in 1951.[267] The wooden buildings at the lighthouse were intentionally burned in 1962 "and the remains were pushed over the cliff." The lighthouse structure itself was "slowly inching down the hillside and succumbing to rust" when in 1998 the lantern room at the top of the tower was removed by helicopter and repositioned down the coast at Point Delgada, adjacent the town of Shelter Cove.[268]

In June 1971 the last of five vessels that had served as the Blunt's Reef Lightship steamed off for San Francisco, replaced by the Blunt's Reef Lighted Horn Buoy (LL 63.10), a much smaller warning system with a much longer name. The 40-foot-diameter buoy flashed a warning light of 6,000 candlepower every two seconds, visible for up to 12 miles. It also sounded a horn blast every 30 seconds.[269] It may have been a technological improvement over the lightship, but it could never offer the succor the vessel provided to the victims of shipwrecks, such as those from the *Emidio*.

The wind still howled and the sea still churned, but there was no one left to complain about it.

# Cape Mendocino Area

Light keeper's house alight, 1962 (CPH, colorized by JR).

### 4. The Blimp That Wouldn't Stay Landed

For years Blunt's Reef had collected sunken ships. Then, in the 1940s, something must have happened to the water, for not once, but twice, the ocean refused to embrace distressed crafts. First came the *Emidio* in 1941, which ignored the torpedo hole in its hull and sailed, without captain or crew, 85 miles to the outskirts of Crescent City. Then, in 1947, came the ZPK-99,[270] better known as Bessie the Blimp.[271]

Bessie unexpectedly alighted on the ocean off Cape Mendocino at 2:50 P.M. on July 14. As the Navy's subsequent report put it, "the ZPK-99 was inadvertently flown into the water, washing her pilot out through a smashed window." Also defenestrated was the copilot. Six others on board "took to the water," leaving three men on board. It was then that Bessie decided to continue her trip. Pilotless, she had risen about 50 feet into the air when the three stragglers leaped out of the gondola, leaving Bessie entirely on her own.[272]

Rancher Joe Russ witnessed these events and promptly called the Coast Guard. A raft was sent from the Blunt's Reef Lightship and picked up the blimp's crew, who "were floating about in their life rafts and Mae Wests,[273] when the big craft bounced up in the air and took off on her own." Just like the S.S. *Emidio* six years earlier, the crewless blimp set out on an unexpected escapade.[274]

While the Coast Guard rescued her crew, Bessie floated off to the northeast. She was done with the ocean but apparently still sought water, for her course headed her directly towards Blue Lake. Since she was unused to flying on her own, the Coast Guard contacted Murray Field and asked that a pilot be sent up to locate the wayward airship. Soon Pete Fleming, accompanied by Pete Sacchi, were airborne. They sighted Bessie and tracked her as she continued her trip.[275]

Bessie had started her solo voyage shortly after 3 P.M. Almost three hours later, according to a *Humboldt Standard* report,

> . . . Blue Lake residents watched the derelict blimp go in and out of the clouds . . . and then gently settle in a fold of the hills.

Ocean House Ranch, onetime blimp sighting station, with the "Canoe" offshore, center. (JR).

> The settling may have appeared gentle from a distance, but the actual impact was severe. As the *Madera Tribune* described it, Bessie "crashed in a stand of second growth timber on Fickle Hill. The fall broke her in two."[276] Both pieces touched ground at Minor's Quarry.[277]
>
> An ambulance sped to the scene, not knowing that no one had been on board. Les Brown, the driver, reported that Bessie "was being looted by souvenir hunters who had broken a trail through the heavy brush and were taking instruments, food rations, and clothing." The looters failed to complete their work, since Navy personnel later found that many items were still on board, including a "machine gun and ammo."[278]
>
> There had been little need for such armament on Bessie's final flight. She'd taken three photographers to Point St. George, where they had photographed sea lions for the California Department of Fish and Game.[279] They must have used up all their film on the assignment, for no photos appeared of Bessie's impromptu landing near Blunt's Reef.

### Appendix A: The Grief of Blunt's Reef

In October 1918 the *S. S. Alaska*, a 3,709-ton ocean liner, "struck a reef near Swanson Bay on the central coast of British Columbia." She worked herself off the reef but was extensively damaged and had to unload her passengers at the nearest port, which was Prince Rupert.[280] The *Alaska* was 29 years old at the time. She would remain afloat just three years longer.[281]

The *Alaska* was long a regular on the Portland-San Francisco-Los Angeles run. She was still at it in May 1921 when the International Seaman's Union went on strike. The Portland Steamship Company (PSC), which owned the *Alaska*, joined other companies in opening a nonunion hiring hall, and within a couple of weeks the PSC had its ships running again with scab crews. The newcomers were a mixed lot. Some had steamship experience, but others had previously only crewed on sailing ships. Another group "had been longshoremen or coal heavers and were now trying to learn more complex jobs." Still others "were not very competent at anything, and would never have been considered for their jobs had the companies not been desperate to break the strike."[282]

On August 5, 1921, a week or so after the strike ended, the *Alaska*, captained by Harry Hovey, left Portland for a trip down the coast. The strikers had not been hired back. The *Alaska*, at 327 feet, was longer than a football field,[283] and the makeshift crew had trouble handling the ship. Edgar Horner, one of the passengers, observed the difficulties with a rising sense of dread:

> It seemed to me at the time that they had a lot of inexperienced men aboard, young kids who couldn't handle the ropes, etc., and they had a difficult time trying to dock the ship at Astoria to take on more passengers and freight, and when they cast loose to leave, they tore away several feet

of the bulwarks on the forward part of the portside boat deck, and the ship swung in on the stern and struck the dock, tearing off some planking and piles.[284]

Five members of the Dyer family were also on board. Besides the parents, Mamie and Uhre, there were their daughter, Arva, and the twins, Duane and Elaine. Before they had left their home in La Grande, Oregon, Duane had shown his grandmother a picture of a rock and told her that their ship would hit something like it.[285] Everyone knew, of course, that young boys craved excitement, so no one paid much attention to his prediction.

Moving out to sea from Astoria, the *Alaska* soon encountered fog. Starting about 8 P.M. the ship sounded her foghorn every couple of minutes, disrupting the passengers' attempts to sleep. Horner took note of the *Alaska's* steering gear, which made a loud banging sound whenever the helmsman altered course. Horner soon developed "an uneasy feeling that everything was not alright."[286]

The following day found calm seas,[287] but enough fog remained to prevent anyone on the *Alaska* from sighting the coast. Horner noted that "there were several children and babies on board" and also "a lot of women passengers."[288] That evening there was "an extra good meal for supper . . . and everyone was feeling in an extra good mood." A number of passengers "were in the smoking room playing cards and dancing." Horner was in the social hall on the main deck, socializing.[289] From time to time he looked out towards the southwest, where he would see the flashing beam of the Blunt's Reef Lightship.[290] At the time he did not realize the significance of the lightship's position relative to that of the *Alaska's*, but he would find out later. Meanwhile the ship's engines throbbed beneath him as the *Alaska* churned through the sea at her top speed of 15 knots.[291]

As evening approached, Second Mate Earl Dupray[292] was called to the bridge by Captain Hovey. According to Dupray, fog had "crept down" over the ocean and Hovey could no longer see the lightship's light. Hovey and Dupray attempted to determine the *Alaska's* position, knowing they were near Blunt's Reef. Twice they altered the ship's direction in an attempt to avoid the reef. Then Hovey thought he heard the lightship's warning whistle. He sent Dupray to the *Alaska's* sounding instruments to determine the direction the whistle came from. Dupray was unable to get an accurate bearing and hurried back to the bridge. Hovey again altered course to take the *Alaska* farther out sea.[293]

As Hovey and Dupray were busy on the bridge, Horner was conversing with about a dozen passengers in the social hall. Presently "someone started joking about a shipwreck and what they would do in case we had a wreck." Horner responded that he "would stay with the ship as long as there was anything sticking out."[294]

At about that same time Margaret Knuth and her husband went to the smoking room to watch passengers who were dancing. Knuth found a happy group that had just put on a 78-rpm record of the popular "Wang Wang Blues," a bouncy foxtrot,[295] on the Victrola. In the middle of the song the *Alaska*, almost as if she was responding to the music, began rocking back and forth. Knuth noted that

> . . . the dancers laughed as they danced on one side of the deck and then were shifted to the other side. Then came a terrible crash! Every piece of wood in the ship seemed to creak and groan and

# Cape Mendocino Area

The doomed S. S. *Alaska* (LC, colorized by JR).

bend. Everyone was thrown to the floor, even those that had been sitting in the chairs. We got up and, just then, another shock, again threw us on the floor.[296]

In the social hall Horner experienced what he called a "terrific jar." The *Alaska's* engines stopped and then "all at once came two more tearing shocks." Horner felt the ship's steel plates being ripped from the bottom of the hull.[297] The *Alaska* had sailed onto the rocks that dotted Blunt's Reef.

Horner promptly went below to his cabin, found his life belt, and put it on. Returning to the deck, he

> . . . saw a steward in uniform . . . and I asked him what we were supposed to do and he looked at me with terror in his face and said god I don't know. So I left him and went forward to where they were lowering one of the lifeboats and helped put the women and children into it.[298]

The *Alaska's* wireless operator tapped out a frantic S.O.S., hoping to reach the Table Bluff station, which was only about 15 miles to the north. The station, however, was receiving another message at the time and did not hear the *Alaska's* call.[299]

But someone else did. About 12 miles distant,[300] the Canadian steamship *Anyox*, with a barge in tow,[301] picked up the message, changed direction, and headed at full speed towards the *Alaska*.[302]

The *Alaska's* S.O.S. was relayed to the wireless station in Portland which in turn sent the report south to Eureka. The Coast Guard station on the Samoa Peninsula finally received the message, not by wireless, but by a telephone call. By then the information was so badly garbled that Coast Guard Captain Laurence Ellison was unclear about what type of assistance was required. He called out his crew at midnight but decided to delay arrival at the site of the incident until daylight.[303]

Unaware that help was on the way, passengers and crew on the *Alaska* were trying to launch her lifeboats. Horner described the inept attempts:

We had to push this boat away from the side as the ship had taken a heavy list to starboard which was making it difficult to stand on the decks. They launched two boats on the port side successfully and two were capsized when they got to the water. I saw the people dumped out into the water and heard the terrible cries as they begged to be helped.[304]

Meanwhile, the *Alaska* tilted ever farther towards starboard. Horner "felt sure it would turn over completely, [for] the decks were almost perpendicular and we had to climb over the rail and stand on the side of the hull. . . ."[305]

About then word came that a ship had answered the S.O.S. call and was coming to the rescue. For a moment this raised everyone's spirits, but the dire condition of the *Alaska* could not long be ignored. As the bow of the ship dipped increasingly deeper into the ocean, the stern correspondingly rose higher and higher. Horner and some 20 to 30 others were clinging to the side of the stern as the *Alaska* "gave a deathly shudder and began to settle with a loud roar of rushing water."[306]

In the engine room, the inexperienced crew had failed to release the boiler's pressure. As soon as the cold seawater hit the superheated boiler plates they ruptured, causing a huge explosion that killed several people outright and hurled others into the sea. The *Alaska*, which had been listing badly, now sank.[307] One highly strung account had Hovey following the "heroic captain" script by stating "I prefer to go down with my ship," but then having the matter decided for him when the *Alaska's* smokestack crashed down on the captain, killing him instantly.[308] The various witnesses, however, make no mention of the manner of Hovey's death.

One of the persons blown into the air by the boiler explosion was Uhre Dyer. H. M. Jensen was floating nearby on a piece of wreckage and spotted Dyer, who was injured by the blast, after he landed in the ocean. Jensen managed to reach Dyer and keep him afloat.[309]

Within the hour the *Anyox* reached the scene. The crew found one lifeboat nearly swamped, but they managed to bring the victims on board; they then emptied the lifeboat of water and went out searching for other survivors. They located about 30 persons who were on makeshift rafts or had been clinging to pieces of wreckage.[310] Among them were Jensen and Dyer.[311]

When the *Alaska* began to sink Horner had leapt from the ship, hit the water, and then swam for all he was worth to avoid the "terrible suction" the sinking created. He had to fight off two men who grabbed onto him in panic and threatened to pull him under. He caught hold of a board and some other bits of wreckage, grasping them until he encountered a stateroom door, which he managed to climb upon. He lay on the door and rested. After a time a man named Springstead drifted by, caught hold of the door, and shared it with Horner.[312]

The men clung to the door for hours. Their legs "became chilled and useless." They shouted at the lifeboats to no effect. They heard other people around them calling. "And," Horner said,

> all night long I heard the cry of a little girl, it was pitiful to hear her, she had been washed overboard without a life belt and . . . Mr. A. J. Franklin . . . picked her out of the water onto some floating wreckage which was filled with big spikes and thrust her clothing onto one of these big nails and there she hung dragging in the cold water all night long crying continually. . . .[313]

Horner and Springstead managed to transfer

from their stateroom door to a piece of the *Alaska's* deck that came floating by. It was about 20 feet square, which allowed room for a boy named Bonnewell to also climb aboard. Bonnewell was covered with oil and so slippery that Horner could hardly grasp him to pull him onto the decking.[314]

The three of them drifted around for about an hour and then came next to an empty life raft, which they managed to climb into. The raft had no oars, so they continued to drift. Soon, however, they encountered another raft that had both oars and passengers: two men who were too sick to paddle. Horner, Springstead, and Bonnewell managed to move onto the new raft, and Horner and Springstead began rowing. According to Horner they rowed for what seemed like "5 or 6 miles," which brought them close to the *Anyox*. With sun rising to their backs they all stood up and were finally seen by the rescue ship. It gave four blasts on its whistle and steamed towards them.[315]

The *Anyox* took them, along with other survivors, to Eureka. There, hundreds of townspeople waited at the dock, ready to help. Horner and several others were taken to "the best hotel in town. Fred Georgeson, the editor of the *Humboldt Standard*,[316] then escorted Horner and Springstead to the newspaper's printing plant, brought them lots of hot water and soap, and let them wash the crude oil from the wreck off their bodies. That done, Georgeson gave them each a set of new clothes and took them out to dinner.[317]

Horner had injured his ankles during his ordeal in the ocean. He was admitted to one of Eureka's hospitals for treatment, where he joined other victims of the wreck. While there, he learned about the fate of the Dyer family. Mamie Dyer and the twins had perished at sea. Mamie's husband, Uhre, was in the same hospital as Horner, "in a private room out of his head most of the time."

Horner learned that the fifth member of the family was four-year-old Arva, the little girl whom A. J. Franklin had pulled out of the water and attached to a piece of wreckage. Arva endured eight hours in the chill ocean. She was then rescued but passed out, regaining consciousness only after a Miss Thompson spent two hours reviving her. She was taken to the same hospital as her father. The nurses brought her to the ward each day where Horner saw "the cute little thing" that he had heard crying throughout the night.[318]

Coincidently, another four-year-old girl had also been rescued. Betty Jean Sanders, coated with oil and wearing a big life belt, was plucked from the sea after spending seven hours in the water. She was numb with cold, but she was soon wrapped in a blanket and pampered by other passengers on her way to Eureka.[319]

The lifesaving crew reached the scene of the wreck just before daylight. They quickly located about a dozen survivors and took them to the *Anyox*. The Coast Guard boat then searched for other victims and found about a dozen more. They were all dead.[320]

By now the fog had lifted, revealing other vessels that had come to help: the Humboldt Bar tug *Ranger*, the lighthouse tender *Sequoia*, and the Coast and Geodetic Survey steamer *Lydonia* were all standing by.[321] They had little to do except retrieve more bodies. By the time the casualty toll was completed, 42 persons were found to have died, while 178 survived.[322]

On Monday, August 8—two days after the wreck—a coroner's jury convened in Eureka. It interviewed three crew members and three passengers. Some of the latter criticized the crew

The *Alaska* makes the front page of the *Humboldt Times* (HT).

for their actions during the wreck. The jury determined those who died in the wreck had drowned.[323] This conclusion, however, ignored the fate of the engine crew, who were killed when the boiler exploded, and that of Captain Hovey, who was crushed by the crashing smokestack.

Two days later federal investigators announced they would charge the *Alaska's* four mates with negligence. The officers were subsequently acquitted of the charges and in fact were commended for their efforts to save those aboard the ship. Condemned instead, "for his negligency in navigating his vessel full speed in a dense fog without taking soundings" was Captain Hovey,[324] who, being dead, could not defend himself.

It was a convenient decision and probably at least partially correct, but it failed to consider the culpability of the Alaska Steamship Company, which first had tried to break a seamen's strike by hiring a makeshift scab crew and then allowed the inexperienced workers to keep their jobs after the strike ended. This created a situation that left no margin for error when the *Alaska* sailed on her final voyage. Then, when Captain Hovey indeed made an error, the disaster was magnified by the crew's fumbling response.

Shortly after the event, the newspapers and the investigators captured one sense of the tragedy in their reports, but a truer understanding of what really happened came only years after the sinking, when an epitaph for the event was published by the *Humboldt Historian*. In part it stated,

> My mother never had a chance as the life boats were over crowded. No one knew how to lower the life boats and people were spilled into the ocean.[325]

The author was Arva Dyer Souders, who recalled that night, 81 years earlier, when she hung from the wreckage of the *Alaska* as her mother, brother, and sister drowned. For years afterward, after she had her own children and then grandchildren, Arva wondered why she had been saved, and finally she realized that "having my own family is my reward after losing my family."[326]

# Chapter 4
# Petrolia

The first white to report about the Mattole Valley was George[327] Hill, who in September 1854 notified the *Humboldt Times* that he had "found a large river hitherto unknown to the people of this section [Humboldt Bay]." Hill thought that the area was filled with promise but in need of the transformative effects that were the province of the recently arrived white population:

> . . . the lands are rich with open prairie sufficient, for a large settlement of farmers—the lands above the river bottoms are open timbered table lands, easy to clear and affording sufficient timber for fencing and firewood for ages to come.[328]

Hill had met the local Mattole Indians, who "had apparently never seen a white man before."[329] The following month the *Times* suggested that the Mattole tribe be given some company—the Indians on Humboldt Bay, who the paper found to be "ill-treated and abused," and who, if they were moved to the Mattole Valley would "get immense quantities of salmon and shell fish, besides game. . . ." Most importantly, the Humboldt Bay Indians would then "be at least twenty to thirty miles from any settlements of whites."[330] The proposal gained no traction at the time, but decades later a version of it came to pass. (See Appendix A.)

The isolation that the *Times* described was soon to end. The Mattole River region was, as the paper claimed, indeed remote, but it had, as Hill indicated, potent attractions for agriculturists. Within two years the lower section of the river saw the start of white occupancy.

In the spring of 1856 two parties converged on the lower Mattole Valley. John Cassard, James Deleseaux, and "Buckskin Jack" Mann impetuously swept down the coast in a small sailboat, landed at the mouth of the river, and walked upstream a short distance. At the future site of Petrolia they met a landward group of explorers consisting of Minor Langdon, J. Avery Langdon, Seth Kinman, and previous visitor George Hill. Three of the seven men decided to take up land in the vicinity. Minor Langdon set up a grist mill, J. Avery Langdon selected a homesite and then went back up the coast, and John Cassard established himself on what became known as Cassard's Flat.[331]

Years later, Kinman described what he had seen on his 1856 visit to the valley. He had found more than fertile farmland:

> The general appearance of the country is mountainous and open, there being timber on some of the gulches. The soil was very fertile and, of course, the grass and clover grew in great abundance. The game was in about the same abundance as that of the Bear River country to which it adjoins. . . . Along some of the streams in numerous places, petroleum oozes out of the ground in quantities [as if] to flow out of a well. Another peculiarity is the innumerable gas jets or springs. By lighting a match to these, they will burn for a considerable length of time.[332]

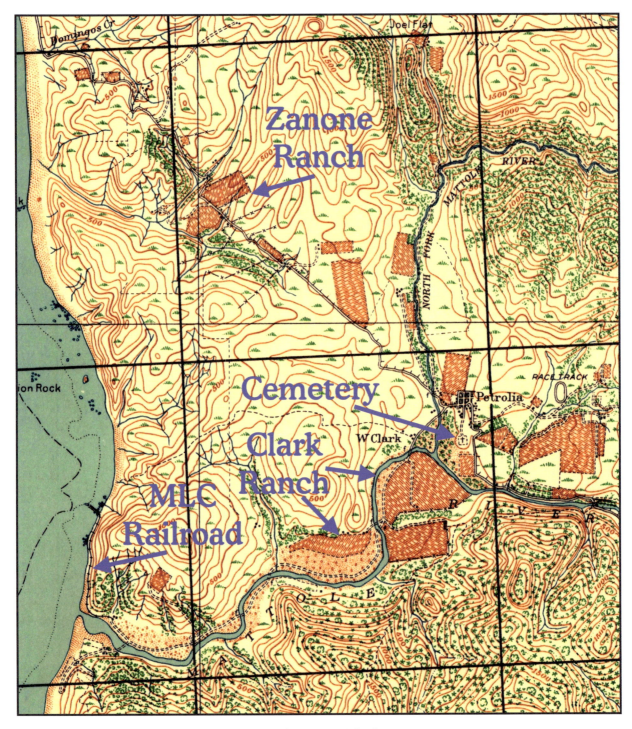

Petrolia area, 1916 (CE).

Rich soil and abundant game were well and good, but for those seeking the main chance, and they were legion in Humboldt County, it was the promise of petroleum production that quickened their pulse. It took a while, however, for word to get out. The usually garrulous Kinman refrained from trumpeting his discovery, and three years passed before mention of the oil encounter oozed into print. Only in 1859 did the *Humboldt Times* run reports about the "rock oil springs" from which "petroleum could be collected in sufficient quantities for putting it up."[333]

But profiting from *any* product found on the Mattole was at the time problematic, since the

# Petrolia

area was far removed from population centers and lacked any effective system of transportation. The same *Times* article indicated that the local farmers owned

> ... very fine places, but [they] pay little attention to farming as there is no market for anything they can raise at home and it will not pay to pack produce away.[334]

Ranching faced the same difficulty. The amount of livestock grazing in the valley was great, but

> ... a market must be found for some of it soon or much of it will have to seek new ranges and the owners of what is left will become poor men.[335]

Nonetheless, whites continued to establish themselves in the valley. Nonhuman forces occasionally caused disruptions. A tree fell on the Mattole schoolhouse, but a new structure was built in the fall of 1860 so that education could continue unabated.[336] In November 1861 an earthquake struck, and "the ground cracked and opened in places a quarter of a mile in length with a tremendous jarring sound." Even more impressively,

> ... in one place the earth opened so much as to let a cow topple over and drop in head first; the opening immediately shut, smashing the whole body of the cow as flat as a pancake, except the tail, which still sticks out as a lasting monument of her latter end."[337]

The earthquake occurred the same month that oil exploration, started that April, was discontinued.[338] Petroleum then passed from the headlines until 1864, when it abruptly appeared that the Mattole would become the oil capital of the West. (See Appendix B.)

To prepare the way for the hoped-for oil boom, James W. Henderson set up a town. In January 1865, he purchased over 1,000 acres of land from Francis Stansberry and Walker S. Hunter near the confluence of the North Fork and main Mattole rivers. Soon thereafter county surveyor J. S. Murray surveyed and mapped a townsite for the community that was intended to serve the local oil industry. The survey map showed the place as Petrolia,[339] and a post office with that name opened there in September.[340]

A letter, probably sent from that selfsame post office, was printed in the *Humboldt Times* on April 14, 1866. It acquainted readers with the recently launched community:

> Petrolia, the future metropolis of Mattole Valley is pleasantly situated on a large flat, near the North Fork of the Mattole River, and is at present but a small town (city, it is called, but it is hardly large enough for that yet,) consisting of a number of dwelling houses, three stores, one hotel, a blacksmith shop, postoffice [*sic*], livery stable, and *one* saloon. The inhabitants number about fifty. The amusements are various. I think the favorites are whisky and "bean poker." They call it bean poker for the reason, I suppose, that they poke beans in a little heap in the middle of the table. . . . The town is rapidly improving in appearance, buildings are being erected, and there are several in contemplation,—a church, two school houses and several dwellings.[341]

Placid Petrolia awaits its first gusher (HCHS, colorized by JR).

The optimism that infused the above account was borne out by recent election statistics: in the 1864 presidential election 26 votes were cast in lower Mattole, while a year later, for the state and county election, the precinct recorded 124 ballots.[342] But the budding enthusiasm of 1866's spring withered over the following months as the oil boom fizzled.[343] In June, Mr. Lane, the local schoolteacher, wrote that "Petrolia is now a rather dry place . . . most of the people are much discouraged in regard to oil."[344]

By then Petrolia, however dry, was *in* place, providing the benevolent benefits of community to all who sought to make a life on the lower Mattole. If oil was not to be the lubricant of local growth, there was still the less spectacular but more reliable enterprise of ranching that spoke seductively of eventual success.

Hearing this sweet call far over the ridges in California's Central Valley, a group of farmers left the Marysville area in 1868 and, with loaded wagons, headed west. For 200 miles a party that included Jacob Miner, Cyrus Miner, and Charles B. Johnston struggled across lands that contained few roads, finally reaching Briceland. Whatever obstacles they had faced so far were dwarfed by what lay ahead—the descent of the Mattole River canyon. One account claims that the group, henceforth known as the "Marysville Settlers," twice had to build rafts and ferry their wagons across the river, and thrice they were forced to cross steep, roadless ridges.[345] At last they reached the hospitable lands of the lower Mattole, and there they busied themselves by "engaging in crop ranching and livestock dealing, and building up large, fertile estates." Over the next eight years, other Marysvillans arrived on the Mattole, the last being Wesley Horton Roscoe in September 1876.[346]

"No oil?" the hard-working Marysville group might have said. "Don't worry, we'll replace it with elbow grease."

But hard work would not be enough for ranching and farming to succeed. The biggest barrier to success, already noted in 1859, was the lack of a road connecting the Mattole with the population centers to the north. The problem had not been solved by the time the first Marysville Settlers arrived in 1868, but presto! the following year a wagon road from the lower Eel River to the Mattole was completed.[347] Now the products of the valley, animal and vegetable, could at last be transported to the eager consumers on Humboldt Bay. And if the area's chief mineral product—oil—could not be successfully marketed, that was no worse a hardship than what the largely oil-less remainder of the county faced.

Lest anyone forget about the improved transportation infrastructure, the *Times* reminded its readers in August 1869 that "a good wagon road connects Mattole and Eel River Valley and this [Humboldt] Bay." The article also mentioned that "Minor Langdon is erecting a new flouring mill in Mattole, near the town of Petrolia," that the "Petrolia Hotel is now under the efficient management of Mr. Charles Doe," that "Schumacher Brothers are doing a good merchandise business," and that "Rudolph Brothers have recently opened a store in Petrolia." Moreover, "the population of the valley has received large accessions during the past twelve months, and business generally seems to be prospering."[348]

Even better news was soon to come. In the summer of 1871 Hurlbutt and Potter announced the opening of a daily stage line between Eureka and Petrolia.[349] As the *Humboldt Times* had predicted when road construction started in 1867,

> ...a line of stages can run...from Eureka to Petrolia in two days, giving us the opportunity to visit that beautiful portion of Humboldt county, and inducing new settlers to take their families there and build their homes.[350]

Indeed, had not the Miners and the Johnstons and the others heard the call, and not waiting for the road to be completed, left Marysville for the Mattole and helped fulfill the prophesy of the *Times*?

A few years passed, and glowing reports continued to emanate from the Mattole area. In April 1875, possibly inspired by the emerald-hued embrace of spring, Mrs. M. A. Chivers signaled the *West Coast Signal* that all was wonderful on the Mattole. Among the manifold attributes of the valley were not only a climate "acknowledged as the best in the world" and agricultural advancement that saw "our hills bespotted with all kinds of stock," but also a natural bounty so fecund that "we are *never* without fish, flesh and fowl," along with an "abundance of fruits, grains, vegetables and delicacies indigenous to the soil." Regarding the populace, "with no hoodlums to disturb or annoy, our children are as well trained and educated as any in California." Both religion and music were well-served, sometimes simultaneously, for:

> There is a good Church building. With a fine organ, and several excellent organists. There are a number of instruments in private families in the town, and more have been ordered.[351]

Swelling to a crescendo, Chivers at last reached the peak of her panegyrical pyramid of prose:

> Does anyone doubt my statement? Come and see for yourself. You need go no further than the hill overlooking the

Progress in Petrolia: a second general merchandise store (HCHS, colorized by JR).

town, from which you can see scenery that surpasses Switzerland—mountains whose heads are crowned with clouds,—others clothed in richest verdure upon whose sides countless herds of cattle graze; valleys green with various grains, fruit trees loaded with blossoms, the river winding in and out like a line of silver, sparkling and dancing on its way; birds caroling the sweetest songs, the musical ring of the anvil stirring the still air; the distant shouts of sportive little ones released from study; the numerous horsemen and pack trains coming and going constantly; and just a little ways off our magnificent redwood forest. What can compare with them?[352]

Perhaps attempting to cool the fires of fulsomeness found in Chivers's paean to Petrolia, the *Signal* then ran a relatively restrained report on the town in July 1876. A rollcall of respected dairy ranchers included Charles S. Cook, Jesse Walker, Mr. Allen,[353] J. W. Henderson & Thomas Hunter, Jacob Miner, Walker S. Hunter, James H. Goff, Elias Hunter, Walter Scott, Mr. Giacomini, and Henry Duff. Besides butter and cheese, other plentiful food products were oats, wheat, Indian corn, potatoes, pumpkins, melons, tomatoes, strawberries, currants, gooseberries, peaches, apples, pears, and grapes. The oil failure was lamented but seen as probably a temporary setback, and even without profiting from petroleum Petrolia had become a good-sized town. There were now two general merchandise stores and two blacksmith shops, along with a hotel, post office, livery stable, church, schoolhouse, Grange hall, Good Templars' hall, saddle and harness shop, boot and shoe shop, carpenter's shop, meat and vegetable shop, saloon, and cooper's shop. About 100 people lived in town with about 800 more in the rest of the valley.[354] Perhaps part of the rising population had been lured by Mrs. Chivers's *Signal* article of the previous year.

In January 1878 the *Humboldt Weekly Times* carried an update on the activity in Petrolia. In the year and a half since the *Signal* printed its list of businesses, the town had added a drug store, doctor's office, and barber shop. M. J. Conklin served as justice of the peace, but with Petrolia holding steady at one saloon, his services were no doubt seldom required.[355]

Life moved ahead as Petrolia reached the end of the decade. Then, for a part of its younger population, it came to a sudden halt. On September 1, 1880, six-year-old Catherine Mackey died of scarlet fever. Two days later her brother Edward, age nine, also succumbed to the illness. Another two days passed and then seven-year-old brother Patrick Mackey died. Then little James Mackey, four years old, was taken by the fever on September 13. Thus within two weeks, four of John and Honorah Mackey's six children were dead. Other families were not spared. On September 29, 1880, siblings Clara Simmons, age 15, and Orson Simmons, age 12, both died. Almon Duff, Elsie Hunter, and Hiram Wright were all two-year-old first cousins who died between October and December. They were buried next to each other in the Petrolia cemetery.[356] A letter from Petrolia published in the *Ferndale Enterprise* on December 9 indicated that over 70 cases of scarlet fever had occurred in the Petrolia area, with 12 fatalities.[357] Later that month the *Humboldt Times* reported that "Mr. T. J. Lannigan of the Eureka Foundry is executing some fine work in the shape of an

Jacob Allen Dudley homestead, southeast of Petrolia, 1886. (DTC, colorized by JR).

iron railing to be placed around the graves of the children of John Mackey of Petrolia, four of whom died recently of Scarlet Fever."[358] Some 70 years later, a fire in the 1950s destroyed most of the cemetery's wooden markers[359] but spared the Mackey children's single headstone[360] and Lanigan's iron railing.

The outer world received an update on Petrolia in 1892, when the *Ferndale Enterprise* carried a report on the town that included a listing of the various businesses. There were:

> . . . two well-stocked merchandising stores, run by J. A. Mackey and Messrs. Hart & Johnston, a first-class hotel with C. M. Averill as landlord, a livery stable run by a Mr. Crawford, . . . a blacksmith shop, with P. J. O'Leary constantly at the forge, a barber shop and barber in the person of John Sanders, a harness shop run by D. L. Marshall, a quiet, orderly saloon conducted by Isaac Brown, and Dr. F. H. Ottmer, one of the most successful practitioners in the county, looks after the health of the town and section. E. McKaig is the handy man of the village, . . . and . . . Charley Conklin serves the people in the capacity of undertaker, carpenter, etc.[361]

Petrolians had 11 years to enjoy the completeness of their community that the *Enterprise* described. Then, in mid-April 1903, a fire started at W. A. Sage's store and spread to nearby buildings, eventually engulfing not only the store but also O'Leary's blacksmith shop, the Petrolia Hotel, and two residences. The leisurely pace of the flames allowed for the rescue of former proprietor Silvia Giacomini's piano from the hotel,[362] but it is doubtful that many happy melodies were forthcoming.

Bad as the fire was, its destructiveness was exceeded just three years later when Petrolia participated in "the greatest earthquake disaster in U. S. history." The 1906 quake, usually associated with San Francisco, also forcefully struck Petrolia with what has been classified as level IX (violent)[363] on the Modified Mercalli Intensity

Petrolia, 1888. (DTC, colorized by JR).

The Petrolia Hotel, sometime before its incineration in the 1903 fire. (CPH, colorized by JR).

scale, "as every structure was severely damaged and several people injured by falling bricks." The Petrolia Hotel was "was off its blocks and badly damaged, though still standing."³⁶⁴ Worse yet, the "Old Saloon" was "broken in two, and the proprietor, Hunter, will quit business."³⁶⁵

Soon, however, happier times returned to the burned and shaken town. In 1907 recently elected Governor James Norris Gillett came to tiny, out-of-the way Petrolia. (See Appendix C.) The *Humboldt Standard* set the stage for the governor's summer visit with a general report on the town in January 1907. The account noted the 1903 fire, which had grown in size in the intervening years so that it had "half destroyed" the town. Also mentioned was the 1906 earthquake that "almost blotted" Petrolia off the map. These diminutions were followed by a frenzy of repairing and rebuilding, so that by 1907 Petrolia

> . . . appears as a new town containing one large general merchandise store and postoffice, two saloons, hotel, livery stable, Sunset telephone office and grocery store run by C. F. Goff, a blacksmith shop, K. of P.³⁶⁶ hall, fifteen or twenty well kept homes, a church, a schoolhouse, [and] a lumber mill two miles from town owned and operated by Reynolds & Etter, who have no trouble disposing of their lumber.³⁶⁷

The article shifted from describing the actual to imagining the possible as it reviewed the area's desultory flirtation with oil drilling and then indicated that Petrolia's namesake industry could be revived with a significant influx of capital, part of which would go towards construction of a "chute for shipping purposes near the mouth of the Mattole River." This facility would not only make the transportation of petroleum possible but would also encourage the exportation of two other local products, apples and tanbark.[368] And indeed, during the following year, such a structure was built. (See sidebar 1.)

Not long after the Mattole Lumber Company built its wharf north of the mouth of the river, another construction project was started a few miles to the south. In 1911 work

---

### 1. The Mattole ~~Lumber~~ Tanbark Company

In 1872 Calvin Cooper Stewart established a shipping point at Newport, a Mendocino County community 12 miles north of Point Arena. Over the next 36 years he gradually moved north, purchasing (with various partners) mills, timberlands, and wharves along the coast. By 1893 he was at Bear Harbor, where he and three co-owners created the Bear Harbor Lumber Company and bought the preexisting wharf and 12,000 acres of timber. Three years later the company incorporated the Bear Harbor and Eel River Railroad. Stewart became a partner in the new Southern Humboldt Lumber Company in 1902, which planned to build a large mill on Indian Creek. He sold his interests in 1903 and focused his attention on tanbark.[369]

There were lots of tanoaks in the Mattole valley, but they were separated from the only shipping point on the southern Humboldt coast, Shelter Cove, by the rugged terrain between Honeydew and Ettersburg. About the time the *Humboldt Standard* was advocating "a chute for shipping purposes at the mouth of the Mattole River," Stewart was envisioning such a facility filled with loads of his tanbark. His vision turned to action in June 1908, when Walter Selvage commenced construction of a 2,000-foot-long wharf to Sea Lion Rock, which lay offshore a mile north of the mouth of the river. The following month Calvin Stewart, Thomas Johnston, and three other Stewarts incorporated the Mattole Lumber Company.[370]

The Mattole Indians called Sea Lion Rock Tci-ya-tci-se. They would swim out to the rock and kill the sea lions by clubbing them on the nose.[371] When the west end of the wharf was built atop their namesake rock, the resident sea lions departed.

In July 1908 Stewart ordered a tiny, saddletank,[372] wood-burning steam locomotive[373] from the Vulcan Iron Works of Wilkes-Barre, Pennsylvania. It did not have to be very big because the loads of tanbark it hauled, while bulky, were light weight. Although the locomotive was shipped in August 1908, it apparent-

The Mattole Lumber Company Wharf to Sea Lion Rock. (MVHS, colorized by JR).

ly entered a time warp en route to its destination, not arriving until July 1909. Accompanying the engine were five flat cars, rails, and ties.[374] The Mattole Lumber Company Railroad (MLCRR) now had much of its equipment.

Presently the MLCRR laid a set of narrow-gauge tracks from the Mattole lagoon northward up the coast and then out along the wharf to Sea Lion Rock. The tracks ran for about a mile and a half, making it the second shortest railroad in Humboldt County.[375] At the end of the wharf the company installed a steam donkey to operate a cable line that took loads of tanbark out to schooners anchored in deeper water west of the rock.

The Mattole Lumber Company built racks with four cornerposts that each held about a cord of tanbark. The racks were loaded onto the flat cars. When a train of flat cars reached the end of the wharf, each rack was attached to the cable line and sent, above the water, to the schooner.[376] On high ground next to the lagoon the company built a cookhouse, bunkhouses, blacksmith shop, barn, and engine house. Just east of the lagoon was property belonging to the Mattole Indian Joe Duncan.[377]

For a decade the MLCRR hauled tanbark along its wharf to Sea Lion Rock, along with apples, wool, and "freight."[378] In 1910 "a large quantity of lighthouse material" was delivered to the wharf for the new facility at Punta Gorda.[379] According to one account, "almost everything" was transported either into or out of the area via the wharf.[380]

MLCRR Engine #1, loaded with tanbark. (CPH, colorized by JR).

Although he had owned various lumber mills during his march up the coast, once he came to the Mattole area Calvin Stewart focused his attention on the harvesting and exporting of tanbark. His choice of the name Mattole Lumber Company harkened back to his earlier interests but did not reflect his new endeavor. By 1918 most of the area's tanbark had been harvested. The wharf, which was regularly ravaged by the sea, had been severely damaged in 1914 and 1916, "then [in 1918] closed down for good."[381]

The company maintained a business office in Petrolia, where it also operated a general merchandise store.[382] It lasted until 1922, when "the company made its last ledger entry."[383]

It took a while for the vestiges of the company's transportation system to vanish. The wooden wharf, regularly battered by the sea, was probably the first to go. The steam donkey on Sea Lion Rock oxidized for 21 years before its last rusty remnants disappeared in 1939, at which time the preternaturally patient sea lions returned to the rock.[384] At the Mattole lagoon, the erosive effects of water were also evident; the Mattole River moved to the north side of its enclosing canyon and washed away much of the Duncan property and the buildings of the Mattole Lumber Company.[385]

The MLCRR's first and only train engine, Mattole Lumber Company #1, had been left in its engine house at the lagoon. It was photographed in 1941, still inside the battered building, and not looking too bad. That had changed by December 1949, when it was no longer within the building and was covered with mud and gravel up to its saddletank. It was then that train buff and railroad historian Henry L. Sorensen learned about the relic, examined it, and then bought it for $1. Sorensen, Gus Haggmark, and a group of cohorts managed to extract the engine from its partial burial, move it to Sorensen's McKinleyville ranch, and restore it. There it remained until 2004, when it was transported to the Valhalla of train engines, the California State Railroad Museum in Sacramento.[386]

Ship passengers rode for free—if they first survived the ride atop a load of tanbark to the ship. (CPH, colorized by JR).

began on a lighthouse facility at Punta Gorda. (See Appendix D.)

A relapse of oil frenzy briefly struck the Mattole in 1920, but it soon passed,[387] joining the other temporary stimulations provided by a decade of tanbark harvesting and the establishment of the Punta Gorda Lighthouse. Petrolia then settled into a prolonged somnolence that is the fate of many middle-aged rural communities. With cattle and sheep ranching the principal economic activities, change came slowly to the area. When *Humboldt Times* feature writer Chet Schwarzkopf visited in April 1949, he found a remote valley reluctant to move into the midcentury present. He stopped to get water for his radiator from "an old sprinkling can under a hydrant" and was surprised to "hear the clang of an anvil!" He found Henry O'Leary still forging horse shoes much as his blacksmith father, Pat, did in the 1870s. "I like horses," O'Leary told Schwarzkopf. "We still use quite a few of them in the valley, both for range riding and for farm work,"[388] he continued, shrinking the decades so it would not seem surprising to see a troop of Petrolia rough riders galloping into town in search of Governor Gillett.

Schwarzkopf noted that Petrolia has "many a new house—as well as an up-to-date motor court," but the photos that accompany his article show the "original John Chambers home, built 1870" and "the Walker mansion of 22 rooms [that] was completed in early 1880s."

Other basic elements of the community included two churches—community and Catholic—and the Petrolia School. The high school, which had been the smallest in the county, had closed the previous year, and there were only 15 pupils in the grammar school.[389] With a population of about 200, Petrolia was "the center of the lower Mattole valley," but, as appraised by Schwarzkopf, it was nonetheless a "tiny town."[390]

If Petrolia was tiny, it was surrounded by decent-sized ranches. Joe Etter had 2,000 acres five miles up the Mattole, where he raised Romney sheep. Knowles Clark filled his 2,800-acre ranch with both Romney and Suffolk sheep. Jim, Francis, and Joe Cook operated a 3,000-acre ranch, while John Edmondson ranched 2,400 acres near Taylor Peak. Five Roscoes owned "enormous areas" some miles above Petrolia, and Clark Rackliff ran both sheep and cattle on his thousand-acre ranch. The Walker family managed both sheep and cattle on their 2,200-acre Sunset View Ranch; decades earlier Abe Walker had brought the first sheep into the valley. But the biggest holding of all was the original Domingo Zanone Ranch, a 6,000-acre spread north of Petrolia near the coast that was being run by various Zanone relatives and descendants.[391]

To hear Schwarzkopf describe it, the Petrolia area was locked into a sort of perpetual golden age of pastoral peace. Yet even at the time of his visit storm clouds were gathering over the sunny Mattole, ready to release their fury in the coming decades. Neb Roscoe, who spent his early years at Upper Mattole, got wind of it when he visited the area in 1953. He found that loggers had pushed a road right up the middle of his favorite fishing stream, Pritchett Creek. Not across the creek, but *up* it, so that the water was diverted into a ditch at the side of the road. When Neb wrote about it, he indicated that "more than forty years have passed, but I never returned to that scene of mindless destruction."[392]

The cutting frenzy that descended upon the Mattole sometimes devastated more than timberlands. (See sidebar 2.)

The logging boom on the Mattole began in 1947, part of a wave of increased lumber production that hit Humboldt County and other timber-rich areas after World War II. The hillsides above the river were incised with miles of logging roads, and cut timber was dragged to landings across the recently denuded slopes. Then the 1955 flood hit:

> Old-timers along the river remember whole log decks showing up, scattered in yards once the flood waters receded—yards that had once sat a half-mile back from the river.[393]

Despite the devastation, heavy timber cutting in the watershed continued:

## 2. Trucking Tragedy

In the 1970s it was still possible to encounter evidence of the intensity with which logging was conducted on the Mattole. Out-of-area motorists driving on the Wildcat Road were shocked to see heavily laden logging trucks laboring up the great grades north of Ocean House Ranch and then observe streams of water spraying from jury-rigged hose systems onto the trucks' overheated brakes during their descent down the opposite side of the ridge.[394]

For truck drivers, getting out the cut could be especially profitable if the rigs were overloaded with logs, thus requiring fewer trips to take the timber to the mills. It was tempting but dangerous for drivers to try this, and sometimes they failed to beat the odds.

That is what happened in May 1957 when two gambling truckers came down the Mattole in short succession. East of Petrolia Sam Brown was maneuvering his "heavily loaded" log truck over the Steel Bridge when he caught the end of one of his logs on a girder, severely damaging the structure. Deputy Sheriff Arthur Eckhardt was called to the scene, where he promptly halted traffic at both ends of the bridge. Richard Shelley drove up in his log truck about 15 minutes after Brown's accident. Shelley took a look at things and said, "I'm light," meaning he didn't have a full load. He added, "I've got to get home for dinner."

Eckhardt was walking back to his patrol car when he heard Shelley's truck start up. Before the sheriff could do anything, Shelley, his truck, and 19 tons of logs were on the bridge.

The bridge collapsed, dropping the truck 35 feet into the river. It landed on its side in some five feet of water. About a third of the cab was visible above the river. Eckhardt shouted down to Shelley, asking if he was hurt. Shelley responded, "No, I'm all right but you have to get a torch to burn me out."

While Eckhardt sped into Petrolia to get the necessary equipment, local resident Art Fisher scrambled down the bank and into the river, where he held the trapped driver's head above the water. Eckhardt returned and called down to Fisher, asking how Shelley was doing.

"I think he's dead," Fisher replied.

And he was right.[395] On time, or late, Shelley never made it to dinner.

The future "Little Golden Gate Bridge" at its original location south of Petrolia, 1957. Damaged by the 1955 flood, it was taken out of service in 1959. Three years later it was offered for sale by Humboldt County. Shirley Gundlach, thinking he had claimed it at auction, dismantled the bridge and moved to the Little Golden Gate subdivision on the Van Duzen River. County officials were surprised to find the bridge missing from the Mattole. Gundlach was even more surprised when told that he was not the high bidder.[396] (MVHS, colorized by JR).

The disaster of 1955 did little to slow the momentum of the logging boom. During the late fifties and early sixties, three sawmills were working around the clock in the lower valley and still could not handle the volume of timber that was coming out of the mountains.[397]

The 1964 flood came and went, but still the loggers kept cutting. Only in 1973, when passage of California's Forest Practices Act limited the level of destruction, did the logging frenzy slow, but by then "most of the largest trees had been taken."[398]

What, we might ask, would George Hill have made of it, had he been transported 119 years into the future? In 1854 he observed the forests on "the lands above the river bottoms" and concluded that there was "sufficient timber for fencing and firewood for ages to come."[399] Perhaps he was correct, given the modest uses he mentioned. But he did not foresee the appetite for trees that was to come later—tanoaks for the bark needed by the leather tanneries, Douglas-fir for the sawtimber needed for new houses. Once methods were found to remove these resources from the Mattole, they were extracted almost completely, leaving a lessened landscape that would have startled and perhaps saddened Hill and his ilk. It was certainly noted by later-day residents of the area, some of whom began restoration work as early as 1978. Eventually two organizations, the Mattole Watershed Salmon Support Group (later renamed the Mattole Salmon Group) and the Mattole Restoration Council, emerged as long-term repairers and protectors of the watershed. Perhaps they are heartened in their work by the conclusion of the poem read to Governor Gillett upon his arrival in Petrolia in 1907:

> Here are no temples grand,
> Joy reigns on every hand,
> Discord has left the land,
> And peace is found.[400]

## Appendix A: Newcomers on the Land

When the *Humboldt Times* suggested moving Humboldt Bay Indians to the Mattole in 1854, the editor had no idea that an actual reservation for that area would be contemplated by the federal government. When such a plan was proposed in 1857, the *Times* did not like it. The Mendocino Reservation had been established in 1856, with its headquarters at the Noyo River, just south of Fort Bragg. Its boundaries were unclear, but in early 1857 Special Agent James Tobin explored up the coast as far as Bear River and reported favorably on the intervening country.[401] Later that year the reservation's subagent, Captain H. S. Ford, wrote to Joel Benton of the Mattole valley that "Congress has appropriated the land from the mouth of Bear River to the mouth of the Noyo River . . . for an Indian Reservation."[402] Ford neglected to mention a Congressional caveat, however, requiring that "such extension shall not interfere with the preemption claims of settlers."[403] The *Times* promptly printed Ford's letter, accompanied by a scathing critique of the "outrage," and sent out copies of a statement of remonstrance to all county election precincts asking that it be signed by the locals on election day and sent to the Commissioner of Indian Affairs.[404]

The statement claimed that the proposed reservation extension would "appropriate more than one-half of our coast" and "lay a very heavy burden upon some sixty or seventy settlers."[405] Thomas J. Henley, the Superintendent of Indian Affairs of California, received the additional written wrath of numerous Humboldt County residents.[406] No mention was made of the burden the 60 or 70 settlers had already imposed on the local Indians.

Although the Mendocino Reservation was never extended up the coast to Bear River, a sort of outpost, called Mattole Station, was established on the north side of the Mattole River about two miles inland from the coast. It was maintained by a reservation employee, James Cunningham, and was about 100 acres in extent.[407]

In early June 1858 a man named Thornton was murdered in the upper Mattole valley. Although he was guilty of no crime himself, the local Indians had reportedly killed him in retaliation for other whites having raped Indian women.[408]

The local whites sought vengeance. Rather than attempting to locate and punish the actual murderers, a group of vigilantes first attacked the easiest target, Mendocino Station, and massacred the peaceful Indians gathered there. Superintendent Henley reported

>...the arrival of James Cunningham from the Mattole Station near Mendocino [sic] with the intelligence that the settlers in that vicinity have attacked, killed or driven away all Indians who had been collected at the station, and are now waging an indiscriminate war upon all who can be found either in the valley or in the mountains. He saw on the day he left for this place several Indians shot without any known provocation. He reports that a party of thirty men were then in readiness to start for Shelter Cove and other places upon the coast for the avowed purpose of attacking and destroying all the rancherias in that vicinity.
>
> Those Indians are peaceable and well disposed, and this is a most outrageous and murderous expedition.[409]

Although it was clear that the Indians had been murdered, no one in authority took action against the vigilantes. Instead the *Humboldt Times* ran an article describing the killing and mutilation of Thornton, calling the ensuing massacre of reservation Indians "a general war," and characterizing the reservation as a "nuisance."

A few months later Special Agent G. Bailey toured the California Indian reservations. He found evidence of fraud and malfeasance, and Henley was removed from his position in the spring of 1859. That December, the government, having reservations about the scope of the Mendocino Reservation, gave up its claim to land in the Mattole valley.[410]

Over the next several years numerous Indians in the Mattole valley were killed by white vigilantes or state militia. A pattern developed where the Indians, deprived of their usual food sources by encroaching whites, killed and butchered cattle, and then Indians were killed in retaliation.[411] According to Seth Kinman, some of the local whites placed a bounty on Indian scalps of $10. Kinman claimed that during the meeting where the bounty plan was discussed, a young white nicknamed "Wild Cat Steve" left the room, killed an Indian who was hoeing potatoes, and brought his scalp back before the meeting adjourned. Kinman thought it a "laughable occurrence" because the victim was a worker for the chairman of the meeting.[412]

In June 1862 Camp Olney was established by Lt. Charles Hubbard at Upper Mattole, making it easier for the military to attack local Indians. Two days later Hubbard's command killed six Indians, including one woman, and took six women and children prisoner. Two weeks later Hubbard sent seven Indians to Fort Humboldt.[413] Time lapsed; then, in May 1864 soldiers from the First Battalion, Mountaineers, chased a band of Indians from the Mattole to the coast. Lt. W. W. Frazier described what happened when the Indians were caught south of Big Flat:

> Two of the Indians commenced shooting arrows at us as soon as they saw us, but they did not last very long, for a well-directed ball from our rifles at each one of them sent them to their happy hunting ground and made good Indians of them. . . . Two bucks and six squaws succeeded in making good their escape, and the other two bucks are lying on the beach, food for bears.[414]

Later in the year troops commanded by Lt. Knyphausen Geer killed and captured other Indians on the Mattole, "thus ending the last physical resistance by Mattoles to White encroachment."[415] A dispatch from October 7, 1864, indicated that the Mattole valley was among the numerous areas in Humboldt County where "there are now but few if any Indians left."[416] According to local historian W. W. Roscoe,

> The year 1864 is generally considered the year of the close of the Indian War in the Mattole Valley. The old settlers here referred to that year as the year of the final round-up of the hostile Indians. During that year troops cornered and captured all the fighting Indians except a few stragglers who were taken into custody the next year. The great majority of the Indians were taken to the Round Valley Indian Reservation. A few were permitted to remain at the mouth of the Mattole River. Conspicuous among those who remained were Indian Jack, Indian Joe, and Indian Major. Some of the Indians sent to the reservation escaped and returned to the mouth of the river where they peacefully reestablished abode for themselves.[417]

Roscoe added that "about the year 1868 an epidemic of measles destroyed a large part of the Indian population at the mouth of the river."[418]

Eventually a few Mattoles returned from their internment on the reservations. They established a new village, called Da-ai-bi, about a mile southwest of Petrolia on the inner side of a large northward bend of the river.[419] A few places in the vicinity were still unoccupied. These were parcels unwanted by the whites, who had by then taken all the choice properties. The leftover land languished until 1887, when Congress passed the Dawes Act. This piece of legislation provided, among other things, a method whereby individual Indians could receive an allotment of surplus land and also be granted United States citizenship.[420] It turned out there were a number of eligible locations in the Mattole valley.

Among the first to receive an allotment was Isaac Joseph Duncan, who claimed a parcel in 1895. His father, Joe Duncan, had purchased land nearby a few years earlier.[421] By 1921 at least a score of Indians owned property within a few miles of Petrolia, most of it in the Shenanigan and Prosper ridge areas. Several of them, including Amos Riley,[422] were not Mattole Indians but instead were from the Wiyot tribe.[423] By then there was little, if any, vacant land left in Wiyot territory to be used for allotments.

Thus, 67 years after the *Humboldt Times* had recommended sending the Indians of Humboldt Bay to the Mattole, some of those selfsame people indeed held land on the river. The allotment of one of them, Jane D. Searson, was of special note. As a girl Searson had witnessed the *General Morgan* enter the Eel River while attempting to find Humboldt Bay, and later she had seen whites massacring Wiyot Indians on the lower river. Her husband told her "that this murdering was done for the purpose [of] getting our land."[424]

And indeed the whites had gotten the Wiyots' land. So much of it, in fact, that Searson and other members of the tribe could only find allotments for themselves far away on the Mattole River.

### Appendix B: The Hundred-Barrel Oil Boom

In July 1864 James W. Henderson visited the Mattole valley for three weeks, filled four or five flasks with oil, and set off by horseback for

Some land regained. In 1895 Ike Duncan claimed an Indian allotment on the flat in the foreground. His father Joe's property lay at the base of the hill across the river (JR).

San Francisco. All went well until Henderson reached Covelo, where his horse fell and all but one of the containers were broken. Down to his last flask, Henderson hesitated but then decided to continue south. Once in San Francisco he was uncertain what to do—how would he find investors for his oil project? Then he learned that Thomas Scott happened to be in town.[425]

By 1864 Scott had already drilled deep into the country's nascent oil industry. He was a man with a rising reputation. Starting as a stationmaster in 1850,[426] by 1853 Scott was a superintendent for the Pennsylvania Railroad. He employed, for $35 a month, a promising telegrapher and personal assistant named Andrew Carnegie.[427] Scott rose to become the first vice-president of the Pennsylvania Railroad and briefly served as Lincoln's Assistant Secretary of War.[428] In 1862 Scott and other Pennsy Railroad officials gained control of the Columbia Oil Company, and Scott took a seat on Columbia's board. The connection between the two companies allowed Columbia to "begin shipping the oil to Philadelphia and other seaboard cities at less than the cost of any other shipper, and the company at once began to make money." In the three months before Henderson met Scott, Columbia Oil had paid its investors $270,000 in dividends,[429] an amount that would be equivalent to about $4,350,000 today.[430]

Henderson located Scott, showed him his solitary remaining oil sample, and told him about the prospects on the Mattole. Scott, as it happened, was already assessing California's petroleum potential. When Josiah D. Whitney, head of the California Survey, determined that the state's asphaltum (a viscous or semisolid form of petroleum)[431] would not produce a viable substitute for whale oil, California petroleum promoters brought in Yale geologist Benjamin Silliman, Jr., who accommodatingly asserted that "the petroleum fields of California . . . were fully as promising as those he had unearthed in Pennsylvania."[432]

This timely pronouncement prompted Scott to engage the services of Levi Parsons as the purchaser of promising California petroleum properties.[433] In 1856 Parsons gained notoriety as part owner of the San Francisco Dock and Wharf Company, which modestly proposed to create a shore-stabilizing bulkhead along the city's waterfront in exchange for an exclusive right to develop and control all the infrastructure—piers, docks, tugboats, etc.—along the bay.

Building an oil derrick during another petroleum phantasy in the early 1950s (CPH, colorized by JR).

As part of the reward for this civic-minded kindheartedness, the company "would be exempt from license fees and almost all taxes forever."[434] The state legislature, its palms greased by the proposal's proponents, readily approved the plan, but Governor John G. Downey demurred, vetoing the bill. Instead, the state built the proposed seawall, and for good measure created the Board of State Harbor Commissioners, whose sole purpose was running the port of San Francisco. This legislation was signed by Governor Leland Stanford in 1863.[435]

Now it was 1864, and Parsons, acting as Scott's agent, purchased or leased some 450,000 acres of "choice localities from Los Angeles northward to the vicinity of Cape Mendocino."[436] For Humboldt County, Henderson received $75,000 from Scott to invest in oil lands.[437] Henderson's trip to San Francisco had proved providential.

The curtain then rose on one of the many stimulating but ultimately sterile speculations for which California became known:

> Chunks of . . . land were sold to hastily formed oil companies both in California and the East. Drillers and equipment were rushed from Pennsylvania across Panama to the West Coast, and an eager public was invited to participate, through the purchase of stock, in the newest of California's exotic treasures.[438]

Humboldt County, on the outer margin of the oil rush, joined in the frenzy. By 1865 more than 50 corporations, with a capitalization "exceeding $35,000,000," were plumbing the depths of the Mattole region in search of a gusher of crude. The three largest operations accounted for about half of the capital. The owners of these companies were from the distant cosmopolitan locations of Liverpool, Philadelphia, and St. Petersburg,[439] where investors should have been more savvy about such speculative schemes but obviously weren't. Even Governor Leland Stanford, who moved within the most exalted levels of capitalism, was susceptible to the buy-quick-and-get-rich bacillus. His Mattole Petroleum Company turned out to be the most successful of the local lot, but that merely meant that its Union Well produced 100 barrels of oil—total—at the stately rate of one barrel per day.[440]

By early 1866 it was clear that, in Humboldt County at least, the oil boom had ended with a thud. That March the Union Mattole Company, considered one of the area's leading producers, shipped out the not-so-grand total of 12 barrels of oil.[441] Reports of last-ditch drilling efforts continued into the fall, but by November the *Humboldt Times* conceded that the work "was doomed to failure."[442]

Years later a review of the oil boom by the California Mining Bureau described the causes of its quick termination on the Mattole. First was the lack of adequate and cheap transportation, not only for conveying the oil from the Mattole area but also for bringing in heavy drilling machinery. Second was a drop in crude oil prices brought about by the numerous discoveries in Pennsylvania. Third was a problem with obtaining proper title to the oil lands. Most of the parcels in the area had been acquired through homesteading, preemption, school warrants, etc. However, after oil was discovered on the properties, all such land was withdrawn by the government from acquisition and converted to mineral land, for which separate title had to be obtained. Many of the oil investors "closed down at once." Others stopped work but obtained proper title to their claims. Among the latter were Thomas Scott and Levi Parsons, who reportedly acquired over

# Petrolia

Waiting for the gusher that never came, c. 1950. (CPH, colorized by JR).

80,000 acres of petroleum property, "which they subsequently sold, reserving, however, the right to bore for oil."[443]

Despite this slowdown on the Mattole, Scott nonetheless had more than enough left on his plate to occupy him for the remainder of his life. Although he shunned the limelight, he increasingly pulled strings in the national puppet show of business and politics. In the 1870s Scott expanded his railroad interests by developing the Southern Railway Security Company as a north-south railroad line. When the Ku Klux Klan began terrorizing black freedmen working on the Southern Railway system, Scott responded by hosting a lavish oyster dinner for assorted wizards and dragons, at which the Klan leaders were offered "positions on the boards of various [railroad] subsidiaries." And when Scott needed more workers to build tracks through the north Georgia hill country, his managers merely "leased the entire population of the state penitentiary—393 convicts—at no charge." Many of the prisoners were former enslaved men who had been convicted of trumped-up offenses.[444]

Then came the presidential election of 1876. A close race between Republican Rutherford B.

Welcoming the latest gusher: how many pints equal a barrel? (FM, colorized by JR).

Hayes and Democrat Samuel Tilden resulted in an electoral college standoff that would be decided by the disposition of three southern states' votes. Scott, again pulling his puppets' strings, reportedly made the "actual determination" that Hayes would receive the votes. Once again, Scott's pursuit of his business interests had harmed the blacks of the South, since a main tenet of the agreement was that Hayes would end Reconstruction by removing Federal troops from the southern states. A lesser-known component of the deal allowed the Texas & Pacific Railroad, another of Scott's revenue-producing playthings, to "receive tens of millions of acres of public lands and huge federal subsidies."445

The capstone of Scott's career, however, was his successful corruption of a portion of the country's corporation law. Scott did this by developing an enshadowed entity known as the holding company, a legal sleight of hand that created a sort of megacorporation that "holds" (owns) the stock of regular corporations. This allowed the "holders" to create multiple corporations, each certified in its own particular state and thus each covered by that state's set of corporation laws. Thus, if a certain corporation was restricted by a certain state regulation, another corporation, based in a less-restrictive state, could be created. Then Corporation A, in the restrictive state, could sell its stock to Corporation B, in the less restrictive state, and conduct operations based on the lax regulations of Corporation B's state.446 It proved to be an extremely effective way to circumvent laws designed to prevent corporate abuse, and the robber barons who controlled much of American business adored it.

**Appendix C: 1907: Petrolia's Banner Year**

It is not often that the trajectories of politics and automotive technology converge, but they did so in the spring of 1907, sparking an outburst of rhapsodic rhetoric that is still startling more than a century later.

It happened in Petrolia.

The episode had its origins in the singular passion with which Petrolians embraced the Republican Party. To say they were loyal to a man barely stretches the truth, as the following account illustrates. A newcomer came to the Petrolia post office to register to vote. The registrar, Gib Langdon, asked the man for his party affiliation. "Democrat," was the reply. To which Langdon reportedly responded, "How do you spell it?"447

In actuality, there were probably three Democrats in town,[448] but in the 1906 general election the Petrolia precinct voted overwhelmingly (some accounts say unanimously) for the straight Republican ticket. This caught the attention of various party bigwigs, including former Eureka City Attorney James Norris Gillett, who had just been elected governor. It had been a difficult campaign, with party boss Abe Ruef orchestrating Gillett's nomination over George Pardee, the Republican incumbent. Pardee was a Progressive and a conservationist. He opposed the Southern Pacific Railroad—the "Octopus"— that dominated California politics and that squeezed every dime it could from the state's farmers and businessmen, who depended on the railroad to ship their produce and goods. The manipulation by Ruef and others galvanized opposition to Gillett, and it appeared that his Democratic opponent, Theodore A. Bell, had a chance of winning.[449] But Bell and the Democrats proved no match for the ego of newspaper mogul William Randolph Hearst, who had created a third party, the Independence League, as a vehicle for him to run for the governorship of New York.[450] League candidates also ran in several other states, including California.[451] There William H. Langdon won 14.4 percent of the vote for Hearst's fledging party, draining off support for Bell, who received 37.7 percent. That was enough to secure a winning plurality for Gillett, even though he received only 40.4 percent of the vote.[452]

Perhaps mindful of Gillett's slim margin of victory, it was arranged that he would travel to Petrolia to reward its voters for their loyalty to the Republican party. Adding interest to the event was the method chosen for getting there—a fleet of that newfangled contraption, the automobile, which would try to traverse the primitive roadway between Ferndale and Petrolia.[453]

Even the prospect of Gillett's trip was enough for the *Humboldt Standard* to loose an outburst of orotundity. Two days before the main event, under the front-page headline "Petrol Wagons for Petrolia," readers were confronted with great blocks of all-but-impenetrable prose:

> On next Saturday Petrolia will be invaded by a squadron of machines, the material for furnishing the power of which, either directly or indirectly, is derived from the natural product after which the town is named—petroleum. . . .
>
> The descent of the petrol wagons on the little town that once aspired to be a rival of Pennsylvania's Oil City, will be on the occasion of the formal presentation of the Republican banner to its citizens for having cast the solidest Republican vote in the county at the last general election.[454]

So it was that on Friday, August 16, 1907, a convoy of "petrol wagons" left the Vance Hotel in Eureka bound for Fortuna, with Governor Gillett occupying "a seat in H. A. Poland's White steamer." Should this vehicle fail to successfully navigate the Wildcat Road on Friday, the governor would be transferred to Fred Smythe's runabout, which apparently was more highly rated for reliability.[455]

On Saturday, "all of the machines behaved well," reaching Capetown at 6:45 A.M., only 45 minutes after leaving Ferndale. Following a quick but "splendid" breakfast, the convoy was off to Petrolia. Arriving about 9:00 A.M., "the

Gillett's auto cavalcade looks sharp, 1907. (JRC, colorized by JR).

string of autos lined up with Governor Gillett's auto in the lead and with banners flying and cannons booming the distinguished guest and his party were royally and cordially received by the reception committee...."[456]

Then, according to the *Standard*, came "the feature of the day . . . [with] the appearance on the scene of fifty mounted rough riders headed by Jim Goff and these knights of the saddle acted as an escort to the governor on the trip to the picnic grounds."[457]

After the two score and ten horsemen evoked recollections of the Rough Rider in the White House, Gillett gave a banner-presentation speech linking the Republican Party with the enforcement of the country's laws, focusing, for the eager ears of the Petrolians, on "the recent persecution of the great corporate interests and the punishing of the Standard Oil Company by the recent fine of nearly thirty millions of dollars." The banner was presented and received, the orchestra provided a cadence to the proceedings, and then everyone—from current rough rider to former oil rig roughneck—turned their attention to the luncheon, which included not one but two barbecued beeves. Those who could subsequently rouse themselves then danced, although this was but a prelude to the grand ball that was staged at the Petrolia town hall that evening.[458]

Two days later the *Standard* published the poem of welcome that had been recited to the governor upon his arrival in Petrolia. It contained the ringing couplet,

# Petrolia

Honor the name "Gillett"—
Our wants he won't forget.⁴⁵⁹

The paper also recapitulated Gillett's cosseted return from Petrolia, first noting that

> . . . the ease with which such cars . . . climb the steepest grades is a revelation to one who has never before sat in a car and found himself lifted at a 7-mile [per hour] clip."⁴⁶⁰

But not all the cars climbed with equal ease. The White steamer that was carrying Gillett "had a break in its condenser."⁴⁶¹ The *Ferndale Semi-Weekly Enterprise*, which also covered the trip, described the problem more elliptically as "a disarrangement of the machinery."⁴⁶² Thus decondensed, the governor, as per the contingency plan, was transferred to F. W. Smythe's Maxwell, there to enjoy the rest of his return trip to Eureka.⁴⁶³ The *Standard's* account implied that only the Sapa Inca, carried on the shoulders

A banner day for Petrolia. (JRC, colorized by JR).

of his subjects, had enjoyed greater solicitude in his mountain travels.

### Appendix D: From San Quentin to Alcatraz

There was no lighthouse at Punta Gorda in 1905, but even if one had been present it would not have prevented the steamer *St. Paul* from hitting a submerged rock a short distance off shore.[464]

On a moonlit summer night the *St. Paul* was running up the coast when the lookout called out, "breakers ahead." It was a message no sailor wanted to hear and normally caused an instantaneous response from the bridge.[465]

But not now.

With the breakers only a half mile away, the *St. Paul* continued straight towards them. The lookout saw "the mate pacing back and forth on the bridge . . . but he just kept pacing." The lookout sang out a second and a third warning but the ship remained headed for the beach.[466]

Suddenly the *St. Paul* stopped. She had hit a submerged rock and caught fast.[467]

The *St. Paul* was only about 200 yards from shore,[468] and taking a lifeboat, the crew and passengers easily reached the beach. Still on board was the ship's cargo, which included a horse belonging to a man named Williamson, and—most important of all—numerous barrels and bottles of whiskey.[469]

Williamson went back to the *St. Paul* and managed to get his horse to jump into the water. The horse started swimming to shore but soon gave up. He finished the trip with Williamson, who was in a life boat, holding the horse's head up by the halter as the semi-submerged steed was floated to shore.[470]

T. K. Clark was eleven at the time. He eventually spent his entire life in the Mattole area. When he was 89 he wrote an account of the *St. Paul's* wreck in which he claimed that

> . . . of the five wrecks that I have attended fairly close by, the St. Paul was the best of all. Seemed to me that this ship which was on its way to Alaska was stocked just about like a store should be. . . .[471]

On Saturday T. K. and his brother Charles went down to see the wreck. The *St. Paul*, still caught on the rock, hadn't gone anywhere. The brothers had only walked a half-mile down the beach when they saw a wooden box floating in the surf. The managed to bring it to shore, opened it, and beheld "twelve quart bottles of Jesse Moore triple AAA whiskey."[472] No wonder the *St. Paul* was T. K.'s favorite wreck.

There was more whiskey still on board the *St. Paul*. It came ashore in a most unusual fashion. The ship had already spent several months stranded on its rock when the ship's insurance company "decided to have the most valuable cargo unloaded." A man named Des Francis was hired to dynamite open a compartment in the *St. Paul* to facilitate the process. The charge went off. It immediately became apparent that Francis had been overexuberant in his use of the explosives. A fire quickly tore through the ship, burning "everything except what was covered by sea water at high tide."[473]

No further attempt was made to remove the cargo, but in anticipation of the high seas of winter, several Mattole men came down to the beach, built small shelters, and waited.[474]

Soon enough a big storm hit. It happened at night when only one man, Rube Hunter, was on watch. While the others slept, Hunter, seeing big oaken barrels washing ashore, went to work. He managed to roll about 40 barrels up to his shelter on the beach. Meanwhile, Grover Gardner woke up, roused his brothers, and together they were able to salvage six barrels.[475]

Word got out about Hunter's find. The county sheriff came down to the beach, impounded the 40 barrels and gave Hunter a receipt. The sheriff indicated that a determination would be made as to who rightfully owned the flotsam whiskey.[476]

Time passed, and when no word was forthcoming about the impounded whiskey, Hunter went to Eureka to see the sheriff. He was told that all the salt water had gotten into all the barrels and the contaminated whiskey thrown out.[477] The explanation may have been inaccurate.

The sheriff never learned about the six barrels the Gardner boys had salvaged. When they were opened later they were all found to have uncontaminated 25-year-old bonded bourbon.[478]

Earlier, three other locals had rowed out to the *St. Paul* and removed some of its cargo. They were caught. One of them, George Titus, turned state's evidence with the result that Bogus Wright spent 13 months in jail while Joe Francisco was sentenced to three years in San Quentin State Prison.[479]

Not far from the *St. Paul's* wreck site another prison, of sorts, was subsequently established. It was the Punta Gorda Lighthouse, whose light was first lit in January, 1912. Situated about three miles south of the mouth of the Mattole River, the lighthouse was about eight miles from town, and the trip between the two places was no picnic. During the summer a team of horses could pull a supply wagon along the beach and over the hills, but in winter the "rushing streams

Punta Gorda houses (HCHS, colorized by JR).

and high surf limited travel to horseback." For years the horse that made the trips was "Old Bill," who was "mean and ornery" and insisted on trying to jump across any puddle he encountered. Lighthouse keeper Wayne Piland braided a small whip and introduced Old Bill to it, after which "Piland and Old Bill got along just fine."[480]

In 1935 the government built a road from the Mattole to Windy Point and then another road that ran south of the point to the lighthouse. This infrastructure improvement was effective during the summer, but in stormy weather Old Bill was reactivated. He was still on duty in 1949, along with two other horses, Tom and Jerry. Technology advanced, the Coast Guard placed a lighted buoy offshore, and in 1951 it closed the station. Old Bill was sold to a woman in Ferndale.[481] By the time of its closure, the difficult-to-access lighthouse had earned the nickname "the Alcatraz of Coast Guard Stations."[482]

Besides the light itself, there were several other structures at the station, including three large houses, a barn, and a blacksmith shop.[483] The sturdy houses and remote location made the lighthouse complex an inviting location for squatters, the last of which were "eight longhair types [who] were politely but firmly ushered off the station"[484] in 1970. A few weeks later the Bureau of Land Management, which by then was in charge of the station, discouraged its further use by burning all the wooden buildings. All that remained were two concrete structures, the lighthouse and the oil house.[485] Photos of these buildings are periodically posted by hikers, who, in emulation of Old Bill, have made their way to the North Coast's abandoned Alcatraz.

# Chapter 5
# Union Mattole and Upper Mattole

Between Honeydew and Petrolia, the Mattole River runs through a fertile valley that proved hospitable both to Indians and to early-day white homesteaders. A branch of the Sinkyone tribe, known only as the "Upper Mattole people," had a string of villages that started near Indian Creek and ran upriver to at least the vicinity of Ettersburg.[486] After whites arrived in the lower portion of the locale, community activities coalesced around two locations, neither having the trappings to be considered a town, but each having enough importance to become a dot on a map. Locals, at least, were cognizant of these stations on the river, understanding the importance of Union Mattole and Upper Mattole.

The first white resident in the Mattole Valley was probably Alfred Augustus ("A. A.") Hadley who, according to various reports, took up land in what came to be called Upper Mattole sometime between 1849 and 1852. He may have been accompanied by a partner, James Young.[487] According to one account, Hadley was present when the Josiah Gregg party came up the valley in early 1850, and Hadley obligingly drew a map for Gregg that showed the way to the Sonoma Trail.[488]

The 1865 county map shows Hadley's property on the south side of the river, across from G. H. Brown's place. A trail that started at the coast ran north-northeast to Hadley's place and then continued north across the mountains to Eagle Prairie (later renamed Rio Dell). Another trail ran southeast from Hadley's 30 miles to the James and John Wood ranch just southwest of the future location of Garberville.[489] The Hadley-Wood connection was strengthened in 1895 when A. A. Hadley's son, Warren, married James Wood's daughter, Ella.[490] Before his own marriage, the elder Hadley had the briefest of courtships. (See sidebar 1.)

Soon after the Hadley marriage, relations on the Mattole between Indians and whites took a turn for the worse. (See sidebar 2.)

Downriver from Hadley's place was a swath of land running from above Squaw Creek down to Indian Creek that was labeled "Jerusalem" on the 1865 county map.[491] The name does not appear on the next county map (1886) but the 1890-1891 county directory lists it under "Towns of Humboldt County."[492] Apparently to avoid confusion with a community half a world away and several thousand years older, the Mattole River location was later referred to as New Jerusalem. The naming of the place reputedly resulted from the fervent gospel singing of the Reverend John Harrow and Asa Harrow families,[493] which was enjoyed by the singers but perhaps a harrowing experience for others. As New Jerusalem grew older, its name was changed to Union Mattole.

In June 1862, the Second California Infantry created a military presence in the Mattole valley by establishing Camp Olney at Upper Mattole.[494] On June 7 a detachment of soldiers attacked an Indian rancheria that was apparently in the canyon of the Mattole, upriver from the future site of Honeydew. Six Indians were killed, five men and a woman. One of the victims was an Indian named Joe, who was identified as the murderer of a Mr. Wise, who'd been killed the

## 1. Table Talk

In 1857 A. A. Hadley stopped at the George Singley ranch (which later became Ocean House) near the mouth of Singley Creek. Hadley took a fancy to Mary Ann Rouche (Annie) Singley, a young Indian woman, who was about 12 or 13[495] and who had been raised by the Singleys. That evening Annie excused herself from the dinner table, gathered her "meager personal belongings," and walked south until she was opposite Steamboat Rock. There Annie waited behind a group of large, honeycomb rocks. A. A. duly appeared on his horse, Annie climbed on behind him, and they rode southward to Upper Mattole and matrimony.[496]

In January 1858 A. A. and Annie Hadley were married in Petrolia[497] and went on to have 11 children.[498] A biographical sketch of A. A. stated:

> On several occasions he had fights with the Indians, and one time had his leg broken and was badly disabled, but he did not lose his grit or courage, and though his companions fled, he drove off the savages single handed with his six-shooter, with which he was an expert.[499]

In the 1930s a Wiyot woman named Carrie Seidner wrote about early-day white men who murdered Indians. Seidner listed a number of

> . . . old Settlers and they were bad ones[;] they kill Indians where they could find one all over the valey [sic] Eureka and mad river Rio Dell. and the worst ones [were] the ones that had Indian women that is how [it] all come out[.] the women [were] told what [the men] would do[.] the men would tell them. and i will tell you the names of the men had Indian women.
> 
> John Duncon, Jack Frassher, Dicke Shaw, Nick Tomkins, John Robison, Haddley, Bill Johnson, Lafferty, Dicker Heffley, Close, John Hasley, Jim Whitman, Joe, and there is a loot [sic] more I did not remember and kill [.] the Indian women are dead now but one Mrs Haddley. . . .[500]

Annie Hadley died in 1937. According to her death certificate, she would have been 91 or 92 years old.[501] In 1907, at age 78, A. A. was killed when his horse threw him, headfirst, into a deep mudslide that had covered the road at Shenanigan Ridge.[502]

Hadley's death came 60 years after Annie had left her dinner at Singleys' to elope with him, ample time for her to listen to all of his table talk.

## 2. "A Treaty of Peace and Friendship"

In the spring of 1858 the remains of a man named Thornton were found in the upper Mattole valley. His body, according to the *Humboldt Times*, had been mutilated "in a horrible manner."[503] The local whites concluded, by a process not reported, that the assailants were Indians and commenced to wage what the *Times* euphemistically called a "general war" against them.[504] Anthony Jennings Bledsoe, no friend of the Indians, predictably claimed that "the settlers in the Mattole valley were incensed beyond forbearance," but he then veered off-script and revealed the true nature of the "war," stating that "for a time there was an *indiscriminate slaughter* of such Indians as could be found by the settlers, twenty being killed in two weeks." [emphasis added].[505]

Bledsoe then returned to his melodramatic apology for the behavior of the whites:

> For the three months succeeding the murder of Thornton there was no sense of security in the Mattole region. The settlers kept their guns within reach at all hours, fearful of the treacherous approach of their treacherous foe. . . . [but] the bloody revenge of the settlers for the murder of Thornton had had a salutary effect on the tribes of the vicinity. They announced their willingness to make a treaty of peace and friendship with the whites.[506]

This was gun barrel diplomacy at its starkest, but the Indians, having just seen a score of their people murdered, had "willingness" forced upon them. The "treaty" made it clear that the whites intended to completely control the behavior of the local Indians. The first clause required the Indians' help in finding "the three Indian murderers now running at large who were concerned in the murder of Mr. Thornton." This was a startling admission that the recent vigilante killings of 20 native people were motivated by blind revenge and a desire to intimidate, for the statement acknowledged that Thornton's murderers were still at large and were not among the victims of the recent white attacks. Other clauses pledged to protect the Indians if they adhered to the terms of the treaty, but those terms were ripe for creating conflict: while one clause permitted the Indians "to return and live in the Valley, collect their wild food, fish, etc.," another section prohibited them from setting fire to the grass, even though prairie burning was a long-used method of preserving their hunting and gathering areas. The same clause required that the Indians "not reside on our claims without our consent," while failing to acknowledge that these "claims" had earlier been taken from the Indians without *their* consent.[507]

Thus half the treaty's title was incorrect from the start, for how could "friendship" exist when one set of "friends" (the whites) had murdered 20 of the other set of "friends" (the Indians), and then created a set of self-serving rules and demanded that the other group obey them?

The second half of the title also proved inaccurate as the whites continued to attack the Indians who, for some reason apparently unanticipated by the whites, continued to remain hostile.[508]

Site of Camp Olney (JR).

previous fall in the Mattole valley. Lt. Charles G. Hubbard, the Camp Olney commander, included an assessment of the local situation in a subsequent report:

> So far as I can ascertain, all the Indians in this portion of the country are hostile; in fact, will ever be so, so long as there are no active and vigorous steps taken to put an end to cold-blooded murder, kidnapping, and treachery. These are in my opinion the sole causes of all these difficulties with the Indians, more especially in this portion of the country and on Eel River. Cold-blooded Indian killing being considered honorable, shooting Indians and murdering even squaws and children that have been domesticated for months and years, without a moment's warning, and with as little compunction as they would rid themselves of a dog. . . . Human life is of no value in this valley, and law seems only to be respected as far as it is backed by visible force. It is well known that kidnapping is extensively practiced by a gang who live in the neighboring mountains . . . [along] with other barbarities, murder, rape, &ct, which no pen can do justice to. If the Indians are hostile they will always be so until some stringent measures are taken to protect them, and to wipe out the perpetrators of these most horrible crimes against humanity.[509]

Thus it was clear that Hubbard realized that the cause of the ongoing Indian-white conflict had its roots in the problematic behavior of many of the local whites. But defining the problem and solving it were two different things, and without a solution, both Indians and whites continued to suffer from the conflict on the Mattole. (See sidebar 3).

As if the massacre at Squaw Creek was not enough, a second murderous attack by whites, date unknown, occurred nearby at the upper Mattole people's village of Ikedin, in the vicinity of Pritchard Creek. "It was here," according to Joe Duncan, that "the white men killed them all when they were catching eels."[510] Duncan also indicated that farther up the river, about a mile west of Honeydew at the village of Lonitci, the whites killed 15 Indians at an undetermined date. A man named Myers rescued one Indian woman.[511]

At one point a young female Indian, who was working for the Pritchett family, was suspected of providing information to the Indian combatants about the movements of the troops at Camp Olney. According to Neb Roscoe, this suspicion was enough for the camp's commander to have her executed without trial.[512]

By September 1864 the conflict in the Mattole area was drawing to a close.[513] According to Lt. Knyphausen Geer of the First Mountaineer Battalion, there was "still one last band, a small party, in the Mattole neighborhood that kept killing, robbing and destroying property." Geer's commander, Col. Henry M. Black, told Geer, "Go and get those Indians, Captain,[514] then knock the dust off your shoes and say 'Goodbye,' that's the last there is here."[515]

According to Geer's account, his detachment found the Indians' trail near Cooskie Peak. They pursued the Indians into the Bear River drainage; then back to the Mattole; then down the coast past Big Flat, Shelter Cove, and Bear Harbor; and then inland to the headwaters of the Mattole. The Indians next went south to the Leggett area. Here Geer's detachment caught up with them. Then, claimed Geer, "Next morning

### 3. Mistaken Identities

At about 7 A.M. on the morning of September 2, 1863, John McNutt left M. J. Conklin's house and rode upriver. A half mile ahead, at Shenanigan Hill, a group of Indians waited in ambush. They were expecting Theodore Aldrich, who was known to "put poisoned grain out for Indians"[516] and "whom they [therefore] hated vehemently." When McNutt rode into view, he was mistaken for Aldrich by one of the Indians, who shot him in the stomach. According to one account, McNutt "reeled in the saddle," exposing his red hair. The Indians, knowing Aldrich had black hair, fled. McNutt made it to a nearby house, where he died about half an hour later. A group of whites formed a posse and tracked down the Indians. The murderer was "betrayed" by the other members of his band, and the whites hanged him from a tree.[517]

Nearly six months later another ambush and fatal shooting occurred. Patrick Mackey and Thomas Lambert were partners in a ranch that ran from Cooskie Peak down to the ocean. One late February day in 1864, they had just finished repairing a corral on Cooskie Creek when Lambert was shot in the back. According to Mackey, the shot had come from one of two Indians, who then shot at Mackey as he ran for cover and who then again shot Lambert where he lay. Mackey subsequently escaped and brought news of the murder to the Mattole.[518]

Again the whites formed a posse. Its intent apparently wasn't to find the perpetrators but simply to heedlessly avenge Lambert's murder, for the whites knew that Indians had a conveniently located rancheria on Squaw Creek about two miles up from its mouth,[519] and they went up there and attacked it. Most of the Indian men were reportedly off hunting,[520] leaving only the group's leader, Snaggletooth, and the women and children. Snaggletooth was killed, depending on the report, either by Bill Roberts or Theodore Aldrich,[521] and the posse murdered all of the women and children. According to one account the most violent killer of the children was Aldrich, the man the Indians had tried to shoot when they mistakenly killed McNutt.[522] It was the massacre that gave the creek its name.[523]

According to Neb Roscoe, after Lambert's death,

> . . . no papers came to light to show that Mackey had ever deeded any part of the property to Lambert. Nothing had been recorded, and the property remained in Patrick Mackey's name thereafter. Naturally there was speculation that he, and not the Indians, had killed Lambert.[524]

Mackey Ranch (HCHS, colorized by JR).

If such speculation was true, it was the second case of mistaken identity on the Mattole within six months. First John McNutt was killed by Indians instead of their intended victim, Theodore Aldrich. Then local whites mistook Indians as the killers of Thomas Lambert instead of his partner, Patrick Mackey. This second mistake led to the massacring of a group of Indians on Squaw Creek, where one of the main attackers was Aldrich, whose life had been spared because of the first mistake. Neither Shakespeare nor the Greeks ever conceived a story more tragic.

we surrounded the Indians and got all but one buck that we wounded. We took all the rest with us back to Fort Humboldt, as prisoners."[525]

It is unclear from Geer's report how many Indians were killed during the engagement. The September 17 *Humboldt Times* ran an article that was more explicit:

> The detachment of troops under Lieut. K. N. Geer, stationed at Mattole, has been doing good work within the last two or three weeks. The remainder of the [Indian] gun party, so called, which has been the scourge and terror of the citizens located in the district of county lying between Eel river and Mattole, has been, it is believed, with a single exception, wiped out.[526]

M. J. Conklin, writing about the end of the conflict, indicated that at some point he had gone to Fort Humboldt and asked Col. Black "that a force of soldiers be stationed in our valley." Black did so. Conklin concluded that "We then, after two years more of war, killed the Indians all off."[527]

With the local Indians mostly either dead or confined to reservations, the whites in the Mattole valley turned their attention elsewhere. In November 1864, less than two months after the conclusion of Geer's Indian hunting expedition, the Mattole Mining District was formed to allow for the orderly development of oil resources. Soon other districts were established along the river, so that by 1865, the Walker, Pennsylvania, Mattole, Frazier, and Upper Mattole districts abutted the river between its mouth and the Honeydew area. Although the oil "boom" busted within two years,[528] in its aftermath the Upper Mattole area maintained its population. In the 1864 election only seven votes were cast at Upper Mattole. This total increased to 21 the following year, at the peak of the boom.[529] In 1875, the oil excitement long past, 24 Upper Mattolians voted.[530] The 1860 presidential race saw the Mattole election district, which ran from Cape Mendocino to Shelter Cove,[531] favoring John C. Breckenridge,[532] the Southern Democratic Party candidate, who subsequently became a brigadier general in the Confederate army.[533]

In May 1866 the *Humboldt Times* received a "Letter from Mattole" that contained an account of New Jerusalem, which contained "six houses, a church, a tannery, and a blacksmith shop." The church, from which the Harrows produced their high-intensity hymns, was "a structure of logs . . . in a rather dilapidated condition."[534]

The author of the letter continued upriver to the next community, which he (or she) called "Brownsville," after G. H. Brown. It was "situated on a high table above the Mattole River" and was "not as large as Petrolia." Its exact size was left to the reader's imagination, as at this point the description ended.[535]

In the spring of 1871 itinerant bookseller John Morris visited Humboldt County. He first canvassed Eureka, which was in the middle of a lumber slump and where he was able to sell only 20 books. This was a discouraging total, but Morris was hopeful that he could do better in the county's agricultural areas, one of which was the Mattole. He was warned against going there, however, because it was believed that "most of the men had married Indian women and that neither the men nor their women could read." Morris went anyway and returned to Eureka with "an order from every family in the Mattole." He encountered one man who claimed he was a graduate of Harvard and who therefore ordered two books. Another man could not read, but he bought a book anyway when his hired hand promised he would read it to him.[536]

Not only books but mail became more accessible in 1871, as that December the Upper Mattole post office opened.[537] The ability of locals to read both books and the mail was enhanced by the establishment of the Upper Mattole School in 1876 and the Union Mattole School in 1879.[538]

Following the upheavals caused by the decade-long Indian-white conflict and the briefer two-year oil boom, the upper Mattole valley settled into the sort of bucolic stability that is the destiny of many areas where ranching predominates. The decades passed, the century turned, and the 1900s finally brought an uptick in news reports from the valley.

In March 1904 sisters Ida and Mary Hadley, along with boatman Jack Harris, drowned in the Mattole while trying to cross the river in a canoe. Harris attempted to save the Hadley women, but both sisters and Harris sank into the river and did not come up.[539]

The *Daily Humboldt Standard* carried a report on Upper Mattole in 1907, indicating that the valley in which it lies

Tanbark convoy along the Mattole (HCHS, colorized by JR).

. . . is about five miles long and is surrounded by fertile hills, containing both open and forest land. The population of the valley and surrounding country is about 200. Stock raising is the principal industry at the present time. Cattle, horses, sheep, Angora goats all thrive on the nutricious [sic] grasses which grow both in the valley and on the surrounding hills.

Our productions consist of all kinds of grain, including Indian corn and all kinds of vegetables, such as potatoes, carrots, beets, rutabages [sic], pumpkins, squash and all other vegetables; also all kinds of fruit, such as apples, pears, peaches, prunes, plums, apricots, and all kinds of berries, which flourish in a temperate climate.[540]

The article also noted "that there are about 80,000 cords of tanbark on the hills surrounding the valley." In addition to the value of its bark, the *Standard* believed that tanoaks could be used for lumber, predicting that

. . . there is little doubt that when the value of this wood becomes better known for commercial purposes that the timber which is now allowed to rot on the ground will be more valuable than the bark which it contains.[541]

To transport the bark, the *Standard* indicated that "a chute or landing near the mouth of the Mattole river is necessary."[542] And indeed, Calvin Stewart and the Mattole Lumber Company created such a device the following year, which ushered in a decade of tanbark harvesting.[543]

In 1913 Joseph Bagley formed the Mattole Valley Orchard Tract Company and bought about 2,000 acres of agricultural land. His plan to subdivide the land into small tracts of five to twenty acres for walnut, apple, and pear orchards never came to fruition,[544] but for a time the business operated an impressive truck.

Located across the Mattole from the Hadley ranch was a large stretch of land belonging to the Roscoe family.[545] In June 1914 Wesley Horton Roscoe and Aramintha Patton Roscoe celebrated their 56th wedding anniversary. The joyfulness of the event was dampened by two unexpected incidents. First, the picnic that had been planned was forced indoors by a steady rain. Second, Roscoes' son, Lewis, and his niece, Frieda, "were ill with the measles, which was not known to some of the relatives until too late to prevent their going."[546]

Wesley and Aramintha had moved to the Mattole in 1876, part of a late wave of the so-called "Marysville Settlers," who had started arriving eight years earlier. By 1919, when Wesley died, their ranch included about 1,500 acres.[547] When Aramintha passed away in 1924, only four of her and Wesley's eight children were still alive.[548] A grandson, Stan Roscoe, his wife Martha, and their son Neb were living with Stan's parents in Upper Mattole in 1922 when the house caught fire. Various Roscoes carried possessions from the house, but the fire spread quickly and little was saved. Among the losses was Martha's collection of 2,000 books. It was the second time a Roscoe house had burned on the same spot.[549] A third structure, described as a "commodious Craftsman home," was then built "at the same spot." It still stands across from a Roscoe barn built in 1880.[550]

In the fall of 1927 a new surge of petroleum interest again surfaced as both the First National Petroleum Company and the North Counties Oil Company began drilling in the Upper Mattole

Bagley's big plans resulted in a big truck but little else (CPH, colorized by JR).

This Roscoe barn dates from 1880 (JR).

area. A flurry of optimistic articles appeared in the local papers for a few months[551] and then, as reality again asserted itself, subsided.

Fire struck Union Mattole in 1934 when its community hall burned down.[552] The slack thus created was soon taken up with the completion of the Mattole Grange Hall in 1935.[553]

In 1937 Ken Roscoe purchased a flock of 150 small Merino ewes that he then bred with Dorset horned rams. He was ridiculed by his cousin for having bought "such poor, little scrub sheep." The winter lambing yielded Roscoe exactly 150 lambs, which, come June, were shipped to the Washburn and Condon Commission Livestock Company in South San Francisco. Later that year the *Western Livestock Journal* reported that Roscoe "had received the highest price paid for a carload of lambs [that year] in the United States."[554] No comment from his cousin was recorded.

Following World War II, timber harvesting came to the Upper Mattole area. In 1950 mills were being built on the Etter and Hadley properties, which brought an influx of loggers and their families. As a result, enrollment was expected to roughly double in the Upper Mattole School, going from 17 students to probably "30 or more." The school district's trustees grappled with the problem of transporting the additional students: "in the past few years a car and later a pickup, driven by Robert Hayter has been satisfactory, but now several trips would be required to haul all the students to the school. . . ." The district considered buying a bus to solve the problem, but many residents felt that the taxation required to fund the purchase was "unwarranted."[555]

Confronted with issues like this, the Upper Mattole area moved, reluctantly, through the middle of the 20th century.

Students at the Upper Mattole School, 1916 (CPH, colorized by JR).

# Chapter 6
# Honeydew

Near the confluence of the Mattole River and Honeydew Creek, there were two Indian villages. They belonged to a tribal group connected with the so-called Sinkyone tribe that is known only as the "Upper Mattole People." One village was near the mouth of the Upper North Fork and was called Nowilkedin ("like a necktie) or Gacdulyaidin; the other was west of the mouth of Honeydew Creek and was called Djegullindin.[556] Nothing more is known about the villages or their inhabitants.

From Honeydew Creek to its mouth, the Mattole River runs through a twisting valley wide enough to allow room for some ranching areas and a road. Above Honeydew Creek the river is confined within a gorge that for miles offers no space for the road to continue, so the route south leaves the river and ascends Wilder Ridge. This arrangement proved tolerable for a time, but with the establishment of a Northwestern Pacific (NWP) train station at South Fork in the 1910s, ranchers from the Mattole area wanted a direct route to the railroad. This meant extending the road that went from the South Fork Eel River up the Bull Creek canyon by switchbacking it up the mountainside to Panther Gap and then zigzagging down the other side of the divide to the vicinity of Honeydew

The George Walker Hunter Ranch, west of Honeydew (CPH, colorized by JR).

The Honey Dew School divided the town's name in two (CPH, colorized by JR).

Creek, where the new road met the road coming up from Petrolia.

Three families—the Hunters, Hindleys, and Etters—were among the early owners of properties in the vicinity of the meeting of the roads.557 While serving as a county supervisor in 1913, George Hindley announced that "a portion of the Mattole Road would be built this fall." Two years previously, county supervisor George Williams had overseen construction of the road ten miles up the canyon of Bull Creek, where it reached the boundary of his district. Now Hindley would take over for the stretch from Panther Gap down to the Mattole.558 Hindley, as it happened, owned a 2,360-acre ranch in Upper Mattole and would be among those benefitting most from easier access to the NWP's station at South Fork. Hindley had scant enjoyment of the fruits of his labors, however, for he died in March 1914.559

The immediate area around the road junction was mostly owned by Emil J. Etter and his wife Minnie.560 Four of his brothers, including the well-known horticulturist Albert, were active in the Etter Brothers' multifaceted businesses at Ettersburg.561 (See Ettersburg chapter.) South and west of the Etter properties was the ranch of George Walker Hunter and May Hunter. The Hunter family had been active on the Mattole since the 1850s.562 Eastward, much of the land around Cathey's Peak and Windy Nip Gap belonged to the heirs of George Hindley. The road from Bull Creek came through a good stretch of Hindley property.563

A function of a junction is often to stimulate community development, which is what happened at the meeting of the roads near the mouth of Honeydew Creek. In March 1915 the "Honey Dew" schoolhouse was completed. The Honeydew Store arrived in 1923, built by Levi Thrap. Three years later the Honeydew

# Honeydew

Post Office opened, with Thrap's son-in-law, Bill West, serving as the first postmaster.⁵⁶⁴

The history of Honeydew is not extensively documented. However, certain significant events have been recorded. For example, at an unknown date, Charlie Etter was using a four-horse team to haul gravel from the riverbar near Honeydew. George Miner found Charlie and his team stopped in their tracks. George ran up to see what was wrong, and Charlie slowly said, "My lead horse dropped dead. Well, he never did that before."⁵⁶⁵

Noteworthy in the architectural annals of Honeydew was the construction of the Mary and Vernile Shinn house in the 1910s. It was a large, squarish structure with a second-story porch that stretched across the front of the building. Inside were ten bedrooms, an abundance of sleeping accommodations for the Shinns and their seven children, which allowed the family to board a succession of local laborers and Honeydew school teachers.

Serving the needs of the house's ten or more residents was but a single bathroom that compensated for its solitariness by being as big as a ballroom. The 20 by 25 foot space had "a claw-foot tub in one corner and a sink and toilet in another corner." The room's users could have played billiards in the vast central area but instead the space was used for drying clothes.⁵⁶⁶

In 1950 Bob Gregg and Bill Smith started the Honeydew Lumber Company "a little north of the Honeydew crossroads." Both owners were Seventh-Day Adventists, and they brought an entire crew of all-Adventist workers with them from Oregon. A small community developed near the mill, including a church, school, and garden. It was probably the dullest location in Humboldt County—the Adventists didn't drink, smoke, or fight. They also did not eat meat, which was just fine with the other residents of the area, most of whom wanted to protect their annual supply of venison.⁵⁶⁷

Looking for a bathroom outside the Shinn House (CPH, colorized by JR).

Only two customers at the Honeydew Store (HCHS, colorized by JR).

John Huntington bought the Honeydew Lumber Company in 1952. Although not an Adventist, he had a similar attitude about certain things and did not allow "drinking, fighting, and swearing around his place." Like the previous owners, Huntington came from Oregon, and he also brought many of his workers with him. The mill burned in January 1954, but it was quickly rebuilt and reopened that June.568

Over time, the community connected with the mill grew in size. Huntington built a large hall for staging social events. Red Hunt, a carpenter, quickly constructed a string of houses for the workers. Hunt built only the shell of each house; the sheet rocking, painting, and wallpapering were done by the women whose families would occupy the structures. An appraisal done in 1959 listed the sawmill, several auxiliary buildings, two halls, and 32 residences.569

Huntington retired in the late 1950s, but the mill stayed in operation until 1966, when it burnt. By then logging in the Mattole area had declined so much that the loss was little felt. After the workers left,

> . . . the townsite just deteriorated until it was gone. As houses sat empty, they were vandalized; then water got in and moisture started to rot them. More vandalism, more rot, until eventually they were burned, and the remains bulldozed away."570

An elegy of sorts for heyday Honeydew appeared in the *Times-Standard* in 1973. It began:

> Driving in from the east, the store and village come as a surprise. Fifteen miles of tortuous mountain road suddenly drop away into a peaceful, willow-shaded valley, with a cluster of buildings nestled in a bend of the Mattole.

> Once Honeydew was a bustling sawmill town.... Now it sleeps quietly, a center for a few dozen ranch families.[571]

By the time of the article, Leonard Meland and his wife had run the store and post office for 25 years. They had taken over from the original postmaster, Bill West,[572] in 1948. During the "sawmill boom" of the early 1950s, the Melands needed to hire three clerks. An awe-struck Meland stated, "you'll hardly believe this, but we grossed $100,000 one year."[573]

We are left to wonder what Meland would have made of the transactions taking place in Honeydew's marijuana-driven economy of the early 21st century.

# Chapter 7
# Ettersburg

The community of Ettersburg lies near the confluence of French Creek and Bear Creek, just west of where the latter meets the Mattole River. In the vicinity was an Indian village called Lenillimi, which in the Sinkyone language appropriately means "flow together in."[574] Also present was a gigantic tree, later known as the Council Madrone, where the local Indians reputedly gathered for meetings.[575] The exact name of the tribal group who lived there has been lost, and they are known today only as "the upper Mattole people." With the river, the creeks, and several nearby prairies, it was a hospitable place—except for the neighbors. There were many grizzly bears in the vicinity,[576] and this reportedly induced the upper Mattole people to establish no villages farther south.[577]

There was an additional problem for the whites who came into the region in the late 19th century. The location lay far from the early transportation corridors, and its remoteness meant that it took a while for the newcomers to establish themselves. By 1874 a route, with an enhancement, was in place—a trail that followed the county's new telegraph line.[578]

Although John Briceland and James Carney had both patented land in the area in 1876, the first property owner whose name appeared on the county maps was J. C. Eriksen, in 1898. He held four parcels centered on the confluence of Bear Creek and the Mattole River; they included the former Briceland and Carney properties.[579] By then two families had arrived that would have a lasting presence in the area. First to come were the Etters. (See sidebar 1.)

The Council Madrone (FC).

The Frenches arrived in the area shortly after Albert Etter.[580] Sara French suffered from asthma, so her husband, James, left his partnership in a Ferndale market and the Frenches moved to the Eriksen home in what was to become Ettersburg. They rented there for five years, during which time James French "ran a hotel and conducted the post office." He also homesteaded 160 acres on nearby Wilder Ridge, where he raised cattle.[581] Subsequently French joined with his brother-in-law, Joseph Pixton,[582] to form French & Pixton, an agricultural enter-

## 1. The "Luther Burbank" of Humboldt County

Albert Etter spent most of his childhood at Coffee Creek, near Ferndale.[583] He showed an interest in plants at an early age, "mastering grafting when a mere child," and started to breed strawberries when he was 12.[584] Albert "believed that school was a waste of time, and that there was nothing to be learned from books because they 'never mentioned nature.'" Accordingly, he abandoned the classroom when he was 14 and began working for local farmers. A few years later, one of his employers sent Albert south to his property on the Mattole River to "bud some nursery stock." The trip turned out to also bud Etter's future.[585]

While

> . . . traveling inland through the hills and beyond the harsh sea winds that plagued his family's farm, Albert thought the sky seemed bluer that he had ever seen it. Throughout the day he dreamed of what he would do with a farm like this, and he vowed that he would somehow make his dream come true. His farm would be called Ettersburg experimental place, and through his hybridizing there he would become famous far and wide.[586]

It was while in this frame of mind that Etter "noticed a lot of unworked land in the area" and decided to acquire some of it. He obtained a map of the locale, "selected a parcel that included a stretch of the Mattole River," and began raising the money to purchase it. Etter accomplished this by cutting 100 cords of firewood at 75 cents a cord. He then walked 25 miles to Eureka to file his land claim and, optimistic that it would be approved, went south and built a log cabin on the property.[587] It was 1894, and Ettersburg had gotten its start.[588]

The Etters were "a numerous family," with Albert having eight brothers and a sister. Three of his brothers—George, Fred, and August—soon joined him in the move to the upper Mattole.[589] In time, they each were "employed in the line for which he is specially fitted by experience and natural endowment." This meant that George and August took care of "the stock and horses, transportation and farm work, while Fred, who was "particularly clever as a machinist" was superintendent of "the sawmills and responsibilities of that nature." The youngest Etter brother, Walter, "though not formally a member of the firm," helped "run the engines and saws, blacksmith shop, donkey engine, etc. Albert, the initiator of the operation, ran the evaporating plant and cannery, along with supervising "the horticultural department."[590] Albert "always made it clear that he was in charge, and he claimed credit for all that was accomplished on the farm."[591]

And it was Albert and his "horticultural department" that put Ettersburg on the map. In 1913 the *San Francisco Bulletin* introduced him to readers in the Bay Area with an article filled with botanical bombast. The first paragraph read:

> Humboldt, home of gigantic redwoods, land of almost unbounded natural resources barely touched, whose fertile valleys have given it high rank among the dairying sections of the State, but in which little attention has been paid to fruit-raising and horticulture, has, strange as it may seem, produced one of the brainiest and most successful horticulturists on the Pacific Coast. He is Albert F. Etter of Ettersburg.[592]

By the second paragraph Etter had risen to the rank of "horticultural wizard," having developed 19 "new and distinct varieties" of strawberries, with possibly 50 more in the offing. Perhaps his most important innovation was the introduction of a local wild strawberry into the mix, which resulted in a berry that was superior for canning. The hero of this hybridization saga was none other than the Cape Mendocino beach strawberry, "originally taken," as the name implies, "from the bluffs at Devil's Gate, south of Cape Mendocino."[593] It was a location that Etter passed every time he traveled between Ettersburg and Ferndale.

Etter introduced the "Rose Ettersburg" hybrid in 1903. This was followed by the Ettersburg 121 in 1907 and his personal all-time favorite, the evocatively named Ettersburg 80 in 1912.[594] The Ettersburg 121 was "a direct cross between two wild species . . . the Cape Mendocino Beach and the Wild Alpine from Europe."[595] A flurry of hybrids in 1913-1914 added 17 more varieties. The pace then slackened, but new introductions continued on into the 1920s and 1930s.[596] In addition to using two strawberries native to the Humboldt area, Etter also worked with wild berries from the alpine areas in France and from the eastern United States. His hybrids became known as the "Ettersburg Family of Strawberries."[597]

But Etter's hybridizing of strawberries was not even the half of it. His 50-acre tract of apples was deemed "the greatest demonstrative experimental apple orchard in Northern California," with "over 500 different varieties of apples . . . [being] fruited here." When samples were entered at the Watsonville Apple Annual, Etter took home 23 first prizes.[598]

Etter also worked with other fruits, most notably creating a plum "that tastes more like an apricot than an apricot itself," and developing "several hundred variations of the wild grape." He also created an experimental plot with "hundreds of beautiful chestnut trees, representing as many different hybrid types."[599]

Numerous articles apprised local readers of Etter's remarkable work. Nearly four months before the *Bulletin* referred to him as a "Plant Wizard," the *Humboldt Times* used the term when describing Etter's receipt of an order for 48,000 strawberry plants from the Pacific Rural Press, which intended to mail its subscribers samples via the new shipping system called parcel post.[600] Etter added to his clippings file in December 1915 when the *Humboldt Times* announced that his "hybred [sic] strawberries had won a gold medal at the Panama Pacific Exposition."[601]

Albert Etter (CNC, partly colorized by JR).

During the 1920s George Darrow, the berry expert at the United States Department of Agriculture (USDA), "made the long and difficult trek to Ettersburg to witness firsthand Etter's breeding program."[602] Much later, in the department's 1937 Yearbook, Darrow listed 52 Etter strawberries and indicated that the Ettersburg 121 was the "best canner in the United States."[603] It was the Ettersburg 450 that was used to breed Darrow's famed Fairfax cultivar, "soon regarded as the best flavored of all strawberries."[604]

Although Etter first gained fame for his work with strawberries, he also found time to experiment extensively with apples. In 1897 he visited Professor E. J. Wickson, who was dean of the Agricultural College at the University of California Davis. Etter wanted to start work on hybridizing apples and asked

# Ettersberg

Albert Etter viewing the fruits of his labors, 1946 (CNC, partly colorized by JR).

Wickson for help. The professor was taken with the "hillbilly" and visited the Ettersburg Experimental Place to see what Etter had done with strawberries and other plants. Wickson counselled Etter, who proceeded to plant "thousands of seedling apple trees that would mature in ten to twenty years." Etter also continued to grow strawberries but came to devote most of his time to apples. By 1930 he had developed "a completely new line of apples," including one he named Wickson in honor of his mentor.[605]

But Etter failed to receive much recognition for his apple hybridization. Although F. F. Flaherty praised Etter's apple activities in an extensive 1934 article in the *Humboldt Times*,[606] word of his work did not reach a national, or even statewide, audience. In an attempt to publicize his apple breeding, Etter sent his USDA friend George Darrow a package containing samples of his best apple varieties. Darrow passed the apples on to his colleague, John Magness, a pomologist who was doing the apple section of USDA's yearbook. Unlike Darrow's comprehensive treatment of Etter's strawberry work, Magness failed to even mention Etter or, for that matter, any California apple-breeder.[607]

Thus consigned to pomological obscurity, by 1940 Etter, who was now 68,[608] found "he had a test orchard full of new apple varieties that he felt were ready to be introduced."[609] However, without a nursery company to grow and sell these apples-in-waiting, it appeared that they would never leave the confinement of his test orchard.

But Etter had one hand left to play. He sent about 40 apple cultivars to George Roedling, Jr., of the highly regarded California Nursery Company. Roedling and his staff studied the samples and in 1944 and 1945 they chose seven Etter varieties for patenting, including the Wickson, Pink Pearl, and Waltana. When Etter died in 1950 it looked as if his apple legacy would be preserved.[610]

Now fate, which seemed to at last be smiling on the Etter apple legacy, did another about-face. According to Etter expert and later-day pomologist Ram Fishman, "the California Nursery Company "suffered a major reversal of fortune not long after Etter's death." The result was that "varietal identities became confused and several Etter identities were lost completely." Back in Ettersburg, the Etter orchard decayed. The trees died, and the area was chiefly used as a sheep pasture.[611]

By the 1970s, however, the Etter pendulum had made another swing. Several apple varieties were available by mail order, and in 1973 Fishman and his family moved to Ettersburg. Fishman soon took up the cause, and in 1983 he and his wife founded Greenmantle Nursery. Eventually they were able to offer a significant selection of Etter apple types, and Ram's research into Etter's work was provided to the public. In a sense, Fishman propagated a new breeding regime that combined the historic Etter stock with Fishman's contemporary experiments, creating a hybrid of pomological wisdom that would have greatly pleased the man who inspired it—Albert Etter.

Back cover, California Nursery Company's 1946 catalogue, featuring Etter's "Pink Pearl" apple, upper left (CNC, partly colorized by JR).

prise that converted goats' milk into cheese in a "factory" near the Eriksen ranch house.[612] The company hired Ed Mixer, an expert from Switzerland, to supervise the cheesemaking.[613] Some of the goats were translated into chevon, or goat meat, which made its way onto dinner tables as an alternative to mutton. One of the Etters claimed that "the cheese produced was strong enough to make Limburger cheese sweet."[614]

Northwest of central Ettersburg the Harrow family took up land. In 1888 Fletcher Harrow gained the distinction of being "the first white child born in that section of the Mattole." Fletcher apparently liked his surroundings; 69 years later it was reported that he "still lives in the house where he was born and has never been further away than to Eureka which he visited a few times."[615] Did Fletcher realize that by traveling only a few miles farther north he could have experienced not only the wonders of Arcata but also of McKinleyville?

John C. Briceland was the opposite of Fletcher Harrow. Instead of staying anchored to one location, he went from Elk Ridge (where he reportedly had a herd of over 500 horses) to Upper Mattole, then to a property near the Eriksen place at Ettersburg, and finally (about 1889) moved southeast about seven miles to the "old Collier place." Here he finally stayed put, ranching and operating a mercantile store at what became known as Briceland.[616]

Another early arrival in the vicinity was Daniel S. Wilder, who lived along the Mattole a short distance west of Honeydew.[617] Little is known about Wilder, other than that he was a farmer from Massachusetts,[618] but he made enough of an impression on the area that the ridge south of Honeydew took his name. Later, a Wilder Post Office operated from 1896 to 1902.[619] Meanwhile, the Wilder School was functioning as early as 1898 but did not have a schoolhouse until 1900. The original school building was "poorly constructed," used a bucket for its water supply, and had no outhouse. In 1909 a new schoolhouse was built "about one and one half miles north of Ettersburg.[620] It was located near the Council Madrone tree.[621] By then the first Ettersburg Post Office had come and gone, lasting only from 1902 to 1906.[622] It was there long enough, however, to give the location what became its lasting name. In 1918 Fred Etter built a new schoolhouse on the Etter Ranch.[623] Yet another school building, this one with a stone front, was constructed in 1931. Apparently the school was sometimes called "Wilder" and sometimes "Ettersburg," although the latter name did not appear in the formal records until 1961. By then it hardly mattered what the school was called, for it closed in 1965.[624] Meanwhile, the deactivated Ettersburg Post Office had resumed operation in 1915.[625] Like the school, it closed in 1965,[626] leaving the community without any public buildings. Then, in 1981, the Ettersburg School reopened in a new building.[627]

Starting in 1915 Ettersburg briefly had a store. It closed at an unknown date.[628] Another store was coming, but it took a long time to arrive. Its gestation began in 1935, when Onofrio "On" Russo[629] and Isabel Russo moved their family from Doody Ridge to Ettersburg so that their three children could attend school. The Russos subsequently left the area, "moved around the state for a time," and then returned to Ettersburg with what were now four Russo kids providing the necessary number of students to keep the school open. There was still no store. Then, in 1942, Les French retired as postmaster and On Russo took over. The post office was a small building but Russo found room inside to start a new Ettersburg store, selling "just a few candy bars and some sundry items." It wasn't much, but it was enough to aggravate Les French, who owned the building and thought that it should only house the post office. Pretty soon it housed nothing, for Russo moved across the road to a larger building that became the Ettersburg grocery, "installing the post office, much to French's chagrin, in a tiny 8-foot by 10-foot room adjoining the store." On Russo added gas pumps. He had his children work at the store. His daughter Bea started so young that she "had to stand on a crate" to see over the counter.[630] It may have seemed to Bea that the business would continue forever, but in 1949 it ended; On Russo closed the Ettersburg store and moved a few miles southward to Whitethorn, where, in 1950, he purchased *that* town's store.[631]

In the 1940s the Walter G. Brix logging company in Briceland purchased Douglas-fir timber from the Ettersburg locals. By the late 1950s most of the accessible trees had been cut, although Les Harrow and Guy Westfall continued small-scale operations. By then, many of Ettersburg's orchards were "overgrown with brush and non productive," and the local ranchers relied "on sheep for their principal income which many supplement by working for the county road department."[632]

After a time, it became hard to imagine the level of activity that once enlivened the Ettersburg countryside. A motorist in search of the town might drive down a narrow dirt road, noticing the profusion of trees that grew close by. Then coming to a gate, there was a glimpse of a large house in

Entrance to Etter's arboretum,
c. 1937 (FMC, colorized by JR).

the shadowed distance. The motorist would turn around, heading back to sunlight and pavement, leaving the Etter ranch without knowing he had seen it. Leaving, without realizing that in some earlier time, they might have encountered, as perhaps Albert Etter once had,

. . . thou, light-winged Dryad of the trees,
In some melodious plot
Of beechen green, and shadows numberless,
Singest in summer in full-throated ease.

               Keats, Ode to a Nightingale

# Chapter 8

# Shelter Cove

This harbor is the best open refuge between Trinidad and Mendocino Bay.
—George Davidson, *Coast Pilot*, 1889

Like Trinidad Head, Point Delgada juts southward from an indented coast, creating to the east a small cove protected from the turbulence of the open sea. Noting this, members of the Coast Survey anchored there in 1853 and came ashore. They found an Indian village nearby and learned from its inhabitants that the name for the cove was the same as that for their tribe—To-not-ken.[633] The surveyors replaced this name with a new one—Shelter Cove—that promised to prove more helpful to English-speaking mariners, especially those in distress.[634]

The To-not-kens had long lived on and near the large flat just north of the cove. At least three locations in the vicinity were occupied at various times by the Indians.[635] In 1881 it was reported that

> Numerous and extensive shell mounds indicated many hundreds of years of feasting upon the shell-fish which abound on the rocks, by the aborigines. Shelter Cove was at one time thickly settled by the Indians.[636]

Delmar Thornbury, investigating the area in the 1910s, found numerous traces of Indian inhabitancy:

> ... there are hundreds of deposits, many of them high upon the encircling hills, some two or three miles from the ocean. They had to pack their food up the steep grades and it is evident from the number and size of the deposits, that a population of hundreds of aborigines lived here at the same time. In fact, Shelter Cove is a native paradise, abounding in abalones, crayfish, clams, fish, and marine food of all kinds.[637]

"Indian Jim," a man who probably lived at To-not-ken, later told of his people first seeing "the boats with sails" passing by the cove generations earlier. Some of the ships may have been Spain's Manila galleons, which came down the California coast after crossing the northern Pacific from the Philippines. Then, many years later, the Indians became "frightened and hid in the willows when they saw "the big boats with the white smoke" go by.[638]

But the first real danger to the To-not-kens came from land, not sea. (See sidebar 1.)

According to the standard received history of the area, Hamilton and Oliver were the first ranchers at Shelter Cove, being replaced when Oliver was killed by Indians and Hamilton traded his ranch to the Ray brothers in 1861.[639] In any event, the Rays shone brightly in their new location; they "commenced dairying and stock raising" and also worked to improve the cove as a shipping point.[640] Then, in 1873, "a family named Yates arrived and formed a partnership with the Ray family." The Yateses reportedly sold out in 1882 and moved to Garberville. Meanwhile a Mr. Childs "built a dairy barn and operated a dairy . . . with the Ray family."[641]

### 1. No Shelter at the Cove

In naming Shelter Cove, the Coast Survey described one of the attractions the location had for the whites. A June 1855 report in the *Humboldt Times* expanded extravagantly on the charms the area offered:

> . . . "Shelter Cove," pronounced to be *the best harbor on the coast.*—Capt. Fisher, of the steamship Humboldt, on the trip before the last, in coming up, had his "smokestack" blown down in a severe blow, and to avoid the gale he ran into Shelter Cove, finding a bluff shore "with any quantity of water," and a land locked harbor, closed to gales from whatever source they might chance to come. The bay is described as an arm of the sea, without the appearance of any bar, and consequently no breakers or "rollers." Parties who have went [sic] down by land report that there are at least twenty thousand acres of the best quality of level prairie land immediately surrounding the bay, with an indefinite amount of gently ascending lands in the back ground, covered with spruce, pine, redwood, alder and other trees. A party from the Sacramento Valley leave here on Monday for Shelter Cove, in company with some of the party who have previously visited it.[642]

There was indeed level land at Shelter Cove, but it covered closer to 200 acres than the 20,000 claimed in the report. Perhaps the parties mentioned in the *Times's* account were disappointed upon discovering this, for it appears that none of their members stayed to settle at the cove. The next year, in July 1856, John Cassad and others from the Table Bluff area took off in the *Quoddy Bell*, bound for Shelter Cove "to found a settlement."[643] The result of this expedition was not mentioned in the press.

By the end of the decade, however, whites had indeed come to stay at Shelter Cove, with the predictable result: conflict with the Indians who had long claimed the area. In December 1859 the *Humboldt Times* claimed that two whites, names unknown, had been killed by Indians at the cove. When other whites located the suspected murderers, they found tools belonging to a shoemaker who had gone missing the previous spring. No mention was made of what then happened to the Indians.[644] The following April, Moses Stafford and a companion were reportedly attacked by Indians while cutting wood near the cove. The fight ended when "Stafford shot one Indian dead and wounded another, and the two [white] men escaped with their lives."[645]

# Shelter Cove

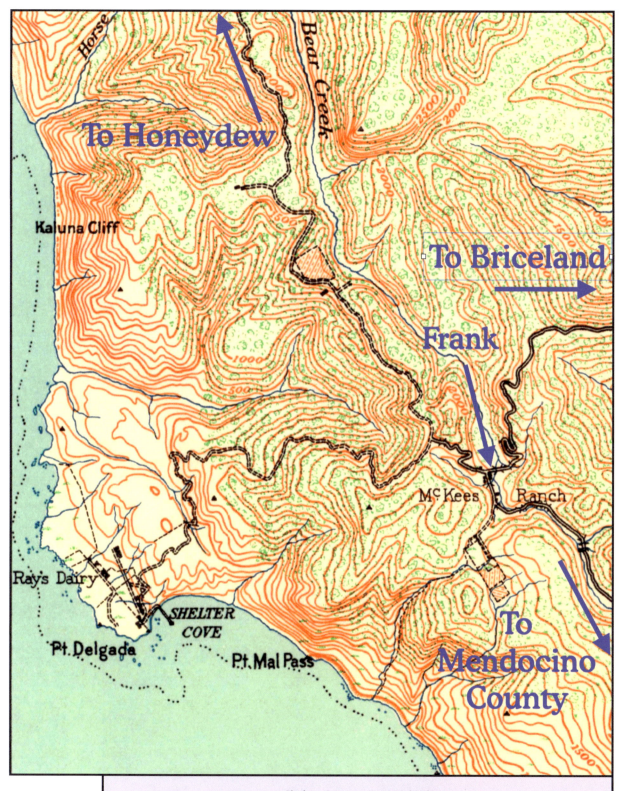

Shelter Cove area, 1916 (CE).

At about this time Lt. William P. Carlin rode north from Fort Bragg to "investigate an alleged Indian attack" at Shelter Cove. Local stockmen claimed that one of their number had been ordered by an Indian leader "to remove cattle and horses from grazing lands adjacent to the Indian settlement." When the stockman went to the village "he was surrounded by Indians who severely wounded him with arrows." Other stockmen came to his rescue, chasing off the Indians and "killing one in the process."[646]

Perhaps unexpectedly, Carlin sought out the Indians, who told a very different story. They claimed the conflict arose when local whites had demanded Indian women and were rejected. Carlin noted evidence that supported the Indians' version: an absence of dead cattle but six very dead Indians, all scalped by the whites.[647]

Carlin was unable to see justice done, but he did attempt to prevent further bloodshed. He secured an agreement from the stockmen that they would allow the Indians to continue living at Shelter Cove "without molestation." For their part, the Indians promised to be peaceful and friendly when encountering whites "passing through their country."[648]

But Carlin's peacemaking came to naught.

In June 1861 word spread that Indians at Shelter Cove had attacked ranchers John[649] Hamilton, S. Smith, and William H. Oliver, killing Oliver. There are several accounts of what happened—all, as usual, told by whites. It appears that Smith shot and killed two Indians before he and Hamilton fled for their lives. The Indians allegedly had recently "killed a man in the employ of Mess. [sic] Hamilton and Oliver." The report added that

> . . . a party of citizens will leave the Noyo [River] . . . in pursuit of and to chastise the Indians. Lieut. Dillon, at Fort Bragg, has been informed of the occurrence and will send out a party of U. S. soldiers as soon as possible.

According to an account written much later,

> Hamilton rode back . . . with a posse of 14 men, including William Shoemake,[650] [and] returned to Shelter Cove. They watched the Indians, who were having a tribal celebration and feast, and when they all lay down to rest the posse attacked. Hamilton led the charge with the cry "Kill them all," and most of the Indians were either driven into the surf with whips and drowned or were shot. The children were put into some sort of stockade for the night, but during the darkness one of the members of the posse, who was classified as a "bad actor," crawled into

the area and cut the throats of most of the children. When Hamilton, who had prevented the rest of the children from being killed, asked the man why he had done such a terrible thing, he replied that the Indians had killed some of his relatives.[651]

Another version of the story leaves out the posse and the massacre, and instead has Hamilton returning alone to bury Oliver, when:

> On his arrival there he heard two small children crying in the nearby woods. Both of the children were Indian boys approximately two and one half years old, abandoned by the Indians as they fled from the battleground.
> Hamilton took the children with him rather than to leave them in the wilderness for it was certain that death from starvation and exposure would be their lot.
> On his way home he met Samuel Bell of Pudding Creek, Mendocino county. Bell took the two boys, naming them Richard and Thomas and raised them as his sons to manhood.[652]

About this time the U. S. Army was also busy in the area killing Indians. A dispatch from Assistant Adjutant-General and Inspector D. C. Buell on July 3 indicated his concern about the extensiveness of the attacks, with one notable exception:

> Upward of 200 Indians (men, with a few accidental exceptions), have been killed by the different detachments. Presuming that this slaughter is to stop at some point short of extermination, for the alleged depredations of the Indians would hardly justify that, I have ventured to advise the officers in command to discontinue it now until other depredations are committed, excepting, however, with reference to the band which recently killed two men (Lewis and Oliver) at Shelter Cove, on the coast. That is a legitimate ground for severe chastisement. . . .[653]

In yet a third version of the Hamilton-Oliver incident, Hamilton was reported fleeing south, whereupon he met the three Ray brothers, John, William, and James, who were coming north "with stock looking for a place to take up." Hamilton on the spot traded his ranch to the Rays for a span of oxen. The brothers then went north to claim their new property and

> . . . did the only sensible thing: they married Indian women and held the Shelter Cove Ranch, ranging their stock on the rich, grassy slopes and increasing their herd of stock.[654]

But the record does not bear this out. Census data from 1880 finds both John and William Ray single, while James Ray had died by then.[655] It is likely that the Rays' "marriages" to Indian women were instances of cohabitation, either forced or unforced, which were common at the time.[656]

If Hamilton indeed swapped his ranch to the Rays, he kept ownership of his cattle. And he kept his hatred of the Indians. In January 1862 he "sent a party of seven men . . . to Shelter Cove, for the ostensible purpose of driving his stock to a safer locality." But there was more to the story than that. As reported by Captain J. B. Moore,

> . . . the real mission was to murder Indians. . . . They had attacked a party of Indians at the Usal River and murdered eleven of them. I say murdered, because they [the Indians] had not made any demonstration against them, nor did they make any defense. . . . I learn . . . that the Indians are doing scarcely any damage. . . . The stories of Indian depredations in this vicinity are all bosh, and . . . I really believe if the Indians were properly treated by the white men they would not in scarcely any instance trouble them. While this party of Hamilton and Smith's were on the trip above mentioned, they failed to even get sight of an Indian at or in the vicinity of Shelter Cove, except one old squaw leading two children, when one of the party named Steve Shannon leveled his rifle and shot her dead while she was trying to get away from them. . . . This same Shannon last summer . . . took a child from a squaw prisoner who happened to be a little to the rear of the party, tied it to a tree, and shot it. . . . Such are a sample of the acts that produce Indian depredations, and such are the men who are anxious to be employed by the Government. We have no power, either civil or military, to successfully prevent or punish these acts of white men, yet we are constantly importuned to punish Indians. . . .[657]

# Shelter Cove

Rangeland on the Shelter Cove flat (CPH, colorized by JR).

But Moore was a low-ranking officer, shouting in the northern California wilderness, and his voice was not heard.

Richard Bell, one of the two boys supposedly saved by Hamilton, had a cousin named Jennie Young who was "born at Upper Mattole." Her obituary stated that "her parents were killed at the Shelter Cove massacre in 1852."[658] The date is probably incorrect, since it is doubtful that whites were present there at the time, but the reference could be to any of the several attacks that came later. Young, along with Richard and Thomas Bell, barely survived the massacres at Shelter Cove. For the Indians, the cove was a place without shelter.

The difficulties that beset Shelter Cove in its early days were compounded by the state legislature, which in 1859 adjusted the Mendocino-Humboldt county line three or four miles northward so that the cove abruptly became a part of Mendocino County. Protests erupted from erstwhile Humboldt County residents and in 1860 the original line, which lay on the 40th parallel, was restored.[659]

Over the next two decades, Shelter Cove developed into the supply port for inland southern Humboldt County, most notably the towns of Briceland and Garberville. Eben Parker and his brothers operated a pack train along the trail that connected these communities. The train reportedly consisted "of anywhere from two dozen to one hundred mules."[660] The mules served long and well, but eventually the need for a wagon road became apparent. A company owned by two Shelter Covians, William Ray and Henry[661] Yates, contracted with Humboldt County to build "the Garberville and Shelter Cove Road" and then subcontracted most of the construction work to S. F. Taylor, who was reportedly "a gentleman who has actively engaged in road building on the coast for many years."[662] Starting at the Garberville end of the route in late August 1878,[663] Taylor, using over 100 workers, headed west and by October 30 had completed 21 3/8 miles, reaching a junction with the Coast Route Wagon Road. Building the remaining three miles of road to Shelter Cove was to be "Mr. Ray's own private enterprise" and was expected to be finished by the end of November.[664]

Even before completion of the road, shipping was in full swing at the cove. About 100,000 pounds of wool were sent from there in 1876, 160,000 pounds in 1877, and 200,466 pounds in 1878.[665] The last year also saw the exportation of numerous other products of southern Humboldt: furs, deerskins, calfskins, dried venison, hides, abalones, abalone shells, eggs, and butter. In 1877 William Ray sold 38 mules, which were shipped from the cove on the steamer Empire for use by the army during the Modoc War.[666]

Elliott's 1881 history provides a wide-ranging account of Shelter Cove:

> It is the natural shipping point for southern Humboldt and northern Mendocino. It has a natural open port, easy of access and vessels often lay here in time of heavy northers. The improvements consist of an ample warehouse and two staunch lighters. It is a strange, weird place, and is well calculated for a seaside resort.
>
> There are about 300 acres of good plowing land, consisting of table-land immediately on the beach and side hill, rising gently above it. Back of this[,] rising higher and more abrupt, higher and higher the grassy hills ascend in a semi-circular form, having the little table flat on the beach for its center, till they reach the timber and chaparral-lined summits of the high ridges.
>
> The sea breaks with awful force upon the rocks north of the harbor and has played some singular freaks. In many places it has cut underground chambers, and when the surf comes rushing in, the angry, boiling and foaming waters may be heard roaring and bellowing through these salty caverns with sullen sound, while the ground quakes with the untold force of the suddenly checked breakers.[667]

The "staunch" lighters were constructed by George Morgan, a retired sea captain who had settled at Shelter Cove. He also built houses for people in the area and at least two wooden peg barns for ranchers on the South Fork Eel.[668]

During the 1880s the port of Shelter Cove experienced further expansion. In 1884 the four Robarts brothers[669] from Ferndale formed the Shelter Cove Warehouse Company, which operated in conjunction with the brothers' Port Kenyon Warehouse Company. The following year the Ray brothers built a wharf at the cove that allowed "deep water steamers and ships" to load.[670] In October 1886, John Ray leased to P. W. Robarts most of Shelter Cove and its appurtenances. Included were "2,760 acres of land, 1,000 head of sheep, lighters, wharves, buildings, etc." The lease was good for five years at $2,000 per annum. Included in the agreement was the hotel building that Ray had constructed earlier that year.[671] (See sidebar 2.)

### 2. Fires by Land, Fires by Sea

John Ray, builder of the Shelter Cove hotel, lived nearby in Humboldt House, a dwelling made from the remains of wrecked ships. The hotel was apparently constructed with more standard materials, for Ray paid $1,000 to have it built. It had two porches and was painted brown. The interior was more exciting: "a brick fireplace from San Francisco, three bedrooms, upstairs, and several bunks in one big room called the 'corral.'" Meals, often featuring salt beef but with home-grown vegetables, were two bits, while a room (whether in the "corral" or not was unspecified) cost fifty cents.[672] Sometime after the Robarts brothers gave up their lease, a blind man named Twilliger took over operation of the hotel. He was "an accomplished musician" and not only held dances at the hotel but gave lessons on his rosewood piano.[673] An earthquake at an unspecified date toppled the hotel's chimney, perhaps damaging the imported fireplace. Then, about the time of the big 1906 earthquake, a fire in the kitchen rapidly expanded and burned the building down.[674]

A new hotel was built. Elizabeth Bowden, who'd worked at the old one when a girl of 15, came back to Shelter Cove to help her husband, William, run the replacement establishment, along with the wharf and store. Her

The post-earthquake, three-year-old hotel (CPH, colorized by JR).

second tenure at the cove proved even more exciting than the first. As Elizabeth told it:

> In 1926, the luxurious yacht called the Nimshaw drifted onto the beach in the Cove. The soft sands did little if any damage, and plans were made to pull the ship off the next day. In the meantime, those aboard came ashore and stayed at the hotel. For some reason the Filipino cook went back on board for something, lit a match, which ignited leaking gas, and the ship blew up, casting him hundreds of feet into the sea. Miraculously he was not fatally injured, but the ship burned. Beachcombers still find part of the ship from time to time, usually pieces of monogrammed silverware from the ornate dining salon.[675]

The second Shelter Cove hotel was remodeled in 1947. In 1958 it too, departed in a blaze of glory,[676] the third serious fire in the vicinity but one certainly less spectacular than the flying Filipino conflagration of 1926, an act that was difficult to follow.

The Robarts brothers gave up their lease in 1887.[677] Perhaps the cove got too hot for them, for in November of that year Percy Robarts reported that:

> . . . the fire in the southern part of this county had reached the Shelter Cove range and burned over part of it and will probably burn over the whole range. When the steamer Hume landed there yesterday, the fire was burning fiercely. Every available man was out fighting the flames. W. McDonald had over 100 cords of tan bark burned, the product of his entire summer's work. Many cattle and sheep will have to be provided with feed in other localities. Many deer and bear have been seen in the burned district with hair all singed by the fire, and bands of deer can be seen along the ocean beach to which they have retreated. Many dead deer have also been found. This is the most disastrous fire which has ever visited our county. . . .[678]

When the flames were finished, they had burnt a swath between Shelter Cove and Petrolia that blackened 10,000 acres of grazing land and 20,000 acres of brush.[679]

Less than two weeks before the blaze, an epistler named "Forrest" wrote to the *Ferndale Enterprise* about the southwesternmost community in Humboldt County:

> Shelter Cove is now a lively germ of a town, being a Sunday rendezvous for muleters [sic], sheep-shearers, bark-peelers, and wagoneers [also sic]. The steamer is now making regular trips to this port. John

# Shelter Cove

> Ray has started a [tan]bark mill, which is doing a great amount of work. . . . Mr. Ray has fifty tons of ground bark ready to ship on the coming steamer.[680]

By 1890 Shelter Cove had indeed germinated, despite the burning of much of the locale, and had solidified its reputation as

> . . . one of the important shipping points for the southern part of Humboldt county. The harbor is partially protected. . . . It is accessible for all crafts the greater part of the year. The water is deep close into the shore, and there is plenty of sea room. Beds of seaweed break the force of the sea when southerly winds prevail. The surrounding country consists of large sheep and stock ranges. . . . Besides grazing, there are large tracts of timber land, chiefly [tan]oak, the bark of which finds its way to the Cove in considerable quantities. The annual export of tanbark from this point amounts to about 2,000 cords. . . . Like all open harbors on this coast, Shelter Cove is only used as a shipping point during the summer months. The exports consists [sic] almost entirely of wool, tanbark and live stock, and the imports of merchandise to supply the wants of the settlers.[681]

Thus enthused Hamm's Humboldt County business directory. But the rosy picture it painted also contained a thorn: in September 1890 the Bank of Mendocino foreclosed on John Ray and took over the Shelter Cove Ranch.[682] Ray accordingly changed his occupation from owner to manager of the ranch, continuing in that capacity until 1894,[683] when George McGowan began leasing the property from the bank. The same month as the foreclosure, the steamer *Ajax* scraped across Blunt's Reef, opening her hull; she proceeded down the coast to a point about ten miles north of Shelter Cove, at which time the wound proved mortal. The passengers and crew, 47 in all, took to the life boats, and all reached the cove safely. They were picked up from this unexpected layover by the steamer *Newport* and taken to San Francisco.[684]

Further excitement ensued. On July 12, 1892,[685] the Shelter Cove Post Office was established with John Ray as postmaster.[686] The following day saw the Frank Post Office open, a mere three miles eastward, at the junction of Shelter Cove-Garberville Road and the Coast Road.[687] Suddenly the isolated southern Humboldt populace had not one, but two places to buy their stamps. Then, in May 1893, a steamer was discharging its cargo when an unruly wave hit the ship, shoving it into the seaward end of the Shelter Cove wharf, which "went down with 50 tons of freight on it." Thus docked of its seaward end, the dock could no longer be reached by steamers, so Ray bought a lighter to carry his tanbark to the offshore ships. In 1894 he eliminated this inconvenience by building 125 feet of replacement wharf. That October a new fire burned 2,000 acres near the cove. Ray must have felt discouragement from this continuum of adversity, but when he died in his mid-50s in 1898, he was still operating his wharf.[688]

The death of John Ray left a vacancy at Shelter Cove that was only filled four years later. In 1902 William and George Notley arrived on the scene, fresh from Notleys Landing near Big Sur, a tanbark and lumber shipping site they had established in the 1890s.[689] The Notleys had been hired by a Santa Cruz tannery to "estimate the tanoak timber on the Shelter Cove Ranch."

Tanbark coming down to the cove (CPH, colorized by JR).

Once at the cove, the brothers exceeded their job description and bought the ranch from the Bank of Mendocino.[690] The Notleys, in conjunction with the Wagner Leather Company, also purchased an additional eight acres that included the wharf.[691]

The Stockton-based Wagner Leather Company wanted an interest in the wharf because they had decided to move their tanbark harvesting operation from the Santa Cruz area to southern Humboldt. The company accordingly built the Pacific Oak Extract Works at Briceland. The plant converted dried tanbark into a syrupy extract that was packed into 50-gallon wooden barrels and hauled to the wharf. According to one report, the influence of the Wagner Leather Company was so great that during its co-ownership of the wharf, Shelter Cove was called Stockton Harbor.[692] Landing at Stockton Harbor was the Wagners' own steam ship, the *Stockton City*.[693] In 1919 the company sold its half interest in the wharf to the Bowden brothers. Three years later, in 1922, the Wagners "ran out of tanbark" and closed their Briceland plant.[694]

The Notley brothers made an unusual acquisition in 1904, buying and moving a herd of cattle from Nevada.[695] Imagine how baffled the bovines were to arrive at Shelter Cove and find not parched desert but the Pacific Ocean and a damp shore. The increase in the cove's cattle population was offset by a decrease in the number of registered voters, which dropped from eleven in 1904 to only seven in 1906. Shelter Cove thereby supplanted nearby Whitethorn as the smallest precinct in the county.[696]

The exodus continued in 1908, when George Notley sold his interest in the ranch to his brother and moved to San Mateo County.⁶⁹⁷ Perhaps he had found recent events at the cove overly stimulating and sought a calmer life. (See Appendix A.)

When George Notley left Shelter Cove, dissolving the partnership with his brother, another pair of brothers promptly filled the vacuum he had left. John W. Bowden and William H. Bowden, whose mother, for what it's worth, was a cousin of Nathaniel Hawthorne, "purchased the one-half interest of the Notley Brothers in the store and wharf at Shelter Cove." The remaining half interest in the property was retained by the Wagner Leather Company. Within a few years the business was incorporated as the Shelter Cove Wharf & Warehouse Company. The wharf was improved so that "steamers of fourteen feet draft can easily and safely dock."⁶⁹⁸

Even after the closing of the extract works, tanbark still left the cove. The grinding mill that John Ray had set up in 1887 gained extra power later that year with the acquisition of a steam engine.⁶⁹⁹ Photos from 1916 show a steam donkey next to a stack of dried bark, along with two "tanbark sheds" near the bluff overlooking the cove. By the early 1930s a gasoline engine was powering the grinder and the ground bark was shoveled into sacks. Workers who had spent a day in the sheds came out covered in brown bark dust and reportedly "sneezed, coughed, and spit brownish fluid for a week."⁷⁰⁰

By the 1910s life at Shelter Cove was stimulated by a new activity—commercial fishing. Humboldt Bay fishermen had worked the waters near the cove for a number of years when, in 1916, they were joined by fishermen from San Francisco. In the summer of 1919 the cove had become a "tent city of 1000," with the temporary populace operating some 200 fishing boats. By early August they had caught over 1,400 tons of salmon, halibut, and rock cod, and they expected to acquire an equal amount before the season closed in November. The total catch was worth approximately $250,000, with the fishermen getting about nine cents a pound for

Barrels of tanbark extract awaiting shipment (CPH, colorized by JR).

salmon, six cents for halibut, and a rock-bottom two cents for rock cod.[701] That same summer a sojourning Eureka resident wrote to the *Ferndale Enterprise*, comparing Shelter Cove's bay to "Naples in miniature with over 200 fishing boats, manned by 90 per cent Italians, mostly from San Francisco." The previous day's catch had run to 55 tons, enough to give a fisherman "a day's wage of $180."[702]

If the fishing paid well, it was also hazardous. Buffalo Nelson, a Sausalito fisherman, discovered this one day while on a small skiff in the cove. Suddenly "the wide open mouth of a monster shark shot up within a foot of his head." Nelson's response was to collect his gear and head back to the safety of Sausalito as quickly as he could. Numerous sharks, ranging from 10 to 25 feet in length, were seen in the cove. They were probably drawn there by the practices of the Western Fishing Company, which mild-cured their catches at the end of the wharf, throwing the heads and guts of the fish into the waters of the cove.[703]

For many fishermen the lure of salmon proved greater than the fear of sharks. In 1925 a combine called the Northern California Fisheries was formed by the San Francisco International Fish Company, The Paladini Fish Company, and the Western Fish Company. The combine leased the Shelter Cove property from Bill Bowden. They used the original warehouse as a fish house and installed a diesel-powered ice plant. The San Francisco International Fish Company became sole owner of the 40-acre shoreside property in 1928, buying it from the heirs of Bill Bowden, who had passed away that year.[704] The bulk of the Shelter Cove Ranch was sold by William Notley to Keith Etter in the 1920s.[705]

Some seafood never left Shelter Cove. Delmar Thornbury, in his travels around the county, stopped at the cove and claimed that he "never shall forget the dinner of abalone served at the hotel." He also noted that earlier inhabitants had partaken of the cove's bounty:

> All over the ranch from the beach to the top of the first range of hills, the black earth and shell mounds indicate the homesites of the aborigines. The number and extent of the kitchen middens, built up from years of feasting on the shell fish indicate a very large population at some time in its history.[706]

Besides food, the cove reportedly became a supply center for beverages. During Prohibition

> . . . tales were told about Mafia connections in Shelter Cove. It was said that cases of liquors were unloaded in the darkness on the pier and transported inland by truck. Mobsters, armed with machine guns, covered the operation and there was no interference by the natives.[707]

Another tale told about the cove was decidedly untrue. It involved a boat from the "Haines Fish Company" depositing a mysterious stranger at "Fisherman Bay," where there were "a few small fishing boats, a tiny storage plant, and a loading pier." The year was 1932, and the locals on shore speculated as to whom the new arrival might be. It took them a long time—most of 309 pages—to find out. Fisherman Bay was of course Shelter Cove, which was the starting point for an adventure that led to the abandoned millsite of Andersonia and the Benbow Inn, and that ultimately involved the Save-the-Redwoods League. The story was *The Man Who Went Away*, the last novel written by best-selling author Harold Bell

# Shelter Cove

Dance band, 1930: (left to right) Sal Russo, guitar; Tony Machi, accordion; Leslie McArthur, violin; Salvatore Pizzimenti, mandolin (MAMC, colorized by JR).

Wright, published in 1942[708] and now all but unknown in Humboldt County.

Meanwhile, back in the real world, the Depression reached Shelter Cove. At summer's end in 1931 "the San Francisco International Fish Company announced that maintenance of the pier had become too costly and that fishing activities would have to be curtailed." After the winter of 1932 the neglected pier already had piling missing, and it was unsafe to walk on the deck. By 1937 there were gaps in the pier. Sections of piling continued to fall into the ocean. With its pier gradually being demolished,

> . . . Shelter Cove became a deserted area. Buildings were empty and an occasional abalone or rock fisherman would pay a visit. Sometimes vacationing groups would use the buildings for a weekend.[709]

Although the Shelter Cove Ranch remained active, the shoreside facilities at the cove slumbered in abandonment until 1941, when the Coast Guard rented the property from owner John Alioto and set up a beach patrol station there. The barn was converted into a stable for the patrol's horses, while the old hotel became the barracks. A kennel was added for the patrol's dogs.[710]

Alioto had been the attorney for the San Francisco International Fish Company. He acquired the fishing facility when the company went bankrupt. After the war he leased the property to three young brothers, and after Alioto's death his widow, Inez, sold it to them. It was the fifth time that a set of brothers had owned or leased land at the cove: first the Rays, then Robartses, then the Notleys, then the Bowdens, and now the Machis—Mario, Tony, and Babe.[711] (See sidebar 3.)

## 3. A Silver, Golden Age at the Cove

When the Machi brothers arrived at the cove in 1946, they had a lease on the fish company's former property and not much else: only "a second-hand jeep, an old battered trailer, a set of carpenter and mechanic tools, a few personal belongings, [and] very little cash." They drove down the "narrow dirt road" from the ridge to find "no caretaker or any sign of inhabitants." But thanks to the Coast Guard, the buildings were still intact, and the brothers also possessed one other, invaluable asset. They remembered the cove when it was a bustling, exciting place.

The brothers' father, Pietro "Pop" Machi, had been a part-owner of the San Francisco International Fish Company.[712] In 1930 Mario came up to the cove to work for his dad. The next year he was joined by Tony and Babe. They were all teenagers at the time.[713]

And what a time they had. The tiny town of Shelter Cove had been transformed into a busy fish-processing facility managed by Sal Russo, who was assisted by such colorful characters as Salvatore Pizzimenti, a 247-pound salmon splitter, and Tony Davi, "the fastest salmon gutter on the coast." The crew lived in the Shelter Cove hotel. The former warehouse became the fish house. Mario's job was moving the salmon 600 feet from the far end of the pier, where the boats unloaded, to the fish house. Other buildings included a grocery store, barn, garage, blacksmith shop, cook shack, and two tanbark sheds. At peak operation, 140,000 pounds of salmon were processed in a day. It wasn't all work. On Saturday nights locals gathered for dancing, with music provided by a four-piece "orchestra" that included the huge Pizzimenti playing a dainty mandolin. Occasionally Salvatore would join the dancers, invariably choosing "a partner that weighed almost as much as he did." As the other musicians played "Over the Waves," the other dancers, like waves, prudently parted for Salvatore and his companion.[714]

At the end of the summer in 1931 the fishing boats left for San Francisco. As they departed, each sounded its whistle three times, signifying "Good-bye, good luck, and God bless you."[715]

A decade later came World War II. All three brothers served in the armed forces. Mario was with the 31st Infantry when it surrendered in the Philippines and survived the Bataan Death March and years in a Japanese prisoner-of-war camp.[716]

Memories run deep, like a current through the sea. In 1946 the Machi brothers had their recollections of the war, but they also had the memories

The Machi brothers: (left to right) Mario, Babe, Tony (MAMC, colorized by JR).

of that earlier time at the cove, when the salmon glinted silver on the sea and the sun set golden in the west. They were fortunate. They knew of a place that could heal the spirit. And when the war was over, they went to it.

With World War II ended, people wanted to enjoy life. The Machi brothers thought that with a few improvements, the cove would be a good place to do that. But how do you improve things with almost no budget?

The war, or rather its end, provided the answer. In 1947 surplus life rafts were cheap, and the brothers could afford to buy ten[717] of them. They started renting the rafts. One day two locals came down the steep road to the cove, bought some salted anchovies, and went out on a raft. Two hours later they had four salmon. Like true fishermen, they bragged about their catch, word spread, and the Machi brothers were in business. Soon they had remodeled the old hotel and began renting rooms in it.[718]

When genial Andy Genzoli of the *Humboldt Times* visited the cove in 1949, he found that in addition to the other improvements,

> . . . the settlement has been converted into a park, where camping facilities are available, and those desiring to fish in the bay will find pleasure awaiting them.[719]

Genzoli also noted that sheep grazed nearby and that "an occasional plane will land on the flat area."[720]

The "flat area" for planes was actually a 1,600-foot landing strip that Harold Lewis had built in 1948. That same year logger Everett Littlefield bulldozed a new road to the beach "down an im-

Shelter Cove town (CPH, colorized by JR).

possible cliff." This allowed for vehicle access so that boats could be launched. The road resurrected the cove: it "was responsible for the start of the growth of Shelter Cove as a sport fishing area."[721]

In 1952 the Machi brothers subdivided 15 lots on their property. The first summer cottage built in the subdivision belonged to George and Lucille Clinkscales. Lucille was the daughter of a former co-owner of the Shelter Cove Wharf & Warehouse Company, Elizabeth Bowden. That same year Babe Machi married another of Bowden's daughters, Marilyn Swithenbank; they moved into one end of the old hotel.[722] Another old-time family reconnected with the cove in 1954 when Bill and Ethel Pass bought two lots in the subdivision and built a summer home. Ethel was a descendant of William Notley.[723]

It was also in 1954 that logging came to the cove. Soon two million board feet of freshly cut timber covered the flat. Some of it was assembled into a log raft for ocean transport to Eureka. The plan did not work. Rough seas at Punta Gorda disrupted the raft, dispersing its cargo across the blue Pacific, and the rest of the logs at the cove were taken inland by truck.[724]

In July 1957 the 110-foot yacht *Flamingo* was hit by a storm southwest of Shelter Cove. By evening she was in danger of sinking. The nearest Coast Guard station was at Humboldt Bay, several hours away. Coast Guard Commander Einar Nelson called the Machis for help and Mario and Tony immediately went into action. Mario, with pilot Don Cummings, took off from the airfield and quickly spotted the *Flamingo*, which had "waves breaking over the pilot house." They returned to the cove and Tony Machi and Dick Marr then set out in a 14-foot skiff. They also mobilized two boats from the cove's fishing fleet to join in the rescue effort. In the dead of night, in a raging sea, Marr and Machi used their skiff to transfer the yacht's six occupants, one at a time, to one of the fishing boats. They finished

# Shelter Cove

the rescue about 2 A.M. and took the victims to the comfort and safety of the Machi brothers' resort. The *Flamingo* sank about four-and-a-half hours later. For their efforts Marr and Tony Machi became the first winners of the Santa Rosa *Press-Democrat's* Heroism Award.[725]

The award was nice, but it didn't help Tony when, a year-and-a-half later, a wind-whipped fire destroyed the brothers' eight-unit motel and Tony's house. The nearest fire equipment was 90 minutes away at Garberville, but there was no way to summon even that distant help as the phone line was down. It didn't matter in any case—the buildings burned in less than an hour.[726]

For more than a hundred years the cove had seen a variety of activities that included ranching, shipping, tanbark processing, commercial fishing, and sports fishing. Throughout this time it had remained isolated and sparsely populated. Then, in 1962, Keith Etter sold his 5,000-acre Shelter Cove Ranch. The property was sold again the following year, and in December 1964 the new owners announced that a "Fifty Million [Dollar] Resort Development is Being Planned at Shelter Cove. 4200 Home Sites, Golf Course, Village. . . ."[727]

The plan was bold, intriguing, and, as soon became apparent, had failed to consider the effects of plate tectonics. The subdivision was bisected by the San Andreas Fault, creator of the 1906 San Francisco earthquake and thousands of other destructive temblors. On each side of the fault line lies a major tectonic plate: the land area to the west consists of a couple of hundred nearly level acres of the Pacific Plate. To the east rise the steep ridge slopes of the North American Plate.[728] If someone bought Pacific Plate property, they were assured of a relatively stable homesite. If they opted for North American Plate land, they obtained a scenic view but also a lot that might slump westward during heavy rains or as the result of a San Andreas

Busy day at Shelter Cove, 1949 (THPO, colorized by JR).

vibration. Many of the lots have proved unbuildable.[729] In 2004 the district manager for the California Coastal Commission indicated that "if the Shelter Cove development were proposed today, it wouldn't be approved."[730]

Thus the troubled history of Shelter Cove land disputes, which found whites confronting Indians a century and half ago, has seen a later chapter that is 50 years old and counting. The land here, like all the impulses it brings forth, may have rested for a bit, but it never sleeps.

## Appendix A: Frail Columbia[731]

It is well known by most mariners, ancient and otherwise, that the gods of the ocean—Poseidon, Neptune, etc.— are notoriously conservative. This is apparent in their maintenance of the *Ledger of the Deep*, a sort of nautical account book wherein the names of all ships are recorded, and which may not be changed (without proper ceremony) except under grave peril.[732] The *Alice Blanchard* proved this when she became the *Chico* ("boy" in Spanish), a change of not only name but also gender.

Retribution occurred off Needle Rock, some four miles south of Shelter Cove, where the Chico foundered in 1906. As late as 1930 her (his?) boiler could still be seen at low tide,[733] a stark warning against angering Neptune, et al. with nomenclatural negligence.

The passenger steamship *Columbia* provoked Poseidon, et al. by different means. She committed the crime of being one of the first ships to have a generator installed that provided electric lights.[734] Apparently this change was not noted in the *Ledger*, and when punishment came it was cruelly ironic. The *Columbia*

Oh boy, is the *Chico* in trouble (CPH, colorized by JR).

became victim to a coastal fog so dense that her enhanced illumination failed to penetrate it.

A series of premonitory problems began on April 18, 1906, when the San Francisco earthquake struck. The *Columbia* was at the time just offshore of the city, being refitted at the Union Iron Works docks. The quake rolled the ship onto her side, causing her to rest uncomfortably against the dock. Her outdated iron-plate hull suffered nine punctures in the process, causing the hold to partly fill with bay brine. As the *Columbia* made its way to Hunter's Point for repairs, rough seas caused her to list heavily, at which time one of her steam pipes burst. That did it for the crew, who promptly abandoned ship, and the stranded steamer then had to be towed to her destination.[735]

Not until January 1907 did the *Columbia* return to service. Soon she was again out of service, spending four days locked in pack ice on the Columbia River.[736] The forced layover, annoying as it was, proved to be a mere squall before the real storm that occurred half a year later.

Saturday, July 20, 1907, began foggy on San Francisco Bay. The weather cleared enough for the *Columbia* to leave port a little before noon, but the inopportune inclemency had delayed the ship's sailing by almost an hour.[737]

The passengers included a contingent of schoolteachers who were returning from a National Education Association convention in Los Angeles. At first the weather was fair with only a light breeze as the *Columbia* steamed up the coast. Later a swell developed, followed in the evening by an enveloping fog. The murkiness intensified, requiring Captain Peter Doran, who had gone to his cabin, to return to the bridge.[738]

The *Columbia's* vaunted electric lights did little good. As the vessel made her way through the fog-shrouded night, lookout S. G. Peterson was able to see "only about two ship lengths off either rail." Nonetheless, the *Columbia* steamed ahead at full speed. Perhaps Doran was trying to make up the time lost in the morning's late departure from San Francisco.[739]

At regular intervals the *Columbia's* fog whistle sounded. Lookout Peterson's watch had barely begun before he heard an answering sound off starboard. He relayed this information to the bridge, but Doran disregarded the warning and maintained top speed. A few moments later Doran and Second Officer Richard Agerup also heard a ship's whistle that was not their own, but the *Columbia* continued steadily ahead. For the next quarter-hour the other whistle continued to sound on the minute, and yet the *Columbia* still sped forward. Then "Peterson saw a ship emerge through the gloom. She was about 150 feet away and was coming 'square on' towards the *Columbia*."

It was the 457-ton steam schooner *San Pedro*, whose hold was filled with 390,000 board feet of lumber belonging to her owner, the Metropolitan Redwood Lumber Company.[740] On deck was a "massive…load of railroad ties and fence posts."[741] A better ocean-going battering ram could hardly be devised. Far too late to be of any use, Doran took remedial action. He ordered the *Columbia* full speed astern, but the ship had already crossed the *San Pedro's* bow, the tip of which presently penetrated the aging iron hull of the *Columbia*. Doran's command to reverse engines then took effect, disengaging the two ships, which began to drift apart. Meanwhile, Doran shouted to the *San Pedro*, "What are you doing, man?"—a question that he could have well asked himself.[742]

Events moved quickly. As the *Humboldt Standard* reported,

> The Columbia, an iron vessel, bore the brunt of the impact, and her iron plates,

Postcard of the *S.S. Columbia*, marked by a victim of the wreck (THPO, colorized by JR).

brittle with age, cracked and the gash, seven feet across the forward hatch, allowed the water free ingress at a great velocity.[743]

The much smaller *San Pedro* was made of wood, but she withstood the collision far better than the *Columbia*. As the *San Pedro* backed away, nursing a badly mashed bow, Captain Magnus Hanson took a quick look at the hole in the hull of the *Columbia* and ordered his schooner's three boats lowered. He knew they would be needed to pick up the *Columbia*'s survivors.[744]

On board the *Columbia*, Captain Doran left the bridge to inspect the damage. As he did so, he too gave orders to ready the lifeboats. Moments later Doran had seen enough. He amended his earlier instructions, shouting "Everyone to the boats!"[745]

The command did not come quickly enough. Some passengers had slept through the collision. Most were in their nightclothes. Many forgot that their life preservers were under their beds. They stumbled about, half dressed, in confusion and panic.[746] The Martindale family, far from the dry lands of their home in Guthrie, Oklahoma, reached the deck. Mr. Martindale put one arm around his wife and held their baby daughter in the other. Together, they jumped into the sea. Martindale's daughter was swept from his arms, never to be seen again. Mrs. Martindale's sister, brother-in-law, and their two children were also lost to the ocean.[747]

Chief Engineer John F. Jackson went to lifeboat #4, which he cut adrift with his knife. He noted that "the steamer was gradually going over to starboard. . . . She was also sinking forward at the same time. She careened over so quickly that our boat commenced to float without lowering it into the water."[748]

Captain Doran, whose earlier heedlessness

had helped cause the collision, attempted to calm the panic-stricken passengers, shouting, "Listen! Listen! Take your time. If you will but take your time all will be safe."[749]

But again Doran was mistaken. There was no time left. The *Humboldt Times* reported that the *Columbia* sank "after barely eight minutes."[750] The *Humboldt Standard* claimed that "it took but eleven minutes."[751] Either way, there was too little time to properly abandon ship. According to the *Standard*, Doran "pulled upon the whistle cord until the rushing water drowned the [boiler] fires."

By then the *Columbia's* crew had succeeded in launching all the starboard lifeboats and all of the life rafts. Doran remained on the bridge. He was heard calling "good bye,"[752] and then the *Columbia's*

> . . . stern went into the air a distance of 50 feet and a great crashing and roaring and hissing sound issued from the mass. . . .
> The mainmast was ripped in two, and the waters were in a few minutes covered with broken bits of wreckage. . . .[753]

Lifeboat #4, with 17 persons aboard, made it to the *San Pedro*. It discharged its passengers and went back to search for more survivors.[754] One of the *San Pedro's* boats, in the command of Second Mate Shaub, first picked up 20 passengers, then 12 more, then 12 again, and finally removed nine victims from one of the *Columbia's* boats. Eventually more than 50 survivors were taken on board the *San Pedro*.[755]

But many did not reach safety, and some made it by the slimmest of margins. Maybelle Watson, a 16-year-old from Berkeley, had boarded one of the lifeboats, but it was overloaded and was sucked into the *Columbia's* vortex when the steamer sank. Watson came to the surface to find many others in the water around her, including Cleveland schoolteacher Emma Griese, who was near to drowning because she "had apparently strapped her life

The *George W. Elder* stands by as the semi-submerged San Pedro decides not to sink (THPO, colorized by JR).

Eighteen of the *Columbia's* passengers (sixteen alive and two dead) made it to shore in this lifeboat (CPH, colorized by JR).

preserver on backward and her head was thrust forward into the water." Watson later said she saw "many men nearby and I called on them to help her." No luck. The men were all intent on saving themselves and were unwilling to direct their energy to aid a damsel in distress. So the other damsel, Maybelle Watson, had to do their job. She swam over to Griese and managed to keep her head above water until the redoubtable lifeboat #4 came by and rescued them both. The then-skipper of the lifeboat, Third Officer Robert Hawse, later said, "To my mind, there is but one heroine in the catastrophe that befell the *Columbia*. That is Miss Maybelle Watson of Berkeley."[756]

Besides the victims who found refuge on the San Pedro, others were taken aboard the passenger ship *George W. Elder*, which had answered the distress call and arrived in time to pluck at least 70 people from the ocean. One lifeboat reached Shelter Cove; it contained 16 survivors and two bodies. The death toll was probably 88 passengers and crew members, one of the highest totals for a wreck on the Pacific Coast.[757]

The owners of the *Columbia*, the San Francisco and Portland Steamship Company, achieved a new level of niggardliness by refusing to refund the full cost of the tickets to the surviving passengers. Instead the company insisted on discounting the refund $2.50,[758] apparently believing that it deserved recompense for transporting the survivors part way to their destination.

Supervising Inspector John Birmingham,[759] after conducting an inquiry into the disaster, found three ships' officers at fault. Mangus Hanson, captain of the *San Pedro*, was suspended from duty for one year, while his chief mate, Ben Hendricksen, was put on the shelf for five years. Peter Doran, captain of the *Columbia*, was also held responsible, but no penalty was levied against him as he was dead and thus unable to receive further punishment. In addition, Birmingham found that the *Columbia's* construction, while conforming to current law, was inadequate for the dangers faced by the vessel, concluding that "A watertight bulkhead extending up to her main deck and fifty feet abaft her collision bulkhead would have saved the ship and all on board."[760]

Within a few years a huge vessel was built that claimed to possess the watertight bulkheads Birmingham had recommended. It had 15 transverse bulkheads that were indeed watertight—as high as they went. Unfortunately, their tops extended only a few feet above the waterline, leaving an open space between them and the bottom of the main deck. If the hull was pierced near either end of the ship, water flowing into the damaged compartments could tip the hull downward enough that the water then flowed into undamaged compartments over the tops of bulkheads. On the night of April 14, 1912, this is exactly what happened when such a ship—which happened to be the S. S. *Titanic*—hit an iceberg in the North Atlantic.[761] The lesson of the *Columbia* had come to naught.

Filling up the front page.

# Chapter 9
# Whitethorn

The "White Thorn valley" made the news in February 1864 when Lt. William E. Frazier and a detachment of 12 men from the Mountaineers Battalion massacred two groups of Indians there, killing 13 men and one woman, while capturing 19 women and two children who were then taken to Fort Humboldt. As the *Humboldt Times* reported it, "the Indians offered no resistance, being completely surprised."[762] This killing of unresisting Indians exceeded even the draconian requirements of Colonel Henry M. Black's subsequent order to troops in the Humboldt Military District "that all Indian men taken in battle shall be hung at once."[763]

A year later the Whitethorn area was held in such little regard that the official Humboldt County map of 1865 covered it over with a chart of county agricultural production.[764] By the time of the next county map, in 1886, enough development had occurred that "White Thorn Station" was shown, located at the end of a road running from the Shelter Cove-Garberville road southward up the Mattole River. From White Thorn Station a trail went west and then south into Mendocino County.[765]

By 1898 the road continued south from what the county map now called "Thorn," following the Mattole upriver across the Mendocino County line to a community labeled "Davis," which was situated about a half-mile south of the line. It appears that Davis had previously been called first Gopherville and then Scottsville. By 1905 Albert Davis was the most important person in town—he owned the saloon—and Scottville became Davis.[766]

From Gopherville-Scottsville-Davis the road continued to follow the Mattole upriver, bending west as it did so, and then reached another tiny community called "French." Here was an intersection with the coastal road. North from here led to "Frank," while the way west went to Bear Harbor and Needle Rock, and the route south went to Kenny, Usal, and on to Fort Bragg.[767]

After the Garberville Mercantile Company (GMC) was formed in 1911, it operated a stage line that ran from Garberville through Whitethorn and southward on to Kenny. The latter was described as "a small place but an important stopover consisting of a one-story hotel, stables, saloon, and post office."[768] Stage passengers who stayed overnight at the Kenny Hotel rose early the next morning, ate a "hearty breakfast and were on the road north by 6:00 a.m."[769] Supplementing the GMC's operation, Joe Thomas provided an early-day taxi service with his team and buggy, taking passengers along the stage route.[770] In addition to transportation, he provided communication; the Garberville-based J. P. Thomas Telephone Company "linked . . . the small towns of Harris, Bell Springs, Ft. Seward, Alderpoint, Blocksburg, Ettersburg, Thorn, Shelter Cove, Redway, Piercy, Leggett, and . . . remote ranches in between."[771]

In 1913 the road that ran through Whitethorn showed its worth when it served as the first link in a multifaceted transportation system that brought an injured wagon driver to medical aid. (See sidebar 1.)

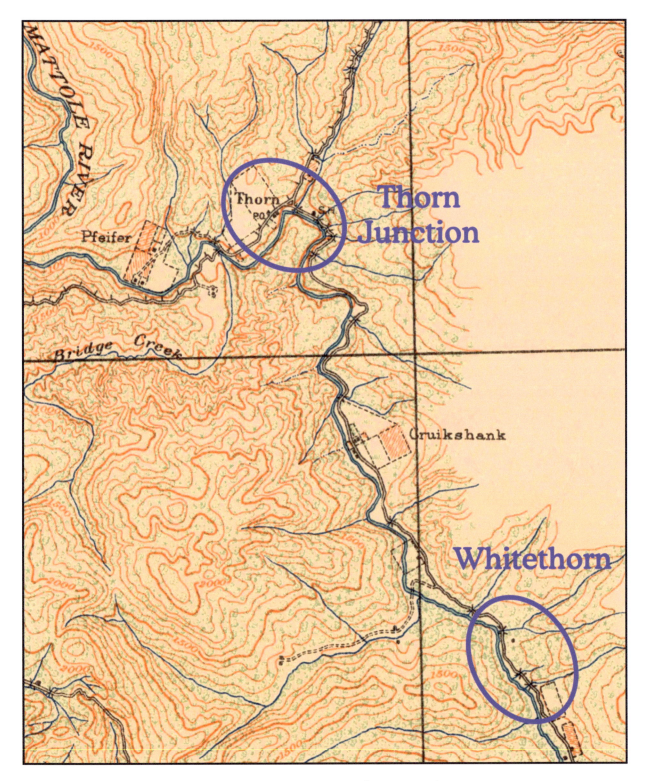

Thorn-Whitethorn area, 1916 (base map: CE).

The area near where McKee Creek meets the Mattole River contains a prairie opening and broad riverside flats. It was here that the road to Whitethorn left the Garberville-Shelter Cove road, and the location came to be called Thorn Junction. In 1884 Don Alonzo McKee homesteaded land there with his wife, Nettie, and in 1889 his mother, Angeline McKee, homesteaded a parcel just to the east.[772] After Don Alonzo's death in 1907, Nettie operated

### 1. Jim Boots's Three-Stage Ambulance Ride

In 1913 the Whitethorn area remained one of the most remote locations in Humboldt County. But when necessity called, its residents could connect surprisingly quickly with the outside world. Wagoner Jim Boots learned this following his misadventure near the Humboldt-Mendocino county line.

One day that spring Boots was driving a six-horse team hauling a load of railroad ties to the landing at Needle Rock. While the team was crossing a gulch just south of the county line, the normally reliable bridge decided to collapse, taking Boots, horses, wagon, and ties to the bottom of the canyon. Arthur Kelsey, who was driving a wagon ahead of Boots, ran back to the scene of the accident to find Boots on the ground with a compound fracture of his shin. Kelsey carried Boots out of the gulch and "sat him down where he could lean up against a tree." Kelsey then rode to Needle Rock to summon help.

Help arrived in the form of Sam Kelsey, Arthur's father. Sam "arrived after

Jim Boots hauling tanbark, 1907 (HCHS, colorized by JR).

> dark that night. He set Jim's broken leg by the light of a coal oil lantern, made a fracture box, [and] filled it with rolled barley, the only thing available that could be used." Sam and a helper, Billy Adams, borrowed a light wagon, put Boots in the back, and set off for Garberville. The trip took them through Whitethorn and Briceland, and by the time they reached Garberville "the team was spent."
>
> Despite the emergency, the Garberville livery stable owner refused to give Kelsey and Adams a fresh team. But a traveling salesman staying at the neighboring hotel heard the anguished argument, "got out of bed and offered to take the group wherever they needed to go." Getting his car, he drove the men all the way down the South Fork Eel and on to the Shively ferry, which they then took, reaching the Shively train station just as the northbound train was leaving. The railway men held the train until they could load Boots into a boxcar, which he rode to Eureka.
>
> Once at the hospital Boots was examined by Dr. Felt, who then told Sam Kelsey, "with all our modern facilities, x-ray and such we cannot improve on the set of that broken bone; we'll leave it just as it is. . . . You did a fine job, Sam."[773]
>
> And the wagon-auto-train transport system didn't do too badly, either.

the ranch on her own until she married Charles Lowrey in 1910. The Lowreys raised cattle and Angora goats.[774]

In February 1888 William T. Cruickshank patented a homestead along the Mattole about a mile south of Thorn Junction.[775] His Whitethorn Ranch became the way station for the Overland Stage and, in August 1888, the site of the Thorn Post Office. Cruickshank served as postmaster until 1910. Nettie McKee Lowrey then became postmaster. By 1923 the recently completed Redwood Highway had caused travel to diminish along the old Fort Bragg-Kenny-Whitethorn route, and the Thorn Post Office was closed. In 1928 Ralph and Lee French obtained the local contract for mail delivery and hired Fred Wolf as the carrier. Previously delivery had been by horse, but Wolf modernized the operation by using an auto.[776] The area's mail was brought to Bertha Lewis's Whitethorn store, where locals would come to collect it. In 1949 Onofrio "On" Russo closed his store in Ettersburg and then bought the Whitethorn store from Lewis in 1950. Russo had been the Ettersburg postmaster, and he apparently missed the job. He sent in a petition to the postal service, and in February 1951, after a 28-year hiatus, a new Whitethorn Post Office opened in his store. Mail delivery, now conducted by Ralph Wilkenson, was still only three days a week, so Russo drove his own vehicle, without compensation, three additional days a week to ensure full service at his post office. In 1966 a separate building for the Whitethorn Post Office was completed. It was run by Russo's wife, Isabel, who had become postmaster in 1962.[777]

Whitethorn's on-again, off-again post office was not the only problematic part of the small, remote community. Its school, while managing to stay open, was fraught with difficulties. (See sidebar 2.)

The post-World War II housing boom led to the establishment of many small sawmills in rural Humboldt County, and the Whitethorn area was no exception. In 1950 five mills lined the west side of Briceland Road: three north of the Whitethorn store and two to the south. Across the road from the store was the still-beleaguered Whitethorn School, inauspiciously flanked by a bar and the town dump.[778]

Ruth Morgan had hoped that the 1934 fire would take out the schoolhouse, forcing the community to construct a new, and hopefully better, building. Instead, Whitethornians had to wait until 1945, when an "emergency structure" replaced the primitive board-and-batten schoolhouse. It did not appear to be an improvement, being clad with rough-cut lumber that looked

### 2. A Thorn in the Side of Whitethorn

Whitethorn had a school at least as early as 1893, when I. Eggler was the teacher and Don Alonzo McKee clerk of the school board.[779] Over the years it had its good times and its bad times, as most institutions do, but it was during the Depression years of the 1930s that it probably hit rock bottom. Thanks to teacher Ruth Morgan, there was an on-site report.

Whitethorn School, no date (HCHS, colorized by JR).

In July 1934 Morgan received a letter informing her that she had been hired as the Whitethorn School teacher and was expected to report the following Monday. Since Morgan had no car of her own, getting there on time proved a challenge. She finally located a friend who was driving to Redway and who agreed to make the side-trip to Whitethorn. Morgan found it to be an unexpected adventure:

> What a trip after leaving Highway 101! The roads were narrow, unpaved, and one series of hairpin turns after another. At the time I vowed I'd never again go over that road.[780]

Another surprise awaited her at the end of the trip:

> My introduction to the school was a ghastly sight. . . . The walls were no more than single boards with some laths over the cracks, and through the years many of these had disappeared. The blackboard was nothing more than a misshapen bulging piece of painted cardboard. The seats were screwed down to the runners and were too big for many of the children. There were narrow windows on three sides causing very poor lighting. Of course there was no electricity or other lighting for that matter. . . . Water was brought up the hill from the river and a bucket placed on a shelf on the porch.[781]

With the onset of winter Morgan learned more about the limitations of the school:

> There was a round iron stove in the building, and in rainy weather I had to start the fire with wet wood after I got to school. Sometimes I'd throw in some floor oil to try to get the fire to burn. . . . When it rained, desks had to be moved to avoid the leaks both from the roof and the side walls. When it was very cold, the ink froze in the wells, and the water froze in the goldfish bowl causing the poor fish to lose their tails.[782]

Later Morgan found that her school was slated for special distinction. When Bertha Murray, the County Superintendent of Schools, and the supervisor, Mrs. Railsbach, paid their annual visit, they proceeded to take a picture of the school. They informed a perplexed Morgan that "the State

Department of Education was publishing a book and wanted a picture of the worst school in California." Murray and Railsbach had brought along their camera because they thought the Thorn School might become the winner.[783]

The students attempted to mitigate the squalor of the school with a series of amusements. They began by bringing Morgan a bouquet of poison oak. She disappointed them by not breaking out in a rash. Next they placed a dead bird in her desk drawer, but this drew no reaction. Then they put some salamanders in the chalk tray below the blackboard. Morgan took the unwanted amphibians down to the Mattole River.[784]

The Whitethorn School, 1930 model, that Ruth Morgan beheld (HCHS, colorized by JR).

Whitethorn School, 1945 model (HCHS, colorized by JR).

Come fall and the school faced greater excitement than at-large salamanders. One of the locals thought to burn some of Whitethorn's ubiquitous brush and the fire got out of control. Students coming to school from Mendocino County reported that the fire was burning on both sides of the road, and that afternoon they had to return home by an alternate route. Three days later the fire was alight in the hills behind the school, and "by noon it was creeping up the road across from the school." Morgan was wondering what action she should take when

> . . . suddenly, a welcome sight appeared—a small fire truck! The fireman drove all the way up onto the grounds and parked right beside the building. I was told to go inside—that everything was under control. What a relief! However, in 15 minutes the fireman came to the door and told me to evacuate the building and remove everything from it.[785]

Wayne Robinson, an eighth-grader, had brought a Ford with a rumble seat to school that day, and the car was quickly filled with books, supplies,

> and the smallest children. The Ford took its cargo to the Robinson house while Morgan walked with the older children to safety. That night she watched as "huge sparks and actual branches on fire were flying everywhere." Morgan thought that the school was a goner, but the wind changed and, for better or for worse, the "worst school in California" was spared.[786]

like it had been salvaged from the scrap heap of a sawmill. The 1945 building was

> . . . divided into two classrooms, both of inadequate size. The primary class was housed in a small building across the creek from the school property in a structure that did not belong to the school district. The water for both buildings was taken from an open creek and presented a health hazard.[787]

Finally, in the mid-1950s a new Whitethorn school was built.[788]

The 1960s saw an unexpected change in the rural fastness of the Whitethorn valley. On Halloween Day in 1962 four nuns from the Cistercian community of Our Lady of Nazareth in Brecht, Belgium, arrived at Whitethorn and proceeded to establish the Redwoods Monastery. Already on hand was Father Roger de Ganck, along with several monks from the Abbey of New Clairvaux, in Vina, California. The monks raised temporary buildings while the sisters "worked on creating the conditions for monastic life." More nuns arrived from Belgium, the monastery and church were completed in 1967, and wood-cabin living quarters were finished in 1976.[789]

As Whitethorn moved through the early 21st century, it recalled its history from more than 80 years ago. In late 2017 the Whitethorn School made the news when the State Water Resources Control Board placed it on a Boil Water Order. As in the 1930s, the school was relying on surface water—always a suspicious source—for its needs. A filtration system was in place, but it was not working properly. A plan to drill a well for a new water supply raised concern when it was pointed out that an underground fuel tank in the vicinity of the school had been found to be leaking 20 to 30 years ago.[790]

Locals may have been shocked by this turn of events, but one former Whitethorn resident would not have been surprised—Ruth Morgan.

# Chapter 10
# Briceland

Briceland was a town with three saloons and no church.
—Helen Thomas Pierce

Long before marijuana became the cash crop for southern Humboldt County, there was another profitable plant that was prevalent in the area. It was the tanoak tree, needed by leather tanneries for its bark. (See Appendix A.) In time the center of the southern Humboldt tanbark industry became Briceland.

Prior to white arrival in the area, there was a large Sinkyone Indian village called To-cho-be northeast of the future site of Briceland. The inhabitants of the village and the surrounding area were known as the To-cho-be ke-ahs.[791] At an undetermined date, but probably in the early 1860s, the village was attacked by a band of rough-hewn whites.[792] To-cho-be was destroyed and its inhabitants either killed or scattered among the hills.

A pack train trail from Shelter Cove to Garberville ran through the area; it was upgraded to a road in 1878. South of Briceland-to-be the route climbed southeast over "Briceland Hill" before descending to cross the Eel just upriver from Garberville.[793] According to one account, a Chinese crew working on the road had a camp just north of the Briceland townsite, and a stream that flowed past the camp was then

The school stands out in Briceland (HCHS, colorized by JR).

named China Creek.[794] The route of the road was such that the townsite "was just right to make it a convenient overnight stop for travelers and freight wagon team, hauling goods from Shelter Cove."[795] Refreshed by their rest, teams and teamsters could then take on the ascent of Briceland Hill.

The first white who moved into the area was reportedly "a man named Collier," who arrived "and built a log cabin and corral in the 1880's."[796] Collier was followed by Jim Filer, who, recognizing the potential of the place, opened a small store.[797]

In 1883 John C. Briceland migrated from the Ettersburg area and moved east. He purchased both Collier's place and Filer's store.[798] Briceland ran the store for three years but then sold it; he had bigger things in mind. For a time he was content to raise horses and livestock, do occasional butchering, and acquire more land. Then he laid out a townsite and built the Briceland Hotel, an ample facility that contained about 25 rooms.[799] In 1889 it was finally time for him to confer immortality upon himself by opening a post office that postal authorities agreed to call Briceland.[800] The town without a name now had one.

Over time, John Briceland lived with three Indian women—Bell, Jennie, and Fanny. They were listed on census rolls as "Housekeepers."[801] According to Della Womack, who was part white and part Indian, "white men took them [Indian women] and worked them like slaves."[802] A brief biography of Briceland indicates that he married the latter two of his "housekeepers," although the account uses euphemisms to avoid identifying them as Indians. Jennie becomes "a native daughter of California," while Fanny "was also born in California."[803] Fanny was designated in Briceland's will as the executor of his estate, one-third of which she was given; the residue was divided among his children, at least three of whom were Fanny's.[804]

In 1896 John Bowden moved from Shelter Cove to Briceland and opened a store. Two years later he not only married Lottie Kehoe but, for good measure, became postmaster. John served two stints in the job, and Lottie did a 19-year stretch. She also found time to teach intermittently at Briceland's school and in the late 1940s was its principal.[805] Della Womack fondly recalled the way John Bowden treated his younger clientele: "He was so nice. I just loved him, he was so good. He gave us kids candy every once and a while. He'd have us say a long word for it."[806]

At one point in the 1890s, some 27 pupils attended the Briceland School. There was a lack of furniture. Fifteen students sat at five double desks, three to a desk. Eight sat on benches around a table. Two (perhaps the misdemeanor troublemakers) were at a small desk in a corner. One sat at the teacher's desk (probably the felony troublemaker). The compiler of the report may have needed to sit at one of the desks for some remedial arithmetic, since only 26 of the 27 students are accounted for. Enrollment increased enough that a new schoolhouse was built in 1907.[807]

Despite the massacre of the village of To-kub-be and other attacks by the whites, a population of Indians remained in the area. John Briceland was but one of several local white men who had relationships with Indian women. The result was numerous children of mixed parentage. Helen Thomas Pierce, who grew up in Briceland in the 1900s, described the situation using a term now considered offensive:

Briceland was a town of halfbreeds. There were more halfbreeds in town

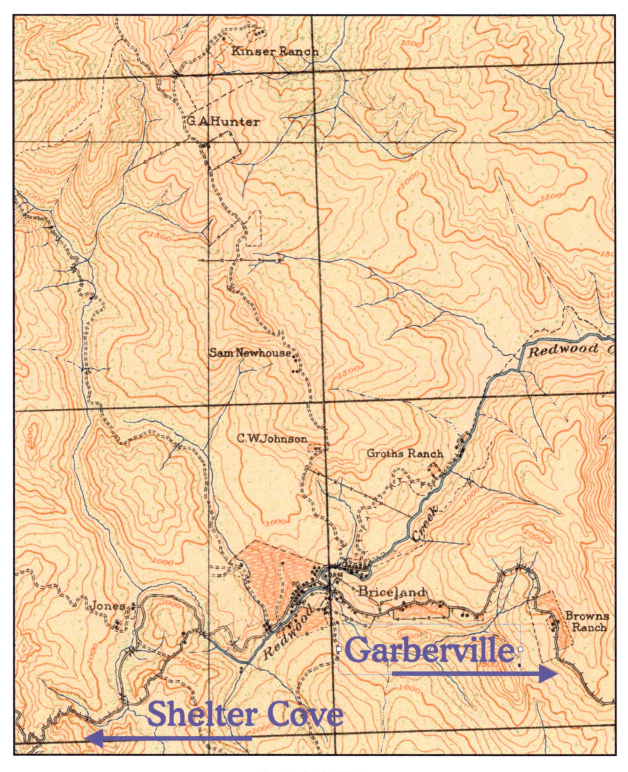

Briceland, 1916 (CE).

than white people, and the two groups lived side by side. And while there was no particular social activity that involved the two groups, when they met at dances and places like that, they were always nice to each other and danced with each other. . . .

I remember Susie Pollock, a halfbreed who was that tall and weighed two hundred pounds, but she could dance

Briceland Hotel, left, and saloon, right (CPH, colorized by JR).

like a dream. All the white people wanted to dance with Susie Pollock because she could dance so well.[808]

In 1910 Margaret Smith Cobb, an author who lived over the ridge at the mouth of Sproul Creek, came out with a novel called *Blaxine: Halfbreed Girl*. According to local historian Mary Siler Anderson, Cobb used the racially mixed Briceland families as "a template for the characters in her novel." Whether or not this was true, Cobb asked fellow author and friend Jack London to provide an endorsement of *Blaxine* and told him of the local reaction to the book:

> . . . they have made some very wicked threats in the Half-breed town of Briceland. I had no time to heed them, but a few days ago while riding home from town, I was dragged from my horse by a half drunken, vicious Half-breed woman and pretty generally mopped around in the road. I believe she would have killed me if it had not been for an old squaw friend of mine. And the old squaw handled me quite as roughly in getting me away from the half-drunken denizen. . . . I got choked, my hair was pulled, but I talked very well whenever I could—and the drunken woman was just something wonderful to look at in her anger.[809]

At least one Indian-white marriage did not go well. In 1903 Hugh P. Robson, "Briceland merchant," violated a court injunction and sold most of his property before fleeing to Canada. The injunction was issued as part of a divorce suit brought by Robson's unnamed "Indian wife" on grounds of cruelty. Before the sale and his subsequent flight, Robson was

> . . . said to have been worth between $10,000 and $15,000, but of this there now remains for his wife and children but a few hundred dollars worth of stock in the store, and a house and lot of small value.[810]

# Briceland

In 1894 Loleta entrepreneurs drilled a well at Briceland in search of oil. They found gas instead, and for a time the well "furnished light and fuel for the whole town." The Briceland store was still using gas fuel in the late 1940s,[811] and its gas lights were available for emergency use as late as 1954.[812]

More important to Briceland than its gas supply was the abundance of tanoaks in the area. In 1900 it was

> . . . reported that nearly every resident of the Briceland section has filed on a tanbark claim and realizes that within a very few years that the tanbark will be worth almost double what it is now. It is the intention of a company below to erect a plant near Briceland for concentrating the bark.[813]

That very year the Briceland Bark Extracting Company began processing tanbark into a "thick, syrupy" liquid. It was sent in 50-gallon barrels to Shelter Cove and then shipped south.[814] Soon a bigger extracting facility was started. It lasted for 20 years, creating Briceland's heyday. (See sidebar 1.)

The closing of the extract plant represented Briceland's third great diminishment. The first occurred in 1908 when the town's women's club disbanded. Their clubhouse served as a community hall for many years but was finally demoted to being a storage space for the grocery store.[815] Loss number two came in July 1914, when a defective stovepipe in the Briceland Hotel allowed an errant spark to land on the underside of the roof of the hotel's kitchen. Soon the roof was aflame, then nearby buildings, and then buildings across the street. There was little wind blowing, but Briceland, like many other rural communities, had neglected to establish a fire department, "and" according to *Humboldt*

No women are seen in front of the festively adorned Briceland Saloon. Perhaps they are too busy maintaining the town infrastructure that allows the male populace to pose at their leisure (CPH, colorized by JR).

Briceland was not short on saloons. Here a well-equipped traveler leaves Billy McGhee's beer parlor (HCHS, colorized by JR).

### 1. The Pacific Oak Extract Works

In 1901 Charles Wagner and his son Edward came through northwestern California looking for a place to process tanoak bark.[816] They owned the Wagner Leather Company, whose tannery in Stockton had started operating in the 1850s.[817] By the turn of the century the Wagners had run out of tanbark from central California, and they decided to obtain bark from Humboldt County. The Wagners were smitten with the Briceland area and consequently did three things. First, they acquired harvesting rights to about 7,000 acres of tanoaks.[818] Second, they bought a half-interest in the wharf and adjacent land at Shelter Cove.[819] Third, they "built a huge extract plant at Briceland, the only one of its kind on the Pacific Coast." The Wagners' Pacific Oak Extract Works[820] began operating in 1902.[821]

At the plant the bark was stored in enormous sheds that could hold at least a thousand cords each.[822] The bark was ground into small pieces. The

Drying shed, Pacific Oak Extract Works (CPH, colorized by JR).

resulting bark chips were placed in a tank, and hot water was repeatedly pumped over them. The liquid was then pumped through five other tanks that each contained fresh tanbark, strengthening the solution. It was then "pumped into a huge copper vacuum where it was boiled down to . . . a thick, molasses-like consistency." This substance was then poured into 50-gallon barrels.[823] Four barrels were loaded onto each company wagon, and six-horse teams then pulled the wagons to a camp about halfway to Shelter Cove. The camp contained a barn, feed for the horses, and relief teams. According to one account, it was called the "Nooning Grounds" because the wagons, which had started at daylight, reached there about noon. They were met by wagons coming up from Shelter Cove. The teamsters would exchange wagons, get fresh horses, and then make the return trip to their starting places.[824]

Tanbark work was seasonal but intense. The road to Shelter Cove was too muddy during the winter for use by the heavily laden wagons, but during the dry months the plant operated full blast and two woods crews worked out of tanbark "camps" peeling the bark and moving it to Briceland.[825] Operating the plant reportedly required the Wagners to employ between 100 and 200 workers.[826] Briceland accordingly grew in size, so that during the days of the extract plant it was a larger community than Garberville.[827][828]

The company eventually bought an Alco truck that was used on the route from Briceland to the Nooning Grounds. Wagner wagons still hauled on the steep, twisting section of road down to Shelter Cove. Next came a four-ton Locomobile truck that was driven by Jim Boots, who had formerly been a teamster for the company. The Wagners later bought two Kleiber trucks,[829] which were kept busy transporting about 3,500 barrels of tanbark concentrate a year.[830]

The Wagner-owned Pacific Leather Company, Stockton (UP, colorized by JR).

In time Edward took over operation of the Wagner Leather Company from his father, Charles. Edward spent part of each summer at the Briceland extract plant, and his wife and two sons came to join him. The family's itinerary for the trip was dictated by the transportation infrastructure of the times, which was primitive but interesting:

> They started their long trip from Stockton to San Francisco where they stayed overnight. Then by train they arrived in Willits where they again spent the night before taking the train to Fort Bragg on the coast. The next day they traveled by horse stage to Usal where they spent the

# Briceland

> night, and the next day to Four Corners where there was a rig waiting to take them to Briceland.[831]
>
> About 1921 the Wagners ran out of tanbark in the Briceland area. They then wanted to relocate their extraction plant closer to the new Redwood Highway, which ran through Garberville and Redway. At the time the road between Briceland and Redway had yet to be built, and the company apparently felt that the aged Briceland-Garberville Road, which went over Briceland Hill and had steep grades, was too challenging a haul. When the county refused to build a road down Redwood Creek to Redway, the Wagners gave up the attempted relocation. Barkless, they shut down the Pacific Oak Extract Works in 1922.[832]

*Times*, "the efforts of the citizens with buckets was of little avail against the onrush of flames." On the north side of the street, the Briceland Hotel, Wood's general store, and three residences were consumed; on the south side, the Williams Hotel, the post office, and Fearrien's butcher shop burnt.[833]

Adding insult to the injury of the 1914 fire, Briceland found itself without supplies in the summer of 1918. Normally goods and trinkets were shipped by boat to Shelter Cove and taken 18 miles by road to end their journey on the shelves of Briceland's store. But a scarcity of ships, perhaps brought on by the country's

Nearing the finish line by the Briceland store (HCHS, colorized by JR).

involvement in World War I, meant that Bricelanders had been waiting for supplies since October 1917. When nothing had arrived by mid-August of the following year, the town's provisionless plight reached such proportions that the distant *Ferndale Enterprise* saw fit to report on the situation. A promise that supplies would arrive by the end of the month hung in the air; if not fulfilled, the town might have to undertake "difficult" transportation from Eureka or "the nearest railroad point" of Alderpoint.[834]

In 1914 Bricelander Bill Luke, who was 18 years old, found a new use for his rifle: use it to club apples out of a tree. This had unintended consequences when the gun discharged a bullet into Bill's right side, "causing a fearful wound." Unable to call 911, young Luke was compelled to "crawl three miles for assistance."[835] He survived the incident but probably lost his fondness for apples.

As if the 1914 fire wasn't enough, another blaze diminished the business district in 1925, taking out another of Briceland's hotels. That was all for a while, but in 1949 the Briceland Lumber Company's mill burned, temporarily putting some 35 workers out of work and causing principal owners A. A. Dimmick and sons to break out the red ink for their bookkeeping.[836]

In 1924-1925 Briceland finally saw a road built that connected directly with Redway.[837] For a time Briceland was still called "the trading center of this whole area," but it was a smaller center than in decades past. By then there was only a store (with its post office), a truck repair garage, a few shops, and a tavern to go with a scattering of dwellings. The town's population was about 250, many of whom were mill workers who came in during the post-World War II lumbering boom. Besides the erstwhile Briceland Lumber Company, there were "several small lumber mills" along the Redway-Shelter Cove road, creating a rambunctious scene with trucks "hurrying back and forth with loads, and numbers of small cabins . . . grouped in strategic places—complete with a collection of automobiles in various stages of repair." Yet travelers would still "frequently . . . see an older house, with its barns and outbuildings, surrounded usually by shade trees, with orchard and garden fenced in against marauding deer." These sheep and cattle ranches recalled an earlier time, before the Redwood Highway was a mere six miles away—before, in fact, there was any highway at all.[838]

By May 1954 the shrunken town was centered on the Bowdens' former store, which was then being operated by Paul Carruth and his unnamed wife. The building's longevity was probably due to its cladding, which was corrugated iron. During the 1914 fire, when many of the town's wooden structures ignited, the ironclad store merely heated up; it grew so hot in fact that a spectator burned himself when he inadvertently leaned against one of its walls.[839]

Briceland continued to count its losses. In the fall of 1954 its school "retired."[840] Then in 1962, the post office followed suit.[841] A book of the past was closed in 1970 when Edward Wagner sold his sheep ranch. It had been 69 years since he first came to the area with his father, Charles, when they were looking for a site for their tanbark plant. Edward had started the ranch in 1944; the sheep probably grazed on open land from which the Wagners had earlier removed the tanoaks.[842]

Briceland's tin store serves a diminishing community (THPO, colorized by JR).

### Appendix A: "Tanbark has big power . . ."

In the late 19th century, leather was an essential commodity. It was used for saddles, bridles, and harnesses; it provided covers for books and travel trunks; it was cut into strips and made into sturdy belts for powering industrial equipment.[843] Its uses were so varied and so frequent that it could be called the rubber, or the plastic, of its day. In 1907 California tanneries turned out 250,000,000 pounds of leather goods, almost all of which were either belting, harnesses, saddles, or shoe and boot soles. The value of all these products was $75,000,000.[844]

An 1867 business directory, when describing leather tanning, noted that the bark of the tanoak "is peculiarly adapted to this purpose."[845] California had vast tracts of tanoak trees, especially north of San Francisco and near the coast, and proved to be an ideal area for leather tanning; the state's moderate Mediterranean climate allowed for a quicker leather production cycle than on the Atlantic Coast or in northern Europe.[846] The California leather industry thrived, with central California tanneries quickly depleting the tanoak supply of the San Francisco Bay Area and the Santa Cruz Mountains. Harvesting then shifted north. With an abundant supply of tanbark close at hand, three leather tanneries were established in Humboldt County. From the late 1880s to the early 1900s, the county's third largest industry was leather manufacturing.[847]

But most tanneries were located in central California. Early-day San Francisco alone had about 50 tanning facilities, which perfumed the city's air with the aromas of the rotting flesh that clung to the animal hides and of the vats of tanbark solution in which the skins were cured for months. Stockton, Santa Cruz, San Jose, Berkeley, Oakland, Santa Rosa, and several other mid-state communities also had one or more tanneries.⁸⁴⁸ Benicia, by no means a metropolis, had three tanneries, including the Kullman and Satz plant that was the largest in California.⁸⁴⁹

The tanoak trees, which can attain a height of 150 feet,⁸⁵⁰ were killed by the bark harvesting process. Bark removal was usually done between about May 15 and July 15, when it was easiest to peel. Tanbark cutters worked in pairs, and peeling a large tree took half a day.⁸⁵¹ A tanbarker cut into the trunk of a tanoak with an ax, girdling the tree near its base. He then made a similar cut about four feet higher on the trunk, and then connected the two horizontal cuts with a single vertical cut. The bark was then peeled back from the vertical cut until it loosened from the entire circumference of the tree. The section of bark was set aside and the tree then cut down. The rest of the trunk was also peeled off in four-foot widths, as were the larger branches. The bark was left at the site for at least two months to dry through the heat of summer, during which time each section "rolled up like a scroll." The bark was then loaded onto pack mules and taken by trail to a landing, where it was either put on sleds and run downhill⁸⁵² or loaded onto wagons and taken out by road.⁸⁵³ At first the fallen tanoak trees were cut up into cord wood and used for heating and cooking. When tanbark harvesting reached its peak between 1900 and 1920, however, there were more downed trees than were needed. Many of them were left on the ground and burned in the fall, a profligate enterprise that disrespected an important member of the forest. Come spring, green tanoak shoots would poke through the ashes and be eaten by the local flocks of sheep,

Tanbarkers rest from tanbarking (CPH, colorized by JR).

thus providing a limited but unexpected use for the trees' remains.[854] Eventually many other uses were found for tanoak wood, including "for flooring, furniture, truck bedding, pallets, veneer, paneling, ties and mine timbers, [and] pulpwood. . . ."[855]

In southwestern Humboldt County most of the tanoak bark made one of three journeys after it was harvested. Bark from the lower Mattole valley was taken by wagon to the Mattole Lumber Company Railroad near the mouth of the river, whence it was carried by a tiny train out to a landing on Sea Lion Rock. Bundles of bark were then sent by cable to schooners that waited in deeper, safer water.[856] Some of the bark from farther south was transported to Shelter Cove, where it was processed by a bark grinder, packed in sacks, and then shipped out on steamers from the Shelter Cove wharf.[857] Other bark first made its way to Briceland, where the Wagner Leather Company's extract plant produced a syrupy tanbark concentrate that was then taken to Shelter Cove and shipped to the company's Stockton tannery.[858]

Although tanoaks ranged over much of Humboldt County, some of the densest stands were in the Mattole drainage. When writing about the "California tanbark oak" in 1911, botanist Willis Linn Jepson reported:

> In southern Humboldt, . . . the tanbark oak belt pushes through the great transverse break in the redwood belt at this point, and an arm extends northward over the Wilder Ridge country to the Rainbow Range. The extensive and virgin body borders the redwood belt on the outside and covers a considerable portion of the Mattole country lying between the redwood belt and the ocean.[859]

Jepson estimated that in 1911 there were about 875,000 cords of unharvested tanoak bark in Humboldt, Trinity, western Siskiyou, and Del Norte counties.[860] Just a decade later, however, the voracious appetite of the leather tanneries had created a shortage of tanbark. Nowhere was this more acutely felt than in Briceland, where the barkless extract plant closed in 1922.

If most southern Humboldt residents lamented the loss of an income-producing commodity, a few others mourned what for them was an even greater diminishment. For the tanoak tree, despite not being a true oak,[861] produced an acorn that was esteemed by the local Indians as the most flavorful.[862] For centuries the tanoak's acorns had provided, along with salmon, the staples of the Indians' diet.

But then the whites came, killing and driving away the Indians and upsetting the Earth. It was after this that Jack Woodman, a Sinkyone Indian who lived north of Briceland, was visited by the tribe's highest spiritual being, Nagaicho, "the great traveler." Woodman related what happened:

> You know Nagaicho passed through Briceland going from north to south; he came over Elk Ridge and he saw where white men had peeled tanbark. He said to me, "It looks just like my people lying around, lying with all their skin cut off." He looked, he looked, he looked once more and he hung his head. He was sad, sad, and he would not look again, he felt so grieved. Tanbark has big power and it all belongs to Nagaicho. He saw men breaking up the rocks and plowing up grass. He saw all thing leaving and going back to where they came from. He felt worst about the tanbark. Then Nagaicho

Mules brought the rolls of dried bark to transfer stations where they were loaded onto wagons (CPH, colorized by JR).

told me that he wanted to make another freshet from the ocean—make everybody die so the world would come back as it used to be. But I said to him, "No, no, I do not want that." I gave him back words, told him not to do that, to leave people alone, they were having a good time, and it couldn't be helped now that they were here. I said, "Don't do that," until Nagaicho said no more about it. You know that this was the third time he wanted to make a freshet because the people are so bad.[863]

Woodman gave this account in 1928 or 1929,[864] just as the Wagner Leather Company, having already shut down its extract plant in Briceland, was closing its tannery. A pretty good-sized freshet came along In 1937. It was followed by even larger floods in 1955 and 1964.

# Chapter 11
# Richardson Grove

If you were someone heading south from Garberville in 1911 and wanted to take your wagon or buggy or stagecoach or car into Mendocino County, you had two choices: you could either go via Sproul Creek on Moody Road southwest to the coast road that ran through Kenny and Usal and on to Fort Bragg, or you could go southeast to Harris and on to Bell Springs and Willits. If you tried to go directly south, up the canyon of the South Fork Eel, you'd have to stop not far past the East Branch, where the road ended and the route narrowed to a trail.[865] Only with the coming of the Redwood Highway at the end of the decade could you follow a road up the South Fork into Mendocino County and points south.

Thus, for more than 60 years, white occupancy of the Richardson Grove area was limited to a few ranches connected to the outside world by rough trails and potentially dangerous water crossings. Although remote, the region was also abundantly scenic, with a twisting, steep-sloped river canyon and nearby flats filled with redwoods. These were sights worth seeing, and when the new highway made them available to travelers, the area became a favored stop for scenery seekers. By the late 1920s the roadside was dotted with tourist attractions that even included a state redwood park.[866]

There is little information about Indian inhabitation of the area. Albert Smith, who belonged to the To-kub-be ke-ah tribal group associated with the Benbow section of the South Fork Eel, said of the vicinity of Joseph D. Smith's[867] ranch, "just that far [upriver] my people live."[868] The

Early day tent camping at Richardson Grove (CPH, colorized by JR).

village there was called Da-tcin-kon-tel-dun.⁸⁶⁹ The Smith Ranch was about two miles south of the East Branch and a mile northeast of Richardson Grove.⁸⁷⁰ Smith added that "the upper part of the South fork river belongs half to coast. Strangers to us."⁸⁷¹ He does not name the group of coastal strangers, although they may have been connected with Indians in the Usal area. George Burtt, a Lolahnkok Indian from Bull Creek, stated that a village called Kahs-cho so-ning-i-be occupied the "large redwood flat known as Richardson Flat," but he did not indicate which tribal group lived there.⁸⁷² Margarite Cook, a southern Humboldt historian who interviewed at least one local Indian, claimed that Kahs-cho so-ning-i-be "was small, with no more than five or six houses." She also indicated that there was another village, which she did not name, about a mile farther upriver at Cook's Valley.⁸⁷³

About a mile downstream from Richardson Grove, where the river bends from east to north, Joseph D. Smith took up 160 acres in 1861,⁸⁷⁴ finally patenting the land in 1889.⁸⁷⁵ Smith was first married to Anna McNeil, who left him in 1883. Eleven years later, on April 16, Smith laconically recorded that "I was home and went to town and got married and came home." His wife, Elizabeth Piercy, apparently came with him.⁸⁷⁶

The Smith ranch served as a food supplier for nearby locales. The couple grew and dried apples, peaches, prunes, and pears. They also cured hams and bacon. Among the communities served were Bear Harbor, Usal, Shelter Cove, and Garberville. The ranch was located next to the trail that ran along the South Fork, and Joseph kept a diary in which he recorded not only his family's activities but the encounters with people who passed by. Even though the route was merely a path and not a road, multiple entries in Smith's diary indicate it was heavily traveled. For example, on October 12, 1895, Smith noted that

> Dyke and Martin went down the river. Jim Weedman went up the river. John Rankin came back with 2 race horses and staid all night and I went down as far as Usal with him and staid all night with Thorn Beldon."⁸⁷⁷

At an unknown date a man named Anderson and his Indian wife Nellie settled on a 120-acre parcel of land on what was later called Hartsook Flat. Anderson drowned in the South Fork Eel, reportedly in 1869,⁸⁷⁸ and Reuben Reed, who knew the family, came over from the Leggett Valley where he was working. He took up the Anderson property and, while he was at it, married Nellie.⁸⁷⁹

The Reeds had little money, but that changed when Reuben made one of his periodic trips to Garberville for supplies. He parked his horse and mule in front of the saloon, made his purchases, and was mounting his steed to leave when several acquaintances invited him to a game of poker. Reuben had $2.50 in his pocket and didn't think he should play, but he permitted himself to be persuaded. It turned out to be quite an event. Reed and the others played all night, and when the game broke up at daybreak Reuben had won $2,600. He used the money to build a "comfortable home" that was also sturdy enough to be in use until 1928 or 1929.

Reuben's younger brother, Ezra, fought in the Civil War and then came west to join Reuben. He first took up 40 acres on Tooby Flat, below Garberville, and then claimed 760 acres east of Hartsook Flat. This property eventually grew to 1,700 acres, co-owned by the brothers, and the high hump of ground in the middle of it became known as Reed Mountain.⁸⁸⁰

# Richardson Grove

Civilian Conservation Corps boys at Richardson Grove (FMC, colorized by JR).

Albert Smith, a local Indian from the Benbow area, indicated that a man named Reed was among the people who attacked Smith's tribal group most often.[881] From the context of his statement, it is almost certain that he meant Reuben Reed.[882]

Reuben and Ezra Reed visited their Kentucky homeland in the 1870s and returned with their father, James Reed, who "homesteaded 160 acres of what is now part of Richardson Grove." The property came to have a cabin on it and also a garden called the "potato patch."[883] Over time the land changed hands, and by 1920 it was owned by Henry Devoy. He leased the redwood grove on the west side of the South Fork to Ed Freeman, who offered the services of a store, dining room, and some 15 cabins for use by tourists who came to camp and fish.[884] In 1922 the State of California purchased 120 acres of the northern part of Devoy's property for about $30,000[885] and used the land to create Richardson Grove State Redwood Park,[886] which was named for politician Friend W. Richardson, who became governor in 1923.[887] The park officially opened the weekend of May 19-20, 1923. The facility upgraded Freeman's operation and featured "several new cabins," "an electric lighting system" and "splendid dining room service."[888]

Richardson Grove was only a year old when four of the leaders of the Save the Redwoods League were called upon to specifically save the park's redwoods. In August 1923 league president John C. Merriam, secretary Newton B. Drury, and members Duncan McDuffie and J. C. Sperry were en route to Eureka when they encountered a fire burning towards the park. Leaving their car,

Stopping at the Richardson Grove Lodge, c. 1945 (JIC, colorized by JR).

the men joined about 30 firefighters in stopping the blaze before it reached Richardson Grove's redwoods.[889]

Freeman continued to operate the park's facilities as a concession until 1932. In the early 1930s the various buildings used by Freeman were dismantled. A striking log lodge, still in use, was built just east of the highway in 1931, followed by a park office south of it.[890]

On the east side of the river John P. Watkins and his wife Ida homesteaded 160 acres. John built a cabin there in 1913 for a family that eventually included 10 kids. They brought in many months of supplies in the fall because when the South Fork rose in the winter, they could not cross it to reach the road. In 1918 the Watkinses moved to Garberville so that their children could regularly attend school. Members of the family lived in the cabin for brief periods until 1934, when they abandoned it. The park took over the property in 1958, and the cabin, which was had remained vacant, was demolished in 1960.[891]

When Henry Devoy sold the northern part of his property to the state in 1922, he also sold the southern portion to Edgar Brown for $10,000. Brown subsequently sold his parcel to Fred Hartsook for $17,000.[892] Soon Hartsook was busy building a roadside resort. It became a place that often filled the pages of the newspapers. (See Appendix A).

In 1933 the civilian Conservation Corps (CCC) mobilized at Richardson Grove, upgrading the park by constructing "campgrounds, picnic facilities, trails, water systems and restrooms."[893] The park office that was built at this time was replaced by a new facility in 1959.[894] In the 1940s visitors had their choice of renting a park cabin or tent (a cabin with bath cost $1 extra), or either staying in their own trailer or camping with their own shelter (or lack thereof).⁸⁹⁵

During the 1950s additions alternated with diminishments. The park brought in sand to create an "instant" beach adjacent the South Fork and offered a "swimming hole with diving board and raft." The river, perhaps outraged by the park's presumptuousness, responded by loosing a massive flood in 1955 that "twisted and demolished buildings, buried campsites with silt, and cause siltation in the Grove." Afterwards the state relocated many of the facilities to higher ground at the edge of the park.⁸⁹⁶

Visitors to Richardson Grove could lunch under the redwoods (JIC, colorized by JR).

Sitting on imported sand at the Richardson Grove "beach" (JRC, colorized by JR).

And so Richardson Grove, with many of its trees perilously near the riverside, moved on through the decades. Bisected by the Redwood Highway, it was seen by many, visited by some, but always a welcome sight for travelers seeking respite from the City, be it for ten minutes or ten days. For the sheltering, thousand-year-old trees it was but an eyeblink either way.

### Appendix A: Hartsook Heartbreak

About 1908 Fred Hartsook could be found, somewhere in California, seated behind a team of mules that was pulling his homemade darkroom. Earlier he had operated a traveling photography studio in Utah with his wife Flossie but, lured by the voice of opportunity, the couple had moved to California to find their fortune.[897]

And find it they did. Fred opened two studios in southern California, closed them and opened one in Los Angeles, and then expanded along the Pacific Coast so that by 1921 there were 20 Hartsook photo parlors in business.[898] People in the public eye flocked to Fred and his studios to be photographed, including Henry Ford, Mary Pickford, John Philip Sousa, Dorothy Gish, and scores of others.[899]

By then Fred had divorced Flossie and married Bess Hesby, who had reigned as "Miss Liberty" at the 1915 Panama-Pacific International Exposition. The newlyweds chose as their honeymoon

The first Hartsook Inn. (HCHS, colorized by JR).

Sinophobia on the South Fork: vigilantes burn the Hartsook Inn (HCHS, colorized by JR).

site a rustic cabin in the redwoods on the South Fork Eel River. Entranced by the location, they purchased the cabin and 37 acres around it and soon went into the resort business.[900]

The *Humboldt Standard* carried a letter from Fred Hartsook in which he informed the Eureka Chamber of Commerce that there were "fifty two mechanics working on the different installations of our electric and ice plants, storeroom, dance floor, and cabins." Of the cabins there were 51, "with or without light housekeeping equipment." The main store building had 12 rooms above it. The ice plant produced "two and one-fourth tons of ice per day," which allowed the resort to make its own ice cream. "A very modern café" was accompanied by a meat market and 20-foot soda fountain, while the store was to carry "a general line of merchandise." Fred asked the chamber's assistance in securing one missing feature: a post office.[901]

And secured it was. Acting with lightning speed for a government agency, the postal service granted an office to "Hartsook" on July 23, 1926[902] —only a year and month after Fred asked for it. By then the Hartsook empire had expanded. He owned 26 photo studios and had also gained attention for his collection of livestock.[903] Hartsook had ranches in Kern County and North Hollywood, where he raised "prize-winning purebred Holstein cattle" as well as goats and hogs.[904] A herd of his dairy cows was in residence at the inn to provide fresh milk for the guests.[905]

A year after Hartsook wrote to the Eureka Chamber of Commerce, someone else sent the chamber a letter regarding the inn. In May 1927 the *Humboldt Standard* reported that Eureka's Federated Trades Council had written to the chamber, "calling attention to the presence of a number of Celestials [Chinese] at Hartsook

Grove." Apparently Hartsook, a relative newcomer to the county, was unaware of one of its prevailing prejudices.

The *Standard* called the letter "the first indication of a Chinese labor problem since the removal of some 20 Orientals about 15 years ago," also recalling the forced expulsion of most of the county's Chinese in 1885. Now Chinese were reportedly working at the inn in the kitchen and other departments. The chamber indicated that the matter was "being looked into."[906]

Spring segued into summer and then, on August 8, the Hartsook Inn again captured the *Standard's* headlines. "Scantily Clad Guests Forced To Flee For Lives" screamed the incongruent heading above a photo of fully dressed vacationers lounging in front of the inn. Apparently no photographer was on hand earlier that morning when the inn burned to the ground, forcing patrons to make a hasty departure from the conflagrating main hotel building. Also destroyed were the ice plant, service station, store, barbershop, post office, and Hartsook's private studio. Among the losses were autographed photos of former presidents Theodore Roosevelt and Warren Harding, "luxurious furnishings," and as much as two and a quarter tons of ice.[907] Bess Hartsook and her three children left "the hotel clad only in their night clothes."[908]

The *Standard's* story indicated that Sheriff J. W. Runner would probe into the cause of the blaze, noting that it was the county's fifth large fire in the last month. Law enforcement officials admitted they had "unearthed nothing tangible in the way of a clue" about any of the blazes.[909] No mention was made about the recent complaint lodged by the Federated Trades Council regarding Hartsook's use of Chinese workers. Undaunted, Hartsook immediately rebuilt.[910]

The fire came while Hartsook was still reeling from an outbreak of hoof and mouth disease that had forced him to destroy his herd of prize Holsteins. This one-two punch to his finances caused him to petition for bankruptcy in April 1928. The photography studios went into receivership,[911] but the new inn remained with the Hartsooks.

In September 1930, Fred Hartsook died of a heart attack in Burbank, California.[912] Bess Hartsook continued to operate the inn. All did not go well. The Depression was in full swing, and tourism slowed to a trickle. In January 1932 the Hartsook Inn went into receivership,[913] although Bess continued to operate it.

In August 1938, the *Humboldt Times* ran an article about her, indicating that "Bess Hartsook, gracious, courageous and undaunted owner of the Hartsook Inn, . . . opened her doors for the finest type of service to the public 14 years ago." Two months later the mortgage on the Inn was foreclosed and the Bank of Eureka claimed the property for $31,470.64.[914] No longer the owner of the inn, Bess Hartsook continued as manager.[915] Another two months passed, and there was a new calamity at the inn; a midnight fire that destroyed the main building and one cottage. By now old hands at such things, the three Hartsook children again made a nighttime escape from the flames. This time Bess Hartsook did not participate, as she was in San Francisco.[916]

Once again the inn was rebuilt—gradually. L. A. Spengler gained control of the partly restored facilities in 1941; three other members of his family assumed operation in 1946, and reconstruction of the inn was finally completed in 1948.[917]

The third inn lasted longer than its two predecessors, but it was erased in 1973 by yet another fire.⁹¹⁸ Chet Willows, the owner, promptly built the fourth incarnation of the Inn. In 1984 his wife sold the property, still called the Hartsook Inn. Several other parties subsequently owned it before it was sold to the Save-the-Redwoods League in 1998.⁹¹⁹ More recently the property became a campus of the Heartwood Healing Arts Center.⁹²⁰

By 1976 Bess Hartsook was living in Mill Valley with her daughter Helen and Helen's husband. Bess was in declining health, suffering from diabetes and having lost a leg as result. Her granddaughter, a well-known tap dancer in the Bay Area known professionally as Rosie Radiator,⁹²¹ decided to create a tribute to her grandmother. On Labor Day that year, Rosie tap danced across the Golden Gate Bridge with her dog, Lu Lu. The *San Francisco Chronicle* picked up the story and a large crowd was on hand to cheer Rosie and Lu Lu on. Rosie proclaimed that it was Tap Dance Day and dedicated the event to her grandmother. As a result of the publicity, Bess Hartsook "was contacted," according to Rosie, "by over three hundred friends and acquaintances that she hadn't seen or spoken with since her days with my grandfather."⁹²²

Beth Hartsook died a few weeks later. She was buried in the Trinidad Cemetery, along with a picture of Rosie tap dancing across the bridge.⁹²³

The second Hartsook Inn (HCHS, colorized by JR).

# Chapter 12
# Benbow

Like so many bucolic locations in southern Humboldt, the confines of the South Fork's lower East Branch were once filled with tumult and sorrow. Here, as elsewhere, a handful of whites swept through the area, leaving a trail of blood and destruction that spread across the landscape like a stain upon a map.

The East Branch and nearby locations on the South Fork were home to a Sinkyone tribal group known as the To-kub-be ke-ahs.[924] A member of this group, Albert Smith, provided the ethnographer Pliny Goddard with detailed information about his people, indicating that there were several villages along the river near Benbow and both villages and summer camps in the East Branch drainage.[925]

Smith also described incidents where whites killed members of his family. Two brothers were shot by soldiers near the headwaters of the East Branch and his mother murdered at a village on the South Fork.[926] Two other Indians, both women, gave accounts of a massacre at Benbow.

According to Nona James, a part-Indian woman whose grandfather was the Indian child-stealer and enslaver James Woods,[927]

Albert and Sally Smith fishing on the South Fork, a mile upriver from Benbow (DTC, colorized by JR).

Sam Piercy was with my grandfather . . . when they were coming through on horseback to clean out the Indians from this part of the country. . . . They found the Indians encamped out by Benbow, where those red rocks are now [1984] that they use for a gravel pit. The Indians used to camp up there when it was wet weather. They was going to clean these Indians out and they cleaned them out all right. They'd kill all the men except the ones that run and hid and then take the women.[928]

The massacre occurred in 1859. Over sixty years later, an Indian woman named Jane Johnson told local historian Margarite Cook that "all of the Indians except several young teenage Indian girls [were] killed." Johnson was one of the girls.[929]

The site of the massacre is visible on the hillside southeast of Benbow above the east side of the river.

At an unknown date a man named "Alfred or Abe Wood" took up property near the mouth of the East Branch. He had a cabin, barn, and large orchard and was apparently the first white to live in the area.[930] In 1872 John and Sarah Davis arrived in the vicinity. They first traveled to the future site of Harris from their former home in Mendocino County; then they promptly headed west, coming "down to a beautiful valley" that contained the East Branch. The Davises borrowed $3,000 from Ben Stoddard and bought Wood's ranch.[931] They failed to pay off the loan and Stoddard took over the ranch. He spent $3,000 building a two-story house and a new barn, thinking this would improve his chances of reselling the property. Sure enough, sometime between 1900 and 1902 Stoddard

On the hillside in the background Sam Piercy, James Wood, and other whites massacred numerous To-kub-be ke-ahs (JR).

sold the ranch to Mel P. Roberts for $8,000. For a time Fred Schumacher lived there, then Fred's brother Ben rented the place.[932] In 1913 Ernest S. Linser acquired the property, which by then totaled 1,288 acres. Linser sold out to the Benbow family in 1922. The hotel the Benbows subsequently built marked a new phase in the area's development. (See Appendix A.)

Upriver about a mile from the Benbow Hotel was the Eel River Lodge, which offered more modest accommodations. Located just southwest of Fish Creek, the lodge was built by Ross Hooper in the late 1920s. It included a main building with restaurant and a set of rustic cabins. The business changed hands several times and was owned by Tom Carp and his wife when the 1955 flood hit. All the cabins were destroyed, and the lodge badly damaged. Slides and washouts to the north and south isolated the lodge from road traffic. Horses, however, could reach the location by coming over Reed Mountain to the east. A group of looters used this route to reach the lodge, from which they took all the liquor, put it on their pack horses, and departed. As if the flood and looting were not enough, someone then set fire to the thrice-afflicted lodge and it burned to the ground. The site later became part of the Benbow Lake State Recreation Area.[933]

In the 1870s the Ray brothers—William, John, and James, who in the previous decade had become the main property owners at Shelter Cove—acquired land along the East Branch about three miles from its mouth. The sheep and cattle ranch they established there eventually grew to include about 6,500 acres. The acquisition was followed by a series of tragedies. On December 6, 1880, another brother, Thomas, drowned in the East Branch when he attempted to cross it during a flood. Eight days later his brother William was also dead, having landed on his head when thrown from his horse. A decade passed, and then Robert Ray was gored and killed by a bull. All three brothers were buried in a family cemetery on the ranch.[934]

Charles and Alice Kinsey bought the property in 1914. Over a hundred years later a third generation of Kinseys were still operating the ranch.[935]

Over time there were two schools that served the area. In 1881 Samuel Dean built the East Branch School on the north side of the river between Buck Mountain Creek and Squaw Creek. The location seems remote now, but in those days it was right on the road that came down from Spruce Grove and then followed the East Branch west towards Garberville. This is the route that Dean, his wife Annie, and their two children took when arriving in Humboldt county in 1878. They knew just where to go, because Annie was the daughter of John and Sarah Davis, the couple that had come to the East Branch in 1872. Samuel Dean was a carpenter by trade, and apparently donated both his labor for building the school and the land it sat on.[936] He had a strong personal interest in the facility because five of his children eventually went there.[937] One of the teachers, Cora Bailey, kept a diary during her time on the East Branch. (See sidebar 1.)

In 1904 the East Branch School was moved a couple of miles south of the river up onto the side of Reed Mountain. It apparently operated there until 1911.[938]

The road that ran up from the East Branch to Spruce Grove is still shown on the 1911 county map, but by then its days were numbered. A new route, now known as Alderpoint Road, had been built east from Garberville to the Mail Ridge road and provided a better connection

Rusticating beside the South Fork at the Eel River Lodge (THPO, colorized by JR).

### 1. Life, and Death, on the East Branch

Life on the East Branch was, according to Cora Bailey, mostly slow-paced and simple, as befit a rural ranching area in the years around 1900. She began a diary on June 1, 1898, noting that it "rained again." The next day also saw "rain again," which meant that Cora "had to ford East Branch on horseback as the water was around the foot log." Two days later the stream had subsided enough that she could go to Garberville in the wagon with school builder Samuel Dean, his wife Annie, and their daughter Izora.

Saturday, June 4: "Mr. Dean put up the new bell-rope at the schoolhouse." The following Monday one of the Deans' sons, Bert, "commenced going to school." During June, Cora mentions, almost always briefly, events such as a sermon given by Mr. Crooks, shopping for clothes in Garberville, and a "social" in town that featured a backward contest where "the ladies drove nails and the men sewed on buttons."[939]

That August, Bert Dean left the East Branch to work at the coast for two or three months. Cora "was very sorry to see Bert quit school, as he was getting along nicely and he is such a nice boy." Another student, Elmer Hurlbutt, missed a week of school because his horse fell on him "as he was riding after cattle."[940]

In September Annie Dean asked Cora to make her daughter Izora a shirtwaist, saying that in return she would give Cora the material to make one for herself. Cora agreed to do it, but lamented that

> . . . I hate to take the other waist for pay. It seems too much, as they are poor people, but Mrs. Dean seems anxious for me to take it and I am sure it is a kind offer."[941]

Annie Dean learned that Bert "can not get his wages over there on the coast for the time he worked," and, Cora wrote, "she seems to feel pretty blue."[942] Cora doesn't provide much information about the Deans, but other sources indicate that Annie was probably too busy to mope for long. The Deans' house was beautifully situated on a flat above the East Branch, and Annie, a gifted gardener, surrounded her home with "flower beds outlined with native rock." She also found time to become "one of the finest horsewomen in all of Southern Humboldt."[943]

Cora finished her second year of school teaching on October 28. The school board (Samuel Dean and a Mrs. Steinbrun) liked her work and promised Cora the job for the next term. Less than a week later, she celebrated her twenty-first birthday while she was home with her family in the Bridgeville area. At Christmas Cora received two presents—a calendar and a tatted collar.[944]

Near the end of March 1899, Cora returned to the East Branch by way of Blocksburg and Harris. A Mr. Reed, probably from nearby Reed Mountain, gave her a ride down the road from Spruce Grove to the East Branch. Cora's valise fell from the buggy and rolled down the hill, "but Mr. Reed got it back entirely uninjured." They met Annie Dean, who was coming in the family's cart for Cora, who then transferred to the cart for the rest of the trip. This was a relief for a friend of Reed's, who had given up his place in the two-seat buggy and had been walking while Cora rode.[945]

The end of May proved especially exciting when the Deans and Cora went to Garberville to see a balloon ascension. Cora didn't report on the event but noted that "Mr. Dean had been drinking, and on the way home, he drove in a very reckless manner."[946]

The summer, fall, and winter came and went without any extraordinary events. Then, on March 25, 1900, while in Eureka, Cora "saw an automobile for the first time this afternoon."[947]

Back at the East Branch in April, John, the Deans' 12-year-old son, "went

Remnant of Spruce Grove to East Branch Road, 2018 (JR).

after the cows and calves and got lost." His older brother Bert and Mr. Hurlbutt looked for him until 3 A.M., waited until daylight, and "found him coming home."[948]

On May 12 there was a "basket social." Bert Dean, who was 17 or 18, paid $2.95 for Maud Reed's basket.[949] While her school was out of session, Cora spent time in Eureka and Bridgeville. She returned to the East Branch in July.[950] Two of the Dean brothers, Sam and Arthur, returned home on May 20, and the next day Arthur visited the school.[951] August 5 found Cora going with Annie, Izora, and John to an evening church service. On the trip home "three drunken shearers rode close behind the wagon on the way back."[952] A dance in Garberville on August 24 was attended by "all the East Branch young folks and Mrs. Dean." Cora danced six waltzes and five quadrilles. She danced with both Bert and Arthur Dean. They stopped about 2 A.M. and got home by 3 A.M.[953]

Cora's entry for September 17 reads:

> Monday. Arthur Dean was killed. He and Bert were out hunting. Bert's horse stumbled (it was dark) and struck his gun against a tree. It went off and shot Arthur through the body killing him almost instantly.[954]

# Benbow 183

> Two days later,
>
> Arthur was buried. Sam Dean arrived in Garberville in time for the funeral by riding twenty-eight hours continuously.[955]
>
> Cora Bailey's diary entries end here.
> Samuel Dean lived until he was 86. His wife Annie, who was 14 years younger, remained at the East Branch ranch. Until she was 82, Annie would walk from the ranch to Garberville. After she came out on the Redwood Highway, south of town, motorists would stop and offer her a ride. Usually she declined, saying the exercise kept her young and fit. Annie died at age 90 in 1942.[956]

between Garberville and the Harris area.[957] By 1921 the middle section of the old East Branch road had reverted to a trail.[958] Several decades later George Cockman was logging in the East Branch drainage and was puzzled by a stone bridge he found part way up the hillside.[959] It didn't seem to connect to anything, but if he had been there 70 years earlier, he might have seen a buggy carrying Reed and Cora Bailey cross that bridge, with another man, on foot, struggling to keep up. The bridge had lasted far beyond the time of those who traveled upon it, and no one was there to apprise George Cockman of its significance.

> Now who will stand on either hand,
> And keep the bridge with me?[960]
>
> Keep it not, as now it is,
> But as it used to be.

## Appendix A: The Benbows Build a Hotel

It's not unusual for a business to be started by siblings; for example, the Hills Brothers' coffee company (brothers Austin Herbert Hills, Earnest Hills, and Reuben Wilmarth Hills) and the Johnson and Johnson bandage company (brothers Robert Wood Johnson, James Wood Johnson, and Edward Mead Johnson).[961] But few, if any, families could top the Benbows' total of nine brothers and sisters who combined to create the southern Humboldt showpiece called the Benbow Inn.[962]

Arthur and Maude Benbow and their family had resided in Humboldt County before moving to Berkeley for ten years, during which time the children decided they wanted "to live out their days in the country" as a family unit.[963] At the time, six of the Benbow children were adults. Joseph, the eldest, had already been a teacher and principal at Franklin School in Eureka, dabbled at being a lawyer, and had started an insurance business. Evangeline was engaged in "a very promising career as a commercial artist and illustrator." Burt was a watchmaker and engraver who had also patented several inventions. Clara was a school teacher. Helen took up drafting and was a "student of architecture." Jessie had "married and seemed ready for a family project." Loleta, Walter, and Robert were "not yet old enough to vote" and had nonexistent resumes.[964]

Evangeline Benbow's artwork
depicted a monumental hotel (JRC).

The Benbows thought they could attain their dream of rural self-sufficiency by raising sheep, so they searched California for the ideal property and found it in the Linser Ranch on the East Branch, which they accordingly bought in 1922 for $45,000. The Benbows spent their collective life savings on just the down payment, which meant that profits from the ranch would go to pay off the mortgage.[965] Soon enough they realized that selling wool and lamb wouldn't pay enough to do this, so they converted the property into a dude ranch.[966]

To raise money for the necessary guest quarters, stables, and horses, the Benbows subdivided part of the ranch property, and the older brothers went to San Francisco to sell the lots. One of the purchasers was Margaret Stewart, owner of the Hotel Stewart. She talked with the Benbow brothers about their project and convinced them "that a hotel would be perfect for the location." The Benbows unanimously endorsed a plan that would include luxury-level accommodations.[967]

They would have to hurry, for in 1923 brothers Oscar and Charles Burris purchased land a few miles down the South Fork and started their own riverside resort at a spot they called Redway.[968] Whichever development was finished first would gain an advantage in claiming the limited supply of high-end tourists.

And hurry the Benbows did. The family "cruised around San Francisco and Oakland," looking for appealing houses and, when they found one, asking the owners the name of their architect. Time and again, they were told "Albert Farr," who had gained fame as the designer of Jack London's Wolf House at Glen Ellen. Soon Farr was drawing up plans for a Tudor-style edifice that was to be called the "Hotel Benbow."[969] As work commenced, Helen Benbow supervised the building crews. Robert "tended to the ranching and the stables." Evangeline did artwork that ranged from sketching the building plans to creating paintings for the walls of the hotel. Walter delivered supplies and became a general handyman. Burt solved a variety of problems "by creating or inventing [tools] to make the job easier." Clara served as the family "peace keeper" who kept the project running smoothly.[970]

The work crew was a diverse lot. The carpenters and plumbers came from San Francisco, while the Scotch stonemason and the wood carver were both specialists trained in Europe.

# Benbow

Most of the other workers were Eurekans. The building materials were usually found locally. The lower part of the hotel was built of stone quarried on the Benbow's property. Wood for the hotel came from two unexpected sources: some timbers were taken from the abandoned Hi Thrap mill, which was located on Benbow property across the South Fork,[971] while other wood was obtained from a bankrupt lumber yard the Benbows had purchased.[972]

Construction started in 1924.[973] With everyone working at top speed, the Hotel Benbow opened on July 17, 1926. Sort of. Only 17 terrace and garden rooms were finished, and guests entered through a temporary side doorway.[974] The adjacent "golf course was completed just in time for the first guests to tee off."[975] By the start of the 1928 season the lobby and the rest of the guest rooms were finished.[976]

Meanwhile, the Burris brothers sold lots in their subdivision, built a primitive golf course and a beautiful sales office, and developed plans for a vast hostelry called the "Redway Tavern." But by then it was 1929, and before work could start on the centerpiece building, the bottom fell out of the stock market. With it went the chance to compete with the Benbows.[977]

As the Burrises' business sank, the Benbows' operation remained afloat, aided by the 1931 addition of a water feature sited across the Redwood Highway from the hotel. The Benbows had contemplated damming the South Fork, but when they received bids for the work, even the lowest was considered "astronomical" by their cash-poor standards. So, with Burt and Helen leading the way, the family members built it themselves. The dam created Benbow Lake, which became a venue for fishing, canoeing, and swimming. To deal with the peak flows of the South Fork, the structure was designed

Hotel Benbow in its early days (THPO, colorized by JR).

Redwood Highway bridge over the East Branch (JRC, colorized by JR).

as "the first all spillway dam in the west." This meant that the entire top of the dam served as the spillway, allowing it to "carry 105,000 cubic feet of flowing water per second."[978]

That same year the California Division of Highways further improved the hotel's ambience by building a magnificent stone bridge that enabled the Redwood Highway to span the East Branch near its mouth. Guests at the Benbow could then look languidly at the bridge arching over the branch's water as they lounged in chairs on the hotel's shaded terrace.[979]

In 1932 the Benbows built a powerhouse atop of the southern end of the dam. They had previously secured a state franchise for supplying electrical power to an area that stretched from the tiny town of South Fork to Laytonville, in Mendocino County. It also meant that the hotel no longer had to rely on diesel generators for its power.[980]

So it was that by the early 1930s the Benbow Hotel offered guests a panoply of outdoor pursuits by providing a riding stable, golf course, hiking trails, and various activities that used the lake and South Fork Eel. Enclosing it all in a verdant embrace of topographical wonder was the beautiful valley of the lower East Branch, part of which was visible from many of the guest rooms. No wonder the hotel register contained signatures often craved by autograph seekers, including those of Spencer Tracy, Clark Gable, Alan Ladd, Charles Laughton, Nelson Eddy, Jeanette MacDonald, Joan Fontaine, and Basil Rathbone.[981] Far from the neon glare of the big California cities, the Hotel Benbow was nonetheless illuminated by the leading lights of Hollywood.

A less flamboyant guest was the author Harold Bell Wright, who stopped at the Benbow with his wife in August 1932.[982] In the 1910s his novels, such as *The Eyes of the World* and *The Winning of Barbara Worth*, had been best-sellers that sold an average of a million copies each.⁹⁸³ Now, in the twilight of his career, Wright relaxed beside Benbow Lake and the Redwood Highway and absorbed the atmosphere of southern Humboldt. Ten years later his final novel, *The Man Who Went Away*, was published.⁹⁸⁴ It didn't take local readers long to realize that Shelter Cove, the timberlands at nearby Andersonia, and the Hotel Benbow itself had all been renamed and reconstituted as part of the book.

The hotel, however, was operating on borrowed time. Although some of the guests were of such lofty financial station as to float above the mundane world of economics, others found that the stock market crash of 1929 had drastically diminished the contents of their pocketbooks. By 1932 the Benbows faced a significant drop in income. The financial situation continued to deteriorate, and two years later a group of Benbow investors decided to foreclose on the property. Burt Benbow, however, quickly organized the Benbow Bondholders' Association, and "at the foreclosure sale on the courthouse steps, Burt Benbow [successfully] bid on the property in the name of the bondholders." The family sold many of their possessions and borrowed on their insurance policies to raise funds to keep from losing the hotel. They then agreed "to continue to operate the property at the most minimum of rates," while they "gradually acquired a majority of bonds in the Association and once again became owners of their hotel."⁹⁸⁵

Despite food rationing, fewer vacationers, and other difficulties, the Benbows kept the hotel open during World War II. In the spring of 1945 the hotel, which was closed for the cold months, suddenly sprang to life when Lord Halifax and other members of the British delegation to the fledgling United Nations called for reservations. The Benbow's chef, who had not planned on returning until summer, came up from San Francisco on a midnight Greyhound bus, bringing with him all the food he would have to cook for the occasion.⁹⁸⁶

A few weeks later the Benbow Hotel opened for its regular season. With a shortage of workers due to the war, two sisters, Naida and

The Redwood Highway passes by the Benbow Inn, 1952 (DTC, colorized by JR).

Betty Olsen, were hired as servers, even though Betty was only 16. They took the Greyhound down from Eureka, carried their suitcases up the steps to the lobby, and were met by one of the Benbow sisters, who told them that the help did not use the main entrance and showed them the servants' entrance. Later that day, they went to lunch in the staff dining room in the Benbow's basement. Sausage patties were the main course. The hotel's gardener, seated next to Naida, advised her not eat them, since the meat had spoiled in the hot weather. The sisters were part of a crew of eight servers, who each worked three shifts per day; breakfast, lunch, and dinner. One evening Naida waited on a man who looked like Clark Gable. He left her a fifty-cent tip, which was a big deal because the servers made only a little more than $4 per day. Naida and Betty had agreed to work until early August. When Naida went to get their wages, the same Benbow sister who had taken them to the servants' entrance refused to pay, perhaps because she hoped to force the sisters to work later into the season. Naida went to an adjacent room and began crying. Another Benbow sister found her, listened to Naida's story, and went next door and got the sisters their money, except the pay for the extra day they had just worked as overtime. The sisters, with most of their wages now in hand, again took the Greyhound, this time to San Francisco, where they intended to do some shopping. Once in the City, they had to take a taxi from the bus station. The cabbie who came to put their suitcases in the trunk was the Benbow guest who looked like Clark Gable.[987]

Naida did not reveal how much of a tip they gave him.

By the early 1950s the Benbows, nine families strong, realized that they "could not survive off the hotel alone."[988] By then called the Benbow Inn, it was sold, then taken back when the purchasers couldn't make a go of it, sold again and taken back, and finally sold for good in 1962.[989] When the inn celebrated its 75th anniversary in 2001, Phyllis Benbow, who was eight when the resort first opened, showed up along with several cousins. Phyllis recalled a visit by Eleanor Roosevelt that resulted in Phyllis bringing her toads up to the First Lady's room and putting them in the bathtub.[990] It was an unusual activity, but not unexpected, for the Benbows always knew how to entertain their guests.

# Chapter 13
# Sproul (Sprowl) Creek Area

In the middle of January 1861, Samuel D. Ross,[991] "widely known as a trafficker with Indians," was traveling up the South Fork Eel when he was "overtaken by a party of rather bold Indians."[992] Their boldness in pursuing an Indian slaver was not surprising; even whites criticized his occupation to the extent that S. D. Ross later defended himself in the *Humboldt Times*.[993] Ross turned on his pursuers and shot one of them, probably fatally. George Woods, who lived on the east side of the river, attempted to raft across the South Fork to help Ross, but the raft became "unmanageable" and Woods debarked onto a mid-river rock. He then tried to swim the remaining distance to shore but drowned in the attempt.[994]

Meanwhile brothers Atwood and Gilbert Sproul, who lived nearby on the west side of the river, came to Ross's aid, "escorting him to their home."[995] The Sprouls may not have known of Ross's occupation, but the Indians apparently thought the brothers, by rescuing him, "shared Mr. Ross' sentiments, and were their enemies."[996]

The Indians bided their time, and then one day, finding the brothers outside dressing a bear they had killed, attacked. As Army Lieutenant D. D. Lynn later reported, "both boys were nearly killed." Despite the Indians' reprimand, the Sprouls continued to offer Ross shelter whenever he passed their way, but Lynn noted that "if the past has anything to do with the future they ought to take warning and eschew all such dangerous hospitality."[997]

The Sprouls did take a precaution; they moved across the South Fork to Gurshorn C. Armstrong's place, where the three men fashioned "a strong stockade . . . as a protection against future attacks."[998] Although the brothers had left the west side of the river, the stream which debouched into the South Fork by their former residence was given the name Sproul Creek. It of course had an earlier name, which was Nas-lin-kok. A Sinkyone tribal group called the Nas-lin-tci kai-a occupied the area, having a village on either side of the creek.[999] Little more is known about the group; Nas-lin-tci kai-a territory may have extended no farther than the limits of their namesake creek's drainage but could have continued farther southward into the fastness of the great redwood forest that ran into Mendocino County.

The creek, sometimes misspelled "Sprawl" on early maps,[1000] achieved a degree of importance in 1898, with completion of Moody Road,[1001] which ran from Garberville to the northern Mendocino coast. It crossed the South Fork near the creek's mouth and then proceeded southward up the eastern side of the Sproul Creek drainage.[1002] Prior to the construction of the Redwood Highway in the late 1910s, the road along Sproul Creek was one of the major routes connecting Humboldt County with points south. It received recognition in 1911 within the pages of *Sunset Magazine*, when Jack London wrote of an extended buggy trip that he, his wife Charmian, and their Japanese servant, Nakata, took that brought them into Humboldt County along the road. Jack had no experience driving a four-horse team, so much of the story dwelt on his learning how to use the reins. Charmian demanded frequent stops to pick berries and once was called on to help Jack untangle the whip from one of the horses'

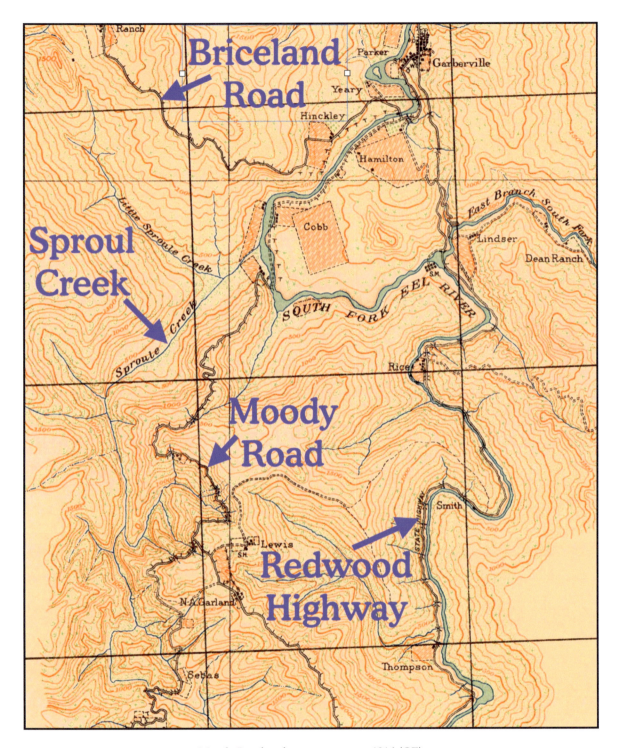

Moody Road and its competitors, 1916 (CE).

harness. Nakata, meanwhile, sat stoically in the back seat holding their most important piece of baggage—Jack's typewriter.[1003] Jack described their approach to Humboldt County:

> At Usal, many hilly and picturesque miles north of Fort Bragg, we turned again into the interior of Mendocino, crossing the ranges and coming out in Humboldt County on the south fork of Eel River at Garberville. Throughout the trip, from Marin County north, we had been warned of "bad roads ahead." Yet we never found those bad roads. We

seemed always to be just ahead of them or behind them. The farther we came the better the roads seemed, though this was probably due to the fact that we were learning more and more what four horses and a light rig could do on a road. And thus do I save my face with all the counties. I refuse to make invidious road comparisons. I can add that while, save in rare instances on steep pitches, I have trotted my horses down all the grades, I have never had one horse fall down nor have I had to send the rig to a blacksmith shop for repairs.[1004]

Coming down to the mouth of Sproul Creek at the South Fork, the Londons reached the ranch of Jack's friend and fellow author Margaret Smith Cobb.[1005] Like London, Cobb wrote fiction, but had she instead written an autobiography it would have been tough to beat. (See sidebar 1.)

Whites were living in the Sproul Creek area before the construction of Moody Road. Among them were Henry and Maria Jane Cox and their family, who had property about two miles southwest of the mouth of the creek.[1006] In 1896 Henry Cox traded part of his land, some 40 acres, for a team of horses. The family that acquired the partial parcel had some children of

### 1. A Story Worth Writing

The sketch of Margaret Smith Cobb that appeared in Leigh Irvine's 1915 history of Humboldt County was one of hundreds that locals paid to have included in the 1,290-page book. Usually Irvine wove together fulsome accounts of his subjects' lives from the ragbag of information they provided. With Cobb, however, Irvine was either inspired to exceed himself or had her participation as coauthor, for the account is as bold and colorful as the best-selling novels of the era, fit to compare with the likes of Harold Bell Wright's *The Winning of Barbara Worth*.[1007]

We are told that "when but a boy," Cobb's father, Thomas Smith, had assisted in "moving the Pottawattamie Indians to the west of the Mississippi," a task that helped to "awaken in him a love for the Indians, to understand something better in their nature than savagery." Smith crossed the plains in 1846 to California, "enlisted under John C. Fremont and served under him during the war with Mexico," and worked "in the timber where Oakland now stands."[1008]

Smith went to Trinity County, found no gold, and left. He and his companions encountered "very troublesome Indians" at the future site of Harris and were forced "to make a stand against them." Continuing south, Smith saw and fell in love with Long Valley in Mendocino County, then came back to it the following year, 1852, and built a log house. Five years later Smith "returned to San Jose for the wife he was to take away to share the wilds with him."[1009]

The woman was Donna Anna Zeparra, granddaughter of Don Juan de Lieva, "a well known figure in Chilean history and one of a long line of Castilian nobility." Don Juan's story, worthy of a book in itself, was reduced to a fragment of a paragraph, crowded out of print by Donna Anna, who "was left an orphan at six years," brought to California by her godparents in 1850, "and soon afterward entered Notre Dame convent at San Jose to be a nun and teacher." Donna Anna had taken her first vows when fate, in the form of an illness that sent her to her godmother's house, intervened. While recovering there, she met Thomas Smith: "it was a case of true love at first sight, the frail Spanish maiden loving the daring blond frontiersman."[1010]

The couple soon married and "set out for the wilds." Thomas and Donna Anna took with them a selection of items to help them tame the Mendocino wilderness:

> The young husband drove a yoke of cattle and carried with him three hundred fruit trees, ornamental trees, and rose cuttings, while the bride carried her great Spanish dictionary and grammar and her finest embroidery and lace needles.[1011]

Once at their home, "the little wife embroidered and wrote Latin poems," while learning that her husband was a "dreamer" who "would never [be] a maker of money." The couple took the time to have eight children, of which Margaret was the sixth. She was born in San Jose and lived there six years, whereupon the family returned with her to their ranch on the South Fork Eel River. Margaret's "opportunities for schooling were very scanty," but she managed to read many of the classics, including all the works of Shakespeare.

Having survived this experience, at age 17 Margaret began to write poems. Ten years later she brought forth "The Drowned Man's Song," which gained the attention of Ambrose Bierce, who arranged for its publication in the *San Francisco Examiner*, "with his praise." Next she won the favor of Jack London, who presented her poem "The Unkissed" to *The Century* magazine. London informed *The Century*

> . . . that I am sending you what I consider, under the circumstances, a most remarkable poem. The author, Margaret Smith Cobb, is a mountain woman, who has lived her life in the most remote mountain districts of California, far beyond the reach of any railroad.[1012]

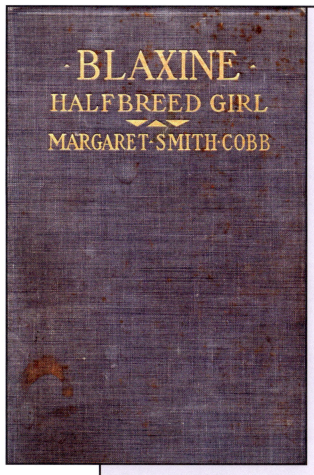

Margaret Smith Cobb's magnum opus (JR).

Perhaps because of this deprivation, London called Cobb a "primitive woman."[1013] Yet it was by choice and not chance that Margaret lacked access to railroads. We learn this from sources other than her laudatory biography. She had grown to adulthood on the Smiths' ranch and then married Harry Greenwell. In 1894 the couple had a daughter, Lillian, while living in the wine country at Asti, in Sonoma County.[1014] Here Margaret had her railroad; it was the San Francisco and North Pacific Railway (SF&NP), which had a station in Asti and by 1898 ran all the way north to Ukiah.[1015]

But something happened. In 1902 Margaret and Lillian left Asti and the SF&NP (and, apparently, Harry Greenwell) and travelled to remote Hollow Tree, near Leggett, where Margaret taught school. There Margaret met Oliver C. Cobb, who had a homestead in the vicinity, and before the year was out they were married. The next year the couple had a daughter, Yvonne, and then the four members of the Cobb family headed north. They took the coast road to Kenny, turned inland to Moody, headed down Sproul Creek past the Sebbas Ranch, and on to the mouth of the creek, where the Cobbs had purchased the 1,600-acre Newton Nunn Ranch for $13,000.[1016] It was a bucolic location, but, like Hollow Tree, a place where a train whistle was never to be heard.

It was there, at the mouth of Sproul Creek, that Cobb embarked on her most ambitious literary project, a novel entitled *Blaxine: Halfbreed Girl*, which was published in 1910.[1017] That April, the *New York Times* reviewed the book, stating in part that:

> Although the author has sometimes lacked the skill to handle with the best effect her difficult theme, a number of the scenes are described with power. The characters though stiff in manner of presentation are informed with much individuality.[1018]

> In 1914 one literary magazine paid Cobb a decidedly left-handed compliment when it related that "Jack London, after reading "Maxine, Halfbreed Girl," [sic] told Miss Cobb that she was a poet . . ."[1019] managing, within the space of one sentence, to get both her marital status and the title of her book wrong while leaving readers to infer that London did not care for her fiction.
>
> By then Cobb's marital status had changed, for her husband Oliver had died earlier that year.[1020] Irvine's biography, which came out the following year, noted his death but indicated that Margaret possessed "unusual" business ability and implied that she would continue to lead the life of author and ranch owner.[1021]
>
> But such was not the case. Although retaining the ranch property, by 1916 Margaret Cobb had moved to Garberville, where she was paid $5 per month as the town's first "library custodian."[1022] From 1919 to 1921 she was the schoolteacher at tiny Sequoia, which was located on the main Eel River northeast of Fruitland.[1023] She reportedly also taught at Garberville and McCann, but her biographical information fades in the 1920s. Margaret Smith Cobb died at her daughter Lillian's house in Piercy in September 1933,[1024] her literary aspirations still awaiting fulfillment.

school age, as did the Coxes. Together the two families possessed enough kids to qualify for an institute of learning, and the Sproul Creek School was duly built on the Cox property. Anita Dale was the schoolteacher in 1897; she had 12 primary students and one grammar school student. There was no library and no outhouse, but the school had seating for 14 students, so there was one empty place.[1025]

Just north of the Coxes lived John Nicholas Meyer and Katherina Meyer[1026] and their children. John Meyer was a carpenter, but to make a living he often split and sold wood and cut and shipped tanbark. His family and neighbors helped with the work.[1027] In 1898, the same year that Moody Road was built, Isaac and Sofia Sebbas had twin boys; eventually they had a total of five sons and three daughters. At the time they "lived between Moody and Thorn"[1028] at an undetermined location, but in the early 1900s the family moved to what was eventually called the "Lower Sebbas Place" on Moody Road just north of the Mendocino County line.[1029] The location was far enough south that in 1903 six of the Sebbas children went to school at Moody, the tiny town on the Bear Harbor & Eel River Railroad about three miles deep into Mendocino County.[1030]

In 1915 Isaac Sebbas was killed when his horse team bolted and threw him from his wagon. That proved to be the first in a string of tragedies to hit the family. One son, William, contracted tuberculosis during World War I and died. His sister, Segred, also sickened with TB and was taken to a sanitarium in Willits. When her health improved, brothers Emil and Victor drove to the sanitarium, picked Segred up, and began driving home. When they reached the South Fork Eel, they had to cross it at Cobb's Riffle, as there was no bridge. The

Thirteen scholars at the Sproul Creek School are enough to fill all but one of the seats (CPH, colorized by JR).

car became stuck in the middle of the river. Victor left the car running and hiked two or three miles to the Beerbower place, where he borrowed a team of horses to pull the car out. When he returned to the river, he found that Emil and Segred had been overcome by carbon monoxide. Victor pulled them out of the car. Emil survived, but Segred didn't. Victor never forgave himself for his sister's death. Thirteen years later, in 1937, he shot himself in the head while in an upstairs room of the Sebbases' ranch house. Still alive, Victor was taken to Willits, where he died.[1031]

That was the end for what became known as the Lower Sebbas Place. Brothers Emil and Walter moved with their mother, Sofia, west to the Bancroft Place,[1032] which from then on was known as the Upper Sebbas Place.[1033] Years after the incident at Cobb's Riffle, Margaret Smith Cobb's daughter Yvonne, who had inherited the Cobb property in 1933, gave Humboldt County a road right-of-way through the Cobb Ranch. This allowed the county to build a connecting route between Briceland Road and Moody Road on the west side of the river, eliminating the crossing at Cobb's Riffle.[1034] In 1934 the county built a covered bridge for the new road across Sproul Creek. Bridge connoisseur S. Griswold Morley called it a "tight, unassuming little bridge," adding, with enlarging eloquence,

Motoring on Moody Road (FMC, colorized by JR).

What an out-of-the-world Eden surrounds it! Alder, bay laurel, and redwood arch the gentle creek; under steep banks the water curls lovingly among mossy stones. . . . Once you have reached this spot you do not soon wish to leave it.[1035]

The Sebbases were not the only family to own more than one location along Moody Road. Nicholas and Katherina Meyer had two "openings"—breaks in the dense forest—called Lower Meyer and Upper Meyer.[1036] Early-day landowner Sylvester Harris gave his name to Upper Harris Place and Lower Harris Place. The Dowell, named for George Dowell, is just a single location but uses George's last name without any further descriptor. Alice and George Boyer had an Upper Place and, on the former Cox property, a lower place simply called the Boyer Ranch.[1037]

As the years passed, Moody Road saw less and less traffic. Ranchers used the north end, as did woodsmen, but destinations to the south were seldom visited. Emil Worda started a split-stuff layout on Sproul Creek in the late 1930s with a cookhouse and small cabins for the workers, while logging for sawtimber began in 1945.[1038] Southward, the dust that had once risen from wagons or buggies bound for Garberville or Fort Bragg lay thick and undisturbed. The Moody School closed in 1912, year after the Londons had driven by.[1039] The hotel at Kenny burned, and in 1924 the town's post office closed.[1040] In 1940 Grace and Forest Moody gave up an attempt to revive their family's namesake town and moved north to the Lower Sebbas Place.[1041] No one from Sproul Creek needed to connect with the coast, and so the south end of Moody Road was abandoned by Mendocino County as a public road, and then Humboldt County abandoned a short stretch from the county line north to the Nielson place in the 1950s.[1042] By then, Moody Road, with its somber history, had lived up to its name.

# Chapter 14
# Garberville

*When did it first start to get civilized around here?*
*Oh, about 16-20 years ago.*

—Nona James, answering in 1984

In 1853 a trapper named Antone Garcia built a "crude log hut" near the southern end of a flat above the South Fork Eel. It was just south of a small stream that, once an actual community developed on the flat, was called Town Gulch. At first the place was uninspiringly called Dog Town or, for a time, South Fork. Only in 1874, with the opening of a post office, did it receive its lasting name—Garberville.[1043]

There are no reports of Indians having occupied the benchland that became Garberville, although a tribal group called Ko-se-ke inhabited the area near the mouth of Bear Canyon, about a half mile to the north. Information about the Ko-se-ke is all secondhand, but it seems clear that they were affiliated with the several other groups both along the South Fork and west of the river that are subsumed under the tribal name Sinkyone.[1044] But questions of Indian nomenclature did not bother early-day whites in southern Humboldt. The newcomers generally lumped all the local Indians together under the name "Wylackie," a term that within Humboldt County, could correctly be applied only to a collection of tribal groups that lived along a short stretch of the main Eel River in the vicinity of Island Mountain.[1045]

At an unknown date before whites arrived in the locale, Indians from the Garberville area went down the South Fork and attacked the Indians at Myers Flat, killing all the men but one, the father of George Burtt. A year later Burtt's father led a group that included allies from other tribes and attacked the Indians from Garberville, killing about 40 of them. According to the Indian informant Briceland Charlie, "George's father took one scalp and brought it back. That made even."[1046]

Some of the early white arrivals brought more trouble to the local Indians. An attack by a group of whites on the village of To-cho-be, near Briceland, found the surviving Indians fleeing up the South Fork. About 150 of them made it to the blufftop site of Garberville, where the whites reportedly caught up with two of them and forced them to jump to their deaths from the bluff.[1047] The flat below the bluff was subsequently claimed by another Indian tormentor. (See sidebar 1.)

For a time nothing much about the area was reported. It was therefore big news in 1864 when H. C. Morse set up a blacksmith shop on what later became Garberville's Main Street. By the following year a store had also appeared.[1048] Three apparently uneventful years passed, and then, in 1868, Jacob Garber and William G. Harris arrived in southern Humboldt together. Harris and his family soon went to Powellsville (later to become Blocksburg) and then headed to the southeastern corner of the county where they established their namesake town of Harris. It took Garber slightly longer to put his name

### 1. "That is all right."

Starting in 1859, James Ervin Wood made three trips into southern Humboldt County, at some point taking up ranchland on the flat southwest of Garberville, probably in 1862.[1049] In October 1861 Wood and two associates, Laurie Johnson and James Freak, were arrested in Colusa, California, and charged with kidnapping Indian children near "Spruce Camp, Eel River, Humboldt County," probably a garbled reference to Spruce Grove, the mail station on the ridge east of Garberville. They were in the process of selling nine young Indians, between three and ten years old, to local ranchers for $55 to $80 each. One of the accused stated that "it was an act of charity . . . to hunt up the children and provide homes for them, because their parents had been killed, and the children would have perished with [sic] hunger." When asked how he knew the fate of the parents, the defendant answered, "because I killed some of them myself." The kidnappers were held in Yuba County but were freed "on bail of five hundred dollars to appear before a magistrate in Humboldt County." Not surprisingly, none of the three made their date with the magistrate, which meant the men's punishment for murder and kidnapping consisted of the forfeiture of the $500 bail.[1050]

The original James Wood Ranch occupied what is now known as Tooby Flat, located in the center of the photo (JR).

> It was a light brush with the law, but it may have convinced Wood to pursue other activities. He was soon found ranching south of the Garberville town site on what later became known as Tooby Flat.[1051] Wood's ranch came to encompass 12,000 acres,[1052] on which he ran some 14,000 head of sheep,[1053] but to reach those totals he had to take a gamble—which he eventually lost.[1054]
>
> Although Wood's first holdings were adjacent the South Fork, his dream was to extend his property all the way east to the main Eel. To help accomplish this goal he purchased ranch land that lay west of Harris, borrowing $40,000 to do so. After a time, a $10,000 mortgage payment came due. Wood reportedly entrusted a relative with the money, asking him to take it to a bank in Eureka. The funds never made it, for it turned out the relative not only had a weakness for gambling but was also a weak gambler. The entire $10,000 moved in the wrong direction across a fateful card table, the bank foreclosed, and Wood lost his entire ranch.[1055]
>
> James Wood was remembered by at least one local Indian, Albert Smith, who grew up on land that later became part of the Wood Ranch. According to Smith, "Jim Woods kill[ed] women and men," and "John Woods [Jim's brother] & Jim and Reed[1056] they fight my people most."[1057] In fact, John Wood had killed Smith's mother south of Benbow, casually turning around and shooting her as he rode uphill from the South Fork.[1058] When Smith was interviewed by Pliny Goddard in 1907 he indicated that he'd kept track of the Wood brothers: "John Woods is in hospital now. Jimmie Woods dead now, that is all right."[1059]

on the map. First he constructed a log cabin north of Bear Canyon that he called the South Fork Trading Post and in 1873 built a general merchandise store up on the flat to the south. The following year he received authorization to use a portion of the store for the new Garberville Post Office.[1060]

Even with this augmentation Garberville wasn't much, but the place held promise. The topography of southern Humboldt was such that several natural transportation corridors met in the vicinity of the town. The county map of 1865 shows some routes already in place. From Hadley's ranch in the Mattole Valley a trail slanted southeast, running between the Mattole River and Elk Ridge, curving through what became the Briceland area and then running southeast again to cross the South Fork at James Wood's ranch. From there another trail ran north, climbing the bluff to Garberville. Trails from the Wood Ranch and Garberville went east to the Spruce Grove mail station, while another route ran southeast to Blue Rock, in Mendocino County. A new trail wound its way northward from Garberville along the east side of the South Fork to connect with the Overland Mail Trail at Camp Grant.[1061]

The land office map of 1875 shows several additional trails approaching the Garberville area from the west. One came down Redwood Creek from the Briceland area and crossed the

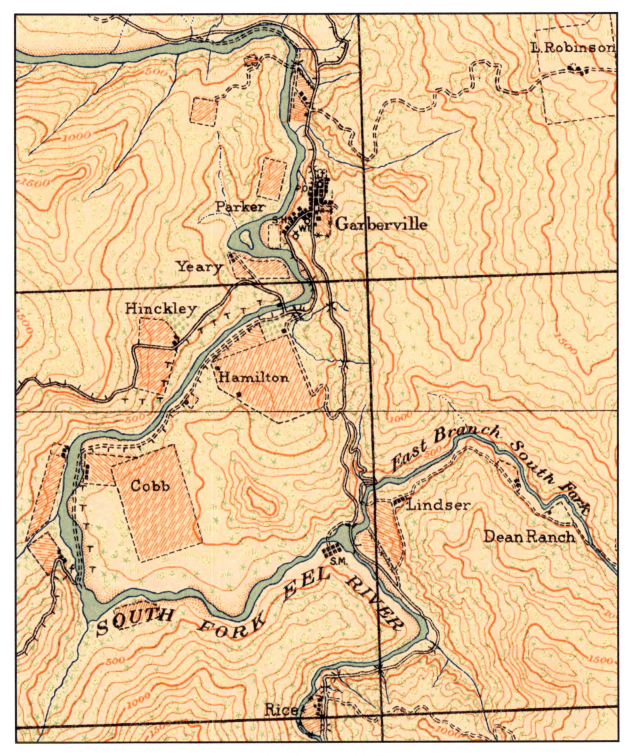

Garberville area, 1916 (CE).

South Fork at the future site of Redway. Another appears to be a variant of the Hadley-Wood trail, crossing over the mountains from the Briceland area. Two other routes converged near the mouth of Sproul Creek, one of which came down the creek's drainage.[1062] In 1950 one early-day trail traveler recalled the excitement of reaching her new home at Garberville. (See sidebar 2.)

In the 1870s Garberville was still a pretty primitive place. John McMillin, who'd arrived in the area in 1870, "purchased most of the land lying on the east side of Main Street" in

# Garberville

1875. He then divided his property into town lots, planting several acres of prune trees[1063] on the vacant property as he waited for the anticipated land boom. The following year, two visitors provided their perspectives on the town's development. A nameless correspondent reported that

Garberville, a town which is situated on the South Fork of Eel river, can only be reached by trail, the nearest wagon road being at Camp Grant, a distance of twenty or twenty-five miles. The town is composed of two hotels, two saloons, one blacksmith shop and a store....

---

### 2. Welcoming the First White Girl to Garberville

During southern Humboldt's pre-road era, the Schumacher family apparently made use of the Hadley-Wood trail in April 1873 when they migrated to Garberville from Petrolia.[1064] Augusta "Gussie" Schumacher was just three at the time, but 77 years later she vividly recalled their arrival, for it was snowing—a meteorological manifestation she had never beheld before.[1065]

Gussie was the first white girl to live in Garberville. Until she was seven all of her playmates were Indian children. "They were kind to me," Gussie said. "Never selfish. The old Indians, too, were kind to me, and I loved all of them." Some of the Indians, whose families had suffered so much at the hands of the whites, "would pick her up and carry her around, giving her dried venison or smoked salmon to chew on."[1066] Anyone who knew the history of the area would have been startled by this response. When James Wood encountered local Indian children, he kidnapped them; when local Indians encountered a white child, they fed her.

Also feeding little Gussie was Jim, the Schumacher's Chinese cook. He made biscuits for her breakfast and then stood by while she ate them. Some of Jim's countrymen helped construct the Shelter Cove road. Until a road was built north to Humboldt Bay, it took an entire week to travel the 83-odd miles from Garberville to Eureka. There were several stopping places along the way, but Gussie's mother, Mary Anne, always took blankets and cooking utensils along in case the family got "caught out."[1067]

Gussie's father, Augustus (usually shortened to "Gus") had attended the University of Heidelberg and had taught school for a year in Arcata. But Garberville had priorities that overshadowed education, and Gus opened a saloon. He built a redwood house for his family and then, sensing another demand, added an addition and turned the building into the Schumacher Hotel.[1068] Mary Anne Schumacher ran the hotel.

The years passed, and when Gussie was 18 she married John Welton Monroe from Eureka. The couple moved to Fortuna, where Monroe had a soft drink

A look at the Garberville business district shows two saloons, and, at the left, the former Schumacher Hotel (HCHS, colorized by JR).

bottling works.[1069] Her second marriage was to William Jones, who operated a stage stop in Miranda, roughly the halfway point between Garberville and Dyerville. It must have been a great comfort to Gussie, when she went to bed beside the road to Eureka, to know that she would no longer be "caught out."[1070]

The principal business is sheep raising, although the country in general is well adapted to, and claims the honor of, production of fleas and ~."[1071]

A few weeks later "Anonymous" noted that although

. . . a few wagons were in use . . . they were brought on the backs of mules, like everything that is imported or exported to and from this place. Shelter Cove is the nearest shipping point, to which a number of pack trains are now running taking wool there and returning with produce and provisions, and their coming and going is looked upon with as much interest as was the arrivals and departures of Ben Holliday's overland coaches in an early day during the great gold fever.[1072]

In addition to wagons, several other interesting objects were brought into Garberville during the town's pre-road days. A buggy was driven up to Harris in the 1870s and brought by trail to Garberville, where it became "a curiosity to the young children." The town's first organ was carried in by mules. The first piano reportedly arrived, remarkably, by boat along the South

# Garberville

Fork River.[1073] However, the transport of certain smaller items was for a time problematic. For years Garberville's mail was dropped off at the little cabin at Center Station, nine miles to the east on the Mail Ridge route. At first it was brought down to town by anyone who happened to pass in that direction. Then a mail carrier was hired to do the job. Sometimes. J. B. Davis, one of the first carriers, "delivered the mail once a week if the weather was pleasant, but if not the patrons had to wait until it cleared up." Only in 1874 did Garberville obtain its own post office and, with it, regular mail delivery.[1074]

For years Southern Humboldt was a Democratic stronghold, with the Republican party only receiving four votes each election. Then one of the Republicans left and the party's tally decreased by 25 percent. By 1907, however, southern Humboldt had fallen in line with most of the county, and the Democrats became the minority.[1075]

By the end of 1878 the trail to Shelter Cove had been graded enough to be upgraded to a road. S. F. Taylor, serving as a subcontractor for William Ray and Henry Yates,[1076] built the "Garberville and Shelter Cove Road" during the fall of 1878;[1077] the eastern end of this route is now known as the Old Briceland Road. Next came a road running from Garberville north, which was started by John McMillin in 1881.[1078] The road was completed as far Phillipsville in 1884.[1079] Meanwhile, a road was built from the mouth of the South Fork to Myer's Ranch (Myers Flat).[1080] The gap between Phillipsville and "the Myers place" was closed in 1885 so that a road then ran from Garberville to the mouth of the South Fork.[1081] This meant that wagons and stages could now travel from Garberville all the way to Humboldt Bay. If this were not enough, a new route to the south was built from Garberville to the coast, via Sproul Creek and Moody, in 1897-1898, which gave access to northwestern Mendocino County and points south.[1082]

Either trail or road would have done for John H. Durst, who wrote of his travels "afoot up the Eel" in 1883. He was not the last visitor to be startled by what he found:

> The road is now to Garberville, the great resort of this whole sheep country, and a rough place. Knives are universally worn by all frequenters of its saloons and hotels. Such villainous whisky is sold, that even Irishmen to whom its virulence is unexpected are disgusted. . . .
>
> Society about Garberville and Blocksburg, a town somewhat farther down, is peculiarly constituted. Many of the substantial residences have for better halves Indian squaws. They were acquired when the country was new and the men poor. But now many of the husbands are rich. The wives dress in silks, but they still have their *bronchos*,[1083] as the roads about Garberville are too limited for their carriage outfits. On the fourth it is customary to have two balls, one for the white women, and on the succeeding night one for the dusky belles. On the latter night appear this dusky aristocracy in all the brilliancy of silk and satins and flaming scarfs. The squaws will not dance with anything less than white partners. The Fourths at these places are revels that draw spectators from fifty miles down the river, at the bay. Indian wives were numerous in times past but they are becoming fewer. Some of the white men after acquiring property have peaceably separated, giving their quondam wives handsome

The Briceland-Garberville Road, seen here crossing the South Fork, replaced part of the trail that ran from Hadley's Ranch on the Mattole (THPO, colorized by JR).

portions, and have taken wives of their own race.[1084]

Durst was a traveler whose superficial impressions of Garberville did not jibe with the deeper reality experienced by people who lived there. Della Womack, who was part Indian, passed on an account from her mother about the treatment of Indian women: "white men took them and worked them like slaves."[1085]

The results of the white male-Indian female relationships had been noted as early as 1871, when a San Francisco newspaper reported that the Garberville school included 27 students, 22 of whom were "half breeds." In one case, a "mother of three children bore her firstborn at the age of twelve, while the father, a white man, was sixty."[1086]

In November 1885 the *Ferndale Enterprise* provided a listing of Garberville's structures, which consisted of "two stores, two saloons, two hotels, two livery and feed stables, one candy store, and eight dwelling houses." Several nearby ranches were mentioned, including those belonging to P. J. Wood and James Wood, L. C. Tuttle, and the heirs of Alex Robertson Jr.[1087] Five years later the *Enterprise* provided an update on the town, which had expanded to include the Turner brothers' blacksmith shop, Stephen Means's "tonsorial establishment," and physician James G. Nellist.[1088] A year later, the Enterprise reviewed Garberville yet again, focusing on selected individuals. Mrs. J. G. Ray shone like a ray of sunshine at her hotel, keeping "a first-class place" with "everything neat and clean." The cook, Jeannie Dahle, knew "just how to prepare a good, wholesome meal." William S. Davis had purchased S. Means's saloon, while Uncle Billy Cornelius could be found at his candy and variety store unless he was at the South Fork Eel fishing. Fred W. Coady operated his drug and stationery store, while Milt Myers was "behind the bar" at the Pioneer Dispensary, which was apparently

Garberville's euphemistically named second saloon. Miss Jessie Daby "had a large number of pupils under her charge at the school." Benton Dahle served as postmaster and with his brother Lemuel ran a "merchandising business." If all this were not enough, Jack O'Conner had come down from Blocksburg to temporarily operate a photography studio in Garberville. The inspection of the town was conducted under thermal duress in August 1891, with "the thermometer registering as high as 112 in the shade."[1089]

Despite it being winter, the following February found times again hot in Garberville, when Grant Myers and J. C. Beerbower, according to their account, "galloped into town," immediately "called for the hostler (more loudly, perhaps, than was necessary)," and then, while in their room at Ray's Hotel, they heard the firing of four or five shots. These activities were enough to have them arrested the following morning and brought before the justice of the peace. To avoid a prolonged stay in the suddenly inhospitable town, the arrestees paid a fine, noting that "the court and committee are welcome to all the glory of the transaction, and to the four dollars also which they unjustly took from us."[1090]

Time fled, and in 1907 the *Daily Humboldt Standard* provided an overview of the Garberville area, noting that the town now had a population of about 300, but that "Jeannie Dahle, and John McMillin, also Reuben Reed are the only old-time settlers left. . . ."[1091]

Although within sight of the South Fork Eel, Garberville is not usually considered a shipping port, but occasionally it served that purpose—and saved a life as a result. About 1910 Adeline Grimes, who lived at the Bell Springs Ranch, was taken sick during the winter, so sick that she needed expert medical attention. With time of the essence, Grimes was taken by sled down to Garberville and then to the nearby South Fork. There she was placed in a flat-bottom boat and taken downriver to Scotia, whence a train took her to Eureka. There one of the doctors Falk operated on her and saved her life.[1092]

A mix of building styles is displayed along the future Redwood Highway (HCHS, colorized by JR).

The yet-to-be-paved Redwood Highway stretches southward from Garberville into the golden haze of summer (THPO, colorized by JR).

Garberville's bygone days were recalled again in 1914, when Eureka's Belcher and Crane Company, a land title business, noted that

> The description in many of the deeds by John McMillin and other former owners are indefinite, inaccurate and do not consistently fit together. Such matters make it impossible to determine definitely the residue of the land under search without an accurate survey of the entire townsite.[1093]

Regardless of any surveying deficiencies, the town was destined to grow, for by 1920 the Redwood Highway was considered "passable" between Sausalito and Eureka,[1094] which allowed Garberville, long off the beaten path, to become the southern entry port of Humboldt County. (See sidebar 3.)

Garberville's growth was interrupted in September 1928, when an entire block of the town was erased one morning by a fast-spreading fire. Among the buildings totally destroyed were the Redwood Supply Company, the J. P.

---

### 3. Stop at the Steaming Cup

By the early 1920s the Redwood Highway was sending a stream of tourists into southern Humboldt County. Even though the highway went through the middle of Garberville, the only place providing meals for the hungry motorists was the Garberville Inn. In 1924 Dwight and Grace Knapp responded to this dining deficiency by opening Knapp's [sic] Restaurant, which featured Dwight's hand-cranked ice cream. Three years later, when Dwight became the Garberville postmaster, the Knapps remodeled the restaurant, adding a gift area and creating a space for the post office in a rear corner of the dining room. They removed two pool tables but kept another type of entertainment—a few slot machines. Knapps' became a perhaps unique business, where patrons could not only have supper but also have access to stamps and slots. Apparently enticed by this trifecta of treats, President Herbert Hoover ate all his meals there when on a week-long fishing trip along the South Fork.[1095]

For a time the restaurant featured a sign that displayed a large bottle of milk, beneath which was the command, "EAT." Then Dwight Knapp was inspired to create an enticing logo featuring a coffee cup. It appeared on his business cards, "on road signs as far away as 75 miles on each side of Garberville," and—displacing the bottle of milk—on one of the signs above the restaurant's entrance. The verisimilitude of the new sign was enhanced by a steam pipe Dwight connected to it, the emissions of which made the sign's coffee appear piping hot. Such marketing enhancements helped the restaurant thrive. The highway was improved in the 1930s, and despite the

Knapps' Restaurant, left, before the milk bottle was replaced by the steaming coffee cup (THPO, colorized by JR).

> Depression, business increased. The restaurant became a regular stop for the Pickwick Stages bus line, and sometimes in summers Knapps' stayed open 24 hours a day. World War II, however, brought shortages of workers and supplies, and part of the dining area was often roped off. In 1945, with the end of the war in sight, Dwight was electrocuted while repairing a leaking faucet. Grace continued on without him for ten years, but finally, in failing health, she closed Knapps'.[1096] On the sign outside the restaurant, the steam went out of the coffee cup, and a little steam went out of Garberville, too.

Thomas store, a garage, and the Sequoia Apartments. The Garberville Inn was scorched but survived. Other entities were not so fortunate. Firefighter L. G. Whiteside died about noon from a heart attack. Another firefighter, C. R. Morales, nearly succumbed from exhaustion, but was revived by Dr. Ernest Smith. Whiteside, 48, had been in Garberville only a month; "he had been ailing for the past two years and came to . . . Humboldt County . . . to regain his health." He had volunteered to fight the blaze because Garberville had no fire department.[1097]

The town may have lacked fire protection, but in another arena it maintained extreme vigilance. (See sidebar 4.)

In August 1931, 79-year-old Dr. Louis P. Rossier was attempting to cross "a dark intersection" in Garberville when he was hit by a car. With the town doctor lying in the street, local medical aid was reduced to zero. Rossier was carried to the nearby home of Elmer Hurlbutt

### 4. Welcome to Humboldt County

Way back in 1880 Eureka's *Democratic Standard* noted, with some syntactical difficulty, that

> Garberville has not a Chinaman within forty miles of it. We venture to assert that no other town in California can make such a boast. The people of this section held a meeting many months ago and determined to give no show for a Chinaman to live, but would deal entirely with white population. . . . Bully for Garberville.[1098]

Fifty years later the town showcased southern Humboldt's continuing intolerance of Asians. In May 1930 William McClure, who was 20 at the time, decided to walk from Redway to Garberville. It was always an interesting trip, but on this day McClure saw more than usual.

The Bear Canyon Bridge (CDH).

He came to the beautiful highway bridge over Bear Canyon and decided to "sit down and loaf." As McClure settled in,

> Suddenly about six or seven cars came up from the direction of Eureka—the bridge was on the old highway from Eureka to San Francisco. They parked their cars to block any traffic—the men got out—about fifteen to twenty of them. They were armed with clubs, baseball bats, axe handles, and guns. They stood around on the south side of the bridge waiting. After a while about five or six cars led by a big limousine of those days, which was a Pierce-Arrow, came from the south toward the bridge. The Eureka men stopped the northbound cars in no uncertain terms— just like a lumber camp brawl of those days. The occupants were forced to get out.[1099]

When the travelers emerged from their cars, the reason for the roadblock became apparent. One of the passengers in the limousine was Katsuji Debuchi, the Japanese ambassador to the United States. He was making a good-will tour from Los Angeles to Vancouver, British Columbia, and had just run into the ill will that certain Humboldt County residents bore towards Asians.[1100] After Garberville reportedly became Chinese free in 1880, Humboldt vigilantes had caught their breath and then in 1885 drove out most of the county's remaining Chinese population. Four years later Eureka's "Japanese colony," 15 in number, also "left, bag and baggage," cheered along by the sentiment in the local press that "we can get along without them."[1101] Either unaware of such sentiments, or unintimidated by them, the Tsuchiya brothers later opened an art supply store in Eureka. They were reminded of the local anti-Asian attitude in late October 1909, when their store was dynamited.[1102] According to local newspaperman Will Speegle, the brothers were seen "disappearing in the fog a couple of blocks away on Fifth Street."[1103] Now, 21 years later, Japanese had again appeared in the county, and some of the locals stood ready at the Bear Canyon bridge to reaffirm Humboldt's aversion to Asians.

Debuchi and his wife were accompanied by State Department officials, who proceeded to argue with the roadblockers. According to McClure, a compromise was reached:

Don't stop in Humboldt: ambassador Katsuji Debuchi, left (LC, colorized by JR).

> The end result was that the ambassador and delegation would be allowed to proceed to Portland only if the ambassador and other Japanese would not get out of the cars to eat or even to use a bathroom until they got to Del Norte County, which was at least ten to twelve hours away in those days. In fact, it took at least four and a half hours to get to Eureka.[1104]

McClure never learned if the edict was enforced all the way to the county line, but several years after the end of World War II, he received a reminder of the incident. A friend passed along a magazine with an article about why Japan had attacked the United States in 1941. Several reasons were given, but the last one jumped out at McClure:

> An incident in Garberville, California . . . where the Japanese Ambassador and other Japanese officials had been stopped and insulted by a bunch of American hoodlums.[1105]

Apparently the bridge blockade had been duly noted.

# Garberville

while someone remembered that another physician was staying at the Benbow Inn. A call was made and soon Dr. L. Mendelsohn of Saratoga arrived to care for his colleague.[1106]

Rossier had begun practicing in Garberville in 1894.[1107] For years he went to patients' homes by horsepower, either riding his horse, Blue Dick,[1108] which took the name of a local wildflower,[1109] or "in a buggy pulled by his faithful old gray mare," which, despite its color, may have been the same animal. Regardless of his means of conveyance, Rossier charged his patients based on the distance he had to travel. Once arrived, "he stayed as long as needed, sometimes a week or more, for this basic charge."[1110] A laudatory biographical account claimed that "in keeping with his Huguenot ancestry he is kind hearted and considerate with all mankind," while noting that "among his patients . . . he has never failed them in their hour of need, whether they have been in need of physics or sympathy, a porous plaster or kindly advice."[1111] None of these treatments would have been of any use to the critically injured Rossier, who died within the hour.[1112]

The *Humboldt Standard*, in 1940, designated Garberville "Humboldt's Vacation Center." The town also had appeal for year-round residents, with the Garberville Civic Club, a Rotary Club with "almost 30 members," a Knights of Pythias Lodge, and "the promotion of a wanted Masonic lodge."[1113] World War II soon intervened, slowing the pace of development, but the subsequent housing boom in the late 1940s jump-started Garberville and other rural communities that partook in the timber trade. Tourism had returned, too, and by 1948 Garberville offered three hotels and eight auto courts. Sheep raising also was big in the region, with Leonard Robertson owning a 10,000 acre ranch, Guy Satterlee and Cal Stewart co-owning one the same size, and Fred Hurlbutt having an 18,000-acre spread.[1114]

Over the last two years Garberville had added four commercial buildings and over 25

Cars galore in Garberville (THPO, colorized by JR).

private homes. The movie theater was poised relocate to a larger building "that will increase the capacity over the present 300"—not bad for a community that had only about twice as many residents. The town's 425 telephones were in use so much that "reports indicate that 24-hour service may be provided." The elementary school, built in 1939, was filled to overflowing with 270 students, which required holding some classes in the Community Church and hiring three new teachers to join the half-dozen already on duty. The only thing slowing the population surge was the area's 100 auto accidents, which claimed five lives.[1115]

In 1951 the first members of the Baby Boomer generation entered the school system, straining the Garberville facilities even more. Three more teachers were added to make an even dozen. They taught 345 students in split shifts, using the school's auditorium and stage and a Quonset hut to house the overflow.[1116] Meanwhile, the building boom continued apace, as lumber mills sprouted up almost as fast as kids. By 1952 the Garberville area had a baker's dozen, plus one at nearby Sproul Creek.[1117]

More kids, more mills, and . . . more tourists. The Redwood Highway had run through the middle of Garberville since its start, and by 1950s the route was lined with businesses catering to the needs of travelers. At the south end of town was Kiessons' Motor Villa, complete with a Standard gas station. The nearby White Motel featured "deluxe stucco cottages" and "tiled showers," while Dinnell's Redwood Gift Shop included novelties and souvenirs fashioned "from the choicest of redwood burls." The Tiskilwa Motel not only had a difficult-to-spell name but also "pre-heated electric units." Bill Sieman's Mobilgas station provided another challenging word as it was ready to provide "Mobi-lubrication for Trucks and Cars." The venerable Redwood Inn was a local landmark dating from 1922 that offered three verandas and a variety of roadside vegetation. Art Johnson's Unique Log

Drugs came early to Garberville (THPO, colorized by JR).

House was built of cross sections from a single redwood tree, distinction enough to merit its inclusion in Ripley's "Believe It or Not." The Eel River Café featured a "landmark sign of a cook flipping flapjacks," which competed with the steaming coffee up at Knapp's Restaurant. For 30 years the Garberville Inn competed with the Redwood Inn for the custom of overnighters, but the contest ended in 1953 when the former was moved around the corner and converted into an apartment house. Look's Restaurant was transformed into the Black and White Café, which lasted until 1960, when, apparently not being colorful enough, it was torn down. The Hotel Lancing was built in 1876, extensively remodeled at least once, and operated until 1968. Four years later it was "demolished." It was probably a victim of the rerouting of the highway, which in 1964 was moved down the hillslope just west of town and converted into a freeway.[1118]

And thus highwayless Garberville now sits upon its blufftop as the world rushes by, visited only by those with great purpose, or great lack of it, watching westward, as if upon a peak in Darien.

# Chapter 15
# Redway

The area near Redway belonged to a tribal group, name unknown, that was part of the Sinkyone tribe. Their only known village was Ltugganobi, which was on the flat on the eastern side of the South Fork Eel opposite the mouth of Redwood Creek.[1119] It was in the area that later became the site of Redway.

North of the flat are steep cliffs that plunge perilously to the South Fork. When John McMillin started building the southern end of the Garberville-Dyerville road in 1881, he chose to avoid the cliffs and bypass the flat by going almost directly north from Garberville. His route crossed over what was later called Buhne's Hill and then regained the river at Dean Creek, where the Buhne family had a ranch.[1120] Allie Buhne, H. H. Buhne's son, owned the thousand-acre-plus property.[1121]

The exact fate of Ltugganobi is unknown, but it may have been destroyed during the circa-1860 rampage of the Asbill brothers and other vigilantes who attacked the village of To-kub-be near Briceland.[1122] In any case, the Indians were probably gone by 1862, when Edward Perrin Gayetty obtained land on the Redway flat. Gayetty sold part of his property to William Carlin in 1876 and more of his land in 1890 to Charles Gustave Lundblade,[1123] keeping only a small parcel at the north end of the flat.[1124] Carlin subsequently sold the remainder of his land to Edwin Ruscoe. The two new owners joined their property into the Ruscoe and Lundblade Ranch, whose northern boundary was adjacent the Buhne Ranch. This was but one of numerous Humboldt County parcels the pair owned, and the ranch was rented out.[1125]

The renters in 1898 were Jacob and Margaret Combs and their family, who came north from Aptos, California. There was no road from Garberville to the property, so the Combses drove their surrey on the South Fork's river bars, fording the river two or three times. The property included an old house, a barn, and a chicken coop, along with an orchard and some chickens. Water came from a spring. The only other family on the flat were the Gayettys. The children from both families attended school in Garberville in the spring and fall but not during winter, when the South Fork was too high to cross. There was a trail to Garberville, but this was traveled only to get mail and supplies.[1126] The two families lived on the flat in near isolation.

Then came the Redwood Highway. Unlike the earlier wagon road, the highway north of Garberville stayed close to the South Fork. It crossed the eastern, more elevated portion of the Redway flat and thereby put the heretofore isolated area right on the new travel corridor. This route avoided the steep climb over Buhne's Hill but faced a different challenge by running across the nearly sheer face of the bluff north of Redway. Grading of the new highway was completed in November 1917, and the beautiful Bear Canyon Bridge, located between Redway and Garberville, was finished in 1921.[1127] This concrete construction was so attractive that the state division of highways chose a full-color painting of it for the frontispiece of its first annual report.[1128]

The placement of the highway was portentous. After languishing as rented ranchland for decades, the flat where Ltugganobi once stood was ready to be repopulated.

And soon this happened. In 1922, while the concrete still hardened on the nearby Bear Canyon Bridge, Lee and Anna Huber purchased a tract of land down near the South Fork and soon thereafter offered lots for homesites at what they called Edgewater Park.[1129] The following year, brothers Oscar and Charles Burris, who had sold their Eureka-San Francisco freight company to Arthur Way, used the money to buy the remainder of the flat.[1130]

Immediately the Burrises began selling lots in their "Redway Summer Homes Subdivision."[1131] This may have been the first use of the name Redway for the flat. It was reportedly coined to indicate that, when coming from the south, it was here that the "road*way*" first started through the "*red*woods."[1132] If so, it was an allusion so cloaked in obscurity as to seldom be appreciated.

For a time, Redway developed swiftly. Summer home seekers from both the Humboldt and San Francisco bay areas bought lots and built houses on them. A direct road from Briceland to Redway was finally constructed in 1924-1925,[1133] and at its junction with the Redwood Highway the Burrises built a "beautiful office [in the style] of English architecture." At first the structure was used as the sales office for the subdivision, but it soon became the pro shop for the Burris-built nine-hole golf course that spread across the eastern side of Redway. Even the best golfers could not avoid the course's sand traps, since a lack of water precluded the growing of any grass, which meant bare earth fairways and "greens" made of "high class sand."[1134] The condition of the course induced serious golfers to travel a few

The dire Redwood Highway cliff route north of Redway (THPO, colorized by JR).

# Redway

A row of madrones at the edge of the Redcrest golf course (FM, colorized by JR).

miles south where the Benbow family, who had a ready water supply, offered a set of golf links with actual grass.[1135]

By 1926 the Benbows also had an inn, magnificently sited at the confluence of the South Fork Eel and its East Branch.[1136] The Burrises saw the new building, and the golf course with its green greens, and they grew green with envy.

During the latter years of the decade, the Burris brothers accordingly drew up plans and drew in investors, and in April 1929 announced, as the *Humboldt Times* vaguely put it, a "Big Project." The centerpiece was to be the "Redway Tavern," modeled on "the comfortable Elizabethan inn of our ancestors." In keeping with its antecedent's architecture, it was to feature a fachwerk façade of stucco and half-timbering but would add the modern amenity of "a private bath and shower" in each of its 140 rooms. Construction would start within 60 days on the $500,000 structure, which would be fitted out with "period furnishings [that] will be designed and made to order especially for this hostelry." Completion was scheduled for New Year's Eve.[1137]

If this were not enough, spring of 1930 would see the opening of a new, "all-grass 18-hole championship golf course," designed "under the direction of noted golf architects." Still straining to surpass the Benbows, the Burrises then delivered their proposed coup de grâce—direct air service to Redway from the Oakland airport using "tri-motored 16-passenger planes."[1138] The site of the Redway Airport was not revealed, but in the past the golf course's long fourth fairway had been used as a landing field.[1139]

The Redway community building (CPH, colorized by JR).

Before the Benbows could thus be put to flight, outside forces intervened. A sum of $2,000,000 was required to complete all of the proposed Redway facilities. It is doubtful that enough of this amount had been raised to start work in late June, as the promotion had promised. What is certain is that on October 29th, the nation's stock market crashed with a force that left many potential investors with little more than a handful of pennies. Less than two years later, on August 26, 1931, the Burris brothers' Redway Summer Homes, sans Redway Tavern, sans 18-hole grass-covered golf course, sans airport, was sold at a foreclosure auction to the Pacific Lumber Company for $16,000.[1140]

Redway residents realized that their community was not to surpass Benbow as a high-toned resort, but they did what they could to make the place enjoyable. Many northern Humboldt families had vacation homes in Redway, and the wives and kids would stay there all summer while the husbands worked in Eureka. Come Friday evening the men would carpool down from Humboldt Bay, often arriving for a midnight dinner.[1141]

Near the junction of the Redwood Highway with Briceland Road was a large barn, old enough to have hand-forged nails. The barn was converted "into a clubhouse with a good size dance floor, kitchen, and large porch with tables, for the nights were hot." Music came from a "loud" phonograph, and people would dance until dawn, go swimming about 6:30 A.M., and then fish for trout. The catch was taken to the clubhouse, cooked for breakfast, and then "everybody was ready to go to work on their lots or houses. NO SLEEP." During the all-night dancing, small children were put to bed in the former barn's hayloft.[1142] It might not have been Benbow, but it was lots of fun.

If you were just passing through, the Redway Lodge, which opened in 1937, provided meals and several cabins in which to stay.[1143] Lots were still being sold, but instead of being offered by the Burrises, the sales were handled at Scotia. The roster of property owners was a geographically varied lot; they came "from Seattle down the Pacific coast to San Diego and east to Kansas City." By 1940 there were 122 property owners in the development. Jack McKenzie was the resident supervisor of the summer home settlement, which, in addition to the club house, included tennis courts, a children's playground, a beach, and a swimming pool. In the off season, when a few winter residents remained, McKenzie was in great demand as a bridge partner.[1144]

The postwar lumber boom brought enough families into the area that the Redway Elementary School opened in 1954. By 1964 the boom was thudding to an end, but then the flood that hit in December oddly rejuvenated the languishing school. It happened thus: the floodwaters severely damaged three southern Humboldt schools: those at Bull Creek, Eel Rock, and Myers Flat. Although only the last was operating at the time, the federal government provided replacement money for all three. Instead of rehabilitating the wrecked buildings, the money was used to add five new classrooms to the Redway School. Subsequently, schools at Garberville, Ettersburg, and Harris were closed and their students sent to Redway. In 1970 the Piercy School, in northern Mendocino County, was also closed and its students added to the rolls at Redway.[1145]

Times had changed. The Redway School occupied the former fairways for the fifth and sixth holes of the Burris brothers' nine-hole golf course.[1146] At recess students might be found unknowingly running around on what had formerly been either greens or sand traps, but even in the course's heyday they couldn't have told the difference.

The Redway Lodge, 1937 (THPO, colorized by JR).

Redway—where sand traps merged with the "greens." (colorized by JR).

# Chapter 16
# Phillipsville

Phillipsville lies within a wide spot in the canyon of the South Fork Eel, where, from Anderson Creek to Fish Creek, the floodplain is bordered by hospitable riverside flats. The local Indians accordingly populated the area with three villages: Kekestci,[1147] Ket-tin-tel-be (Kutduntelbi), and Sa-be-ye (Sebiye).[1148] Then came the Indian holocaust, which meant some 17 years of attacks by whites across much of Humboldt County. The whites took over the land, and except for some housepits and perhaps a scattering of artifacts, the villages vanished. For a time a store occupied the site of Kekestci, while Sa-be-ye was plowed up and replaced by fruit trees and a garden.[1149] Ket-tin-tel-be, which was "said to have been a large village,"[1150] later became an "orchard & ranch."[1151]

The 1865 county map showed three residents in the area.[1152] Living at what would become the northern outskirts of Phillipsville was John Marshall.[1153] At some point he captured an Indian from Kontelkyodun, a village at the future site of Myers Flat. Marshall "sold him to George Woodman of Long Valley who was pretty mean." The Indian was given his slave owner's last name and became Jack Woodman,[1154] who was Gladys Ayer Nomland's main informant for her "Sinkyone Notes."[1155] Marshall's property later became the Combs Ranch.

Aaron Chaffin owned most of what became the Phillipsville townsite.[1156] He remained longer than either of his original neighbors.[1157]

South of Chaffin was George Phillips. He was probably one of the vigilantes who earlier massacred the Indians from the village of To-kub-be at Briceland.[1158] Phillips Flat was perhaps named for him, but another resident of the area, Simon Phillips, is sometimes awarded the honor. Both men lived with Indian women, and each couple had a son. Given such similarities, historians have been unable to reach a firm conclusion about which man was the community's namesake.[1159]

By the 1870s the area was a transportation hub. No roads were present, but a trail ran through the site of Phillipsville on the flats along the east side of the South Fork,[1160] while another trail, near the southern end of the future town, took off to the northeast, running up a ridge spur to connect with the "Mail Trail" atop Mail Ridge.[1161] At the north end of the community a trail branched northwest from the river trail and crossed the South Fork, while a half mile farther north, another trail took off from the river trail, running northward into the mountains towards Mail Ridge and Fruitland.[1162]

In 1881 an epistolist writing as "Nomad" found that the location was gradually filling up with people, but it was still simply called Phillips Flat:

> This place is on the south fork of Eel River, seventeen miles from Camp Grant. It is a beautiful little valley, divided into four farms, and owned respectively by C. M. Bailey, A. Chaffin, E. J. Dean and Albert Logan. There is one store here, owned by Thomas Perkins,

who keeps a general assortment of dry goods and groceries.[1163]

Nothing unusual so far. But then Nomad revealed a surprise:

> C. M. Bailey is building a house, which, I am informed, is to be used as an observatory. The glasses have not arrived yet, but as soon as they come he will put them in position. Customers can look through one of them for a "bit," or two looks for a quarter.[1164]

There were no subsequent reports of anyone observing an observatory on Phillips Flat.

The establishment of the Phillips*ville* Post Office in 1883 was indicative of the growth of the town; no longer a nearly empty "flat," it was now a populated "ville."[1165] Abetting the community's development was the completion, in 1885, of a road that ran from Garberville all the way to the mouth of the South Fork Eel. A road coming up the river from its mouth had been built as far as Myers's Ranch (Myers Flat) by 1879,[1166] while a road going down the South Fork from Garberville reached Phillipsville in 1884.[1167] In 1885 the intervening eight-mile stretch, between Myers Flat and Phillipsville was completed,[1168] so that the 1886 county map showed a road along the east side of the South Fork from Garberville all the way down to the main Eel, where the route connected to the West Side Road that ran along the main Eel from Grizzly Bluff to Camp Grant.[1169]

That same year a stage operated between Rohnerville and Phillipsville, closing down for the winter in mid-December.[1170] In 1887 A. W. Johnson advertised for what may have been the same enterprise, his "Rohnerville and Phillipsville Stage Line,"[1171] but he was apparently uninterested in running the remaining few miles to Garberville. The following year, however, Garbervillians were pleased to learn that Albert Logan was conducting a semiweekly stage run from Rio Dell to their distant town. In fact, it was noted that "already there is a great increase in travel along Eel River and the possibilities are . . . [that] Mr. Logan will have to get a bigger wagon soon."[1172]

When Logan's stage plied the route between Rio Dell and Garberville, it passed through a third ville—Sliverville—which was described as being "a beautiful green spot on the bank of the South Fork, eighty-five feet above the level of the river at low tide." It was two miles south of Phillipsville.[1173] As of April 1885 Sliverville (also called Silverville, Soonerville, and Gasbag) contained "a blacksmith shop and twelve stakes, drove in the ground sixty feet apart, indicating the town lots." One of the parcels already possessed a building that had once been "used as a saloon. But it was too close to the river and too far from San Francisco." All of this information was contained in a letter to the *Humboldt Times* from "Nacilbuper," whose name later-day historian and anagramist Andy Genzoli determined was "Republican" spelled backwards.[1174] The county directory from the same year indicated that in addition to the blacksmith shop there was a feed stable and also "a hotel in the course of construction."[1175]

The most noteworthy resident of the Sliverville area[1176] was William B. Mudd, whose ranch in 1885 had about 1,000 head of sheep and a "choice" orchard.[1177] A decade earlier, however, Mudd had gained even greater notoriety. The story went back to August 1875 when, at Garber and Martin's store in Garberville, M. J. Byrnes shot and instantly killed W. S. Greenwood.

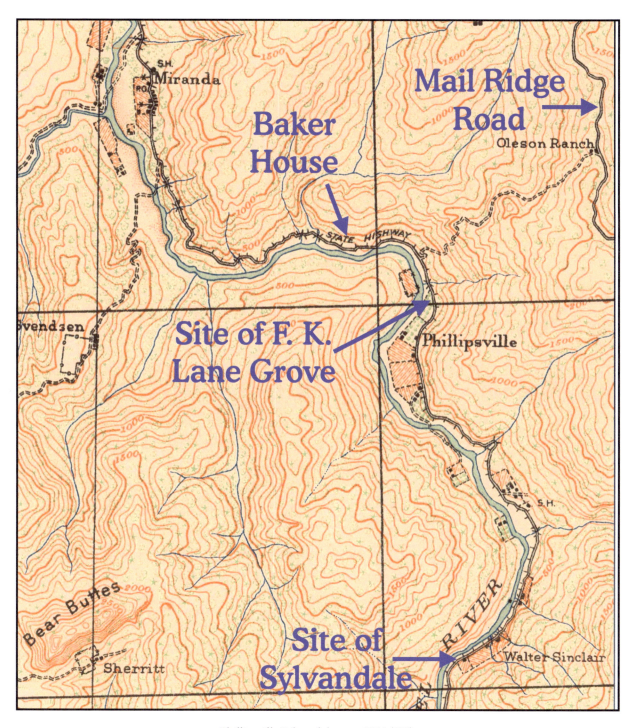

Phillipsville-Sylvandale area 1916 (CE).

A coroner's jury ruled the killing "justifiable homicide" since Byrnes reportedly fired in self-defense.[1178] Two and a half years passed and then Byrnes was on the other end of a fatal bullet's trajectory when he was shot by William B. Mudd. It then came out that Byrnes had shot Greenwood not in self-defense but rather at the behest of "local cattlemen."[1179] Apparently the shooting of Byrnes was also ruled justifiable, because seven years later Mudd was receiving guests at his well-stocked ranch.

Mudd fared better than the local community, for Sliverville faced the fate of most slivers and was soon removed; by 1890 it had vanished from the pages of the county directory.[1180] Years later, another tiny town developed in the area. (See sidebar 1.)

Some two months after Nacilbuper's 1885 letter to the *Humboldt Times*, the *Humboldt Standard's* traveling correspondent, McTavish, sent in an account of Phillipsville, making no mention of the nearby town of the 12 stakes.

Instead readers learned that "the next place in importance to Garberville, on the South Fork, is Phillipsville." E. J. Dean, the postmaster, had 20 acres of good bottomland "under cultivation in grain and orchard." Aaron Chaffin, the town's old-timer with 20 years in residence, had 30 acres cultivated. He lamented the recent rise in sheep ranching, stating "that before cattle

### 1. From Sliverville to Sylvandale

The exact location of Sliverville is now unknown, but it must have been close to where, years later, a successor with a similar name developed. In 1902 Walt and Voreh Sinclair planted a small redwood at their honeymoon cottage beside the South Fork. The tree flourished and so did the location, which became known as Sylvandale.[1181]

The Sinclairs owned property that included the river bar west of the highway. Anglers went there to drop a line in Sylvandale Hole, while the highway department came there to relieve the riverbed of some of its gravel.[1182] In time the adjacent townlet came to include a Shell gas station and a combination motor court[1183] and bar. The latter two businesses were for a time operated by Virginia Walker, who would "run out loggers who got fresh," and who "could swear with the best of them."[1184]

In 1952 Leo and Lucille Hull purchased the property from the Sinclairs. Lucille promised Voreh Sinclair that she would care for the "Honeymoon" redwood, which by then was 150 feet tall. The Hulls and two of Leo's relatives operated a nursery and gift shop. The nursery stocked both native and tropical plants.[1185]

During the 1950s Sylvandale was a small but diversified community. It featured the Hulls' nursery and gift shop called the "Redwood Jewel Box," the Phippses' gas station, and Virginia Walker's motor court-bar-grocery store combine.[1186] An outlandish ornament just to the northeast was the "Sylvandale sycamore,"[1187] a beautiful broadleaf that was native to the Central Valley, the Transverse Range, and coastal areas south of San Francisco Bay. Nowadays northbound motorists departing Highway 101 see it on their left at the end of the offramp.

The 1955 flood rushed through Sylvandale, taking out the Hulls' house. The bridges were out on the Redwood Highway, so the Hulls and others

> crossed nearby Rocky Glen Creek on planks before being transported to Phillipsville, where the Salvation Army had set up a facility at the Riverwood Inn. The night after the height of the flood, Leo Hull suffered a severe heart attack. The Hulls sold their Sylvandale property in July 1959 and Leo Hull died two months later.
>
> Lucille Hull, who later became a noted Sierra Club activist, recalled her time at Sylvandale fondly. During the summers she witnessed bumper-to-bumper traffic on the highway, once having to wait 10 minutes for a break to appear so she could cross the road. It was a wonderful time. "The world came to my door," Lucille said. "I loved every minute of it."[1188]

were superseded times were better, money more plenty." A Captain Stinson made up for part of this deficiency by having 100 acres under cultivation, 40 acres "of splendid redwood timber," and not only "a large orchard in full bearing" but also "a young prune orchard, put out one year ago." Stinson also had "accommodations for travelers and a stable for teams." Lastly, Thomas Perkins kept the town's store, inside of which he was "doing a good business."[1189]

By 1890 Phillipsville had attracted the attention of another newspaper; the *Ferndale Enterprise* indicated that Uriah Beerbower was both "post master and landlord at that village," and that Joseph Stockel "conducts a general merchandise store on the place." Compared to the previous year, Beerbower had less land to lord over, as "about 1 acre of the ranch was carried away by the river last winter."[1190] The county directory from the same year cast a wider net than the *Enterprise* and found "eight or ten families, a schoolhouse, store, postoffice, livery stable, etc. Here we find more orchards, and more are being planted each year."[1191]

Not to be outdone, the *Enterprise* provided an addendum the following year, noting that Beerbower's ranch "is dotted with fig, walnut, olive, prune, almond, nectarine, cherry, peach, apple, pear, apricot, quince and orange trees." If this were not enough, "a small vineyard is also one of the successful experiments at this place, grapes in large clusters and of different varieties being grown."[1192] It was a remarkable showing of productivity for someone who did not own the property. Beerbower conducted his ranching on land leased from Ferndale businessman Arnold Berding[1193] that was located at the north end of Phillipsville on what had been John Marshall's property.[1194]

When David E. Gordon came along the South Fork in the fall of 1899, he noted that "there are few wayside homes after leaving Garberville until Phillipsville is reached." Only one exception was mentioned, "the old Mudd place at Dean Canyon," which lay nearly three miles north of Garberville and was reached only after a steep climb and descent of the ridge that lay between. Long ago the name Mudd had dried up, replaced by "Camp Solitude," the "fine mansion and the elegantly arranged surroundings" of the late Captain H. H. Buhne and his family.[1195] William Mudd had sold his thousand-acre ranch to Buhne in 1888, who wanted an inland retreat free of the "rheumatic twinges which the damp bay atmosphere inevitably visits upon him" at his ranch at the edge of Humboldt Bay. Buhne built a "handsome residence" at Camp Solitude, stayed at the ranch intermittently for several years, and died there in October 1894.[1196]

Gordon determined that "Phillipsville is emphatically a place of homes and orchards, and from here goes some of the finest early fruits that are disposed of in Eel river valley and Eureka." He found Henry Freeman, M. P. Alexander, Levi Chadbourn, and John Weeks and sons all with "productive places in or in the immediate vicinity of Phillipsville." Also noteworthy was John W. Logan's farm. Gordon indicated that the "new cut-off road" that came down from Olsen's, a stage stop on the Mail Ridge road, might provide an important link to Garberville.[1197] This prediction has yet to be fulfilled.

By 1900 Uriah Beerbower was gone from Berding's ranch property, but his daughter, Mrs. Alexander (her first name sacrificed upon the altar of male dominance) and her husband's family were now renting it from Berding, who for a time owned "most of Phillipsville."[1198] That summer, new renters took over. They were Jacob and Margaret Combs and their three children. The log house on the property still contained the Phillipsville Post Office that Beerbower had once been master of.[1199]

The post office wasn't much—just nine boxes in a corner of the house—but the ranch became a rest stop for travelers on the Garberville-Dyerville road. Margaret Combs started cooking meals for those who came by, and there was a four-room cottage on the property if the stoppers wanted to stay overnight.[1200]

In 1907 the *Daily Standard* had upgraded the status of the Combses' stopping place, calling it the "Phillipsville Hotel." Not to be outdone, the post office boasted a long-distance telephone for those who found communication by letter too slow. The summer weather struck a nice

The Combs Ranch sits above the pale-blue South Fork (CPH, colorized by JR).

balance, being "hot enough to sun dry prunes and other fruits while not so dry but that several crops of alfalfa can be raised without irrigation." All types of fruit and vegetables were grown by Phillipsville's farmers, but peaches were singled out for special distinction. For relief from toiling in the fields there was both an "ideal picnic ground" and "a hall suitable for dance or entertainments."[1201] By 1911 the Combses had bought Berding's ranch.[1202] The following year the property lost one of its attractions when the Phillipsville Post Office was discontinued and merged with Miranda's.[1203]

If Phillipsville lost its post office, it had by then gained another public building. It was a school that opened in 1901 near Ohman Creek, about a mile and a half south of town. The Phillipsville School was notable for its large library—a whopping collection of 444 books—and for its lack of playground equipment, which chiefly consisted of a large pepperwood tree that was "an integral part of the many games the children played."[1204]

About a mile northwest of Phillipsville, just east of Fish Creek, an interesting intersection of lives occurred. (See sidebar 2.)

Phillipsville was one of a string of small communities along the lower part of the South Fork Eel devoted to agriculture, local commerce, and the care and feeding of travelers. For three decades the Dyerville-Garberville road along the South Fork contended for primacy with the overland routes to the east. Then in the late 1910s came the Redwood Highway. It swept down the South Fork through the small riverside communities, which were never the same again. (See Appendix A.)

As automobilists drove the new Redwood Highway, towns such as Phillipsville found themselves catering to a new set of needs. Motorists required oil, gas, and garages, not the feed, stables, and blacksmiths that served the horse-drawn age. The visitors came increasingly to spend time among the redwoods or beside the streams and rivers. Communities that were once mere stopping places for travelers could now serve as tourist centers, with a clientele that measured their stay not in hours but in days or even weeks. In the decades following the completion of the highway, Phillipsville became a town transformed by the exigencies of modern transportation.

### 2. A Picture-Perfect Spot

From 1904 to 1910 Ray Jerome Baker owned a photography studio at 5th and F streets in Eureka. At a Socialist meeting in 1906 he met a local school teacher, Edith Frost, and they soon married. During these years Baker acquired a light-weight motorcycle,[1205] which he used to reach photography locations in rural parts of the county. His images sometimes showed more than outdoor scenery, for in August 1908 Baker was convicted of "taking obscene photographs," for which he was fined $50. In 1910 Baker, his wife, and her son Earl moved to Hawaii, perhaps hoping that the land of the hula was more accepting of the depiction of scantily clad locals. In any case, the islands remained Baker's home until his death in 1972.[1206]

Dan Merrifield was a farmer who lived in the Upper Mattole area during the 1860s. He and an Indian woman, name unknown, had a son, Truman, who was born about 1865.[1207] By 1879 Dan Merrifield, his name shown on the government map as "Mayfield," had a house on the west side of Grasshopper Peak in the upper Bull Creek drainage.[1208] In 1889 he received a land patent on the property,[1209] which later became part of the Hazelton Ranch.[1210]

Truman Merrifield married Maggie May Burns in 1903. Truman was about 42 and May, as she was often called, was 16 at the time of their marriage. The couple began having children[1211] and moved to an old house near the county wagon road between Miranda and Phillipsville. The dwelling was next to land that belonged to Edith Frost Baker's family.[1212]

Ray Jerome Baker began building an imposing but rather charmless log cabin on the Frosts' property.[1213] The site was called Oak Terrace. On trips back to California from Hawaii, he spent considerable time working on the cabin. Baker received some help with the construction when a "Mr. Hill, bricklayer from Eureka," came down to Oak Terrace and gave instructions for building a stone fireplace.[1214] Various members of the Hill family had done brickmaking in Eureka since the 1870s.[1215] With Hill supervising, Baker did the heavy lifting—hauling rocks, mixing concrete, etc. The fireplace was finished in August, 1923.

During his trips to Oak Terrace, Baker would visit the Merrifields, whose "split lumber" house was located about 200 yards from the Bakers' log cabin. In November 1919 he had a "good dinner" at the Merrifields', that included "most likely deer out of season." Afterwards "the youngsters brought out their musical instruments and did their best to entertain."[1216] On one of his visits in about 1917 Baker, ever the photographer, lined up the Merrifield family outside their house with a fruit tree in the background. Truman stands to the left, wearing what appears to be a military uniform, arms akimbo. Next to him is May, holding their baby, Woodrow. On May's right are the other six Merrifield children, standing in descending order according to height. It is a perfectly conceived photograph—everyone attentive and at ease, everyone looking either handsome or beautiful, everyone appearing happy or at least contented. Baker captured a moment when the members of this family seemed to be hearing the chords of some vital harmony, when, for a moment at least, the arc of their lives had brought them above the enshadowed low places of everyday concerns, and where the sun shone golden all around them.

Ray Jerome's visits to Oak Terrace continued for many years. Edith Baker

Baker's motorcycle, often seen in his rural Humboldt photographs (CPH, colorized by JR).

came in 1930 and exclaimed, "Oh I do like this house."[1217] But something was amiss with the Bakers' marriage. In 1934 Ray Jerome wrote stiffly from Oak Terrace to "Dear Wife," and that same year confided to his journal that their relationship had deteriorated. He also believed that Edith's son, Earl, "clung to her and despised me."[1218]

Also deteriorating were the fortunes of the Merrifield family. Truman Sr. was arrested in Blocksburg in the summer of 1920 for taking a deer out of season and for failing to provide for his family. Later that year Truman Sr. attempted to have his 15-year-old daughter, Viola, placed in a reform school rather than marrying Aaron Ensey, which had been her intent.[1219] In 1921 Harold, the infant son of Truman and May, died when only two weeks old. Then, in September 1923, Truman Sr. succumbed to tuberculosis.[1220]

Ray Jerome Baker was working at Oak Terrace in July 1934 and one day drove May Merrifield and two of her children to Eureka to see the eldest Merrifield daughter, Rhoda, who had married and had six children. Baker found Rhoda's home "a picture of misery, filth and poverty." Her husband, Carl Nelson, "was about somewhere but drove off in his car without coming in. He may have had a good reason," Baker continued, "for I believe that Mrs. Merrifield took a couple of shots at him when he visited her hillside home some time ago." Baker then took May to the house of her second oldest daughter, Viola, whose wedding Truman had tried to stop. Viola was now a widow with two children, and she had to work as a cook in the tanbark camps and as a house cleaner to support her small family. Unlike her sister Rhoda, Viola "looked clean and had fresh, clean clothes."[1221]

The downward spiral of the Merrifield family continued. In July 1937 Truman Jr. died at the age of 28. Two weeks later his mother, May, pled guilty to burglary and served 30 days in the county jail.[1222]

After his 1934 visit Baker did not return to Oak Terrace until 1947. His journal mentioned the Merrifields' house but he did not indicate that he'd seen any of the family. In 1961, on another visit to Humboldt County, Baker called on May Merrifield, who by then had left the rental and owned a home of her own. That same year Earl Baker died. He had inherited the house from his mother and deeded Oak Terrace to his wife.[1223]

About a year later the log house burned. Baker wrote that the cause was "negligence," but he did not elaborate.[1224] In 1967 May Merrifield died on the first of May. She was 79 years old.[1225]

Ray Jerome Baker died in 1972 in Honolulu. He was 91 years old and had left a large legacy of photos taken in both Humboldt County and Hawaii.[1226]

Today Oak Terrace is part of Humboldt Redwoods State Park. The site is

The Merrifield family, photographed by Ray Jerome Baker (CPH, colorized by JR).

> easily recognized because of the tall stone fireplace that stands, monument like, above the Avenue of the Giants.
>
> The fireplace, which Baker built for the log house he never owned, recalls Oak Terrace's unfulfilled hopes. And there is another object of recollection associated with the place. It is Baker's photograph of the nine Merrifields, all in a row, looking towards his camera at a moment when the future, with all the tragedy it held, was as yet unanticipated and instead there was only Baker and the Merrifields, coming together to create a masterpiece of the photographer's art.[1227]

Franklin K. Lane monument (JIC, colorized by JR).

One of the first changes came at the north end of town, where the new Humboldt State Redwood Park established a memorial grove honoring Franklin K. Lane. While serving as Woodrow Wilson's Secretary of the Interior, Lane had run afoul of conservationists by supporting the controversial plan to create the Hetch Hetchy Reservoir in Yosemite National Park,[1228] but he balanced this affront to the environment by later becoming the first president of the Save-the-Redwoods League. In August 1924, some three years after his death, the Franklin K. Lane Memorial Grove was dedicated in what was called "a magnificent redwood tract at Kettintelbe, Humboldt County, California."[1229] Various sources at the time used the name for the nearby Indian Village, Ket-tin-tel-be, as the town's name, rather than Phillipsville.[1230]

In 1926 the Combses' log cabin "hotel," which contained the former post office, burned to the ground.[1231] Another reduction of the Combs Ranch came with the realignment of the Redwood Highway at the north end of Phillipsville in the late 1930s; it moved the roadbed westward out of the Franklin K. Lane Grove so that it obliterated much of the Combs orchard.[1232] Walnut trees were thus sacrificed to save redwoods.

At the time of the realignment, the only business shown in Phillipsville was the Deerhorn Lodge,[1233] which had a store, cabins, and gas pump. The Deerhorn had started operation in the 1920s.[1234] As tourism increased, Phillipsville expanded northward so that by 1949 travelers would first encounter the Adele Stennett service station and motor court, followed by the Fountain Hut. Then came what was probably Phillipsville's most striking business building, the Riverwood Inn.[1235] It offered "choice steak, pan-fried chicken, and other specialties" plus dancing, hotel rooms, and "beautiful oil paintings of the redwoods."[1236] Not to be outdone was the "fine cuisine" of Shelton's, where Fred Shelton began serving meals in 1940.[1237] Among the other lodging facilities was the Tad-Jo Rancho Motel and the Madrona Motel,[1238] the latter offering "private tile showers,"[1239] a necessity for those who did not like showering in public.

On August 1, 1948, Phillipsville regained its lost post office. For a time it was located "in an old home." Twenty years later a real post office was finally built, a small (12 foot by 26 foot) building at the north end of Phillipsville just south of the Combs Ranch. It had 83 boxes, a ninefold-plus increase over the nine that were lodged in a corner of the Combses' cabin. In a

For travelers on the Redwood Highway, it was easy to sleep or eat in Phillipsville (THPO, colorized by JR).

# Phillipsville

Phillipsville's pint-size post office (THPO).

sense, however, the new post office harkened back to its primitive predecessor, for the postmaster was Ruth Beasley, whose husband Darrell was the grandson of Jacob and Margaret Combs.[1240]

The new post office served a community of about 200 people. Phillipsville had claimed a population of about 250 as recently as 1964, but many residents left after that year's flood.[1241] During that December deluge a dramatic story unfolded north of the Combs Ranch. (See sidebar 3.)

---

### 3. "Hurry, I can't last much longer . . ."

It isn't often that someone must decide—in a matter of seconds—whether they will risk their life in order to perhaps prevent someone else's death, but that is what Jack King faced on the night of December 22, 1964.

King, who lived north of Phillipsville, was removing possessions from his flood-threatened home when he and helper Art Morgan heard a cry for help. They stopped working and listened. The call came again from the direction of the river, nearly drowned out by the roaring water.

King had a small skiff close at hand. He kicked off his boots, stripped to his shorts, and armed with a single paddle and a flashlight, launched his boat into the flood.

He shouted, "I'm coming with a boat." Back came the shouted information that there were two people, a man and a woman, who were standing in water up to their necks. King decided that if his boat tipped over in the swift current, he would swim to them instead.

King heard the woman's voice. She shouted, "Hurry, I can't last much longer." Her companion was treading water, trying to hold her up. The couple had tried driving their pickup through a straight stretch of the highway near the Franklin K. Lane Grove, hit a low spot, and the floodwater swept them off the road. Somehow they had strayed several hundred feet from the highway.

Now the man shouted, "Hurry up, she can't swim."

King reached the couple. Though of "slight build," he was able help the woman into the boat without capsizing it. Then he turned to assist the man, who weighed "around 200 pounds or more." Somehow King was able to also pull him aboard, but the skiff tipped enough to also allow a large amount of water to flow onboard.

Now King reversed course, paddling the heavily laden boat directly against the current. Several cars had stopped on a higher part of the highway and were illuminating the scene with their headlights.

Slowly King made headway. Finally he reached low water, got out of the boat and began pulling it towards safety. Art Morgan and others waded out to help King, hauling the skiff and its occupants to high ground and safety.

Morgan then put the couple in his car and headed over a back road to Garberville. Midway his engine died, but another car came up and took the couple the rest of the way.

He was already a hero, but Jack King wasn't done yet. The next day he and Leonard Lawson tried to reach Miranda by boat. They were forced to turn back when they encountered a mass of debris and floating logs. The water was 30 feet deep. On their return to Phillipsville the men passed a tree whose top protruded about a foot above the floodwaters. In its topmost branch was a cottontail rabbit. King and Lawson stopped their boat, picked up the rabbit, and took it to safety in Phillipsville.

King didn't discriminate. He'd rescue all creatures, great or small.[1242]

## Appendix A: The Route Through the Redwoods

Well before a highway into Humboldt County was given serious consideration, its course through southern Humboldt was determined by the "Three Bills," a trio of engineers with specific expertise in the routing of . . . railroads.

Bill Hood was chief engineer for the Southern Pacific Railroad. Bill Storey held the identical position with the Santa Fe. Bill Edes had recently taken the same job with a newly created entity, the Northwestern Pacific Railroad (NWP). The NWP had been formed in January 1907 by the Southern Pacific and Santa Fe with the intent of using it to build a single line connecting Humboldt and San Francisco bays rather than having each of the railroad giants construct their own, separate, competing line.[1243]

Both parent companies had previously sent their surveying crews into the river canyons to determine the best route. The Santa Fe engineers had chosen the South Fork Eel. Those of the Southern Pacific thought the main Eel was preferable. Now the experts conferred, compared, and unanimously decided on the main Eel. Thus, that October work started at Willits aiming towards the main Eel, a project that culminated seven years later with the completion of the line at Cain Rock.[1244]

Meanwhile, another transportation route was being planned. In November 1910 the State Highway Act was approved, providing partial funding for a system of California state highways. Among the proposed routes was one running north from San Francisco Bay. The five counties through which it would pass—Marin, Sonoma, Mendocino, Humboldt, and Del Norte— agreed to contribute the remainder of money necessary for the project.

Surveying the northern portions of the route proved to be an exciting experience. The survey crews often found themselves in daunting terrain that lacked even a trail to follow:

> Sometimes the slopes along the route were so steep that the surveyors could not even use animals to carry their equipment but had to pack it on their own backs. Often they had to feel their way around the side of a perpendicular cliff, where later a ledge would be carved out to carry the road.[1245]

The highway surveyors, like those from the Southern Pacific Railroad, determined that the canyon of the main Eel provided the best transportation corridor through northern Mendocino and southern Humboldt counties. But the railroad interests had acted more quickly, pre-empting the route for train traffic.[1246] Thus the decision made by the "Three Bills" determined the course of not only the Northwestern Pacific Railroad but also that of the Redwood Highway, which was forced to take the second-best route that ran along the South Fork.

Even second-best would be a considerable improvement over the existing north-south route, the Overland Road, which crossed the mountains of eastern Humboldt County only to confront motorists with what the *California Highway Bulletin* called "the terrors of the Bell Springs Grade," a climb into northern Mendocino County that had an uphill angle of a car-stopping 30 degrees. The new highway, in following the canyon of the South Fork Eel, would avoid the entire mountain upon which Bell Springs sat while never ascending a grade of more than six percent.

Contracts for portions of the highway work were let starting in 1912,[1247] but progress was

Railroad surveyors, left, near Fort Seward (DTC, colorized by JR).

slow. By the end of 1916 only 6.93 miles of roadway had been graded in Humboldt County. Even that was better than the record in Del Norte and Mendocino counties, each of which had a total mileage of zero.[1248]

The most difficult section of highway construction lay between the Humboldt-Mendocino county line and the tiny community of Cummings, 29.3 miles to the south, where the infamous Bell Springs Grade began on the old Overland Road.[1249] For the new highway, three major bridges were required to cross chasms through which the Eel and its tributaries flowed. To make matters even more difficult, there was no preexisting supply route into the area. Accordingly, an "emergency haul road had to be built from the Leggett Valley to Westport," which could receive highway building material and equipment brought by coastal steamer.[1250] Union Landing, Hardy Creek, and Fort Bragg also served as supply ports. The road between Leggett and the coast required wire suspension bridges at several locations. A 45-mile-long telephone line was run along the supply route.[1251]

For two years, road work in the Leggett area was performed exclusively by pick and shovel. Once a trail reached Cummings, horse teams brought from the south could do part of the work. Only in 1918 did the "first steam shovel get on the job."[1252]

The entry of the United States into World War I made the highway work even more difficult. The shipment of construction materials was restricted by the War Industries Board, and the channeling of young men into the armed services created a highway labor shortage. The latter deficiency was partly offset by implementation of the state's Convict Act of 1915, which allowed prison crews to be deployed for work on the highway.[1253] Several convict camps

# Phillipsville

were established between Cummings and the Humboldt County line. They each housed a contingent of 125 or more prisoners who were supervised by an unarmed head guard and two assistants.[1254]

Bolstered by the prison workforce, the highway gradually took shape. Foot by foot, mile by mile, a roadway was cut through the wilderness. Between September 20, 1915, when convict labor began, and December 31, 1918, the prisoners:

> . . . excavated of solid and loose rock 411,125 cubic yards, and of earth and clay 336,375 cubic yards, a total excavation of 747,500 cubic yards, the expense involved being $500,077.10, and average cost of only sixty-seven cents per cubic yard, which it may be stated for the information of the uninitiate is scandalously cheap.[1255]

The scandal, if there was one, consisted of the prisoners not being paid for their work. The men were "housed in tents and frame buildings," and their food was reportedly ample and good. In lieu of any cash payment, the convicts had their sentences commuted one day for every two they spent on the job. Assignment to the road crew was voluntary. As an added inducement, the prisoners were given free tobacco.[1256] Not listed among the benefits was the transition from a small cell at San Quentin to the spectacular coastal mountains of the South Fork Eel's upper drainage.

Work on the highway had progressed enough that in February 1917 car dealer Axel[1257] Hermanson "drove a Maxwell car from Eureka to Sausalito in the 'unheard-of time' of 18 hours and five minutes."[1258] By August 15 "the

"On the Redwood Highway" says the post card. "*Staying* on the Redwood Highway" was the challenge (THPO, colorized by JR).

road was completed to a width of 12 feet" and Governor William D. Stephens, exactly five months in office,[1259] "made an official inspection of the road."[1260] An image from the times shows Stephens exiting his open-topped car at Garberville,[1261] gripping the car's door tightly after enduring the cliff-clinging route through the South Fork's daunting gorge. Work continued on the highway, extending it to a "proper width" and otherwise reducing the rigors of the road experienced by such driving daredevils as Hermanson and Stephens, and on July 1, 1918 it was opened for general travel.[1262] In fact, the final improvements were so significant that five days later Hermanson, anticipating the

Redwood Highway near Phillipsville (THPO, colorized by JR).

increased demands of Eureka drivers, bought the entire supply of Maxwell autos available in San Francisco—three, to be exact.[1263]

The new highway arrived just in time to meet the needs of a populace swept up in the singular passion of automania. In 1919 there were slightly less than 7 million families in the United States who owned cars. By 1923, a mere four years later, the total was 23 million.[1264] Many thousands of those millions lived in the San Francisco Bay area, and many of those thousands sought stimulation or relaxation by driving away from the bayside cities to the oak woodlands, redwood forests, and twisting rivers that lay to the north—that lay along the new Redwood Highway.

The ranks of such travelers were legion. In March 1925 the *Arcata Union* reported that "more than 50,000 persons often leave Sausalito on Sundays and holidays, bound northward on the start of the Redwood Highway." Many of them were day trippers who might go no farther than San Rafael or Santa Rosa, but others were intent on reaching the highway's namesake redwoods and continued on into Mendocino and Humboldt counties.[1265] Traffic at the other end of the highway, with no San Francisco-like metropolis nearby, was noticeably sparser but was gradually increasing. While some 681 Redwood Highway-bound cars per day departed Grants Pass in the summer of 1923, that total had risen to "over 1,000" two years later.[1266]

During its early days the highway created an intimate relationship with the motorists who traveled it. No one knew this better than Esterfay McBride Pfremmer, who, decades later, recalled the high, and low, points of her travels. She first described her trip along the route in 1918, when she was 6 years old:

# Phillipsville

The Redwood Highway was a narrow, winding, dirt road and I remember my brother and I reaching out from the car to grab wild berries as we drove along. Also, it was not unusual for someone living along the way to stop us and ask us to post a letter for them at the next town, or for some other small favor.

Nine years later she drove the highway[1267] in a "stripped-down" Model T Ford that lacked a windshield and forced Pfremmer to "wear goggles to protect my eyes." She could have used more protection:

Between Garberville and Eureka the road was being oiled and graveled for some distance and by the time I reached Eureka my face and hair was [sic] covered with oily gravel, with only the area behind my goggles left clean. A barber in Eureka washed my hair, and fortunately for him, and for me, my hair was quite short.[1268]

More than oil and gravel covered some sections of the highway. In 1932 a terrific windstorm dropped 32 big redwoods on the roadway between Miranda and Stafford. Mel Martin, who worked for the highway department, removed them using a ponderous Wade drag saw that bucked up the trees into movable slices. The work was no picnic as the Wade

Resurfacing the Redwood Highway (CPH, colorized by JR).

weighed between 400 and 500 pounds and had to be wrestled into place for every cut. Martin preemptively fell 114 "leaners" during the 1930s—redwoods whose trunks angled out over the highway and threatened to fall at inopportune times.[1269]

In the late 1930s the aging highway was modernized by widening and straightening the roadbed. In one nine-mile stretch 209 curves were eliminated. In two instances, at the Franklin K. Lane Grove north of Phillipsville and the Nelson Grove east of Myers Flat, the highway was rerouted rather than cutting into heavy stands of redwoods.[1270]

By the 1950s the Redwood Highway had gained fame as one of a select group of great travel routes. In the words of Donald Culross Peattie, it was "unlike any other in the world. It's more than a motor trip; it's a pilgrimage to the most awesome temple raised by any mortal creature— if you can say that a redwood tree, *Sequoia sempervirens*, the ever-living sequoia, is mortal."[1271] If Peattie's admiration for the highway, and the redwoods, seems extreme, it should be noted that two of his most popular books were about trees.

At the time of Peattie's article the road was lined with a string of redwood groves and parks that delighted tourists and became destinations for vacationers. Few people who enjoyed the beauty of the Redwood Highway would have agreed with the "Three Bills" that it was only the "second-best route."

# Chapter 17
# Bear Buttes

When seen from the south, the Bear Buttes present a striking image: a sawtooth line of small jagged peaks ominously dominating the horizon. They constitute the tallest landform in the area, rising some 2,600 feet above the flat at Phillipsville, which lies some three miles to the northeast. Why is it then, we might ask, that the first white explorers to come through the area—half starved and fully lost—chose to expend their flagging energy on climbing to this rugged ridgeline in the middle of winter? Why, indeed. (See Appendix A.)

The Bear Buttes area is indeed rugged, with steep slopes plunging to the river and the creek canyons that surround it. The government survey map of 1873 shows trails approaching the buttes from Briceland on the southwest, up Butte Creek from the north, and from the Dean Creek-Redway area on the southeast.[1272] Prairies to the southeast of the buttes were homesteaded by Lewis Stump,[1273] David and Sarah Teel,[1274] and Benjamin and Margaret Hale,[1275] among others. West of the buttes Henry and Sadie Tosten homesteaded another prairie area.[1276]

In early days, there was a very small school southeast of the buttes on the Joseph Swithenbank Ranch.[1277] The property was purchased in the 1860s[1278] and Joseph, his wife, and three sons took up residence. Mrs. Swithenbank (the account fails to give her first name) "sent to Boston for a school marm to teach in the private school she had built on the ranch." This arrangement tended to keep

Beautiful background: the Bear Buttes (HCHS, colorized by JR).

their boys out of circulation, but the Swithenbanks also had a store in Garberville, and it was there that one son, Charlie, met Elizabeth "Gussie" Miller, with the result that she eventually enlarged the size of her last name to Swithenbank.[1279]

The Bear Butte [sic] School operated from at least 1889 to 1898. For the first two years it was on the Stump property, and then it was moved to the east side of the Teel Ranch. There was no outhouse for the first school—perhaps a reason for moving to the Teel property, where, by 1897, "there was one good outhouse." At the second school the boys all sat in one row of desks, the girls in another. The pedagogical effect of this arrangement is unknown. The school was of odd construction, with windows along only one side of the building. Perhaps the brightest scholars were allowed to study there. Students had to provide their own textbooks, although by 1898 the school library had 123 books. On Sunday evenings the schoolhouse was used for church services, with the pastor crossing the South Fork by boat from Miranda.[1280]

The rugged landscape of the Buttes attracted adolescent adventurers, such as Bud Scott, his brother, and other youngsters who attended a YMCA camp on the west side of the South Fork. Both in 1921 and 1924, Bud and his friends explored the area around the Buttes and admired the view from near the top. In the late 1940s Bud returned to climb the miniature mountains again. His brother-in-law, Adolph Coffey, went along, liked the area, and subsequently purchased the Weeks property on the northeast side of the Buttes. Coffey subsequently sold out, and when Scott visited the locale again in 1955, he found a very different place:

> A friend and I had trouble finding our way through a logged-off area. The old road had been obliterated and a jumble of slash remained. The [Weeks'] cabin had been burned to the ground. The pristine serenity of the area was just a memory, but the Buttes themselves remained rugged and stately against the blue of the summer sky.[1281]

Much indeed had been lost on the buttes, but there was one instance of retrieval. (See sidebar 1.)

---

**1. The Return of the Lambkiller**

On June 7, 1931, at an elevation of about 2,500 feet on the west side of the Bear Buttes, rancher Henry Tosten collected a sample of a "tall, robust, leafy perennial" that his lambs had been eating. Many of the lambs subsequently died, and Tosten suspected that the plant was the culprit.[1282]

The "leafy perennial" turned out to be *Astragalus agnicidus*, common name Humboldt milkvetch, nickname lambkill milkvetch. Suspicion confirmed, the Tostens "vigorously attacked" the plant. When botanist and astragalus expert Rupert C. Barnaby visited the ranch in 1954, the lambkiller had itself been nearly killed off. Shortly thereafter came word that it had entirely disappeared. As the Tosten Ranch was the only location where the Humboldt milkvetch grew, this meant that the California Native Plant Society subsequently placed

# Bear Buttes

The lambkiller in solitary confinement (SM).

the species on its dire List 1A: "plants presumed extinct in California."[1283]

List 1A was where the Humboldt milkvetch remained until 1987, when two state biologists, Ken Berg and Karen Bittman, attempted to confirm the plant's extinction. They contacted a southern Humboldt conservation biologist, Robert Sutherland, who had been interested in the milkvetch "for a decade and had searched for it earlier." Sutherland communicated with the Tosten family, who still owned the Bear Buttes property, and was invited to visit the ranch. When Berg, Bittman, and Sutherland arrived, the Tostens showed them the site where they recalled seeing the lambkiller more than 30 years earlier. The location had "grown back to dense evergreen forest." It seemed unlikely that any milkvetch would be present there.[1284]

The biologists looked at other locations on the ranch, areas that were "a mosaic of non-native grasslands and second-growth mixed evergreen forest." They returned to their starting point without finding anything. Then,

> . . . just before dark we found a logging trail leading to an area where the Tostens had removed a Douglas-fir snag several years earlier; this had opened the canopy and scarified the ground. There in the clearings were small herbaceous plants resembling a milk-vetch. We counted fewer than twenty-five plants, and all appeared to be either young or badly browsed; the tallest one was only six inches high.[1285]

The Humboldt milkvetch that had gone missing for over 30 years had returned. How?

*A. agnicidus* is part of the Leguminosae family, the members of which are known for "impermeable seed coats [that] allow the seeds to remain viable in the soil for many years." In this case the lambkiller seeds had waited patiently for over three decades, until a tree removal unearthed them and allowed them to germinate.[1286]

The Tostens no longer ran sheep. They enthusiastically embraced the idea

> of protecting the site, which was then fenced off. When the biologists later returned to the ranch, they found many additional seedlings and plants in a nearby clearing, bringing the total number of Humboldt milkvetches to over a hundred.[1287]
>
> The 1987 rediscovery of the lambkiller at the Bear Buttes was soon followed by sightings at several other locations. By 2011 A. *agnicidus* had been found on various Humboldt County timberlands, including a site near Larabee, and also at the Jackson Demonstration Forest in Mendocino County. Secreted in subsurface seed banks, colonies of lambkiller had awaited the soil disturbance caused by logging to activate their potential.[1288]
>
> Little lambkiller who made thee?
> Dost thou know who made thee?
> Gave thee life and bid thee feed.
> By the stream and o'er the mead,
> Left thee there so safely hidden,
> Showing yourself only when bidden.
>
> (With apologies to William Blake.)

### Appendix A: Three Stories, One Truth

And diff'ring judgements serve but to declare
    That truth lies somewhere, if we knew but where.
    —Thomas Cowper

A core story in the lore of Humboldt County is the summary of an exploration escapade in 1849-1850 that led to the "rediscovery" of Humboldt Bay by a party of adventurers who had come from the Trinity gold fields. An account by one of the participants, L. K. (Lewis Keysor) Wood, was written up from his notes by Walter Van Dyke,[1289] editor of the *Humboldt Times*, and published in that paper in 1856.[1290] It was reprinted in the *Weekly Humboldt Times* in 1863[1291] and in the *West Coast Signal* in 1872.[1292] Both Elliott's 1881 county history[1293] and Irvine's 1915 biographical history[1294] included it. An extensively annotated version appeared in 1966 in *The Quest for Qual-A-Wa-Loo*,[1295] a collection of reports about and from early explorers of the Humboldt Bay region. It is almost impossible for local history enthusiasts to avoid encountering the account.

Wood's story has almost all the attributes of a best seller—an expedition into an unknown land, contact with people from another culture, conflicts with difficult comrades and dangerous animals—everything but the requisite romantic interest that would add dimension to the image of adventurers adrift in a wilderness they were poorly prepared to navigate. Small wonder that it became part of the bedrock upon which Humboldt County history was built.

Except that it is almost certainly false.

According to the Wood-Van Dyke account, L. K. Wood was part of the Josiah Gregg party, a group of eight men who left the Trinity River gold fields in November 1849. They were in search of a large bay on the coast that might serve as a supply port for the miners, who were already running low on provisions and had no other prospect of being resupplied. After an exhausting journey to the shores of the Pacific, the Gregg party succeeded in locating not one bay, but two: Trinidad and Humboldt. The group then headed south to bring news of their accomplishment to San Francisco. But dissention among the party members, long simmering, boiled over at the Eel River, and the group split in two. Gregg and three others headed for the coast, while Wood and the remaining three went up the Eel. According to Wood, his party found rough going along the river, at one point ascending Monument Peak in hopes of easier traveling. Instead they were caught in a blizzard and forced down to the Eel at the future site of Redcrest. Continuing upriver, they reached the confluence with the South Fork, whose course they then began to follow. Food was scarce. At the mouth of Salmon Creek, they encountered a group of five grizzly bears, one of which they wounded. The bears escaped, leaving the men still hungry. The party trudged farther upriver to the mouth of Butte Creek, where they "ascended a divide between Butte Creek and south fork of Eel River, and continued southward along the divide through an open grass-clad country."[1296]

The next day, while still in the mountains, the men "espied" a group of eight grizzlies. Here was a second chance to obtain some bear meat. Wood fired his rifle and dropped one bear, while Isaac Willson shot another. Five of the remaining bears ran off up the mountainside. The last bear, unhurt, stayed behind, "looking first upon her fallen companions," according to Wood, "and then upon us."[1297]

At this point Willson took the hint and headed for a nearby tree. Meanwhile, Wood was trying to reload his rifle but had difficulty ramming the ball down the barrel. He also began to realize the folly of shooting into a sleuth[1298] of bears. Wood now followed Willson's example and ran for a tree, the unhurt bear not far behind. Unfortunately, Wood chose a small California buckeye to clamber up. The bear proceeded to batter the buckeye, with, as Wood put it, "the purpose of breaking it down or shaking me out of it." Suddenly, reinforcements appeared. Wood watched in horror,

> . . . when to my astonishment the bear I had shot down, having recovered sufficiently from the effects of the wound, came bounding towards me with all the violence and ferocity that agony and revenge could engender. No blow that I could inflict with my gun upon the head of the maddened monster could resist or even check her.[1299]

Wood's new assailant then lunged at the buckeye and broke it down. As the tree fell to earth, Wood managed to land on his feet and begin running for another small tree that stood about 30 yards away. Wood expected to be caught at any moment, since he "could distinctly feel the breath of wounded bear as she grabbed at my heels."[1300]

With the bear literally breathing down his neck,[1301] Wood managed to reach the tree, grab it, and swing himself around to the opposite side of the trunk. The wounded bear, taken by surprise, continued down the hillside "some twenty paces" before she could stop and turn around. Wood began to climb the tree, but now angry bear #2 caught up with him, grabbed Wood by the ankle, and pulled him down to the ground. Bear #1, having clambered back up the hill, rejoined the fracas and caught hold of Wood's left shoulder. The two ursine tormentors then engaged in a tug of war, one pulling at Wood's shoulder, the other at his leg.[1302]

His clothing probably saved Wood's life. Instead of clawing at his flesh, the bears tore away Wood's pants and part of his shirt and coat. They also scratched him up pretty thoroughly and dislocated his hip, but that seemed to be enough to satisfy them. Leaving Wood battered and bleeding on the ground, the unwounded bear left the area, while the wounded one ambled up the hillslope about a hundred yards and, as Wood put it, "deliberately seated herself and fastened her gaze upon me."[1303]

The excitement subsided but did not end. After lying still for several minutes, Wood "ventured to move." Bingo. The bear stormed down from her grandstand seat and, as Wood recounted,

> . . . no sooner had reached me than she placed her nose violently against my side and then raised her head and gave vent to two or three of the most frightful, hideous and unearthly yells that were ever heard by mortal man.[1304]

Eventually the loud bear left. Wood found that his injuries "became momentarily more painful." His comrades took him down the hillslope to a camping area. There they waited 10 or 12 days for Wood's condition to improve. When it didn't, they bargained with some local Indians to care for him while they went for help. The Indians took the goods they'd been offered and promptly left, not to be seen again. Wood's companions then debated what to do with him. It was a long discussion. Finally Wood heard Willson shouting, "No! I will not leave him! I'll remain with him, if it is alone, or I will pack him if he is able and willing to bear the pain!"[1305]

Willson's outburst settled the matter. His companions placed Wood on his horse and he rode, in great pain, all the way to Guadalupe West's ranch[1306] in the Sonoma Valley, where he was cared for until he recuperated.[1307]

According to Wood's journal, he left the West ranch on April 1, 1850, went to Sonoma for a few days, and then arrived in San Francisco on April 7.[1308] By then his companions had spread word of their discovery and several ships had sailed north in search of Trinidad and Humboldt bays. One of the vessels, the *Laura Virginia*, entered Humboldt Bay on or about April 14.[1309] On April 19 Wood met with W. B. Young, an official of the Laura Virginia party, in San Francisco. Young had heard of Wood's recent travails and responded sympathetically, granting Wood the deed to a "good lot" in the town that the party was establishing on Humboldt Bay. Wood then went to San Jose where, on August 5, he somewhat redundantly bought three lots in that community. He subsequently left for Humboldt Bay. Wood arrived at the brand-new town of Union on September 9 and the next day had a cabin built on the property Young had provided for him.[1310]

The above account became part of the standard received history of the white occupancy of Humboldt County. Wood's story was considered an eyewitness report of early events and thus a solid foundation upon which to place the progression of activity that followed. In serialized form it was available to readers of the *Humboldt Times* in May 1856. This was, however, not the first time that a newspaper had published an article about the expedition that had traveled from the Trinity mines to Sonoma County. Some six years earlier, on April 9, 1850, the *Daily Alta California*, a San Francisco newspaper, had carried a report from its Sonoma correspondent, Veritas. The author, whose nom de plume implies truthfulness, had interviewed a member of the party who, although unnamed, almost certainly was L. K. Wood.

According to Veritas's version, a group of men had left Sacramento the previous fall to "explore the country watered by the Trinity river and possess themselves of information relative to the richness of its gold washings." They reached the headwaters of the Trinity and did some mining, making "upwards of two hundred dollars per day." Having confirmed the existence of a gold strike, the men proceeded to travel down the river. Then one of the party, the interviewee, became ill, and "was advised to repair to sea coast." He did so, accompanied by two other members of the group. The three men had a daunting trip, enduring "many fatiguing marches, scaling mountains and descending abrupt canon [*sic*] sides." They had difficulty finding food and, after traveling for nearly two months, were nearly starving. It was then that they encountered "a herd of grizzly bears," and promptly shot at them, killing one of the animals. At that point "a wounded bruin and its full grown cub made directly at one of the men." This man was the interviewee, who threw down his gun and tried to climb a sapling. One of the bears caught him and dragged him to earth, dislocating his hip in the process and otherwise injuring him. Once on the ground, "the bears lacerated his flesh, and stripped his clothing

> fast becoming exhausted. One morning, while searching for acorns or ground nuts, they observed a herd of grizzly bears, intent upon making a similar morning meal. The sight of fresh animal food tempted the poor travellers to expend a portion of their scant ammunition in an endeavor to bring down one of these formidable beasts, and they discharged their pieces, without counting upon the result in the event of wounding one of them. One shot inflicted a mortal wound, while a wounded bruin and its full grown cub made directly at one of the men. Our informant had thrown down his rifle, and was in the act of climbing a sapling, when the bears turned from his comrade upon him. He was too weak to escape them, and the foremost dragged him to the earth. His hip joint was dislocated by the fall, and he was otherwise severely injured. He remained with his face downward, while the bears lacerated his flesh, and stripped his clothing from him, after which they left him, and he was found by his companions in a dreadful state of suffering. His wounds were dressed, and after a short time he was enabled to proceed slowly on the journey. The second day after, they reached the sea coast, at a point which they judged to be above the bay of Trinidad. They

From "A Journey Overland," *Daily Alta California*, April 9, 1850, page 1. Note that in this version the bear attack occurred before the party reached Trinidad.

from him, after which they left him, and he was found by his companions in a dreadful state of suffering."[1311]

His two friends dressed his wounds, and the three men then continued on towards the coast, which they reached two days later. Near Trinidad Bay, they turned north and followed the coast to what they thought was the mouth of the Trinity River but which actually was the Klamath. Then they reversed course, arriving "in a couple of days" back at Trinidad Bay. The three men continued south past Humboldt Bay and "came upon a beautiful stream, along which great numbers of Indians lived, who took fish from its waters in astonishing abundance." They named the river the Eel, and proceeded to travel along it for almost 200 miles. Frequently avoiding parties of Indians that they judged to be hostile and "suffering severely from hunger, they struck the 'home trail,' and the three companions in this arduous journey separated." The interviewee, "after leaving his comrades, came on to the 'rancho of the widow West,' and shortly thereafter arrived in Sonoma."[1312]

This account, communicated shortly after the trip was completed, not only has the bear attack occurring many miles north of the Bear Buttes, but it also reduces the size of the party from four to three and makes no mention of the other original expedition members after they separated on the Trinity River. In Wood's 1856 version, all eight men stay together until a quarrel at the crossing of the Eel River causes them to split into two groups of four, the one led by Wood and the other led by the party's original leader, Josiah Gregg. The Gregg party reportedly encountered great difficulties on its trip south, and Gregg died of starvation near Clear Lake.[1313]

Wood's 1856 account also includes a description of encounters with the Indians around Humboldt Bay, most especially a friendly meeting with the leader of the Humboldt Bay Indians, Ki-we-lat-tah.[1314]

It appears that for decades no one conversant in Humboldt County history was aware of the *Daily Alta California* article and the discrepancies between it and the Wood account that was published four times before the turn of the century. Then, in November 1901, a short item appeared in at least three local papers that alluded to yet another version of the story.

The *Loleta Record*, the *Arcata Union*, and the *Ferndale Enterprise* all ran articles "in regard to the approaching death of Indian Coonskin Dick."[1315] The reports stated that

The Indian referred to is the son of old Coonskin, mentioned in L. K. Wood's narrative of the discovery of our bay. The Indian name of the old man was Kiweelattah, and it was he who cared for and saved the life of Mr. Wood after being torn by a bear, *on Eel river*, while on his way out from here in 1850. Mr. Wood had a picture painted of Kiweelattah, which is still in possession of David Wood at his home near Arcata.[1316] [emphasis added]

There was no mention that this report was directly at odds with the account Wood had published, and apparently no one who read the article remarked about it at the time. Perhaps it would have received greater attention if information from yet another source had been available—an account by someone who had actually observed Wood and the others on their journey to the south.

A Wiyot woman named Jane Sam was interviewed in the early 1920s when she was about 88 years old.[1317] She had been about 16 when she saw what she called the "L. K. Wood party" coming to Table Bluff from Humboldt Bay. Sam indicated that:

White men had 8 mules first whit[e] men seen that came to county came down through little River, came down to-word mad River, down to Penn [peninsula]. Was seen across the bay on North Jetty side could not get across went back by way of Mad River. Indians showed them trail to bucksport. another Indians took them to Eel River country from bucksport. When they got on Table

Ki-we-lah-tah, aka Coonskin (CPH, colorized by JR).

Jane Sam describes L. K. Wood being attacked by a bear on Table Bluff (JR).

bluff near singleys they was attacked by a grizzly bear L. K. Wood was this mans name, news spread around Humboldt bay that L. K. wood was bitten by a bear. Some Indians came back to see him. Was brought down to old singleys ferry now and was treated, doctored with Indians medicine by a Coonskin Indian, L. K. Wood after he got well came to Arcata (now) and made his home there. The rest of the man left and left L K wood alone here.[1318]

Jerry James, a noted Wiyot leader and Jane Sam's nephew,[1319] was interviewed about the same time as his aunt. Although not alive at the time of Gregg party's visit, he related that he had "heard" about L. K. Wood and other white people coming through "with mules or horses," and that L. K. Wood "was bitten by a grizzly bear and was treated by one Indian 'Coonskin' afterward."[1320]

In Sam's account, the Indian Ki-we-lat-tah that Sam refers to as "Coonskin" meets and cares for Wood at the future site of Singley's Ferry, a location on the Eel River near today's Fernbridge. Wood, however, claimed that the expedition met Ki-we-lat-tah farther to the north at the future site of King Salmon and found him to be a "very dignified and intelligent Indian." Wood added that in 1872 Ki-we-lat-tah was "still . . . living on the bay and has always been known as a quiet and friendly Indian."[1321] By then Wood had named his Arcata farm Kiwelattah and had commissioned a painting of the Indian leader by Stephen W. Shaw.[1322] Wood was also master of the Kiwelattah Grange, which was based in Arcata and whose name was probably chosen by Wood.[1323] These actions suggest that Wood felt something more than mere admiration for Ki-we-lat-tah. Based on Jane Sam's account, Wood's overriding motivation would have been gratitude, for the Indian had saved his life.

The Union Company that Wood joined was a troubled and troubling group. It included several members, one of whom was Captain Smith, who had been arrested for a murderous rampage in Napa and Sonoma counties that killed numerous peaceful Indians.[1324] Some of the arrestees had then jumped bail, joined the Union Company, and headed to Humboldt Bay.[1325] Speaking of the company, Wood in 1872 claimed that

> . . . four of the recruits were arrested for murder (Indian killing,) which delayed us. (Six should have been arrested, and

five of the six hanged, as they never quit Indian killing, but kept it up after reaching here, which was the first cause of our Indian troubles.)¹³²⁶

In 1851 Captain Smith, freed from his incarceration after being charged with murder and now living on Humboldt Bay, led an unprovoked attack on a Wiyot village that killed most or all of the inhabitants, leaving one Indian "perforated with sixteen bullets."¹³²⁷ By then, another member of the Union Company, W. H. Sansbury, had shot and killed two Indian boys on the shore of the bay.¹³²⁸ Among the various groups of whites who had come to establish themselves on Humboldt Bay, L. K. Wood had managed to affiliate with the most problematic one of all.

Over 170 years have passed since L. K. Wood and his companions made their trip from the Trinity River. During that time one account, Wood's narrative, has been used almost exclusively to describe events along the way. But what of the other reports, which contradict Wood's published version and raise questions about why he would have told the story he did? There are reasons why Wood may have trod lightly on the truth. Foremost is the series of murderous activities conducted by members of the Union Company, both before the group's formation and afterward on Humboldt Bay. Wood's "official" history of these events distances him from the perpetrators but may have also been an attempt to obscure his complicity. We are also left to wonder if Wood knew more about Josiah Gregg's death than he revealed in his account, which is the only report we have of the event.

In the end, two questions are left unanswered. First, why would Wood give two vastly different stories about his trip and his encoun-

The Bear Buttes, where L. K. Wood was almost certainly not attacked by bears, punctuates the skyline north of Garberville (JRC).

ters with the bears? Second, why would a 16-year-old Wiyot woman have concocted another contradictory account that was identical to what three local newspapers printed as known fact? Accepting either Veritas's information or Jane Sam's report requires a huge paradigm shift in most people's understanding of Humboldt history. But how, after reading them, can we still believe the carefully calibrated story that Wood presented to us as fact?

As Thomas Cowper reminds us, the "truth lies somewhere," but all too often lies have lain closer at hand. We now have reason to believe that Wood's words, like a faulty compass, are not to be trusted within the geography of the past.

# Chapter 18

# Miranda

*Meet me on my vast veranda*
*My sweet, untouched Miranda*
*"We Both Go Down Together"*
      —The Decemberists

Were it not for some calligraphic confusion on the part of the United States Postal Service, the town of Miranda would have been called Mirada, as applicant Augusta "Gussie" Schumacher Monroe[1329] had (perhaps with overly ornate handwriting) requested. Instead, the small town on the South Fork Eel has had to endure being confused with the fifth largest moon of the planet Uranus, which does not even have a zip code.

The elevated, open flat upon which Miranda developed indeed left the town (and her verandas) untouched by floods. It was earlier the site of Tcis-tci-bi, a Sinkene village "opposite [the] mouth of Salmon creek." The Sinkene Indian named Briceland Charlie told Goddard that "this is the last [village] south of Charlie's people."[1330] After Charlie returned from the reservation he built a ne-gik here; this was "a large, round, conical house used for dancing."[1331]

The early history of white occupancy of the area is muddled. A family named Sanford are the first named white residents but their all that is known about their arrival date is that it preceded that of the Logan family, which arrived in 1874.[1332] Various sources claim the location was initially called Jacobson Valley,[1333] but that name doesn't appear in print until July 1889.[1334] Jacobson himself is mentioned in 1885 as having "valuable timber" there. He reportedly had tilled the nearby ground and was "putting out . . . the most choice varieties of fruit." A Mr. Williams resided on the farm. Adjacent to Jacobson's parcel on the north was the property of James and Melissa Wilds, who already had "an excellent orchard and a good grain farm well cultivated; also valuable timber lands."[1335] Melissa Wilds had previously been Melissa Sanford;[1336] she was probably part of the family that had been the first whites to live in the vicinity.[1337] Jacobson is not given a first name in the 1885 report but he is mentioned as being from Eureka.[1338] This probably makes him Meyer Jacobson, who "for a number of years" had a "boot and shoe business in Eureka." He died in Portland in 1894.[1339]

Clarity comes to the area's history only after several members of the Logan family arrived in the 1870s and developed ranches in the area. (See sidebar 1.)

In 1876 the first Miranda schoolhouse was built "on the bank of the South fork of the Eel River." The location may have been too close to the river for wintertime comfort, for 1888 a new school was established high on the Miranda flat.[1340] Building it became a community event. According to Jane Logan:

> The few neighbors got together and selected a site for a school. Then they got out lumber and planed it, got windows and built a school house and made good desks and [a] blackboard.[1341]

A far cry from Jacobson's Valley: Miranda as a tourist stop on the Redwood Highway and hangout for South Fork High School students (THPO, colorized by JR).

### 1. The Logans Take the High Ground

In 1870 Albert Logan came west on horseback. He was 21. He rode to the South Fork Eel, claimed some land across the river from the future site of Phillipsville, and went to work. Within four years he "had built a good house and barn and out-houses, fenced a field, and digged [sic] a well. He [also] had an orchard started." Later Albert fetched his brother, Chester, from Illinois.[1342]

Another Logan brother, John Wesley, and his wife, Amanda Ruth, decided in 1874 to join the precursor brothers in southern Humboldt. John "had farmed at home from the time he could reach up to the plow handles." Before they left Illinois the couple sold most of their possessions, including horses, cattle, and a gang plow. Besides John and Amanda the party included Martha McDaniel, Amanda's mother; three Logan children, Arthur, Martha, and Foster; and a woman named Burdine Riggs. They traveled with an emigrant train for "nearly a month" before they reached San Francisco:[1343]

Thence they made their trip up the coast in the old steamboat "Pelican," and from there proceeded by stage to Rohnerville, continuing from that point as far as Rio Dell in a lumber wagon. The Rohnerville teamster who had brought them so far would not go on, being afraid of being caught in a winter storm.[1344]

The Logans were still miles from their destination, but then, according to one account,

. . . Uncle Albert and a couple of Indians came in a big dug-out boat 36 feet long. The river was high. They had to pole the boat and it was very slow going. Grannie and Arthur and Martha walked along the bank much of the time. It was December 15th when they got to Uncle's farm home which was across the river from what is now the Combs place.[1345]

John Logan then considered "two prospective places for a home." One was on the west side of the South Fork, about a mile southwest of the Miranda townsite. The second was on the east side of the river, just north of what would become downtown Miranda. Logan chose the latter "because he thought the school would be on this side of the river." He bought the property from Bill Sellars, a "young bachelor [who] was homesick for the East." By the following July, Logan "had the house built, a good garden raised, the wheat cradled, and bound in sheaves and some land cleared for a vineyard."[1346]

Miranda Post Office, 1908. Jane Logan long served as postmaster[1347] ( JR).

This bridge across the South Fork, shown in 1925, connected Miranda with Salmon Creek and other locations west of the river (FMC, colorized by JR).

It was now 1875. There was another resident in the newly built Logan house, a daughter named Jane,[1348] who became the family's first Humboldt County native. Eighty-nine years later she wrote an account of the Logans' first quarter century on the South Fork that forms the basis for much of this account. Even as a child Jane was attentive and retentive, so that she could recall such events as when a

> . . . crowd of Indian women came and sat on the ground and threshed wheat with their fingers. Father fastened a handmill on the wall where he ground the wheat. Mother had a round wooden sieve which she shook the flour through. I ground many a pan of wheat when I was small. The next year the sheaves of wheat were laid on a clean-swept barn yard and the horses went round and round and tramped out the wheat. Father used to take a pack-load of farm produce to Garberville or to Blocksburg (two horses packed) and bring home needed supplies such as nails, windows, coffee (beans), brown sugar, salt, shirting, lead, calico and thread.[1349]

On one occasion John Logan took a single pack horse named Bill to Blocksburg, traded his produce for two 50-pound sacks of flour and a keg

> of syrup, loaded them on Bill and headed for home. All went well until "Bill reached for a bite of poison oak leaves when the shaley rock caused him to slip on the steep hillside." Down tumbled Bill, over and over, until "there was nothing left of his pack but splinters and a coat of syrup and flour." The next day the Logan children came out to see the disheartening mess, realizing that for a while this was as close as they would get to having pancakes. But "anyhow," Jane said, "we were glad Bill got home alive.[1350]
>
> The 1880s saw significant developments on the elevated flat. The Reverend Joel Burnell arrived by horseback from the Hydesville area and organized a church. The date he did so is uncertain, but beginning in 1882 camp meetings were conducted in the vicinity; the first of these sent its hymns soaring over the South Fork from "a big grove of redwoods at the mouth of Salmon Creek." Subsequent revivals were held on the riverside flat north of, and 113 feet below, the Miranda townsite at what later became the Stephens Grove. For these events the Logans would take the family organ down the hillslope to buttress the singing.[1351]
>
> The road between the mouth of the South Fork and Garberville was completed in 1885,[1352] providing access by wagon to the population centers of the lower Eel and Humboldt Bay. John Logan promptly bought a wagon. Not only could he now transport his produce to faraway destinations, but he could also take far larger loads than when he was limited to Bill and other pack horses.[1353] Living high on the Miranda flat now revealed another of its advantages, for the start of the trip was all downhill.

But Logan indicated that there was soon trouble at the new school:

> The first teacher was Miles Dean from Boston, a fine, frail, elderly single man. Because he was against the idea of "squaw men" a bunch of big "bullies" . . . rode up to school one day, booted and spurred and armed with clubs or guns, and beat the teacher until he was no longer able to keep school. The older boys raised a window and helped the children out [who were] so scared they ran all the way home. There was no more school for quite a while. . . .[1354]

By 1887 a new activity had developed on the South Fork Eel: selling timberland. According to an October report:

> The Eel River country is attracting a great deal of attention just now. Every claim worth taking for its timber seems to have been filed on. A number of claims have been sold at prices from $3,000 to $6,000. Among those who have parted with good redwood claims recently is Mr. John Logan. . . .[1355]

Not all the interest was in timber claims. In the 1890s John W. Monroe and his wife

As the road through Miranda improved, roadside businesses popped up (RGC, colorized by JR).

Gussie purchased 540 acres on the Miranda benchland that included what later became the business district of the town.[1356] At least part of the property had earlier belonged to Jacobson. Gussie had been the first white girl to live in Garberville, arriving there in 1873 at the age of three.[1357] In 1889[1358] she married John Monroe, who owned a soda bottling works in Fortuna.[1359] His father, Alonzo Judson Monroe, served a term a Humboldt County District Attorney.[1360] In October 1899 newspaperman David Gordon traveled down the South Fork, taking note of the Monroe property, which had grown to 800 acres. The ranch was run by Oscar Kerry, and Gordon indicated that

> . . . the apple crop is large this year, and if it was nearer to Mr. Monroe's Fortuna cider mill and bottling works it could be made a very profitable one. But as the distance between the two points is over 40 miles the expense of transportation will absorb much that would otherwise go to the profits side of the enterprise. It is presumed that much of the crop will be stored at or near the mouth of the South Fork and from thence [sic] be taken by boat to Scotia landing, or perhaps only to the new one opposite Pepperwood bottom.[1361]

John W. Monroe died in 1902,[1362] leaving Gussie with seven children and the Miranda property. Gussie rented all but three acres of the ranch to the Garberville Mercantile Company (GMC) after it was formed in 1911. The GMC operated a stage line between Garberville and Dyerville; Miranda, which was roughly the

# Miranda

route's halfway point, became the changeover stop for the horse teams. The company had barns and sheds and used the ranch's acreage to provide hay for the stage horses.[1363] William R. Jones, who had resided in Miranda since 1888, married the widowed Gussie Monroe in 1910.[1364] He subsequently served as the GMC's Miranda hostler.[1365]

August 26, 1905, was a red-letter day for the community, since as of that date locals could send or receive letters, red or otherwise, from their own post office.[1366] The mix-up that resulted in the office being called Miranda rather than Mirada actually proved fortuitous in the 21st century, by which time "mirada" had become an offensive slang term meaning "chick, babe, hot, sexy."[1367] Far better to live in Miranda, with its obscure but bland reference to a Uranian moon and to a character in Shakespeare's *The Tempest*.

Quietly, newly named Miranda had snuck into the 20th century. Like other towns along the South Fork, the opening of the Redwood Highway and the accompanying influx of automobile tourists changed the business dynamic of Miranda, so that by the 1920s, food and lodging accommodations had popped up along the roadside like mushrooms after a fall rain. It helped that the Stephens Grove, on the flat just north of town, was added to Humboldt State Redwood Park in 1922 to honor Governor William D. Stephens. In 1921 Stephens was confronted with the Redwoods Preservation Bill, which provided $300,000 for purchasing southern Humboldt timberlands. He vacillated about approving it, claiming the money was needed for education. Finally, an exasperated William Kent, congressman and member of the Save-the-Redwoods League, roared at him, "Hell, Bill! Close the schools. The kids would

Gray's, surrounded by Redwood Highway greenery. Pies from Miranda-grown apples were probably served for dessert (THPO, colorized by JR).

A later version of the Miranda Post Office, 1910 (CPH, colorized by JR).

love it, and they'd make up the work in a couple of years. If we lose these trees, it will take 2,000 years to make *them* up!" Given this new perspective on state funding priorities, Stephens signed the legislation, helping to assure that redwood groves, like the one to be named for him, would be added to the park.[1368]

By the late 1920s the highway near Miranda featured both the Maple Hills Cabins, with 1.5 miles of river frontage, and the Miranda Auto Camp at the center of town. In 1929 the Miranda Store took up residence in a new building, and in the 1930s the Mountain Coffee Shoppe and service station, Maple Hills Cabins, and Riley's Redwood Resort (later called Forest of Arden) were added to the local lineup. Later additions included Faulkner's Redwood Lodge and the Whispering Pines Motel. And, for those who wanted more rustic accommodations, there was still camping at the Stephens Grove. Being situated on lower ground than Miranda, the grove was damaged by the 1955 flood, and then the 1964 flood obliterated 99 percent of the campground,[1369] which was never rebuilt.[1370]

By 1925 Miranda was attracting more than tourists. That fall, the South Fork Union High School opened with students attending classes in four tents. An actual schoolhouse was completed in 1929. It was torn down in 1955 and replaced a structure still in use in 2020.[1371] The 1888 elementary school operated until 1935, when it burned down. A preexisting one-room frame structure was pressed into school service; first one room was added, then another. By 1954 there were so many students that some were taught in the Miranda Grange Hall and at Payne's Restaurant. Later that year a new, six-classroom schoolhouse was completed.[1372]

Governor William D. Stephens's reward for approving $300,000 to purchase southern Humboldt redwoods: a grove just north of Miranda (THPO, colorized by JR).

The Forest of Arden Resort offered spartan seating and an outdoor fireplace (THPO, colorized by JR).

The high school district was large. It served students from as far away as Shelter Cove, Ettersburg, Dyerville, Blocksburg, and Whitlow, and it extended southward into Mendocino County to reach Piercy and Reynolds.[1373] If students complained about the long bus ride, they needed only to be reminded of John Cathy, who lived with his family on the outskirts of Miranda in the 1880s. Once a year he drove his team and wagon along the primitive roads into Springville (Fortuna) for the family's annual shopping trip. It took John two days to reach town, one day to do all the shopping, and two more days to get back. On the fifth day of his trip his children "waited patiently for the sound of the wagon and horses coming up the hill," because they knew they would each get a bag of candy. Decades later John's daughter Rose recalled the trips, and the reward—for it was a sweet memory.[1374]

# Chapter 19
# Salmon Creek Area

Salmon Creek, one of the main tributaries of the lower South Fork Eel, never contained a town, but its topography dictated that an enclosed community would develop there once ranchers discovered the area's attributes. Seen on a map, the drainage resembles an outstretched hand reaching westward, with the north and south forks of the creek and their offshoots representing the fingers, which seem to be clawing their way up the eastern side of Elk Ridge.

The watershed was long a part of the homeland of a Sinkyone tribal group called the Sinkenes. Most of their villages in the drainage were either along the main stem (or South Fork) of Salmon Creek or on its North Fork.[1375] To the west were upland prairies—hunting and gathering areas—that rose to the top of Elk Ridge (called Dja-tcun-kuk by the Sinkenes)[1376] and then spilled over the western side of a ridgeline that was punctuated by a series of picturesque buttes. A system of trails, mapped in 1874 but probably dating back to Sinkene times, crossed the ridge and also ran along its top, connecting the Mattole and South Fork Eel watersheds.[1377]

Briceland Charlie, who was Pliny Goddard's Sinkene informant, mentioned three locations along Elk Ridge: Dickson Butte (Ses-tco), "rock stand up" (Kin-nah-das-ste), and Kos-kus-tco-tug-gut. At the last, ". . . they burn dead. Burn in one hour. Pile up all kinds of dry wood."[1378]

Charlie also indicated that the "soul" of a dead Sinkene went to a specific location based on the type of death:

> When they die with sickness the soul goes ba gan way across the ocean. . . . When get killed with arrow they go ya bi toward east. . . . When snake bite he goes same place. Don't know what place go when drowned. They say got a great big valley full of acorn soup. The dead folks come there to eat.[1379]

The Sinkenes, who lived in proximity to Elk Ridge, developed a very successful strategy for hunting the ridge's namesake species. According to Charlie, his people

> Used to run after elk. Big one he gives up about noon. Little one about 4 o'clock. Sometimes little one he get away. All [of the Sinkenes] run after and holler, 5, 10, 20 miles then [the elk] stand still let man come up slope and shoot him. He gives out he can't run anymore. Don't chase deer just elk.[1380]

Another hunting technique, used for both deer and elk, was to fence a quarter-mile section of trail with brush and then tie to trees about 40 ropes across the trail. The deer and elk were then driven along the trail and, tripped by the ropes, "several were sometimes caught at [on] one drive."[1381]

Among the first whites to acquire land at Salmon Creek were brothers David and William Dixon, who patented their first parcels in 1876. A portion of Elk Ridge came to be known as Dickson Butte, probably an imperfectly spelled attempt to honor the brothers.[1382]

Salmon Creek canyon, looking towards the buttes, 1908 (EDC, colorized by JR).

Over the next few decades, a handful of ranching families came to own most of the land in the upper Salmon Creek drainage. The 1911 county map shows large parcels belonging to L. M. Burnell, George Washington Hunter, John Nelson, Sarah Kinsey, and Waddington and Samuels.[1383]

There were also some smaller holdings. In 1906 Fred Duckett patented 160 acres north of Salmon Creek and west of Mill Creek.[1384] His sister, Annie,[1385] had married John Henry Hunter,[1386] whose brother, George Washington Hunter, was once the Humboldt County District Attorney and later a superior court judge. In 1900 Judge Hunter purchased 1,700 acres of grazing land on Elk Ridge, at the top of the Salmon Creek drainage, along with all the stock that were grazing on it.[1387] The judge, "with the assistance of his brother John . . . [carried] on a very extensive sheep and cattle raising business."[1388] The Ducketts, however, lived in a rustic shingle and lapboard cabin that suggests a financial struggle for a family trying to make do on a 160-acre ranch. Their neighboring rancher Judge Hunter, on the other hand, lived in Eureka, where he and his family occupied a monumental Queen Anne-Eastlake mansion that still stands, albeit in disarray, to this day.[1389]

The Ducketts lived about three miles up the Salmon Creek canyon. Above them were lots of livestock but few people. Charles Myers became aware of this one day in March 1912 when on his way down from Elk Ridge. At about 3 P.M. his Colt revolver fell from his holster, struck a rock, and discharged, the bullet striking him in the right leg. Myers needed to find help, but his leg was broken and it was slow going. His wound forced him to lie on his back and push himself over steep and rugged terrain. Twice Myers had to crawl across Salmon Creek. At 1:30 the next morning, Myers finally "reached a cabin where he was given all possible aid" and then taken to first to Phillipsville, then to Miranda, and lastly to the Union Labor Hospital in Eureka. He was attended by two doctors and was expected to soon recover. It had taken Myers over ten hours to reach help.[1390]

Although there were few inhabitants in the Salmon Creek drainage, there were enough families to require a school. Helen Thomas Pierce recalled her days as a student in the 1910s:

> Our first school was held in an old pioneer cabin on the Samuels ranch. It was about a mile and a half from our house and Bill [her brother] and I walked to and from school. Sometimes there would be deep snow or mud, and sometimes dust. . . . Our schoolhouse was one room and small. The roof leaked and the walls were falling apart, but no one criticized it, and in the warm spring months we really liked it, and liked playing on the shore of the pretty little pond nearby. . . . This lasted for a whole year and then something happened to the school—either it fell down or was burned—I don't remember which, but the next year we went to school in Lindley's barn. In the wintertime a horse or two shared it with us. We had no school furniture, but disposed of ourselves along the manger or wherever we could find a place to sit. We had no blackboard, no stove, no seats, no nothing! At recess on a cold day we would run to the house and

The young Duckett sisters have their hands full (CPH, colorized by JR).

warm up. It got pretty chilly after winter started, so the parents got busy and started a schoolhouse. . . .[1391]

It is unclear what this school was called. In 1929 the Oakdale School, located on the flat between Mill Creek and Salmon Creek, began operation.[1392] Jim Thomas attended the Oakdale School in the 1930s. Jim and two other boys rode horses to school, as did June Lindley. Gordon Tosten rode a mule.[1393] For some it was a three-hour ride, and the tired animals were kept in a three-sided barn. All of the other students walked to the school. Jim claimed that "we always had good teachers. . . . We were there to learn. . . . The Ten Commandments were on the wall and we had to know them."[1394] He also recalled school sports:

We didn't have much of an area to play baseball. If the ball wasn't hit foul, it either went over the fence into the road or over the bank into Salmon Creek. . . . We had what was called a "playday" with all the other schools at South Fork. Once every year we gathered and competed in running, jumping, etc. They laughed at our little bunch as some didn't have track shoes and still other of us went barefoot, but we always came away with the majority of the ribbons.[1395]

Helen and Jim Thomas were part of a family that lived in Salmon Creek for decades. It took considerable effort, however, for the Thomases to obtain their ranch. (See sidebar 1.)

Not many windows on one side of the Oakdale School (HCHS, colorized by JR).

## 1. Where there's a will . . .

John Nelson acquired a small ranch three miles west of Bear Buttes[1396] in about 1879. He added to the property until he owned some 1,700 acres. Around 1890 Charles Seymour Thomas and his wife Ella went to work for Nelson, who was a bachelor. Charles, a carpenter, built barns, outbuildings, and fences, while Ella became the cook and housekeeper. A year later the Thomases moved to Briceland, where Charles built a big house for their family. He also did carpentry for others and became both a notary and a justice of the peace.[1397] According to his daughter Helen, Charles Thomas

> . . . had a whole set of law books and he'd read all of them, and everybody had the greatest faith in his ability to decide what was right. He was called Judge Thomas but he wasn't really a judge.[1398]

Nelson and Thomas developed a close and trusting relationship, and for several years "Nelson would sign without reading any paper Thomas might present to him." By December 1913 "Nelson was single, about 68 years of age, and in poor health." He decided he couldn't stay on the ranch. Thomas offered to try to find a tenant, but when that attempt failed, he arranged to rent the ranch himself. Thomas had also "invited Nelson to come and live with him as one of the family" and this Nelson promptly did. Since Thomas was a notary public, he drew up the lease agreement. Nelson then asked Thomas to prepare his will. It stipulated that two of Nelson's friends should be given $500 each, that the Thomases' children were each to receive $1,500 each, and that Charles and Ella were to have "the residue of the estate," which of course included the ranch.[1399]

At Nelson's suggestion, two of the Thomases' sons, Adrian and Rex, moved to the ranch to run it. They were still fairly young, so their parents came up from Briceland every couple of weeks to check on their work.[1400]

So things went for about 15 months. Then Nelson heard from a friend "that Thomas was claiming to have a deed to the property." Nelson asked Thomas for the document and was told that it was at a bank in Eureka. Nelson, by now apprehensive, saddled up, and "although feeble, rode 90 miles on horseback to the bank, only to be "denied inspection of the document." After riding back the 90 miles to Briceland, Nelson checked with a second notary, who had also been involved in the completion of the legal documents, and learned that one of the papers had indeed been a deed. Nelson, who had believed he had only signed the rental agreement and the will, promptly moved from the Thomases' house and contacted an attorney.[1401]

On May 10, 1915, Nelson conveyed his property to Charles Lowrey, a bartender in Briceland,[1402] and the deed was recorded the next day. On May 21 the Thomases recorded their deed, which Nelson had signed in December 1913. Four days later Nelson sued the Thomases to invalidate their deed.[1403]

Nelson won his case in the trial court. The Thomases then appealed the verdict, but the District Court of Appeal affirmed the lower court's decision. By now it was March 1918. The Thomases asked for a rehearing; it was denied in April.[1404] A month later John Nelson died.[1405]

Helen Thomas was a young girl when these events transpired, but 60 years later she provided her family's version of the events. She indicated that Nelson had talked with the Briceland storekeeper, whose brother "was a lawyer of somewhat doubtful character." The brother learned about the deed that Charles Thomas held, but which had not been recorded. The brother then convinced Nelson that Thomas "had contrived to get Nelson's ranch away from him." The brother then talked Nelson into signing a paper that he claimed would force Thomas to give the ranch back to him. The paper was actually a deed to the ranch.[1406] The Briceland storekeeper was F. L. Kehoe, and in Eureka there was indeed a lawyer named William Kehoe, who, with his partner, J. F. Coonan,[1407] and two other attorneys represented Nelson in his lawsuit.[1408] If Helen Thomas's story is correct, William Kehoe had named the Briceland bartender, Charles Lowrey, as the only person listed on the second deed in order to shield the identity of the person who would actually take over the property, which was Kehoe himself.

Now Nelson was dead, and it was time to settle his estate. There were two wills to probate, the one from 1913 that left almost everything to the Thomases and a will from 1915 that was apparently executed after Nelson came under the influence of William Kehoe.[1409] The 1915 will gave the estate to Fred Fearrien, Leopold Grothe, Charles Lowrey, and William Kehoe.[1410] Fearrien and Grothe had testified at the Nelson-Thomas trial.[1411] They were both Briceland residents.[1412]

Litigation resumed, and in February 1919 the 1913 will was declared valid. By then, the Thomases had reportedly paid over $10,000 in legal fees to obtain most of Nelson's estate.[1413] Now the rest of the Thomas family moved from Briceland to Salmon Creek and joined Adrian and Rex, who had continued running the ranch through almost four years of litigious turmoil.[1414]

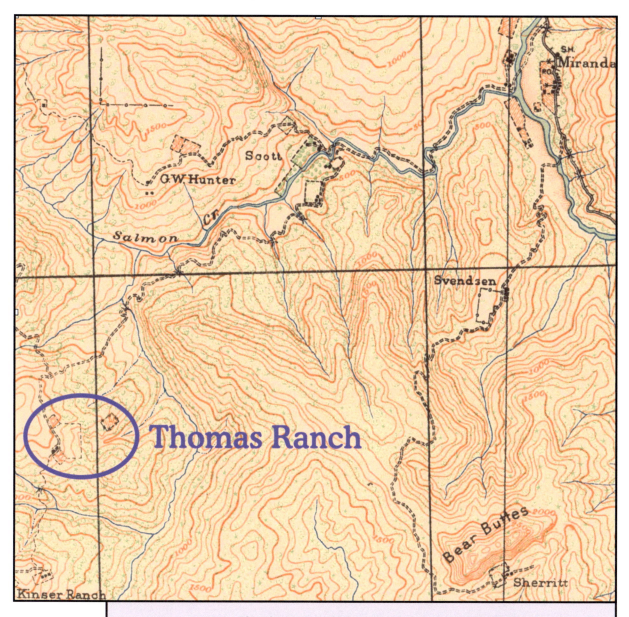

The Thomas Ranch, far up Salmon Creek, 1921 (CE).

The Thomases were left to wonder how much they had gained in the process. Helen Thomas recalled that

> . . . the house we were to live in was <u>OLD</u>. It was built on a steep sidehill of pure rock. In the winter the rain would run straight down this hill, across the back porch, and into the kitchen, but when we moved there, it was the dry season, so we gave that no thought. From the back porch you entered a dark little kitchen, simply furnished with a lopsided wooden sink and a huge black stove.[1415]

The fireplace chimney was made of sticks, rocks, and clay. There were only two bedrooms, and according to Helen, they were "<u>Small</u>." One of them had no windows. Carpenter that he was, Charles Thomas soon enlarged the house with his sons' help.[1416]

It took years for the Thomases to pay off the $10,000 they owed for the lawsuit. Charles contracted diabetes and died. None of the family could go to the funeral in Eureka because the Thomases had no car and it was too expensive for any of them to make the trip. Needing money, the family sold the bark from the tanoaks that dotted the ranch. They bought a car and for a time used it to deliver beef from cattle that they slaughtered.[1417] The Thomases ran also sheep, and to open up rangeland for a flock in the 1930s, they girdled and killed the Douglas-firs on the property, only to learn a decade later they had destroyed tens of thousands of dollars' worth of sawtimber.[1418]

Despite these difficulties, the Thomases hung onto the ranch for several decades. In the late 1960s two local men, Jim Johnson and Kenny Wallen, bought the ranch and subdivided it. Their timing was just right. The back-to-the-land movement was heading into high gear, and many young people wanted to move from the city to the country. The Thomas Ranch parcels became a popular destination.[1419]

In 1968 JoAnn and Don Bauer drove up from Berkeley during spring break. They liked the location, and joining with another couple, they bought the first 40-acre parcel in the new subdivision. There was a sheep barn on the property, likely built by Charles Thomas some 70 years ago. The barn later blew down during a "terrible wind storm."[1420]

A San Francisco commune called the Magic People bought 40 acres up the road from the Bauers' place.[1421] It included the old Thomas ranch house, but the Magic People spread out and lived "all over" the property. Among the residents were brothers John and Peter Kaufhold and their partners, Julie and Barbara. The brothers "built simple, beautiful wood cabins and raised their kids on the land."[1422]

In the 1970s, when Helen Thomas, by then Helen Pierce, looked back on her years at the ranch, she recalled memories of a mostly happy childhood. When her carpenter father built a large dining room on the south side of the house, he filled the wall with dozens of small window panes and built shelves in front of them. Helen's older sister Marguerite loved flowers, and

> . . . one year she bought cyclamen seed, and at the end of the second year all these shelves were filled with flowering plants in shades of red, pink, and white. One of the loveliest sights I've ever seen.[1423]

# Chapter 20

# Myers Flat

The "flat" at Myers Flat is bounded on three sides by the South Fork Eel. It points southwestward, not too high but high enough to require the river to loop around it. The flat was called Ken-tes-cho-be by George Burtt, a Lolahnkok Indian who was born at Bull Creek. Burtt indicated that unlike many other flats along the main Eel and South Fork, this one was "never forested."[1424]

On the northwestern part of the flat was a Sinkene village called Todunni ("water sings"). A large California laurel grew at Todunni, but the entire site was washed away. Across the South Fork from the flat was another Sinkene village, Gutta-bun-dun, where there was a deep hole in the riverbed. There was "a yitco [dance place] and a large hollow tree in which a family used to spend the winter." Pliny Goddard's Sinkene informant Briceland Charlie lived at Gutta-bun-dun when a boy.[1425]

Gladys Nomland's main Sinkyone informant, Jack Woodman, told her that

> Once there was a big camp at Myers because we were told there was a war coming soon. All my people gathered there. The enemies came up on the upper side of the river and the chiefs talked, but while they were talking all their men began to shoot bows and arrows and the fight began. All the women and children ran down the sandspit on the lower side of the river and jumped in the river and tried to get away, but there was a high bank across the river on the other side and they couldn't get out. Some of them drowned, but most of them the enemy shot down while they were in the water. A few escaped, but it was a big killing, a big war. I don't know what they fought about, but my mother told me about it and every time she told it she cried, because all her people were killed there.[1426]

Charlie told of a battle at Myers Flat that was probably the same fight that Woodman described. In Charlie's version,

> One time Garberville fellows came to Myer's [sic] place and killed . . . all but George's [Burtt] father. After a year George's father gathered up eel river, Mattole & Blocksburg Indians and went over there and made even. They killed about 40 Garberville Indians. George's father took one scalp and brought it back. That made even.[1427]

Woodman also mentioned three fights between his Sinkyone tribe[1428] and whites—at Dyerville Flat, Bull Creek Flat, and an unnamed location about four miles downriver from Myers Flat. There was also a battle between the Sinkyones and "the Harris people and the Wailaki near the mouth of South fork."

In 1868 Elias and Sarah Myers paid $1,000 to a pair of men named Farris and Brock for squatter's rights to 160 acres on the South Fork Eel, and, using a 22-mule pack train,[1429] moved their possessions from Rohnerville to their new property.¹⁴³⁰ The land they acquired took up most of the Ken-tes-cho-be flat. By the time of their arrival, there were few Indians left in southern Humboldt County and apparently none at what eventually became known as Myers Flat.

Elias and Sarah had six children. Elias's bachelor uncle, Andrew, also lived with them. Five of the children eventually left the flat, but one, named U. S. Grant Myers¹⁴³¹ (he was born in 1864, during the high point of his namesake's military career), went to Heald's Business College in San Francisco in 1884 and then returned to live and work on the Myers homestead.¹⁴³²

In 1885 roaming reporter McTavish provided the *Humboldt Standard* with an account of the South Fork Eel. At "the Meyers [*sic*] Place," McTavish found a "farm owned by Mrs. S. D. Meyers containing 500 acres" that included a five-acre orchard and vineyard. In addition to the grapes in the vineyard, there were "peaches, apples, pears, figs and stone fruits of all kinds," along with "corn, wheat, oats and sweet potatoes in the fields." The "comfortable buildings" on the Myers farm made it "a good stopping place."¹⁴³³

The Myers ranch continued to make the news, both as a source of produce and as a source of comfort to travelers. An 1887 account mentioned "A. J. Myers [Uncle Andy] and Mrs. Sarah Myers, who keep the deservedly popular stopping place above the mouth of Canoe Creek...."¹⁴³⁴ The following year the *Rohnerville Herald* noted "the handsome and delicious fruit grown on the Myers farm ... [that] were sent to the Mechanics' Fair exhibit in San Francisco last autumn."¹⁴³⁵ In 1890 it was the *Ferndale Enterprise* proclaiming that

Myers Flat School, 1899 (HCHS, colorized by JR).

... the Myers farm . . . is a beautiful piece of property, as well as an excellent place to rusticate, and some of the finest fruit and vegetables, raised on Eel river are produced here.[1436]

The next year found Uncle Andy, Grant, and his brother Christy all busy on the farm,[1437] but Grant would leave before the end of the decade. (See sidebar 1.)

Sarah Myers died in 1903,[1438] followed by Uncle Andy in about 1907.[1439] Grant and Mattie worked at building up the farm and building a family. Of their five children, three were given unusual names. At least part of their daughter's name—Nevada California Myers—can be explained by the date of her birth, which was California Admission Day.[1440] U[lysses] S[idney] Grant Myers, Jr perpetuated a name that was common only in Myers Flat, but he asserted

### 1. Grant Goes North

In February 1898 Grant Myers took a leave of absence from the family farm and sought his fortune in the far north, traveling first to Tacoma, Washington, and then on to Skagway, Alaska, en route to the Klondike gold fields. He made friends with a man named Perry who had a 115-pound dog. Steamer fare between Tacoma and Skagway was $35 for humans and $8 for dogs, a bargain rate for large canines like Perry.[1441] Rather than crossing the daunting Chilkoot Pass, Myers went through nearby White Pass, a less demanding route that was nonetheless so hard on pack animals that it was known as the "Dead Horse Trail." White Pass also presented another danger: a criminal element that may have included the notorious Soapy Smith gang. Smith himself was killed the year of Grant Myers's trek during the so-called Shootout on Juneau Wharf.[1442]

Myers sledded over the mountains to a location he incongruously called "Windy oven," built his own boat, and came down the Yukon River, arriving in Dawson on June 18, 1898. There he took up placer mining.[1443]

In September 1899 the *Daily Standard* reported that "Uncle Andy" Myers was busy toiling in his vineyard by the South Fork, where he was raising a half-dozen varieties of grapes. The "tenants" of Andy's hillside grapery included "Sweetwaters, Catawbas, Muscats, Black Hamburgs, Isabellas and Missions." They were prolific producers: "clusters weighing three to six pounds are not uncommon," went the report, but on another subject the article was strangely silent.[1444] What of Andy's gold-seeking nephew, Grant?

The suspense ended exactly one week later when the *Enterprise* published a lengthy article entitled "Returned Klondiker," in which Grant Myers, having just arrived in Eureka on the *Pomona*, told of his experiences in the wilds of

U. S. Grant Myers (colorized by JR).

the Canadian north. Readers learned that Myers, while there, paid $1 for any of the three principal meats—beef, moose, or caribou—and that one miner friend "secured a claim which may make him a millionaire." Of his own finances, however, Myers said nothing. He also related that he had taken two dogs with him from Humboldt County to help in conveying his supplies from Skagway. One dog had contracted pneumonia and died, but the second, named "Rowdy," was "made of better stuff" and took the entire round trip with Myers, costing his master $4 for a railroad ticket back to Skagway while Grant paid $10 for his. It was unclear if Myers brought any gold back with him, but he did return with "a petrified mastodon's tooth weighing about five pounds."[1445]

Before Myers left for the frozen north, he had become betrothed to Mattie Smith. In March 1901, with Grant returned from the Klondike, they were married. Years later Grant admitted to having "met with an appreciable amount of success, clearing several thousand dollars" during his Klondike caper.[1446] The money apparently served as a sort of reverse dowry that he brought to the marriage.

That, and a dog named Rowdy and a petrified mastodon tooth.

his individuality by going by "Sid." Andrew Fay Myers's name no doubt honored "Uncle Andy," but in so doing it became the only "normal" name of the first four. Next came perhaps the oddest of the lot. Although his gravestone in the Myers Flat Cemetery shows him as "Leslie R. Myers," his true name was Lesser Roosevelt. He was born in 1910, when Teddy the Roughrider was the most famous man in the country, so it is easy to understand why someone named U. S. Grant Myers would want to honor another Republican president, adding the qualifier "Lesser" as a sign of respect for the "Greater" Roosevelt. Lesser dealt with his unusual name by becoming known as Les.[1447] Last came Willis Wayne Myers, born in 1915[1448] at a time when his parents' nomenclatural inspirations had apparently been exhausted.

By the time of Willis's birth, the Myers farm had "one-hundred acres under a high state of cultivation, with seven hundred bearing apple trees, and a young orchard of three hundred Bartlett pear trees." The Myerses also raised sweet potatoes, sweet corn, other vegetables, small fruits, and berries, along with having a dairy ranch, chickens, and hogs.[1449] To go with all this, in 1915 Grant and Mattie replaced their overnight stopping place with the Myers Hotel,[1450] the construction of which was probably stimulated by knowledge that the nascent Redwood Highway was routed directly through the Myerses' property.[1451] In fact, any road along the South Fork had to pass through the Myers family's domain, for their land stretched across almost the entirety of the flat, from the riverside up onto the hill slope to the northeast. In 1914 the only other property owner shown in the vicinity was Joe Stockel, whose small farm was wedged into the extreme eastern corner of the flat, with most of his parcel on the far side of the river.[1452]

The highway was built, and soon Grant Myers developed a plan to take advantage of his propinquity to the increased traffic that passed by his doorstep. (See sidebar 2.)

By 1927 Myers, as the place was then called, had become a tiny community, its business district including the Myers Hotel, the Myers Auto Camp, and the Myers Store,[1453] the latter operated by G. F. Cloney, who had bought the building and rebuilt it in 1925.[1454] The auto camp offered a row of small cabins nestled next to the redwoods at the north end of the flat. The store, as befit its location on the Redwood Highway, had a single gas pump.[1455] The hotel had ten guest rooms, ladies' and gentlemen's

### 2. The Imbiber's Badge

With the highway came more traffic—and an irresistible opportunity for Grant, who accordingly bought himself a tin sheriff's badge. Any time he needed money for a drink—which was often—he would put on his badge and wait behind a roadside redwood. When a car approached, Grant would jump out from behind the tree and block the road. He would confront the startled motorist, whip back the lapel of his coat to briefly show the badge, announce that he was the local sheriff, and inform the now nervous driver that he had been speeding. The driver now had a choice, according to "Sheriff" Myers. He could either come to court the next day, which meant an unexpected overnight stay at the Myers Hotel, or he could forfeit bail and give the $5 fine to Myers, who would deliver it to the court. Needless to say, the motorists always chose to hand over a five-spot to Myers. As the abashed automobilist drove off, Grant would amble over to the Myers store, hand the "fine" over to storekeeper G. F. Cloney, and be given a bottle of whiskey as his reward for catching another "car-driving criminal."[1456]

parlors separated by a double fireplace, and a single bathroom. Users of the solitary facility needed to be "quick about it." Grant Myers, who had acquired the nickname "Pap," regaled visitors with tales of variable veracity.[1457]

The years passed, and Myers expanded to accommodate the interests of tourists. By the 1940s Cloney's Cottages offered not only "ten new modern cottages all made from select redwood," but also "gas, oil, groceries, also eats." The "Myers Hotel and Restaurant" provided dining service, "detached showers and toilets," and "trailer space with showers, toilets, wash trays, water and electricity." At an unknown date a goosepen redwood near the northern end of the flat became an attraction first known as the "Doust Tree" and later as the "Shrine Tree," where motorists paid for the privilege of driving their cars through the narrow passageway at the base of its trunk. The River Vista Lodge provided not only proximity to the tree but also "completely renovated units, kitchens, gas heat . . . novelty store, fountain, [and] gas station."[1458] The facility was purchased in 1948 by two sea captains, Homer Gillette and Walter Nilson. Explaining the change of occupation, Gillette said,

> The sea is no place for family men. So we decided to sail a motor court for a change, and take our families along![1459]

Co-captain Nilson added,

> Running a place like this requires a somewhat different type of navigation, you might say, but we like it fine.[1460]

Myers Store: U. S. Grant Myers in front of gas pump (HCHS, colorized by JR).

# Myers Flat

Little did the captains realize that their nautical experience would put them in good stead when the South Fork washed across the flat twice in the coming decades.

A short distance south of the sea captains' lodge was the lumber business of four landlubbers. The Morrison and Jackson lumber company was started in 1947[1461] by two pairs of brothers. Harry Jackson conducted the logging operations, while brother Elbert supervised shipping. Harlan "Duke" Morrison managed the planing mill and his brother Walter ran the sawmill. The foursome were all former logging truck drivers. They logged about 90 percent redwood timber and 10 percent fir, doing selective cutting. Their main mill was at Salmon Creek, with a planing mill near the Shrine Tree at Myers Flat.[1462] The business was big enough that Morrison and Jackson shared a loading dock at the South Fork train station with several other mills.[1463] By 1952 there were nine mills in the general area.[1464]

Much later than many of the county's rural communities, Myers obtained a post office in 1949. It also received a change in its official name as it became Myers Flat.[1465] The 1950s saw the flat subdivided, and about 90 homes were built.[1466] Entertainment for the enlarged community was provided by a drive-in movie theater, installed near the center of the flat.[1467] By the mid-1950s Myers Flat had a population of about 475, served by two grocery stores, a hardware store, motel, restaurant, post office, school, church, and—a sure sign of success—a liquor distributorship and warehouse.[1468]

Just as Myers Flat hit its stride, the town was washed off its feet by the 1955 flood. Duke Morrison and family had a house at the northwest corner of the flat, near the river. As the rain came down in torrents and the river rose up, the family tarried. By the time the Morrisons

Tight fit in the Shrine Tree (JRC, colorized by JR).

decided to head for higher ground, the flood was washing across the lower flat. It was nearly half a mile to safety.[1469] The Morrison children held hands as they plunged into the swirling water. Carol "Mori" Morrison was a small child at the time. As she walked towards safety, the water rose to her armpits. The line of Morrisons held, and finally the family, including little Mori, made it to high ground near the highway.[1470]

Like the Morrisons, the planing mill survived the 1955 flood and also the larger one that came in 1964. But a couple of years later the wooden mill caught fire and burned down in about three hours. It was replaced by a steel structure and continued operation. In 1972 the Morrisons and Jacksons sold out to Fred Holmes, who kept the mill for two years before selling to Georgia-Pacif-

The boys at the Morrison-Jackson Mill, 1948 (HCHS, colorized by JR).

ic. The mill subsequently gained attention when it employed Lucille Arnot as general manager; it was a rarity to have a woman fill that position in the lumber industry. In 1978 Georgia-Pacific closed the mill, and the company auctioned off the buildings and equipment.[1471]

The Myers Resort Hotel also closed in the 1970s, finally reopening in 1990[1472] as the community focused increasingly on the tourist trade.[1473] The refurbished hotel was modernized to keep pace with the times. Instead of a single bathroom for all the guests, all the rooms now had en suite facilities. The his-and-hers parlors had been converted, along with the dining room, into a single large lobby.[1474] The conviviality engendered by the comingling of the sexes was tempered, however, by the absence of Grant Myers and his stories about the Klondike. Aware of this diminishment, the new owners of the hotel did the next best thing—they hung a large portrait of Grant in the new lobby.[1475]

And so, in a sense, there still was a Myers on the flat.

# Myers Flat

Pick-up sticks at the Morrison-Jackson Mill after the 1964 flood (HCHS, colorized by JR).

# Chapter 21
# Burlington

In 1878 Jimmy Carothers moved from Rohnerville to the South Fork Eel, taking up land at what would later be the north end of Burlington. He was then in close proximity to his father, Tom, who had homesteaded at the future site of Weott.[1476] A neighbor of Jimmy's, Nancy Burnell, recalled decades later that as a child she and her family "looked forward to his visits with delight, hoping he would bring his accordion and play. He often did."[1477] Jimmy, however, was noted by the locals for more than his musicianship. (See sidebar 1.)

In 1882 an interesting logging experiment occurred south of Jimmy Carothers's property, near the mouth of Canoe Creek.[1478] John Mowry, who held 160 acres of land there,[1479] and a partner named Randall began cutting redwood timber at a small steam-powered mill that received its water from a half-mile-long flume. Randall and Mowry cut the wood into cants and dumped them into the South Fork, the idea being that these relatively small sections of redwood timber would then float all the way to a point on the main Eel River near its mouth. From there the cants would be

> **1. Poor Man, Rich Man: Jimmy Carothers Insulates His Shack**
>
> When calling on neighbors near his homestead at Burlington, Jimmy Carothers cut a strange figure. His battered hat had lost all sense of shape, and the faded shirt he wore was so big it had to be tucked in folds and pinned together. His baggy, oversized trousers hung precariously by one strap of his suspenders. On his feet were a pair of mismatched shoes, one black, one tan, each a different size and both too large. It wasn't surprising that during his visits, Jimmy would claim any discard in sight: old bailing wire, frayed rope, dusty bottles, rusty tin cans and buckets, and especially pieces of string. He would carry off any and all such objects, muttering to himself that they were "valuable . . . very valuable."[1480]
>
> Jimmy took these items to his property, where he stored them in and around a weather-beaten hut that was nearly obscured by a thicket of brush and young redwoods. The shelter was a patchwork of boards and flattened tin cans; its dirt floor was covered by a selection of the stuff he'd collected.[1481] Nearby, Jimmy maintained a garden and apple orchard.[1482]
>
> The locals must have smiled when a sketch of Carothers appeared in Leigh Irvine's 1915 history of Humboldt County. It was the kind of vanity publication that charged a fee for printing someone's biography, and there, amazingly,

James (Jimmy) Carothers (LI, colorized by JR).

was a story about Jimmy, complete with a photo of him casting a bewildered glance at the camera. What a tale he had told the author, something about coming from a prominent family and being heir to a fortune. The most surprising thing of all was that he'd somehow found enough money to have the account printed in the book.[1483]

It was only much later that the skeptics got their comeuppance. When Jimmy eventually passed away, someone began searching around his shack. Hidden among its nooks and crannies were hundreds of gold pieces: $5, $10, and $20 coins. The hoard amounted to about $60,000, all of it sharing space with his "valuable" string and tin cans. It thus turned out that Carothers's story was true. His reclusive sister had similar tendencies. She had died in her run-down Eureka mansion two years earlier, leaving an estate that no one claimed. Either her brother had never learned of her death or felt that he had no need for additional wealth.[1484]

So it was that Jimmy had died far richer than anyone thought, poor only in the esteem of his friends.

taken to mills in Eureka for final sawing into lumber. But the cants didn't perform as expected; they grounded in the riverbed, requiring a team of horses to enter the river and pull them free. The work was dangerous for the horses, frustrating for the teamster, and expensive for Randall and Mowry. Soon the experiment was abandoned,[1485] thus for a time sparing some of the riverside redwood forest.

William Robinson patented land just south of Jimmy Carothers's place in 1884.[1486] Robinson had "a small water mill" on the 160-acre property and lots of redwoods. In the fall of 1887 he sold 150 acres of the parcel for $4,000, "keeping two houses

Burlington CCC camp, 1936 (HRSP, colorized by JR).

and [the] mill and perhaps a million [board] feet of timber."[1487] Robinson took some trees from the property but in exchange left his name; Robinson Creek flows through a gulch just north of Burlington campground. By 1914, when the route of the Redwood Highway was being mapped, A. Harden owned most of the Burlington flat. At the north end was a property owned by "Mrs. L. R. Carland" through which ran Robinson Creek. South of the stream Carland had an oat field; north of it she had an orchard, house, barn, and outbuildings. On her property, straddling

Early Burlington (CPH, colorized by JR).

Robinson Creek, was the "Old Saw Mill" that had belonged to Robinson. The original county wagon road, which on its way from Weott ran part way up the hill slope, dropped southwardly to run through Carland's property. When the Redwood Highway was built in the late 1910s, it was located closer to the river, just west of the mill.[1488]

With the new highway running through it, the location that later became Burlington got its start as a town about 1917. For a time it was known as "Tighe and Green's Camp,"[1489] a probable reference to the local logging operation. The first businesses, all in the vicinity of today's state park headquarters, were a general store, stage stop, butcher shop, and pool hall. R. C. Chapman logged the area in the 1920s, while Lawrence G. Chapman operated a tie camp, store, garage, and trucking business. Also present were a Pacific Gas and Electric substation and a Division of Highways maintenance station.[1490]

By 1925 there was enough activity in the general area to merit establishment of a post office. The contending locations were McKee's Mill and Tighe and Green's Camp, which were both located on the east side of the South Fork about a mile and half apart. McKee's Mill proved the winner, with the post office taking the name Weott in 1925.[1491] Then the Depression came, business was bad, and in 1931 with no post office to draw locals, Lawrence G. Chapman declared bankruptcy and sold what became known as Burlington to the State of California.[1492]

Following the 1937 flood the Civilian Conservation Corps (CCC) camp at Dyerville was moved to Burlington. Eighteen years later, after the next big flood, in 1955, the Humboldt Redwoods State Park headquarters followed the example of the CCC camp and made the same move.[1493]

When the CCCs arrived at Burlington, they realized they needed a recreation hall, but there wasn't money for one in the budget. A CCC building in Eureka that was serving as a warehouse was moved to Burlington to provide the shell of the recreation hall, but there was no floor. Captain Ennis, a resourceful officer, took matters in hand. First,

> . . . Ennis called the Holmes-Eureka Lumber Company, and told them that the Pacific Lumber Company was donating half the lumber for flooring if Holmes Eureka would donate the rest. They agreed, and then Captain Ennis called Pacific Lumber Company and told them that Holmes Eureka was donating half of the flooring if PL would donate the rest, which they did.[1494]

The Burlington CCC camp had four barracks to house 250 workers, many of them from Missouri. In addition to the recreation hall with its dazzling redwood floor, there was a cookhouse, dining room, bath house, hospital with resident doctor, and a library. At first some of the CCC workers from the Ozarks could make no use of the library because they couldn't read. So the CCCs hired Louis Soto as a part-time literacy instructor to teach them. While the CCC was at Burlington, its workers built what became the state park headquarters building and park staff houses.[1495]

By 1940 the park had a campground at Burlington, with a ranger assigned to supervise it.[1496] The facility was located just north of the town, with campsites placed among the stumps of an early-day logging operation. Today a row of bigleaf maples stands along the roadway in front of park headquarters, replacing, in a way, the missing redwoods. Nearby, the bustle of recreational vehicles has replaced the softer sounds of Jimmy Carothers's accordion music.

Cottage at Burlington, 1940 (HRSP, colorized by JR).

# Chapter 22
# Weott

About three miles upstream from its mouth, the aggradational activities of the South Fork Eel River created a broad alluvial flat above its east bank. Perhaps 300 yards wide, the flat meets a rapidly ascending slope that climbs eastward to the ridgetop. Somewhere on the flat was a Sinkene village called Sosnoibundun, the site of which was still marked by five housepits when the ethnographer Pliny Goddard and the Sinkene Indian Briceland Charlie visited the area in 1903. Charlie indicated that there was once a yitco, or dance house, at Sosnoibundun that he had danced in.[1497] When another ethnographer, C. Hart Merriam, drove by the locale with the Lolahnkok Indian George Burtt 20 years later, Burtt told him that the spot was called To-be-ah.[1498]

Thomas Carothers took up land on the flat in 1868,[1499] obtaining a patent for it in 1883. His property included most of the central portion of what later became the town of Weott. Thomas's son Jimmy patented land a short distance to the south in 1889.[1500] Thomas Carothers died in 1899 and Jimmy subsequently sold much of his father's property to Eureka attorney Louis M. Burnell.[1501]

It took a while for the locale to become a community. When Dwight Felt, Sr., traveled down the South Fork from Garberville in September 1895, he found "nothing in Weott except the homestead cabin of Jimmy Carothers,"[1502] which was actually located closer to Burlington than to Weott. In 1911 or 1912 a temporary town transpired about a quarter-mile north of the flat when a tanbark operation, known as Helm's [sic] Camp, began cutting tanoaks from there northward to the future site of the Women's Federation Grove. The cut bark was taken by wagon to South Fork where, with the rail line south still uncompleted, it was instead transported by train northward to Fields Landing, whence it was shipped by ship southward to ports on San Francisco Bay.[1503]

Information is sparse, but it appears that Helm's Camp was either taken over by one of the McKee brothers, either Bert or Ernest, or operated under contract with one of the McKees by John F. Helms, who co-owned a shingle mill at Holmes, on the main Eel River.[1504] In any event, Ernest McKee subsequently purchased "a 40 acre property at what would become the town of Weott." McKee, who previously operated tie camps in the Santa Cruz mountains and at Fruitland, not only produced railroad ties[1505] from his Weott property but also "operated a fairly good-sized shingle mill there." The flat was given the informal name of McKee's Mill.[1506]

McKee hauled his redwood products[1507] from Weott to the South Fork train station. As he levelled the redwoods on his Weott tract, McKee blasted out the resultant stumps and subdivided his property for home sites.[1508] Some of the new arrivals started with more modest accommodations; Walter J. Curry, who took over McKee's mill, began residency in Weott in 1916 while living in a tent. Eventually he came to own the mill and much of the town. Bob Johnson, who later owned Weott's store, also at first tent camped after he arrived in 1918.[1509]

A highway view of Weott, showing Schelling's packing house with its long roof at rear left (CPH, colorized by JR).

By the late 1910s the locale gained the first trappings of a town with the opening of two stores. At first both of them were in tents. Frank and Camelia Souza seemingly had an advantage with their general merchandise business, since Camelia was part of the Young family that had already established stores in Pepperwood and McCann. But they "lasted quick" and after starting 1917 they folded up their tent the following summer.[1510] Lasting longer was the J. E. Johnson store, which at first also had canvas walls when it opened some time between 1917 and 1919.[1511] Johnson supplemented his McKee's Mill business by driving a peddler's wagon to outlying locations and did well enough to move from his tent into an actual building. The Johnson family ran the store for decades, eventually relocating eastward a short distance up the hillside.[1512]

The Redwood Highway brought more business and more businesses to the flat. In 1923 Walter Schelling's hotel, a shoe repair shop, Joel Burnell's Shell gas station, and a combination ice cream-confectionary parlor lined the roadway. Just north of town, Shelling had an apple-packing house that when vacant was used as a dance hall. In 1924 came a sure sign of community success—a movie theater.[1513] That same year the McKee's Mill School opened.[1514] Then, inexorably, 1924 was followed by 1925, and with it came the community's great identity crisis. (See sidebar 1).

Having received its name and post office in 1925, Weott continued growing, so that by 1927 it had added a pair of barbershops, a dress shop, Harry and Mac Willet's grocery store, two butcher shops, and two additional service stations run by the Pesulas and the Frasers.[1515] Balancing these additions were two subtractions: in late July M. P. Dugan's shingle mill and 800,000 shingles burned up,[1516] and a few days later Schelling's hotel went up in flames.[1517]

At an unknown date Ernest McKee expanded

## 1. Losing Sight of Redview

On July 22, 1923, ethnographer C. Hart Merriam and his two daughters picked up George Burtt in Fortuna and drove south with him on the Redwood Highway. It was to become the most significant auto trip in the annals of Humboldt County ethnography, for along the way Burtt provided the names and descriptions of 62 places of significance for his Lolahnkok tribal group and the larger Sinkyone tribe of which it was a part.[1518] One of the first entries was for "To-be-ah," which Merriam recorded as the Sinkyone name for "Schelling Camp Flat," a "lumber camp, garden and orchard."[1519] It is likely no white had ever heard the Sinkyone word spoken before this.

Those whites who came to occupy the area had difficulty settling on *their* name for the place, having tried out Helm's Camp and McKee's Mill when those woods operations were the main activities on the flat. By the time of the Merriam and Burtt trip, Schelling Camp had joined the designation competition.

Two years later, despite the Schelling Camp attempt, McKee's Mill remained the preferred name, but that would not continue for long. The locals had applied for a post office and held a contest to decide what it should be called. Accordingly "the citizens put names of their choice in a ballot box in Johnson's store." The winning entry was suggested by none other than W. H. Schelling, but it was not his name nor that of his camp or his flat; instead it was "Redview."[1520]

Redview? The *Humboldt Times* article that disclosed this information also carried the dateline "Redview," yet nary a line of print was devoted to explaining the choice. Green there was aplenty to see in the foliage that dominated the area, and there was some blue if you went over and looked at the South Fork Eel. But there was no red visible anywhere unless it was the paint on some of the town's buildings. "Redwoodview" would have made sense, but "Redview" certainly didn't.

For the next few weeks the *Times* continued to carry stories from Redview, but apparently the Redviewians were having second thoughts. This led them to have a second naming contest, and this time a youngster, little Arabella McKee, came up with winner—she suggest calling the place Weott. Arabella believed she had chosen an Indian word meaning "the river," and she was partly right.[1521] The Wiyot Indians called the lower Eel River "Wiyot," and indeed the water that flowed past the newly named town of Weott indeed did eventually become part of the Wiyot River on its way to the sea.

The Weott post office was duly established on September 23, 1925, but during

Looking south through Weott to the wall of redwoods (THPO, colorized by JR).

the preceding two months Redview, on paper at least, maintained its tenuous existence. "Redview Child Fractures Arm" blared a *Times* headline on August 19;[1522] "Noted Musicians Camp at Redview" the *Times* told readers on August 25;[1523] "Noted Painter in Visit to Redview" was the report from August 29.[1524]

And then, except for an ad mentioning Redview on September 1, nothing. No announcement that Redview had ceased to exist. No advisory that the former town of Redview would henceforth be called Weott. And still no hint of where, in the vicinity, anyone could view anything red.

On September 22, 1925 the many-named community officially became Weott.[1525] There was no mention of the event in the *Humboldt Times*.

his Weott operations by adding a saw mill near his shingle mill. The mills were located at the eastern edge of the flat just south of Newton Road.[1526] Both were destroyed by a fire in July 1933.[1527] The losses were later balanced, after the repeal of Prohibition that December, when two saloons opened, along with a pool hall operated by Mae and Monte Wright.[1528]

In the 1930s Weott defied the Depression by being one of the liveliest spots on the Redwood Highway. Ed and Agnes Johnson's business was the "largest mercantile store in the area," with

No one went hungry in Weott (THPO, colorized by JR).

customers coming from Bull Creek, South Fork, Myers Flat, McCann, and other nearby communities. It also housed the post office. Their building was two stories tall, with groceries on the first floor and work clothes and shoes upstairs. For good measure, Johnson added a soda fountain later in the decade. Another multipurpose establishment was the Davises' Loma Vista, which contained the telephone switchboard, another soda fountain, an upstairs rooming house, and the "smallest bar on the north coast," which consisted of "six stools and no tables." Of larger capacity was Monty's Bar, considered the main watering hole for both highway travelers and locals. A seasonal regular was Charley "Wildcat" Kenny, who spent his summers atop nearby Grasshopper Peak as the fire lookout. While there he would let his fingernails and big red beard grow and then descend to Weott in the winter, where he would enliven the night life at Monty's by telling stories. If anyone disturbed his performances, "Wildcat"

would reach over and rake their necks with his clawlike nails. "Wildcat," indeed.[1529]

If someone wanted more than a liquid lunch, there was Mel Cotter's restaurant, John the Greek's café, Sam Wilkinson's Fireplace Restaurant, and a dining facility run by Arline and Reese Cathy. The tiny Loma Vista also served food in addition to alcohol; owners Ed and Nancy Davis imported attractive young women from Eureka to serve as waitresses,[1530] thereby making sure that all six barstools stayed occupied. Later came Parlotto's, which got its start in Weott before moving to Fortuna.[1531]

Other businesses active during the 1930s included Jim Cara's barbershop, the Park Edge Auto Court, the Burgess Shingle Mill, Bertha Prust's dress shop, and Frank Roberts's butcher shop. Bill Kearns operated a trucking service that served all of southern Humboldt. He started with Kleiber trucks that still used solid-rubber tires and then switched to Macks, which featured their distinctive bulldog hood

Bill Kern's truck carrying a full load, 1940 (THPO, colorized by JR).

ornament.[1532] Weott even had its own baseball team, appropriately called the "Tie Makers."[1533]

Besides baseball, there were other entertainments. One of the town's younger residents made sure of that. (See sidebar 2.)

Post-World War II Weott was noted for the appeal of the nearby redwoods and the South Fork Eel. Rambling reporter Chet Schwarzkopf noted that:

. . . at either end of the town, its main street . . . becomes a highway passing between massive fluted columns. . . . You literally can step out of Weott into the forest primeval in moments—nay seconds. Or you can meander through fragrant gardens and fruit orchards in back of the business district, down to the river, in almost as quick time.[1534]

### 2. Harold Fisher Put the "Whee!" in Weott

The Depression meant hard times for many folks along the South Fork. But those who lived in and around Weott could always look forward to various entertainments provided by one of the younger residents, Harold Fisher. The entire lower river was his stage. His productions were always comedies.

During his early years Fisher honed his skills so that by high school he was ready to reel off a string of mischief masterpieces. Two of these involved getting to the school itself. Fisher would delay the trip by stuffing a large potato in the school bus's exhaust pipe. When the driver, Al "Hefty" Johnson, would start the engine, Fisher's airflow impediment would stall it. Johnson was bald-headed, and once he got the bus in motion, the back of

The Maribel Theater staged Harold Fisher's impromptu productions (HCHS, colorized by JR).

his head proved an irresistible target for Fisher and friends, who would use it for spitball target practice.

Once at the school, other opportunities for amusement presented themselves. When the typing teacher once left class, Fisher proceeded to grab Tom Milligan, take him to the window, and dangle him upside down outside the window while holding Tom by his heels. The teacher's sudden reappearance prompted Fisher to hide the evidence of his prank; he simply let go of his friend's feet, causing Tom to drop headfirst to the ground.

In addition to such school-related escapades, Fisher found a venue in downtown Weott. First he would visit the old Weott water tank, which had become the home of numerous bats. He would catch several of the less-agile ones and put them in a paper bag. Then he proceeded to the Mirabel Theater, which showed nightly double features. The second picture was always a B-movie that often tended to drag. During a particularly dull stretch, Fisher would reach under his seat, retrieve his paper sack, open it, and liberate the bats. For a few glorious minutes, the bats would careen around the theater, often flying in front of the screen and superimposing their shadows upon the far less lively celluloid images. Tiring, the bats would retreat to the balcony, where they rested after their aerial acrobatics. The performance was such a great hit that Fisher subsequently repeated the performance. Once.

Fisher seemed always ready to take advantage of an opportunity for amusement. But when fate favored him with a chance to create a climax to his comedic productions, he refused to accept it.

Fisher was about 15 when he got a job helping Bill Fraser maintain the Weott waterworks. Fraser needed an assistant because the waterline started across the river on the steep slope of Grasshopper Peak and Fraser was none too nimble—he had a peg leg.

The day of the pivotal event, Fisher drove Fraser's vehicle, a Cadillac car, across a riffle in the South Fork at Gould Bar. On the west side of the river, a trail led past Forest Lodge and up the mountainside to the intake for the pipeline. On the way up Fraser's peg leg became detached and rolled down the steep slope. Fraser was immobilized. Finding the artificial limb was up to Fisher.

What an opportunity! How easily could Fisher have reported that he couldn't find the wooden leg, although that would mean he'd have to help Fraser down the trail and back to his car. Still, Fraser's discomfort would probably be no greater than that of Tom Milligan's when he was dropped out of the typing class window.

Soon enough Fisher trudged back up the trail, bringing, to Fraser's immense relief, the missing wooden leg. Fisher never explained his motivation for bypassing his chance for a prank, but it was well known that he preferred performing before a larger audience.[1535]

Redwoods ahead. Looking north through town (THPO, colorized by JR).

The nearby South Fork offered summer water warm enough to swim in, while in

> . . . fall and winter the salmon and steelhead come up from the sea, and last summer's swimming pools become fishing holes for some of the world's greatest game fish.[1536]

The main residential district was on the steeply sloping mountainside east of town, "where [in 1948] numbers of new homes are under construction." There were already about 450 people living in Weott. The school drew on outlying areas and had about 75 students. The business district served the widely scattered residents of the lower South Fork region along with tourists and travelers driving the Redwood Highway. There were a number of "really excellent motels," in addition to "several restaurants and taverns, market and garage facilities, souvenir shop . . . and the best in fishing gear for the sports fisherman."[1537]

Weott's riverside location, which made it so attractive to swimmers and anglers, also meant that it felt the full effect of the mid-century floods. The town was "virtually destroyed" by the 1955 freshet, and then, in 1964, residents saw the South Fork run 35 feet deep on the Redwood Highway, taking out 54 buildings.[1538] For good measure, Weott managed a good-sized flood between the two really big ones when the South Fork sloshed through town in February 1960.[1539]

Two months after experiencing this junior flood, Weott was again in the news when a jury from Eureka traveled there to view the property of Chauncey and Mabel Gould, which lay just south of town. The state of California had condemned the parcel for use as a road. The

Battering the batteries—the 1955 flood (HSU, colorized by JR).

state offered $4,200, but the Goulds wanted a bit more—$25,000. The jurors returned to court, deliberated, and decided that neither amount represented the correct value of the property. Deeming it "logged over land for which there would be no homesite demand," the jury determined that it was worth only $3,500.[1540] This meant the Goulds would receive $700 less than if they had accepted the state's offer. Added to that loss was an undisclosed amount they had to pay in attorney's fees.

Sometimes it is best to leave well enough alone.

# Chapter 23
# Bull Creek

In times past the stream now known as Bull Creek was called Lolahnkok, as were the people who dwelt beside it.[1541] The canyon it flowed through must have been a nearly perfect place to live, with a grove of Kahs-cho, the giant redwoods, near its mouth that gave way to mixed forest and prairies farther up the drainage. On the enclosing hillslopes the Lolahnkoks could gather Sah-chung, the acorns of the tanoak, prized above all others. Nearby was Sil-tse, the huckleberry, and lower down was Lah-chin-te, the hazel nut. Game animals like In-che, the deer, abounded, and each year the creek would fill with Klo-kuk, the salmon.[1542]

About halfway up the drainage was the canyon's only known Lolahnkok village, Kahs-cho-chin-net-tah.[1543] This was the birthplace of a boy named Ah-dah-dil-law.[1544] He was destined to become the only link with the Lolahnkoks' past. (See sidebar 1.)

The first reports about events at Bull Creek all involve the conflict between Indians and whites. (See sidebar 2.)

As happened throughout most of Humboldt County, the combination of massacres and

---

### 1. Ah-dah-dil-law

In 1850 much of the Mattole River drainage was occupied by a Sinkyone Indian group now known only as the "Upper Mattole People." Their southernmost village was Lenillimi, located near the future site of Ettersburg.[1545] It was probably from Lenillimi that a couple named Los-ki-ta and Betsey[1546] traveled to the canyon of Bull Creek, crossing over Elk Ridge as they moved from the Mattole River drainage to that of the South Fork Eel. Either Los-ki-ta or Betsey or perhaps both of them had a family connection with the Lolahnkok tribal group that occupied the canyon. Now that connection became stronger with the birth of their son, Ah-dah-dil-law, which occurred sometime in the 1850s.[1547]

At an unknown date, some Indians from the Garberville area (an unnamed group of the Sinkyone tribe) came down to Ken-tes-cho-be (Myers Flat) and killed all the Indians there except Los-ki-ta. Sometime later he gathered together allies from the Eel River, the Mattole River, and Blocksburg. They went south and killed about 40 of the Garberville Indians. Los-ki-ta took one scalp and "that made even."[1548] The Sinkyones were the only southern Humboldt tribe that took scalps.[1549]

Over time the Humboldt County Indian genocide reached the South Fork of the Eel, and Ah-dah-dil-law's "father and uncle were killed while fishing near Dyerville by a party of white men."[1550] For a time Ah-dah-dil-law was in the lower Eel River valley, where he witnessed the 1861-1862 flood, stating many years later that "when I was a boy whole valley covered by water."[1551] Ah-dah-dil-law was still a child when he was taken to the Smith River Reservation. He was later moved to the Hoopa Valley Reservation.[1552] At some point he took the name George Burtt, which he used for the rest of his life.[1553]

Burtt married a Nongatl woman named Tu-ha-kah.[1554] She was the cousin of the Nongatl Indian named Van Duzen Pete, and one of her parents was from the Nongatl tribal group called the Kit-tel.[1555] Tu-ha-kah had lived for a time in Kit-tel territory on the Van Duzen River, a few miles above Bridgeville.[1556] She took the name Susie.[1557] By 1885 George and Susie Burtt were living at Sa-bug-gah-nah, a village on the South Fork Eel upriver from Myers Flat. It was then and there that their first son, Guy, was born.[1558]

George also spent time farther up the South Fork, so that when the ethnographer Pliny Goddard interviewed him in 1907, he was able to provide information about the Redway-Garberville area.[1559] In addition, Burtt gave Goddard several short tales, or stories, that Alfred L. Kroeber published in 1919.[1560]

Although Ah-dah-dil-law had left Bull Creek when he was young, the lure of his home canyon must have been compelling. For a time he may have lived in a "goosepen" redwood[1561] on the Bull Creek Flat.[1562] In 1896 he is listed as "George Burt" in the Humboldt County Precinct Register, making him one of the first local Indians eligible to vote. His occupation is given as rancher, his age is 37, and he is five feet, eight inches tall. His post office address is Dyerville, so by then the Burtts were probably living in the canyon of Bull Creek.[1563]

A newspaper report from October 1899 indicated that "Indian George & family" were "back in their home on Bull Creek, 10 miles above its mouth." He and his household, "numbering a little less than a dozen," had spent the summer in Mendocino County, where George had harvested tanbark. He earned enough money that he returned "with ballast in both trousers' pockets."[1564] The location given for the Burtts' home indicates that they were by then living high up on one of the forks of Cuneo Creek. For a time five of the Burtt children, three boys and two girls, hiked down the canyon each day to attend the Bull Creek School, which was located near the site of Kahs-cho-chin-net-tah, their father's birthplace.[1565] Burtt patented the 80-acre property on upper Cuneo Creek in 1907.[1566] That same year two of the Burtts' sons, Walter and Elmer, died within a week of each other during a tuberculosis epidemic at the Chemawa Training School in Oregon.[1567]

Although they lived in a remote side canyon, far above the town of Bull Creek,

Susie and George Burtt and probable granddaughter (MCNAP, colorized by JR).

the Burtts were well-known in the white community. George would sometimes hike several miles up to and around Thomas Hill to visit the Crismon family at Fox Camp, where he would "bum things" from Arch Crismon.[1568] Burtt was "great friends" with Bruce Lewis, who had a ranch near the mouth of Cuneo Creek. When the Burtts stopped living year round at their place farther up the creek, they would come back each spring, and George would have Bruce haul his goods on a sled up to the Burtts' cabin. One year, Albert Lewis, a little boy at the time, scratched a "111" on his chin with charcoal to imitate Susie Burtt's tattoo.[1569]

In their later years the Burtts spent part of their time on the lower Eel River, either at Loleta or Fortuna.[1570] One year Susie Burtt was "taken sick" at Loleta. George paid two Wiyot shamans, a man and a woman, $15 and a horse to cure Susie. The woman shaman was a "sucking doctor" and sucked out disease "objects" from Susie's head and stomach. Susie then recovered.[1571] In April 1930 the Burtts' five-year-old grandson, Clarence, drowned in Rohner Creek.[1572] A few days later, Nora Coonskin, a Bear River (Nekanni) shaman, conducted a healing ceremony near Fernbridge for a tubercular Indian boy about 16 years of age. During the ceremony, Coonskin twice brought a little girl into the ceremony to help. The girl, it turned out, had been accused of pushing Clarence Burtt off a pier, which had led to his drowning. Coonskin showed that the girl was innocent because she had been able to help remove the "pain" from the tubercular boy's body.[1573]

Each summer between 1921 and 1923, the ethnographer C. Hart Merriam visited the Burtts at their home in Fortuna. Each time he collected information from both of them, but mostly from George.[1574] On the morning of July 22, 1923, Merriam and his two daughters, Dorothy and Zenaida, picked up George at his home, and Zenaida drove them south on the Redwood Highway. Starting at Dyerville, Burtt began pointing out and naming locations along the road as Merriam noted the mileage from Dyerville.[1575] It was probably the lengthiest ethnogeographical account Merriam ever recorded and was reminiscent of the trips Pliny Goddard documented in the 1900s with Van Duzen Pete and the Mattole Indian Joe Duncan.

In 1928 George and Susie Burtt sold their property on Cuneo Creek. The deed transfer indicates they received $10 for the property, although one of the purchasers claimed the Burtts were paid $10 per acre. The deed definitely contained at least one discrepancy, calling Susie Burtt "Sadie," which was the name of one of the Burtts' daughters. Both George and Susie signed the document with an "X," indicating they were unable to read what they were signing.[1576]

A group of six persons bought the Burtt place, including four members of the Wrigley family from Elk River. One of them was Irving Wrigley, who later became a noted local apple grower. He called the Cuneo Creek property "the Indian's." It had a small apple orchard on the north side of the cabin, but Wrigley became fascinated with a solitary apple tree south of the dwelling that produced a pink-fleshed apple.[1577] Wrigley was sure all of Burtt's apple trees had been started as seedlings.[1578] It should be recalled that George Burtt's parents had come from the Ettersburg area, where Albert Etter later conducted his fruit hybridization experiments. The apple that Wrigley and others found at the Burtt property bore great similarity to one of Etter's apples, the Pink Pearl. Although the Pink Pearl was not developed until about 1944, Etter had been working with apples since about 1900 at his experimental station in Ettersburg,[1579] and it is tempting to consider the possibility that George Burtt, on his travels through southern Humboldt, had acquired his seeds there. Wrigley attempted to grow the same pink-fleshed apple but never succeeded. He did develop a new apple variety that he called the "George Burtt" but its flesh was cream-colored, not pink.[1580]

When Irving Wrigley went to "the Indian's" in 1929, the cabin had fallen down. Wrigley's brother-in-law, Lloyd Russell, who had property to the north of the Burtts' at the head of Bear River, had visited the cabin years earlier. He noted that the structure was made of split lumber but framed with peeled logs. No one had lived there "for many years." Russell went inside and found the floor strewn with "love letters from a boyfriend of one of the Burtts' daughters—"much love, much kisses"—messages that had been written prior to World War I.[1581]

The Burtt homestead lay far up in the Cuneo Creek drainage, upper right (JR).

In the late 1930s, Burtt, then approaching his eighties, was interviewed yet again, this time by University of California Berkeley graduate student Harold Driver. Burtt told of his tribe's ways of life. The Sinkyones held a world renewal or "Big Time" ceremony irregularly: there was no particular month or season, but when it happened it lasted for seven days.[1582] There was no private ownership of land. Food was "free, like with air and water."[1583] Among the southern Humboldt tribes, only the Sinkyones used otter, fisher, and raccoon fur as part of their regalia.[1584] These were all little pieces of information that Driver collected, but there were many of them, like the folkloric tales Burtt had told to Goddard and the various village locations he had given to Merriam. They added up.

In March 1940 George Burtt died in Fortuna.[1585] That December Susie Burtt passed away in Rohnerville.[1586] They are buried next to three of their grandchildren in the Sunrise Cemetery on Newburg Road in Fortuna.[1587]

Many years later the Cuneo Creek property became part of Humboldt Redwoods State Park. For a time a backpack camping site was maintained at what was by then called the "Indian Orchard,"[1588] but no one at the park knew which Indian was meant. The orchard itself was just a few untended apple trees, with a narrow gully running between them—just as a story, by then long obscured, ran through the orchard.

deportation to reservations removed the Lolahnkoks from their Bull Creek homeland, creating multiple opportunities for whites to take up land there. Among the first to do so were Tosaldo and Addie Johnson, who arrived in 1872 or 1873, establishing themselves on a hillside prairie north of the Bull Creek Flat redwoods. Tosaldo reportedly built up a flock of some 2,000 sheep,[1589] but "bears, panthers, and other such beasts of prey killed off a thousand head in one season. This," his biography drily states, "led him to engage in hunting."[1590] Tosaldo obtained some hounds and focused on killing deer and bears. He tanned the deer hides, and Addie converted them into pants and moccasins. The bear hides became rugs.[1591]

While searching for a lost lamb one day, Addie came upon a lovely location above Johnson Prairie. She was so taken by the spot that she told Tosaldo that she wished to be buried there when she died. Only a few months later, Addie failed to survive the birth of their second child

---

**2. "Joseph Russ and his men caught up with the Indians at the creek...."**

In January 1863 a group of Indians was busy building a winter village in the redwoods of lower Bull Creek. For the last six months, they had reportedly moved about southern Humboldt, raiding ranches and taking food, guns, and clothing. There were, however, no accounts of them having harmed any whites. They now had with them a supply of wheat and grain, and about 400 pounds of dried meat. Most of the men were out looking for more cattle that they might convert into beef, but about 10 remained in camp to help the women make the conical frames for their winter houses and then cover them with slabs of bark. They had finished eight so far; then the air was rent with the cracks of rifle shots, and the Indians began falling to the ground. Two of the men escaped, but five lay dead among the houses. Three more died while trying to cross the creek. The women were shot, too. Many were killed, but several were only wounded.

Jerry Whitmore and nine other white vigilantes moved out from the trees and surveyed the carnage their guns had wrought. They had been following the Indians for more than a week and had finally caught them at Bull Creek. Whitmore and his men burnt the half-built village and destroyed the food and other goods. They took four of the women with them to Fort Humboldt, but some of the ones they had shot were left behind. Whitmore thought that the band "cannot move the wounded [that] they have to take care of without making a large trail." He indicated that he intended "to spend the winter in assisting to exterminate this band if not sooner done."[1592] It was probably this attack, which saw a number of wounded Indian women left at the site, that generated the location's offensive name of Squaw Creek. Robert Look, a member of the family that later lived on Look Prairie, a half mile north of the mouth of the creek, provided corroborating information by indicating that there was an Indian massacre downstream from the Flatiron Tree that gave Squaw Creek its name.[1593]

Whitmore's attack was indeed a massacre, but according to the Sinkyone Indian Jack Woodman there was also an actual battle between Indians and whites "on the flat at Bull creek." Woodman claimed that "I cannot say what it was about, but I know that the Mattole and Bear River people joined with us against the whites."[1594] Woodman made no mention of the outcome.

There was at least one other related event at Bull Creek during the Indian genocide of the 1850s and 1860s. There are several accounts of what happened. They diverge widely in what they claim.

The incident started when a group of Indians rustled a bull from a ranch that was located either in the Mattole area, or on Bear River, or on Rainbow Ridge. In any case, the Indians took the bull eastward. The rancher and some other whites followed the Indians' trail to a secluded canyon where they found the bull and its captors. The animal had been butchered and was either being cooked or being eaten. At this point the various stories, already in disagreement, split far apart. Two accounts, one quoting the other, state that "a battle followed. Who ran, we don't know."[1595] Another version insists that the Indians "succeeded in making a complete get-away by fleeing in all directions."[1596] A fourth statement indicates that "the Indians were pursued and killed by a group of settlers."[1597] None of these reports provided sources, but in two other cases the names of the reporters are known. Robert Look wrote in his diary that the creek got its name when "Indians killed a bull and took it from Mattole—carcass found at Bull Creek. Killings also a fact."[1598]

And Caroline Edeline Rumrill provided another version of the story. This one involved her husband, George:

> During George Rumrill's employment with the Russ company, a small bunch of Indians did some "bull napping," which was an expensive prize bull that Joseph Russ had imported to improve stock. He called together some of his riders, seventeen of them counting George, and they trailed the Indians. Joseph Russ and his men caught up with the Indians at a creek, which later was referred to as Bull Creek, still named so today."[1599]

Caroline Rumrill did not say what happened to the Indians when Russ and his 17 men caught them at the creek.

The Look Prairie Barn stood on land once owned by the Johnsons (JR).

and her grieving husband complied with her request.[1600]

Three years after Addie's death, Tosaldo married Roxanne Jean Hanlon. Ranch life continued at Johnson Prairie. Tosaldo raised corn, potatoes, and other garden vegetables. He knew how to bud and graft trees, and Roxanne was the teamster who took the resultant apples to market. They raised horses, cattle, hogs, and chickens on their small ranch, and Tosaldo made bacon and hams, including deer ham. To obtain cash, Tosaldo cruised timber[1601] and sheared sheep. He served as the local deputy sheriff and constable.

Tosaldo and Vic Pedrotti played fiddles at dances. Once Roxanne and Mandy Pedrotti found that their husbands had left (without permission) for a dance at the Hindley Ranch in distant Honeydew. The women saddled up, took their four or five children with them over Panther Gap, and surprised their fiddling husbands at the dance.[1602]

In 1875 Noah and Mary Turner bought 240 acres that straddled Bull Creek downstream from its confluence with Cuneo Creek.[1603] By then S. P. Clark owned land west of the creek between the properties of Francis M. How and J. M. Whitlow,[1604] and William Millsap had acquired a parcel known as Fox Camp on the ridge west of Bull Creek.[1605]

By 1876 enough families had moved into the canyon that the Bull Creek School was established. The first class had nine boys and seven girls.[1606] In August 1878, a dance was given in the new schoolhouse to raise funds for improving the furnishings, at which about 20 couples attended.[1607] Time elapsed, and then, in December 1885, the Bull Creek school teacher, Oscar H. Bryan, drowned while trying to ford a winter-high Bull Creek on horseback. His horse survived and was found next to the creek. For a time, the scene of the teacher's death was called Bryan's Ford.[1608]

Another family established itself in Bull Creek when, in 1878, James and Mary Hamilton bought the Whitlow property, located near the confluence of Mill Creek and Bull Creek.[1609] Daniel Merrifield subsequently claimed land in the upper Bull Creek drainage; his property appears on the 1879 government map of the area.[1610] Directly southeast of Merrifield was a larger parcel that Lemuel and Harriet Hazelton acquired.[1611] In September 1899, a fire at the head of Bull Creek burned through their ranch, but the buildings were saved.[1612] Lemuel died in October 1901, and Harriet married M. P. Endicott in 1904.[1613] Endicott had previously "sold his valuable place in Eureka to use the money to stock his ranch in the Bull Creek section with cattle, hogs, and goats."[1614] One of the Hazeltons' daughters, Eunice, married Amos Cummings, and they moved to Bull Creek in 1907. They bought land northwest of the Turners and southwest of the Hamiltons and added to the four-acre orchard already present. Amos exhibited his King and Jonathan apples at the 1914 San Francisco apple show, winning a gold medal for his Kings.[1615]

Artemus Howard Lewis and Sarah Reed Lewis purchased 150 acres on Cuneo Creek in 1890. Their son, Abner Bruce Lewis (known as Bruce), married Noah and Mary Turner's daughter, Ida May. Bruce continued the ranch operation that his father had started,[1616] and he and his family raised pears, peaches, apples, and nuts. The apples were sold in Eureka. They also ran cattle, sheep, and hogs.[1617] Bruce added to the ranch property, paying neighbor Annie Stansberry "350 gold coins for 160 acres." For years Bruce's "outside" job was falling timber for the Pacific Lumber Company (PL). He would travel

Abner Bruce Lewis, Ida May Lewis, and Arthur Howe[1618] (HRSP, colorized by JR).

"between Scotia and Bull Creek [by] walking over the hill," actually a bit of a trip since it involved crossing Monument Ridge. In about 1906, Bruce was cutting timber in the Shively area when a big storm forced the crew to stay in camp. Bruce sat in on a poker game, went on a hot streak, and wound up winning $85. He promptly

> . . . bought a team of horses and a wagon, drove to Scotia, filled the wagon full of lumber, went home to Bull Creek and never worked for anybody but himself again.[1619]

By May 1902 Bull Creek was busy enough that it was allocated its own post office. It was hard for outsiders to tell, however, because it operated under the mystifying name "Helper." Rose Taylor, the postmaster, had chosen the name because she "thought it would be a great help to the residents of the valley to have their own post office." Apparently it wasn't helpful enough, for it closed two years later.[1620] During its brief heyday, its name was used for newspaper datelines, providing at least one memorable journey into print:

**Flames Stopped by Prayer**

HELPER, September 23–

The ensuing article made it clear that it was a special HELPER indeed who extinguished the fire.[1621]

For years a county road connected Bull Creek with the West Side Road at Dyerville, but it ended midway up the canyon. In 1911 county supervisor George Williams oversaw the road's extension ten miles farther, which carried it to the rim of the drainage at Panther Gap. Roy Poland was the contractor for the job, with the result that a dramatic hairpin turn on the route was named Poland's Elbow. In 1913 George Hindley, the county supervisor to the west of Williams's district, oversaw the road's next and final section, which brought it down to Honeydew, on the Mattole.[1622]

The Bull Creek community of ranchers took on the trappings of a town in about 1918, when Jasper Turner sold 10 acres on the west side of the Bull Creek road to Art Johnson, who promptly placed a home, store, dance hall, several rentals, and a baseball field on the property, which was located next to the Bull Creek School. Johnson would have overbuilt if he had only the locals to rely on, but families from Eureka, Fortuna, and other communities came to Bull Creek on weekends and holidays, swelling his trade. At the time the PL owned the Bull Creek Flat and

William B. Shively's work crew building the Mattole Road, 1911 (HRSP, colorized by JR).

# Bull Creek

allowed free camping there. The campers found that Art Johnson's store was a handy place to meet their needs, and the flat became a busy place. As one local described it, "if you drove from Dyerville to Bull Creek Flat at night, you might think you were driving through a long city because of all the lights from the camps."[1623]

On weekends Johnson offered a range of entertainments at his store-ballfield-dance-hall complex, starting with a baseball game on Saturday afternoon, followed by a dance that night. On Sunday there was a barbecue and another ball game, sometimes a double header. No box scores remain, but it is known that on July 4, 1932, the Weott Pastimers defeated the Carlotta Cubs 12 to 7.[1624] Children competed for prizes in foot races and other events. The men could win an award for the most trout caught, while the women could compete in "rolling pin throwing"—always a useful skill.[1625]

Bull Creek residents found their own form of entertainment in following the escapades of one of the locals. (See sidebar 3.)

The 1920s brought a surge of forest-related activity in Bull Creek. By 1918 most of the tanoaks in the Mattole valley had been cut for their bark,[1626] and by 1921 the same was true in the Briceland area.[1627] There were still tanoaks in the Bull Creek drainage, however, and at least two tanbark harvesting operations sprang up. In addition to the DeYoung operation, where Dave Chadbourne encountered his "enemy tree," the Sunset Trading and Land Company of Willits had several bark camps, including one on the side of Grasshopper Peak. This remote location was supplied by Weott grocer Tom Hill, whose elderly truck labored up the steep grade from Bull Creek once or twice a week carrying canned "fruit in gallons, wooden buckets of apple jam, and . . . barrels of flour, sugar, beans, and so forth."[1628]

For a time autos could depart Mattole Road and drive among the Bull Creek redwoods (THPO, colorized by JR).

### 3. Death-Defying Dave Chadbourne and His Dangerous Dodge

On March 12, 1922, the *Humboldt Times* reported that

> David Chadbourne and Walter Briceland, both of Dyerville, suffered a narrow escape from drowning a few days ago when a footbridge over Bull Creek, which was swelled by heavy rains, broke under them, precipitating them into the raging stream. Both are expert swimmers and succeeded in making their way to the score [sic] after a struggle and suffered no bad effects from the ducking [sic].[1629]

Two months later came another report on Chadbourne's well-being, this time from the Dyerville-Bull Creek column in the *Humboldt Beacon*:

> D. Chadbourne is just recovering from a very bad hand, caused by a scratch.[1630]

With the onset of summer Dave's courtship with danger hit its stride, and the *Beacon* was there to follow it.

June 30:

> David Chadbourne was hurt quite badly Sunday in the ball game at Mattole when the pitcher hit him in the head with the ball. He has fully recovered from the blow.[1631]

A more dire incident on July 7 made the *Beacon's* front page:

> David Chadbourne and Jesse Ridley narrowly escaped death while falling tan bark in the DeYoung bark woods. In falling a large Tan Oak, the tree struck a large Madroni [sic] but feeling sure that the tree was safe they began trimming. Soon they heard some queer noises and concluded that it must be the same tree. While trimming another limb from their tree Jesse glance[d] up at this huge big tree it was coming toward them. Calling Dave's attention immediately, they both scampered for a get away. As it was heading toward them. Jesse had good clear sailing but Dave had very little chance of escaping the death that awaited him. But his first, last, and only chance was just one and he dashed into the gulch and below the embankment just in time to hear the crash and report of the enemy which fell directly where the boys were working.[1632]

August 11:

David Chadbourne had his leg crushed quite badly one day recently while peeling bark, one of the mules became frightened and on turning around caught one of his legs between the load of bark and a tree, he is doing nicely.[1633]

September 8:

What might have resulted in a very serious accident Monday evening, occurred near the Bull creek store, when David Chadbourne just backed his car out of the road after taking his folks and the W. W. Taylor family to Church. Just as he stopped his car one of the wheels dropped off. Had he been traveling along a dangerous bank with the heavy load he had there might have been more to tell.[1634]

There *was* more to tell on October 20:

While driving about 25 miles an hour, David Chadbourne and Addie Taylor [came] very near being seriously hurt when one of the wheels of his automobile came off the machine, forward skidding about 10 feet, fortunately [n]either one were hurt.[1635]

March 23, 1923:

David Chadbourne cut his hand quite badly Monday when he accidentally threw his hand against an axe blade while carrying it on his saddle.[1636]

May 11, a front-page story:

David Chadbourne was quite ill on Monday evening.[1637]

May 18, relegated to page 7:

David Chadbourne has fully recovered from his sick spell.[1638]

By September, Dave's flirtations with disaster seemed to be dying down, but they hadn't quite ended:

"Auto in red, trouble ahead," if it was Dave Chadbourne's detrimental Dodge (colorized by JR).

Word was received by friends of David Chadbourne that Dave was in an automobile accident and narrowly escaped injury.[1639]

And that was it for the year.

Perhaps Dave had become more careful, for he had recently gotten married. His bride was Addie Taylor, who also happened to be the *Beacon's* Bull Creek and Dyerville correspondent. For two years Dave had obliged Addie by periodically providing her with exciting material for her weekly newspaper column, but in the course of his escapades, the accident victim and the accident reporter had fallen in love.[1640] Now Dave's safety was paramount, and rather than careening around the corners of the Bull Creek road in his dangerous Dodge,[1641] he could devote his spare time to safer activities, such as playing violin and guitar at local dances while Addie accompanied him on the piano.[1642]

While readers of the *Beacon* could easily keep up with the couple by reading the paper's weekly Bull Creek column, both Addie and Dave had lesser known, but highly interesting backstories. Addie made her debut in print when she was 13. She had sent a letter to the *Humboldt Times* that generated an article with the following headline:

**Little Mountain Girl Is**
  **Unable to Get Schooling**
    **But Writes Interestingly**

Enclosed in the letter was a short account called "Our Camping Trip," which told of Addie, her parents, and Mr. and Mrs. Barkdull vacationing on the Mattole River. Also along was their transportation; three horses and two mules, with Addie riding "the little buckskin mule Jack." Four dogs made up the rest of the party: Jock, Paddy, Peddro, and Blondey. There were two excitements on the trip. First, when "Papa & Mr. Barkdull went fishing again and they got just lots of fish and Papa killed a rattlesnake and two scorpions." Then, while Annie was riding her mule, Jack, the group came to a bad place where there was a deep hole in the trail, and the "horses went over it all rite but my mule both front feet went into a hole and [Jack] very nearly went on his head."[1643]

Enclosed with article was a note:

> Dear Editor:—Just a few lines as I am sending you a story I wrote for your paper. I live way   up in the mountains where there is no children and I can't go to school but mama teaches me and I learn myself. I hope you will put my letter in with the rest of the letters.
>
> Addie Louise Taylor[1644]

Decades later Addie Chadbourne wrote what was probably her last published report. In a letter to the editor of the *Humboldt Historian*, she gave a brief account of her family's time in Bull Creek. She also wrote about her husband and his family:

> There, at Bull Creek, I met my future husband. He was a young half-breed Indian man. Well, I fell in love with him and in two years we were married. His name was David Chadbourne. His grandmother on his mother's side was a full blood Indian who had been found in a papoose basket by some white people. It was after the last massacre at Big Flat on the other side of Kings Peak.
>
>   They heard a baby crying and there she was floating on the waves of the ocean, so they kept and raised her. When she grew up she married a man whose name was Daniel Anderson Sutherland. . . .[1645]

It was obvious that Dave Chadourne wasn't the only member of his family who knew something about survival.

On the north side of Grasshopper Peak, Enoch Johnson ran a tie camp, where sections of redwood were hand split to create railroad ties.[1646] For many years afterward, four of the camp's shacklike cabins gradually decayed in the shadows of the second-growth woods.[1647] Mason Livingston operated another tie camp opposite the mouth of Albee Creek on the lower slopes of Grasshopper Peak,[1648] while in 1922 Howard Barter's crew split railroad ties and grapestakes in the Albee Creek drainage.[1649] That same year the Danielson and Turner Mill was operating in the same area, cutting not redwood but Douglas-fir (for two-by-fours) that grew on the hillslope above the Bull Creek Flat.[1650]

A third enterprise made use of some of Bull Creek's old-growth redwoods but allowed them to remain in place. During Prohibition, "chimney trees" whose interiors had been burned out by fires, were utilized by moonshiners as locations for their stills. Smoke from the still's boiler would rise up the "chimney" and be dispersed in the overstory foliage, masking the smoke from detection. The best-documented operation was Don Turner's. Don was the grandson of early Bull Creek arrivals Noah and Mary Turner, and he knew the area well. He picked a location on Squaw Creek Ridge that "had the best quality water in the country," found a suitable chimney tree, and went to work. Don grew his own corn, and after using the mash in his still, took it back to his ranch, where he fed it to his pigs. According to Don, they "loved the mash and acted just like people when they got a snoot full." Don's whiskey cost "seventy cents a gallon to make and we sold it for seven fifty a fifth." That meant a huge profit, but it was diminished slightly "because we had to pay the DA fifty gallons a month to stay in business."[1651]

The Grasshopper Peak Lookout, 1935 (HRSP, colorized by JR).

Ed Davis, another Bull Creek moonshiner, had the same agreement with District Attorney Stephen Metzler, but this failed to give him protection from the Dry Squad. Davis was caught and taken to jail, and the squad broke up four of his Bull Creek stills. He had been unable to buy off the other important link in the enforcement chain, Sheriff Jack Runner.[1652]

William Turner made both moonshine and split stuff, the latter of which he hauled to the South Fork train station for shipment to distant locations. In 1925 Turner acquired a baby bear whose mother had died. He named the bear "Bear," which although an uninspired choice was at least easy to remember. Bear grew large and was given away and then, growing larger still, given away again, the last time to the captain of a ship. Bear sailed off into the west and was never heard of again.[1653]

By 1921 PL owned the lower three miles of the Bull Creek Flat and most of the hillslopes above it.[1654] During much of the decade, the fate of the flat's magnificent redwood forest was uncertain, as the Save-the-Redwoods League and the Humboldt Women's Save the Redwoods League attempted, in near desperation, to protect the trees from being cut.

In July 1926 the embattled Bull Creek and Dyerville flats received an important set of visitors: John D. Rockefeller Jr. and part of his family came to look at the redwoods. They arrived at the South Fork train station in a private railcar, where they were met by Newton B. Drury, secretary of the Save-the-Redwoods League, and were transferred to an open-air Cadillac and a Lincoln touring car. Seated in the back of the Cadillac, Rockefeller could lean back and stare skyward towards the tops of 300-foot-tall redwoods.[1655] That afternoon the Rockefellers enjoyed an al fresco picnic lunch at Bull Creek Flat. Rockefeller had already donated a million dollars to help save the forest before he ever saw it, but his open-air drive and redwood-shaded luncheon further stimulated his interest to the extent that in 1930 he contributed another million.[1656]

Finally, in August 1931, PL sold both the Bull Creek and Dyerville flats, which soon became part of the Humboldt Redwoods State Park.[1657] At about the same time, 320 acres of adjacent upstream redwoods was acquired from the Metropolitan Lumber Company, a tract that included a trio of striking redwoods: the Tall Tree, the Giant Tree, and the Flatiron Tree.[1658] In 1952 the redwood grove on Bull Creek Flat was named the Rockefeller Forest.[1659]

As the fight to save the Bull Creek redwoods moved through the 1920s, farther up the canyon part of the forest was lost. The event focused on the Fox Camp area that lay across the ridgeline west of Bull Creek. (See sidebar 4.)

In defiance of the Great Depression, Irving Wrigley and Lloyd Russell set up a small circular mill on Bull Creek in 1936. They cut

A giant in the Rockefeller Forest (THPO, enhanced by JR).

### 4. From Fire to Snow—Max Crismon Finds Excitement

Max Crismon knew a bit about long rides—while living at the Fox Camp Ranch in 1922, he rode an hour and a half each way to the Bull Creek School. Then, in 1929 he had a chance for a *really* long ride. Irv Kelley had 25 bucking horses, which he used in the Fortuna rodeo, pastured at Fox Camp. One day a fire broke out on the hillslope between Bull Creek and the ranch. Kelley had to get the horses out in a hurry, and Crismon and a herding dog helped him. They drove the horses north, taking a trail on the Bull Creek side of Big Hill and then going through an opening in the ridge by Thomas Hill.[1660] This brought them into the Bear River drainage, where they forded the river near its headwaters and then climbed up Brushy Ridge, crossed over Monument Ridge, and then dropped towards the Eel through Giacomini Prairie. They stayed west of Rio Dell on their way to a large pasture west of Howe Creek. There the horses vacationed in safety while the fire blackened he landscape from Fox Camp all the way west to Rainbow Ridge. According to Crismon, the "fire burned [the] country to a frazzle."[1661]

Crismon had more excitement during the hard winter of 1937-1938. He was living in the log cabin at the old Hazelton place pretty far up the Bull Creek drainage. Max ran a trap line that winter, and while out with his dog checking it one day, he saw a bear walking in front of him. He followed the bear over the ridge into the Canoe Creek drainage. Max was a good shot but his weapon was deficient—a 0.22 rifle that he loaded with 0.22 longs. Max fired and hit the bear in the neck; he fired twice more, hitting the bear in the shoulder and back. The bear kept going and went back across the ridge to the vicinity of the Hazelton place. Max lost sight of the bear but finally found him while the wounded and winded animal was lying down. Max shot him at close range in the head and chest. The bear responded by snapping his jaws. Max's next shell jammed in the chamber. Now the bear, with five bullets in him but still feeling frisky, jumped up and ran down the hillslope, growling all the way. Max and his dog set out in pursuit and caught up with the querulous quarry yet again. As the dog kept the bear at bay, Max was able to get off two more shots. One hit the bear between the eyes, the other in one of the eyes. That finally did it. Max would have bear meat on his menu for a while, for the victim weighed over 200 pounds.[1662]

both Douglas-fir and redwood and did some custom milling for Humboldt Redwoods State Park, sawing long, thick planks for tables and benches at the Women's Federation Grove. Next door to Wrigley and Russell's mill, the Redwood Products Company built both a sawmill and shingle mill in 1939. That same year the company's president, A. L. Nelson, was appointed to the State Parks Commission, offering him the opportunity to cut and save redwoods simultaneously.[1663]

If the nationwide economic crisis wasn't problem enough, Bull Creek suffered two localized difficulties that affected ranching and farming. First came the deathly cold winter of 1937-1938, which froze much of the livestock. The Pedrotti family saw their herd of about 35 Herefords diminish to fewer than ten before the winter ended.[1664] Then, in the early 1940s, Washington State began marketing its visually beguiling but insipid red delicious apples, leaving Humboldt County growers in the lurch. Even Bull Creek apples, with their prize-winning pedigree, were in scant demand. Bruce Lewis "loaded his old truck with apples, wrapped in paper [and] packed in new boxes, headed for town and could not sell one box."[1665]

Chauncey and Mabel Gould bought the old Hazelton Ranch, the last place up the Bull Creek drainage, in the middle of World War II. At the war's end, their son Don left the service, returned home, and began supervising road building on the ranch. The most import project was connecting the ranch with Mattole

The Wrigley-Russell Mill, c. 1939 (FMC, colorized by JR).

Road at a point opposite the site of the second Bull Creek cemetery. The new road went up the west side of the Bull Creek drainage, crossed the creek at a constriction in the canyon called the Narrows, and then continued to the hillside site of the ranch house. Other ranch roads were built up the west and south sides of Grasshopper Peak.[1666]

A certain degree of turbulence marked the Goulds' time at the ranch. There was no electricity at the property, so the family had a freezer that was powered by coal oil. Mabel Gould filled the tank with gasoline by mistake; the freezer responded by catching fire, and the ranch house burned to the ground.[1667] Wildfires sometimes erupted on the property, reportedly started by Don Gould, "either because he was drunk or to improve deer hunting."[1668] Don may have had help, since he often invited his buddies up to partake of parties at the ranch.[1669] The most noted Gould escapade, however, involved Don's dad, Chauncey. He was a large man, weighing some 265 pounds, and had a tremendous temper.[1670] Once Chauncey hired a timber faller who was also a preacher. Chauncey observed the man's work and didn't like it. He confronted the preacher, shouting, "if you can't fall trees any better than that, get the hell out!" The preacher responded, "you can't talk to me like that, I'm a man of the cloth." To which Gould replied, "if you can't fall trees any better than that, you can *damn well* get the hell out!" Forthwith did the maligned minister depart, leaving, however, his name upon the landscape, which ever since has been called Preacher's Gulch.[1671]

Although by 1931 the redwoods on the Bull Creek Flat were safely within the bounds of Humboldt Redwoods State Park, the forest farther up the drainage was still in private ownership. The mills of the 1930s and early 1940s processed a small portion of the unprotected trees, but it was only in 1947 that "logging was initiated on a large scale." Timbermen found they could pay for the redwood on a site and be given the now-millworthy Douglas-fir for free.[1672] The Bear River Lumber Company ran a mill just upstream from the Rockefeller Forest, employing about 15 men to cut some 71,000 to 72,000 board feet of lumber per day. As the mill's name implied, its logs came from near the head of Bear River, just over the ridge from Bull Creek.[1673]

In 1953 Hershell D. Wheeler packed up his mill equipment and a half-dozen of his top workers and moved them—lock, stock, and saw blade—from Mississippi to Bull Creek, where he took over and upgraded the old Littlepage Mill near the mouth of—what else?—Mill Creek.[1674] A mile down the stream, the Bee River Mill employed a dozen workers to cut as much as 50,000,000 board feet of sawtimber in a single year.[1675]

As logging progressed, the hillsides above Bull Creek were crisscrossed with skid roads, where Caterpillar tractors "skidded" logs down 60- or 70-degree slopes, tearing up the ground and any small vegetation that was in their path. The skid roads connected to a network of haul roads, where several logs could be loaded onto a single truck and then moved to the mill.[1676] Photos from the 1940s to the 1960s show darkened areas of primeval forest transformed into spiderwebs of devastation, as if part of a war zone.[1677]

By 1954 half of the upper watershed had been cut over. Added to that was the destruction of some 7,000 acres by wildfires.[1678] Incredibly, some of the fires were intentional, set by Bull Creek residents as a form of entertainment. Townsfolk would watch the flames burn up the

# Bull Creek 317

Wheeler Mill, c. 1954. Bull Creek in foreground (HRSP, colorized by JR).

hillside and wait for the state fire crew from Weott, their engines' lights flashing and sirens blaring, to arrive and put it out. As a result, the Weott state fire station had one of the highest incident rates in the state.[1679]

What had been a sleepy ranching community became a roughshod boom town. By 1955 there were 87 families comprising between 260 and 265 individuals living in Bull Creek.[1680] Many had come there to get the timber out, and according to one report, the town "was dependent entirely on logging." The canyon was filled with smoke from the mills' conical burners so that "your eyes would burn all day long."[1681] Dust from the log and lumber trucks lay "two feet thick on the road," requiring motorists to turn on their headlights in the middle of the day.[1682] June Ruggles, who lived in Bull Creek but taught at the Larabee School, encountered on her commute as many as 17 logging trucks driving the one-lane Mattole Road that wound through the Rockefeller Forest.[1683]

Some of the Bull Creek wildfires were small, such as the two that burnt in September

1952, neither one of which was larger than 30 acres.[1684] But as the decade progressed, there was an ominous increase in the severity of the blazes. The filing room of the Bear River Lumber Company, just west of the Rockefeller Forest, caught fire in November 1954, and soon flames engulfed almost the entire mill. Owner Howard Trimble suffered a $100,000-plus loss, which was especially annoying because he had purchased the mill little more than a month earlier.[1685] Then in early September 1955 came a much larger fire that burned through the Bull Creek area, charring over 5,800 acres and incinerating several houses and cabins.[1686]

With the slopes of the upper drainage laid bare by logging and fires, and with skid roads and haul roads creating ready-made drainage channels, Bull Creek was a disaster waiting to happen. The wait ended in late December 1955. (See sidebar 5.)

The December 1955 flood that nearly destroyed the town of Bull Creek wreaked additional havoc in the canyon. On the Bull Creek Flat, the flood-engorged stream had cut deeply into its banks, sawing off sections of the flat that then dropped into the water, carrying with them scores of ancient, streamside redwoods. What had been a 50-foot-wide creek had "quadrupled in width with steepened, raw-earth banks."[1687] More subtle but equally pernicious was the layer of silt that the floodwaters then deposited on the flat, a sometimes lethal covering of alluvium

Mattole Road in the Rockefeller Forest, 1958 (HRSP, colorized by JR).

### 5. Runaway Runoff

Crenellating the southwestern edge of the Bull Creek drainage is Panther Gap, a dip in the ridgeline where Mattole Road, heading west, crosses over to its namesake watershed. The gap is also the wettest spot around, with an average annual rainfall of about 115 inches. In the middle of December 1955, the area was hit by a good-sized storm, but by the morning of the twenty-first it had tapered off and locals were hopeful they would have a dry Christmas.

By that evening, they knew they wouldn't. A new, regionwide rain event had swept in from the coast, and it soon became a record-setter. At the tiny town of Honeydew, which sits in the Mattole valley west of Panther Gap, the pluvial assault pounded down in torrents, and then, instead of subsiding, actually intensified. When the gauge was checked for the day's total, it registered 21.2 inches, an incredible rate of nearly an inch an hour. There was still plenty of precipitation left when the storm crossed over Panther Gap—enough to inundate Bull Creek with three *feet* of water.

In much of the upper drainage, those three feet were dropping on recently burned or logged hillslopes, pounding into the barren earth like tiny artillery shells, washing loose the soil and turning skid roads into cascades and haul roads into miniature rivers. Sometimes a pile of logging debris briefly stopped the onrush, but then it was washed away, and the water gathered behind it swept downward with increased power, amplifying the storm's effect. Before long, Bull Creek had jumped its banks and expanded to fill the canyon, sweeping away whatever stood before it.

Don Gould was at his ranch house, high up in the drainage, when he realized he'd better get out. He decided to head for the family's riverside vacation home at Weott, some 15 road miles away.

Behind him came the flood.

Gould drove down the canyon, turned onto Mattole Road, and crossed the Cuneo Creek bridge. Did he feel it quiver as debris from the heavily logged side canyon slammed into the structure? There was no time to think of that, for soon he was passing the Bull Creek School and the town's store, and then he was on the first Bull Creek bridge. Muddy water covered the roadway, but Gould made it across the creek and was on the flat where stood the Bee River Mill. By now the surging creek had swept into the mill's log deck, jumbling two million board feet of timber into an impromptu dam, causing the water to back up into the main part of town.

Suddenly the jam broke loose, but just as quickly it reformed opposite

Edgar and Marie Moore's house (and son) after the flood (HRSP, colorized by JR).

Albee Creek. With the new jam dam now impounding the stream's water, Gould may have felt a momentary sense of relief as he approached the second Bull Creek bridge. He crossed the temporarily diminished creek and had just reached the Rockefeller Forest when the Albee Creek jam broke loose, sending hundreds of logs and a wall of water hurtling against the wooden bridge, knocking it down the canyon.[1688] Gould would be the last person to escape from Bull Creek on Mattole Road.

But some residents remained in the town, or what was left of it, and the damage wrought by the flood compelled them to stay there. Emergency supplies were flown into the canyon and dropped by parachute, and then teams of volunteers packed in food by hiking across the mountains from Rio Dell. Lloyce Chadbourne carried in 15 dozen eggs, reached the town, and promptly fell into a side stream. Quickly a pair of hands plunged into the water and pulled up—the eggs. Only then was Lloyce removed from the creek, learning that all 180 eggs had survived intact.

# Bull Creek

> Teenager Bill Beat lived in Weott but decided he just had to go see how things stood in Bull Creek. His plan was simple, and simply dangerous. He went to the bank of the still-raging South Fork Eel River, and, with the nimbleness of youth, pulled himself up onto the town's water line, a pipe that connected to a supply source across the river on Grasshopper Peak. Beat then propelled himself along the water pipe, doing a sort of South Fork shimmy, until he reached the Bull Creek side of the river. He then picked up an old trail that ran along the side of Grasshopper Peak and hiked it into town.
>
> Or what was left of the town. About 35 houses had washed away, and most of the rest were filled with mud. The store was gone too, and farther up the canyon the Bull Creek Cemetery had ceased to exist. Many of its coffins had floated downstream on the flood and were now lodged in the limbs of redwoods in the Rockefeller Forest.
>
> In Bull Creek, the flood had truly raised the dead.[1689]

that choked the life out of additional dozens of old-growth giants. By 1961 the California Division of Beaches and Parks had determined that over 10 percent of the Bull Creek Flat had been washed away and that 524 large (more than four feet in diameter) redwoods had been lost.[1690]

Like the redwoods, the community of Bull Creek continued to suffer the aftereffects of the flood. The silt that covered the Bull Creek Flat also filled the creek itself, so that the water found new routes that continued to disrupt the town. By March 1957, more than a year after the flood, the creek was flowing down the middle of Mattole Road. Hershell Wheeler's mill, which the flood had buried in mud, was below the new elevation of the silt-enhanced creek, protected only by a gravel dike. The dike soon washed out, allowing the creek to flow "unimpeded through the lumber yards, making operations impossible." Downstream, the Bee River Mill was also partly underwater. The mill owners and the residents of Bull Creek were outraged that no level of government had stepped in to solve the problem, failing to note the irony of a situation that had been caused by the very lumbering activity that was now stymied.[1691]

And the government *had* tried to help. In the spring of 1956, the Bull Creek channel had been cleared of alluvium and debris so that the creek flowed eight feet below the deck of the Bull Creek bridge. But rainstorms still sent silt streaming down the hillsides, and a year later the creek's clearance beneath the bridge had been reduced to eight inches instead of eight feet.[1692]

But new forces were soon to be deployed.

The damage to the redwoods on Bull Creek Flat caught the attention of park officials and of both the Save-the-Redwoods League and the Sierra Club.[1693] Existing restrictions on timber harvesting had failed to prevent the destructive debacle of the 1955 flood, and the league and the State of California determined that the only way to secure protection of the old-growth forest on Bull Creek Flat was to stop any logging of the upper watershed. Regulatory action was not considered an option, so instead the league raised money for the purchase of all private land in the drainage and the transfer of its ownership to Humboldt Redwoods State Park.[1694] Laurence Rockefeller, the son of John D. Rockefeller Jr., continued a family tradition by contributing $500,000 to help fund the effort.[1695] So it was that by late 1963 the league had purchased, and then transferred to the state, some 18,000 acres in the Bull Creek drainage "at a cost of just over $1 million."[1696] By the early 1980s, the acquisition was complete; all of the watershed was within the park.[1697]

Many Bull Creek residents resisted their removal from the canyon,[1698] but they could not withstand the power of eminent domain, and everyone eventually left. In the late 1960s and early 1970s the state bulldozed and burnt buildings until almost all of the structures within the canyon were obliterated.[1699] Decades later, Amos Cummings's apple orchard still turned white with sweet-scented blossoms in the spring, but a hundred years after the trees had won him his medal, they struggled for survival, their story all but forgotten—victims of the same fate as George Burtt's village of Kahs-cho-chin-net-tah that once stood not far from the orchard.

Nearby, Bull Creek ran relentlessly down the canyon, murmuring its mantra that, sooner or later, water is always stronger than earth.

Amos Cummings's apple orchard 75 years after its prime (JR).

# Chapter 24
# Dyerville

In times past, the place where Tah-cho (the main Eel River) was met by Sin-ke-kok (the South Fork Eel)[1700] had a name of its own. The mingling of the waters was called Lel-lin teg-o-be,[1701] perhaps to indicate that it was not merely one of the many confluences on the river but a unique location where two powerful aqueous forces met. On the benchland to the northwest lay a village belonging to the Sinkyone tribe. George Burtt, from the Lolahnkok tribal group in Bull Creek, called the village Chin-tah-te.[1702] Briceland Charlie, from the neighboring Sinkene group centered in Salmon Creek, gave the name as Ltcin-ta-din.[1703] The village was probably in Lolahnkok territory but the evidence isn't conclusive[1704]

On September 7, 1851, the Redick McKee Expedition arrived at Lel-lin teg-o-be on their journey north from Sonoma. George Gibbs, who kept the party's journal, noted that the two rivers each "contained nearly the same amount of water."[1705] He also reported that

> Near the forks, we met a canoe, the first seen on our journey. It was a dug-out, square at both ends, and sufficiently rude and clumsy. The river was now filled with stakes, driven into the sand at pretty regular intervals, to which the Indians fasten baskets of wicker-work to take the eels, and which at certain seasons it abounds, and which have given their name to the stream. These, smoked and dried, constitute a principal article of food among the natives.[1706]

No more is heard about the Indians of Ltcin-ta-din. It is likely they suffered the fate of most of their people and were either killed by whites or sent to reservations during the 1850s and 1860s. The presence of a military installation at nearby Camp Grant all but assured this outcome, especially given the genocidal intent of the militia that was stationed there. Early in 1864, for example, Captain William E. Hull of the Second California Volunteer Infantry was ordered by the commander of Camp Grant "to take the field and capture or kill all Indians found between the northern boundary of the Mendocino Reservation and Bear River, in Humboldt County."[1707]

Thus the Indians were quickly removed from the locale, but whites were slow to then occupy it. The government mapping done in 1869 shows no cultural features at the future site of Dyerville, the closest such being Dobbins's house, garden, and ferry at Camp Grant, two miles up the main Eel.[1708]

The construction of the West Side Road in 1877 transformed the area. Previous travel had either been by a low-water-only wagon route that often used the bed of the Eel or by a trail that stayed on the east side of the river. Now came a road that followed the west side of the Eel, crossing the South Fork on its way to nearby Camp Grant.[1709] With the new road came development; the following year, a letter to the *Humboldt Times* mentioned a store at the mouth of the South Fork, where

> Geo. Harrington keeps on hand a fair supply of boots and shoes, ready made clothing, dry goods and groceries which

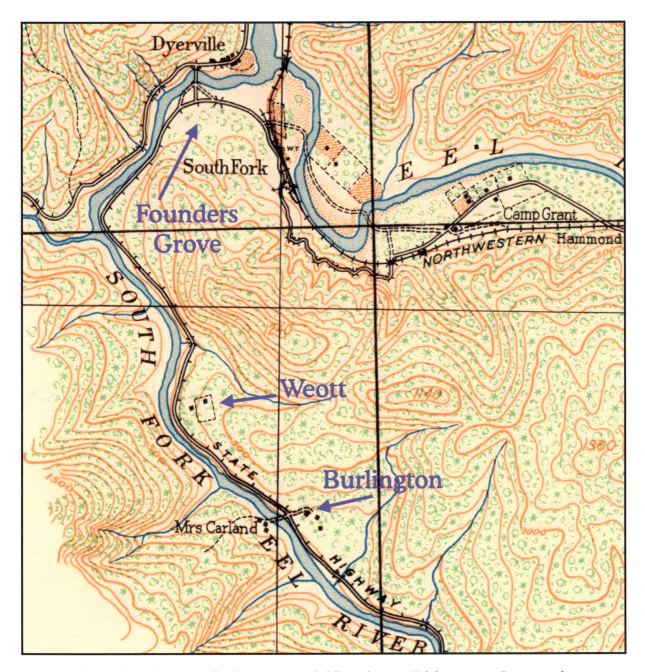

Road radiate from Dyerville, 1916: going north follows the main Eel downriver to Pepperwood, Scotia, etc.; east leads to Camp Grant and the Mail Ridge road; south goes up the South Fork Eel to Garberville and Mendocino County; west runs up the Bull Creek canyon (CE).

he sells from ten to twenty five cents cheaper than others—taking in exchange all manner of family supplies and pays cash prices for all the surplus eggs, butter, bacon, etc. the farmers and stock raisers can produce.[1710]

Harrington was apparently a squatter. In 1881 the Pacific Lumber Company (PL) purchased 3,241 acres of state lands around the confluence of the South Fork and main Eel that included the location of Harrington's store. Three years later PL sold 30 of these acres at the mouth of the South Fork to James Cartwright for $10 but retained the timber rights. In 1888 Cartwright sold the property to William B. Mudd for $2,500—a tidy 25000% profit. Later that year Mudd sold it to Charles Vinson Dyer for $3,500.[1711] This

# Dyerville

proved to be a timely transaction, for when a post office was established in April 1890, it was called Dyerville rather than Muddville.¹⁷¹²

In July 1879, less than two years after the completion of the West Side Road, a road going up the South Fork had been built from the river's mouth to Myer's [sic] Ranch (later to become Myers Flat).¹⁷¹³ In 1881 construction began on a road running down the South Fork from Garberville.¹⁷¹⁴ Work continued, and in 1885 the two roads met somewhere "between Phillipsville and the Myers place."¹⁷¹⁵ This meant a wagon could now travel all the way from Humboldt Bay to Garberville, with the road junction at the mouth of the South Fork a key link in the route. In May 1888 Albert Logan drove his semiweekly stage from Rohnerville to Garberville, part of "a great increase in travel along Eel River," prompting the prediction that "there is little doubt that a village is about to spring up at the mouth of the South Fork of the Eel River."¹⁷¹⁶ Within the week, H. Chadbourne, a blacksmith who already ran a hotel there, was preparing to build a shop that would allow him to return to his main line of work, while E. S. Townsend was about to open a general merchandise store. Prognostication escalated, so that the barely begun town was expected "in a very few years . . . [to be] much larger than Rio Dell is now."¹⁷¹⁷

Perhaps. But certainly not for a while. The county directory of 1890 listed only seven citizens of the Dyerville area: the saloon keeper, the hotel operator, two road overseers, two constables, and one justice of the peace.¹⁷¹⁸ According to one account, it may have been activities at the saloon that required the residency of not one but two constables *and* a justice of the peace. Evi Straton "Pap" Townsend ran the saloon, which

Dyerville's saloon of the holey ceiling (HSU, colorized by JR).

contained the strange architectural embellishment of a ceiling with holes in it. This feature was the result of certain customers' displeasure with Townsend's late-night attempts to close the bar. If Pap announced his intention to do so, some of the boys would take out their revolvers and fire a few perforating shots roofward, with the result that Pap would serve up another round of whiskey or beer.[1719]

Although the abundant forces of law and order at the mouth of the South Fork appeared justified by such antics, other important components of a community came only with the stately progression of the decade. Dyerville eventually came to have a hotel, store, saloon, livery stable, blacksmith shop, ferry, and post office.[1720] There was no public school but "Miss E. Logan teaches a small private school."[1721] In October 1905 one business was temporarily subtracted from the list, when the Dyerville hotel incinerated in spectacular fashion:

Charley Million, stage driver for the South Fork line did heroic work to save P. E. Carland's store, which was in danger of catching fire. He climbed to the roof in his bare feet, leaving the marks of his toe nails on the side of the building. Charley says fighting fire is not pudding, especially in your bare feet.

John Dijekes of Phillipsville was a guest at the hotel, and escaped in his underclothes, carrying his trousers under his arm. He lost his fine gold watch in the fire. "Pap" Townsend, an old pioneer of Dyerville, was staying at the hotel and slept so soundly that escape was cut off. He had to be thrown out of a window into a blanket held by four men. The building was a total loss and was owned by P. E. Carland who will erect another as soon as possible.[1722]

Dyerville's replacement hotel, built after the 1905 fire (THPO, colorized by JR).

# Dyerville

Carland may have had an ash heap instead of a hotel, but thanks to barefoot Charley Million, he still had the Dyerville store.[1723] This he sold in 1909 to PL, which enfolded the business into its Eel River Mercantile Company, adding it to their main store in Scotia and branches at Shively and Field's Landing. Temporarily storeless, Carland moved to Scotia and became manager of the entire Eel River Mercantile operation.[1724]

By 1898 additional road building had solidified Dyerville's position as a transportation hub. The West Side Road entered town from the north, exited to the southwest, and almost immediately met a spur road that ran some seven miles up the Bull Creek canyon. The West Side Road then dropped down to the South Fork ferry. On the south side of the river there was an almost immediate junction: the Garberville road headed up the South Fork, while the West Side Road turned east to reach its original destination of Camp Grant. Now, however, the latter road had been extended up the main Eel, eventually leaving the river to switchback up to Fruitland and then continue south along Mail Ridge.[1725] Thus, by 1907 it was reported that "the overland stage passes . . . [through Dyerville] twice per day and changes horses at the stable. The Garberville stage stops over night in Dyerville and transfers the mail and passengers to the overland stage to be taken on to Camp Five [Elinor]."[1726]

While most traffic went *near* the Eel, some went *on* the river as Dyerville became a "port." Shipping activity from there did not always go smoothly. (See sidebar 1.)

When Harriet Morris Tracy took the stage up the West Side Road in 1905, she noted that

> At Dyerville I had the finest breakfast, fried chicken, potatoes, hot biscuits, preserve sauce, and everything well cooked and clean.[1727]

If travelers found the food good at Dyerville, traveling in the neighborhood could be downright awful. This Willis Nichols learned when he and his buggy met with a remarkable string of misfortunes north of town. (See sidebar 2.)

Buggy rides were not the only dangerous Dyerville activity in 1911. At the end of March Klippel and McLean's paddle-wheeler, the *Poison Oak*, was towing a supply boat loaded with rails and powder upriver to the current construction site for the Northwestern Pacific rail line. About two miles below Dyerville, the supply boat was caught in an eddy and capsized, spilling its cargo into a deep hole before righting itself. Also lost was the only passenger on board, a horse used for helping to tow the supply boat up certain stretches of the river.[1728]

For years the crossing of the South Fork from Dyerville required either going by ferry or, if conditions were favorable, the use of a low-water ford. J. S. Story and E. S. Ingersoll of Eureka tried the latter method in December 1886—always a dangerous month. They drove their buggy into the river, which promptly caught up the vehicle and propelled it downstream. Disaster was avoided when "John Myers . . . dodging the drifting trees and logs, made his way in a boat toward them, and barely succeeded in rescuing the whole outfit."[1729] On another occasion Jim Boots was driving the overland stage from Harris. He "found that the South Fork was bank to bank and plenty of driftwood coming down." It was too high for the ferry to operate, so Boots and another man started across in a row boat. Their progress was slowed when one oar broke; Boots then

Dyerville became a major stop on the West Side Road (HCHS, colorized by JR).

**1. The Late, Not So Great, Maria**

The Eel and the South Fork seasonally carried lots of water between their banks. For a time they also carried boats. Families had small crafts that met their modest transportation needs, but commercial enterprises required larger vessels, one of which was the 40-foot "schooner" *Great Maria*. She had three means of propulsion: the flow of the river for downstream runs, a sail to catch the wind that often blew upstream, and a three-man crew that pushed long poles into the riverbed when going in either direction. Occasionally a fourth propellant was used: a horse to help pull the boat over riffles. The *Great Maria* was owned by Grant Myers of Myers Flat. She journeyed up the South Fork as far as Phillipsville and up the main Eel at least to McCann.[1730]

The *Great Maria* and her cohort boats carried various cargoes: groceries, meats, household goods, and farm supplies went to families and towns along the rivers, while fresh and dried fruits, produce, wool, hides, etc. were brought down towards the coast. Other vessels were sometimes needed. Once two strong-backed oarsmen in a rowboat took Charlie Myers to the Scotia hospital "in record time" after he had accidentally shot himself in the leg on Salmon Creek.[1731]

> That was an exciting trip, but it was rivaled by the voyage of the *Great Maria* on December 18, 1901. She was filled to the gunwales with 200 boxes of apples from Camp Grant, had just stopped at Dyerville, and then continued downriver in the evening.[1732]
>
> But not for long. After about five minutes, the boat encountered waves some three feet high. These promptly filled the *Great Maria* with water. Captain Nelson, at the steering oar, was washed overboard but made his way back on board by clinging to a floating box of apples. The crew—Joe Stockel, Vic Pedrotti, and a Mr. Martin—stayed with the boat but were gradually immersed in the Eel as the *Great Maria* slowly sank. At this point a dugout canoe was dispatched from shore to attempt a rescue. Captain Nelson, with a tow line in hand, jumped into the Eel and brought the line to the canoe. Upon reaching dry ground Nelson found, however, that the tow line was not fastened to anything, let alone the *Great Maria*. By now crewman Martin had jumped ship, landed in shallow water, and struggled to shore.[1733]
>
> That left Pedrotti and Stockel on board. They stayed with the vagrant vessel for about half a mile, at which point the boat lodged in a drift of logs. The men clambered out upon the logs and made it to safety. By now most of the apples had floated free from the boat and continued their trip by bobbing down the Eel. Few were recovered by Stockel, the rightful owner, but families downriver soon experienced an unanticipated apple harvest.[1734]
>
> The *Great Maria* had, in a sense, delivered her cargo, but it was to the wrong recipients. She remained stuck in the drift where it appeared doubtful "that she can ever be recovered from under those logs."[1735]
>
> And for a time there was one less boat to crowd the port of Dyerville.

paddled for dear life with the remaining oar. They were close to being swept into the main Eel when Grant Myers, "who'd been holding a lantern to guide them to shore, threw the men a line and then hauled them to safety."[1736]

In 1913 the county commenced building a bridge across the South Fork as part of the nascent Redwood Highway.[1737] When construction began on the bridge, the ferry ceased operating. This loss of revenue could have impacted the former ferry keeper, Gafford Myers, but he built a temporary toll bridge across the South Fork to reclaim some of his lost income. Certain travelers, however, preferred to ford the river at a riffle rather than pay the toll. To counteract this, Myers periodically borrowed a pair of horses from Vic Pedrotti, the Dyerville blacksmith, and used them to plow the riffle out. This inevitably led to someone's wagon or auto becoming stuck in the suddenly deeper river. Out came Myers, driving Pedrotti's horses, ready to pull free the victim's vehicle for a two- or three-dollar fee.[1738] During the 1915, flood Pedrotti's team was of

## 2. Rough Times along the Road

On July 28, 1911, Willis Nichols of Camp Grant set a record for accident efficiency by being involved in three mishaps in one hour. Nichols had gone to Shively to consult with a physician about an attack of rheumatism. Within a short time the ailment became the least of his worries.[1739]

Returning to Camp Grant, Nichols encountered an inebriate staggering along the road in the vicinity of Englewood (Redcrest). Nichols, in Good Samaritan fashion, offered the man a ride in his buggy. The offer was accepted, and Nichols then drove through town and started down the grade to the south. The descent proved too much for the passenger, who promptly tumbled out of the buggy, contriving as he did so to grab the reins away from Nichols. This abrupt maneuver startled the horse, which promptly bolted down the road. With the reins trailing in the dust, Nichols watched in horror as the buggy careened downhill until it turned on its side, depositing him heavily on the ground. Still dragging the battered buggy, the horse disappeared down the road.[1740]

Nichols was disabled by his mishap, but help was at hand; he called to his erstwhile passenger and asked him to go to the Pedrotti place for aid. Still befuddled, the drunken hitchhiker "dashed off in a frenzied manner toward Dyerville, covering about 200 yards only to fall into the dust where he was later discovered slumbering soundly, an automobile having barely missed running over him."[1741]

But assistance, nonetheless, soon appeared. Good Samaritan #2, Alonza Smith, happened by, and he secured another horse and buggy to take the injured Nichols to Dyerville. This plan worked—temporarily. After about a mile the rescue outfit encountered a passing automobile. This overstimulated the new horse, which lunged suddenly, propelling Nichols for a second time into the road, an event that allowed him to sustain fresh injuries.[1742]

Back into the buggy went the twice battered Nichols. For another period of time, all went well in the attempt to reach Dyerville, but then the new horse encountered the handiwork of the first horse, which had distributed parts of Nichols's buggy along the road. Upon seeing a piece of linoleum(!) from the wreck, horse #2 immediately had a second panic attack, jerking the buggy about in a manner that rendered Nichols upon the road for a third time. Again Nichols was returned to the buggy, which finally brought him to Dyerville. Here he was eventually examined by Dr. Falk, who found no broken bones but did discover "numerous bruises and cuts." There was also some painful ligament damage.[1743]

# Dyerville

A peaceful buggy ride near Dyerville (JR, colorized by JR).

Nichols was then taken to his home at Camp Grant, from which he should never have left. His misadventure apparently cast a miasma upon the road, for the next day the mail stage, after leaving Dyerville, had *its* horses startled into a stampede that resulted in the stage being wrecked about two miles from town.[1744]

It was a new roadway rumpus that thrice-wounded Willis Nichols, now safely ensconced at Camp Grant, was happy to miss.

little use, as Vic instead required a rowboat to rescue his family's washing, which hung outside above the water rising over Dyerville.[1745] Pedrotti maintained an alfalfa field above the confluence of the South Fork and main Eel. Each year, after the alfalfa was cut and harvested, the field was temporarily converted into the Dyerville baseball diamond.[1746] The ball filed survived the 1915 flood and lasted 40 longer before a bigger freshet removed it.[1747]

The roadbed for the Redwood Highway was graded through Dyerville in 1914.[1748] The highway's planning map at the time showed that the town had a store, hotel, shop, two barns, and three houses. The alignment of the new highway ran close to the hillslope on the west, requiring the removal of almost all of Dyerville's structures.[1749] Some of the buildings were now no longer needed, since auto and truck traffic on the new state highway made different demands than did wagon or buggy traffic on the old West Side Road. Motor vehicles required a gas pump and garage, not a blacksmith and livery stable. Travelers no longer found them-

A teamster (probably Gafford Myers) uses horses and wagon (probably Vic Pedrotti's) to pull a luckless motorist's auto from the secretly sculpted South Fork (HCHS, colorized by JR).

selves having to stop for the night because the ferry wasn't operating or because a full day of riding had brought them only to the South Fork. Thus, when the highway was rerouted in 1931 to accommodate a new bridge across the river, a diminished Dyerville consisted of only a garage, store, and three houses, all of which were on the east side of the roadway.[1750]

By then attention had shifted to the south side of the South Fork, where the redwood-rich Dyerville Flat stood. (See Appendix A.)

The Bull Creek and Dyerville flats became part of Humboldt Redwoods State Park when they were dedicated at Bull Creek at 11:00 A.M. on September 13, 1931. A second dedication took place at 2:30 P.M. that afternoon. On the Dyerville Flat, the Founders Tree was named in honor of Madison Grant, John C. Merriam, and Henry Fairfield Osborn, the three men deemed most responsible for the formation of the Save-the-Redwoods League.[1751]

The acquisition of the Bull Creek and Dyerville flats represented a huge expansion of Humboldt Redwoods State Park. It also doomed what was left of the town of Dyerville. The new bridge across the South Fork soon took travelers past a town transformed into the park's headquarters. The erstwhile store became the park's main building, with offices, a museum, and a visitor center. Some of the dwellings were converted into housing for park employees. Several superannuated buildings were torn down and replaced by garages and maintenance areas. The California Division of Forestry put in a dispatch center and fire station. In 1933 the federal government added to the state's facilities by establishing a Civilian Conservation Corps (CCC) camp at the Dyerville townsite.[1752]

Then came the near-biblical year of 1937. Reversing that book's prognostication of disasters, a summer and fall of huge forest fires that engaged the CCC boys as firefighters was followed by a December flood that cut away part of riverside shelf upon which Dyerville stood. The Division of Forestry promptly decamped, moving its headquarters to Fortuna and its fire station to Weott, while the CCC camp moved up the South Fork to Burlington, a couple of miles upriver from Weott.[1753]

The wisdom of these moves was proved on December 20, 1955, when park superintendent James Warren watched while the flooding South Fork rose 19 feet in one hour as its waters rushed by Dyerville. Three days later the river tore out the town's one-time alfalfa field and former baseball diamond while filling the state buildings with a surfeit of silt. The destruction was intensified by the activities of the hillslope above the highway, which cut loose with an avalanche of alluvium that attacked the park buildings from the opposite direction. Finally the park took the hint and relocated its headquarters to Burlington.[1754]

Buildingless, Dyerville became the site of a northbound on-ramp when the Redwood Highway was converted to freeway. The park eventually built an overlook that allowed scenery seekers to view the mingling of the waters once known as Lel-lin teg-o-be. And, miraculously, buildings reappeared at Dyerville. Brigadoon-like, the annual Avenue of the Giants Marathon saw a row of 50 or more portable toilets temporarily lining the roadside for the convenience of the runners. Some of them were placed close to the site of the Dyerville saloon, but unlike their predecessor, they each had only a single hole in their ceiling.

Dyerville, 1915 (DTC, colorized by JR).

### Appendix A: The Three Telegrams

On page 36 of the 1895-1896 Humboldt County Business Directory is a listing for "McGaraghan, P, speculator."[1755] He is the only person in the entire directory with this occupation.[1756]

Speculators invest in commodities, such as stocks, that they believe will gain substantial value, at which time they can be sold for a handsome profit. McGaraghan speculated in land. George Washington, who is more famous for other endeavors, did likewise, purchasing 1,459 acres in rural Virginia in 1752. By 1800, when he executed his will, he owned 52,194 acres "to be sold or distributed."[1757]

It is unclear how much land McGaraghan amassed in his role as a speculator, but by 1898 he had claimed one especially interesting parcel: a 160-acre piece of heavily forested hillslope, a half-mile square, that lay between the main Eel and South Fork Eel rivers about three-quarters of a mile south of Dyerville.[1758] The property, however, was not to remain in McGaraghan's possession for long.

In 1898 much of the Bull Creek and Dyerville flats already belonged to PL, but there were several small holdings, like McGaraghan's, and a large tract belonging to the Western Redwood Company that were not theirs. By 1911 many of these parcels, including McGaraghan's, were in PL's hands. The company owned much of the land on both sides of the main Eel from Scotia all the way upriver to Camp Grant. It owned part of the north slope of Grasshopper Peak. And it owned the Dyerville and Bull Creek Flats.[1759]

Willis Lynn Jepson, probably the most famous botanist in the state, had "described the Bull Creek redwoods as the best of their kind."[1760] Now PL could fondly contemplate the day when these "best" redwoods would be transported to their mill at Scotia and transformed into the best-quality lumber.

In 1911, though, the trees weren't going anywhere because there was no effective way to move logs from Bull Creek to Scotia. It would take a major change in the county's transportation infrastructure before anything could happen.

The necessary transition came in 1914 when the Northwestern Pacific Railroad (NWP) completed its line from Sausalito to Trinidad. Among the stations along the way was one called South Fork, which lay a few hundred feet east of the Dyerville Flat. It would be easy for PL to run a short spur line from the NWP tracks to the tract of towering redwoods.

But not yet.

Between Scotia and Dyerville, PL had been clearing redwoods for almost three decades, gradually cutting their way south as they followed the extension of the railroad. By 1916 they operated several logging camps in the Larabee Creek area,[1761] some four miles north of South Fork, while large tracts of uncut timber lay in three drainages between Larabee Creek and South Fork. Unless PL changed its logging strategy, it would be years before it got to Dyerville Flat.

But then another transportation transformation intervened. In 1917 three members of the patrician Bohemian Club decided to play hooky from the group's summer high jinx on the Russian River and drive up the new Redwood Highway to see the forests of southern Humboldt County.[1762]

The three Bohemians carried with them some impressive credentials: Madison Grant was chairman of the New York Zoological Society, Henry Fairfield Osborn was president of the American Museum of Natural History, and John C. Merriam was a professor of paleontol-

Building the railroad near South Fork (CPH, colorized by JR).

ogy at the University of California Berkeley.[1763] Less impressive, at least by later standards, were other portions of their resumés. All three were prominent supporters of the eugenics movement, which exalted the so-called "Nordic" race and promoted discrimination against other racial groups, including bans on interracial marriage, limits on immigration from non-European countries, and the involuntary sterilization of certain non-Nordic women.[1764] In 1916 Grant wrote *The Passing of the Great Race*, a white supremacist screed that Adolph Hitler subsequently called "my Bible."[1765] For Osborn, Merriam, and Grant, it was only a short step from this tainted theorizing to anointing the coast redwood as the sylvan representative of the "master race."

The trio's 1917 trip took them through the redwood forests along the South Fork and main Eel rivers, areas that until recently had been reachable only by wagon road. Merriam later described their descent from the roadway into the forest:

Suddenly we swung from the highway, dropping down a steep slope into primeval redwood timber. The car quieted as its wheels rolled over the leafy carpet. The road soon ended in a trail, and the party proceeded on foot. . . .

As we advanced, the arches of foliage narrowed above us and shade deepened into night. . . . Like pillars of a temple, the giant columns spaced themselves with mutual support, producing unity and not mere symmetry. . . .

But woven through this picture was an element which eludes the imagery of art. The sense of time made itself felt as it can but rarely be experienced. While ancient castles may tell us of other ages in contrasts of the seemingly fantastic architecture, living trees like these connect us by hand-touch with all the centuries they have known. The time they represent is not merely an unrelated, severed past;

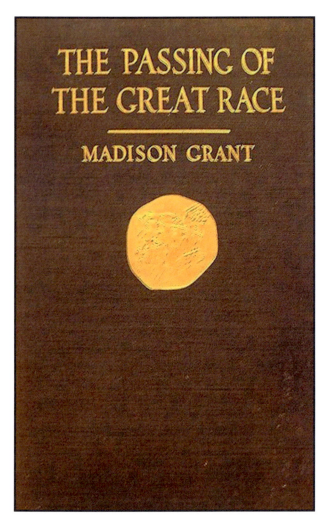

Hitler's Bible (WP).

it is something upon which the present rests, and from which living currents seem to move.

We realized that the mysterious influence of this grove arose not alone from magnitude, or from the beauty of light filling deep spaces. It was as if in these trees the flow of years were held in eddies, and one saw together past and present. The element of time pervaded the forest with an influence more subtle than light, but that to the mind was not less real.[1766]

After subsequently arriving at the Arcata Hotel, Osborn and Grant sent off a letter to governor William D. Stephens informing him that "the superb woods of Bull Creek flats are incomparably grand" and indicating that creating "a Redwood Park of Humboldt County . . . would be one of the most gratefully received and long remembered acts of your administration."[1767]

The days passed, and Governor Stephens governed, but no park was forthcoming. In 1918 Grant returned to California and "endeavored to interest the California Highway Commission in securing a strip of timber along the new highways." When no strip was secured, Grant and Merriam spent the winter of 1918-1919 "enlisting the support of a patriotic group of Californians" in creating a new conservation organization.[1768]

The support was successfully enlisted, and in April 1919 the just-formed Save-the-Redwoods League (SRL) hired brothers Newton and Aubrey Drury "to handle advertising, publicity and a direct-mail membership drive."[1769] Newton became the SRL's first executive secretary[1770] and soon had much more to "handle," including an attempt to protect the Bull Creek and Dyerville flats.

In June Madison Grant again drove up the Redwood Highway. Along the South Fork he found a string of "small lumber camps" on 40-acre parcels, where the roadside trees were "doomed to the ignoble fate of being riven for railroad ties, for shakes or shingles, and perhaps worst of all, for grape stakes." If this were not bad enough, Grant discovered that the California Highway Commission had indeed bought a hundred-foot-wide band of redwoods along the highway, but instead of protecting the trees had "actually contracted with the [previous] owners for the removal of the timber."[1771]

It hadn't taken long. The railroad, less than five years old, and the highway, still under construction, had been yoked together in a system

# Dyerville

that all but guaranteed the destruction of southern Humboldt forest. "Tie hacks" could cut and split the roadside redwoods, take them by truck a few miles along the highway to the South Fork train station, and load them aboard the NWP's railcars for transport to the lumber yards of San Francisco and the wineries of the Napa Valley. Grant, after his drive through the highwayside desolation, had sounded the alarm just as the brand-new SRL began to mobilize, but could a single organization move quickly enough to stem the tide?

The answer was no, a single organization couldn't. But two could.

On August 2, 1919, the first meeting of the SRL's board of directors was held in Parlor B of San Francisco's Palace Hotel.[1772] A week later, after a visit to Eureka by SRL leaders Grant and Steven Tyng Mather, the various local women's clubs formed the Humboldt County Women's Save-the-Redwoods League (HCWSRL). Within three months, it was 800 members strong.[1773]

At its start the SRL was led exclusively by men, most of whom were wealthy and held positions of power. They could reach out to others of their station not just in California but throughout the nation. They could speak the language of bankers and businessmen and could look a timber company owner in the eye as an equal. Their first president was Secretary of the Interior Franklin K. Lane; their first secretary and treasurer was Robert Gordon Sproul, who later became the president of the University of California at Berkeley.[1774]

Contrastingly, the HCWSRL consisted chiefly of women, but "admitted men who were willing to work alongside [not above] them." The organization was locally based and meagerly funded; its initial dues of 50 cents a year was soon reduced to 25 cents.[1775] For some observers, the potential of new organization may have raised doubts, but there were reasons to believe the group might be effective. Two decades earlier, the San Jose Woman's Club had shown its strength when it supported the newly formed Sempervirens Club in a successful drive to establish Big Basin Redwoods State Park in the Santa Cruz Mountains.[1776] Now, in 1919, women flexed their political muscle nationally by gaining Congressional approval of the 19th Amendment, which secured for women the right to vote.[1777]

On September 6, 1919, the HCWSRL made the news when the *Humboldt Standard* ran a photo of four well-dressed elderly women in front of a car displaying a banner with the slogan "SAVE THE REDWOODS." As impressive as the sentiment were the pedigrees of the matrons ex-

Newton B. Drury (CSP, colorized by JR).

Four doughty dowagers enter the fray. Left to right: Lucretia Anna Huntington Monroe, Kate Harpst, Mary Anne Atkinson, Ella Georgeson. Driver Frank Silence sits quietly in the car (CPH, colorized by JR).

pressing it: Lucretia Anna Huntington Monroe was a school teacher whose husband was a notable local attorney; Kate Harpst, who owned the car, was the widow of an Arcata lumberman; Mary Anne Atkinson was the wife of the owner of the Metropolitan Lumber Company; and Ella Georgeson's husband was publisher of the *Humboldt Standard*, bank president, and former Eureka mayor.[1778]

The same week as the HCWSRL car photo, a meeting of the preservation allies took place in Eureka. Madison Grant and other members of the SRL met with Laura Perrott Mahan, recently elected president of the HCWSRL, and other members of her group. Out of the meeting came a plan to prevent further roadside redwood cutting by paying the cutters $60,000 to put down their axes.[1779]

The groups had only two days to savor their accomplishment before PL began logging Dyerville Flat. PL president John Emmert claimed that winter weather made the steep slopes of the Larabee Creek drainage, where the company had been cutting, too slippery to continue, whereas the "nature of the topography" at Dyerville Flat permitted logging during the rainy season. This, Emmert claimed, would keep PL's Scotia mill open and 800 to 1,000 employees at work.[1780]

Emmert was attempting to cast the situation as a simple adherence to the dictum of "business as usual," but from the preservationists' perspective, it was an immediate crisis. The Dyerville and Bull Creek flats were the jewels in a crown of riverside redwoods that would soon, hopefully, become a state or national park. Each stroke of the woods-

# Dyerville

man's ax, each kerf cut by a PL worker's saw was damaging one of the jewels and diminishing the chances that a crown worth saving would remain. The threat was felt so acutely that the "Humboldt County Chamber of Commerce . . . implored Emmert to stop the cutting," and more than 50 of its members telegrammed him to that effect. Emmert's response was to send five additional logging teams to Dyerville Flat.[1781]

The *Humboldt Times* raged against Emmert's latest act, claiming that soon the flat would be "ruined for National Park purposes."[1782] Whether knowingly or not, the paper had revealed what was probably the true aim of PL. Where a Laura Mahan might see the trees as monuments to immortality and thrill to the vertical beauty of the tall trunks rising into the verdant overstory, a John Emmert might long to view them laid horizontally, sawed into sections, and sent off as the largest logs ever to be cut by PL's mill. By beginning the cutting now, PL could inch its way across Dyerville Flat and on to the even larger grove at Bull Creek. Just a narrow corridor, with a rail line built along it, might be enough to ruin the flats for park status and thus ensure that PL's lust for lumber would be fully satisfied.

With the SRL and the HCWSRL struggling to organize their campaigns, it was the Humboldt County Chamber of Commerce that rode to the redwoods' rescue. They produced testimony by

> . . . experienced loggers [who] were confident that even during the winter, other timber owned by Pacific Lumber could be cut without damaging the prospects for a national park.[1783]

With his credibility challenged, Emmert at first held fast to his plan, but he then agreed to reduce the Dyerville cutting.[1784] He indicated that the greatest part of the logging "was to come from the sidehills and not the flat," that no logging would occur between the South Fork train station and the Redwood Highway at the Dyerville bridge, that PL would cut only enough timber for the winter, and that "a timber cruiser chosen by the Save the Redwoods committee . . . [would] lay out the timber to be cut."[1785]

In this way 1919 passed into 1920. Logging on Dyerville Flat stopped, at least temporarily, as the preservationists expanded their efforts to save endangered redwoods. In August 1921 the SRL dedicated the Bolling Memorial Grove at Elk Creek on the South Fork Eel[1786] between Myers Flat and Miranda. It was the first in a long series of memorial groves, which were purchased with funds donated to honor particular individuals.[1787] It was also the first parcel of land in what was to become Humboldt State Redwoods Park,[1788] which opened in June 1922.[1789]

At the time of its dedication, the Bolling Grove preserved 35 acres of redwoods.[1790] It was a pretty, streamside location, but, in comparison to the entire South Fork redwood forest, it was tiny, protecting just a few dozen trees out of the thousands that lined the riverside highway.

And the rest of the forest would not be there forever. By 1921 some 21% of Humboldt County's redwoods had already been cut. PL was logging its timberlands at an even faster rate: it had leveled 26,000 of its 69,000 acres of redwoods[1791] and was closing in on the South Fork.

But the tree-savers were making progress. By 1923 the SRL had acquired all but two parcels along the 14-mile stretch of highway between Miranda and Dyerville.[1792] In 1924 the league announced an expansive four-project program that included saving redwoods at locations

Dedication of the Bolling Grove, 1922: Madison Grant, second from left; Henry Fairfield Osborn, fourth from left; John C. Merriam, to right of monument; Newton B. Drury, far right (SRL, colorized by JR).

distant from the South Fork: at Prairie Creek, along the Del Norte coast, and at Mill Creek and the Smith River in Del Norte County. At the top of the list, however, was the grail of the preservationists—the Bull Creek and Dyerville flats.[1793]

Four years had passed since PL had briefly logged on Dyerville Flat. Then on the evening of November 23, word reached Laura and James Mahan—the choppers were back! The next morning the Mahans drove south to see if the information was accurate.[1794]

Neither of the Mahans left a detailed account of what they found, but 15 years later George Waldner, the editor of the *Ferndale Enterprise*, wrote a vivid description of the event that is worth repeating, even though it mixed fact with folklore:

> Parking their car just inside the fringe of the grove their ears caught the unmistakable sound of workmen not far ahead. Hurrying toward their objective near the east side of the forest they saw sharp sunshine where, they knew, only the semi-darkness of deep redwoods had prevailed since time immemorial. Unbelievably before them were the results

of logging operations. Huge redwoods stretching flat through the clutching underbrush, the fragrance of undisturbed sorrel replaced by the acrid fumes of gasoline, the flash of a double-bitted ax arcing swiftly through the air.

In another moment they reached the foreman of the crew. Excitedly they demanded he stop his men from further work of destruction. The foreman had his orders and intended to carry them out. They cajoled. But the work must go on. In desperation Mrs. Mahan climbed to the flat surface of a freshly cut stump. There she stood and defied the men to proceed. Only then did the work cease for she stood in the path of certain death had work continued.[1795]

Laura Perrott Mahan (HCHS, colorized by JR).

No Hollywood writer could have scripted the scene any better, but people familiar with logging and with the Dyerville Flat would have quickly noted at least one or two deviations from the truth. First, the Mahans would probably have approached the logging site from the Redwood Highway and therefore would not have encountered any downed trees along their route; the loggers had started from the opposite side of the flat and were cutting towards, not away from, the highway. Second, no chopping boss would have let his crew drop a redwood onto a stump, whether or not it was one upon which Laura Mahan stood. The impact of the falling tree hitting the stump would have shattered part of the trunk, costing PL a substantial sum in lost lumber. Even if Laura Mahan did manage to position herself in actual path of the tree, the choppers could have simply moved on to another redwood. But images can be powerful, and the one Waldner created stood like a giant falsifying tree within the forest, shutting out the sunlight of the truth.

What actually happened was dramatic enough. After conducting "a personal investigation on the ground," Laura Mahan reported the result to the Eureka papers, managing to meet the deadline of the *Humboldt Standard*, the city's afternoon paper. The result was a small front-page article, "Dyerville Flat Redwoods Being Cut By Loggers,"[1796] which was being read hours after the Mahans made their discovery. The next morning, subscribers to the *Humboldt Times* were greeted with a double-banner headline that shouted, "HUMBOLDT COUNTY IN FIGHT WITH LUMBER CO. FOR TREES."[1797]

Before their coffee grew cold, breakfast-time readers learned that not only were the "axes and

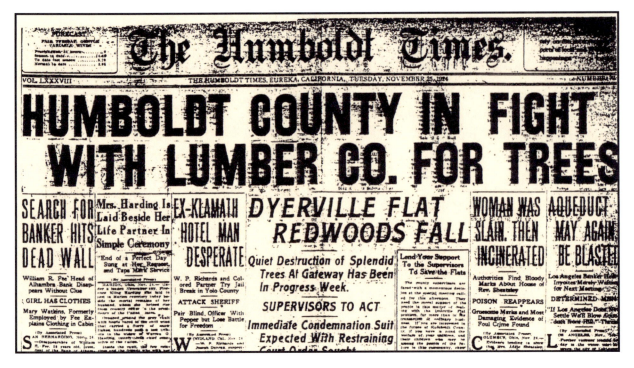

Big news at breakfast (colorized by JR).

saws of the Pacific Lumber Company" destroying the "hope of generations yet unborn," but that within a few hours the Humboldt County Board of Supervisors were to meet in special session to decide what they would do about it.[1798]

When the board convened, its five members faced a room filled with concerned citizens. Laura Mahan was there with a delegation from the HCWSRL. Many allies from the Eureka Woman's Club sat nearby, and there were contingents from the American Legion, the Rotary Club, the Elks Club, and the Humboldt State Teachers College. Residents from Ferndale, Loleta, Trinidad, Fortuna, Rohnerville, Garberville, and even tiny Carlotta were present. Newton Drury, secretary of the SRL, had come up from San Francisco along with Frederick Erskine Olmstead, who was preparing a plan for the league to buy 3,000 acres of the Dyerville and Bull Creek flats.[1799]

The board viewed this staunch coalition of preservationists, considered the issue, and then voted unanimously to buy 160 acres of Dyerville Flat from PL and to seek an injunction to halt the logging. The board also instructed Humboldt County District Attorney Arthur W. Hill to begin condemnation proceedings against PL as the first step in acquiring the acreage.[1800]

These actions inflamed Fred Murphy, a member of the family that owned PL. When, following the county supervisors' action, the SRL asked PL for a meeting to attempt a non-confrontational solution to the conflict, Murphy not only opposed the SRL's offer but also instructed PL's attorneys to seek a temporary restraining order to prevent the condemnation of Dyerville Flat. The request was granted, but when it became apparent that the court would not make the restraining order permanent, PL dropped the case.[1801]

Instead, PL switched to a new, more subtle tactic. It offered to allow perpetual public use of the southern portion of the Dyerville Flat in exchange for a pledge from the county to file no further condemnation suits. PL also indicated it would sell 300-foot-wide corridors on either side of the highway along the stretch that passed through the flat.[1802]

The offer was designed to appeal not to the SRL and the HCWSRL but to a portion of their supporters. PL believed that the board of supervisors, local business interests, and a significant part of the general public would be satisfied with access to a small, cost-free portion of the Dyerville Flat rather than insisting on having the county purchase a larger, expensive parcel. If this wedge that PL was trying to drive into the preservationist movement was not powerful enough, they company attempted to strengthen it by including the following statement:

> We appreciate the love of the beautiful which actuates those who would prevent any of the redwood trees of this state from being cut or destroyed. But we believe that such aestheticism should not be allowed to be carried to the extent where it destroys the property rights of others and prevents the carrying on of ordinary business operations according to the law of the land.[1803]

The appeal by a large business concern to the gospel of property rights had been used before and would be used many times later. But Laura Mahan and the HCWSRL were having none of it. They promptly made their opposition known and gathered the support of several sympathetic organizations. But other community groups, and most especially the Humboldt County Board of Supervisors, wavered. Newton B. Drury found that only one supervisor remained steadfast in his support of acquiring the flat.[1804]

On February 11, 1925, the situation reached a climax. That day the supervisors met to consider PL's offer, which had gained enough traction within the community to put the preservationists on the defensive. If the SRL and the HCWSRL ever needed help, the time was now.

Unknown to almost everyone, they had it.

Back in 1923 the SRL was informed that John D. Rockefeller Jr. was interested in establishing a memorial redwood grove in honor of his mother. Quietly the league pursued the lead, learning that Rockefeller's interest might exceed the purchase of a single parcel. Negotiations ensued, and in November 1924 Rockefeller sent the SRL a check for a sizable sum—$1,000,000.[1805] The next year, when Drury came up to Eureka for the February board of supervisors meeting, he knew he would be gambling on the future of the Dyerville Flat,

Barely room for all the numbers (JRC, colorized by JR).

but he now had a few extra chips to throw in the pot.

Three weeks earlier, the SRL had received Olmstead's study of possible redwood acquisitions. Olmstead indicated a preference for the purchase of three parcels: the Dyerville Flat, a series of small groves along the highway, and the *entire* 2,290-acre Bull Creek Flat. Based on this, the SRL prepared a resolution for the Humboldt County Board of Supervisors urging them to reject PL's proposal and indicating that the league "had over three-quarters of a million dollars available for the purchase of [the flats at] Dyerville and Bull Creek."[1806]

February 11 arrived. At ten that morning, as the *Humboldt Times* reported,

> Grandad and Grandchild, mother and father and young folk, thronged Judge Murray's chambers at the courthouse... when the momentous question of the condemnation of Dyerville Flats by the Humboldt board of supervisors was to be discussed and decided upon in open meeting. Officials of the Pacific Lumber Company sat in a little group to the right of the courtroom, and on the left sat the members of the district attorney's party, representing the board of supervisors and the people of Humboldt county. An air of expectancy hovered over all.[1807]

Even the most extravagant expectations were fulfilled by what followed.

As the *Times* saw it, Senator H. C. Nelson, PL's attorney, "presented his side of the contention in a logically clear and imposing manner." In fact, the *Times* noted, "none other could have presented the case better, few so well." However, Nelson "was pitting cold, unpalpitating [sic] legal lore against public sentiment, and that proved an insurmountable barrier."[1808]

No wonder then that District Attorney Hill gave what was considered "a wonderfully forceful presentation of the people's side of the controversy." Hill must have sensed that the audience saw him, a mere county official, riding knight-like to the rescue of the Humboldt populace, for he

> ... made it known in plain, unvarnished language, and in a ringing voice that carried conviction with it to every man and woman in the court room, that if The Pacific Lumber Company, or its legal representatives, insisted on throwing down to him, and the people of Humboldt County, and the nation the gauge of battle, that they would find him willing to take up the people's standard and the people's fight as far as it was necessary to take it to a successful conclusion.[1809]

By the *Times's* standard this should have proved the death knell to PL's cause, yet the debate continued. Nelson and Hill each fired another salvo. Irwin T. Quinn offered the Humboldt American Legion's support for saving the redwoods. Donald MacDonald, PL's treasurer, talked "about how large a payroll the company carried." Later MacDonald "wagged and shook his finger" at James Mahan, who shook his finger back.[1810]

At a morning break Arcata businessman Henry Brizard had warned Drury that PL had succeeded in raising doubt among the supervisors as to the SRL's ability to buy the Bull Creek and Dyerville redwoods and that Drury needed to "do something to offset the effect of that argument." Drury had immediately phoned his brother Aubrey in San Francisco, asking for help in supplying proof of the SRL's financial resources. Now the lunch break came and went with no word from Aubrey.[1811]

Back in the courtroom, the MacDonald-Mahan finger fight escalated. Mahan accused MacDonald of duplicity when the PL treasurer had earlier said that the company would sell the north Dyerville Flat if the necessary money was raised, but was now saying that PL wouldn't do it. Drury, seated nearby, intensely wished that he'd heard back from his brother, but this thought was shelved as MacDonald and Mahan "approached each other, MacDonald stiffening and straightening and Mahan shaking his fist." Quickly Drury "interposed . . . that all should be amiable and no personalities indulged in."[1812] What MacDonald and Mahan intended to do next will never be known for, as the *Humboldt Times* reported,

> At this dramatic moment three telegrams in rapid succession were handed to Drury, who read:
> "$700,000 in funds on hand to save redwoods."
> "$750,000 in funds on hand to save redwoods."
> "$750,000 in funds on hand to save redwoods."[1813]

The messages came from William H. Crocker, president of the Crocker National Bank; J. D. Grant, SRL vice-president and a director of a half-dozen banks; and James C. Sperry, "a prominent figure in California financial circles."[1814] The audience was thunderstruck. Drury later said "you could have heard a pin drop."[1815]

Aubrey Drury had come through, perhaps more so than he realized. It appears that Newton Drury wanted three telegrams, all confirming that the SRL had a *total* of $750,000 available to buy redwood timberlands. But one of the three responders telegraphed the figure of $700,000 instead. When Drury read the telegrams to the audience, this discrepancy in the amount of available funds apparently created the impression that each telegram was about a *separate* pledge of money. This led to the conclusion that the SRL had not a mere $750,000 on hand but a whopping $2,200,000 instead.

Fortified by the dramatic, if somewhat misleading, impact of the telegrams, the board of supervisors voted unanimously[1816] to accept the SRL's proposal, "calling for amicable negotiations if at all possible, condemnation proceedings if necessary, and league acquisition of Bull Creek and Dyerville Flat [sic]."[1817]

The miracle of the three telegrams was not the only pivotal event of the day. A typical Humboldt County winter rainstorm provided a second situation that greatly benefitted the SRL. After the supervisors' meeting concluded, Newton Drury and Albert W. Atwood, who was writing about the redwoods for *The Saturday Evening Post*, boarded the evening train for San Francisco. The torrential rain, however, had blocked the tracks and so the men deboarded in Scotia, where they planned to stay overnight in PL's Mowatoc (later renamed Scotia) Inn. PL president John Emmert learned of their arrival, and, in an act of unexpected but fortuitous hospitality, invited Drury and Atwood to dinner. The meal, according to Drury, was "wonderful," and Emmert was "particularly friendly." The result was that the SRL and PL were able to defuse their confrontational relationship and embark on more amicable negotiations for

The Mowatoc Inn, site of Drury's delightful dinner (JRC colorized by JR).

the league's acquisition of the Bull Creek and Dyerville flats.[1818]

That evening at Scotia, neither Drury nor Emmert had any idea how long those negotiations would last. As it turned out, they were prolonged beyond the most pessimistic projections. Six months after dining with Drury, Emmert met with John C. Merriam, the SRL president and proposed that the league consider acquiring some 10,000 to 12,000 acres in Bull Creek rather than the 2,000-plus that was the SRL's current objective. Merriam left the meeting convinced that PL "would not willingly sell a smaller area."[1819]

The league was trapped. Here was an offer of a tract of redwoods whose size vastly exceeded their expectations, but the cost of which would be far beyond the funds they could reasonably expect to generate. Agreeing to the proposal might strain the SRL beyond the financial breaking point, but the only other option, instituting condemnation proceedings for the smaller block of land, was something the SRL was unwilling to attempt. The league decided to accept PL's offer.[1820]

PL and the SRL agreed to have a three-person arbitration board determine the value of the forestland, which would then form the basis for negotiations about the final price. In 1927 the arbitrators returned a figure of $5,600,000, far higher than the league had hoped. With certain ancillary costs added, the final cost would be $6,000,000.[1821]

Raising the money was a daunting task, but events soon transpired to make it easier. In November 1928 California voters approved a $6,000,000 state park bond that would match

# Dyerville

public contributions, dollar for dollar, up to that limit, so that the combination of donations and bond money would equal $12,000,000. The bond measure passed statewide by nearly a three-to-one margin. Laura Mahan noted that in Humboldt County the margin was five to one.[1822] Two months later Rockefeller, having visited the Bull Creek and Dyerville flats in 1926,[1823] indicated that he would donate another million dollars to the cause if the SRL could match it by the end of 1930. This meant that any donation to the league would, up to a point, effectively be quadrupled—doubled by Rockefeller's pledge and that amount then doubled by the state bond money. The SRL's fundraising goal finally appeared reachable.[1824]

Now the main hurdle was having PL agree on a price. From 1928 to 1930, while the flats at Bull Creek and Dyerville remained uncut but vulnerable, the issue remained unresolved. As the impasse became apparent, the recently formed State Park Commission became involved in the negotiations. Then, in 1930, A. Stanwood Murphy, soon to become president of PL, joined Emmert at the meetings. At first his presence had no effect, and the SRL edged toward the solution it had long dreaded, condemnation proceedings.[1825] But Arthur E. Connick, Eureka bank president and future SRL president, began talking with Murphy. Connick knew the temper of Humboldt County preservationists and their allies, and he warned Murphy that a refusal by

Dedication of the Bull Creek-Dyerville forest, September 13, 1931 (IA, colorized by JR).

PL to settle would probably result in a boycott of redwood lumber, abetted by articles in the *Saturday Evening Post* and other magazines condemning the "wanton devastation and destruction" of the redwood forests.[1826]

Murphy blinked. In April 1931 Connick and Murphy announced a compromise. The purchase area was reduced by nearly a third, from 13,239 to 9,000 acres, and the price would be substantially less than what PL wanted: $3,212,220. A survey of the forest showed what the preservationists were getting for their money: "105,392 redwoods of a diameter of more than 20 inches" plus 34,836 smaller redwoods and 21,313 Douglas-fir trees.[1827] If the purchase price was applied solely to the larger redwoods, the cost came to $30.48 per tree, by anyone's standards a stupendous bargain.

By June PL had signed off on the sale, followed by the approval of the State Parks Commission. The transaction, six years in the making, was completed in August, and on September 13, 1931, over a thousand celebrants gathered beside the Bull Creek road for the dedication of the Bull Creek-Dyerville forest.[1828] It had taken the efforts of two Save-the-Redwoods leagues, two $1,000,000 donations—and three timely telegrams—but the greatest redwood forest on earth had finally been protected.

# Sources

A. J. J. [pseud.]
    1878a  A Visit to Petrolia and Upper Mattole. Ferndale Enterprise, June 8, 1878:3.

America's Story
    2020  Andrew Carnegie Grows Up Working. Web page. Electronic document, http://library.humboldt.edu/humco/holdings/photodetail.php?S=spott&CS=All%20Collections&RS=ALL%20Regions&PS=Any%20Photographer&ST=ALL%20words&SW=&C=52&R=15 accessed on July 19, 2020

American Lumberman
    1912a  Among the Northern Redwoods. American Lumberman, March 30, 1912.
    1912b  Among the Northern Redwoods. American Lumberman, April 27, 1912:55.

American Philosophical Society
    2020  American Council of Learned Societies Committee on Native American Languages, American Philosophical Society [ACLS Collection]: Detailed Inventory. Web page. Electronic document, https://search.amphilsoc.org/collections/view?docId=ead/Mss.497.3.B63c-ead.xml accessed on January 4, 2020.

Anderson, David
    2000  Russ Family Roots Run Deep. Times-Standard, May 29, 2000.
    2001a  The story of a Bridge, a boat, and a budget. Times-Standard, February 5, 2001:A1, A8.

Anderson, Kat
    2005  Tending the Wild: Native American Knowledge and the Management of California's Natural Resources. Berkeley: University of California Press.

Anderson, Mary
    1984a  Nona James at 80 Descended from Genuine Pioneer Stock. Redwood Record, September 20, 1984.
    1985a  Chinese in Southern Humboldt. Redwood Record, April 11, 1985:A-6.
    1987a  A lifetime of hunting, trapping. Humboldt Historian, March-April 1987:4-6.
    2006  Backwoods Chronicle: A History of Southern Humboldt 1849 – 1920. N. p.

Anonymous
    1987  Mount Pierce. Humboldt Historian, November-December 1987:12.
    N.d.a.  Fragment of map of ranches in Bear River valley. Photocopy in author's possession.
    N.d.b.  Interview by Jerry Rohde with unnamed resident of Eel Rock, ca. 2000.

Anonymous [pseud.]
    1876a  Notes from Anonymous. Humboldt Times, July 21 1876:1.

Anster, John
    2019  Poems: With Some Translations from the German. Web page. Electronic document, https://books.google.com/books?id=DVhMAAAAcAAJ&pg=PA216&dq=%22the+black+jager%27s+song%22&hl=en&sa=X&ved=0ahUKEwi5r6bWo-fjAhVKDq0KHZeHDHsQ6AEIMjAB#v=onepage&q=%22the%20black%20jager's%20song%22&f=false accessed on August 3, 2019.

anthromuseum.ucdavis.edu
    2021a  Clinton Hart Merriam 1855-1942 American Naturalist and Ethnographer. Web page. Electronic document, http://anthromuseum.ucdavis.edu/c-hart-merriam-biography.html accessed on June 12, 2021.

Arcata Leader
    1879a  Overland. Arcata Leader, December 6, 1879:3.

Arcata Union
    1901a  Good Old Indian. Arcata Union, November 9, 1901:5.
    1913a  Interesting Account of Trip by Delegates to Redding. Arcata Union, July 10, 1913.
    1919a  Bowden Brothers Take Over Shelter Cove Wharf Property. Increased Shipping Activity Looked For. Arcata Union, October 23, 1919.
    1925a  Redwood Highway article. Arcata Union, March 12, 1925:4.
    1926a  Redwood Highway article. Arcata Union, July 29, 1926:6.
    1927a  Another Oil Well for Upper Mattole. Arcata Union, September 29, 1927.
    1933a  McKee Saw Mill Burns at Weott. Arcata Union, July 7, 1933.

Arceneaux, Marc
    2013  Best Western Plus Humboldt House Inn Presents Stories of the Inn's Founders & Early Garberville. Garberville: Best Western Plus Humboldt House Inn, 2013.

Arms, L. R.
    N.d.  A Short History of the US Army Noncommissioned Officer. Webpage. Electronic document, http://www.armystudyguide.com/imagesvr_ce/1203/a-short-history-of-the-us.pdf accessed on August 21, 2016.

Asbill, Frank
    1953  The Last of the West. Manuscript photocopy: Humboldt State University Library, Arcata.

Asbill, Frank, and Argle Shawley
    1975  The Last of the West. New York: Carlton Pres, Inc.

askArt
    2019a  Margaret Smith Cobb. Web page. Electronic document, http://www.askart.com/artist/Margaret_Smith_Cobb/11181975/Margaret_Smith_Cobb.aspx accessed on July 30, 2019.

Aspen Daily Times
    1888a  Facts about Wool. Aspen Daily Times, October 16, 1888:3.

Atherton, Gertrude
    1945  Golden Gate Country. New York: Duell, Sloan & Pearce.

Atkinson, Theodora Kaspar
    2019  Recollections of Stafford. Photocopy in possession of author.

avalon.law.yale.edu
    2016  General Orders No. 100: The Lieber Code. Web page. Electronic document, http://avalon.law.yale.edu/19th_century/lieber.asp#sec3 accessed on August 28, 2016.

aveofthegiants.com
    2016a  Redcrest. Webpage. Electronic document, http://www.aveofthegiants.com/on-the-avenue/redcrest/ accessed on July 10, 2016.

Ayer, N. W., and Son
    1921  N. W. Ayer and Son's American Newspaper Annual and Directory. Philadelphia: N. W. Ayer & Son.

B [pseud.]
    1878  Letter from a Traveler. Ferndale Enterprise, June 28, 1878.

Bailey, Cora
    1900  Cora Bailey Diary: June 1, 1898 through September 19, 1900. Copy on file at the Humboldt County Historical Society, Eureka.

Bair, Marie Melanson
    1989a  Summer fun at Boehne's river camp. Humboldt Historian, September-October 1989:11.

Baker, Ray Jerome
    1934a  Letter to "Wife." Original in the Bishop Museum Archives, Honolulu, Hawaii; filed as MS GRP 16, Box 9.5.
    2006  Ray Jerome Baker information from Bishop Museum: photographs with identifying information and selection of memoirs, diaries, and correspondence. Copy on file in the Humboldt County Collection, Humboldt State University Library, Arcata, CA

Baldo, Chris, and Theron Brown
    2005  Fred C. Holmes – Redwood in His Blood. Roots of Motive Power, Inc. Newsletter 23 no. 3.

Bancroft, Hubert Howe
    1888a  History of California, Vol. VI. San Francisco: The History Publishers
    2015  Humbert Howe Bancroft's History of Utah 1540-1886. Web page. Electronic document, http://www.utlm.org/onlinebooks/bancroftshistoryofutah_chapter22.htm accessed July 31, 2015.

Bancroft Library
    1997  A. L. Kroeber Papers, 1869-1972. Bancroft Library, University of California, Berkeley.
    2020  Guide to A. L. Kroeber Papers. Web page. Electronic document, https://oac.cdlib.org/findaid/ark:/13030/tf3d5n99tn/entire_text/ accessed on January 2, 2020.

Barber, Mrs. Enos (sic)
    1937  Aged Indian Woman Passes at Blue Lake. Humboldt Times, April 1, 1937:4.

Baratti, John L.
    N.d.  History of Rio Dell 1850 – 1959. Photocopy available at the Humboldt State University Library, Arcata.

Barnum, Robert
    2017  Interview with Jerry Rohde on May 24, 2017.

Bassett, Vicki
    2015  Causes and Effects of the Rapid Sinking of the Titanic. Undergraduate Engineering Review. Web page. Electronic document, http://writing.engr.psu.edu/uer/bassett.html accessed on November 24, 2015.

Bauer, JoAnn
    2020a  Personal communication with the author, November 2, 2020.
    2020b  Personal communication with the author, November 3, 2020.

Baumgardner, Frank H.
    2006  Killing for Land in Early California. New York: Algora Publishing.

Baumhoff, Martin
    1958  California Athabascan Groups. Anthropological Records 16, no. 5.
    1963  Ecological Determinants of Aboriginal California Populations. Berkeley: University of California Press.

Baxter, Grace Johnson
    1987a  A Railroad Track and a Hobble Skirt. In *Humboldt County the Way It Was*, volume IV, edited by Gayle Karshner. Arcata: The Union.
    1987b  Tosaldo Johnson, a Pioneer and his Family. In *Humboldt County the Way It Was*, volume IV, edited by Gayle Karshner. Arcata: The Union.

Beal, Scoop
    1941a  Men Tell Of Attack. Humboldt Standard, December 22, 1941:1, 15.

Bean, Walton
    1973  California: An Interpretive History, 2nd ed. New York: McGraw-Hill.

Bear River Band
    2021  Wiyot/Mattole History. Web page. Electronic document, http://www.brb-nsn.gov/our-story/wiyot-mattole-history/ accessed on June 28, 2021.

Belcher, Jerry
    1970  U. S. Ousts Youthful Colony from Humboldt County Haven. Photocopy contained in the Petrolia file at the Humboldt County Historical Society, Eureka, CA.

Belcher Abstract & Title Co.
    1921-1922  Atlas of Humboldt County, California. Eureka: Belcher Abstract & Title Co.

Belyk, Robert C.
    2001  Great Shipwrecks of the Pacific Coast. New York: John Wiley & Sons, Inc.

Benbow, Michael J.
    2005  A Family's Quest for a Piece of Paradise: The Benbow Hotel as a Symbol of the First Modern Era. M. A. thesis, Humboldt State University.

Bencie, Robin
    1997 Genetic Variation and Inbreeding Depression in the Rare California Endemic, *Astragalus agnicidus* (Leguminosae). M. A. Thesis, Humboldt State University.
    2021a Personal communication with Jerry Rohde, February 8, 2021.

Berg, Ken, and Roxanne Bittman
    1988 Rediscovery of the Humboldt Milk-Vetch. Fremontia, April 1988.

Bess, Carol Robertson
    2020 Alexander Robertson. Web page. Electronic Document, https://web.archive.org/web/20041110213233/http://www.blocksburg.com/robertson_comments.php?id=P31_0_15_0_C accessed via Wayback Machine on August 15, 2020.

Bevington, Douglas
    2009 The Rebirth of Environmentalism: Grassroots Activism from the Spotted owl to the Polar Bear. Washington: Island Press.

Big Trees
    1952 The Big Trees. Web page. Electronic document, https://www.youtube.com/watch?v=UWcMg-yohJs accessed on May 19 2019.

Bishop, Verda
    1991 Interview with Jerry Rohde, May 18, 1991.

Bittermann, Rusty
    2010 The Remarkable Saga of the Coopers of Coopers Mills, Hydesville. Humboldt Historian, Summer 2010:8-16.

Black, Patricia
    2007 Interview with Jerry Rohde.

Blackie, W. G.
    MDCCCXCIX (1899) Literary Pastimes of Early Life. Glasgow: Blackie and Son Limited.

BlackPast.org
    2016 Fort Pillow Massacre (1864). Web page. Electronic document, http://www.blackpast.org/aah/fort-pillow-massacre-1864 accessed on September 3, 2016.

Bledsoe, A. J.
    1885 Indian Wars of the Northwest. San Francisco: Bacon & Co.

Blue Lake Advocate
    1900a Article on Judge Hunter's land purchase in Salmon Creek. Blue Lake Advocate, April 17, 1900:3.
    1902a Dance at Porter's hall article, Blue Lake Advocate, May 24, 1902:1.
    1903a Social time at Porter's hall article, Blue Lake Advocate, April 18, 1903:1.
    1904a Social dance at Porter's hall article, Blue Lake Advocate, July 23, 1904:1.

Blue Lake Advocate
    1893a Harris-Dyerville road story. Blue Lake Advocate, November 4, 1893:2.
    1898a Pedrotti wounding story. Blue Lake Advocate, August 8, 1898:2.
    1898b Mail routes story. Blue Lake Advocate, October 22, 1898:1.
    1900a The Cream of Country News. Blue Lake Advocate, July 14, 1900:2.
    1904a Mrs. Grant Johnston bear story. Blue Lake Advocate, April 30, 1904:2.
    1914a To Build Yager Creek Bridge. Blue Lake Advocate, February 28, 1914:1.
    1920a From Hydesville and Vicinity, Blue Lake Advocate, February 7, 1920:4.
    1930a Dinsmore cattle article. Blue Lake Advocate, December 13, 1930:3.
    1931a Fred Bair Sells Maple Creek Ranch. Blue Lake Advocate, August 1, 1931:2.
    1937a Mollie Brock Died Sunday. Blue Lake Advocate, April 3, 1937:1.

BoatSafe.com
    2015 Ceremony for Renaming Your Boat. Web page. Electronic document, http://www.boatsafe.com/nauticalknowhow/rename.htm accessed on November 27, 2015.

Book Review Digest
    1910a Review of Blaxine. Book Review Digest, vol. 6:79.

Boots, Jim
    1964 The Life of an Old Stage Driver and Mule Skinner. Humboldt Historian, January-February 1964:7.

Borden, Stanley T.
    1949a The Pacific Lumber Co. Western Railroader 12, no. 8 (1949):7-11.
    1958a NWP's Carlotta Branch . . . the California Midland RR. Western Railroader, February 1958.
    1963a San Francisco & Northwestern. Western Railroader, January 1963.
    1968a Traffic Stopped When Logs Crossed Highway at Brown's Mill. Humboldt Historian, May-June 1968:2.

Bowcutt, Frederica
    2015 The Tanoak Tree. Seattle: University of Washington Press.

Branscomb, Ernie
    2009a "Enoch Percival French and Newton Bishop Drury," Ernie's Place (blog), http://ernielb.blogspot.com/2009/07/enoch-percival-french-and-newton-bishop.html accessed on August 5, 2020.

Brekke, Joann Smith
    1990 Interview with Jerry Rohde.

bridgemeister.com
    2022a (suspension bridge) Petrolia, California, USA – Mattole River. Web page. Electronic document, https://www.bridgemeister.com/bridge.php?bid=2143 accessed on January 20, 2022.

Britannica
    2021a Sioux. Web page. Electronic document, https://www.britannica.com/topic/Sioux accessed on February 15, 2021.

Brown, Jim
    2008 Folsom Prison. Charleston, SC: Arcadia Publishing Co.

Brown, Salmon
    1879a Letter from Bridgeville. Daily Humboldt Times, March 7, 1879:3.

Bruff, J. Goldsborough
    1949 Gold Rush. New York: Columbia University Press.

Buxton, Katie
    1989 Capetown traced from 1854. Humboldt Historian, May-June 1989:22-23.

Calflora
    2021a Astragalus agnicidus. Web page. Electronic document, https://www.calflora.org/app/taxon?crn=795 accessed on December 23, 2021.

California Board of Bank Commissioners
    1900 Report of the Board of Bank Commissioners. Sacramento: State Printing.

California Bricks
    2018a John B. Hill. Web page. Electronic document, http://calbricks.netfirms.com/brick.hill.html accessed on September 22, 2018.

California Department of Engineering, State Highway Commission
    1914a Plan and Profile of Proposed State Highway in Humboldt County, from Shively to Jordan Creek.

California Department of Natural Resources, Division of Forestry
    1949a [Map of] South Half of Humboldt County.

California Department of Public Works, Division of Highways
    1933a Plan and Profile of State Highway in Humboldt County between Jordan Creek and South Scotia Bridge.

California Highway Bulletin
    N. d. Eliminating the Terrors of the Bell Springs Grade. Excerpt without full citation, found in the "Transportation-Highway 101" file at the Humboldt County Historical Society, Eureka, California.

California Military History
    2020a Fort Iaqua. Web page. Electronic document, http://www.militarymuseum.org/FtIaqua.html accessed on July 4, 2020.

California State Agricultural Society
    1891 Transactions of the California State Agricultural Society During the Year 1890. Sacramento.

California State Mining Bureau
    1886 Sixth Annual Report of the State Mineralogist, Part I. Sacramento.
    1896 Thirteenth report of the State Mineralogist. Sacramento.

California State Parks
    2022a Richardson Grove State Park. Web page. Electronic document, https://web.archive.org/web/20071025161142/http://www.humboldtredwoods.org/images/richardsongrove.pdf accessed on January 11, 2022.

California State Railroad Museum
    2018 Master Railroad Equipment Roster. Web page. Electronic document, https://www.californiarailroad.museum/assets/carousels/CSRM-Public-Roster-7-19-2016.pdf accessed on August 9, 2017.

Californian
    1910 Ad for Fort Seward. The Californian, December 24, 1910.
    1914 Eel Rock Springs. The Californian, August 22, 1914.

Calisphere
    2018a Front view of Tom and Sally Bell. Web page. Electronic document, https://calisphere.org/item/ark:/13030/kt35800395/ accessed on January 6, 2019.

Canfield, John H.
    2015 The Enduring Lesson Of A Little Log Bridge. Web page. Electronic document, https://mattolehistory.wordpress.com/2011/04/23/bear-river-bridge-building-lesson/ accessed on August 9, 2015.

Caro, Robert
    1975 The Power Broker: Robert Moses and the Fall of New York. New York: Vintage Books.

Carr, Ezra S.
    1875 The Patrons of Husbandry of the Pacific Coast. San Francisco: A. L. Bancroft and Company.

Carr, John
    1891 Pioneer Days in California. Eureka: Times Publishing Company.

Carranco, Lynwood
    1982 Redwood Lumber Industry. San Marino, CA: Golden West Books.
    1984a No. 1–the born-again engine. Humboldt Historian, May-June 1984:3-5.

Carranco, Lynwood, and Estel Beard
    1981 Genocide and Vendetta: The Round Valley Wars of Northern California. Norman, OK: University of Oklahoma Press.

Carranco, Lynwood, and Henry L. Sorensen
    1988 Steam in the Redwoods. Caldwell, ID: The Caxton Printers, Ltd.

Carranco, Ruth, and Links Carranco
    1977 Briceland Once Center of Thriving Tanbark Industry. Humboldt Historian, November-December 1977:1-2.

Carter, Ernest
    1983a "American Tank" was once a place in Humboldt life. Humboldt Historian, May-June 1983:7, 16.

CCH2 Portal
    2021 Specimen Records Table for *Astragalus agnicidus*. Web page. Electronic document, https://www.cch2.org/portal/collections/listtabledisplay.php?db=all&taxa=Astragalus+agnicidus&usethes=1&taxontype=2 accessed on February 8, 2021.

Census Online
    2018a 1860 Federal census – Pacific T[o]w[nshi[p]. Web page. Electronic document, http://files.usgwarchives.net/ca/humboldt/census/1860/pg00001.txt accessed on December 17, 2018.

Chadbourne, Addie
    N. d. Letter to the Editor. Humboldt Historian. Photocopy of a single page which shows no date.

Chadbourne, David
    1991 Interview with Jerry Rohde, May 21, 1991.

# Sources

Chase, Alice Davis
    1986 Recollections of a journey to a 'strange land.' Humboldt Historian, July-August 1986:21-22.

Chernow, Ron
    2017 Grant. New York: Penguin Press.

Childs, Richard, et al.
    1991a Richard Childs, Robert Childs, and Velma Childs, interview with Jerry Rohde.

Childs, Velma
    1986 100-year-old log school restored in Redcrest area. Humboldt Historian, May-June 1986:3-4.

Chivers, Mrs. M. A.
    1875 A Lady's Defence of Petrolia. West Coast Signal, April 28, 1875:3.

Christensen, Carl
    1989 Surfman describes rescue. Humboldt Historian, March-April 1989:5.

Clark, Julia Steere
    N.d.a. A Bit of Background. Copy on file at the Humboldt County Historical Society, Eureka.
    N.d.b. A Bit of Conclusion. Copy on file at the Humboldt County Historical Society, Eureka.

Clark, T. K.
    1983a Regional History of Petrolia and the Mattole Valley. Eureka: Miller Press.
    1983b Wreck of the St. Paul—1908 [sic]. Humboldt Historian, September-October 1983:10-11.

Clever, Fran
    1982 Southern Humboldt town names outlive communities. Humboldt Beacon, March 11, 1982:3.
    1998 Before the Floods: Early memories of Dyerville, South Fork, Weott, and Burlington. N. p.

Coast and Geodetic Survey
    1909 United States Coast Pilot: Pacific Coast, 2nd ed. Washington DC: Government Printing Office.

Cobb, Margaret Smith
    1910a Blaxine: Halfbreed Girl. New York: The Neal Publishing Company.

Cockman, George
    N.d.a. Personal communication with Jerry Rohde.

Coe, Frederick
    2019 The Madrones. Web page. Electronic document, https://www.pacifichorticulture.org/articles/the-madrones/ accessed on September 12, 2019.

Colbruno, Michael
    2020 Walter Van Dyke. Blog. Electronic document, http://mountainviewpeople.blogspot.com/2011/05/walter-van-dyke-1823-1905-california.html accessed on August 24, 2020.

Conklin, J. M.
    1882 Judge J. M. Conklin Tells About Neighbors of the Mattole Valley. Ferndale Enterprise, April 28, 1882.

Cook, Margarite Drucella
    1974a Schumacher story. In The Trail Back:B-19.
    1997 The Southern Humboldt Papers. 16 volumes. Photocopy: Humboldt County Library, Eureka.

Cook, Margarite, and Diane Hawk
    2001 A Glance Back: Northern Mendocino County History. Piercy, CA: Hawk Mountaintop Publishing.
    2006 In the Early Days: Southern Humboldt History 1853-1920. Piercy, CA: Hawk Mountaintop Publishing.

Cooskey, Laura Walker
    2004a Honeydew this and Honeydew that . . . . Now . . . and Then: The Journal of the Mattole Valley Historical Society 5(3);1-2.
    2004b Honeydew Milltown Swept Away like Sawdust. Now . . . and Then: The Journal of the Mattole Valley Historical Society 5(4);1-4.
    2004c Oil Dream creates Petrolia in Lower Mattole. Now . . . and Then: The Journal of the Mattole Valley Historical Society 6(1):1-3.
    2011a A Guide to the Petrolia Cemetery Burials. Now . . . and Then 9(2):5-14.
    2017a Mattole Lumber Company: A Man, A Plan, and Tanbark. Now . . . and Then: The Journal of the Mattole Valley Historical Society 10(4):1-6.
    2017b Mattole Lumber Co., Pt.2: The Wharf 1908-18: Opening the Valley. Now . . . and Then: The Journal of the Mattole Valley Historical Society 10(4):1-3.
    2018a Personal communication from Laura Cooskey to Jerry Rohde, May 23, 2018, 1:08 A. M.
    2018b Personal communication from Laura Cooskey to Jerry Rohde, May 23, 2018, 9:28 A. M.
    2018c Personal communication from Laura Cooskey to Jerry Rohde, May 22, 2018, 10:12 P. M.
    2019a The "other" Native Land Grab. Now . . . and Then 11(4).
    2020a So . . . what happened to the Natives here? Web page. Electronic document, https://web.archive.org/web/20110719234842/http://www.mattolehistory.org/Mattole_Natives.pdf accessed on July 24, 2020.
    2022a Personal communication with the author, February 18, 2022.
    2022b Personal communication with the author, February 15, 2022.

Cornford, Daniel A.
    1987 workers and Dissent in the Redwood Empire. Philadelphia: Temple University Press.

Coy, Owen C.
    1923 California County Boundaries. Berkeley: California Historical Survey Commission.
    1982[1929] The Humboldt Bay Region 1850 – 1875. Eureka: Humboldt County Historical Society.

Cozzens, Peter
    2016a The Earth Is Weeping: The Epic Story of the Indian Wars for the American West. New York: Alfred A. Knopf.

Crain, Jim
1977 Historic Country Inns of California. San Francisco: Chronicle Books.

Crane, William B.
2012 Franz and Bear River Horse, 4th ed. Ferndale: Ferndale Museum.

Crichton, R. Chalmers
1988a Arthur Way: civic leader and racer. Humboldt Historian, July-August 1988.

Crismon, Max
1991a Interview with Jerry Rohde, May 29, 1991.
N.d.a Interview with Jerry Rohde.

Crocker, Clarence E.
2016 Post Offices and Postal Officials: Bivingsville and Glendale, South Carolina 1837-2010. Web Page. Electronic document, http://glendalesc.com/postoffice.html accessed on December 4, 2016.

Crow, Leslie
2017 Pacific Tannery, Wagner Leather Company and Pacific Storage Company: Finding Success in Business for 138 Years. Web page. Electronic document, http://www.leathersmithe.com/california-historical-tanne/the-pacific-tannery-wagner.html accessed on August 12, 2017.

CRTANCS (California Retired Teachers Association North Coast Section), eds.
1989 History of Humboldt County Schools: Volume II - Eureka Area. Eureka: Humboldt County Office of Education.
1993 History of Humboldt County Schools By High School Districts: Volume III - Ferndale Area. Eureka: Humboldt County Office of Education.
1999 History of Humboldt County Schools: Volume IV - Fortuna Area. Eureka: Humboldt County Office of Education.
2001 History of Humboldt County Schools By High School Districts: Volume V - Southern Humboldt Area. Eureka: Humboldt County Office of Education.

Cuddeback Union School District
2019 Area History. Web page. Electronic document, http://www.humboldt.k12.ca.us/cuddeback_sd/area_history.php accessed on March 19, 2019.

Cunningham, Mary Louise
2000a One man's Dream: George Young Builds a Store and a Family in Pepperwood. Humboldt Historian, Winter 2000:15-21.

Curtin, Jeremiah
1940 Memoirs of Jeremiah Curtin. Madison: State Historical Society of Wisconsin.

Curtis, Edward S.
1970[1924]a The North American Indian, Vol. 13. New York: Johnson Reprint Corporation.
1970[1924]b The North American Indian, Vol. 14. New York: Johnson Reprint Corporation.

Daigh, Michael
2015 John Brown in Memory and Myth. Jefferson, NC: McFarland & Company, Inc.

Daily Alta California
1850a Humboldt Correspondence. Daily Alta California, September 20, 1850.
1850b Trinidad—A Journey Overland. Daily Alta California, April 9, 1850.
1850c The Indian Outrages in Napa Valley. Daily Alta California, March 19, 1850:2.
1851a The Eel River Valley. Daily Alta California, August 26, 1851:3.
1864a The Klamath Indian War: Capture and Execution of Two Indian Chiefs. Daily Alta California, April 19, 1864:1.

Daily Evening Bulletin
1871a Schools—Halfbreeds. [San Francisco] Daily Evening Bulletin, November 11, 1871.

Daily Humboldt Standard
1890a Steamer Ajax Wrecked. Daily Humboldt Standard, September 20, 1890.
1907a Promotion Work In Humboldt County. Daily Humboldt Standard, February 5, 1907:3.
1907b Promotion Work in Humboldt County. Daily Humboldt Standard, February 6, 1907:3.
1907c. Promotion Work in Humboldt County. Daily Humboldt Standard, February 11, 1907:3.
1907d Promotion Work in Humboldt County. Daily Humboldt Standard, January 23, 1907:6.
1907e Promotion Work in Humboldt County, Daily Humboldt Standard, February 26, 1907:2.
1907f Fatal Landslide at Upper Mattole. Daily Humboldt Standard, March 29, 1907:2.
1907g Promotion Work in Humboldt County. Daily Humboldt Standard, February 17, 1907:3.
1907e Garberville. Daily Humboldt Standard, April 6, 1907:7.
1910a Steamer Del Norte Rams Lightship. Daily Humboldt Standard, January 5, 1910:1.
1911a Flat Boat Upset in Eel River. Daily Humboldt Standard, March 31, 1911:1.

Daily Humboldt Times
1888a In Memoriam. Daily Humboldt Times, September 20, 1888.
1908a Railroad Work Monday. Daily Humboldt Times, March 29, 1908.

Daily Standard
1895a At Fort Iaqua. Daily Standard, July 19, 1895.
1899a Humboldt Vineyard. Daily Standard, September 26, 1899:3.
1899b Returned Klondiker. Daily Standard, October 2, 1899:3.

2016b Ulysses S. Grant Launched an Illegal War Against the Plains Indians, Then Lied About It. Web page. Electronic Document, http://www.smithsonianmag.com/history/ulysses-grant-launched-illegal-war-plains-indians-180960787/ accessed on November 12, 2016.

1899c Blocksburg Scorching. Daily
Humboldt Standard, September 25,
1899:3.
1903a. Carlotta New Railroad Town.
Daily Humboldt Standard, August 29,
1903:4.
1911a Flat Boat Upset in Eel River.
Daily Standard, March 31, 1911:1.
Daily Star
2020a Twenty Lives Lost. Web page.
Electronic document, https://news.
google.com/newspapers?nid=1297&-
dat=19020104&id=0H8TAAAA-
IBAJ&sjid=kooDAAAAIBAJ&p-
g=6762,66972&hl=en accessed on May
30, 2020.
Daily Times-Telephone
1883a Rohnerville Programs. Daily
Times-Telephone, April 1, 1883:3.
Dana, Charles A.
1902 Recollections of the Civil War. New
York: D. Appleton and Company.
David Rumsey Map Collection
2019 [Map of] San Francisco and North
Pacific Railway. Web page. Electronic document, https://www.
davidrumsey.com/luna/servlet/detail/
RUMSEY~8~1~26792~1100604:San-
Francisco-and-North-Pacific-Rai accessed
on July 27, 2019.
Davidson, George
1889 Coast Pilot of California, Oregon,
and Washington. United States Coast
and Geodetic Survey. Washington, DC:
Government Printing Office.
Davis, Samuel
2019 Miscellaneous poems, chiefly on
divine subjects. Published for the reli-
gious entertainment of Christians in
general. Web page. Electronic document,
https://quod.lib.umich.edu/cgi/t/text/
text-idx?c=evans;cc=evans;view=text;id-
no=N05397.0001.001;rgn=div2;node
=N05397.0001.001:4.1 accessed on
August 4, 2019.
Davy, Marguerite Ross
1950a First White Girl Tells Garberville
Story. Humboldt Times, September 3,
1950.
1950b Humboldt County's Redwood
Parks. Humboldt Times, July 23, 1950.
Dawson, William Leon
1923 The Birds of California, vol. 3. San
Diego: South Moulton Company.
Deering, E. R.
1966 The Maple Creek Willie Indian
Scholarship Fund. California Education,
April 1966:3.
DeLong, Harriet
1971 Book Agent of the 1870's. Humboldt
Historian, November-December 1971:1, 9.
Democratic Standard
1880a Garberville has not a Chinaman . . . .
Democratic Standard, March 27, 1880:3.
Dengler, Lori
2006 The 1906 Earthquake on
California's North Coast. Humboldt Histo-
rian, Winter 2006:27-34.

Denny, Edward
1911 Denny's Official Map of the County
of Humboldt California. San Francisco:
Edward Denny & Co.
Deseret News
1975a Scholar fund running dry. Deseret
News, December 26, 1975:4.
Dictionary.com
2019a Firkin. Web page. Electronic
document, https://www.dictionary.com/
browse/firkin accessed on July 21, 2019.
Dinsmore, Muriel
1975a City "dudes" restore rural lodge.
Times-Standard, January 12, 1975:15, 18.
Dinsmore, Trustom R.
1961 John Dinsmore. Humboldt County
Historical Society Newsletter, May 1961.2
Director of the Census
1907 Official Register: Persons in the
Civil, Military and Naval Service of the
United States and List of Vessels. Washing-
ton: Government Printing Office.
Dixon, Roland B.
1930 Pliny Earle Goddard (1869-1928).
Proceedings of the American Academy of
Arts and Sciences 34(12):526-528.
Dolfini, Sally
2004 Good Times at the Stafford Inn.
Humboldt Historian, Summer 2004:22-26.
Doolittle, A. J.
1865 Official Township Map of Humboldt
Co., Cal. San Francisco: A. J. Doolittle.
Driver, Harold E.
1939 Culture Element Distributions: X:
Northwestern California. Anthropological
Records 1(6).
Durst, John H.
1883 Afoot up Eel River. Overland
Monthly (1)3:250-255.
Easthouse, Keith
2017a School Board Opts to Drill A Well
at Whitethorn School. Humboldt Indepen-
dent, December 12, 2017:1, 5.
E. B. C. (pseud.)
1892 Bear River Jottings. Ferndale
Enterprise, March 18, 1892:5.
EcoTopia
2106a Julia Butterfly Hill. Web page.
Electronic document, http://ecotopia.org/
ecology-hall-of-fame/julia-butterfly-hill/
accessed on January 3, 2016.
Eddy, J. M.
1893 In the Redwood's Realm. San
Francisco: D. S. Stanley & Co.
Edeline, Denis P.
1978 At the Banks of the Eel. N.p.
N. d. The Edeline Family. Excerpt
photocopy in possession of author.
Eel Valley Advance
1970a Bark camp article. Eel Valley
Advance, April 27, 1980:8.
1970b Route 36: Redwood Empire's
Conversation Piece. Eel Valley Advance,
November 23, 1970.
Eich, Glenyth L.
1978 "Punkin Center" Researched by
Present Resident. Humboldt Historian,
January-February 1978:1, 4.

1984 Robinsons' link to Shively goes back four generations. Humboldt Historian, July-August 1984.

Egan, Timothy
   2012 Short Nights of the Shadow Catcher. Boston: Houghton Mifflin Harcourt.

Eggenberger, David
   1985 An Encyclopedia of Battles. New York: Dover Publications, Inc.

Elliott, Helen, and Fred Elliott
   N. d. The Story of Bull Creek. Photocopy in author's possession.

Elliott, Wallace W.
   1881 History of Humboldt County, California. San Francisco: Wallace W. Elliott & Co.

Elsasser, Albert B.
   1978 Mattole, Nongatl, Sinkyone, Lassik, and Wailaki. In Handbook of North American Indians, vol. 8: California. Robert F. Heizer, ed. Pp. 190-204. Washington: Smithsonian Institution.

Elvidge, Lois
   1974 Dobbyn School History Tells of Past Educational Era. Humboldt Historian, November-December, 1974:10.
   N. d. Memories of Fort Seward. In The Trail Back 1974:A-21.

Empty Road
   2015 Ledger of the Deep: The Mythology of Renaming a Boat. Web page. Electronic document, http://www.theemptyroad.com/ledger-of-the-deep-the-mythology-of-renaming-a-boat/ accessed on November 27, 2015.

Encyclopædia Britannica
   2016a Nathan Bedford Forrest. Web page. Electronic document, https://www.britannica.com/biography/Nathan-Bedford-Forrest accessed on October 10, 2016.
   2018a John C. Breckenridge. Web page. Electronic document, https://www.britannica.com/biography/John-C-Breckenridge accessed on August 19, 2018.

Encyclopedia.com
   2015a Kroeber, Alfred L. Web page. Electronic document, http://www.encyclopedia.com/doc/1G2-3045000665.html accessed on June 8, 2015.

Engbeck, Joseph H. Jr.
   2018 Saving the Redwoods. San Francisco: Save the Redwoods League.

Essene, Frank
   1942 Cultural Elements Distributions: XXI: Round Valley. Anthropological Records 8:1.

Ethnological Documents
   2002 Ethnological Documents Collection of the Department and Museum of Anthropology, University of California, Berkeley, 1875-1958. Berkeley: Bancroft Library. Microfilm: Humboldt State University Library, Arcata.

Eureka Heritage Society
   1987 Eureka: An Architectural View. Eureka: Eureka Heritage Society.

Eureka-Humboldt Library
   N.d. Index to 1860 Humboldt County census. Photocopy in author's possession.

Eureka Independent
   1952a First Truck Freight in Humboldt in 1912. Eureka Independent, March 19, 1952:6.

Eureka Newspapers, Inc.
   1949a 1949 Classified Business Directory. Eureka: Eureka Newspapers, Inc.
   1965a The One Thousand Year Flood. Eureka Newspapers, Inc., February 15-16, 1965.

Evans, George S.
   2007 [1904?] Wylackie Jake of Covelo. Nevada City, CA: Mountain House Books.

Evans, J. Ray
   1978 Old Humboldt Paper Company Born of A Shipwreck. Humboldt Historian, January-February 1978:3.

Evans, Raymond
   1999 When Fast Food Was A Rabbit. N.p.

Evening Star
   1877a Communication. Evening Star, February 21, 1877:3.
   1877b Ad for Larabee Hotel. Evening Star, July 25, 1877:1.
   1877c Ad for Overland stages. Evening Star, July 25, 1877:1.
   1877d From the South. Evening Star, May 10, 1877:1.

Falk, Peggy
   2018 Interview with Jerry Rohde, December 5, 2018.

Farager, John Mack, ed.
   1998 The American Heritage Encyclopedia of American History. New York: Henry Holt and Company.

Faulkner, Jessie
   2002a One Foggy Night . . . The Final Tale of the Alaska. Humboldt Historian, Fall 2002:20-23.
   2003a Turbulent times in Shively: Residents recall commute by boat. Times-Standard, November 24, 2003.
   2004a Harvest Home. Humboldt Historian, Fall 2004:32-35.

Felt, T. D.
   1869 Another Indian Depredation—Heroic Conduct of Mrs. Bowman. Humboldt Times, April 3, 1869.

Ferndale Enterprise
   1878a Hansell article. Ferndale Enterprise, August 30, 1878:3.
   1878b The Beaumont Bro's. Ferndale Enterprise, July 10, 1878:3.
   1880a Article about Blocksburg's Overland Hotel. Ferndale Enterprise, September 10, 1880:3.
   1881a A Four Day's Journey Southward. Ferndale Enterprise, August 11, 1881:3.
   1882a Editorial Notes. Ferndale Enterprise, July 21, 1882:2.
   1884a Mazeppa. Ferndale Enterprise, March 29, 1884:5.
   1885a Letter from Garberville. Ferndale Enterprise, December 5, 1885:5.

1885b A Sad Fate. Ferndale Enterprise, November 29, 1885:1.
1886a Death of Joseph Russ. Ferndale Enterprise, October 15, 1886:3.
1886b Local News. Ferndale Enterprise, December 17, 1886:5.
1887b Local News. Ferndale Enterprise, February 11, 1887:5.
1889a An Act of Bravery. Ferndale Enterprise, May 1889.
1890a South Fork Notes. Ferndale Enterprise, June 27, 1890:5.
1891a Upper Eel River and Garberville Notes. Ferndale Enterprise, August 21, 1891:5.
1892a The Town of Petrolia. Ferndale Enterprise, May 13, 1892:1.
1892b Communicated. Ferndale Enterprise, April 1, 1892:4.
1892c From the Alton Journal of Oct 15th. Ferndale Enterprise, October 10, 1892:1.
1893a Over the Grade. Ferndale Enterprise, December 22, 1893:5.
1894a Notice of foreclosure. Ferndale Enterprise, March 30, 1894.
1899a Indian George and family article. Ferndale Enterprise, October 6, 1899.
1899b Bull Creek forest fire article. Ferndale Enterprise, September 1, 1899.
1901a Here and There. Ferndale Enterprise, April 26, 1901:1.
1906a Humboldt Registration. Ferndale Enterprise, October 9, 1906:8.
1909a Death of Judge C. G. Stafford. Ferndale Enterprise, July 9, 1909:1.
1912a Crawled Ten Hours With Broken Leg. Ferndale Enterprise, March 29, 1912.
1913a Another Wizard Works Miracles with Plants. Ferndale Enterprise, April 25, 1913.
1913b Writes of Overland Auto Trip. Ferndale Enterprise, July 22, 1913.
1914a Article on Roscoe wedding anniversary. Ferndale Enterprise, June 30, 1914.
1918a Briceland Now Isolated Town. Ferndale Enterprise, August 20, 1918.
1919a Shelter Cove A Lively Town. Ferndale Enterprise, August 15, 1919:7.
1919b Frank Johnson Meets Death in Train Accident. Ferndale Enterprise, September 6, 1919:1.
1921a Made Capetown in One Hour 38 Min. Ferndale Enterprise, March 4, 1921:1.
1924a Grandma Roscoe is Called to Rest. Ferndale Enterprise, June 6, 1924.
1940a Mr. and Mrs. J. Mahan's Part in "Save-the-Redwoods" History is Reviewed. Ferndale Enterprise, January 19, 1940.
1941a June 14 Marks 25th Anniversary of S. S. Bear Wreck. Ferndale Enterprise, June 13, 1941.
1941b Jap Submarine Attacks Tanker Near Cape Mendocino. Ferndale Enterprise, December 26, 1941:1.
1955a Worst Flood! Ferndale Enterprise, December 23, 1955:1.
1955b Eel Valley Swimming Through the Deluge. Ferndale Enterprise, December 23, 1955:1.

Ferndale Semi-Weekly Enterprise
1897a Local Items. Ferndale Semi-Weekly Enterprise, September 24, 1897:4.
1901a Here and There. Ferndale Semi-Weekly Enterprise, April 26, 1901:8.
1901b Under the head of "Good Old Indian. . . ." Ferndale Semi-Weekly Enterprise, November 12, 1901:5.
1903a Killed It With a Hammer. Ferndale Semi-Weekly Enterprise, November 26, 1903:4.
1903b Despite the Superior Court injunction . . . . Ferndale Semi-Weekly Enterprise, April 10, 1903:5.
1904a Triple Drowning in the Mattole River. Ferndale Semi-Weekly Enterprise, March 15, 1904:4.
1907a Banner Presented. Ferndale Semi-Weekly Enterprise, August 20, 1907:4.
1914a Local Notes. Ferndale Semi-Weekly Enterprise, September ***, 1914:5.

Find A Grave
2017 Anna "Annie" Duckett Hunter. Web page. Electronic document, https://www.findagrave.com/cgi-bin/fg.cgi?page=gr&GSln=Hunter&GSiman=1&GScnty=194&GRid=138328341& accessed on April 30, 2017.
2019a Augusta Phillipina *Schumacher* Jones. Web page. Electronic document, https://www.findagrave.com/memorial/155396461/augusta-phillipina-jones accessed on December 18, 2019.

Finn, J. D. John
2018 Cockiness, incompetence and a labor strike led to a shipwreck. Offbeat Oregon. Web page. Electronic document, https://offbeatoregon.com/1512a.alaska-shipwreck-368.html accessed on December 4, 2018.

Fisher, Harold
1989 Weott had its own heyday. Humboldt Historian, March-April 1989:20.

Fisher, Harold, and Jane Bryant Fisher
1991 Interview with Jerry Rohde, May 22, 1991.

Fishman, Ram
2006a Albert Etter: The Legacy of a Fruit Explorer. Now . . . and Then: The Journal of the Mattole Valley Historical Society (7)2.
2019 The Ettersburg Apple Legacies. Web page. Electronic document, http://www.greenmantlenursery.com/fruit/etter-apples.htm accessed on September 10, 2019.

Flaherty, F. F.
1934 Etter Brothers Create Earthly Paradise. Humboldt Standard, June 24, 1934.

Fletcher, Randol B.
2011 Hidden History of Civil War Oregon. Charleston, SC: History Press.

Foner, Eric, and John A. Garraty eds.
    1991 The Reader's Companion to American History. Boston: Houghton Mifflin Company.
Forbes, Stanly
    1886 Official Map of Humboldt County, California. San Francisco: Stanly Forbes.
    1896 Official Map of Humboldt County, California. San Francisco: Stanly Forbes
Forest Lookouts
    2020a Iaqua Buttes. Web page. Electronic document, https://californialookouts.weebly.com/iaqua-buttes.html accessed on July 8, 2020.
Forrest (pseud.)
    1887 From Forrest. Ferndale Enterprise, October 21, 1887:4.
Fountain, Susie Baker
    1960a Strong's Station. Humboldt County Historical Society Newsletter, March 1960:5-6.
    1964a The Settlement of the Humboldt Bay Region in 1850. Blue Lake Advocate, December 24, 1964:3.
    1965a The Settlement of the Humboldt Bay Region in 1850. Blue Lake Advocate, February 18, 1965.
    2001 Susie Baker Fountain Papers. 128 volumes. Microfilm: Humboldt State University Library, Arcata.
freepages.rootsweb.com
    2018 Frank Kanning Mott. Web page. Electronic document, http://freepages.rootsweb.com/~npmelton/genealogy/lamott.htm accessed on November 22, 2018.
French, George
    1997 Any Weott Pastimers Left? Humboldt Historian, Summer 1997:39.
Frickstad, Walter N.
    1955 A Century of California Post Offices. Oakland: Philatelic Research Society.
Friend, George
    1939 Hardships and Dangers of Early Humboldt Life Told by Pioneer of Section. Humboldt Times, December 17, 1939:13-14.
Fritz, Emanuel
    1922a A pile of railroad ties.... Webpage. Electronic document, https://digicoll.lib.berkeley.edu/record/15277?n=en#?c=0&m=0&s=0&cv=0&r=0&xywh=0%2C-100%2C1500%2C1407 accessed on October 22, 2020.
    1922b Thousands of split redwood grape stakes.... WebpageElectronic document, https://digicoll.lib.berkeley.edu/record/15280?n=en#?c=0&m=0&s=0&cv=0&r=0&xywh=0%2C-95%2C1500%2C1407 accessed on October 22, 2020.
    1922c A small sawmill on Bull Creek.... Webpage. Electronic document, https://digicoll.lib.berkeley.edu/record/16076?n=en#?c=0&m=0&s=0&cv=0&r=0&xywh=-328%2C0%2C2155%2C1155 accessed on October 22, 2020.
    1939a Sawmill of Wrigley and Russell.... Webpage. Electronic document, https://digicoll.lib.berkeley.edu/record/16066?n=en#?c=0&m=0&s=0&cv=0&r=0&xywh=-725%2C-12%2C2875%2C1542 accessed on October 22, 2020.
Fritz-Metcalf Photograph Collection
    2016a Large stump . . . on Holmes Flat. Accession # 4879. Webpage. Electronic document, http://dpg.lib.berkeley.edu/webdb/metcalf/search?keyword=reback&dates=&location=&photographer=&photono accessed on May 18, 2016.
    2016b Truck hauling. Jordan Creek. Accession # 3091a. Webpage. Electronic document, http://dpg.lib.berkeley.edu/webdb/metcalf/search?keyword=&dates=&location=&photographer=&photono=3091a accessed on May 17, 2016.
    2016c Selective logging by Pacific Lumber Company on north slope of Jordan Creek. Accession # 3964. Webpage. Electronic document, http://dpg.lib.berkeley.edu/webdb/metcalf/search?keyword=&dates=&location=&photographer=&photono=3964 accessed on May 17, 2016.
    2016d Fire in logging slash on Bridge Creek. Accession # 1146. Webpage. Electronic document, http://dpg.lib.berkeley.edu/webdb/metcalf/search?keyword=&dates=&location=&photographer=&photono=1145 accessed on May 18, 2016.
    2016e Camp Coolen . . . at top of Bridge Creek incline. Accession # 1421. Webpage. Electronic document, http://dpg.lib.berkeley.edu/webdb/metcalf/search?keyword=&dates=&location=&photographer=&photono=1421 accessed on May 18, 2016.
    2016f Fire prevention signs used by the Pacific Lumber Company.... Webpage. Electronic document, http://dpg.lib.berkeley.edu/webdb/metcalf/search?keyword=&dates=&location=&photographer=&photono=2483 accessed on May 19, 2016.
Frost, Ralph C.
    1966 How Showers Pass Was Named. Humboldt County Historical Society Newsletter, January-February 1966:2.
Fuller, A. A.
    1873a Upper Eel River. West Coast Signal, September 17, 1873:2.
Fugit, Tempus III (pseud.)
    1935 Early History of the Beautiful Mattole Valley in Southern Humboldt. Humboldt Times, December 29, 1935.
Fumiko Cahill, Jennifer
    2021a Removing a Monument to a Eugenicist Nazi Collaborator. Web page. Electronic document, https://www.northcoastjournal.com/humboldt/removing-a-monument-to-a-eugenicist-nazi-collaborator/Content?oid=20899165 accessed on January3, 2021.
Gaffney-Gorman, Bertha
    1976 Willie Was His Name, And He Had A Vision. Sacramento Bee, January 5, 1976:B4.

Gardner, Susan
  2001  Family member reflects bask on history of grand hotel; What happened to the dude ranch? Redwood Times, August 17, 2011.
Garner, Bryan A.
  2016  Garner's Modern English Usage. Oxford: Oxford University Press.
Garner, James G.
  1965  General Order 100 Revisited. Military Law Review 27:1-48.
Gates, Leroy J.
  1883  A Frightful Accident and One of the Most Miraculous Escapes from Death on Record. Unattributed clipping in the J. W. Henderson biography file at the Humboldt County Historical Society, Eureka. Grizzly Creek Lower Blackburn Carlos Arturo
Gates, Paul W.
  2002  Land and Law in California. West Lafayette, IN: Purdue University Press.
Gates, Thomas M.
  N.d.  [Map of] Yurok Aboriginal Territory. Photocopy in author's possession.
Geer, Knyphausen
  1948  Captain Knyphausen Geer: His Life and Memoirs. Humboldt County Historical Society Journal.
Genealogy.com
  2018a  The Christopher Erin Lindstrom of Roseville, CA: Information about Mary Anne Roche Singley. Web page. Electronic document, https://www.genealogy.com/ftm/l/i/n/Christopher-Erin-Lindstrom/WEBSITE-0001/UHP-0454.html accessed on August 20, 2018.
  2019a  Register Report of John Putnam. Web page. Electronic document, https://www.genealogy.com/ftm/p/u/t/Ed-Putnam/BOOK-0001/0043-0275.html accessed on August 12, 2019.
Geni
  2018a  Willis Wayne Myers. Web page. Electronic document, https://www.geni.com/people/Willis-Myers/6000000014826422079 accessed on November 29, 2018.
  2019a  Jane Susanna Logan. Webpage. Electronic document, https://www.geni.com/people/Jane/6000000041891851055 accessed on August 11, 2019.
Geniella, Mike
  2001  Benbow turns 75. Press Democrat, July 18, 2001.
Genzoli, Andrew
  1949a  Shelter Cove—Humboldt's Land of Paradise. Humboldt Times, September 11, 1949:17, 23.
  1952a  There Was More Than Weather in Sgt. McLean's Log Pages! Humboldt Times, April 6, 1952:6.
  1952b  Story of the Walla Walla. Humboldt Times, January 6, 1952.
  1971a  Automation Ends Era of Lightship. Times-Standard, June 12, 1971:3.
  1972a  Eel River Country. Fresno, CA: Mid-Cal Publishers.
  1977a  Redwood County: With the passing of time. Times-Standard, April 15, 1977:28.
  1979a  Bridgeville was a lively trip. Times-Standard, March 5, 1979.
  1982a  Wreck of the S.S. Bear. Humboldt Historian, May-June 1982:3-7.
  1982b  'The Poison Oak'—Disappointment on the Eel River—. Humboldt Historian, March-April 1982:8-9.
  1982c  Apples and the 'Great Maria.' Humboldt Beacon, January 7, 1982:5.
  1982d  Redwood Country. Humboldt Beacon, May 12, 1982:5.
  1983a  Remembering a daring transition from Sail to Steam . . . . Humboldt Historian, January-February 1983:18-19.
Genzoli, Andrew M., and Wallace E. Martin
  1972  Redwood Pioneer—a frontier remembered. Eureka: Schooner Features.
Gibbs, George
  2016  George Gibbs' Journal of Redick McKee's Expedition Through Northwestern California in 1851. Web page. Electronic document, http://klamathbucketbrigade.org/Gibbs_1851JournalMcKeeExpedition040406.htm accessed on August 12, 2016.
Gibbs, James S., Jr.
  1957  Shipwrecks of the Pacific Coast. Portland, OR: Binfords & Mort.
Gifford, E. W.
  1939  The Coast Yuki. Anthropos (34)1:292-375.
Gift, Harry E.
  1987  Ship knees harvested in Iaqua area. Humboldt Historian, March-April 1987:17.
Gipson, Naida Olsen
  2005  Babes In Benbow. Humboldt Historian, Summer 2005:28-31.
Goddard, Pliny E.
  1903a  #1 Sinkyone Notebook. In Selected Notebooks of Pliny Earle Goddard Relating to Humboldt County Tribes. Jerry Rohde, ed. PDF file archived at the Cultural Resources Facility, Humboldt State University, Arcata, CA.
  1906a  Redwood Creek & Mad River Notebook. In Selected Notebooks of Pliny Earle Goddard Relating to Humboldt County Tribes. Jerry Rohde, ed. PDF file archived at the Cultural Resources Facility, Humboldt State University, Arcata, CA.
  1906b  Lassik 1906 Names of Places Names of Plants. [Lassik notebook #2]. Original at Special Collections Division, University of Washington Libraries.
  1907a  Mattole Notebook #1, P. E. Goddard, October 1907. In Selected Notebooks of Pliny Earle Goddard Relating to Humboldt County Tribes. Jerry Rohde, ed. PDF file archived at the Cultural Resources Facility, Humboldt State University, Arcata, CA.
  1907b  Places V[an] Duzen to Mad River Pete [Notebook] #21. In Selected Notebooks of Pliny Earle Goddard Relating to Humboldt County Tribes. Jerry Rohde, ed. PDF file archived at the Cultural Resources Facility, Humboldt State University, Arcata, CA.

1907c [Untitled] Sinkyone Notebook II Albert Smith and George Burt [sic]. *In* Selected Notebooks of Pliny Earle Goddard Relating to Humboldt County Tribes. Jerry Rohde, ed. PDF file archived at the Cultural Resources Facility, Humboldt State University, Arcata, CA.

1907d Untitled Sinkyone Notebook 1 Albert Smith and Sallie [Sally] Bell Interviews. *In* Selected Notebooks of Pliny Earle Goddard Relating to Humboldt County Tribes. Jerry Rohde, ed. PDF file archived at the Cultural Resources Facility, Humboldt State University, Arcata, CA.

1907e 1 Nongatl Peter Van Duzen 1907 [Notebook]. *In* Selected Notebooks of Pliny Earle Goddard Relating to Humboldt County Tribes. Jerry Rohde, ed. PDF file archived at the Cultural Resources Facility, Humboldt State University, Arcata, CA.

1907f Mattole [Notebook] #2. *In* Selected Notebooks of Pliny Earle Goddard Relating to Humboldt County Tribes. Jerry Rohde, ed. PDF file archived at the Cultural Resources Facility, Humboldt State University, Arcata, CA.

1908a Yager 1908 Village Sites copied on cards [Notebook]. *In* Selected Notebooks of Pliny Earle Goddard Relating to Humboldt County Tribes. Jerry Rohde, ed. PDF file archived at the Cultural Resources Facility, Humboldt State University, Arcata, CA.

1908b Sinkyone Notebook IV, July 1908. *In* Selected Notebooks of Pliny Earle Goddard Relating to Humboldt County Tribes. Jerry Rohde, ed. PDF file archived at the Cultural Resources Facility, Humboldt State University, Arcata, CA.

1908c Duzen Mrs. Pete (~ and Mad River) June 15, 1908. PDF file archived at the Cultural Resources Facility, Humboldt State University, Arcata, CA.

1908d Nongatl Van Duzen Pete [Notebook] 18[.] June 17, 1908. *In* Selected Notebooks of Pliny Earle Goddard Relating to Humboldt County Tribes. Jerry Rohde, ed. PDF file archived at the Cultural Resources Facility, Humboldt State University, Arcata, CA.

1908e Peter V. D. June 20 1908 Nongatl [Notebook] 19. *In* Selected Notebooks of Pliny Earle Goddard Relating to Humboldt County Tribes. Jerry Rohde, ed. PDF file archived at the Cultural Resources Facility, Humboldt State University, Arcata, CA.

1908f [Untitled Sinkyone Notebook Charlie Interview July 1908] *In* Selected Notebooks of Pliny Earle Goddard Relating to Humboldt County Tribes. Jerry Rohde, ed. PDF file archived at the Cultural Resources Facility, Humboldt State University, Arcata, CA.

1913a Wayside Shrines in Northwestern California. American Anthropologist (15)4:702-703.

1914a Notes on the Chilula Indians of Northwestern California. University of California Publications in American Archaeology and Ethnology (10)6:265-288.

1914b Chilula Texts. University of California Publications in American Archaeology and Ethnology (10)7:289-379.

1919a Letter from P. E. Goddard to Dr. C. Hart Merriam dated February 25, 1919. Copy in author's possession.

1922a [Untitled Notebook Bear River and some Wailaki, August to September 1922.] *In* Selected Notebooks of Pliny Earle Goddard Relating to Humboldt County Tribes. Jerry Rohde, ed. PDF file archived at the Cultural Resources Facility, Humboldt State University, Arcata, CA.

1923 The Habitat of the Wailaki. American Archaeology and Ethnology, vol. 20. University of California Press.

1929 The Bear River Dialect of Athapascan. University of California Publications in American Archaeology and Ethnology (24)5.

N.d.a Van Duzen [Notebook] #20. *In* Selected Notebooks of Pliny Earle Goddard Relating to Humboldt County Tribes. Jerry Rohde, ed. PDF file archived at the Cultural Resources Facility, Humboldt State University, Arcata, CA.

N.d.b V[an] D[uzen] Songs [Notebook] #23. *In* Selected Notebooks of Pliny Earle Goddard Relating to Humboldt County Tribes. Jerry Rohde, ed. PDF file archived at the Cultural Resources Facility, Humboldt State University, Arcata, CA.

N.d.d #2 Sinkyone [Notebook]. *In* Selected Notebooks of Pliny Earle Goddard Relating to Humboldt County Tribes. Jerry Rohde, ed. PDF file archived at the Cultural Resources Facility, Humboldt State University, Arcata, CA.

N.d.e. Lassik Misc. [Lassik notebook #1]. Original at Special Collections Division, University of Washington Libraries.

N.d.f. Bald Hills [Notebook]. *In* Selected Notebooks of Pliny Earle Goddard Relating to Humboldt County Tribes. Jerry Rohde, ed. PDF file archived at the Cultural Resources Facility, Humboldt State University, Arcata, CA.

Goetzmann, William H., and Kay Sloan
  1982 Looking Far North: The Harriman Expedition to Alaska, 1899. Princeton, NJ: Princeton University Press.

Goldberg, Ami
  1985 Fascinating years at the Ettersburg Ranch. Humboldt Historian, September-October 1985:6-9.

Golla, Victor
  2011 California Indian Languages. Berkeley: University of California Press.
  2015a Personal communication with author regarding Goddard notebook #22, April 30, 2015.
  2015b Personal communication with author regarding certain Athabascan language terms, July 10, 2015.

Golla, Victor, and Sean O'Neill, eds.
  2001 The Collected Works of Edward Sapir. Vol. 14: Northwest California Linguistics. Berlin: Mouton de Gruyter.

Gomez, Melissa
    2021 UC Berkeley removes Kroeber Hall name, citing namesake's 'immoral' work with Native Americans. Web page. Electronic document, https://www.latimes.com/california/story/2021-01-27/uc-berkeley-kroeber-hall accessed on February 2, 2021.

Google Patents
    2019a Gradometer. Web page. Electronic document, https://patents.google.com/patent/US1219341 accessed on April 10, 2019.

Gordon, David E.
    1899a Old Camp Grant. Daily Standard, October 13, 1899:3.
    1899b Over the River. Daily Standard, October 16, 1899:3.
    1899c Along the Road. Daily Standard, October 17, 1899:3.
    1899d Along the River. Daily Standard, October 18, 1899:3.

Grant, Bonnie
    2005 Bonnie Henderson Grant *in* Children from our One-Room Schools. Blocksburg, CA: Blocksburg Town Hall Association.

Grant, Madison
    1919 Saving the Redwoods. Zoological Society Bulletin, September 1919:92-118.

Gravelmap
    2019 Gravel Routes in California: Whitethorn. Web page. Electronic document, https://gravelmap.com/browse/california accessed on June 23, 2019.

Greenmantle Nursery
    2020a The Ettersburg Apple Legacies. Web page. Electronic document, http://www.greenmantlenursery.com/fruit/etter-apples.htm accessed on September 2, 2020.

Greenson, Thaddeus
    2006a 'Simpler ways of life.' Times-Standard, October 19, 2006.

Gregory, Tom
    1911 History of Sonoma County California with Biographical Sketches of The leading men and women of that county, who have been identified with its growth and development from the early days to the present time. Los Angeles: Historic Record Company.

Greig, Rusty
    1964a Brice's Ferndale – Petrolia Stage Line. Humboldt County Historical Society Newsletter, July-August 1964:1.

Griggs, Gary, and Deepika Shrestha Ross
    2014 California Coast from the Air. Missoula, MT: Mountain Press Publishing Company.

Gudde, Erwin Gustave
    1969 California Place Names. Berkeley: University of California Press.

Guinn, J. M.
    1904 History of the State of California and Biographical Record of Coast Counties, California. Chicago: The Chapman Publishing Co.

Gurnon, Emily
    2004a Buyer Beware. North Coast Journal, April 22, 2004.
    2004b Gem on Ocean Quickly Loses Its Brilliance. Web page. Electronic document, https://www.latimes.com/archives/la-xpm-2004-jun-21-me-sheltercove21-story.html accessed on July 3, 2020.

Hackett, Bob, and Sander Kingsepp
    2019 INJ Submarine I-17. Tabular Record of Movement. Web page. Electronic document, http://www.combinedfleet.com/I-17.htm accessed on June 24, 2019.

Hagemann, David
    N.d. Sam Stockton 1905-1983. Photocopy on file under "Biographies" at the Humboldt County Historical Society, Eureka, California.

Hale, J. J.
    1879a Card of Thanks. Daily Humboldt times, March 12, 1879:3.

Hamm, Lillie E.
    1890 History and Business Directory of Humboldt County. Eureka: Daily Humboldt Standard.

Hanson, Buck
    1962 The Called Me A "Mule-Skinner." Humboldt County Historical Society Newsletter, March 1962:8.

Hanson, Buck, and Jim Boots
    1963 Memories of the Pacific Oaks Extract Works. Humboldt County Historical Society Newsletter, January-February 1963:13.

Harrington, James Peabody
    1983 The Papers of John P. Harrington in the Smithsonian Institution 1907 – 1957. Microfilm: Humboldt State University Library, Arcata.

Harville, Richard
    1985a Joseph Russ: A noted pioneer of Humboldt. Humboldt Historian, March-April 1985:4-7, 26.

Harville, Ronald P.
    1982 Letter to editor. Humboldt Historian, July-August 1982:17.
    1988 The Story of the Fort Baker Ranch. Santa Barbara: Ronald Patrick Harville.

Hawk, Diane
    2004 Touring the Redwood Highway: Humboldt County. Piercy, CA: Hawk Mountaintop Publishing.

Healdsburg Tribune
    1924a Large Crowd At Grove Dedication. Healdsburg Tribune, August 26, 1924:1.
    1936a Mrs. Georgeson, Ill Few Weeks, Dies in Eureka. Healdsburg Tribune, Enterprise and Scimitar, May 14, 1936:7.

Heartwood
    2018 Heartwood Mountain Sanctuary. Web page. Electronic document, https://www.heartwoodhub.com/emerald-springs-spa-wellness-center/ accessed September 26, 2018.

Heinbach, Orpha
    1986 A child's view of the Shively tunnel project. Humboldt Historian, July-August 1986:12-13.

Heizer, Robert F.
    1993 The Destruction of California Indians. Lincoln NB: University of Nebraska Press.

Heizer, Robert F., ed.
    1972 George Gibbs' Journal of Redick McKee's Expedition Through Northwestern California in 1851. University of California Berkeley, Archaeological Research Facility, Department of Anthropology.
    1978 Handbook of North American Indians, vol. 8: California. Washington: Smithsonian Institution.

Heizer, Robert F. and Alan J. Almquist
    1971 The Other Californians. Berkeley: University of California Press.

Heizer, Robert F. and Albert B. Elsasser, eds.
    1963 Aboriginal California: Three Studies in Culture History. Berkeley: University of California Press.

Heller, David
    2020a Personal communication with the author, October 30, 2020.
    2020b Personal communication with the author, October 31, 2020.

Hendricks, Karen Campbell
    2013 Bull Creek Memorial Cemetery. N. p.
    2015 Redway. Humboldt Historian, winter 2015:20-23.

Hewes, Gordon W.
    1940 Notes, Book III. Photocopy of hand-written notebook in author's possession.

Hill, Hazel
    1954a Briceland Is Filled With Treasured Memories. Humboldt Times, May 16, 1954: 10.
    1955a Blocksburg Life Was Rough, Ready, Happy. Humboldt Times, December 18, 1955:9.

Hill, Jesse Kaufhold
    2020a John Kaufold: "A Hipster before They Existed." Web page. Electronic document, https://kymkemp.com/2020/02/21/john-kaufhold-a-hipster-before-they-existed/ accessed on November 12, 2020.

Hillman, Raymond W.
    2007 Fog-bound tragedy remembered. Times-Standard, July 20, 2007: A1, A8.

History and Happenings
    2017a Eel Rock. Web page. Electronic document, http://historyandhappenings.squarespace.com/humboldt-county/2016/12/12/eel-rock.html accessed on December 23, 2017.
    2019a Island> Irma> Island Mountain. Web page. Electronic document, http://historyandhappenings.squarespace.com/trinity-county/2016/2/3/island-irma-island-mountain.html accessed on February 16, 2019.

History Vault
    2016 Nathan Bedford Forrest. Web page. Electronic document, http://www.history.com/topics/american-civil-war/nathan-bedford-forrest accessed on October 10, 2016.

HNSA
    2018a Lightship *Swiftsure*. Webpage. Electronic document, https://archive.hnsa.org/ships/swiftsure.htm accessed on December 19, 2018.

Hodge, Frederick W., ed.
    1910a Handbook of American Indians North of Mexico, part 2. Washington: Government Printing Office.

Holland, Herb
    1948a Garberville—*The Heart of the Redwoods*. Humboldt Times, September 19, 1948:9.

Home Herald
    1893a Lamb Bro's ad. Home Herald, March 3, 1893.

Hosmer, Frances Dinsmore
    N.d. Humboldt Days: Recollections of Frances Dinsmore Hosmer, as set down by her daughter Anne Hosmer Wrightson. Photocopy located in the biography files of the Humboldt County Historical Society, Eureka.

Hotchkiss, George W.
    1898 History of the Lumber and Forest Industry of the Northwest. Chicago: George W. Hotchkiss & Co.

House, Freeman
    1999 Totem Salmon. Boston: Beacon Press

HSU Special Collections
    2018 Swanlund-Baker Photograph Collection - Biography. Web page. Electronic document, https://en.wikipedia.org/wiki/Ray_Jerome_Baker accessed on August 22, 2018.

Humboldt & Trinity Toll Road Company
    N.d. Prospectus letter. Copy in possession of the author.

Humboldt Beacon
    1910a The Passing of Wm. B. Dobbyn of Rohnerville. Humboldt Beacon, May 27, 1910:7.
    1910b Capitalists Invest in So. Humboldt. Humboldt Beacon, May 27, 1910:4.
    1916a The Pacific Lumber Company To Have Four Stores In Woods. Humboldt Beacon, March 17, 1916.
    1916b "Budds", the Well Known Indian Dies at Shively. Humboldt Beacon, March 24, 1916.
    1922a Redwood Park Is Now Open To The Public. Humboldt Beacon, June 16, 1922:4.
    1922b Dyerville and Bull Creek. Humboldt Beacon, May 20, 1922:2.
    1922c Bull Creek Dyerville Items. Humboldt Beacon, June 30, 1922:6.
    1922d Dyerville and Bull Creek. Humboldt Beacon July 7, 1922:1.
    1922e David Chadbourne leg injury article. Humboldt Beacon, August 11, 1922.
    1922f What might have resulted in a very serious accident . . . . Humboldt Beacon, September 8, 1922:7.
    1922g Dyerville Items of Interest. Humboldt Beacon, October 20, 1922:2.

# Sources

    1923a  Dyerville and Bull Creek Items. Humboldt Beacon, February 23, 1923.
    1923b  Bull Creek Items. Humboldt Beacon, May 11, 1923:1.
    1923c  Chadbourne has fully recovered . . . . Humboldt Beacon, May 18, 1923:7.
    1923d  Word was received by friends . . . . Humboldt Beacon, September 14, 1923:3.
    1967a  Old Pepperwood Mill. Humboldt Beacon, January 5, 1967.
    1967b  Shively's "Indian Buds." Humboldt Beacon, January 26, 1967:15.
    1997a  Carlotta's Plans for Fire Hall Are Temporarily in Limbo. Humboldt Beacon, March 20, 1997.
    N.d.  The Killer Eel. Fortuna, CA: Humboldt Beacon, n.d.

Humboldt County Clerk
    1896  Precinct Registers of Humboldt County, State of California. Eureka.

Humboldt County Deeds
    N.d.  Humboldt County Recorder's Office, Eureka, CA.

Humboldt County Department of Community Development Services
    2003  Humboldt 2025 General Plan Update: Agricultural Resources and Policies.

Humboldt County Historical Society Newsletter
    1960a  The Old-Timer's Corner. Humboldt County Historical Society Newsletter, May 1960:11.

Humboldt County Schools
    1944  Directory of Public Schools Humboldt County 1944-1945. Eureka: County Superintendent of Schools.

Humboldt Historian
    1965a  In Memoriam. Humboldt Historian, July-August 1965.
    1968a  Article containing information about Redwood House. Humboldt Historian, July-August 1968:1.
    1981a  Photo of Young's Store, Pepperwood. Humboldt Historian, July-August 1981:11.
    1987a  U. S. Grant—the West Coast Years. Humboldt Historian, November-December 1987:11-13.
    1987b  In Memory. Humboldt Historian, March-April 1987:24.
    1995a  On The Right Track: Raleigh Christopher. Humboldt Historian, Winter 1995:22.
    1996a  In Memory: Margaret (Peggy) Satterlee. Humboldt Historian, Fall 1996:46.
    1999a  Obit for Louise Read Paine. Humboldt Historian, Spring 1999:45.
    2002a  Southern Humboldt Schools. Humboldt Historian, Spring 2002:6-14.

Humboldt Standard
    1883a  A. J. Huestis. Humboldt Standard, March 24, 1883.
    1907a  First Wreck News. Humboldt Standard, July 22, 1907:1.
    1907b  Promotion Work in Humboldt County. Humboldt Standard, January 14, 1907:6.
    1907c  Petrol Wagons for Petrolia. Humboldt Standard, August 15, 1907:1.
    1907d  Banner Presentation and Rally at Petrolia. Humboldt Standard, August 16, 1907:1.
    1907e  A Gala Day at Petrolia. Humboldt Standard, August 17, 1907:1.
    1907f  Automobiling in the Mountains. Humboldt Standard, August 18, 1907:1.
    1907g  A Welcome to Governor Gillett. Humboldt Standard, August 18, 1907:2.
    1907h  Fatal Landslide at Upper Mattole. Humboldt Standard, March 29, 1907:2.
    1908a  Indian's Death Creates A Stir. Humboldt Standard, January 17, 1908.
    1908b  Humboldt and Trinity County Toll Road. Humboldt Standard, February 1, 1908.
    1910a  Daylight Through Bryan Bluff Tunnel. Humboldt Standard, July 19, 1910:1.
    1912a  Geo. Tooby Buys A Locomobile. Humboldt Standard, September 19, 1912.
    1914a  $5,000 Fire Rages at Briceland. Humboldt Standard, July 14, 1914.
    1915a  Canoe from Fort Seward. Humboldt Standard, August 2, 1915.
    1916a  S. S. Bear Lost—Survivors Here. Humboldt Standard, June 15, 1916:1-2.
    1916b  Show 1200 Ft. Depth. Humboldt Standard, June 15, 1916:1.
    1916c  Tell of Night at Sea. Humboldt Standard, June 15, 1916:1-2.
    1916d  Alder Point Is Charming Village And Summer Camp. Humboldt Standard, December 13, 1916:1.
    1918a  Hermanson Signs Up Three Autos. Humboldt Standard, July 6, 1918:4.
    1919a  School of Sharks Attracted To Shelter Cove Alarm Fishermen. Humboldt Standard, September 20, 1919.
    1919b  Chester Denmark article. Humboldt Standard, July 26, 1919.
    1919c  Salmon Brown Is Dead; Kills Self. Humboldt Standard, May 13, 1919.
    1919d  Gasoline Gave Fury to Fire at Bridgeville. Humboldt Standard, December 16, 1919.
    1920a  Well Known Indian Woman, 90 Years of Age, Died Mon. Humboldt Standard, January 29, 1920.
    1920b  Death of Emerson recalls Story Of Early Murder Here. Humboldt Standard December 10, 1920.
    1921a  Death of Mrs. Martha Cuddeback Recalls Stories of Pioneering. Humboldt Standard, January 22, 1921.
    1921b  Woodshed Being Repaired for School Use; Fire. Humboldt Standard, August 30, 1921.
    1921c  Iaqua Dog Guard Sheep Night and Day, Saves Tiny Lamb in Underbrush. Humboldt Standard, September 27, 1921.
    1921d  Article about Hazeltons. Humboldt Standard, November 2, 1921.
    1922a  Incendiarism Causes Loss of Over $10,00 On Two Ranches at Fruitland. J. Lower Jailed. Humboldt Standard, September 1, 1922.

1923a Lawyer and Lumberman. Humboldt Standard, November 1, 1923.
1923b Queer Pranks of Wind Work Destruction at Brown's Mill. Humboldt Standard, August 22, 1923.
1923c Dr. J. C. Merriam Fights Fire at Redwood Grove Near Garberville. Humboldt Standard, August 6, 1923.
1924a Franklin K. Lane Memorial Redwood Grove To Be Dedicated In Humboldt On August 24. Humboldt Standard, August 5, 1924.
1924b Over 350 Men Are Employed in Mill and Woods of the Holmes-Eureka [sic] Company. Humboldt Standard, December 24, 1924.
1924c Dyerville Flat Redwoods Being Cut By Loggers. Humboldt Standard, November 24, 1925
1925a Crew of 50 [sic] Men at Work on Fred Hartsook Resort. Humboldt Standard, June 16, 1925.
1925b Founder of Fruitland Succumbs. Humboldt Standard, March 10, 1925.
1926a Man Who Lived Ten Years in Hollow Tree Is Burned to Death in South Fork Cabin. Humboldt Standard, February 13, 1926.
1926b "Hoop Skirt" Saves Pioneer; Miss Cuddeback Tells Story. Humboldt Standard, July 30, 1926.
1927a George Tooby, Pioneer Resident Of County, Dies In This City. Humboldt Standard, August 3, 1927
1927b New Oil Company Will Drill in Mattole Area. Humboldt Standard, October 27, 1927.
1927c Employment of Chinese at Hartsook's Draws Protest. Humboldt Standard, May 27, 1927.
1927d Sheriff Will Probe Mysterious $200,000 Highway Hotel Blaze, Humboldt Standard, August 8, 1927.
1927e Hartsook's Inn Soon to Reopen. Humboldt Standard, November 21, 1927.
1927f Weott Shingle Mill Destroyed by Fire. Humboldt Standard, July 29, 1927.
1927f Weott Hotel Destroyed by Blaze. Humboldt Standard, August 3, 1927.
1927g Indian Charged with Beating up an Indian Woman. Humboldt Standard, July 20, 1927.
1928a Jennie Sands, Aged Indian Woman, Dies. Humboldt Standard, July 28, 1928:9.
1928b Third Well to Be Sunk at Mattole. Humboldt Standard, January 13, 1928.
1928c One Dead from Fighting Conflagration; Woman is Burned in Oil Explosion. Humboldt Standard, September 29, 1928.
1930a N. W. P. Closes Shively Station. Humboldt Standard, March 13, 1930.
1930b 20,000 Arce Timber Area To Be Opened. Humboldt Standard, December 4, 1930.
1931a Pioneer Doctor of County Dies in Auto Crash. Humboldt Standard, August 21, 1931.
1931b Summer Home Area Sold on Bids. Humboldt Standard, August 26, 1931.
1931c 10,000 Acres of Giant Tres Added to State Parks; Dream Realized. Humboldt Standard, September 14, 1931.
1931d Bull Creek and Dyerville Redwood Forests Purchased for State's Park System. Humboldt Standard, June 22, 1931.
1932a Receiver Named for Hartsook Inn. Humboldt Standard, January 29, 1932.
1934a Mrs. Minnie Peet Succumbs in Arcata. Humboldt Standard, June 4, 1934:9.
1935a New Mattole Grange Hall Is Dedicated. Humboldt Times, August 12, 1935.
1935b New Logging Operations at Carlotta. Humboldt Standard, August7, 1935.
1937a Rites Held for Indian Woman. Humboldt Standard, April 1, 1937:7.
1937b Conductor and Two Itinerants Escape Death Near Shively. Humboldt Standard, August 6, 1937:1.
1937c Former Humboldt Resident Succumbs. Humboldt Standard, August 28, 1937.
1938a Victim Falls Off Narrow Span. Humboldt Standard, May 30, 1938.
1938b Find Body of River Victim. Humboldt Standard, May 31, 1938.
1938c M'Cann Truck Driver Shot in Skid Chain Row. Humboldt Standard, January 21, 1938.
1938d Hartsook Inn Is Auctioned. Humboldt Standard, October 10, 1938.
1938e Flames Sweep Hostelry to Resist Efforts of Garberville Firemen.
1939a Death Closes Long, Active Career. Humboldt Standard, October 5, 1939.
1939b New Shively Span Opened For Traffic. Humboldt Standard, January 25, 1939.
1939c Helmke Store Name Restored To Alderpoint. Humboldt Standard, June 6, 1939.
1940a Humboldt's Vacation Center Boasts Interesting History. Humboldt Standard, March 30, 1940.
1940b George Burtt, 94, Taken By Death. Humboldt Standard, March 18, 1940.
1940c Death Claims Mrs. Susie Burt, 92. Humboldt Standard, December 13, 1940.
1941a Pioneer, Age 90, Remains Active. Humboldt Standard, April 9, 1941.
1941b Daniel J. East of Iaqua Dies. Humboldt Standard, October 21, 1941.
1947a Prompt Action By Humboldt Ranch Owner Credited With Saving 11 Lives In Blimp Crash. Humboldt Standard, July 15, 1947.
1955a Old Eel Rock School Must Serve Again. Humboldt Standard, August 15, 1955:26.
1964a Eye-Witness Story from Stafford Told Standard. Humboldt Standard, December 26, 1964.

# Sources

1964b  Pepperwood Wiped Out, Other Towns Crushed!! Humboldt Standard, December 23, 1964:1.

N.d.a  Bull Creek Redwood Park to be Dedicated Sunday. Undated clipping in author's possession.

Humboldt State University Library

2020a  [Photo of] Three States Good Roads Rally, Dinsmore en route to Eureka. Special collections photo #1999.07.3157. Web page. Electronic document, http://library.humboldt.edu/humco/holdings/photodetail.php?S=dinsmore&CS=All%20Collections&RS=ALL%20Regions&PS=Any%20Photographer&ST=ALL%20words&SW=&C=14&R=1 accessed on August 2, 2020.

Humboldt Times

1854a  Mattole River and Valley. Humboldt Times, September 23, 1854:2.

1854b  Indians. Humboldt Times, October 28, 1854:2.

1855a  Immigration. Humboldt Times, July 21, 1855:2.

1855b  Humboldt County Lands. Humboldt Times, June 9, 1855:2.

1855c  Indian Hostilities—Three Men Killed. Humboldt Times, January 20, 1855:2.

1856a  Eel River Correspondence. Humboldt Times, November 1, 1856:2.

1856b  For Shelter Cove. Humboldt Times, July 19, 1856:2.

1856c  Murder of J. P. Albee by Indians. Humboldt Times, November 15, 1863:2.

1857a  A Digger Shot by Diggers. Humboldt Times, September 26, 1857:2.

1857b.  Mendocino reservation Again. Humboldt Times, September 5, 1857:2.

1858a  Serious Indian Troubles—Removal or Extermination. Humboldt Times, September 18, 1858:2.

1858b  Indian Excitement.—Two White Men Wounded.—Two Indians Killed. Humboldt Times, June 12, 1858:2.

1858c  More Indian Outrages.—Man Shot Down in the Trail. Humboldt Times, June 26, 1858:2.

1858d  Mad River Indians. Humboldt Times, June 26, 1856:2.

1858e  Our Indians. Humboldt Times, July 17, 1858:2.

1858f  Fight with the Indians.—One White Man Killed.—Ten Mules Scattered and Missing. Humboldt Times, July 17, 1858:2.

1858g  Fight with Indians.—One Man Killed and One Wounded. Humboldt Times, August 7, 1858:2.

1858h  What's to be Done? Humboldt Times, August 7, 1858:2.

1858i  Horrible Murder by Indians. Humboldt Times, September 18, 1858:2.

1858j  Serious Indian Trouble.—Removal or Extermination. Humboldt Times, September 18, 1858:2.

1858k  Indian Troubles. Humboldt Times, September 18, 1858:2.

1858l  Action of the Citizens of Union. Humboldt Times, September 18, 1858:2.

1858m  Gone to Work Right. Humboldt Times, September 18, 1858:2.

1858n  No Authority. Humboldt Times, September 25, 1858:2.

1858p  Movement of Troops. Humboldt Times, October 23, 1858.

1858q  Fight with the Indians. Humboldt Times, October 30, 1858:2.

1858r  Ranch Burned by Indians. Humboldt Times, October 30, 1858:2.

1858s  Indian Matters. Humboldt Times, November 20, 1858:2.

1858t  The Volunteer Expedition in this County. Humboldt Times, November 27, 1858:2.

1858u  Volunteers. Humboldt Times, December 4, 1858:2.

1858v  Mass Meeting in Mattole Valley. Humboldt Times, September 18, 1858:2.

1858w  Trouble with the Indians in Mattole. Humboldt Times, June 19, 1858:2.

1858x  Letter from Yager Creek. Humboldt Times, October 9, 1858:2.

1859a  The Murdered Men. Humboldt Times, December 24, 1859:2.

1859b  From the Volunteers. Humboldt Times, January 1, 1859:2.

1859c  Another Volunteer Wounded. Humboldt Times, January 29, 1859:2.

1859d  Fight with Indians.—Three Men Severely Wounded. Humboldt Times, January 29, 1859:2.

1859e  Our Indian War. Humboldt Times, January 29, 1859:2.

1859f  Indian War. Humboldt Times, March 12, 1859:2.

1859g  Send Them Out. Humboldt Times, April 23, 1859:2.

1859h  More Trouble with Indians. Humboldt Times, May 14, 1859:2.

1859i  Another Volunteer Company. Humboldt Times, May 28, 1859:2.

1859j  One of the Redwood Indians . . . . Humboldt Times, June 4, 1859:2.

1859k  Mattole Valley. Humboldt Times, November 19, 1859:2.

1860a  House Burned by Indians. Humboldt Times, October 13, 1860:2.

1860b  Re Built. Humboldt Times, September 16, 1860.

1861a  Cleaned out Again. Humboldt Times, June 15, 1861:3.

1861b  Another White Man Murdered by Indians in the County. Humboldt Times, June 29, 1861:2.

1861c  A Large Haul. Humboldt Times, February 9, 1861:3.

1861d  Apprenticing Indians. Humboldt Times, March 9, 1861:2.

1861e  Kidnapping. Humboldt Times, November 2, 1861:2.

1861f  Lieutenant Collins' Command. Humboldt Times, June 22, 1861:2.

1861g  Attack by Indians. Humboldt Times, January 19, 1861:2.

1861h Massacre and Plunder by Indians on Upper Eel River and Van Duzen's Fork. Humboldt Times, February 3, 1861:2.
1861i Article about Indians killing cattle on Cooksey Ranch. Humboldt Times, October 12, 1861:3.
1861j Indian Difficulties. Humboldt Times, December 14, 1861:2.
1862a Rain at Hoopa. Humboldt Times, July 12, 1862:3.
1862b Fort Seward. Humboldt Times, February 15, 1862.
1862c Court-Martial. Humboldt Times, July 26, 1862:3.
1862d Murder of J. P. Albee by Indians. Humboldt Times, November 15, 1862:2.
1862f Indian Outrages. Humboldt Times, July 12, 1862:3.
1862g Two Citizens Murdered by Savages. Humboldt Times, July 12, 1862:3.
1863a All Right. Humboldt Times, January 3, 1863:3.
1863b Revenge. Humboldt Times, January 24, 1863:2.
1863c Took in Twenty. Humboldt Times, March 7, 1863:2.
1863d Two Indians Killed. Humboldt Times, January 11, 1863:2.
1864d Good Haul of Diggers. Humboldt Times, January 11, 1863:2.
1864a Our Indian War. Humboldt Times, April 2, 1864:3.
1864b Our Mails Again. Humboldt Times, December 3, 1864:2.
1864c Hard on the Indians. Humboldt Times, February 20, 1864:3.
1864d Murdered by Indians. Humboldt Times, March 5, 1864:2.
1864e Indian Matters at Mattole. Humboldt Times, September 17, 1864:2.
1864f Iaqua Correspondence. Humboldt Times, August 27, 1864:2.
1866a Letter from Mattole. Humboldt Times, April 14, 1866:2.
1866b Letter from Mattole. Humboldt Times, May 28, 1866.
1866c Abandoned. Humboldt Times, September 15, 1866:3.
1867a Hog Ranch For Sale [ad]. Humboldt Times, May 18, 1867:2.
1867b Road Improvements. Humboldt Times, July 6, 1867:3.
1869a After the Redskins. Humboldt Times, April 3, 1869.
1869b Mattole Items. Humboldt Times, August 28, 1869:3.
1869c Another Indian Depredation. Humboldt Times, January 23, 1869:3.
1874a Hydesville and Van Duzen Road. Humboldt Times, March 4, 1874:3.
1874b A New Enterprise. Humboldt Times, February 7, 1874:3.
1875a The Kneeland Prairie and Round Valley Road. Humboldt Times, May 18, 1875.
1876a Letter to editor. Humboldt Times, July 7, 1876.
1877a Notes from Hydesville. Humboldt Times, December 1, 1877:1.

1878a Exports from Shelter Cove. Humboldt Times, September 14, 1878:3.
1878b Petrolia Is Swept By Flame. Humboldt Times, April 27, 1878.
1879a Supervisors. Humboldt Times, May 14, 1879:3.
1880a Camp Grant. Humboldt Times, February 25, 1880.
1880b Iron Railing for Mackey graves article. Humboldt Times, December 18, 1880.
1880c Pleasure Resort. Humboldt Times, July 14, 1880.
1881a Strong's Summer Resort. Humboldt Times, June 25, 1881.
1883a Legal notice of property sale. Humboldt Times, August 11, 1883.
1883b News summary including Collier-Briceland land transaction. Humboldt Times, August 16, 1883.
1889a Notice for Camp Meeting at Jacobson Valley. Humboldt Times, July 11, 1889:3.
1891a Fruitland article. Humboldt Times, September 2, 1891:3.
1891b Bank of Eureka foreclosure article. Humboldt Times, June 23, 1891:3.
1892a The Fruitland Company, Incorporated. Humboldt Times, February 27, 1892:2.
1892b Real Estate Transfers. Humboldt Times, March 27, 1892:2.
1892c Humboldt's Orchards. Humboldt Times, August 21, 1892:4
1894a Article about the Fruitland Company. Humboldt Times, February 11, 1894:4.
1894b Allard ad for Fruitland property. Humboldt Times, October 10, 1894:2.
1894c Death of a Former Eurekan. Humboldt Times, May 4, 1894:4.
1895a Lawsuit article. Humboldt Times, February 16, 1895:4.
1896a Enterprise Etchings. Humboldt Times, February 2, 1896:1.
1903a Asbill-Ellery. Humboldt Times, June 7, 1903:9.
1906a Petrolia Badly Hit. Humboldt Times, April 20, 1906:8.
1907a Columbia's Dead Number 90. Humboldt Times, July 23, 1907:1, 3.
1907b Shelter Cove Survivors. Humboldt Times, July 23, 1907:3.
1907c Blames Officers of Both Boats. Humboldt Times, September 7, 1907:1.
1907d Officiated at Two Weddings. Humboldt Times, September 5, 1907.
1909a Old Pioneer Is Dead. Humboldt Times, October 31, 1909.
1911a Victim of Three Painful Accidents in One Hour. Humboldt Times, July 11, 1911.
1911b Leaves Bequest To Mrs. Tooby. Humboldt Times, January 8, 1911.
1911c Entire Town of Carlotta Is Sold. Humboldt Times, March 29, 1911:1.
1911d Cherries Are Now Ripe . . . . Humboldt Times, June 11, 1912:3.

# Sources

1912a Modern Hotel at Fort Seward Will Be Opened Within Ninety Days. Humboldt Times, August 7, 1912.
1913a Chico Construction Co. Is Awarded Contract to Build Dyerville Bridge. Humboldt Times, March 12, 1913.
1913b Humboldt Strawberries to go by Parcels Post. Humboldt Times, January 5, 1913.
1913c Hindley Will Build Bull Creek-Mattole Road. Humboldt Times, August 29, 1913.
1913d Boys Testify for Father in $5000 Suit. Humboldt Times, November 5, 1913.
1913e Dinsmores Deny Story of Plaintiff. Humboldt Times, November 6, 1913.
1913f Young Homesteader Is Awarded $2,500 Damages by Jurors. Humboldt Times, November 7, 1913.
1913g Earl Burns' Young Son Commences Suit against Dinsmores for $10,000. Humboldt Times, November 8, 1913.
1913h Albert Schmidt Postmaster for Eighteen Years. Humboldt Times, March 15, 1913.
1914a Old Timer! Do You Remember When~ . Humboldt Times, May 31, 1931.
1915a Albert F. Etter Gets Gold Medal. Humboldt Times, December 21, 1915.
1916a Vessel is Looted of Articles of Value by Crew. Humboldt Times, June 18, 1916:1.
1918a "Hobo Jack" Trainman's Mascot Pays Visit to Eel Rock People. Humboldt Times, July 22, 1918:6.
1919a Shelter Cove Is Now Tent City of 1000. Humboldt Times, August 8, 1919.
1919b Brief Outline of the Life of W. H. Roscoe, Pioneer of Mattole. Humboldt Times, January 18, 1919.
1919c Indians Stole Durham Bull and Held Potlach; Bull Creek Named. Humboldt Time, March 23, 1919.
1920a Blaze Destroys Blocksburg Store. Humboldt Times, July 18, 1920.
1921a Shively Burns As Firemen Work. Humboldt Times, September 22, 1921.
1922a Boys Thrown into Creek by Old Bridge. Humboldt Times, March 12, 1922.
1923a Garberville News Briefly Told. Humboldt Times, May 23, 1923:8.
1924a Humboldt County in fight with Lumber Co. for Trees. Humboldt Times, November 25, 1924.
1925a Highlights on Contest over Redwoods Seen in Court Room. Humboldt Times, February 12, 1925:2.
1925b People Win Redwoods in Days Fight. Humboldt Times, February 12, 1925:1-2.
1925c McKees Mill to be Known as Redview. Humboldt Times, July 3, 1925:2.
1925d Noted Musicians Camp at Redview. Humboldt Times, August 14, 1925.
1925e Redview Child Fractures Arm. Humboldt Times, August 20, 1925.
1925f Noted Painter in Visit to Redview. Humboldt Times, August 29, 1925.
1929a Burris Bros. Announce Big Project. Humboldt Times, April 23, 1929.
1930a Anthropologist Conducts Indian Research Work. Humboldt Times, August 16, 1930:7.
1930b Shively Ferry Cable Snaps. Humboldt Times, March 2, 1930.
1930c Inquest Held for Clarence Burt. Humboldt Times, April 14, 1930:3.
1931a Humboldt Tomatoes Shipped. Humboldt Times, September 12, 1931.
1931b Eureka Firm To Build New Dyerville Bridge. Humboldt Times, April 30, 1931.
1931c Naming of World's Tallest Tree to Feature Dedication of Dyerville Redwood Park. Humboldt Times, September 10, 1931.
1932a When Shively Ferry Sank. Humboldt Times, February 16, 1932.
1932b Old Timer Do You Remember When. Humboldt Times, September 1, 1932.
1932c Famous Author Visits Benbow. Humboldt Times, August 3, 1932.
1935a Will Visit Old Home in Walls, Shetland Islands. Humboldt Times, May 10, 1935.
1935b Grange Hall Burns in Upper Mattole. Humboldt Times, January 1, 1935.
1935c Young and Ambitious at 76. Humboldt Times, September 12, 1935.
1935d Young and Ambitious at 76. Humboldt Times, September 12, 1935.
1937a Survivor of Massacre Dies. Humboldt Times, January 24, 1937.
1937b Well Known Members of N.W.P. Meet Terrible Fate; Locomotive Turns Over. Humboldt Times, August 7, 1937:1.
1938a "A Poet of the Redwoods." Humboldt Times, June 10, 1938.
1939a Death of Thomas Bell Brings To Light Strange Early Day Story. Humboldt Times, May 14, 1939:12.
1940a Last Survivor of Pioneer Days Massacre Succumbs. Humboldt Times, January 20, 1940.
1940b Yager and Jordan Creeks to be Future Log Source. Humboldt Times, October 4, 1940.
1948a Shively Maps Bridge Drive. Humboldt Times, January 25, 1948:1.
1949a Workman Washed Off Shively Span. Humboldt Times, February 23, 1949.
1952a Directory of Humboldt County Lumber Mills. Humboldt Times, January 13, 1952:8, 10.
1955a Blocksburg article. Humboldt Times, August 18, 1955.
1956a Blaze Destroys Historic Hotel in Fort Seward! Humboldt Times, April 29, 1956:1.
1957a Mattole Bridge Collapses. Humboldt Times, May 12, 1957.
1960a Ft. Seward Lumberman Bids High. Humboldt Times, August 5, 1960.

1960b  Five Injured When Train Hits Truck Near Fort Seward. Humboldt Times, October 8, 1960:1.
1962a  Maple Creek Willie's Generosity Provides Indian Scholarships. Humboldt Times, October 11, 1962:17.
1964a  Warehouse, Gasoline Station, 3 Homes Burn; One Man Hurt. Humboldt Times, February 22, 1964.

Humboldt Weekly Standard
1891a  Assessment Notice. Humboldt Weekly Standard, August 13, 1891:2.
1891b  Notice of Assessment. Humboldt Weekly Standard, July 9, 1891:3.

Humboldt Weekly Times
1874a  Wagon Road Bill. Humboldt Weekly Times, March 7, 1874:2.
1874b  Wagon Road Bill. Humboldt Weekly Times, March 7, 1874:2.
1875a  Van Duzen bridge article. Humboldt Weekly Times, January 2, 1875:3.
1881a  Tan bark article. Humboldt Weekly Times, July 30, 1881.

Hunt, Aurora
1962  The Army of The Pacific And the Unsung Valor of its Men. Montana: The Magazine of Western History, Spring 1962:49-61.

Hunt, Chris
1998  Ettersburg: Nothing Left Today. Times-Standard, August 28, 1998.

Hunt, L. C.
1982  Report on six-month's old Fort Humboldt. Humboldt Historian, May-June 1982:12.

Inforuptcy.com
2021a  Case number: 1:19-bk-10071 – Fruitland Vineyards LLC Northern California Bankruptcy Court. Web page. Electronic document, https://www.inforuptcy.com/browse-filings/california-northern-bankruptcy-court/1:19-bk-10071/bankruptcy-case-fruitland-ridge-vineyards-llc accessed on May 26, 2021.

Impr. [pseud.]
1858  Indian Women.—Their Treatment. Trinity Weekly Journal, January 9, 1858:2.

Indian Historian
1965  Maple Creek Willie . . . . The Indian Historian, February 1965:8.

Indian War Papers
1860a  Affidavit of James McAtee . . . March 8, 1860. Inventory of the Military Department. Adjutant General. Indian War Papers, folder F3753.555.
1860b  Petition by citizens of Yager Creek and Van Dousnes [sic] Fork to Governor Downey to call to active service the Humboldt Cavalry Company of volunteers to protect citizens from Indians. Written in Hydesville, Humboldt County, February 23, 1860. Inventory of the Military Department. Adjutant General. Indian War Papers, folder F3753.439.

International News Service
1915  Press Reference Library. New York: International News Service.

Irvine, Leigh H.
1915  History of Humboldt County, California. Los Angeles: Historic Record Co.

"J"
1880  Letter from Petrolia. Ferndale Enterprise, December 9, 1880:3.

Jackson, Dorothy
1984  Letter to the Editor. Humboldt Historian, November-December 1984:27.

James, Jerry
1921[?]a  Statement regarding L. K. Wood and Gregg Party. Photocopy available, as part of the "Wiyot History Papers," in the Special Collections, Humboldt State University Library, Arcata.

James, Nona
1984  Interview with Mary Anderson, September 12, 1984. Photocopy in possession of author.

Jameson, B. T., T. D. Felt, and Kennerly Dobyns
1852  Letter to "Fellow Citizens," January 15, 1852. Original at the Humboldt County Historical Society, archived as object # 2014.054.07.

Jeans, Ivan
1984  Pete McCloud: Mad River Recluse. Trinity [Yearbook] 1984.

Jepson, Willis Linn, et al.
1911  California Tanbark Oak. U. S. Department of Agriculture, Forest Service, Bulletin 75.

Johnson, Lauren M.
2021  UC Berkeley removes the name on a school building over an anthropologist's controversial past. Web Page. Electronic document, https://www.cnn.com/2021/01/27/us/uc-berkeley-removes-kroeber-from-anthropology-building-trnd/index.html accessed on June 28, 2021.

Johnson, Warren B.
1887  From the Pacific to the Atlantic: Being and Account of a Journey Overland from Eureka, Humboldt County, California, to Webster, Worcester Co., Mass., with a Horse, Carriage, Cow and Dog. Webster, MA: John Cort.

Johnston, Richard
1882  Narrative. Transcription, produced by Richard Roberts, available at the Ferndale Museum, Ferndale, CA.

Join California
2018a  November 6, 1906 General Election. Web Page. Electronic document, http://www.joincalifornia.com/election/1906-11-06 accessed August 2, 2018

Jones, Alice Goen, ed.
1981a  Trinity County Historic Sites. Weaverville, CA: Trinity County Historical Society.

Jordan, Mike
1947a  Rolling, Pitching Lightship Marks 'Sign Post' To Protect Shipping. Humboldt Times, February 9, 1947.

Jorgensen, Skip, and Mary Ellen Boynton
2019  When butter was gold. Our Story, March-April 2019.

Kanahele, Charlene
    1990  Renfroe's mountain hospitality. Humboldt Historian, January-February 1990:12-13.

Karshner, Gayle, ed.
    1987a  The Way It Was, Humboldt County Volume IV. Arcata: The Union.

Kaufman, George S., and Edna Ferber
    N.d.  Dinner at Eight. New York: Samuel French, Inc.

Keesey, Beatrice
    1982  Letter to the Editor. Humboldt Historian, November-December 1982:21.

Kelsey, C. E.
    1971  Census of Non-reservation California Indians, 1905 - 1906. Berkeley: Archaeological Research Facility, Department of Anthropology.

Kelsey, Arthur
    1982  Emergency—Mountain-country style . . . . Humboldt Historian, September-October 1982:9.

Kemp, Bruce
    1983  Native American History: The Lolangkok Sinkyone *in*: Humboldt Redwoods State Park General Plan Cultural Resources Element.

Kilkenny, Matina
    N.d.  Note regarding the name "Redway." Photocopy in author's possession.

Kinman, Seth
    2010  Seth Kinman's Manuscript and Scrapbook. Ferndale, CA: Ferndale Museum.

Kircher, John C. and Gordon Morrison
    1993  Ecology of Western Forests. Boston: Houghton Mifflin Company.

Kneiss, Gilbert
    1956  Redwood Railways. Berkeley: Howell North.

Knight, Mrs. John [Topsy]
    [1921?]a  Statement regarding reservations and attacks by whites on Indians. Photocopy available, as part of the "Wiyot History Papers," in the Special Collections, Humboldt State University Library, Arcata.
    [1921]b  Statement regarding reservations and attacks by whites of Indians living on Eel River. Photocopy available, as part of the "Wiyot History Papers," in the Special Collections, Humboldt State University Library, Arcata.

Knuth, Margaret
    1989  Shipwreck survivor tells her story. Humboldt Historian, March-April 1989:3-5.

Krei, Melvin A.
    N.d.a  Sinking of the Emidio. Copy of typescript in author's possession.

Kroeber, A. L.
    1908a  Notes on California Folk-Lore. Journal of American Folk-Lore xxi:37-38.
    1919  Notes and Queries: Sinkyone Tales. Journal of American Folk-Lore, April-June 1919.
    1925  Handbook of the Indians of California. Washington: Government Printing Office.
    1929a  Pliny Earle Goddard. American Anthropologist, New Series, (31)1:1-8.
    2021a  The Nature of Land-Holding Groups in Aboriginal California. Web page. Electronic document, https://digitalassets.lib.berkeley.edu/anthpubs/ucb/proof/pdfs/ucas056-003.pdf accessed on February 2, 2021.
    1976b  Yurok Myths. University of California Press, Berkeley and Los Angeles, California.
    1997  Papers, 1869-1972. Microfilm available at the Humboldt State University Library, Arcata.

Kühl, Stefan
    2000  Nazi Connection: Eugenics, American Racism, and German National Socialism. Oxford: Oxford University Press.

L. [pseud.]
    1877a  Communication. Evening Star, July 24, 1877:1.

Lacey, James, and Williamson Murray
    2013  Moment of Battle: The Twenty Clashes That Changed the World. New York: Bantam Books.

La Motte, H. D.
    N.d.  Statement of H. D. La Motte. Original at the Bancroft Library, University of California Berkeley.

Larribie [pseud.]
    1877a  From the South. Evening Star, May 10, 1877:1.

Larson, William E. et al.
    2011  Archaeology of the Smith Creek Watershed, Humboldt County, California. Archaeological Research Center, Department of Anthropology, California State University, Sacramento.

LeBaron, Gaye
    2019a  Glory days of North Coast railroads are history. Web page. Electronic document, https://www.pressdemocrat.com/news/2962068-181/glory-days-of-north-coast accessed on April1, 2019.

Leeper, David Rohrer
    1950  The Argonauts of 'Forty-Nine. Columbus, OH: Long's College Book Company.

Legier, Jules
    1958  Mattole Indians: 1854 to the Present. Photocopy of paper for History 198 class, on file under "History—Settlement Period 1850-75 Indian Wars" in the Humboldt County Collection, Humboldt State University Library, Arcata, CA.

Lentell, J. N.
    1898  Official Map of Humboldt County California. N. p.
    1901  Map of Humboldt County 1901. San Francisco.
    1905  Map of Mendocino County. San Francisco.

Lewis, Al, et. al.
  1991 Interview by Jerry Rohde with Al Lewis, Ed Lewis, and Blanche Lewis Tompkins, July 29, 1991.

Lewis, Ed
  2001 Bull Creek, as I saw it in 1931. Photocopy in possession of author.

Lewis, Oscar, ed.
  1966 The Quest for Qual-A-Wa-Loo. Oakland, CA: Holmes Book Company.

Library of Congress
  2019a Washington as Land Speculator. Web site. Electronic document, https://www.loc.gov/collections/george-washington-papers/articles-and-essays/george-washington-survey-and-mapmaker/washington-as-land-speculator/ accessed on July 20, 2019.

library.humboldt.edu
  2016 Tooby and Prior Photo Album – Finding Aid. Web page. Electronic document, https://library.humboldt.edu/humco/holdings/ToobyAid.htm accessed on October 31, 2016.

lighthousefriends.com
  2018 Punta Gorda Lighthouse. Web page. Electronic document, http://lighthousefriends.com/light.asp?ID=63 accessed on August 10, 2018.
  2019 Cape Mendocino Lighthouse. Web page. Electronic document, http://www.lighthousefriends.com/light.asp?ID=25 accessed on June 24, 2019.

Literary Digest
  1918 A Million from Novels. Literary Digest, March 2, 1918:32-33.

Logan, Jane
  1964a Memories of Jane Logan. Humboldt County Historical Society Newsletter, May-June 1964.

London, Jack
  2019 Navigating Four Horses North of the Bay. Sunset Magazine Web page. Electronic document, https://www.sunset.com/travel/california/jack-london-archival-essay accessed on February 7, 2019.

Long, Clarence D.
  1960 Wages and Earnings in the United States 1860-1890. Princeton, NJ: Princeton University Press.

Look Robert C.
  N.d. Diary. Notes made from original by author on February 1, 1992.

Lost Coast Outpost
  2015a Karuk Leader Amos Tripp Passes; Services at Redwood Acres Monday. Web page. Electronic document, http://lostcoastoutpost.com/2014/apr/12/karuk-leader-amos-tripp-passes-services-redwood-ac/ accessed on April 26, 2015.

Loud, Llewellyn L.
  1918 Ethnogeography and Archaeology of the Wiyot Territory. University of California Publications in American Archaeology and Ethnology 14:3.

Lowry, Mabel
  1982 The History of the Telephone in Bear River Valley. Photocopy in author's possession.
  1986 Early Ranch Days in Bear river Valley. Humboldt Historian, November-December 1986:12-13, 16-17.
  N.d. The Big Bear River Fire of 1945. Photocopy in author's possession.
  1995 Bear River School. Humboldt Historian, Fall 1995:17-18.

lyricsplayground.com
  2018 Lyrics to Dardanella. Web Page. Electronic document, https://lyricsplayground.com/alpha/songs/d/dardanella.html accessed on December 5, 2018.

M. H. [pseud.]
  1877 From "The Island" to Eagle Prairie. West Coast Signal, August 15, 1877:1.

Machi, Mario
  1984 Gem of the Lost Coast: A Narrative History of Shelter Cove. Eureka: Eureka Printing Co., Inc.

Machi, Mary Ann
  2012a The Sinking of the Yacht *Flamingo*. Humboldt Historian, Fall 2012:36-38.
  2015a Email communication with Jerry Rohde dated October 19, 2015.
  2015b Shelter Cove Chronology. Copy in possession of author.
  2015c Robarts Family Info. Copy in possession of author.
  2015d Email communication with Jerry Rohde dated November 10, 2015.
  2015e Email communication with Jerry Rohde dated November 26, 2015.

Machi, Mike
  2012a Ray family tree. Copy in possession of author.

Madera Tribune
  1924a Memorial to Franklin Lane. Madera Tribune, August 25, 1924:3.
  1947a Bessie Blimp Bangs Hilltop. Madera Tribune, July 15, 1947:1.

Madley, Benjamin
  2016a An American Genocide: The United States and the California Indian Catastrophe, 1846-1873. New Haven: Yale University Press.

Makepeace, Anne
  2002 Edward S. Curtis: Coming to Light. Washington DC: National Geographic Society.

Malte-Brun, Conrad
  2015[1824] Universal Geography: or A Description of All Parts of the World, on a New Plan, According to the Great Natural Divisions of the globe; Accompanied with Analytical, Synoptical, and Elementary Tables. Web page. Electronic document, https://archive.org/details/universalgeograp07malt accessed on August 5, 2015.

Margolin, Malcolm
  1981 The Way We Lived. Berkeley: Heyday Books.

Marine Insight
  2020 Dry Docking of Ships – Understanding Stability and Docking Plan. Web page. Electronic Document, http://ernielb.blogspot.com/2009/07/enoch-percival-french-and-newton-bishop.html accessed on August 5, 2020.

Mark West Area Chamber of Commerce
    2020  Mark West Area History. Web page. Electronic document, https://markwest.org/chamber-history/ accessed on December 23, 2021.

Martin, Mel
    N.d.  Interview with Jerry Rohde

Martin, Wallace
    1983  Sail and Steam on the Northern California Coast 1850 – 1900. San Francisco: National Maritime Museum Association.

Mathison, Ray
    1998  The History of Alderpoint. Eureka: Eureka Printing Co.

Mattole Restoration Council
    2018  Mission and History. Web page. Electronic document, http://www.mattole.org/about/mission-history/ accessed on August 12, 2018.

Mays, Tom
    2018  "The California Mutiny." Unpublished manuscript, January 11, 2018. Microsoft Word file.

McBride, Viola Russ
    1995a  How Ranches Got Their Names. N.p.: Viola Russ McBride.
    1998a  Settlers and Indians on Bear River: Tales Remembered. Humboldt Historian, Summer 1998:20-25.

McCloskey, Bruce
    1982  Letter to editor. Humboldt Historian, September-October 1982:16.

McClure, William, and Ruth McClure
    2013  The Japanese Ambassador's Visit. Humboldt Historian, Winter 2013:34-37.

McCormick, Evelyn
    1963a  Dwight Felt Sr. article. Humboldt Times, June 2, 1963:7.
    1986a  Locomotive proved fatal to nine men. Humboldt Historian, March-April 1986:7-8.
    N.d.a  Living With The Giants. Rio Dell: Evelyn McCormick.

McGuire, Michael
    1979  Petrolia cemetery is being brought back to life. Times-Standard, June 5, 1979.

McKinney, John
    2018  Wildest Coastline in California. Web page. Electronic document, http://articles.latimes.com/1992-08-09/travel/tr-6108_1_king-range-coast accessed on June 1, 2018.

McLean, Louise
    1917  Discovery of Humboldt Bay. Overland Monthly (LXX) 2.

McMorris, Christopher, and Steven J. Melvin
    2013a  Historical Resources Evaluation Report: Honeydew Bridge Replacement Project. Humboldt County.

McNamara, Robert
    2015  Doughface. Web page. Electronic document, http://history1800s.about.com/od/1800sglossary/g/Doughface.htm accessed on August 9, 2015.

McTavish [pseud.?]
    1885a  Down the Coast. Daily Humboldt Standard, September 30, 1885:3.
    1885b  Englewood to Rio Dell. Daily Humboldt Standard, July 21, 1885:3.
    1885c  Camp Grant. Daily Humboldt Standard, July 16, 1885:3.
    1885d  On the Road. Daily Humboldt Standard, June 3, 1885:3.
    1885e  Phillipsville. Daily Humboldt Standard, June 30, 1885:3.
    1885f  By Rail. Daily Humboldt Standard, May 27, 1885:3.
    1885g  Blocksburg. Daily Humboldt Standard, June 2, 1885:3.
    1885h  Bridgeville. Daily Humboldt Standard, May 29, 1885:3.
    1885i  Down the South Fork. Daily Humboldt Standard, June 19, 1985:3.

measuringworth.com
    2016a  Web page. Electronic document, https://www.measuringworth.com/uscompare/relativevalue.php accessed on July 28, 2016.
    2016b  Web page. Electronic document, https://www.measuringworth.com/uscompare/relativevalue.php accessed on August 21. 2016.
    2016c  Web page. Electronic document, https://www.measuringworth.com/uscompare/relativevalue.php accessed on October 31, 2016.
    2017a  Web page. Electronic document, https://www.measuringworth.com/uscompare/relativevalue.php accessed on August 7, 2017.
    2018a  Web page. Electronic document, https://www.measuringworth.com/calculators/uscompare/result.php?year_source=1864&amount=270000.00&year_result=2017 accessed on March 27, 2018.
    2020a  Web page. Electronic document, https://www.measuringworth.com/calculators/uscompare/relativevalue.php accessed on November 16, 2020.

Melendy, Howard B.
    1962a  The Overland Automobile Stage: 1908-1914. Blue Lake Advocate, November 1, 1962:2.
    1962b  The Overland Automobile Stage: 1908-1914. Blue Lake Advocate, October 25, 1962:2.
    1962c  The Overland Automobile Stage: 1908-1914. Blue Lake Advocate, November 22, 1962:2.
    1962d  The Overland Automobile Stage: 1908-1914. Blue Lake Advocate, November 29, 1962:2.
    1962e  The Overland Automobile Stage: 1908-1914. Blue Lake Advocate, November 8, 1962:2.

Merriam, C. Hart
    1918a  The Acorn, a Possibly Neglected Source of Food. National Geographic Magazine (34)2 (August 1918):129-137.
    1921a  California Journal 1921, vol. 1. Photocopy at the Cultural Resources Facility, Humboldt State University, Arcata.
    1922a  California Journal 1922, vol. 1. Photocopy at the Cultural Resources Facility, Humboldt State University, Arcata.

1923a California Journal 1923, vol. 1. Photocopy at the Cultural Resources Facility, Humboldt State University, Arcata.

1923b Application of the Athapaskan Term Nung-kahhl. American Anthropologist, vol. 25:276-277.

1966 Ethnographic Notes on California Indian Tribes. Berkeley: University of California Archaeological Research Center 68, part 1.

1976 Ethnogeographic and Ethnosynonymic Date from Northern California Tribes. Contributions to Native California Ethnology from the C. Hart Merriam Collection 1.

1993 C. Hart Merriam Papers Relating to Work with California Indians, 1850-1974. Berkeley: University of California Library Photographic Service, 1993.

Merriam, C. Hart, and Zenaida Merriam Talbot
1974 Boundary Descriptions of California Indian Stocks and Tribes. Berkeley: Archaeological Research Facility, Department of Anthropology.

Merriam, John C.
1938 "Forest Windows" in Published Papers and Addresses of John Campbell Merriam, vol. 3. Washington: The Carnegie Institution of Washington, 1897-1903.

Merriam-Webster
2019a Jehu. Web page. Electronic document, https://www.merriam-webster.com/dictionary/jehu accessed on June 24, 2015.

Metsker, Charles F.
1949 Metsker's Atlas of Humboldt County, California. Tacoma, WA: Charles F. Metsker.

militarymuseum.org
2019a The Attack on the SS Emidio. Web page. Electronic document, http://www.militarymuseum.org/Emedio.html accessed on June 24, 2019.
2016a Humboldt Volunteers. Web page. Electronic document, http://www.militarymuseum.org/ accessed on October 9, 2016.

Mills, Ellen L., ed.
1985 The Papers of John Peabody Harrington in the Smithsonian Institution: 1907 – 1957, Volume 2. White Plains, New York: Kraus International Publications.

Milota, Marilyn Keach
1993a Humboldt County California Abstracts of Death Records 1873-1925, vol. I. Photocopy available at the Humboldt Room, Humboldt County Library, Eureka.
1993b Humboldt County California Abstracts of Death Records 1873-1925, vol. II. Photocopy available at the Humboldt Room, Humboldt County Library, Eureka.
2001a Humboldt County California Abstracts of Death Records 1926-1935. Photocopy available at the Humboldt Room, Humboldt County Library, Eureka.
2003a Humboldt County California Abstracts of Death Records 1936-1947. Photocopy available at the Humboldt Room, Humboldt County Library, Eureka.

Miner, George "Buck"
1996 The Origin of the Mattole: Through the Eyes of a Salmon. Petrolia, CA: George "Buck" Miner.

Monroe, George
1981 Letter to the Editor. Humboldt Historian, November-December 1981:19.

Monroe, Thomas H.
1962 Notes on the Albee Family. Transcription of a speech given to the Humboldt County Historical Society, on file in the Biography collection at the Humboldt County Historical Society, Eureka, CA.

Morgan, Ruth E.
1982a Thorn had the 'worst' school building in California . . . . Humboldt Historian, January-February 1982:16.
1982b Kids tried to terrify their teacher. Humboldt Historian, July-August 1982:15.
1982c Fire came close but it just wouldn't take Whitethorn School. Humboldt Historian, May-June 1982:16.

Morley, S. Griswold
1938 The Covered Bridges of California. Berkeley: University of California Press.

Morrison Carol "Mori"
1991 Interview with Jerry Rohde, March 7, 1991.

Morrison, Clyde
1960 Discrepancies and Corrections: Captain Knyphausen Geer's Memoirs. Humboldt County Historical Society News Letter, May 1960.
1962a Silas W. Morrison: Part III. Humboldt County Historical Society Newsletter, January 1962:9-10.
1962b Silas W. Morrison: Part IV. Humboldt County Historical Society Newsletter, March 1962:13-14.

Morrison, Sid
1979 Ranches in Bear River. Photocopy in possession of author.

Mortenson, Alice
1990 Interview with Jerry Rohde on December 14, 1990.

Moungovan, Mrs. T. O.
1964a Shelter Cove Scalping. Mendocino County Historical Society Newsletter (3)1:7-8.

Mountaineer (pseud.)
1864 Camp Grant Correspondence. Humboldt Times, December 3, 1864:2.

Mulcahy, J. A.
1970 Letter to the Editor. Humboldt Historian, January-February 1970:2.

Mulley, Alice Y.
1999 Wild River. Humboldt Historian, Fall 1999.

Murphey, Edith V. A.
1941 Out of the Past: A True Indian Story. California Historical Society Quarterly 20(4):349-364.

Murray, Ellen
1987a The hazards and joys of ranch life. Humboldt Historian, July-August 1987:10-13.

1987b Adventure started in Redway. Humboldt Historian, July-August 1987:14-17.
Myers, Geraldine
1992 Phone interview with Jerry Rohde.
Nace, Ted
2003 Gangs of America: The Rise of Corporate Power and the Disabling of Democracy. San Francisco: Berrett-Koehler Publishers, Inc.
Nash, Glen
1985a Blue Slide bridges and their builders. Humboldt Historian, March-April 1985:21-22.
1988a Benbow: the place and family. Humboldt Historian, January-February 1988:3-8.
1988b The triumphs and trials of Benbow. Humboldt Historian, March-April 1988:14-19.
1989a Blake's colorful role in phone history. Humboldt Historian January-February 1989:3-5
1996a Making a Living, Making a Life in Humboldt County. Eureka: Globe Properties.
Neibur, H.
1867 Another Route for the Proposed Wagon Road. Humboldt Times, December 7, 1867:2.
Neiss, Gilbert H.
1956 Redwood Railways. Berkeley: Howell-North.
Nelson, Byron Jr.
1988 Our Home Forever: The Hupa Indians of Northern California. Salt Lake City: Howe Brothers.
New York Botanical Garden
2020 Astragalus agnicidus Barneby. Web page. Electronic document, http://sweetgum.nybg.org/science/world-flora/monographs-details/?irn=16879 accessed on May 9, 2020.
New York Historical Society
2016 What does the 'S' in Ulysses S. Grant stand for? Web page. Electronic document, http://blog.nyhistory.org/ulysses-grant/ accessed on October 4, 2016.
New York Lumber Trade Journal
1917 Obituary of John Sedgwick Noyes. New York Lumber Trade Journal, September 15, 1917:28B
New York Times
1864a The Fort Pillow Massacre. New York Times, May 3, 1864.
2020a Pacific Steamship Walla Walla Wrecked. Web page. Electronic document, https://timesmachine.nytimes.com/timesmachine/1902/01/04/issue.html accessed on May 30, 2020.
Nixon, Stuart
1966 Redwood Empire. New York: E. P. Dutton.
Noble, Nancy Burnell
1980 Letter Box. Humboldt Historian, September-October 1980:15.

Nomad (pseud.)
1881 Notes from South Fork. Humboldt Times, April 22[?], 1881:3.
Nomland, Gladys Ayer
1931a A Bear River Shaman's Curative Dance. American Anthropologist, New Series, January-March, 1931:38-41
1935 Sinkyone Notes. University of California Publications in American Archaeology and Ethnology (36)2.
1938 Bear River Ethnography. Anthropological Records (2)2.
Nomland, Gladys Ayer, and A. L. Kroeber
1936 Wiyot Towns. University of California Publications in American Archaeology and Ethnology (35)5.
North Coast Journal
2021a Notice of Impending Power to Sell Tax-Defaulted Property. North Coast Journal, May 27, 2021:32-33.
Northern Californian
1858a Indian Affairs. Northern Californian, December 15, 1858:2.
1860a Hydesville Volunteers. Northern Californian, February 8, 1860:3.
Northrup, Cynthia Clark, and Elaine C. Prange Turney
2003 Encyclopedia of Tariff and Trade in U. S. History. Westport CT: Greenwood Publishing Group.
Norton, Jack
1979 Genocide in Northwestern California: When Our Wolds Cried. San Francisco: Indian Historian Press.
nps.gov
2016a About the Homestead Act. Webpage. Electronic document, https://www.nps.gov/home/learn/historyculture/abouthomesteadactlaw.htm accessed on July 13, 2016.
OAC
2018a Guide to C. Hart Merriam Papers, Vol. 2. Web page. Electronic document, http://www.oac.cdlib.org/findaid/ark:/13030/tf1z09n5qh/entire_text/ accessed on April 2, 2018.
Obarr, O. W.
1999 Little Histories of the Road: Carlotta. The Northwesterner, Spring-Summer 1999:26.
Ober, James
1973 Humboldt History. Photocopy of student paper in Rio Dell file at the Humboldt County Historical Society, Eureka.
O'Hara, Susan Pritchard
N. d. History of Humboldt Redwoods State Park. Photocopy available at Special Collections, Humboldt State University Library, Arcata.
O'Hara, Susan J. P., and Alex Service
2013 Northwestern Pacific Railroad: Eureka to Willits. Charleston, SC: Arcadia Publishing.
O'Hara, Susan J. P., and Dave Stockton
2012 Humboldt Redwoods State Park. Charleston, SC: Acadia Publishing.

Olsen, Michele
    2020a  The First Netherland Fruit & Land Culture Association. Copy of manuscript in author's possession.

Ommen, Terry L.
    2012  Wild Tulare County: Outlaws, Rogues & Rebels. Charleston, SC: The History Press.

Open Jurist
    2015  223 U. S. 365 –Metropolitan Redwood Lumber Company v. Charles P. Doe. Web page. Electronic document, http://openjurist.org/223/us/365/metropolitan-redwood-lumber-company-v-charles-p-doe- accessed on November 11, 2015.

Oregon Daily Journal
    1920  Sad Story of Man Who Saved Bulb Industry is Told. Oregon Daily Journal, November 28, 1920:4.

Oregon Encyclopedia
    2020a  Chemawa Indian School. Web page. Electronic document, https://oregonencyclopedia.org/articles/chemawa_indian_boarding_school/#.X1UWsi2z13Q accessed on September 6, 2020.

Oregon Historical Quarterly
    2001  Edgar Horner and the Wreck of the *Alaska*. Oregon Historical Quarterly 102(1):72-85.

Orton, Richard H.
    1890  Records of California Men in the War of Rebellion, 1861 To 1867. Sacramento: State Printing Office.

Osgood, Wilfred H.
    1944  Biographical Memoir of Clinton Hart Merriam 1855-1942. Web page. Electronic document, http://nau.edu/uploadedFiles/Centers-Institutes/Merriam-Powell/_Forms/cmerriam_Osgood_bio_NAS.pdf accessed on July 6, 2015.

OSU
    2017  Tanoak. Oregon State University, Oregon Wood Innovation Center. Web Page. Electronic document, http://owic.oregonstate.edu/tanoak-lithocarpus-densiflorus accessed on September 13, 2017.

Ott, Melissa
    2017  The Tanoak (Notholithocarpus densiflorus), A Significant Santa Cruz Native Plant. Web page. Electronic document, https://ventana2.sierraclub.org/santacruz/node/216 accessed on August 4, 2017.

Pacific Reporter
    1901  Pacific Reporter, volume 62. St. Paul: West Publishing Company.
    1918  Nelson v. Thomas et al. Web page. Electronic document, https://www.google.com/books/edition/The_Pacific_Reporter/rvQ7AAAAIAAJ?hl=en&gbpv=1&dq=%22C.+S.+Thomas%22+Ella+Thomas%22%22John+Nelson%22&pg=PA398&printsec=frontcover accessed on October 31, 2020.

Paddock, Sterling, and Bill Paddock
    2001  Interview with Jerry Rohde, September 29, 2001.

Palmer, Henrietta
    1879a  Letter to Aunt Mary, April 2, 1879. Copy on file at the Humboldt County Historical Society, Eureka.
    1879b  Letter to Aunt Mary, April 30, 1879. Copy on file at the Humboldt County Historical Society, Eureka.
    1879c  Letter to Aunt Mary, May 5, 1879. Copy on file at the Humboldt County Historical Society, Eureka.
    1879d  Letter to Aunt Mary, June 6, 1879. Copy on file at the Humboldt County Historical Society, Eureka.
    1879e  Letter to Aunt Mary, June 25, 1879. Copy on file at the Humboldt County Historical Society, Eureka.
    1879f  Letter to Aunt Mary, August 3, 1879. Copy on file at the Humboldt County Historical Society, Eureka.

Palmer, T. S.
    1954  In Memoriam: Clinton Hart Merriam. The Auk 71:2.

Palmrose, Robert
    2013  Where Is Sherwood? A History of the Overland Auto Stage Company. Humboldt Historian, Winter 2013:10-19.

Pardee, Mike
    1951  Garberville—Center of Eel river Industry. Press-Democrat, December 2, 1951:1,3.

Parker, Stanley
    1984  Brown's Camp and its gentleman boss. Humboldt Historian, July-August 1984:18-20.
    1988a  Reflections of Holmes Lumber Company. Humboldt Historian, May-June 1988:3-7, 14.
    N.d.  Palco Past: A Social History of Scotia and the Pacific Lumber Company: Neighbors—Brown's Camp. Photocopy on file at the Humboldt County Historical Society, Eureka, CA.

parks.ca.gov
    2020a  Richardson Grove State Park. Web page. Electronic document, https://www.parks.ca.gov/?page_id=422 accessed on August 20, 2020.

Parrish, Justine
    1965  Harrowing Rescues Along Southern Humboldt Flooded Areas Brought Out Best. Humboldt Standard, January 7, 1965.

Parsnips, Louella [pseud.]
    2013a  Captain Marble's Matrimonial Mania. Humboldt Historian, Spring 2013:26-28.

Pavlik, Bruce, et al.
    1992  Oaks of California. Los Olivos, CA: Cachuma Press.

PBS
    2015a  Harriman Expedition Retraced: The 1899 Expedition. Web page. Electronic document, http://www.pbs.org/harriman/1899/1899.html accessed on July 6, 2015.
    2015b  Harriman Expedition Retraced: C. Hart Merriam 1855-1942. Web page. Electronic document, http://www.pbs.org/harriman/1899/1899_part/participant-merriam.html accessed on July 6, 2015.

Peattie, Donald Culross
    1954 Avenue of the Giants. Holiday, March 1954.
    1991 A Natural History of Western Trees. Boston: Houghton Mifflin Company.

PeopleLegacy
    2022 Where is George Newton Rumrill Buried? Web Page. Electronic document, https://peoplelegacy.com/george_newton_rumrill-276f4k1 accessed on February 20, 2022.

Peterson, Stirling
    1984. Personal communication with the author.

Pfremmer, Esterfay
    1976 Letter to the Editor. Humboldt Historian, May-June 1976:33.

Phegley, Milton
    1991 Rain or shine, the Harris Post Office delivered. Humboldt Historian, September-October 1991:18-20.

Pierce, Helen Thomas
    1976 The Thomas-Wimer Family. Photocopy in the biography files, Humboldt County Historical Society, Eureka.

Pinches, Bill
    2006 In-person interview with Jerry Rohde, November 3, 2006.

Platt, Tony
    2019a. Saving the Redwoods: The Eugenic Connection. Web page. Electronic document: https://www.homeworkmarket.com/sites/default/files/qx/16/02/16/03/platt_saving_the_redwoods_the_eugenic_connection.doc accessed on December 5, 2019.

Polk
    1950 Polk's Eureka (California) City Directory 1949-1950 Including Arcata and Humboldt County. San Francisco: R. L. Polk & Co.

Polk-Husted
    1914 Eureka City and Humboldt County Directory 1914-15. Web page. Electronic document, https://www.google.com/books/edition/Polk_Husted_Directory_Co_s_Eureka_City_a/pMZLAQAAIAAJ?hl=en&gbpv=1 accessed on November 1, 2020.

postalhistory.com
    2016a Post Offices California Redcrest. Webpage. Electronic document, http://www.postalhistory.com/postoffices.asp?task=display&searchtext=redcrest&state=CA&county=&searchtype=word accessed on July 10, 2016.

Powers, Alfred
    1949 Redwood Country. New York: Duell, Sloan & Pierce.

Powers, Stephen
    1872a The Northern California Indians, No.1. Overland Monthly (8)4.
    1872b Afoot and Alone; A Walk from Sea to Sea by the Southern Route. Hartford, CT: Columbian Book Company.
    1976[1877] Tribes of California. Berkeley: University of California Press.

Pritchard, Margaret
    1987a Dyerville gone but its history lives. Humboldt Historian, March-April 1987:9-13, 16.
    1987b Business end of Dyerville experience. Humboldt Historian, May-June 1987:18-21.
    1987c Dyerville crossing had its perils. Humboldt Historian, July-August 1987:18-21.
    1987d Dyerville: stage roads to highway. Humboldt Historian, September-October 1987:22-24.

Pritchard, Margaret, and Susan Pritchard O'Hara
    1991 Interview with Jerry Rohde, April 30, 1991.

Pro-Football-Reference-Com
    2015a Dave Lewis. Web page. Electronic document, http://www.pro-football-reference.com/players/L/LewiDa22.htm accessed on April 26, 2015.

pythias.org
    We serve our community across the United States, Canada, and the world. Web page. Electronic document, https://www.pythias.org accessed on January 20, 2022.

Rambler [pseud.]
    1887a Notes from Southern Humboldt. Daily Humboldt Times, July 19, 1887:3.

Randles, Anthony
    1966 Punta Gorda Lighthouse article. Humboldt Times, April 17, 1966:17.

Raphael, Ray, and Freeman House
    2011 Two Peoples, One Place. Revised edition. Eureka: Humboldt County Historical Society.

Rathjen, Mark
    1989 New life for aging hotel. Times-Standard, September 10, 1989.

Rayle, D. E.
    2014. The Golden Spike Story. The Northwesterner, Fall-Winter 2014:7-15.

readtheplaque.com
    2019 Cape Mendocino Lighthouse. Web page. Electronic document, https://readtheplaque.com/plaque/cape-mendocino-lighthouse accessed on June 26, 2019.

Redwood Coast
    2012 Redwood Coast City Street Map. Burnaby, BC: GM Johnson & Associates Ltd.

Redwood Monastery
    2017 A Short History. Web page. Electronic document, http://www.redwoodsabbey.org/Life/History/ accessed on December 10, 2017.

Reed, Anna
    1986a Anna Reed describes 1872 horseback trip to Humboldt. Humboldt Historian, March-April 1986:18-20.
    1904a A Heroine of Humboldt. Northern Crown, May, 1904:7-10.

Reger, June
    2005 The Murphy Family. *In*. Children from our One-Room Schools. Blocksburg, CA: Blocksburg Town Hall Association.

Reichard, Gladys
    1922 Wiyot, Yurok Texts. *In*. Gladys Reichard filed notebooks on Wiyot Indians, [ca. 1920-23]. Bancroft Library microfilm, collection number: BANC MSS 2004/111c.

Reis, Peggy
    2005 Margaret "Peggy" Woodman Reis. *In*. Children from our One-Room Schools. Blocksburg, CA: Blocksburg Town Hall Association.

Richardson, Claude
    2002 Interview with Jerry Rohde on November 2, 2002.

Rigby, Ken
    2016. Phone interview with Jerry Rohde on December 2, 2016.

Ringwald, George
    2003a The Shelter Cove Saga: From land scam to popular resort. North Coast Journal, August 28, 2003. Web page. Electronic document, http://www.northcoastjournal.com/082803/cover0828.html accessed on December 2, 2015.
    2003b Boom Time: Its troubled past largely forgotten, Shelter Cove is going gangbusters. North Coast Journal, September 4, 2003. Web page. Electronic document, http://www.northcoastjournal.com/090403/news0904.html#anchor272215 accessed on December 2, 2015.

Roberts, Ann
    2009 Kiwelattah Through the Eyes of Seven Settlers. Humboldt Historian, Spring 2009:24-27.

Robinson, John
    1964a The Redwood Highway: Part II— Building the Road. California Highways and Public Works, July-August 1964:24-33.
    1964b The Redwood Highway: Part I— Early history of Transportation in the Northern Coastal Counties. California Highways and Public Works, May-June 1964:2-11.

Robinson, W. W.
    1948 Land in California. Berkeley: University of California Press.

Rochester Democrat and Chronicle
    1903 Obituary of Col. Henry T. Noyes. Rochester Democrat and Chronicle, December 1, 1903:12.

Rohde, Jerry
    1991a Taking a long ride through local history. Redwood Record, October 29, 1991:3.
    1992a Elinor Elegy: Part I. Redwood Record, May 12, 1992:3.
    1992b Two families endure a S. Humboldt flood. Redwood Record, May 19, 1992:3.
    1992c Elinor elegy: The Conclusion: The waters recede. Redwood Record, May 26, 1992:3.
    2000a Alice, Elinor, and the Great Flood. Humboldt Historian, Winter 2000:4, 36-37.
    2001a Benbow SRA Campground Cultural Resources Investigation: Historical Review. Copy in author's possession.
    2002a Bull Creek Beginnings. Humboldt Historian, Summer 2002:36-37.
    2005a Field notes of interview by author with Henry and Billye Tsarnas at the Tsarnas mill site, July 22, 2005.
    2005b Phone interview by author with Billye Tsarnas, July 19, 1905.
    2008a The Sonoma Gang. Web page. Electronic document http://www.northcoastjournal.com/humboldt/the-sonoma-gang/Content?oid=2127928 accessed on October 22, 2013. Also available in: North Coast Journal, September 11, 2008:14-15, 17-19.
    2010a Genocide & Extortion. Web page. Electronic document http://www.northcoastjournal.com/news/2010/02/25/genocide-and-extortion-indian-island/ accessed on October 29, 2011. Also available, without endnotes, in: North Coast Journal, February 25, 2010:10-17.
    2014a Both Sides of the Bluff. Eureka: MountianHome Books.
    2016a An American Genocide. Web page. Electronic document, https://www.northcoastjournal.com/humboldt/an-american-genocide/Content?oid=4116592 accessed on February 28, 2021.
    N.d.a. Notes copied from ornithological display at Eureka High School, Eureka.

Rohde, Jerry, and Gisela Rohde
    1992 Humboldt Redwoods State Park: The Complete Guide. Eureka, CA: Miles & Miles.
    1994 Redwood National & State Parks: Tales, Trails, & Auto Tours. McKinleyville, CA: MountainHome Books.

Rohde, Jerry, and Donald Verwayne
    2005 Tsarnas Mill Site. State of California—The Resources Agency, Department of Parks and Recreation Primary Record.

Rohnerville Herald
    1887a The *Standard* of Monday says: . . . Rohnerville Herald, November 2, 1887:2.
    1887b Stage Line ad. Rohnerville Herald, November 2, 1887:2.
    1888a Samples . . . . Rohnerville Herald, January 18, 1888:3.
    1888b Ed. B. Barnum . . . . Rohnerville Herald, February 22, 1888:3.
    1888c A Summer Resort. Rohnerville Herald, February 29, 1888:3.
    1888d Drowning of G. W. Charles. Rohnerville Herald, February 29, 1888:3.

Romo, Cheryl
    1998 The Mystery of Hans Weisel and the Bar-W. American West, September-October:66-71.

Roscoe, Ken
    1991. Heydays in Humboldt. N. p.: ILLIANA Limited.

Roscoe, Neb
    1996. Heydays in Mattole. McKinleyville, CA: ILLIANA Limited.

Roscoe, James
    1985a The days of Chief Lassik and his people were sadly numbered. Humboldt Historian, March-April 1985.

1985b An Ethnohistory of the Mattole. Photocopy of a Humboldt State University paper in possession of author.

rosieradiator.com
    2018 The Guinness Book of World Records. Web page. Electronic document, http://rosieradiator.com/id3.html accessed on September 26, 2018.

Rowley, Max
    2004a tracing the Sonoma trail. Humboldt Historian, Spring 2004:29-33.

Rubalcava, Leann
    1999 A Walkway to the Giants: Phillipsville in focus. Humboldt Historian, Winter 1999:26-30.

Ruggles, June
    1990 Interview with Jerry Rohde, April 30, 1990.

Russell, Angus
    1991 Interview with Jerry Rohde, May 25, 1991.

Sacramento Daily Union
    1863a Alleged Kidnapping in Mendocino. Sacramento Daily Union, March 26, 1863:2.

Sacramento Union
    1921 Forty-Eight Are Lost In Shipwreck. Sacramento Union, August 8, 1921:1-2.

Sam, Mrs. Jane
    1921a Revised statement regarding Indian Island Massacre, date March 27/21. Photocopy available, as part of the "Wiyot History Papers," in the Special Collections, Humboldt State University Library, Arcata.
    1921b Original statement regarding L. K. Wood and Gregg Party. Photocopy available, as part of the "Wiyot History Papers," in the Special Collections, Humboldt State University Library, Arcata.
    [1921?]b Statement regarding Indian Island Massacre. Photocopy available, as part of the "Wiyot History Papers," in the Special Collections, Humboldt State University Library, Arcata.
    [1921?]c Taken to Reservation. Photocopy available, as part of the "Wiyot History Papers," in the Special Collections, Humboldt State University Library, Arcata.
    [1921?]d Revised statement regarding L. K. Wood and Gregg Party. Photocopy available, as part of the "Wiyot History Papers," in the Special Collections, Humboldt State University Library, Arcata.
    [1921?]e Taken to Reservation [revised version]. Photocopy available, as part of the "Wiyot History Papers," in the Special Collections, Humboldt State University Library, Arcata.

San Jose Woman's Club
    2019 San Jose Woman's Club. Web page. Electronic document, https://sjwomansclub.org/all-about-sjwc/ accessed on December 7, 2019.

San Francisco Call
    1895a The Horrible History of Round Valley. San Francisco Call, October 21, 1895:8-9.
    1902a George White, Round Valley King, Is Dead. San Francisco Call, June 10, 1902:4.
    1911a Change at Postoffice, Irma, Trinity County. San Francisco Call, October 26, 1911:9.

San Francisco Chronicle
    1983a California's Oil History. San Francisco Chronicle, March 21, 1983.

San Francisco Daily Alta
    1867a The Late Terrible Slaughter in Mendocino County. San Francisco Daily Alta, October 26, 1867.

Saul, Barbara Canepa
    1992a Alfred Augustus (A.A.) Hadley. Humboldt Historian, July-August 1992:8-13.

Save-the-Redwoods League
    1931 Annual Report. Copy on file at Special Collections, Humboldt State University Library, Arcata.
    1939a Annual Report. Copy on file at Special Collections, Humboldt State University Library, Arcata.

Schwarzkopf, Chet
    1948a Weott—Town with Olympic Setting. Humboldt Times, December 5, 1948:5.
    1948b Miranda—Town With A Unique School. Humboldt Times, November 21, 1948:15,17.
    1949a Bridgeville—Heart Of The Upland Empire. Humboldt Times, May 1, 1949:32.
    1949b Pepperwood—Resorts and Gardens Join. Humboldt Times, March 6, 1949:13, 17.
    1949c Holmes And Larabee—Live And Let Live. Humboldt Times, June 12, 1949:17, 28.
    1949d Redcrest-Englewood—People Return. Humboldt Times, April 3, 1949:13, 17.
    1949e Shively—A Man Said It Was Paradise. Humboldt Times, February 6, 1949.
    1949f South Fork - McCann - Dyerville—Big Land. Humboldt Times, July 24, 1949:13, 15.
    1949g Ettersburg and Briceland—Smiling Land. Humboldt Times, June 26, 1949:17, 31.
    1949h Phillipsville—Climate and Setting Lure. Humboldt times, August 14, 1949:13, 15.
    1949i Petrolia—The Heart of a Hidden Valley. Humboldt Times, April 17, 1949:13, 17.
    1949j Myers Flat—Business And Living Are Good. Humboldt Times, May 15, 1949: 17, 21.
    1949k Carlotta—A Pioneer Family named It. Humboldt Times, March 20, 1949:11, 15.
    1949l Bridgeville—Heart of the Upland Empire. Humboldt Times, May 1, 1949:32, 16.

Scott, Jeremiah, Jr.
    1997a Curless Family Leaves a Legacy. Humboldt Historian, Fall 1997:22-26.

Scott, Lynford (continued)
   2018a The Ray Brothers, the Kinsey Family, and Boy Scout Troop 54. Humboldt Historian, Summer 2018:28-33.

Scott, Lynford
   1985a The Great Maria used sail and push on the Eel. Humboldt Historian, May-June 1985:9.
   1986a A summer outing and climb up Bear Buttes. Humboldt Historian, March-April 1986:12-13.
   1989 Family album of early railroad images. Humboldt Historian, July-August, 1989:3-7.
   1999 Looking Back at 90 Years.... Eureka: Lynford Scott.

Searson, Mrs. [Jane Duncan]
   [1921?]a Statement regard early Indian-white relations, murders by whites, massacre at Rio dell. Photocopy available, as part of the "Wiyot History Papers," in the Special Collections, Humboldt State University Library, Arcata.
   [1921?]b Revised statement regard early Indian-white relations, murders by whites, massacre at Rio dell. Photocopy available, as part of the "Wiyot History Papers," in the Special Collections, Humboldt State University Library, Arcata.

seasky.org
   2019a Miranda. Web page. Electronic document, http://www.seasky.org/solar-system/uranus-miranda.html accessed on August 9, 2019.

Secrest, William B.
   2004 California Feuds. Sanger, CA: Quill Driver Books/Word Dancer Press.

Seidner, Carrie
   1939a Letter to "Friend" [Lucy Allard], dated July 24, 1939. Photocopy available, as part of the "Wiyot History Papers," in the Special Collections, Humboldt State University Library, Arcata.
   N.d.a. Portion of letter [page 1 is missing] to Mrs. Allard. Photocopy available, as part of the "Wiyot History Papers," in the Special Collections, Humboldt State University Library, Arcata.

Shelton, Heather
   2001a The Benbow tradition. Times-Standard, July 22, 2001.

Shepherd, Marvin
   2011 The Sea Captain's Odyssey: A Biography of Captain H. H. Buhne 1822-1895. Walnut Creek, CA: Georgie Press.

Shields, David S.
   2013 Still: American Silent Motion Picture Photography. Chicago: University of Chicago Press.

Shipyard Log
   2020 Knees from Trees. Web page. Electronic document, http://boothbayharborshipyard.blogspot.com/2008/09/knees-from-trees.html accessed on July 8, 2020.

Silvey, Jack
   1985a Living Legends: Dr. Niles dedicated to students, science. Humboldt Historian, July-August 1985:3-5.
   1995a A Tribute to Dr. Doris Kildale Niles. Humboldt Historian, Fall 1995:37-38.
   1998a Bridges Span Time in Mountain Community. Humboldt Historian, Winter 1998:32-39.

Slocum, Bowen & Co.
   1881 History of Napa and Lake Counties, California. San Francisco: Slocum, Bowen & Co.

Smith, Clara
   N.d. Elinor. Section of photocopy of Smith family history in possession of Jerry Rohde.

Smith, Eric Krabbe
   1990 Lucy Young or T'tcetsa: Indian-White Relations in Northwest California, 1846-1944. M. A. thesis, University of California, Santa Cruz.

Smith, Gladys
   1995 Albert Felix Etter, Hybridizer. Pacific Horticulture, Summer 1995:16-22.

Smith, Jean Edward
   2001 Grant. New York: Simon and Schuster.

snac
   2018. Baker, Ray Jerome, 1880-1972. Web page. Electronic document, http://snaccooperative.org/view/9988283 accessed on August 22, 2018.

Snyder, John w.
   1984 The Bridges of John B. Leonard 1905 to 1925. Concrete International, June 1984:58-67.

Sonoma Democrat
   1867a The Little Lake Vendetta. Sonoma Democrat, November 2, 1867:1.

Southern Humboldt Life and Times
   1997a Eel Rock/Fruitland Ridge. Southern Humboldt Life and Times, July 29, 1997:12.

Sparks, Virginia
   1986 Memo on Larabee, Weott, and Fruitland. Photocopy on file at the Humboldt County Historical Society, Eureka.

Spartacus Educational
   2016 Fort Pillow Massacre. Web page. Electronic document, http://spartacus-educational.com/USACWpillow.htm accessed on September 3, 2016.

Speece, Darren Frederick
   2017 Defending Giants. Seattle: University of Washington Press.

Speegle, Will N.
   1931a Benbow Dam article. Humboldt Times, October 4, 1931.
   1945a Hospitality De Luxe. Humboldt Times, April 7, 1945.
   1947a Early Days in Blocksburg. Humboldt Times, July 6, 1947.

Spencer, Ed B.
   1895 Business Directory of Humboldt Count: 1895-6. Eureka: E. B. Spencer.

St. John, Fern
   1959 Some Like It Englewood, Some Like It Redcrest—It's the Name That Matters. Humboldt Times, November 7, 1959.

1968a Shively Ferry Stirs Memories. Humboldt Historian, November-December 1968:3, 6.
1968b Wagon Freighters Helped Create N. W. P. Humboldt Historian, July-August 1968:3.
1969 Historic Old Bridges Part of Humboldt's Past. Humboldt Beacon, May 1, 1969.
N.d.a Saga of Henry Millsap's 75 Years In Pepperwood; He's Still Alive, Stayed to the Last, Ready to Fight, in The Killer Eel. Fortuna, CA: Humboldt Beacon, n.d.
N.d.b [Article on Englewood School]. Photocopy with date and title missing, located in the Eureka clipping file in the Humboldt Room, Eureka Main Library.

Standard Publishing Co.
1893 Eureka Business Directory 1893-4. Eureka: Standard Publishing Co.

Stansberry, Linda
2016 Bridgeville. Web page. Electronic document, https://www.northcoastjournal.com/humboldt/bridgeville/Content?oid=3552638 accessed on April 8, 2019.

Startare, Lillie
2015 Personal communication with Jerry Rohde, October 16, 2015.

State of California, California Highway Commission
1914a Plan and Profile of Proposed State Highway In Humboldt County from Dyerville to Shively. As Built Plans.
1914b [Plan and Profile of Proposed State Highway In Humboldt County from Miranda to Dyerville.] As Built Plans.
1922a First Biennial Report of the Division of Highways. Sacramento.
1928a Sixth Biennial Report of the Division of Highways. Sacramento.
1931a Plan and Profile of Proposed State Highway In Humboldt County from Dyerville to
Shively. As Built Plans.

State of California, Department of Engineering
1912 Third Biennial Report. Sacramento.

State of California, Department of Natural Resources, Division of Forestry
1949a [Map of] South Half Humboldt County.

State of California, Department of Public Works, Division of Highways
1937 Plan and Profile of State Highway in Humboldt County, between Stegemeyer Bluffs and Myers. As Built Plans.

State of California, Resources Agency, Department of Water Resources, Northern District
1975 Van Duzen River Basin Environmental Atlas. Sacramento, Calif.

Stindt, Fred A.
1987 The Northwestern Pacific Railroad. Kelseyville, CA: Fred A. Stindt.
1988 The Northwestern Pacific Railroad 1964-1985 vol. 2. Kelseyville, CA, Fred A. Stindt.

Strobridge, William F.
1994 Regulars in the Redwoods: the U. S. Army in Northern California, 1852-1861. Spokane, WA: Arthur H. Clark Co.

Stockton, Dave
2004 The Man from Whiskey Flat. Humboldt Redwoods Interpretive Association Newsletter, Summer 2004.

Stone, A. K.
1913 Fort Seward—The Embyro Metropolis. Eureka Herald, December 7, 1913:33.

Stuart, John D., and John O. Sawyer
2001 Trees and Shrubs of California. Berkeley: University of California Press.

Subcommittee of the Committee on Indian Affairs: House of Representatives
1926 Hearing . . . on H. R. 8036 and H. R. 9497. Washington DC: Government Printing Office.

Sunset
1951 Article on Eel River. Sunset, March 1951.
2021a Wine Tasting in Humboldt County. Web page. Electronic document, https://www.sunset.com/travel/california/humboldt-county-wine accessed on May 24, 2021.

Surveyor General's Office
1858a [Map of] Township Nº 1 North Range Nº 3 West, Humboldt Meridian. San Francisco: Surveyor General's Office.
1858b [Map of] Township Nº IV North Range Nº II East, Humboldt Meridian. San Francisco: Surveyor General's Office.
1871a [Map of] Township Nº 1 North Range Nº 1 East, Humboldt Meridian. San Francisco: Surveyor General's Office.
1871b [Map of] Township Nº 1 North Range Nº 2 East, Humboldt Meridian. San Francisco: Surveyor General's Office.
1871c [Map of] Township Nº 1 South, Range Nº 2 East, Humboldt Meridian. San Francisco: Surveyor General's Office.
1872a [Map of] Township Nº 1 South, Range Nº 3 East, Humboldt Meridian. San Francisco: Surveyor General's Office.
1872b [Map of] Township Nº 1 North, Range Nº 5 East, Humboldt Meridian. San Francisco: Surveyor General's Office.
1872c [Map of] Township Nº 1 North, Range Nº 3 East, Humboldt Meridian. San Francisco: Surveyor General's Office.
1872d [Map of] Township Nº 2 North, Range Nº 5 East, Humboldt Meridian. San Francisco: Surveyor General's Office.
1872e [Map of] Township Nº 1 North, Range Nº 5 East, Humboldt Meridian. San Francisco: Surveyor General's Office.
1873a [Map of] Township Nº 2 South, Range Nº 4 East, Humboldt Meridian. San Francisco: Surveyor General's Office.
1873b [Map of] Township Nº 3 South, Range Nº 5 East, Humboldt Meridian. San Francisco: Surveyor General's Office.
1873c [Map of] Township Nº 2 South, Range Nº 5 East, Humboldt Meridian. San Francisco: Surveyor General's Office.

1873d [Map of] Township N⁰ 1 South, Range N⁰ 4 East, Humboldt Meridian. San Francisco: Surveyor General's Office.

1873d Map of] Township N⁰ 2 South, Range N⁰ 4 East, Humboldt Meridian. San Francisco: Surveyor General's Office.

1874a [Map of] Township N⁰ 3 South, Range N⁰ 2 East, Humboldt Meridian. San Francisco: Surveyor General's Office.

1875a [Map of] Township N⁰ 4 South, Range N⁰ 3 East, Humboldt Meridian. San Francisco: Surveyor General's Office.

1875b [Map of] Township N⁰ 3 South, Range N⁰ 3 East, Humboldt Meridian. San Francisco: Surveyor General's Office.

1875c [Map of] Township N⁰ 4 South, Range N⁰ 1 East, Humboldt Meridian. San Francisco: Surveyor General's Office.

1876a [Map of] Township No. 2 South, Range No. 3 East, Humboldt Meridian. San Francisco: Surveyor General's Office.

1876b [Map of] Township N⁰ 4 South, Range N⁰ 4 East, Humboldt Meridian. San Francisco: Surveyor General's Office.

1876c [Map of] Township N⁰ 3 South, Range N⁰ 4 East, Humboldt Meridian. San Francisco: Surveyor General's Office.

1876d [Map of] Township N⁰ 2 North, Range N⁰ 2 East, Humboldt Meridian. San Francisco: Surveyor General's Office.

1879a [Map of] Township N⁰ 2 South, Range N⁰ 2 East, Humboldt Meridian. San Francisco: Surveyor General's Office.

1885a [Map of] Township N⁰ 1 South, Range N⁰ 2 East, Humboldt Meridian. San Francisco: Surveyor General's Office.

Swales, Thomas
  1863 Last Will and Testament. Photocopy in "Probate Papers," accession number 83:39.4, Ferndale Museum archives.

Swanlund-Baker
  2018a Photo of Albert and Sallie Smith at Briceland Store. Web page. Electronic document, http://library.humboldt.edu/humco/holdings/photodetail.php?S=Albert%20smith&CS=All%20Collections&RS=ALL%20Regions&PS=Any%20Photographer&ST=ALL%20words&SW=&C=6&R=1 accessed on January 8, 2019.
  2018b Photo of Albert and Sallie Smith at Briceland. Web page. Electronic document, http://library.humboldt.edu/humco/holdings/photodetail.php?R=0&S=Albert%20smith&CS=All%20Collections&RS=ALL%20Regions&PS=Any%20Photographer&ST=ALL%20words&SW=&C=6 accessed on January 8, 2019.

Sweasey, Earla Reynolds
  1975 School Story Brings Memories. Humboldt Historian, January-February, 1975:5.

Tam, J. H.
  1885 Humboldt County, California Directory, 1885-1886. N.p.

tapdanceroom.com
  2019 Meet the Tap Dance Director. Web page. Electronic document, http://www.tapdanceroom.com/Tap-Dance-Instructor-About-Us-San-Francisco-CA.html accessed on March 31, 2019.

Taussig, F. W.
  1893 The Duties on Wool and Woolens. Oxford: Oxford University Press.

Taylor, Addie Louise
  1917 Little Mountain Girl Is Unable To Get Schooling But Writes Interestingly. Humboldt Time, February 4, 1917.

Taylor, Maralee
  1980 Where Is Weott? Humboldt Historian, July-August 1980:3-5.

Teague, Vera Snider
  1975. From Buckskin to Team Bells. Ukiah, CA: The Letter Shop.

The Writer
  1914a. Writers of the Day. The Writer, vol. XXVI.

thespruce.com
  2021 9 Heirloom Potato Varieties for Your Garden. Web page. Electronic document, https://www.thespruce.com/heirloom-potato-varieties-for-organic-garden-2539922 accessed on December 31, 2021.

Thomas, John L.
  1968 Kunz, [sic] Ben Arthur Trials In Ericson Case Recalled. Trinity 1968 Yearbook.

Thornbury, Delmar L.
  1923 California's Redwood Wonderland: Humboldt County. San Francisco: Sunset Press.

Timberman
  1920a Stockton. The Timberman, September 1920:48.

Times-Standard
  1968a New Phillipsville P. O. Is in Service. Times-Standard March 5, 1968.
  1973a There's something for every citizen at Honeydew store. Times-Standard, May 16, 1973:2.
  1973b Fire ravages Hartsook Inn. Times-Standard, June 13, 1973.
  1990a. Its 1906 Again. Times-Standard, July 6, 1990:A-1.
  1993a Richard Redwood Childs obit. Times-Standard, September 23, 1993:B-11.
  1995 Historical Hotel Burns. Times-Standard, June 29, 1995:1.
  2009a Jay Martin Dinsmore obit. Times-Standard, May 24, 2009:C-6.
  N.d.a. Article on Dinsmore Lodge. Undated clipping located in the "Dinsmore" file in the Special Collections at the Humboldt State University Library.

Tooby, Arthur N.
  1983 Memories of old Harris hotel. Humboldt Historian, July-August 1983:12.

Townes, John E.
  1850. Letter to editor. Daily Alta California, June 26, 1850:2.

Townsend, Charles H.
    1886  Four Rare Birds in Northern California: Yellow Rail, Emperor Goose, European Widgeon, and Sabine's Ruffed Grouse. The Auk, vol. 3. New York: L. S. Foster.

Tracy, Eleanor Ethel
    1992a  Schoolma'am: The Letters of Eleanor Ethel Tracy: Alder Point, California March-June 1903. Compiled by Harriet Tracy DeLong. Eureka: Eureka Printing Co.
    1993a  Schoolma'am: The Letters of Eleanor Ethel Tracy: Harris, California 1905-1906. Compiled by Harriet Tracy DeLong. Eureka: Eureka Printing Co.

Tracy, M. D.
    2018  17 Dead; 43 Missing; when Steamer Alaska Sank Saturday Night. Web page. Electronic Document, https://www.wrecksite.eu/docBrowser.aspx?1361?5?1 accessed December 11, 2018.

Trail Back
    1974  The Trail Back 100 Years. Garberville, CA: Redwood Record.

Trinity Journal
    1860a  The dwelling of old Seth Kinman . . . . Trinity Journal, July 14, 1860:2.

Trinity Weekly Journal
    1858a  Organization of Indian Fighters. Trinity Weekly Journal, October 16, 1858:2.
    1859a  More Humboldt Indian Troubles. Trinity Weekly Journal, May 21, 1859:2.

tuccycle.org
    2015a  Tour of the Unknown Coast. Web page. Electronic document, http://www.tuccycle.org/ accessed on December 15, 2015.
    2015b  Ride Information. Web page. Electronic document, http://tuccycle.org//rides/100_mile_route accessed on December 15, 2015.

Turk, E. E.
    1861a  Lieut. Collins' Command. Humboldt Times, June 15, 1861:3.

Turner, Dennis W. and Gloria H. Turner
    2010  Place Names of Humboldt County, 2nd Ed. California. Orangevale, CA: Dennis W. & Gloria H. Turner.

Tuttle, Don
    1982  Investigation of Coastline Retreat at Shelter Cove, California. Copy on file at Humboldt County Natural Resources, Public Works.
    2016a  Personal communication with Jerry Rohde regarding Shively Road, August 2, 2016.

Tyrrell, A. J.
    1932  The Pioneers Reach Humboldt. Ferndale Enterprise, March 18, 1932.

Urban Dictionary
    2019a  mirada. Web page. Electronic document, https://www.urbandictionary.com/define.php?term=mirada accessed on August 13, 2019.

Underwood, Emily
    2020  An Unlikely Resurrection. Flora (3)2.

US Bureau of the Census
    1860a  Federal Census, Humboldt County, California, Mattole Township.
    1900a  Federal Census, Indian Population, Humboldt County, California, South Fork Township.
    1900b  Federal Census, Indian Population, Humboldt County, California, Mattole Township.
    1910a  Federal Census, Indian Population, Humboldt County, California, Van Duzen Township.

US Bureau of Land Management
    2016a  General Land Office record for Township 3 South, Range 4 East, Section 17, Humboldt Meridian. Web page. Electronic document, http://www.glorecords.blm.gov/results/default.aspx?searchCriteria=type=patent|st=CA|cty=023|twp_nr=3|twp_dir=S|rng_nr=4|rng_dir=E|sec=17|m=15|sp=true|sw=true|sadv=false accessed on December 15, 2016.
    2016b  General Land Office record for Township 3 South, Range 4 East, Section 8, Humboldt Meridian. Web page. Electronic document, http://www.glorecords.blm.gov/results/default.aspx?searchCriteria=type=patent|st=CA|cty=023|twp_nr=3|twp_dir=S|rng_nr=4|rn-dir=E|sec=8|m=15|sp=true|sw=true|sadv=false accessed on December 15, 2016.
    2016c  General Land Office record for Township 2 South, Range 5 East, Section 20, Humboldt Meridian. Web page. Electronic document, http://www.glorecords.blm.gov/results/default.aspx?searchCriteria=type=patent|st=CA|cty=023|twp_nr=2|twp_dir=S|rng_nr=5|rng_dir=E|sec=20|sp=true|sw=true|sadv=false accessed on December 16, 2016.
    2016d  Record of Land Patents for "Kneeland" in Township 2 South, Range 5 East. Web page. Electronic document, http://www.glorecords.blm.gov/results/default.aspx?searchCriteria=type=patent|st=CA|cty=023|ln=kneeland|twp_nr=2|twp_dir=S|rng_nr=5|rng_dir=E|m=15|sp=true|sw=true|sadv=false accessed on December 18, 2016.
    2016e  Record of Land Patents for "Hoglen" in Township 2 South, Range 5 East. Web page. Electronic document, http://www.glorecords.blm.gov/results/default.aspx?searchCriteria=type=patent|st=CA|cty=023|ln=hoglen|twp_nr=2|twp_dir=S|rng_nr=5|rng_dir=E|m=15|sp=true|sw=true|sadv=false accessed on December 18, 2016.
    2017a  Patent records for T1S, R2E, Humboldt Meridian. Web page. Electronic document, https://glorecords.blm.gov/results/default.aspx?searchCriteria=type=patent|st=CA|cty=023|twp_nr=1|twp_dir=S|rng_nr=2|rng_dir=E|sec=10|sp=true|sw=true|sadv=false accessed on April 10, 2017.

2017b Patent records for "Stump" in T3S, R3E, Humboldt Meridian. Web page. Electronic document, https://glorecords.blm.gov/results/default.aspx?searchCriteria=type=patent|st=CA|cty=023|ln=stump|twp_nr=3|twp_dir=S|rng_nr=3|rng_dir=E|m=15|sp=true|sw=true|sadv=false accessed on December 2, 2017.

2017c Patent records for "McKee" in T4S, R2E, Humboldt Meridian. Web page. Electronic document, https://glorecords.blm.gov/results/default.aspx?searchCriteria=type=patent|st=CA|cty=023|ln=McKee|twp_nr=4|twp_dir=S|rng_nr=2|rng_dir=E|m=15|sp=true|sw=true|sadv=false accessed on December 4, 2017.

2017d Patent records for "Cruickshank" in T5S, R2E, Humboldt Meridian. Web page. Electronic document, https://glorecords.blm.gov/results/default.aspx?searchCriteria=type=patent|st=CA|cty=023|ln=cruickshank|twp_nr=5|twp_dir=S|rng_nr=2|rng_dir=E|m=15|sp=true|sw=true|sadv=false accessed on December 8, 2017.

2017e Patent records for "Filkins" in T2S, R4E, Humboldt Meridian. Web Page. Electronic document, https://glorecords.blm.gov/results/default.aspx?searchCriteria=type=patent|st=CA|cty=023|ln=filkins|twp_nr=2|twp_dir=S|rng_nr=4|rng_dir=E|m=15|sp=true|sw=true|sadv=false accessed on December 13, 2017.

2018a Patent records for Township 3 South, Range 2 East, Humboldt Meridian. Web page. Electronic document, https://glorecords.blm.gov/results/default.aspx?searchCriteria=type=patent|st=CA|cty=023|twp_nr=3|twp_dir=S|rng_nr=2|rng_dir=E|m=15|sp=true|sw=true|sadv=false#resultsTabIndex=0&page=4&sortField=11&sortDir=0 accessed on March 19, 2018.

2018b Patent records for Township 2 South, Range 2 West, Humboldt Meridian. Web page. Electronic document, https://glorecords.blm.gov/results/default.aspx?searchCriteria=type=patent|st=CA|cty=023|twp_nr=2|twp_dir=S|rng_nr=2|rng_dir=W|m=15|sp=true|sw=true|sadv=false#resultsTabIndex=0&page=6&sortField=11&sortDir=0 accessed on August 13, 2018.

2018c Patent records for "Carothers" in Township 2 South, Range 2 East, Humboldt Meridian. Web page. Electronic document, https://glorecords.blm.gov/results/default.aspx?searchCriteria=type=patent|st=CA|cty=|ln=carothers|twp_nr=2|twp_dir=S|rng_nr=2|rng_dir=E|m=15|sp=true|sw=true|sadv=false accessed on November 11, 2018.

2018d Patent records for "Mowry" and "Robinson" in Township 2 South, Range 2 East, Humboldt Meridian. Web page. Electronic document, https://glorecords.blm.gov/results/default.aspx?searchCriteria=type=patent|st=CA|cty=023|twp_nr=2|twp_dir=S|rng_nr=2|rng_dir=E|sec=12|m=15|sp=true|sw=true|sadv=false accessed on November 12, 2018.

2018e Patent records for Section 29, Township 2 South, Range 3 East, Humboldt Meridian. Web page. Electronic document, https://glorecords.blm.gov/results/default.aspx?searchCriteria=type=patent|st=CA|cty=023|twp_nr=2|twp_dir=S|rng_nr=3|rng_dir=E|sec=29|m=15|sp=true|sw=true|sadv=false accessed on November 28, 2018.

2018f Record of Land Patents for Section 18, Township 2 South, Range 2 East, Humboldt Meridian. Web page. Electronic document, https://glorecords.blm.gov/details/patent/default.aspx?accession=CA1090__.232&docClass=STA&sid=dbz2g1e3.v55 accessed on September 21, 2018.

2018g Record of Land Patent for Joseph D. Smith in Section 1, Township 5 south, Range 3 East, Humboldt Meridian. Web page. Electronic document, https://glorecords.blm.gov/details/patent/default.aspx?accession=CA1090__.201&docClass=STA&sid=qnscm2jw.fsw#patentDetailsTabIndex=1 accessed on September 24, 2018.

2019a Patent records for Section 12, Township 3 South, Range 3 East, Humboldt Meridian. Web page. Electronic document, https://glorecords.blm.gov/results/default.aspx?searchCriteria=type=patent%7Cst=CA%7Ccty=023%7Ctwp_nr=3%7Ctwp_dir=S%7Crng_nr=3%7Crng_dir=E%7Csec=12%7Cm=15%7Csp=true%7Csw=true%7Csadv=false accessed on August 9, 2019.

2019b Patent for Melissa J. Wilds, formerly Melissa J. Sanford, for property in Section 3, Township 3 South, Range 3 East, Humboldt Meridian. Web page. Electronic document, https://glorecords.blm.gov/details/patent/default.aspx?accession=CA0990__.202&docClass=STA&sid=mm3cmhby.c4w#patentDetailsTabIndex=1 accessed on August 11, 2019.

2019c Patent records for Section 3, Township 3 South, Range 3 East, Humboldt Meridian. Web page. Electronic document, https://glorecords.blm.gov/results/default.aspx?searchCriteria=type=patent|st=CA|cty=023|twp_nr=3|twp_dir=S|rng_nr=3|rndir=E|sec=3|m=15|sp=true|sw=true|sadv=false accessed on August 11, 2019.

# Sources

2019d Patent records for Section 1, Township 4 South, Range 1 East, Humboldt Meridian. Web page. Electronic document, https://glorecords.blm.gov/results/default.aspx?searchCriteria=type=patent|st=CA|cty=023|twp_nr=4|twp_dir=S|rng_nr=1|rndir=E|sec=1|m=15|sp=true|sw=true|sadv=false accessed on August 28, 2019.

2019e Patent records for Section 6, Township 4 South, Range 2 East, Humboldt Meridian. Web page. Electronic document, https://glorecords.blm.gov/results/default.aspx?searchCriteria=type=patent|st=CA|cty=|twp_nr=4|twp_dir=S|rng_nr=2|rng_dir=E|sec=6|sp=true|sw=true|sadv=false accessed on August 28, 2019.

2019f Patent records for Section 7, Township 4 South, Range 2 East, Humboldt Meridian. Web page. Electronic document, https://glorecords.blm.gov/results/default.aspx?searchCriteria=type=patent|st=CA|cty=|twp_nr=4|twp_dir=S|rng_nr=2|rng_dir=E|sec=7|sp=true|sw=true|sadv=false accessed on August 28, 2019.

2020a Patent for south half of Section 29 and north half of Section 32, Township Three North Range Three East. Web page. Electronic document, http://www.glorecords.blm.gov/details/patent/default.aspx?accession=CA0910__.076&docClass=STA&sid=kcs4oubq.wgn#patentDetailsTabIndex=1 accessed on July 8, 2020.

2020b Patent for George Bert, for property in Section 27, Township 1 South, Range 1 East, Humboldt Meridian. Web page. Electronic document, https://glorecords.blm.gov/details/patent/default.aspx?accession=0658-425&docClass=MV&sid=p-v5d21n5.f13#patentDetailsTabIndex=1 accessed on August 17, 2020.

2020c Patent records for Section 6, T3S, R3E, Humboldt Meridian. Web page. Electronic document, https://glorecords.blm.gov/results/default.aspx?searchCriteria=type=patent|st=CA|cty=023|twp_nr=3|twp_dir=S|rng_nr=3|rndir=E|sec=6|m=15|sp=true|sw=true|sadv=false accessed on August 30, 2020.

2020d Patent records for Section 18, T2S, R2E, Humboldt Meridian. Web page. Electronic document, https://glorecords.blm.gov/results/default.aspx?searchCriteria=type=patent|st=CA|cty=023|twp_nr=2|twp_dir=S|rng_nr=2|rngdir=E|sec=18|m=15|sp=true|sw=true|sadv=false accessed on September 20, 2020.

2021a Patent record for Charlie Briceland, for property in Section 33, T2S, R2E, Humboldt Meridian. Web page. Electronic document, https://glorecords.blm.gov/details/patent/default.aspx?accession=0658-424&docClass=MV&sid=mss-0dzab.rk5 accessed on March 4, 2021.

US Circuit Courts of Appeals Reports, vol. 11
    1895 Noyes et al. v. Barnard. Web page. Electronic document, https://books.google.com/books?id=f-JNAQAAIAAJ&pg=PA425&lpg=PA425&dq=alger+noyes+van+duzen&source=bl&ots=RM_ag_V6UU&sig=ACfU3U3PhqthBlyojY0VcYliF2HzaSOA8g&hl=en&sa=X&ved=2ahUKEwi61vWlkLjiAhULWK0KHXTACFcQ6AEwC3oECAcQAQ#v=onepage&q=alger%20noyes%20van%20duzen&f=false accessed on May 26, 2019.

US Coast Survey
    1854 Preliminary Survey of Harbors of the Western Coast of the United States: Crescent City Harbor, Harbor of Mendocino City, Shelter Cove, Port Orford on Ewing Harbor. Web page. Electronic document, http://historicalcharts.noaa.gov/historicals/preview/image/CP367C accessed on November 30, 2015.
    1870a Part of Humboldt Bay, California. Register N° 1176.
    1870b Part of Humboldt Bay, California. Register N° 1174.

US Coast & Geodetic Survey
    1940 Cape Mendocino and Vicinity. Washington, DC.

US Congress, House of Representatives
    1897 Tariff Hearings before the Committee on Ways and Means. Congressional serial set issue 3543. Washington: Government Printing Office.
    2015 Ex. Doc. 282. Congressional Edition, vol. 2561:1-21. Web page. Electronic document, https://books.google.com/books?id=LT9HAQAAIAAJ&q=282#v=snippet&q=282&f=false accessed on August 3, 2015.

US Department of Agriculture
    1920a Trinity National Forest, California: 1920 [map]. Washington DC: United States Department of Agriculture, Forest Service. [A version of this map, catalogued at the Bancroft Library as G4362.T7E1 1920; .U5; Case XD, contains annotations and hand colorings done by C. Hart Merriam to show the names of Indian tribes and their boundaries in the Humboldt-Mendocino-Trinity area.]
    1937a Yearbook of Agriculture 1937. United States Department of Agriculture.
    2015a Clinton Hart Merriam. Web page. Electronic document, http://www.aphis.usda.gov/wps/portal/aphis/ourfocus/wildlifedamage/sa_programs/sa_nwrc/sa_history/ct_clinton_hart_merriam/!ut/p/a0/04_Sj9CPykssy0xPLMnMz0vMAfGjzOK9_D2MDJ0MjDzd3V2dDDz93HwCzL29jAwMTfQLsh0VAXWczqE!/ accessed on June 2, 2015.
    2015b Tanoak. Web page. Electronic document, US Department of the Interior

1978a National Register of Historic Places Inventory–Nomination Form: Carlotta Hotel. Web page. Electronic document, https://npgallery.nps.gov/NRHP/GetAsset/34762081-f74c-4bea-88d0-f54eb89a48c3 accessed on May 19, 2019.

1981a National Register of Historic Places Inventory–Nomination Form: Lower Blackburn Grade Bridge. Web page. Electronic document, https://npgallery.nps.gov/NRHP/GetAsset/NRHP/81000148_text accessed on May 19, 2019.

US Department of the Interior, Geological Survey
    1949a Garberville, California. Quadrangle.
    1949b Alderpoint, California. Quadrangle.
    1940a Iaqua Buttes, California. Quadrangle.
    1951a Scotia, California. Quadrangle.
    1969a Redcrest, California. Quadrangle.
    1969b Weott, California. Quadrangle.

US Department of the Interior, Office of Indian Affairs
    1929a Application for enrollment for George Burt [sic], #4461.

US House of Representatives
    1858 Executive Documents . . . During the First Session of the Thirty-Fifth Congress 1857-'58. Washington: James B. Stedman.

US Office of Education
    1910 Annual Report of the Commissioner of Education, vol. 1. Washington DC: Government Printing Office.

US Senate
    1890. Executive Documents of the Senate of the United States for the First Session of the Fifty-First Congress 1889-'90. Washington DC: Government Printing Office.

US War Department
    1897a The War of the Rebellion: A Compilation of the Official Records of the Union and Confederate Armies; Series 1 - Volume 50 (Part I). Washington DC: Government Printing Office.
    1897b The War of the Rebellion: A Compilation of the Official Records of the Union and Confederate Armies; Series 1 - Volume 50 (Part II). Washington DC: Government Printing Office.

uscglightshipsailors.org
    2018 Blunt's Reef Lightship. Web page. Electronic document, http://www.uscglightshipsailors.org/blunts_reef_lightship_lv83_wal508.htm accessed on December 19, 2018.

Van Deliner, Bernice
    1984 James Ervin Wood–Garberville/Ranch Founder. Humboldt Historian, January-February 1984:3-7.

Van Dyke, Walter
    1891 Early Days in Klamath. Overland Monthly, vol. XVII, No. 104 Second Series, August 1891.

Van Kirk, Susie
    2019a National Register of Historic Places Inventory–Nomination Form for Carlotta Hotel. Web page. Electronic document, https://npgallery.nps.gov/NRHP/GetAsset/34762081-f74c-4bea-88d0-f54eb89a48c3 accessed on April 1, 2019.
    N.d.a. Merrifield Family. Copy in author's possession.

Vatnsdal, Russell L.
    1957 Ettersburg: A History of Humboldt County, California. Unpublished paper located in the "Ettersburg" file in the Humboldt County Collection, Humboldt State University Library, Arcata.

Verdi, Anne F.
    1974 William F. Notley: Early Californian. Noticias del Puerto de Monterey (18)10:17-21.

Vincent, Paul
    1983 A Tale of Tanbarking: What Happened at Briceland and Shelter Cove. Humboldt Historian, January-February 1983:3-8.

Vinyard, Lucille
    1990. Interview with Jerry Rohde, December 20, 1990.

Volunteer [pseud.]
    1862 From Fort Seward. Humboldt Times, March 22, 1862:3.

"W"
    1859a Letter from Cape Mendocino. Humboldt Times, November 12, 1859:2.
    1859b Mattole Valley. Humboldt Times, November 19, 1859:2.

"W" (2)
    1864a Iaqua Correspondence. Humboldt Times, July 26, 1864:2.

Walker, Laura
    1996 The Early Days of Mattole Road. Mattole Restoration Newsletter, Winter 1996.

Waltmann, Henry G.
    1971 Circumstantial Reformer: President Grant & the Indian Problem. Arizona and the West 13(4):323-342.

Ward, Charles Willis
    1915a Humboldt County California. Eureka: Ward-Perkins-Gill Co.

Wasserman, Laura, and James Wasserman
    2019 Who Saved the Redwoods? New York: Algora Publishing.

Water Resources Control Board
    2017 Executive Director's Report, September 19, 2017.

waterboards.ca.gov
    2016a In the Matter of Water Quality Certification for Shively Community Bridge – Low-Flow Railcar Crossing, Eel River Project. Web page. Electronic document, http://www.waterboards.ca.gov/northcoast/board_decisions/water_quality_certification/pdf/2014/140407_ShivelyCommBridge_401.pdf accessed on July 28, 2016.

Waterman, T. T.
    1992[1920] Yurok Geography. Trinidad, CA: Trinidad Museum Society.

Way, Dave
    1947a J. Fairhurst Says Industry is Permanent. Humboldt Standard, November 17, 1947.

waymaking.com
    2019 SS Emidio Memorial. Web page. Electronic document, http://www.waymarking.com/waymarks/WMF8RW

SS_Emidio_Memorial_Crescent_City_CA accessed on June 24, 2019.

WeatherDB
  2016  Alderpoint, California Average Rainfall. Web page. Electronic document, https://rainfall.weatherdb.com/l/562/Alderpoint-California accessed on November 14, 2016.

Weekly Humboldt Times
  1858a  Indian Matters—Movement of the Volunteers. Weekly Humboldt Times, November 20, 1858:2.
  1860a  Indian Hostilities—Volunteer Company. Weekly Humboldt Times, February 4, 1860:2.
  1860b  Volunteer Company—Immediate Action Necessary. Weekly Humboldt Times, February 11, 1860:2
  1863a  Good Haul of Diggers. Weekly Humboldt Times, January 17, 1863:2.
  1879a  Our Wool Interest. Weekly Humboldt Times, November 8, 1879.

Weigel, Lawrence E.
  1976  Pre-Contact Cultural Ecology of the Nongatl Indians of Northwestern California. Humboldt Journal of Social Relations 4:1.

Werelate.org
  2017  John Henry Hunter. Web Page. Electronic document, http://www.werelate.org/wiki/Person:John_Hunter_(55) accessed on April 30, 2017.

West Coast Signal
  1871a  Stage line ad. West Coast Signal, September 20, 1871:3.
  1874a  Stage Line Extended. West Coast Signal, September 30, 1874:3.
  1875a  Completed. West Coast Signal, August 4, 1875:3.
  1875b  From the Bay to Yagerville. West Coast Signal, September 29, 1875.
  1876a  Ad for B. Blockburger. West Coast Signal, January 12, 1876:4.
  1876b  Mattole Valley. West Coast Signal, July 26, 1876:3.
  1876c  From the Wagon Road. West Coast Signal, December 16, 1876.
  1876d  Good Road. West Coast Signal, November 1, 1876:3.
  1876e  Bullard & Sweasey stage line ad. West Coast Signal, August 16, 1876:1.
  1877a  Ad for Eel River House. West Coast Signal, September 5, 1877:4.
  1877b  Splendid Road. West Coast Signal, August 15, 1877:1.
  1878a  Completion of the Garberville and Shelter Cove Road to the Coast Route Road. West Coast Signal, November 6, 1878:3.
  1878b  Overland from San Francisco. West Coast Signal, September 4, 1878:1.

Western Directory Co.
  1920  Eureka City Directory. Long Beach: Western Directory Co.

Wheeler, Jessie
  1997a  Bridge Speech. Photocopy on file at the Humboldt County Historical Society, Eureka, CA.
  2014a  Interview with Jessie Wheeler, October 31, 2014.
  2015a  Phone interview with Jerry Rohde, May 31, 2015.
  2017a  The Heyday of Bridgeville. Sr. News, June 2017:1, 4.

Whistle Punk
  2005  Metropolitan Redwood Lumber Company. Whistle Punk, July 2005:6.

White, Ralso
  N.d.  Ralso White Collection, College of the Redwoods Library, Eureka, CA.

White, Ronald C.
  2016  American Ulysses: A Life of Ulysses S. Grant. New York: Random House.

Whiteshot, Charles A.
  1905.  The Oil Well Driller. Mannington, WV: Charles A. Whiteshot.

Wichels, Ernest D.
  2017  How it all began. Web page. Electronic document, http://www.solanoarticles.com/history/pdf/pdf_files/how_it_all_began.pdf accessed on August 6, 2017.

Wikimedia Commons
  2018a  Category: Fred Hartsook. Web page. Electronic document, https://commons.wikimedia.org/wiki/Category:Hartsook_Photo accessed on September 25, 2018.

Wikipedia
  2015a  Dave Lewis (punter). Web page. Electronic document, http://en.wikipedia.org/wiki/Dave_Lewis_(punter) accessed on April 26, 2015.
  2015b  Pliny Earle Goddard. Web page. Electronic document, http://en.wikipedia.org/wiki/Pliny_Earle_Goddard accessed on June 1, 2015.
  2105c  Clinton Hart Merriam. Web page. Electronic document, https://en.wikipedia.org/wiki/Clinton_Hart_Merriam accessed on July 4, 2015.
  2015d  Ticino. Web page. Electronic document, https://en.wikipedia.org/wiki/Ticino accessed on August 5, 2015.
  2015e  Sylvanus Morley. Web page. Electronic document, https://en.wikipedia.org/wiki/Sylvanus_Morley accessed on August 7, 2015.
  2015f  Cadastre. Web page. Electronic document, https://en.wikipedia.org/wiki/Cadastre#Cadastral_surveys accessed on August 9, 2015.
  2015g  Public Land Survey System. Web Page. Electronic document, https://en.wikipedia.org/wiki/Public_Land_Survey_System accessed on August 9, 2015.
  2015h  Historical ranking of Presidents of the United States. Web page. Electronic document, https://en.wikipedia.org/wiki/Historical_rankings_of_Presidents_of_the_United_States#2013_Gallup_poll accessed on August 9, 2015.
  2015i  Cordelia Botkin. Web page. Electronic document, https://en.wikipedia.org/wiki/Cordelia_Botkin accessed on November 9, 2015.

2015j Notleys Landing, California. Web page. Electronic document, https://en.wikipedia.org/wiki/Notleys_Landing,_California accessed on November 10, 2015.

2015k Hail, Columbia. Web page. Electronic document, https://en.wikipedia.org/wiki/Hail,_Columbia accessed on November 25, 2015.

2016a Julia Butterfly Hill. Web page. Electronic document, https://en.wikipedia.org/wiki/Julia_Butterfly_Hill accessed on January 3, 2016.

2016b Luna (tree). Web page. Electronic document https://en.wikipedia.org/wiki/Luna_(tree) accessed on January 3, 2016.

2016c Fort Humboldt State Historic Park. Web page. Electronic document, https://en.wikipedia.org/wiki/Fort_Humboldt_State_Historic_Park accessed on August 25, 2016.

2016d Albert Sidney Johnson. Web page. Electronic document, https://en.wikipedia.org/wiki/Albert_Sidney_Johnston accessed on August 25, 2016.

2016e Lieber Code. Web page. Electronic document, https://en.wikipedia.org/wiki/Lieber_Code accessed on August 28, 2016.

2016f Department of the Pacific. Web page. Electronic document, https://en.wikipedia.org/wiki/Department_of_the_Pacific accessed on August 30, 2016.

2016g Battle of Fort Pillow. Web page. Electronic document, https://en.wikipedia.org/wiki/Battle_of_Fort_Pillow accessed on September 3, 2016.

2017a Northwestern Pacific Railroad. Web page. Electronic Document, https://en.wikipedia.org/wiki/Northwestern_Pacific_Railroad#cite_note-6 accessed on November 25, 2017.

2017b List of English terms of venery, by animal. Web page. Electronic document, https://en.wikipedia.org/wiki/List_of_English_terms_of_venery,_by_animal accessed on November 27, 2017.

2017c Black Friday (1869). Web page. Electronic document, https://en.wikipedia.org/wiki/Black_Friday_(1869) accessed on December 6, 2017.

2018a White Motor Company. Web page. Electronic document, https://en.wikipedia.org/wiki/White_Motor_Company accessed on January 6, 2018.

2018b Great Flood of 1862. Web page. Electronic document, https://en.wikipedia.org/wiki/Great_Flood_of_1862#Northern_California accessed on January 14, 2018.

2018c Franklin Knight Lane. Web page. Electronic document, https://en.wikipedia.org/wiki/Franklin_Knight_Lane#Later_life_and_legacy accessed on April 1, 2018.

2018d Thomas A. Scott. Web page. Electronic document, https://en.wikipedia.org/wiki/Thomas_A._Scott accessed on May 27, 2018.

2018e Asphalt. Web page. Electronic document, https://en.wikipedia.org/wiki/Asphalt accessed on July 29, 2018.

2018f James Gillett. Web page. Electric document, https://en.wikipedia.org/wiki/James_Gillett accessed August 2, 2018.

2018g. Independence Party (United States). Web page. Electronic document, https://en.wikipedia.org/wiki/Independence_Party_(United_States) accessed on August 2, 2018.

2018h Tank Locomotive. Web page. Electronic document, https://en.wikipedia.org/wiki/Tank_locomotive#Saddle_tank accessed on August 9, 2018.

2018i. Dawes Act. Web page. Electronic document, https://en.wikipedia.org/wiki/Dawes_Act accessed on August 13, 2018.

2018j Mercalli intensity scale. Web page. Electronic document, https://en.wikipedia.org/wiki/Mercalli_intensity_scale accessed on August 19, 2018.

2018k Ray Jerome Baker. Web page. Electronic document, https://en.wikipedia.org/wiki/Ray_Jerome_Baker accessed on September 23, 2018.

2018l Fred Hartsook. Web page. Electronic document, https://en.wikipedia.org/wiki/Fred_Hartsook accessed on September 24, 2018.

2018m Frank K. Mott. Web page. Electronic document, https://en.wikipedia.org/wiki/Frank_K._Mott accessed on November 22, 2018.

2018n Tudor Revival architecture. Web page. Electronic document, https://en.wikipedia.org/wiki/Tudor_Revival_architecture accessed on November 24, 2018.

2018o White Pass. Web page. Electronic document, https://en.wikipedia.org/wiki/White_Pass accessed on November 28, 2018.

2018p Shootout on Juneau Wharf. Web page. Electronic document, https://en.wikipedia.org/wiki/Shootout_on_Juneau_Wharf accessed on November 28, 2018.

2018q Wang Wang Blues. Web page. Electronic document, https://en.wikipedia.org/wiki/Wang_Wang_Blues accessed on December 10, 2018.

2019a History of California's state highway system. Web page. Electronic document, https://en.wikipedia.org/wiki/History_of_California%27s_state_highway_system#cite_note-1907-117-39 accessed on April 6, 2019.

2019b Russell A. Alger. Web Page. Electronic document, https://en.wikipedia.org/wiki/Russell_A._Alger accessed on May 26, 2019.

2019c Aaron T. Bliss. Web page. Electronic document, https://en.wikipedia.org/wiki/Aaron_T._Bliss accessed on May 26, 2019.

2019d Pottawatomie massacre. Web page. Electronic document, https://en.wikipedia.org/wiki/Pottawatomie_massacre accessed on June 21, 2019.

## Sources

    2019e  Common Carrier. Web page. Electronic document, https://en.wikipedia.org/wiki/Common_carrier accessed on October 17, 2019.
    2019f  List of Governors of California. Web Page. Electronic document, https://en.wikipedia.org/wiki/List_of_governors_of_California accessed on November 5, 2019.
    2019g  Nineteenth Amendment to the United States Constitution. Web page. Electronic document, https://en.wikipedia.org/wiki/Nineteenth_Amendment_to_the_United_States_Constitution accessed on December 7, 2019.
    2020a  Pink Pearl. Web page. Electronic document, https://en.wikipedia.org/wiki/Pink_Pearl_(apple) accessed on Sedan Day, September 2, 2020.
    2021a  Lakota people. Web page. Electronic document, https://en.wikipedia.org/wiki/Lakota_people accessed on February 14, 2021.
    2021b  George Hearst. Web page. Electronic document, https://en.wikipedia.org/wiki/George_Hearst accessed on June 12, 2021.

WikiTree
    2017a  Frederick Alexander Duckett. Web page. Electronic document, https://www.wikitree.com/wiki/Duckett-858 accessed April 30, 2017.

Wildwood, Nellie
    1876a  The Bear River Region. West Coast Signal, October 11, 1876:3.

Wilson, Melinda, and Jerry Lesandro
    2004  Milking Cows at Bear River. Humboldt Historian, Summer 2004:28-33.

Womack, Della
    1985  Interview with unnamed interviewer. Copy in author's possession.

Wood, Lewis K.
    1856  Northern Coast of California—Its Early Settlement. Humboldt Times, April 26, 1856.
    1863  Northern Coast of California—Its Early Settlement. Humboldt Times, February 7, 1863.
    1872a  Discovery of Humboldt Bay: L. K. Wood's Narrative. West Coast Signal, March 20, 1872:1.
    1872b  The Discovery of Humboldt Bay—Letter from Lewis K. Wood, Esq. West Coast Signal, March 20, 1872:2.

Work Projects Administration
    1940a  The National Guard of California 1849-1880, Part 1. Sacramento.
    1940b  The National Guard of California 1849-1880, Part 2. Sacramento.

WorthPoint
    2018  RPPC Phillipsville Garberville CA Resort Lodge Humboldt Redwood Hwy Eureka Photo. Web page. Electronic document, https://www.worthpoint.com/worthopedia/rppc-phillipsville-garberville-ca-22056928 accessed on April 2, 2018.

Worthen, Evelyn Shuster
    1996  The Unfolding Drama of Bridgeville, a Former Stagecoach Town: As Told By a Country School Teacher. Eureka: E. S Worthen.

Wrecksite
    2018a.  S S Alaska (+1921). Website. Electronic document, https://www.wrecksite.eu/wreck.aspx?23643 accessed on December 13, 2018.

Wright, Harold Bell
    1942  The Man Who Went Away. New York: Harper & Brothers.

Wrigley, Irving
    1991  Interview with Jerry Rohde, May 31, 1991.
    N.d.  Interview with Jerry Rohde

www.flickr.com
    2016a  1913 Locomobile. Web page. Electronic document, https://www.flickr.com/photos/carlylehold/29364889913/ accessed on October 31, 2016.

Wright, Warren B.
    1975  Sheep shearing time at the Drewry Ranch.

Yarborough, Bridget M.
    1976  "S.S. Emidio" Ends Voyage In CC Port. Del Norte Triplicate Bi-Centennial Edition:193.

Y. Z. (pseud.)
    1859  Letter to the Editor. Northern Californian, December 28, 1859:2.

Zachary, Jean
    1986  Some glimpses of history from Moody Road areas. Humboldt Historian, January-February 1986:16-21.

# Endnotes

1. Coy 1982:6.
2. Daily Alta California 1851a:3.
3. Morrison identifies him as "Dobbins or Dobbyns . . . [who] was living near Alton in 1851" (Morrison1962a:10). In January 1852 Kennerly Dobyns was a resident of the Eel River valley (Jameson, Felt, and Dobyns 1852).
4. Daily Alta California 1851a:3.
5. Goddard 1929:323.
6. Merriam 1993:reel 31, frame 247.
7. The name is given as Hoaglen in Clyde Morrison's account, but as Hoghland (Geer 1987:10) or Hoagland elsewhere (Turner and Turner 2010:124, Worthen 1996:25, Schwarzkopf 1949a:32). Although Morrison claims that Hoaglen "appears on deed recordings in the Trinity County records" (Morrison 1960), most later recordings of the name have it as Hoagland.
8. Morrison 1962a:10.
9. Accounts about who arrived when at Bear River are fragmentary and sometimes contradictory. Mabel Lowry states that "the first families were the Morrisons and the Lowrys and others came soon after," (Lowry 1986:12) but she doesn't provide the sources of her information. The names and sequence provided in this chapter are incomplete, but they are based on a variety of published sources, most notably the biographical accounts of Irvine's 1915 Humboldt County history.
10. Irvine 1915:445.
11. Harville 1985a:5.
12. Irvine 1915:446; Leeper 1994:138.
13. Irvine 1915:798.
14. Harville 1985a:5.
15. Irvine 1915:446.
16. Harville 1985a:5. Viola Russ McBride states that "the Lone Star [Ranch] was probably the first property acquired by Joseph Russ on Bear River Ridge if not the entire Bear River area." (McBride 1995:1). However, the Lone Star property included Kinman Pond, a location that Seth Kinman occupied until at least 1860, when his cabin there was burned (Trinity Journal 1860a:2). This was three years after the time that Harville claims Russ established the Spicy Breezes Ranch.
17. Humboldt Times 1855a:2.
18. Kinman 2010:1, 26.
19. Turner and Turner 2010:142-143.
20. Wilson and Lesandro 2004:29-31.
21. Irvine 1915:1144.
22. Geer 1948:20.
23. Irvine 1915:351.
24. Irvine 1915:616.
25. Irvine 1915:764.
26. Johnston refers to Olmstead by only his last name, but other documents indicate that he was William T. (Irvine 1915:1143-11450.
27. Johnston 1882:65.
28. Johnston 1882:66.
29. Johnston 1882:66.
30. Johnston 1882:66.
31. Johnston 1882:66-72. Rohde 2014a:88-89.
32. Johnston 1882:74-75.
33. Johnston 1882:76-77.
34. Johnston 1882:78.
35. Russ is always referred to as "my neighbor" by Johnston, but his identity becomes clear when Johnston mentions that he "was named for the Assembly" (Johnston 1882:82). It was actually the state senate that Russ first served in, being elected in 1877. Only three years after Johnston's narrative, in 1885, was Russ elected to the state assembly (Irvine 1915:446). Johnston was understandably reluctant to name the powerful individual with whom he had a series of difficult financial entanglements. Further confirmation of the identity of Johnston's "neighbor" was provided by Johnston descendant Patricia Black (Black 2007).
36. Johnston 1882:80.
37. Johnston 1882:80.
38. Only Brown's last name is given by Johnston, but we know that James D. Henry Brown was a landowner on Elk River at the time (Irvine 1915:770; Humboldt County Deeds Book G:282). In 1860 Brown was a leader in the Indian Island Massacre (Rohde 2010a).
39. Johnston 1882:82-84.
40. Johnston 1882:85-89.
41. Johnston 1882:89-95.
42. Johnston 1882:95.
43. Irvine 1915:446.
44. Black 2007.
45. Ferndale Enterprise 1894a.
46. McBride 1998a:20-21.
47. Lowry 1995:17.
48. McBride 1998a:21.
49. McBride 1998a:21-22.
50. McBride 1998:22.
51. McBride 1998:22.
52. McBride 1998:22.
53. Humboldt Times 1856a:2.
54. Geer identifies the physician as Dr. Phelps (Geer 1948:19) but Kinman, in his account, says it was "Dr. Simpson from Fort Humboldt" (Kinman 2010:29).
55. Geer 1948:18, 20. Hawley's imprecation is not fully spelled out in Geer's manuscript but it has been unbowdlerized here. Geer calls Hicks's partner "Holly," but Morrison corrects this to "Hawley," citing deed records (Morrison 1960).
56. Geer 1928:20.
57. Kinman 2010:30.
58. McBride 1998:20.
59. Raphael and House (2011:174-178) list over 30 massacres of Indians in Humboldt County between 1860 and 1864. See Rohde 2010a for a description of the multiple massacres of February 1860.
60. Trinity Journal 1860a:2.
61. Kinman 2010:31. The melted butter incident may well have started Kinman down the slippery slope of exaggeration that marked his later accounts.
62. Seidner n.d.a. 3; McLean 1917:137.
63. Humboldt Times 1860a:2.
64. Humboldt Times 1861a:3.
65. Coy 1982:197. It is surprising that author Coy, who was both Professor of History at the University of Southern California and Director of the Cal-

ifornia State Historical Association when he wrote this, provided no source for his claim, nor did he describe the situation with any precision. In fact, Coy later unfocusedly confuses Humboldt County's Bear River with a stream of the same name in Idaho, claiming that "a colony of Morrisites, a branch of the Mormon faith," settled on Humboldt's Bear River in 1863 (Coy 1982:200). The Morrisites were actually a heretical offshoot of the Mormon Church who became involved in a battle with the Salt Lake County sheriff and his posse that left ten Morrisites and two members of the posse dead (Bancroft 2015:615-621). Humboldt County's Bear River residents, already embroiled in a deadly white-Indian conflict, had no need of Utah's malcontented Morrisites being added to their community.
66. McBride 1998:24.
67. US War Department 1897b:740.
68. US War Department 1897a:296.
69. US War Department 1897a:297
70. McBride 1998:4.
71. Goddard 1929:291.
72. Nomland 1938:Map 1.
73. Coy 1982:236.
74. Coy 1982:map between pages 198 and 199. The patent process in early day California is described as follows: "By an act of April 4, 1863, California authorized individuals seeking land to file applications with state locating agents. The state agent then would apply to the register [registrar] of the federal land office who would check his records to determine whether the land applied for was subject to location by the state, was not mineral, and had no other claim, railroad, preemptor, or otherwise—and, if he found it open for selection, he notified the surveyor general, who made the same checks the register had already made, and then, if the application was approved, sent it back to the state agent. The patent ultimately came from the state, theoretically, only after the federal government had issued its patent to California for the land in question" (Gates 2002:235).
75. Coy 1982:map between pages 198 and 199.
76. Coy 1982:243.
77. Wildwood 1876a:3.
78. Fountain 2001:(110)106.
79. Fountain 2001:(113)57.
80. The figure of 81 dairies probably came from Russ. It may be too high. Wilson and Lesandro state that "from 1870 to 1900 there were as many as twenty-five dairies at Bear River" (Wilson and Lesandro 2004:30). Rancher Sid Morrison mapped 52 ranches (and one schoolhouse) in the general Bear River-Capetown area but does not give the dates of their operation nor indicate if they all had dairies (Morrison 1979).
81. Elliott 1881:135-136.
82. An interesting fictionalized account of Bear River in the 1880s is Franz and Bear River Horse, which uses actual Bear River residents as characters (Crane 2012).
83. Johnston's statistics are in keeping with those provided by Bear River rancher Mabel Lowry a century later: "An 80-cow dairy took 4 men to run it. Each man had a string of 20 cows to milk and soon knew his string from all the others" (Lowry 1986:12).
84. Elliott 1881:136.
85. Jorgensen and Boynton 2019:11.
86. Elliott 1881:136.
87. Mulcahy 1970:2.
88. Lowry 1986:17. Lowry, ever-loyal to Bear River, fails to note that it was Johnathan Lyons's sheep, from the Bald Hills in northern Humboldt County, that won a gold medal from the Exposition Universelle de Paris in 1900 (Rohde and Rohde 1994:124).
89. Humboldt County Department of Community Development Services 2003:1-2.
90. Fountain 2001:(31)280.
91. Anderson 2000. Another source puts the figure at 180,000 acres (Raphael and House 2011:255).
92. Raphael and House 2011:332, note 48.
93. Ferndale Enterprise 1882a:2.
94. Rohde and Rohde 1994:15-20.; Shepherd 2015; US Congress, House of Representatives 2015:1-21.
95. Ferndale Enterprise 1886a:3. Shepherd 2015:138.
96. McBride 1995.
97. Wikipedia 2015d.
98. Malte-Brun 2015:579.
99. Irvine 1915:506, 709, 803-804, 813, 849-850, 895, 937-938, 945, 977-978, 980, 988, 1094-1095, 1101-1102, 1106-1107, 1109, 1111, 1116, 1118, 1120-1121, 1159-1160, 1185. Irvine lists many other dairymen from the Ticino canton who located elsewhere in Humboldt County.
100. Irvine 1915:1106-1107
101. Irvine 1915:977-998.
102. Irvine 1915:810.
103. Richardson 2002.
104. Ferndale Semi-Weekly Enterprise 1903a:4.
105. The newspaper article referred to the couple as "Mr. and Mrs. Chipperiano Ambrozini," but it appears their actual names are as stated in the text (Irvine 1915:1111).
106. Fountain 2001:(110)108.
107. Belcher Abstract & Title Co. 1921:1.
108. St. John 1969.
109. His full name was Sylvanus Griswold Morley, the older maternal cousin of another scholar of the same name. The younger Sylvanus Griswold Morley became an archaeologist specializing in the Maya. During World War I he used his research activity as a cover for espionage work he did for the U. S. Government in Mexico (Wikipedia 2015e). A carelessly compiled Morley bibliography might sandwich The Covered Bridges of California (1938) between An Introduction to Mayan Hieroglyphs (1915) and The Ancient Maya (1946). Readers of this esoteric endnote will know the difference, however.
110. Morley 1938:18.
111. St. John 1969.
112. Canfield 2015.
113. Anonymous n.d.a.
114. Belcher Abstract & Title Co. 1921:1; US Department of the Interior, Geological Survey 1951a.
115. Chase 1986:22.
116. US Department of the Interior, Geological Survey 1951a.
117. A cadastral survey is used to "document the boundaries of land ownership." In the United States, this was required in 1785 legislation that

# Endnotes

established the Public Lands Survey System. The surveys divided areas into townships, which were square units of six miles to a side. Within each township were 36 one-mile-square units called sections. Such surveys required the establishment of an initial point, usually a mountain peak, from which were plotted a principal meridian (north-south line) and a baseline (east-west line). All townships were plotted from the principal meridian (measured as the range) and baseline (measured as the township). Thus a township three miles north of the initial point and two miles east would bear the designation "Township 3 North, Range 2 East" (Wikipedia 2015f, 2015g). For Humboldt County and nearby areas, these determinations were based on the initial point of Mount Pierce.
118. Anonymous 1987:12.
119. McNamara 2015.
120. Wikipedia 2015h.
121. Turner and Turner 2010:170-171.
122. Lowry 1986:17.
123. CRTANCS 1993:2-4.
124. This was probably Peter, the solitary Bear River Indian that Goddard found in the valley in 1907 (Goddard 1929:292).
125. CRTANCS 1993:3.
126. Lentell 1898; Ferndale Enterprise 1889a.
127. Ferndale Enterprise 1889a.
128. CRTANCS 1993:4.
129. Lowry 1995:18.
130. Lowry 1995:18.
131. Lowry 1982:1-2.
132. Lowry n.d.:1.
133. Lowry n.d.:1-4.
134. Fountain 2001:(48)65.
135. Lowry 1982:3.
136. Lowry 1986:17.
137. Wilson and Lesandro 2004:31-33.
138. Frickstad 1955:43.
139. Wildwood 1876a:3.
140. Turner and Turner 2010:106-107.
141. Turner and Turner 2010:90.
142. Frickstad 1955:43.
143. Frickstad 1955:42.
144. Goddard 1929:291.
145. Nomland 1938:91.
146. Irvine 1915:1033.
147. Wildwood 1876a:3.
148. Surveyor General's Office 1858a.
149. Swales 1863.
150. Fountain 2001:(86)48.
151. Doolittle 1865.
152. Elliott 1881:1889.
153. Blue Lake Advocate 1904a:2.
154. Fountain 2001:(110)97.
155. Fountain 2001:(106) 269.
156. CRTANCS 1993:10-11.
157. Elliott 1881:189.
158. Fountain 2001:(106)269.
159. CRTANCS 1993:2-5.
160. CRTANCS 1993:10.
161. Solanum tuberosum "peach blow" was native to South America
162. CRTANCS 1993:11.
163. CRTANCS 1993:12.
164. CRTANCS 1993:12; Irvine 1915:999.
165. CRTANCS 1993:12.
166. Forbes 1886.
167. Ferndale Enterprise 1884a:5.
168. Ferndale Enterprise 1884a:5.
169. A firkin is either "a small wooden vessel or tub for butter, lard, etc." or "a British unit of capacity usually equal to a quarter of a barrel" (Dictionary.com 2019a). It is therefore possible for a cooper to make a container that fulfills both definitions.
170. Another source spells his last name Bernardasher (E. B. C. 1892:5).
171. Boynton 2019a:13-14.
172. McTavish 1885a:3.
173. McTavish 1885a:3.
174. McTavish 1885a:3.
175. E. B. C. 1892:5.
176. Another source spells his last name Bernardasie (Boynton 2019a:
177. E. B. C. 1892:5.
178. Buxton 1989:22.
179. Buxton 1989:23.
180. Clark 1983a:91.
181. Humboldt Standard 1907e:1.
182. Thornbury 1923:93.
183. He was at the time Superintendent of Eureka Schools (US Office of Education 1910:612).
184. Thornbury 1923:96.
185. Genzoli 1982a:4.
186. Genzoli 1982a:4.
187. Genzoli 1982a:4.
188. Genzoli 1982a:4-5.
189. Genzoli 1982a:5.
190. Humboldt Standard 1916a:1.
191. HNSA 2018.
192. Humboldt Standard 1916a:1. Another account indicates uncertainty about the number of lifeboats that were involved (Genzoli 1982a:6).
193. Humboldt Standard 1916a:1; 1916c:1
194. Humboldt Standard 1916a:1, 1916b:1.
195. Genzoli 1982a:3.
196. Humboldt Times 1916a:1.
197. Evans 1978:3.
198. Evans 1978:3.
199. Harville 1982:17.
200. Crichton 1988:6, 9.
201. Harville 1982:17; McCloskey 1982:16; Crichton 1988a:6.
202. McCloskey 1982:16.
203. Buxton 1989:23. Buxton states that the latter three establishments were the only hotels in Capetown's history, but this claim is contradicted by the other reports given above.
204. Ferndale Enterprise 1921a:1.
205. CRTANCS 1993:12. The authors conclude their account of the school by stating that "we do not know whether it was in 1951 or 1959" that it closed, leaving an eight-year lacuna in the possible closing dates.
206. tuccycle.org 2015a.
207. tuccycle.org 2015b.
208. "Thus passes the glory . . ."
209. Powers 1949:23-25.
210. Powers 1949:25.
211. The Mattole Indians in fact called Sugarloaf the "Sealion's Sweathouse" (Harrington 1983a:reel 2:599).
212. "W" 1859a:2.
213. Coast and Geodetic Survey 1909:102.
214. Martin 1983:98.

215. Rohde 2014a:204-28.
216. Martin 1983:92.
217. Martin 1983:151.
218. Martin 1983:204-205.
219. Martin 1983:40, 42-43.
220. "W" 1859a:2.
221. Fountain 2001:(96)13.
222. Ferndale Enterprise 1881a:3.
223. Ferndale Enterprise 1881a:3.
224. An obscure reference to either the ninth century B.C.E. king of Israel or "a driver of a coach or cab" (Merriam-Webster 2019a), in this case probably the latter.
225. Ferndale Enterprise 1881a:3.
226. Harrington 1983:(1)503 left.
227. Harrington 1983:(1)434 right.
228. Driver 1939:415; Harrington 1983:(2):707 right-708 left. See my Southern Humboldt Indians for details.
229. Harrington 1983:reel 2, frame 606 right. Harrington quotes the Mattole Indian Johnny Jackson, who stated that "the Ind[ian]s lived on both side of Davis C[ree]k."
230. Greig 1964a:1.
231. Genzoli 1952a:6.
232. Genzoli and Martin 1972:32.
233. Parsnips 2013a.
234. Parsnips 2013a.
235. Ferndale Enterprise 1893a:5.
236. Genzoli 1952b.
237. New York Times 1902:1.
238. Daily Star 2020a.
239. New York Times 2020a.
240. Genzoli 1952b.
241. Genzoli 1952b.
242. HNSA 2018a.
243. US Coast & Geodetic Survey 1940.
244. Thornbury 1923:99-100.
245. uscglightshipsailors.org 2018.
246. Daily Humboldt Standard 1910a:1.
247. uscglightshipsailors.org 2018
248. Roscoe 1996:3.
249. lighthousefriends.com 2019.
250. The article is noteworthy for its scant use of the definite article.
251. Jordan 1947a.
252. Krei n.d.a.
253. Krei n.d.a.
254. Krei n.d.a.
255. Krei n.d.a; militarymuseum.org 2019a.
256. Hackett and Kingsepp 2019.
257. militarymuseum.org 2019a; Beal 1941a:1. Note: the different sources of information about the Emidio often vary in their details. I have focused on two retrospective accounts, Hackett and Kingsepp 2019 and militarymuseum.org 2019a, that had the dual advantages of collecting information from numerous sources and of focusing on the vessels involved, which was a part of the story I chose to emphasize. Beal 1941a has the immediacy (and the occasional inaccuracy) that comes from interviewing participants shortly after the event.
258. militarymuseum.org 2019a.
259. militarymuseum.org 2019a.
260. Ferndale Enterprise 1941b:1.
261. Hackett and Kingsepp 2019.
262. Hackett and Kingsepp 2019.
263. Yarborough 1976:193; militarymuseum.org 2019a.
264. Yarborough 1976:193.
265. waymaking.com 2019.
266. Nash 1996a:107.
267. Madera Tribune 1947a:1.
268. Nash 1996:106-107.
269. These were inflatable life vests named for the highly inflated movie star.
270. Madera Tribune 1947a:1; Humboldt Standard 1947a; Nash 1996a:106-107.
271. Madera Tribune 1947a:1; Humboldt Standard 1947a; Nash 1996a:107.
272. Madera Tribune 1947a:1.
273. Humboldt Standard 1947a.
274. Nash 1996a:107.
275. Nash 1996a:106-107.
276. www.lighthousefriends.com 2019.
277. readtheplaque.com 2019.
278. www.lighthousefriends.com 2019.
279. Genzoli 1971a:3.
280. Belyk 2001:192.
281. Finn 2018.
282. Finn 2018.
283. Not counting the end zone.
284. Oregon Historical Quarterly 2001:74-75.
285. Souders 2002:5.
286. Oregon Historical Quarterly 2001:75.
287. Faulkner 2002a:20
288. Oregon Historical Quarterly 2001:75.
289. Oregon Historical Quarterly 2001:77.
290. Oregon Historical Quarterly 2001:78.
291. Finn 2018.
292. Faulkner 2002a:23; Tracy 2018. Faulkner gives the last name as "Duprec."
293. Tracy 2018.
294. Oregon Historical Quarterly 2001:77.
295. Wikipedia 2018q.
296. Knuth 1989:4
297. Oregon Historical Quarterly 2001:77.
298. Oregon Historical Quarterly 2001:77.
299. Gibbs 1957:214.
300. Sacramento Union 1921:1.
301. Oregon Historical Quarterly 2001:82; Faulkner 2002a:22; Sacramento Union 1921:1; Christensen 1989:5. Horner called the Anyox a tug, but Faulkner, Christensen, and the Sacramento Union described her as a steamship, which is how she appears in a photo accompanying Faulkner's article. Faulkner and Horner claimed that the Anyox was towing a sailing ship, while the Sacramento Union and Christensen indicated that it was the barge Henry Villard. It seems most likely that the last two sources were correct, inasmuch as Christensen was an experienced seaman who observed the rescue ship and its tow after the chaos of the situation had diminished.
302. Gibbs 1957:214.
303. Christensen 1989:5
304. Oregon Historical Quarterly 2001:77. Knuth reported that three boats were lost and three, including the one she was in, got away safely (Knuth 1989:4), but Faulkner indicated that only the first and fourth boats capsized (Faulkner 2002a:21), which coincides with Horner's account.
305. Oregon Historical Quarterly 2001:77.
306. Oregon Historical Quarterly 2001:78.
307. Finn 2018.

# Endnotes

308. Gibbs 1957:214-216.
309. Souders 2002:5.
310. Gibbs 1957:216-217; Faulkner 2002a:22.
311. Souders 2002:5.
312. Oregon Historical Quarterly 2001:78.
313. Oregon Historical Quarterly 2001:78-79.
314. Oregon Historical Quarterly 2001:79, 81.
315. Oregon Historical Quarterly 2001:81.
316. Ayer and Son 1921:77.
317. Oregon Historical Quarterly 2001:83.
318. Oregon Historical Quarterly 2001:84; Souders 2002:5.
319. Sacramento Union 1921:2.
320. Christensen 1989:5.
321. Christensen 1989:5.
322. Wrecksite 2018a. Faulkner reported 132 passengers and 82 crew members, for a total of 214, rather than Wrecksite's 220 (Faulkner 2002a:20).
323. Faulkner 2002a:23.
324. Faulkner 2002a:23.
325. Souders 2002:5.
326. Souders 2002:5.
327. Fountain 2001:(48)32.
328. Humboldt Times 1854a:2.
329. Humboldt Times 1854a:2.
330. Humboldt Times 1854b:2.
331. Tempus Fugit III 1935. The names of several of the men are rendered differently in Fugit's account, perhaps because time moved so quickly for him or her. The versions that appear in this text have been provided by Mattole historian Laura Cooskey (Cooskey 2018b).
332. Kinman 2010:56. Regarding the long-winded Kinman and the gas jets, it might be said that "it took one to know one."
333. "W" 1859b:2.
334. "W" 1859b:2.
335. "W" 1859b:2.
336. Humboldt Times 1860b.
337. Fountain 2001:(48)47. This account may, however, be simply a tall tail tale.
338. Coy 1982:229.
339. Cooskey 2004c:6-7, 9.
340. Frickstad 1955:45.
341. Humboldt Times 1866a:2.
342. Coy 1982:236.
343. Coy 1982:235-236.
344. Cooskey 2004c:11.
345. At a spot on the Mattole several miles below Ettersburg, later called Sterrit Hole, the Marysville Settlers may or may not have encountered excitement. According to accommodating Andy Genzoli, who seldom heard a tale he didn't want to retell, the Marysville Settlers reached Sterrit Hole and "at this point the wagon train was halted. The water was deep, swift, and the pool one hundred yards long. Several rafts were constructed, and a wagon placed on each. Cyrus Miner, serving as teamster, drove each raft, bearing a wagon through the chasm to a flat north of the pool" (Fountain 2001:(48) 327). However, Buck Miner, a descendant of Cyrus's, gave a far less dramatic account: the Marysville Settlers "faced a narrow rock chasm with water too swift and deep for their wagons to negotiate. This gorge had to be avoided by the wagon train." The real excitement, according to Miner, came a few years later, when local resident Frank Sterrit, skeptical of the risk posed by the chasm, "attempted to ride his horse through the gorge, and was drowned" (Miner 1996:130-131). Sterrit's posthumous reward for determining the extent of the danger was having the hole named for him.
346. Children and Teachers of the Mattole Union School 1962:46-48; Roscoe 1991:vii; Fountain 2001:(48)274; Cooksey 2022. Cooksey has supplied a detailed account of who some of the Marysville Settlers were and when they arrived on the Mattole. She also summarized the lack of agreement among sources about who arrived when and suggested that only those Marysville individuals whose credentials are undisputed be mentioned. I have heeded her advice.
347. Coy 1982:280. The road, which began at the mouth Oil Creek five miles south of Centerville, had been started in 1867 (Humboldt Times 1867b:3). Between Centerville and Oil Creek the route was not by road but along the beach (Rohde 2014a:200-201).
348. Humboldt Times 1869b:3.
349. West Coast Signal 1871a:3.
350. Humboldt Times, 1867b:3.
351. Chivers 1875a:3.
352. Chivers 1875a:3.
353. Mattole Valley historian Laura Cooskey is puzzled by the reference to "Mr. Allen" as she is unaware of anyone by that name living in the area at the time of the newspaper article. She suggests that it may refer to either Allen Miner or his son, Henry Allen Miner (Cooskey 2022a).
354. West Coast Signal 1876b:3.
355. Humboldt Weekly Times 1878a:2.
356. Cooskey 2011:5-14.
357. "J" 1880:3.
358. Humboldt Times 1880b.
359. Cooskey 2011a:1.
360. McGuire 1979.
361. Ferndale Enterprise 1892a.
362. Ferndale Semi-Weekly Enterprise 1903c:4.
363. Wikipedia 2018j.
364. Dengler 2006:27-31.
365. Humboldt Times 1906a:8.
366. This was the Knights of Pythias, a fraternal organization founded in 1864 (pythias.org 2022a).
367. Daily Humboldt Standard 1907d:6.
368. Daily Humboldt Standard 1907d:6.
369. Carranco and Sorensen 1988:162-166.
370. Carranco and Sorensen 1988:167-168.
371. Goddard 1907f:18-19.
372. A saddletank locomotive has its water tank sitting "on top of the boiler like a saddle sits atop a horse" (Wikipedia 2018h).
373. Carranco and Sorensen 1988:168.
374. Cooskey 2017a :4-5.
375. Belcher Abstract & Title Co. 1921:4. Carranco and Sorensen claim the length was two miles, but this distance is not supported by the Belcher map. Up until 1907 the Metropolitan Redwood Lumber Company Railroad had the shortest line—about a mile from its mill to the San Francisco and Northwestern Railway. But then Metropolitan built a wooden trestle across the Eel and extended rails into its timberlands along Slater Creek, adding two miles to its trackage (Whistle Punk 2005:6).Thus, briefly, the MLCRR gained the coveted honor as the county's shortest rail

line, only to lose the title in 1908 when a new diminutive rail line appeared. This was the Haw Quarry Railroad that ran to the head of Fay Slough and was one mile long (Daily Humboldt Times 1908a). Still secure for the MLCRR was another vaunted title: it remained the county's westernmost railroad.
376. Clark 1983a:102.
377. Clark 1983a:101-103; Carranco and Sorensen 1988:168.
378. Roscoe 1996:120; Carranco and Sorensen 1988:168; Cooskey 2017b:2.
379. Cooskey 2017b:2.
380. Carranco and Sorensen 1988:168.
381. Cooskey 2017b:2; Carranco and Sorensen 1988:168.
382. Cooskey 2017b:3.
383. Carranco and Sorensen 1988:168.
384. Clark 1983a:100-101.
385. Clark 1983a:101-103.
386. California State Railroad Museum 2018.
387. San Francisco Chronicle 1983a.
388. Schwarzkopf 1949i:13.
389. Schwarzkopf 1949i:13.
390. Schwarzkopf 1949i:13.
391. Schwarzkopf 1949i:17.
392. Roscoe 1996:98.
393. House 1999:41-42.
394. I was surprised to witness this in 1979 when making my first trip through the area.
395. Humboldt Times 1957a:1, 3.
396. bridgemeister.com 2022a.
397. House 1999:41-42.
398. House 1999:42.
399. Humboldt Times 1854a:2.
400. Humboldt Standard 1907g:2.
401. Coy 1982:152-153.
402. Humboldt Times 1857b:2.
403. Coy 1982:153.
404. Humboldt Times 1857b:2.
405. Humboldt Times 1857b:2.
406. Coy 1982:153.
407. Humboldt Times 1858w:2, 1859k:2; United States House of Representatives 1858:183.
408. Roscoe 1985b:30.
409. Quoted in Heizer 1993:34-35.
410. Coy 1982:153-155.
411. Roscoe 1985b:38.
412. Kinman 2010:59.
413. United States War Department 1897a:73.
414. United States War Department 1897a:299.
415. Humboldt Times 1864e:2; Coy 1982:190-191; Geer 1948:29; Roscoe 1985b:49-50.
416. United States War Department 1897b:1005.
417. Roscoe 1940:13-14.
418. Roscoe 1940:14; Fountain 2001:(32)342.
419. Ethnological Documents 2002:reel 12(4)103; Goddard 1907f:72-74.
420. Wikipedia 2018
421. BLM 2018b.
422. Harrington 1983:(reel 1)frame 371 left.
423. Belcher Abstract & Title Co. 1921:4.
424. Searson 1921a:1.
425. Fountain 2001:(48)24; Genzoli 1991:16.
426. Nace 2003:59.
427. America's Story 2020.
428. Wikipedia 2018d.
429. Whiteshot 1905:62.
430. Measuringworth 2018
431. Wikipedia 2018e.
432. Lavender 1987:282-284.
433. Lavender 1987:284.
434. Nolte 2018.
435. Nolte 2018.
436. Lavender 1987:284.
437. Irvine 1915:741. Irvine's account erroneously gives the year as 1874 rather than 1864.
438. Lavender 1987:284.
439. Coy 1982:234.
440. McKinney 2018. Coy cites production by the Union Mattole Company that ran as high as 850 gallons for one month but gives no overall total (Coy 1982:234).
441. Coy 1982:235.
442. Coy 1982:236.
443. California State Mining Bureau 1886:198-199. An interesting side story is the use, by Henderson, of "Indian script" to obtain title to the Mattole oil lands. It is far beyond the scope of this book to describe the intricacies of the original issuance of the script (which was intended to serve in lieu of land allotments to certain Indians in Minnesota and Wisconsin) and the predatory acquisition of such script and its subsequent misuse by gluttonous grifters of the Henderson-Scott ilk. A detailed account of the script's connection with the Mattole oil fields is provided in Cooskey 2019a.
444. Nace 2003:64.
445. Nace 2003:64-65.
446. Nace 2003:65-68.
447. Clark 1983a:64-65.
448. Clark 1983a:64-65.
449. Wikipedia 2018f.
450. Bean 1973:321.
451. Wikipedia 2018g.
452. Join California 2018a. Two minor party candidates, Socialist Austin Lewis and James H. Blanchard of the Prohibition party, garnered 5.1 percent and 2.4 percent of the vote respectively.
453. Humboldt Standard 1907c:1.
454. Humboldt Standard 1907c:1.
455. Humboldt Standard 1907d:1.
456. Humboldt Standard 1907e:1.
457. Humboldt Standard 1907e:1.
458. Humboldt Standard 1907e:1.
459. Humboldt Standard 1907g:2.
460. Humboldt Standard 1907f:1.
461. Humboldt Standard 1907f:1
462. Ferndale Semi-Weekly Enterprise 1907a:4.
463. Humboldt Standard 1907f:1.
464. Roscoe 1996:68.
465. Roscoe 1996:68.
466. Roscoe 1996:68.
467. Roscoe 1996:68.
468. Clark 1983b:10.
469. Roscoe 1996:70, 74.
470. Roscoe 1996:71-72; Clark 1983b:11.
471. Clark 1983b:10.
472. Clark 1983b:10.
473. Roscoe 1996:74.
474. Roscoe 1996:74.
475. Roscoe 1996:74-75.
476. Roscoe 1996:75.
477. Roscoe 1996:75.
478. Roscoe 1996:75.
479. Roscoe 1996:72-74.

# Endnotes

480. lighthousefriends.com 2018.
481. lighthousefriends.com 2018.
482. Randles 1966:17.
483. Randles 1966:17.
484. Belcher 1970.
485. lighthousefriends.com 2018.
486. Ethnological Documents 2002:12(4) 113-124, 196-206). The confusion about this tribal group's identity is longstanding and complex. See Southern Humboldt Indians by this author for a detailed explanation.
487. Neb Roscoe gives 1850 as the year (Roscoe 1996:1); Cooskey says that Hadley descendants claim it was the winter of 1849-1850 (Cooskey 2018c); the Humboldt Standard gives 1851 or 1852 (Humboldt Standard 1907h:2); Saul states that Hadley and Young lived on the Mattole during the winter of 1848-1849, left for the Sierra Nevada gold mines, and then both returned in 1850 (Saul 1992a:8). Mattole old-timer M. J. Conklin, however, lists the first Mattole Valley settlers as "John Cassard, James Delesaux, John LeMan and another man whose name I've forgotten" (Conklin 1882). W. E. Roscoe claims that Hadley did not move to Upper Mattole until 1857 (Roscoe 1940:18).
488. Cooskey 2004c:1. Neb Roscoe believes that Hadley encountered the L. K. Wood party (Roscoe 1996:1) but the prevailing belief is that Wood's group came up not the Mattole but the South Fork Eel. Cooskey indicates that it was the Gregg party, on their way up the Mattole, that Hadley met, and this is the version given here.
489. Doolittle 1865.
490. Irvine 1915:683.
491. Doolittle 1865.
492. Hamm 1890:14.
493. Turner and Turner 2010:138, 175.
494. US War Department 1897a:73. The camp was named for Col. James N. Olney. Soldiers from Company A of the 2nd Infantry Regiment of the California Volunteers, commanded by Lt. Charles G. Hubbard, were the first troops stationed there (Turner and Turner 2010:48).
495. Her death certificate indicates she was born in 1845, but the event was not documented at the time since no whites were present yet on the North Coast and no records of this sort were kept (Milota 2003a).
496. Roscoe 1996:2; Irvine 1915:682; Cooskey 2022b.
497. Genealogy.com 2018a.
498. Roscoe 1996:2.
499. Irvine 1915:682.
500. Seidner n.d.a.
501. Milota 2003.
502. Daily Humboldt Standard 1907f:2; Saul 1992a:13; Cooskey 2022b.
503. Humboldt Times 1858 :3.
504. Humboldt Times 1858w:2.
505. Bledsoe 1885:285.
506. Bledsoe 1885:285.
507. Humboldt Times 1858v:2.
508. US War Department 1897a:73-74.
509. US War Department 1897a:73-74.
510. Goddard 1907f:61-62. Ethnological Documents 2002:reel 12(4)120.
511. Ethnological Documents 2002:reel 12(4)122; Goddard 1907f:64.
512. Roscoe 1996:6-7.
513. Humboldt Times 1864e: 2.
514. The reference to Geer as "Captain" is puzzling. Nowhere in the War of the Rebellion records of army dispatches is he referred to by that title; rather, he is always mentioned as "lieutenant."
515. Geer 1948:27.
516. Fountain 2001:(117)179.
517. Fountain 2001:(48)130.
518. Humboldt Times 1864d:2; Roscoe 1996:7.
519. Roscoe 1940:12.
520. Roscoe (1996:8) indicates that most of the men and older children were at the camp at the time of the attack but "ran away." Cooskey (2022b) believes that "the men were off on a hunting expedition." I have gone with Cooskey's account as she had access to more sources of information than Roscoe, who used Charley Krill as his sole source.
521. Neb Roscoe says it was Roberts (Roscoe 1996:8), while W. E. Roscoe claims it was Aldrich (Roscoe 1940:12).
522. Roscoe 1996:7-8.
523. Roscoe 1940:13.
524. Roscoe 1996:8-9.
525. Geer 1948:27-29.
526. Humboldt Times 1864e:2.
527. Conklin 1882. Conklin gives the date of his meeting with Black as May 10, 1864, but the year must have been 1862 if two years elapsed before the local conflict ended.
528. Coy 1982:229-235.
529. Coy 1982:236.
530. Coy 1982:243.
531. Coy 1982:242.
532. Coy 1982:301.
533. Encyclopædia Britannica 2018a.
534. Humboldt Times 1866b.
535. Humboldt Times 1866b.
536. DeLong 1971:1.
537. Frickstad 1955:47.
538. CRTANCS 1993:74, 77.
539. Semi-Weekly Enterprise 1904a:4.
540. Daily Humboldt Standard 1907e:2.
541. Daily Humboldt Standard 1907e:2.
542. Daily Humboldt Standard 1907e:2.
543. Carranco and Sorensen 1988:168.
544. McMorris and Melvin 2013a:4.
545. Forbes 1886; Lentell 1898; Denny 1911.
546. Ferndale Enterprise 1914a.
547. Humboldt Times 1919b.
548. Ferndale Enterprise 1924a.
549. Roscoe 1996:101-102.
550. Cooskey 2022b.
551. Arcata Union 1927a; Humboldt Standard 1927b; Humboldt Standard 1928b.
552. Roscoe 1996:47-48.
553. Cooskey 2022b.
554. Roscoe 1996:114-115.
555. Fountain 2001:(110)100: Cooskey 2022b.
556. Ethnological Documents 2002:12(4)123-124.
557. Forbes 1886; Lentell 1898; Denny 1911.
558. Humboldt Times 1913c; Fountain 2001:(91)66.
559. Irvine 1915:485.
560. Belcher Abstract & Title Co. 1921:5.

561. Irvine 1915:631-633.
562. Irvine 1915:814-815.
563. Belcher Abstract & Title Co. 1921:4.
564. Cooskey 2004a:1.
565. Walker 1996:5.
566. Franklin 2020:4-5.
567. Cooskey 2004b:1-2.
568. Cooskey 2004b:3.
569. Cooskey 2004b:4.
570. Cooskey 2004b:4.
571. Times-Standard 1973a:2.
572. The article refers to him as "O. W. West," but the initials were reversed and the reference was to "William O. West" (Cooskey 2004a:1).
573. Times-Standard 1973a:2.
574. Ethnological Documents 2002:(12)4:206.
575. Coe 2019.
576. Ethnological Documents 2002:(12)4:206.
577. Goddard 1908b:94. Goddard's village notecard for Lenillimi states: "There were formerly many grizzlies there of which the Indians were afraid (Ethnological Documents 2002:(12)4:206). However, his field notes, referenced here, read: "That is all nobody lived above were afraid of grizzlies," which indicates that the presence of bears upriver from Lenillimi prevented Indian occupation of the area.
578. Surveyor General 1875c; Coy 1982:286.
579. Lentell 1898; BLM 2019d, 2019e, 2019f.
580. Goldberg 1985:6.
581. Irvine 1915:628.
582. The story of the Etters establishing themselves at what became Ettersburg uses Gladys Smith's account, which she indicates was based on Albert Etter's autobiographical notes (Smith 1995:22). Other versions, such as Schwarzkopf's (Schwarzkopf 1949g:17), tell a somewhat different story.
583. Smith 1995:16-17.
584. Smith 1995:17.
585. Schwarzkopf 1949g:17.
586. Irvine 1915:631.
587. Irvine 1915:633.
588. Smith 1995:17-18.
589. Ferndale Enterprise 1913a. The Enterprise reprinted the recent San Francisco Bulletin article.
590. Ferndale Enterprise 1913a.
591. US Department of Agriculture 1937a:490.
592. Irvine 1915:630.
593. US Department of Agriculture 1937a:490-491; Smith 1995:18.
594. Smith 1995:19.
595. Ferndale Enterprise 1913a.
596. Flaherty 1934.
597. Humboldt Times 1913b.
598. Humboldt Times 1915a.
599. Fishman 2006a:2.
600. US Department of Agriculture 1937a:490-491.
601. Fishman 2006a:2.
602. Smith 1995:20.
603. Flaherty 1934.
604. Fishman 2006a:2.
605. Smith 1995:16.
606. Fishman 2006:3.
607. Fishman 2006:1, 3. In this account Fishman gives the number of cultivar samples as "some three dozen." In another article, Fishman sets the number at "some 40" (Fishman 2019).
608. Fishman 2006:5.
609. Vatnsdal 1957:8.
610. Irvine 1915:886-887.
611. US Bureau of Land Management 2019d.
612. Vatnsdal 1957:
613. Goldberg 1985:7.
614. Vatnsdal 1957:8.
615. Vatnsdal 1957:9
616. Vatnsdal 1957:9-10
617. Doolittle 1865; US Bureau of the Census 1860a:7.
618. US Bureau of the Census 1860a:7.
619. Frickstad 1955:48.
620. CRTANCS 2001:110.
621. Goldberg 1985:9. Goldberg calls it the "Indian Council Tree."
622. Frickstad 1955:43.
623. Goldberg 1985:9.
624. CRTANCS 2001:110, 113.
625. Frickstad 1955:43.
626. Wikipedia 2019
627. CRTANCS 2001:106.
628. Vatnsdal 1957:10-11.
629. Cook 1997:(12)67.
630. Hunt 1998.
631. Cook 1997:(12)67.
632. Vatnsdal 1957:12-13.
633. Davidson 1889:303. Sally Bell, a member of the To-cho-be ke-ah tribal group from the Briceland area, indicated that Shelter Cove was called Tahng-ah-tah and that the people from there were the Tahng-I ke-ah (Merriam 1993:(30)495-497). Davidson's account is based on information that the 1853 survey expedition obtained directly from the Indians living there at the time, while Bell's interview occurred nearly seventy years later. The two renderings appear to be slightly different versions of the same name.
634. Davidson 1889:302.
635. Machi 2015a.
636. Elliott 1881:160.
637. Thornbury 1923:31.
638. Cook 1997:(10)81.
639. Humboldt Times 1855b:2.
640. Humboldt Times 1856b:2.
641. Humboldt Times 1859a:2.
642. Bledsoe 1885:317.
643. Strobridge 1994:177, 199.
644. Strobridge 1994:199.
645. Strobridge 1994:199.
646. Moungovan 1964a:7.
647. This may actually be "Shoemaker," a far more common last name, but such a rendering does not appear in the record.
648. Moungovan 1964a:7. Moungovan adds: "This information concerning the murder of the Indian children was learned by Les Hamilton while working with John Hamilton's sons in the Shelter Cove area as a young man. He had talked with one of the Indians there who was one of the children whose life had been spared."
649. Humboldt Times 1939a:12. Tom Bell later married Sally Bowles, who became the noted Sinkyone informant then known as Sally Bell.
650. United States War Department 1897a:527.
651. Cook 1997:(10)81.
652. Machi 2012a.
653. Seidner 1939a.

# Endnotes

654. United States War Department 1897a: 835.
655. Humboldt Times 1937a.
656. Cook 1997:(10)81. This account, by Ernest McKee, is retold by other authors (Machi 1984:12-13; Cook and Hawk 2006:85; Anderson 2006:33).
657. Fountain 2001:(89)402.
658. Cook and Hawk 2006:85.
659. Coy 1923:110.
660. Cook and Hawk 2006: 57. Another source gives the pack train size as "100 to 150 mules" (Machi 2015b).
661. Machi 2015b.
662. West Coast Signal 1878a:3. A later report claims that John McMillin, using Chinese labor, built the Garberville to Briceland section of the road (Cook and Hawk 2006:9, 56) but the source for this information is not documented.
663. Cook 1997:(10)83.
664. West Coast Signal 1878a:3.
665. Humboldt Times 1878a:3.
666. Cook and Hawk 2006:85.
667. Elliott 1881:159-160.
668. Cook 1997:(7)118.
669. There were four Robarts brothers: James T., Robert Wilkinson, Percival Wright, and William H., all born in England. William H. Robarts had the distinction of marrying Ada Brown, whose sister-in-law, Cordelia Botkin, was the notorious "Poisoned Chocolate Murdress" (Machi 2015c). In the 1890s Botkin engaged in an affair with John Dunning, a reporter for the Associated Press. Both Botkin and Dunning were married at the time, but not to each other. In 1898 Dunning set off for Cuba to cover the Spanish-American War. When he departed he told Botkin that he would not return to her as he had reconciled with his wife. In July, Dunning helped save survivors from Spanish ships sunk at the Battle of Santiago de Cuba. In August, Botkin sent Dunning's wife a box of chocolates, "With love to yourself and baby." Dunning ate at least three pieces and shared the candies with others. Three days later, she and her sister, Harriet Deane, died in agony from arsenic poisoning. The handwriting on the note matched that in letters previously sent by Botkin. The chocolates were traced back to a San Francisco candy shop, and from there the trail led to Botkin as the purchaser. Cordelia Botkin was tried for murder in December 1898 and convicted. She was again convicted at a retrial in 1904. She died in San Quentin Prison in 1910 (Wikipedia 2015i). It could be said that Botkin received her just desserts.
670. Cook and Hawk 2006:86.
671. Cook and Hawk 2006:86.
672. Cook 1997:(10)88.
673. Cook 1997:(10)81.
674. Cook 1997:(10)88.
675. Cook 1997:(10)88.
676. Cook 1997:(10)88.
677. Cook and Hawk 2006:86.
678. Rohnerville Herald 1887a:2.
679. Machi 2015b.
680. Forrest 1887:4.
681. Hamm 1890:109.
682. Machi 2015b, 2015d.
683. Cook 1997:(10)81.
684. Daily Humboldt Standard 1890a.
685. Frickstad 1955:46.
686. Machi 2015b.
687. Machi 2015b; Frickstad 1955:43; Lentell 1898.
688. Cook 1997:(10)82; Machi 2012a.
689. Verdi 1974:18; Wikipedia 2015j.
690. Cook 1997:(10)82; Verdi 1974:18. Verdi claims that the ranch was acquired from the "Bank of Fort Bragg," but this is contradicted by at least four newspaper articles that indicate it was the "Bank of Mendocino" (Machi 2015d).
691. Cook 1997:(10)82.
692. Crow 2017.
693. Timberman 11920a:48; Cook and Hawk 2006:77.
694. Carranco and Carranco 1977:1-2; Bowcutt 2015:44, 48; Genzoli 1983:19; Arcata Union 1919a. For an in-depth history of the Wagner Leather Company, see Crow 2017.
695. Cook and Hawk 2006:89.
696. Ferndale Enterprise 1906a:8. Whitethorn's voter cohort had expanded from six to fourteen.
697. Cook 1997:(10)82.
698. Irvine 1915:975-976.
699. Forrest 1887:4.
700. Cook 1997:(10)86.
701. Humboldt Times 1919a. A vacationer at the cove, citing the same source, claimed the catch was only 140 tons (Ferndale Enterprise 1919a).
702. Ferndale Enterprise 1919a:7.
703. Humboldt Standard 1919a.
704. Machi 1984:28; Cook 1997:(10)88; Verdi 1974:21.
705. Verdi 1974:21. The date of this sale is uncertain. Various sources give 1924 and 1929 as the year (Machi 2015b).
706. Thornbury 1923:116.
707. Machi 1984;28-29.
708. Wright 1942.
709. Machi 1984:38-39.
710. Machi 1984:42, Machi 2015b.
711. Machi 1984:42; Machi 2015b.
712. Machi 1984:29-30.
713. Machi 1984:29-30; Machi 2015e. In another account, Mario Machi says that his brother Tony was already at the cove in 1930 when Mario arrived (Cook 1997:(10)86). The brothers came up on the fishing boat S. F. International No. 3. As of 2015 the boat was still afloat and could be found in recently restored condition at the Wharfinger docks in Eureka as the Stephanie (Machi 2015e). Hopefully the name change has been recorded in the Ledger of the Deep.
714. Machi 1984:30-31.
715. Machi 1984:37-38.
716. Machi 1984:Preface, 42.
717. This is the number Machi gives in his book. In another account, he puts the number at five (Cook 1997:(10)87).
718. Machi 1984:44, 48.
719. Genzoli 1949a:17.
720. Genzoli 1949a:17.
721. Machi 1984:51.
722. Machi 1984:51; Cook 1997:(10)88.
723. Machi 1984:52.
724. Machi 1984:52.
725. Machi 2012:36-38.
726. Fountain 2001:(96)316.

727. Machi 1984:58.
728. Griggs and Ross 2014:25; Ringwald 2003a, 2003b.
729. Gruron 2004a.
730. Gurnon 2004b.
731. The reference is to the patriotic song "Hail, Columbia," the official anthem of the Vice-President of the United States (Wikipedia 2015k).
732. BoatSafe.com 2015; Empty Road 2015.
733. Machi 1984:21.
734. Machi 2015b.
735. Belyk 2001:154-155.
736. Belyk 2001:155.
737. Belyk 2001:156.
738. Belyk 2001:156.
739. Belyk 2001:156; Open Jurist 2015.
740. Open Jurist 2015; Belyk 2001:157.
741. Hillman 2007:A1.
742. Belyk 2001:157-158.
743. Humboldt Standard 1907a:1.
744. Belyk 2001:158.
745. Belyk 2001:159.
746. Belyk 2001:159-160.
747. Humboldt Standard 1907a:1.
748. Belyk 2001:158, 160-161.
749. Humboldt Standard 1907a:1.
750. Humboldt Times 1907a:1.
751. Humboldt Standard 1907a:1. A subsequent inquiry set the time at "between eight and nine minutes" (Belyk 2001:170).
752. Humboldt Standard 1907a:1; Humboldt Times 1907a:1.
753. Humboldt Times 1907a:1, 3.
754. Belyk 2001:163.
755. Humboldt Times 1907a:3. The Times estimated that 75 to 80 survivors reached the San Pedro, but these figures may be too high.
756. Belyk 2001:164-165.
757. Humboldt Times 1907b; Gibbs 1957:219-220: 3; Belyk 2001:170; Hillman 2007a. The various sources disagree about the number of both survivors and deaths. Belyk and Hillman both give the death total as 88; Gibbs puts it at 87. I have gone with the majority.
758. Belyk 2001:168.
759. The Humboldt Times article misspells the name as "Bermingham." Another source spells it "Birmingham"(Belyk 2001:171). The latter is the correct spelling as confirmed by the Official Register (Director of the Census 1907:62).
760. Humboldt Times 1907c:1.
761. Bassett 2015.
762. Humboldt Times 1864c:3.
763. Humboldt Times 1864a:3.
764. Doolittle 1865.
765. Forbes 1886.
766. Cook and Hawk 2001:40-41.
767. Lentell 1898; Lentell 1905; Cook and Hawk 2001:28.
768. Cook and Hawk 2006:21.
769. Cook and Hawk 2006:57.
770. Cook and Hawk 2006:47.
771. Cook and Hawk 2006:48.
772. BLM 2017c.
773. The above account summarizes Kelsey 1982:9.
774. Irvine 1915:1214-15.
775. BLM 2017d.
776. Irvine 1915:1214-1215; Frickstad 1955:46; Cook 1997:(12)67.
777. Cook 1997:(12)67.
778. Standard Publishing Co. 1893:94.
779. Morgan 1982a:16.
780. Morgan 1982a:16.
781. Morgan 1982a:16.
782. Morgan 1982a:16.
783. Morgan 1982b:15.
784. Morgan 1982c:16.
785. Morgan 1982c:16.
786. Scott 2019a.
787. Cook 1997:(10)13.
788. Cook 1997:(10)13.
789. Redwoods Monastery 2017.
790. Easthouse 2017a:1, 5; Water Resources Control Board 2017:3.
791. Merriam 1993:(9)194, (30)416. This Sinkyone tribal group is not be confused with the To-kub-be ke-ahs of the Benbow area.
792. Asbill 1953:109-118, 122-123. A detailed account appears in chapter 3 of Southern Humboldt Indians.
793. Lentell 1898; Cook and Hawk 2006:56.
794. Cook and Hawk 2006:56. This account claims that John McMillin was the construction boss, but a newspaper article from the time states that it was S. F. Taylor (West Coast Signal 1878a:3). Another source indicates that the road "was constructed by Chinese laborers" (Anderson 2006:69).
795. Hill 1954a:10.
796. Cook 1997:(2b)29.
797. Hill 1954:10.
798. Humboldt Times 1883a, 1883b; Hill 1954a:10. Irvine's brief biography of Briceland gives the year as "about 1889," (Irvine 1915: 1190) but the six-year discrepancy with the notices in the Times strains, by too great an extent, the leeway provide by the word "about."
799. Irvine 1915:1190-1191; Hill 1954:10; Cook and Hawk 2006:70.
800. Frickstad 1955:41.
801. Anderson 2006:45.
802. Anderson 2006:45.
803. Irvine 1915:1191.
804. Anderson 2006:45-46.
805. Schwarzkopf 1949g:17; Hill 1954a:10.
806. Womack 1985.
807. Hill 1954a:10.
808. Anderson 2006:62.
809. Anderson 2006:58-59.
810. Ferndale Semi-Weekly Enterprise 1903b:5.
811. Schwarzkopf 1949g:17.
812. Hill 1954a:10.
813. Fountain 2001:(70)53.
814. Vincent 1983:3-4; Fountain 2003:(70)53.
815. Carranco and Carranco 1977:1.
816. The tannery had operated under various names but was incorporated as the Wagner Leather Company in 1895 (Crow 2017).
817. Carranco and Carranco 1977:1.
818. Cook 1997:(10)82.
819. Cook and Hawk 2006:76.
820. Carranco and Carranco 1977:1.
821. Anderson gives the 1,000-cord figure (Anderson 2006:66), while Carranco and Carranco claim the capacity was 3,000 cords (Carranco and Carranco 1977:1).

# Endnotes

822. One source states that when full the barrels weighed 300 pounds each (Carranco and Carranco 1977:4.); another source gives the weight as "from 500 to 600 pounds . . . ." Humboldt Standard 1907b:6). The horses pulling the wagons would have noticed the difference.
823. Carranco and Carranco 1977:1,4; Cook and Hawk 2006:79, 82. Carranco and Carranco make the claim regarding the naming of the Nooning Grounds. It is also possible that the name was applied because the wagoners ate their lunch, or, in the argot of the time, "nooned," there.
824. Carranco and Carranco 1977:4.
825. One source gives the figure as 100 (Carranco and Carranco 1977:4.), while another says "from 150 to 200" (Humboldt Standard 1907b:6).
826. Carranco and Carranco 1977:4.
827. In 1906, for example, Briceland had 80 registered voters while Garberville had 70. The leader among far southern Humboldt communities was Blocksburg, with 105 (Ferndale Enterprise 1906a:8).
828. Cook and Hawk 2006:82.
829. Schwarzkopf 1949g:17.
830. Carranco and Carranco 1977:4.
831. Carranco and Carranco 1977:4; Anderson 2006:67.
832. Hill 1954:10.
833. Humboldt Standard 1914a; Fountain 2001:(70)55.
834. Ferndale Enterprise 1918a.
835. Ferndale Semi-Weekly Enterprise 1914a:5.
836. Schwarzkopf 1949g:17.
837. Cook and Hawk 2006:77.
838. Schwarzkopf 1949g:17.
839. Hill 1954:11.
840. Cook 1997:(10)12.
841. CRTANCS 2001:42.
842. Carranco and Carranco 1977:4.
843. Bowcutt 2015:34-35.
844. Jepson et al. 1911:6. The value in 2016 dollars would be $1,980,000,000 (Measuringworth 2017). On this basis, it would be interesting to compare the relative value of tanbark with its later-day replacement, marijuana.
845. Ott 2017.
846. Bowcutt 2015:35.
847. Bowcutt 2015:35, 38-39; Carranco and Carranco 1977:1. The Carrancos do not reveal what the first and second largest industries were, but the production of redwood products was certainly one of them.
848. Bowcutt 2015:39-40.
849. Wichels 2017.
850. The maximum recorded height is 208 feet (Bowcutt 2015:10). A small stand of very tall, old-growth tanoaks is found on Peavine Ridge, above Albee Creek, in Humboldt Redwoods State Park.
851. Jepson et al. 1911:11.
852. Vincent 1983:4-6.
853. Bowcutt 2015:41.
854. Anderson 2016:65, 68.
855. OSU 2017.
856. Carranco and Sorensen 1988:168.
857. Forrest 1887:4; Cook 1997(10)86.
858. Carranco and Carranco 1977:1, 4.
859. Jepson et al. 1911:8.
860. Jepson et al. 1911:9.
861. Pavlik et al. 1992:8.
862. Merriam 1918a:134: Bowcutt 2015:22.
863. Nomland 1935:169-170.
864. Nomland 1935:149.
865. Denny 1911.
866. Hawk 2004:vii, 2, 4-6, 8-10, 15-16.
867. Albert Smith calls him "Charlie John Smith" (Goddard 1907c:47), and Cook and Hawk have him as Jose "Chandler" Domingo Smith (Cook and Hawk 2001:192), but his 1889 land patent gives his name as Joseph D. Smith (US Bureau of Land Management 2018b).
868. Goddard 1907c:47.
869. Goddard 1907d:12.
870. Joseph D. Smith's ranch was situated in the north half of the southeast quarter of Section 12, Township 5 South, Range 3 East, Humboldt Meridian (Belcher Abstract & Title Co. 1922:11).
871. Goddard 1907c:46.
872. Merriam 1923a:60.
873. Cook and Hawk 2001:198.
874. Cook and Hawk 2001:192.
875. US Bureau of Land Management 2018g.
876. Cook and Hawk 2001:192-193.
877. Cook and Hawk 2001:192, 193, 196.
878. Elsewhere Cook and Hawk state that Reuben Reed was the first settler in the area, arriving in 1865 (Cook and Hawk 2001:198). This, however, conflicts with their account of Reed arriving after Anderson's drowning in 1869.
879. Cook and Hawk 2001:185-186.
880. Cook and Hawk 2001:187.
881. Goddard 1907c:49.
882. Smith stated that "Reed [was] alive yet" (Goddard 1907c:49). Smith was interviewed in 1907, by which time Ezra Reed was again living in Kentucky, so that Smith would have had no knowledge of whether he was alive or dead. Therefore Smith must have been referring to Reuben Reed, who was living within a few miles of Smith in 1907 and did not die until 1918 (Cook and Hawk 2001:189).
883. Cook and Hawk 2001:198.
884. Cook and Hawk 2001:198.
885. In one instance Cook and Hawk give the price as $30,000, but in another place they give it as $32,000 (Cook and Hawk 2001:199, 204).
886. parks.ca.gov 2020a.
887. Cook and Hawk 2001:198-199.
888. Humboldt Times 1923a:8.
889. Humboldt Standard 1923c.
890. Cook 1997:(8)95, 105; Cook and Hawk 2001:198-199. Cook and Hawk claim the lodge "was built around 1931," but on her own, Cook indicates that it "was completed between 1928 and 1930." Cook and Hawk caption a picture of the lodge with the date as 1929. The California State Parks website is much more definite, giving the year as 1931 (California State Parks 2022a).
891. Cook and Hawk 2001:202-203.
892. Cook and Hawk 2001:204.
893. California State Parks 2022a.
894. Cook 1997(8)95.
895. Cook and Hawk 2001:2001.
896. Cook and Hawk 2001:201.
897. Wikipedia 2018l.
898. Wikipedia 2018l.
899. Wikimedia Commons 2018a.

900. Wikipedia 2018l.
901. Humboldt Standard 1925a.
902. Frickstad 1955:44.
903. Cook and Hawk 2001:208.
904. Wikipedia 2010l.
905. Cook and Hawk 2001:208.
906. Humboldt Standard 1927c.
907. Humboldt Standard 1927d.
908. Humboldt Standard 1938e.
909. Humboldt Standard 1927d.
910. Humboldt Standard 1927e.
911. Shields 2013:90.
912. Wikipedia 2018l.
913. Humboldt Standard 1932a.
914. Humboldt Standard 1938d.
915. Humboldt Standard 1938e.
916. Humboldt Standard 1938e.
917. Cook and Hawk 2001:209.
918. Times-Standard 1973b.
919. Cook and Hawk 2001:210.
920. Heartwood 2018.
921. Otherwise known as Bess Bair (tapdanceroom.com 2019).
922. Rosieradiator.com 2018.
923. Rosieradiator.com 2018.
924. Merriam 1993:(30)416, (31)102. Merriam, who interviewed Smith briefly (1993:(30)416), obtained the tribal group name from the Lolahnkok Indian George Burtt (1993:(31)102).
925. Goddard 1907c:35-48.
926. Goddard 1907c:50-51, 53, 57.
927. Heizer and Almquist 1971:45-46.
928. Anderson 1984a.
929. Cook 1997:(6)108.
930. Cook 1997:(2)123.
931. Cook 1997:(3)114-115; Cook and Hawk 2006:36.
932. Cook 1997:(2)123.
933. Cook 1997:(3)114-115.
934. Scott 2018:29-30.
935. Scott 2018:30-31.
936. Cook and Hawk 2006:36-37.
937. CRTANCS 2001:90.
938. Bailey 1900.
939. Bailey 1900.
940. Cook and Hawk 2006:37.
941. Bailey 1900.
942. Bailey 1900.
943. Bailey 1900.
944. Bailey 1900.
945. Bailey 1900.
946. Bailey 1900.
947. Bailey 1900.
948. Bailey 1900.
949. Bailey 1900.
950. Bailey 1900.
951. Bailey 1900.
952. Bailey 1900.
953. Cook and Hawk 2006:38.
954. Belcher Abstract & Title Co. 1922:11; CRTANCS 2001:88-91.
955. Denny 1911.
956. Belcher Abstract & Title Co. 1921:3.
957. Bailey 1900.
958. Bailey 1900.
959. Cockman n.d.a.
960. Macaulay, Lays of Ancient Rome.
961. With three brothers joining together, it should have been Johnson and Johnson and Johnson.
962. Nash 1988a:3.
963. Nash 1988a:3-4.
964. Benbow 2005:5.
965. Nash 1988a:3-4; Benbow 2005:4-6.
966. Benbow 2005:6.
967. Benbow 2005:6-7.
968. Nash 1988a:6.
969. Nash 1988a:6; Benbow 2005:11.
970. Benbow 2005:6-7.
971. Cook 1997:(2)124.
972. Nash 1988a:6-7.
973. Shelton 2001a.
974. Nash 1988a:8.
975. Crain 1977:24.
976. Nash 1988a:8.
977. Humboldt Times 1929a.
978. Speegle 1931a; Nash 1988b:14-15.
979. Nash 1988b:14.
980. Speegle 1931a; Nash 1988a:8.
981. Benbow 2005:66.
982. Humboldt Times 1932c.
983. Literary Digest 1918:32.
984. Wright 1942.
985. Nash 1988b:16.
986. Nash 1988b:17-18.
987. Gipson 2005.
988. Gardner 2011.
989. Geniella 2001.
990. Shelton 2001a.
991. Fountain 2001:(99)104.
992. US War Department 1897a:8.
993. Humboldt Times 1861d:2.
994. Humboldt Times 1861g:2.
995. US War Department 1897a:8.
996. US War Department 1897a:8.
997. US War Department 1897a:8.
998. Bledsoe 1885:337; Fountain 2001:(31)143.
999. Goddard 1907c:48.
1000. Forbes 1886.
1001. Zachery 1986:16. The northern end is now called Sprowl Creek Road.
1002. Lentell 1898; Daily Humboldt Standard 1907g:3.
1003. London 1911.
1004. London 1911.
1005. Denny 1911.
1006. Lentell 1898; Irvine 1915:766.
1007. Irvine 1915:953.
1008. Irvine 1915:953.
1009. Irvine 1915:953.
1010. Irvine 1915:953.
1011. Irvine 1915:954.
1012. Irvine 1915:954.
1013. The Writer 1914a:165.
1014. Cook and Hawk 2001:149.
1015. David Rumsey Map Collection 2019.
1016. Denny 1911; Irvine 1915:954; Cook and Hawk 2001:149..Cook and Hawk give the acreage as 1,400 acres, but Irvine, who received information directly from Margaret Smith Cobb, indicated it was 1,600 acres.
1017. Cobb 1910a.
1018. Book Review Digest 1910:79.
1019. The Writer 1914a:165.
1020. Cook and Hawk 2001:149.
1021. Irvine 1915:956-957.
1022. Cook 1997:(VII)42.
1023. CRTANCS 2001:215, 219.
1024. Cook 1997:(3)15.

1025. Lentell 1898; CRTANCS 2001:248.
1026. There is disagreement regarding the spelling of Nicholas and Katherina's last name. I have used "Meyer" as it appears here, based on the 1907 wedding announcement for Mary Myers in the Humboldt Times (Humboldt Times 1907d).
1027. CRTANCS 2001:248.
1028. Zachary 1986:18.
1029. Denny 1911; Zachary 1986:18. Zachery states that Isaac Sebbas and his older sons cut tanbark and hauled it south to "the railroad on Indian Creek." They could have reached the Bear Harbor & Eel River Railroad (BH&ERRR) at tiny Moody, several miles to the south, or where the road to Andersonia met the rail line (Borden 1964a:2). However, the BH&ERRR was severely damaged by the 1906 earthquake ("two locomotives were left stranded at Moody with no way out") and apparently ceased operating at that time (Cook and Hawk 2001:66). It is doubtful that any of the Sebbas boys were old enough to help with the hauling prior to the earthquake, so Zachary's account is baffling.
1030. Borden 1964a:2; CRTANCS 2001:168.
1031. Zachary 1986:18.
1032. Belcher Abstract & Title Co. 1922:11.
1033. Zachary 1986:18.
1034. Zachary 1986:19-20.
1035. Morley 1938:38.
1036 Zachary's article, from which the information in this paragraph was taken, mistakenly spells the name Meyer as "Myers." I have corrected the spelling of the family's name and that of the two "openings." However, I have been unable to find any official spelling for the openings.
1037. Zachary 1986:20-21.
1038. Barnum 2017.
1039. Cook and Hawk 2001:54.
1040. Cook and Hawk 2001:28-29.
1041. Zachary 1986:16.
1042. Metsker 1949:58; Zachary 1986:21; Barnum 2017.
1043. Turner and Turner 2010:105; Cook and Hawk 1997:2; Anderson 2006:41; Arceneaux 2013:19.
1044. Merriam 1993:(30)416. The linguist Victor Golla indicates that the "Sinkyone dialect was spoken along the South Fork of the Eel River," specifically including Garberville (Golla 2011:79).
1045. Goddard 1923:95.
1046. Goddard 1903a:49. Charlie indicated that the local Indians "didn't always take scalp when killed. If one party kill and scalped then they made even and took scalps in return. Probably when scalp was taken settlement with money couldn't be made" (Goddard 1903a:36).
1047. Asbill 1953:111.
1048. Cook and Hawk 1997:3; Arceneaux 2013:19; Anderson 2006:42; Van Delinder 1984:3; Irvine 1915:1254. Van Delinder gives "1859 or 1860" as the year Wood started his ranch, Arceneaux says "late 1862," and Cook and Hawk offer "the spring of 1862-1863"—a time that does not exist. Anderson gives no date, and the biography of Charles W. Wood, James's son, only states that James came to Humboldt County in 1859.
1049. Heizer and Almquist 1971:45-46; Humboldt Times 1861e:2.
1050. Turner and Turner 2010:236. The 1875 Land Office map shows "Woods Field" straddling the line between sections 25 and 26, T4S, R3E (Surveyor General's Office 1875a), which would place it about one-half mile east of the Garberville Airport.
1051. Cook and Hawk 2006:4.
1052. McTavish 1885d:3.
1053. Cook and Hawk 1997:4.
1054. Cook and Hawk 1997:4.
1055. The reference is almost certainly to one of two local brothers, namely Reuben Reed. Smith stated that "Reed [was] alive yet" (Goddard 1907c:49). Smith was interviewed in 1907, by which time Reuben's brother, Ezra, had returned to Kentucky, so that Smith would have had no knowledge of whether he was alive or dead. Reuben Reed did not die until 1918 (Cook and Hawk 2001:189), and in 1907 he was living within a few miles of Smith.
1056. Goddard 1907c:49-50.
1057. Goddard 1907c:50.
1058. Goddard 1907c:49.
1059. Arceneaux 2013:19.
1060. Arceneaux 2013:19; Anderson 2006:46; Cook and Hawk 1997:6.
1061. Doolittle 1865.
1062. Surveyor General's Office 1875a.
1063. According to one account it was not "a well-defined trail," but their route took them "by way of Elk Ridge and Bear Buttes," which is roughly where the Hadley-Woods trail is marked on the 1865 map (Cook and Hawk 1997:11; Doolittle 1865).
1064. Davy 1950a:7.
1065. Davy 1950a:7.
1066. Davy 1950a:7.
1067. Cook 1974a:B-19.
1068. Cook 1974a:B-19.
1069. Cook 1974a:B-19.
1070. Cook and Hawk 2006:8.
1071. Humboldt Times 1876a. It is not clear who—the writer or the editor—was afraid to use the missing four-letter word.
1072. Anonymous 1876a:1.
1073. Daily Humboldt Standard 1907g:3. If the report is accurate, this is the farthest upriver any boat is known to have traveled on the South Fork. "Ahoy, Garberville!"
1074. Daily Humboldt Standard 1907g:3.
1075. Daily Humboldt Standard 1907g:3.
1076. Machi 2015b.
1077. West Coast Signal 1878a:3; Cook 1997:(10)83. Another account claims that John McMillin, using Chinese labor, built the Garberville to Briceland section of the road (Cook and Hawk 2006:9, 56), but the source for this information is not documented.
1078. Cook and Hawk 2006:56. The authors also claim that McMillin used Chinese workers on this project, but the Democratic Standard reported in March 1880 that the Chinese had been expelled from Garberville (Democratic Standard 1880:3).
1079. McTavish 1885i:3.
1080. Fountain 2001(70)165).
1081. McTavish 1885i:3.
1082. Daily Humboldt Standard 1907g:3.

1083. An alternate spelling for broncos.
1084. Durst 1883:255.
1085. Anderson 2006:45.
1086. Daily Evening Bulletin 1871.
1087. Ferndale Enterprise 1885a:1.
1088. Ferndale Enterprise 1890a:5.
1089. Ferndale Enterprise 1891a:5.
1090. Ferndale Enterprise 1892b:4.
1091. Daily Humboldt Standard 1907g:3.
1092. Cook 1997:(7)88.
1093. Cook 1997:(7)64.
1094. Cook and Hawk 1999:76.
1095. Knapp and Knapp 1988:12-13, 17.
1096. Knapp and Knapp 1988: 17.
1097. Humboldt Standard 1928a.
1098. Democratic Standard 1880a:3.
1099. McClure and McClure 2013:35.
1100. McClure and McClure 2013:34, 36.
1101. Fountain 2001:(103)213.
1102. Fountain 2001:(80)329.
1103. Fountain 2001:(80)273.
1104. McClure and McClure 2013:36.
1105. McClure and McClure 2013:36. McClure indicated that he later tried to buy a copy of the magazine but it had sold out. He subsequently forgot the name of the publication, and even though he later searched for the article he never found it.
1106. Humboldt Standard 1931a.
1107. Cook and Hawk 2006:27.
1108. Cook 1997:(VII)88.
1109. Blue dicks is the common name for the wildflower Dichelostemma capitatum, formerly known as Dichelostemma pulchellum or Brodiaea pulchella, none of which would have been a useful name for a horse.
1110. Trail Back 1974:10.
1111. Irvine 1915:489.
1112. Humboldt Standard 1931a.
1113. Humboldt Standard 1940a.
1114. Holland 1949:9.
1115. Holland 1949:9.
1116. Pardee 1951:1.
1117. Humboldt Times 1952a:8, 10.
1118. Cook and Hawk 2016:23-29, 32-33, 38-39.
1119. Ethnological Documents, 2002:12(4)138.
1120. Lentell 1898; Denny 1911; Cook and Hawk 2006:56. Forbes's 1886 map shows the road following the later Redwood Highway route and thus crossing the Redway Flat, but this is contradicted by both the Lentell and Denny maps, which show the Buhne Hill route described in the text.
1121. Ferndale Enterprise 1891a:5.
1122. Asbill 1953:110-111.
1123. Hendricks 2015:20.
1124. Lentell 1898.
1125. Lentell 1898; Hendricks 2015:20-21.
1126. Murray 1987b:14-15.
1127. California Highway Commission 1928a:170.
1128. California Highway Commission 1922a:frontispiece.
1129. Cook 1997:(8)60; Hendricks 2015:21-22. Hendricks claims that the Hubers purchased the land from the Burris brothers, but Cook's information indicates that the Burrises did not buy land at Redway until 1923.
1130. Cook 1997:(8)60; Hendricks 2015:21.
1131. Hendricks 2015:21.
1132. Kilkenny n.d.
1133. Cook and Hawk 2006:77.
1134. Cook 1997:(8)63. The author has assumed that the fairways were simply dirt, but they may have been covered with "low class" sand.
1135. Hendricks 2015:21.
1136. Trail Back 1975:C-16.
1137. Humboldt Times 1929a.
1138. Humboldt Times 1929a.
1139. Cook 1997:(8)63.
1140. Humboldt Standard 1931b.
1141. Cook 1997:(8)61.
1142. Cook 1997:(8)61.
1143. Cook 1997:(8)65.
1144. Cook 1997:(8)67.
1145. CRTANCS 2001:204-205.
1146. Cook 1997:(8)63.
1147. This is Pliny E. Goddard's rendering of the name (Ethnological Documents 2002:12(4):129).
1148. C. Hart Merriam's versions of the last two names are given first (Merriam 1922a:58), while Goddard's are given in parentheses (Ethnological Documents 2002:12(4):130-131).
1149. Ethnological Documents 2002:12(4):129, 131.
1150. Ethnological Documents 2002:12(4):130.
1151. Merriam 1922a:58. The property Merriam refers to was eventually known as the Combs Ranch.
1152. Doolittle 1865.
1153. Fountain 2001:(96)22.
1154. Goddard 1903a:69.
1155. Nomland 1935:149. Nomland claims that Woodman was "born and always lived in his own culture at Briceland." Given that Goddard's source, Charlie, was a reliable informant and that a George Woodman indeed lived in Long Valley (US War Department 1897a:651-652, Charlie's account is given preference here (Goddard 1903a:69).
1156. Fountain 2001:(96)22.
1157. Nomad 1881:3.
1158. Frank Asbill's account of the massacre mentions a George Phillips as being part of the raiding party but provides no more details about him (Asbill 1953:123).
1159. Turner and Turner 2010:187; Rubalcava 1999:27.
1160. Surveyor General's Office 1875b.
1161. Surveyor General's Office 1876c.
1162. Surveyor General's Office 1875b, 1876a.
1163. Nomad 1881:3.
1164. Nomad 1881:3. This may be the same C. M. Bailey who in 1896 owned the Bailey Mine near Seiad Valley on the Klamath River (California Division of Mines and Mining 1876:387), but unless proof is forthcoming this speculation will remain confined to these endnotes.
1165. Frickstad 1955:45.
1166. Fountain 2001(70)165).
1167. McTavish 1885i:3.
1168. McTavish 1885i:3.
1169. Forbes 1886; Rohde 2014:48-51. Forbes, however shows the road bending west through what was later Redway although the route actually went to the east over what was called Buhne's Hill.
1170. Ferndale Enterprise 1886b:5.

# Endnotes

1171. Rohnerville Herald 1887b:2.
1172. Fountain 2001:(70:165).
1173. Tam1885:62.
1174. Cook 1997:(8)14.
1175. Tam 1885:62-63.
1176. Lentell 1898.
1177. McTavish 1885i:3.
1178. Fountain 2001:(17)283.
1179. Cook 1997:(IV)27.
1180. Hamm 1890.
1181. Vinyard 1990.
1182. Vinyard 1990.
1183. Hawk 2004:49.
1184. Vinyard 1990.
1185. Vinyard 1990.
1186. Vinyard 1990.
1187. It is a California sycamore (Platanus racemosa Nutt.).
1188. Vinyard 1990.
1189. McTavish 1885:3.
1190. Ferndale Enterprise 1890a:5.
1191. Hamm 1890:123.
1192. Ferndale Enterprise 1891a:5.
1193. Ferndale Enterprise 1891a:5.
1194. Lentell 1898. Land patent records indicate that John Marshall and Nancy Marshall claimed adjoining 160-acre parcels in 1876 (US Bureau of Land Management 2019a). The relationship between the Marshalls is not known, although an 1875 listing of the "Estate of J. C. Marshall" includes both parcels (Fountain 2001:(96)22.
1195. Gordon 1899c:3.
1196. Shepherd 2011: 336-337, 362-363.
1197. Gordon 1899c:3.
1198. Schwartzkopf 1949h:13.
1199. Murray 1987b:16.
1200. Murray 1987b:16.
1201. Daily Humboldt Standard 1907c:3.
1202. Denny 1911.
1203. Frickstad 1955:45.
1204. CRTANCS 2001:188.
1205. HSU Special Collections 2018. Baker's motorcycle appears, like trademark, in several of his photographs.
1206. HSU Special Collections 2018.
1207. Van Kirk n.d.a.
1208. Surveyor General's Office 1879a.
1209. US Bureau of Land Management 2018f.
1210. Lentell 1898; Denny 1911.
1211. Van Kirk n.d.a.
1212. Baker 2006.
1213. Wikipedia 2018k.
1214. Baker 2006.
1215. California Bricks 2018a.
1216. Baker 2006.
1217. Baker 2006.
1218. Baker 2006; 1934a.
1219. Van Kirk n.d.a.
1220. Milota 1993b:476.
1221. Baker 2006; Van Kirk n.d.a.
1222. Van Kirk n.d.a.
1223. Baker 2006.
1224. Baker 2006.
1225. Van Kirk n.d.a.
1226. Wikipedia 2018k.
1227. Here is Baker's original black and white image:
1228. Wikipedia 2018c.
1229. Humboldt Standard 1924a.

1230. Healdsburg Tribune 1924a:1; Madera Tribune 1924a:3; Turner and Turner 2010:142. According to California Place Names, "C. Hart Merriam changed the name [from Phillipsville] to Kittentelbe [sic] after the Indian village at the site, but when the post office was reestablished, August 1, 1948, the old name was again chosen" (Gudde 1969:244). Merriam was in fact chairman of the U. S. Board on Geographic Names from 1917 to 1925 (Online Archive of California 2018a).
1231. Cook 1997:(8)20.
1232. State of California, Department of Public Works, Division of Highways, 1937:4-5; Save-the-Redwoods League 1939a.
1233. State of California, Department of Public Works, Division of Highways, 1937:4-5.
1234. WorthPoint 2018; Schwartzkopf 1949h:13; Hawk 2004:54.
1235. Schwartzkopf 1949h:13.
1236. Hawk 2004:56.
1237. Schwartzkopf 1949h:13.
1238. Schwartzkopf 1949h:13.
1239. Hawk 2004:56.
1240. Times-Standard 1968a.
1241. Times-Standard 1968a.
1242. The entire account is based on Parrish 1965.
1243. Kneiss 1956:133-134.
1244. Kneiss 1956:133-134.
1245. Robinson 1964a:25-26.
1246. Robinson 1964a:26.
1247. Robinson 1964a:24-25.
1248. Robinson 1964a:26.
1249. Also called the "Rattlesnake Grade" (California Highway Bulletin, n.d.).
1250. Robinson 1964a:26-28.
1251. Cook and Hawk 2001:73.
1252. Robinson 1964a:26-28.
1253. Robinson 1964a:27-28.
1254. Cook and Hawk 2001a:74.
1255. Blow 1920:45.
1256. Blow 1920:41-44.
1257. Western Directory Company 1920:109. Axel Hermansen is listed as owning a garage at the corner of 4th and I streets in Eureka. Given his first name, his occupation is appropriate.
1258. Fountain 2001:(120)37.
1259. Wikipedia 2019f.
1260. Cook and Hawk 2001:76.
1261. Rohde and Rohde 1992:91.
1262. Cook and Hawk 2001:76.
1263. Humboldt Standard 1918a:4.
1264. Caro 1975:144.
1265. Arcata Union 1925a:4.
1266. Arcata Union 1926a:6.
1267. Attentive readers will have noted that Pfremmer would have been 15 at the time, an unexpectedly young age to be driving the Redwood Highway. However, Pfremmer points out that her aunt, Fay Aldrich, was "the first woman driver in Humboldt County," so audacious automobiling apparently ran in the family (Pfremmer 1976a:33).
1268. Pfremmer 1976a:33.
1269. Martin 1991.
1270. Rohde and Rohde 1992:110-111; State of California, Department of Public Works, Division of Highways 1937:5-9.
1271. Peattie 1954a:58.
1272. Surveyor General's Office 1875b.
1273. US Bureau of Land Management 2017b
1274. Cook 1997:(XI)97-98.
1275. Cook 1997:(V)24.
1276. Humboldt Historian 1987b:24; Metsker 1949:60 .
1277. Forbes 1886.
1278. The source gives the time as "just before the crash following the Civil War," which probably refers to the "Black Friday" gold panic of September 24, 1869 (Wikipedia 2017c).
1279. Cook 1997:(11)52, 56.
1280. CRTANCS 2001:19-20.
1281. Scott 1986:12-13.
1282. New York Botanical Garden 2020.
1283. Berg and Bittman 1988:13; Bencie 1997:4; New York Botanical Garden 2020; Underwood 2020:40; Calflora 2021a.
1284. Berg and Bittman 1988:13-14.
1285. Berg and Bittman 1988:14.
1286. Bencie 1997:4.
1287. Berg and Bittman 1988:14.
1288. Bencie 2021a; CCH2 Portal 2021.
1289. Fountain 1965a:3; Bancroft 1888a:501.
1290. Wood 1856 et seq.
1291. Wood 1863 et seq.
1292. Wood 1872 et seq.
1293. Elliott 1881:83 et seq.
1294. Irvine 1915:28 et seq.
1295. Lewis 1966:111 et seq.
1296. Lewis 1966:111-145.
1297. Lewis 1966:145-146.
1298. The collective noun for a group of bears is either sleuth or sloth (Wikipedia 2017b). Sleuth is used here as these bears were anything but slothful.
1299. Lewis 1966:146.
1300. Lewis 1966:146.
1301. For once this hackneyed phrase is actually apt.
1302. Lewis 1966:146-147.
1303. Lewis 1966:147.
1304. Lewis 1966:147.
1305. Lewis 1966:147-152.
1306. The property is usually referred to as the Mark West Ranch. Mark was Guadalupe's husband. His name was given to various features of the local landscape (Mark West Area Chamber of Commerce 2020), a biased beneficence that ignored his wife.
1307. Lewis 1966:152-156.
1308. Lewis 1966:171-172.
1309. Coy 1982:44-47.
1310. Lewis 1966:172-175.
1311. Daily Alta California 1850b.
1312. Daily Alta California 1850b.
1313. Lewis 1966:156-158.
1314. Lewis1966:137-142.
1315. The nigh-onto-death Indian actually lived until August 1903 (Humboldt Times 1903b).
1316. Ferndale Semi-Weekly Enterprise 1901b:5; Arcata Union 1901a:5. No copy of the third paper, the Loleta Record, is known to exist. That the Coonskin article appeared there is confirmed only because the other two papers so stated.
1317. Humboldt Standard 1928a.

# Endnotes

1318. Sam 1921b. There is a second version of Sam's statement that includes additional information and has greater clarity. Both versions were written by a younger Wiyot, Warren Brenard, who had recorded the statements of several Wiyot elders in the 1920s. The revised statement mentions a companion of Wood's named Smith, who stayed with him after he was wounded. In Wood's long-accepted narrative, there is no one in the party named Smith. However, one of the members of the Union Company, which established the town of Union (Arcata) and of which Wood was also a member, was a Captain Joseph Smith (Lewis 1966:167; Fountain 1964a:3).
1319. Humboldt Standard 1928a.
1320. James 1921[?]a.
1321. Lewis 1966:140.
1322. Roberts 2009:25.
1323. Carr 1875:135, 241.
1324. Daily Alta California 1850c:2
1325. For a more detailed account of Union Company's members and their activities, see Rohde 2008a.
1326. Wood 1872a:2.
1327. Leeper 1950:132-133.
1328. La Motte n.d.:7-8; Lewis 1966:167.
1329. Cook 1997: (X)51. An alternate but less plausible explanation claims that postal authorities made no mistake, for Gussie Monroe had actually submitted the name Miranda, mistakenly believing that this was the first name of Amanda Ruth Logan (CRTANCS 2001:161).
1330. Goddard 1908f:65; Ethnological Documents 2002:12(4)62). Merriam, using information from the Lolahnkok George Burtt, gives the name for Miranda as "Kahs-cho-boo-ah-me (Merriam 1993:(30)420).
1331. Ethnological documents 2001:12(4)62; Goddard n.d.d:12. Apparently Charlie's construction of the ne-git was uncharacteristic of someone from his Sinkene tribal group. Sam Suder, whose Tsis-tci kai-a tribal group was just south of the Sinkenes, told Goddard that his people had ne-gits but that Charlie's people used an open brush enclosure for their dancing.
1332. Cook and Hawk 2006:133.
1333. Cook and Hawk 2006:133; Turner and Turner 2010:137.
1334. Humboldt Times 1889a:2.
1335. McTavish 1885e:3; BLM 2019c.
1336. US Bureau of Land Management 2019b.
1337. Eureka Newspapers Inc. 1949:81.
1338. McTavish 1885e:3.
1339. Humboldt Times 1894c:4.
1340. Logan 1964a.
1341. Logan 1964a:1.
1342. Logan 1964a; Irvine 1915:917.
1343. Irvine 1915:917.
1344. Logan 1964a. The author of this account, Jane Logan, was not alive at the time but had access to information from family members who made the trip. A second account, probably based on information from Jane's mother, Martha Logan, differs in some details (Irvine 1915:917). The Combs property was in Phillipsville, several miles southeast of Miranda.
1345. Logan 1964a.
1346. Geni 2019a.
1347. Logan 1964a.
1348. Logan 1964a.
1349. Logan 1964a.
1350. McTavish 1885i:3.
1351. Logan 1964a.
1352. CRTANCS 2001:159.
1353. Logan 1964a.
1354. Logan 1964a.
1355. Fountain 2001:(70)209.
1356. Cook and Hawk 2006:133; Lentell 1898.
1357. Davy 1950:7.
1358. Genealogy.com 2019a.
1359. Hamm 1890:49.
1360. Irvine 340-341.
1361. Gordon 1899c:3.
1362. Genealogy.com 2019a.
1363. Cook and Hawk 2006:21, 133.
1364. Find A Grave 2019a.
1365. Cook and Hawk 2006:21.
1366. Frickstad 1955:45.
1367. Urban Dictionary 2019a.
1368. Rohde and Rohde 1992:99; Engbeck 2018:226-227, 232. Engbeck provides a slightly different Kent quote than the one given here.
1369. As of 1992 the stonework from two small bridges still marked the route of the original pathway through the campground (Rohde and Rohde 1992:116).
1370. Hawk 2004:58-66.
1371. CRTANCS 2001:237-239.
1372. CRTANCS 2001:159.
1373. Schwarzkopf 1948b:15; CRTANCS 2001:235.
1374. Cook 1997:(7)114.
1375. Ethnological Documents 2002:63-79.
1376. Goddard 1903a:19.
1377. Surveyor General's Office 1874a.
1378. Goddard 1903a:59.
1379. Goddard 1903a:60. Briceland Charlie added that "Old folks say they never hear they eat anything when they die quick and go ya bi. But when they die slow of sickness they eat acorns" (Goddard 1903a:62).
1380. Goddard 1903a:66, 68.
1381. Goddard 1903a:34.
1382. Turner and Turner 2010:72; Bureau of Land Management 2018a.
1383. Denny 1911; Fountain 2001:(48)259.
1384. BLM 2020c.
1385. WikiTree 2017a; Find A Grave 2017a.
1386. Irvine 1915:1247; werelate.org 2017.
1387. Blue Lake Advocate 1900a:3.
1388. Fountain 2001:(48)259.
1389. Eureka Heritage Society 1987:61.
1390. Ferndale Enterprise 1912a.
1391. Pierce 1976:19.
1392. CRTANCS 2001:177, 180.
1393. CRTANCS 2001:181-182.
1394. CRTANCS 2001:182.
1395. CRTANCS 2001:182.
1396. Lentell 1898.
1397. Pacific Reporter 1918; Pierce 1976:1, 3.
1398. Anderson 2006:64.
1399. Pacific Reporter 1918. The account comes from the testimony of witnesses at the subsequent trial.
1400. Pierce 1976:13.
1401. Pacific Reporter 1918.
1402. Polk-Husted 1914:200.
1403. Pacific Reporter 1918.
1404. Pacific Reporter 1918.

1405. Heller 2020a.
1406. Pierce 1976:14.
1407. Polk-Husted 1914:165, 200.
1408. Pacific Reporter 1918.
1409. Heller 2020a.
1410. Heller 2020b.
1411. Pacific Reporter 1918.
1412. Polk-Husted 1914:200.
1413. Heller 2020a.
1414. Pierce 1976:14.
1415. Pierce 1976:15.
1416. Pierce 1976:15-16.
1417. Pierce 1976:18.
1418. Heller 2020a.
1419. Bauer 2020a.
1420. Bauer 2020a, 2020b.
1421. Bauer 2020b.
1422. Hill 2020a.
1423. Pierce 1976:15.
1424. Merriam 1993:(30)420.
1425. Ethnological documents 2002:12(4)64, 66.
1426. Nomland 1935:166.
1427. Goddard 1903a:49.
1428. Neither Nomland nor Woodman ever specified what tribal group he came from. Nomland (1935:149) lumped all the groups in the area under the general tribal name Sinkyone.
1429. Two animals better than the famed "20-mule train" that transported borax across the wastelands of the Mojave Desert.
1430. Irvine 1915:901; Trail Back 1974:C-8.
1431. His biographical sketch in Irvine's history lists him thus, although the 1896 precinct register gives his name as Ulysses Sidney Grant Myers (Humboldt County Clerk 1896).
1432. Irvine 1915:901-902.
1433. McTavish 1885:e3.
1434. Fountain 2001:(70)180.
1435. Rohnerville Herald 1888a:3.
1436. Ferndale Enterprise 1890a:5.
1437. Ferndale Enterprise 1891a:5.
1438. Fountain 2001:(52)124.
1439. Wikipedia 2018o. Despite its name, Juneau Wharf is in Skagway's harbor. It appears that the shootout left Soapy all washed up (Wikipedia 2018p).
1440. Irvine 1915:902.
1441. Daily Standard 1899a:3.
1442. Daily Standard 1899b:3
1443. Irvine 1915:902.
1444. Trail Back 1974:C-8.
1445. Humboldt County Clerk 1896; Trail Back 1974:C-8.
1446. Myers 1992.
1447. Irvine 1915:902; Myers 1992; Rohde and Rohde 1992:106-107.
1448. Geni 2018a.
1449. Irvine 1915:302.
1450. Schwarzkopf 1949j:17.
1451. California Highway Commission 1914b.
1452. California Highway Commission 1914b; Belcher Abstract & Title Co.:1921:2.
1453. Martin 1991; Pritchard and O'Hara 1991. Martin said that the "fine" was $5.00, Pritchard and O'Hara claimed it was $10.00. I have used Martin's figure since was alive during the last years of Myers's career and probably had first-hand information about the scheme.
1454. Myers 1992.
1455. Schwarzkopf 1949j:17; Hawk 2004:68.
1456. Hawk 2004:68-71.
1457. Rathjen 1989; Myers 1992; Hawk 2004:69.
1458. Hawk 2004:68-71.
1459. Schwarzkopf 1949j:17.
1460. Schwarzkopf 1949j:17.
1461. Rathjen 1989.
1462. Rathjen 1989.
1463. Schwarzkopf 1949j:17.
1464. Humboldt Times 1952a:8.
1465. Frickstad 1949:45.
1466. Myers 1992.
1467. Rohde and Rohde 1992:122.
1468. Rathjen 1989.
1469. Metsker 1949:61.
1470. Morrison 1991.
1471. Rathjen 1989.
1472. Rathjen 1989.
1473. Morrison 1991.
1474. Rathjen 1989.
1475. Rathjen 1989.
1476. Lentell 1898; Taylor 1980:3; US Bureau of Land Management 2018c. Jimmy Carothers's property originally ran from the area west of today's Burlington campground to the ridgeslope east of Weott.
1477. Noble 1980:15.
1478. Teague 1975:115.
1479. Teague 1975:115-117.
1480. Taylor 1980:3.
1481. Irvine 1915:700.
1482. Teague 1975:117.
1483. It is unclear from the account which side of the river Randall and Mowry logged on, as Mowry owned property on both sides (Lentell 1898).
1484. US Bureau of Land Management 2018d.
1485. Fountain 2001:(126)284.
1486. US Bureau of Land Management 2018d.
1487. Fountain 2001:(70)213.
1488. California Highway Commission 1914b:18.
1489. Taylor 1980:5.
1490. Pritchard n.d.
1491. Frickstad 1955:47; Taylor 1980:5.
1492. Pritchard n.d.
1493. Pritchard 1987d:24.
1494. Clever 1998:23-24
1495. Clever 1998:22-24.
1496. Pritchard n.d.
1497. Ethnological Documents 2002:12(4)61.
1498. Merriam 1923:55.
1499. Fountain 2001:(70)202.
1500. US Bureau of Land Management 2018c.
1501. Irvine 1915:700; Taylor 1980:3; Fountain 2001:(70)202. Taylor incorrectly gives Burnell's name as "Burcell."
1502. McCormick 1963a:7.
1503. Eel Valley Advance 1970a:8; Taylor 1980:3; Fountain 2001:(47)202; Turner and Turner 2010:121; Pritchard n.d. Taylor and the Turners claim that the camp split redwoods for railroad ties; the other sources state that tanbark was harvested. The detailed information provided by Fountain and the Eel Valley Advance makes it virtually certain that it was a tanbark camp.
1504. Irvine 1915:872; Eel Valley Advance 1970:8; Taylor 1980:3.
1505. Brown and Baldo 2010:7-8.

# Endnotes

1506. Fountain 2001:(112)92.
1507. Only the transport of ties is mentioned, but it seems probable that shingles from his mill were also sent to South Fork.
1508. Brown and Baldo 2010:7-9.
1509. Schwarzkopf 1948a:15.
1510. Cunningham 2001:21.
1511. There is disagreement about the starting date for Johnson's store. Taylor, citing information from local old-timers, puts it as "about" 1917 (Taylor 1980:4). Schwarzkopf recorded family member Bob Johnson indicating that the family arrived in 1918 (Schwarzkopf 1948a:15). O'Hara and Stockton claim it was 1919 when "Johnson arrived in Mckee's [sic] Mill to open a store (O'Hara and Stockton 2012:17).
1512. Taylor 1980:4; O'Hara and Stockton 2012:17.
1513. Pritchard n. d.; Taylor 1980:4-5; Clever 1998:17.
1514. CRTANCS 2001:263.
1515. Merriam 1923a:55-60.
1516. Merriam 1923a:55.
1517. Humboldt Times 1925c:2.
1518. Humboldt Times 1925e.
1519. Humboldt Times 1925f.
1520. Frickstad 1955:47.
1521. Taylor 1980:5.
1522. Humboldt Standard 1901:27e.
1523. Humboldt Standard 1927f. A subsequent edition of the paper, which reported the burning of the Hartsook Inn, made reference to the Weott hotel fire but did not mention the Dugan Mill conflagration, substituting instead the burning of the Walden brothers' mill at Holmes (Humboldt Standard 1927d).
1524. Clever 1998:28.
1525. Arcata Union 1933a.
1526. O'Hara and Stockton 2012:17.
1527. Humboldt Times 1925d.
1528. Taylor 1980:5.
1529. Fisher 1989:20; Fisher and Fisher 1991.
1530. This was the term that applied to them at the time.
1531. Fisher 1989:20; Fisher and Fisher 1991; Clever 1998:17-18.
1532. Fisher 1989:20; Clever 1998:17.
1533. Cook 1997:(8)11. One wonders how often the Tie-Makers' games went into extra innings.
1534. Schwarzkopf 1948a:15.
1535. Fisher and Fisher 1991.
1536. Schwarzkopf 1948a:15.
1537. Schwarzkopf 1948a:15.
1538. Fountain 2001:(96)386.
1539. Fountain 2001:(96)389.
1540. Fountain 2001:(79)309.
1541. Merriam 1993:(30)420, 422.
1542. Merriam 1993:(30) 26, 28; (52)116, 130, 132, 133, 136.
1543. Merriam 1993:(30)413.
1544. The information appears on Ah-dah-dil-law's headstone at the Sunset Cemetery near Fortuna.
1545. Ethnological Documents 2002:12(4)206.
1546. United States Department of the Interior, Office of Indian Affairs 1929:2. This document is Burtt's application for enrollment as a California Indian. It indicates that Burtt was born "on Mattole River," which disagrees with Merriam's and Driver's statements that have Burtt born on Bull Creek. I have given Bull Creek as his birthplace in my account since I have higher confidence in the veracity of Merriam's information, which came from extensive contact with Burtt, than I do with the Department of the Interior form that shows his birthplace as being on the Mattole.
1547. Driver 1939:308; Merriam 1993:(30)413.
1548. Goddard 1903a:49.
1549. Driver 1939:358.
1550. Humboldt Standard 1940b.
1551. Mulley 1999:23.
1552. Driver 1939:308.
1553. This is the spelling that appears on his headstone and which is also given in his obituary (Humboldt Standard 1940b). His last name is sometimes rendered as Burt or Bert, and he was also known as "Indian George."
1554. The information appears on Tu-ha-kah's headstone at the Sunset Cemetery near Fortuna.
1555. Goddard 1908a:31-32.
1556. Goddard n.d.a.:57.
1557. The information also appears Tu-ha-kah's headstone at the Sunset Cemetery near Fortuna.
1558. Merriam 1923a:56; Humboldt Standard 1927g.
1559. Goddard 1907c.
1560. Kroeber 1919:346-350.
1561. "Goosepen" redwoods are mature trees with burned-out interiors. By putting a bit of fencing across the opening, geese and other farm animals could be kept inside.
1562. Crismon 1991a.
1563. Humboldt County Clerk 1896.
1564. Ferndale Enterprise 1899a.
1565. Martin n.d.
1566. Denny 1911; US Bureau of Land Management 2020b.
1567. Daily Humboldt Standard 1907e:7; Oregon Encyclopedia 2020a.
1568. Crismon 1991a.
1569. Lewis et al. 1991.
1570. Merriam 1923a:54; Martin n.d. Apparently the Burtts did not live at the Rohnerville Rancheria, at least not when Merriam visited them, as he mentions his time at the rancheria as being separate from his time with the Burtts (Merriam 1923a:61).
1571. Kroeber 1908a:37-38.
1572. Humboldt Times 1930c.
1573. Nomland 1931:38-41.
1574. Merriam 1993:(30)346, 508.
1575. Merriam 1923a:54-60.
1576. Humboldt County Deeds, Book 187:372; Wrigley n.d.
1577. Mel Martin called it a "perfectly cream apple" that turned purple in December (Martin n.d.).
1578. Wrigley 1991, n.d.
1579. Wikipedia 2020a; Greenmantle Nursery 2020a.
1580. Wrigley n.d.
1581. Wrigley n.d.
1582. Driver 1939:364-365, 422.
1583. Driver 1939:358, 415.
1584. Driver 1939:332, 395.
1585. Humboldt Standard 1940b.
1586. Humboldt Standard 1940c.
1587. Author's observation of the grave site.
1588. Rohde and Rohde 1992:234-237.

1589. Weekly Humboldt Times 1863a:2. A second-hand account of what might be the Whitmore-led attack states that "about 300 Sinkyone were believed to have been massacred somewhere along Bull Creek; and Captain Wright may have been in charge of the 'soldiers.'" According to this same source, "among the few who survived were several women who were taken prisoner and sold as indentured servants ("slaves") to local white people. When they later ceased being servants, they committed suicide" (an account by Alberta Price reported in Kemp 1983:13). The figure of 300 deaths would far exceed that of any other Humboldt County massacre; it is highly unlikely that so many Indians were found in a single location, let alone that such a number was killed. The mention of a "Captain Wright" probably refers to a vigilante expedition led by "Captain" Seman Wright in February 1860 that resulted in the killing of about 40 Indians on the South Fork of Eel River (Heizer 1974:156). Members of Wright's company were subsequently implicated in the series of massacres, including one on Indian Island, that took place a few weeks later (Rohde 2010a).
1590. Look n.d.
1591. Nomland 1935:166.
1592. Humboldt Times 1919c:9.
1593. Gilligan n.d.
1594. Look n.d.
1595. Edeline n.d. George Rumrill was born in 1851 (PeopleLegacy 2022), which would indicate that bull incident probably occurred no earlier that the late 1860s, given that Rumrill must have been at least in his late teens to be working for Russ.
1596. His daughter, Grace, puts the figure at 200 (Baxter 1987b:19).
1597. Irvine 1915:1032.
1598. Baxter 1987b:19.
1599. Baxter 1987b:19.
1600. Genzoli 1972a:49; Elliott and Elliott n.d.
1601. This process involves estimating the volume of timber in a specific plot of ground.
1602. Baxter 1987b:19.
1603. Lentell 1898; Irvine 1915:1219-1220.
1604. Fountain 2001:(70)204.
1605. Fountain 2001:(89)389.
1606. CRTANCS 2001:54.
1607. Fountain 2001:(24)3.
1608. Ferndale Enterprise 1885b:5; CRTANCS 2001:60.
1609. Hendricks 2013:33.
1610. Irvine 1915:947.
1611. Surveyor General's Office 1879a; BLM 2020d.
1612. Lentell 1898;
1613. Ferndale Enterprise 1899b.
1614. Humboldt Standard 1921d.
1615. Fountain 20001:(62)248.
1616. Lentell 1898; Denny 1911; Irvine 1915:1029; Humboldt Standard 1921d.
1617. Irvine 1915:893-894.
1618. Lewis et al. 1991.
1619. Lewis 2001:5.
1620. Frickstad 1955:44.
1621. Daily Humboldt Times 1903a:2.
1622. Humboldt Times 1913c; Clark 1983:71; Fountain 2001:(91)66.
1623. Lewis 2001:9.
1624. French 1997:39.
1625. Lewis 2001:10.
1626. Humboldt Times 1922a.
1627. Humboldt Beacon 1922b:2.
1628. Fountain 2001:(112)92.
1629. Humboldt Beacon 1922c:6.
1630. Humboldt Beacon 1922d:1.
1631. Humboldt Beacon 1922e.
1632. Humboldt Beacon 1922f:7.
1633. Humboldt Beacon 1922g:2.
1634. Humboldt Beacon 1923a:6.
1635. Humboldt Beacon 1923b:1.
1636. Humboldt Beacon 1923c:7.
1637. Humboldt Beacon 1823d:3.
1638. Rohde 2002a:37; Chadbourne n.d.
1639. Chadbourne 1991.
1640. Bishop 1991.
1641. Taylor 1917.
1642. Taylor 1917.
1643. Chadbourne n.d.:2.
1644. Carranco and Sorensen 1988:168.
1645. Carranco and Carranco 1977:4.
1646. Bishop 1991; Pritchard and O'Hara 1991.
1647. Rohde and Rohde 1992:258.
1648. Lewis 2001:1.
1649. Fritz 1922a, 1922b.
1650. Fritz 1922c.
1651. Stockton 2004a.
1652. Lewis n.d.:31.
1653. Lewis n.d.:32.
1654. Belcher Abstract & Title Co. 1921:2.
1655. Humboldt Times 1926a; Engbeck 2018:272-273.
1656. Engbeck 2018:274.
1657. For a detailed account of this stirring struggle see the Dyerville chapter.
1658. Save-the-Redwoods League 1931:8; US Department of the Interior, Geological Survey 1969b.
1659. Pinterest 2020a.
1660. Crismon 1991a.
1661. West Coast Lumberman 1939a; Wrigley 1991.
1662. Crismon 1991.
1663. This is the name of a landform, not a person.
1664. Crismon 1991a, n.d.a.
1665. Lewis 2001:8-9.
1666. Gould n.d.
1667. Gould n.d.
1668. Pritchard and O'Hara 1991.
1669. Russell 1991.
1670. Grossenheider 1998.
1671. Rohde and Rohde 1992:262; Gould n.d.
1672. Beat 1991.
1673. Humboldt Standard 1948a.
1674. Rohde and Rohde 1992:221.
1675. O'Hara and Stockton 2012:40.
1676. The description of the Bull Creek logging roads is based on field observations by the author in the 2000s.
1677. Drury 1960:11.
1678. Wayburn 1960:10.
1679. Pritchard and O'Hara 1991.
1680. Jackson 1956.
1681. Beat 1991.
1682. Beat 1991.

# Endnotes

1683. Ruggles 1990.
1684. Blue Lake Advocate 1952a:6.
1685. Blue Lake Advocate 1954a:3.
1686. Blue Lake Advocate 1955a:1. Another source gives the acreage for this fire as 5,600 acres (Gilligan 1966:54).
1687. Engbeck 2018:372.
1688. The sidebar account is based on Rohde and Rohde 1992:48-51.
1689. Gilligan 1966:55.
1690. Traynor 1961a.
1691. Griffith 1957:9.
1692. Griffith 1957:9.
1693. Wayburn 1960; Traynor 1961; Gilligan 1966:55.
1694. Gilligan 1966:51, 54-55.
1695. Engbeck 2018:373.
1696. Engbeck 2018:373.
1697. Schrepfer 1983:112.
1698. Johnson 1960.
1699. O'Hara and Stockton 2012:123-124.
1700. Merriam 1993:(30)414. The information comes from George Burtt, a Lolahnkok Indian who came from nearby Bull Creek.
1701. Merriam 1993:(9)155. The information again comes from George Burtt.
1702. Merriam 1993:(30)413.
1703. Goddard 1903a:55.
1704. Briceland Charlie was a Sinkene Indian from Salmon Creek, a few miles up the South Fork. Pliny Goddard's field notes for one of his interviews with Charlie states "Dyerville Ltcin ta din Used to be village just below house our kind people" (Goddard 1903a:55). Goddard takes this to mean that the village belonged to Charlie's Sinkene group (Ethnological Documents 2002:12(4):57). However, it appears that the rest of Sinkene territory lay somewhat to the south, and was probably separated from this village by Lolahnkok territory at the mouth of Bull Creek. This suggests that the village near Dyerville was Lolahnkok.
1705. Gibbs 2016:25-26.
1706. Gibbs 2016:26.
1707. US War Department 1897b:740.
1708. Surveyor General's Office 1885a.
1709. Rohde 2014:48-50.
1710. Pritchard 1987a:13. In 1987 Pritchard wrote a four-part series on Dyerville that is a masterpiece of thoroughness.
1711. Pritchard 1987a:13, 16.
1712. In point of fact, the Western Watchman reported in March 1888 that a post office was in the offing, but indicated that it would be named either South Fork or Crismon (Fountain 2001:(70)184). The latter was the name of a family that lived in the area.
1713. Fountain 200:(70)165).
1714. Cook and Hawk 2006:56.
1715. McTavish 1885i:3.
1716. Fountain 2001:(70)165.
1717. Fountain 2001:(70)165.
1718. Hamm 1890:146.
1719. Pritchard 1987b:19.
1720. Pritchard 1987b:18-19.
1721. Gordon 1899d:3.
1722. The Humboldt Daily Standard of October 14, 1905, as quoted in Pritchard 1987b:19.
1723. While Carland's store didn't burn, it did suffer other difficulties. In 1906 the Eel rose high enough to reach both the store and stables; the water went "nearly a foot deep" in the store, and Carland was forced to turn his horses out of the stables to let them seek safety. That same year the San Francisco Earthquake shook Dyerville enough that the twice-blighted Carland lost "$300 or $400 worth of goods in his store and saloon." (Pritchard 1987c:21).
1724. Pritchard 1987b:19-20.
1725. Lentell 1898.
1726. Daily Humboldt Standard 1907a:3.
1727. Scott 1985a:9.
1728. Scott 1985a:9.
1729. Genzoli 1982a:5.
1730. Genzoli 1982a:5.
1731. Genzoli 1982a:5.
1732. Tracy 1993a:66.
1733. Humboldt Times 1911a.
1734. Humboldt Times 1911a.
1735. Humboldt Times 1911a.
1736. Genzoli 1982a:5.
1737. Humboldt Times 1911a.
1738. Humboldt Times 1911a.
1739. Daily Standard 1911a:1.
1740. Pritchard 1987c:18.
1741. Boots 1964:7.
1742. Humboldt Times 1913a.
1743. Karshner 1987a: 192-193.
1744. Clever 1998:9.
1745. Humboldt Times 1911a.
1746. Clever 1998:13.
1747. Pritchard 1987d:24.
1748. State of California 1928a:170.
1749. State of California 1914a:2.
1750. State of California 1931a:3. An alternate map of the project shows one house-size building on the west side of the highway becoming victim of the new alignment (Humboldt Times 1931b).
1751. Humboldt Times 1931
1752. Pritchard 1987d:24.
1753. Pritchard 1987d:24.
1754. Pritchard 1987d:24.
1755. Spencer 1895:36.
1756. The 1893-1894 directory listed three other speculators. By 1895 one of them had become a woodsman, one a "general trader," and one was no longer listed (Standard Publishing Company 1893:25, 49, 54, 75.)
1757. Library of Congress 2019a.
1758. Lentell 1898.
1759. Denny 1911.
1760. Engbeck 2018:242-243.
1761. Belcher 1921:2.
1762. Engbeck 2018:198.
1763. Wasserman and Wasserman 2019:27.
1764. Platt 2019a.
1765. Kuhl 2000:85. In June 2021 the California Department of Parks and Recreation removed a monument dedicated to Grant from Prairie Creek Redwoods State Park (Cahill 2021a). At the Founders Grove on the Dyerville Flat in Humboldt Redwoods State Park, two signs were replaced with a single sign that acknowledges the racism of two of the "founders," Grant and Henry Fairfield Osborn (Carter 2022).

1766. Merriam 1938:1898-99.
1767. Engbeck 2018:201-202.
1768. Grant 1919:116.
1769. Engbeck 2018:212.
1770. Savetheredwoods.org 2020.
1771. Grant 1919:99, 103.
1772. Engbeck 2018:214.
1773. Wasserman and Wasserman 2019:36-38.
1774. Grant 1919:115.
1775. Wasserman and Wasserman 2019:37.
1776. San Jose Woman's Club 2019.
1777. Wikipedia 2019g. The amendment required approval by three-fourths of the states. It became law the next year when ratified by Tennessee, the 36th state to do so.
1778. Irvine 1915:285; Healdsburg Tribune, Enterprise and Scimitar [!] 1936a:7; Wasserman and Wasserman 2019:37-38.
1779. Engbeck 2018:218-219.
1780. Ferndale Enterprise 1940a; Engbeck 2018:219.
1781. Engbeck 2018:220.
1782. Engbeck 2018:220.
1783. Engbeck 2018:220.
1784. Engbeck 2018:220.
1785. Ferndale Enterprise 1940a.
1786. Engbeck 2018:233.
1787. Engbeck 2018:233, 235.
1788. The name was later changed to Humboldt Redwoods State Park (Rohde and Rohde 1992:36).
1789. Humboldt Beacon 1922a:4.
1790. Wasserman and Wasserman 2019:52.
1791. Wasserman and Wasserman 2019:49, 53. The rate here was almost 38%.
1792. Engbeck 2018:238.
1793. Engbeck 2018:240-241.
1794. Humboldt Times 1924a:1.
1795. Ferndale Enterprise 1940a.
1796. Humboldt Standard 1924c.
1797. Humboldt Times 1924a:1.
1798. Humboldt Times 1924a:1.
1799. Wasserman and Wasserman 2019:97.
1800. Engbeck 2018:250; Wasserman and Wasserman 2019:97.
1801. Engbeck 2018:251.
1802. Engbeck 2018:251.
1803. Wasserman and Wasserman 2019:100.
1804. Wasserman and Wasserman 2019:101-102.
1805. Engbeck 2018:248-249; Wasserman and Wasserman 2019:104.
1806. Engbeck 2018:252.
1807. Humboldt Times 1925a:2.
1808. Humboldt Times 1925b:1-2.
1809. Humboldt Times 1925b:2.
1810. Humboldt Times 1925b:2.
1811. Engbeck 2018:254.
1812. Humboldt Times 1925b:2.
1813. Humboldt Times 1925b:2. Drury, in an interview 47 years after the fact, gave a much less dramatic account, claiming that the telegrams arrived at intervals of several minutes and that he only read them aloud "when there was a pause." (Engbeck 2018:254). It is thus uncertain as to what actually happened, but I have chosen to use the Humboldt Times version, which was written at the time of the event and of course is much more exciting. Readers of this endnote can choose which version to believe.
1814. Engbeck 2018:255.
1815. Engbeck 2018:255.
1816. Humboldt Times 1925b:2.
1817. Engbeck 2018:255.
1818. Engbeck 2018:255.
1819. Engbeck 2018:256.
1820. Wasserman and Wasserman 2019:117-118.
1821. Engbeck 2018:272; Wasserman and Wasserman 2019:117-118.
1822. Wasserman and Wasserman 2019:119-120.
1823. Humboldt Times 1926a.
1824. Engbeck 2018:274.
1825. Engbeck 2018:274-275; Wasserman and Wasserman 2019:140.
1826. Humboldt Standard 1931d; Engbeck 2018:274-275; Wasserman and Wasserman 2019:140.
1827. Humboldt Standard n.d.a.
1828. Humboldt Standard 1939c; Engbeck 2018:274-275; Wasserman and Wasserman 2019:14

# About the Author

Jerry Rohde has been researching Humboldt County history and writing about it for over 30 years. He has been the ethnogeographer and historian for Humboldt State University's Cultural Resources Facility for over 20 years and has authored or co-authored previous six books and written more than 500 reports for state and local agencies and various Indian tribes. His History of Humboldt County People and Places series is planned to include seven books, of which *Southwest Humboldt Hinterlands* is the third. Jerry and his wife Gisela live in South Stumpville, a Eureka suburb.

Made in the USA
Columbia, SC
22 October 2024

22139f54-d8c0-4b2d-a19d-28d2f328b20dR03